Sourcebook on
VIOLENCE
AGAINST
WOMEN

Editors

Claire M. Renzetti
Jeffrey L. Edleson
Raquel Kennedy Bergen

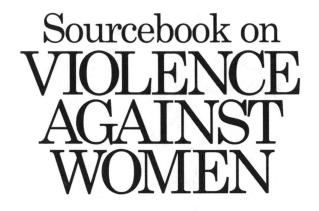

Sourcebook on
VIOLENCE AGAINST WOMEN

Sourcebook on VIOLENCE AGAINST WOMEN

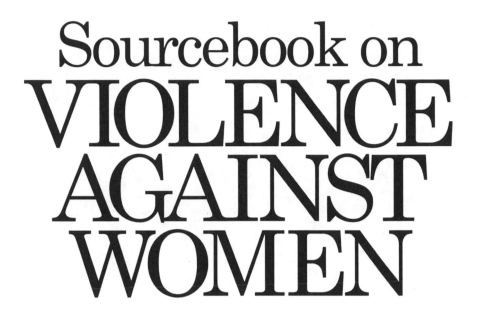

Editors

Claire M. Renzetti
Jeffrey L. Edleson
Raquel Kennedy Bergen

Sage Publications
International Educational and Professional Publisher
Thousand Oaks ■ London ■ New Delhi

For information:

Sage Publications, Inc.
2455 Teller Road
Thousand Oaks, California 91320
E-mail: order@sagepub.com

Sage Publications Ltd.
6 Bonhill Street
London EC2A 4PU
United Kingdom

Sage Publications India Pvt. Ltd.
M-32 Market
Greater Kailash I
New Delhi 110 048 India

Printed in the United States of America

Library of Congress Cataloging-in-Publication Data

Main entry under title:

Sourcebook on violence against women / edited by Claire M. Renzetti,
Jeffrey L. Edleson, and Raquel Kennedy Bergen.
    p. cm.
Includes bibliographical references and index.
  ISBN 0-7619-2004-8 (cloth) — ISBN 0-7619-2005-6 (pbk.)
  1. Women—Crimes against. 2. Abused women. 3. Family violence. 4.
Sex discrimination against women. I. Renzetti, Claire M.
II. Edleson, Jeffrey L. III. Bergen, Raquel Kennedy.
  HV6250.4.W65 S68 2000
  362.82'92—dc21   00-010215

Printed on acid-free paper.

        03   04   05   06   07   7   6   5   4   3   2

Acquisition Editor:	Nancy Hale
Editorial Assistant:	Heather Gotlieb
Production Editor:	Diana E. Axelsen
Editorial Assistant:	Candice Crosetti
Typesetter/Designer:	Marion Warren
Indexer:	Jeanne Busemeyer
Cover Designer:	Michelle Lee

Contents

Foreword   ix
    Senator Paul D. Wellstone and Sheila Wellstone

Preface   xi

PART I   **Theoretical and Methodological Issues in Researching Violence Against Women**   **1**

Chapter 1.   Theoretical Explanations for Violence Against Women   5
    Jana L. Jasinski

Chapter 2.   Definitional Issues   23
    Walter S. DeKeseredy and Martin D. Schwartz

Chapter 3.   Measurement Issues for Violence Against Women   35
    Sujata Desai and Linda E. Saltzman

    SPECIAL TOPIC: Men Researching Violence Against Women   53
    Neil Websdale

Chapter 4.   Ethical Issues in Research on Violence Against Women   57
    Jacquelyn C. Campbell and Jacqueline D. Dienemann

Chapter 5. Collaborating for Women's Safety: Partnerships Between
Research and Practice   73
Jeffrey L. Edleson and Andrea L. Bible

PART II   **Types of Violence Against Women**   **97**

Chapter 6.   Victimization of Female Children   101
Kathleen A. Kendall-Tackett

SPECIAL TOPIC: Female Genital Mutilation   115
Tamar Diana Wilson

Chapter 7.   From Prevalence to Prevention: Closing the Gap Between
What We Know About Rape and What We Do   117
Karen Bachar and Mary P. Koss

Chapter 8.   Violence Against Women by Intimate
Relationship Partners   143
*Patricia Mahoney, Linda M. Williams, and
Carolyn M. West*

Chapter 9.   Violence Against Older Women   179
Linda Vinton

Chapter 10. Mainstreaming Immobility: Disability Pornography
and Its Challenge to Two Movements   193
R. Amy Elman

Chapter 11. Sexual Harassment: Violence Against Women at Work   209
Phoebe Morgan

PART III   **Prevention and Direct Intervention**   **223**

Chapter 12. Services for Sexual Assault Survivors:
The Role of Rape Crisis Centers   227
Rebecca Campbell and Patricia Yancey Martin

SPECIAL TOPIC: Sexual Assault Nurse Examiner
(SANE) Program   243
    Linda E. Ledray

Chapter 13. Shelters and Other Community-Based Services for
Battered Women and Their Children   247
    Cris M. Sullivan and Tameka Gillum

Chapter 14. Intervention Programs for Men Who Batter   261
    Larry W. Bennett and Oliver J. Williams

Chapter 15. The Violence Against Women Act of 1994: The Federal
Commitment to Ending Domestic Violence, Sexual
Assault, Stalking, and Gender-Based Crimes of Violence   279
    Roberta L. Valente, Barbara J. Hart, Seema Zeya,
    and Mary Malefyt

Chapter 16. Criminal Justice System Responses to Domestic
Violence: Law Enforcement and the Courts   303
    LeeAnn Iovanni and Susan L. Miller

Chapter 17. Advocacy on Behalf of Battered Women   329
    Ellen Pence

Chapter 18. Health Intervention With Battered Women: From
Crisis Intervention to Complex Social Prevention   345
    Evan Stark

Chapter 19. Religious Issues and Violence Against Women   371
    Marie M. Fortune

Chapter 20. School-Based Education and Prevention Programs   387
    Mary K. O'Brien

Chapter 21. Getting the Message Out: Using Media to Change
Social Norms on Abuse   417
    Marissa Ghez

PART IV **Continuing and Emerging Issues**   **439**

Chapter 22. Domestic Violence as a Welfare-to-Work Barrier:
             Research and Theoretical Issues   443
             Jody Raphael

             SPECIAL TOPIC: Criminalization of Pregnancy   457
             Drew Humphries

Chapter 23. Prostitution, the Sex Industry, and Sex Tourism   459
             Jody Miller and Dheeshana Jayasundara

Chapter 24. Violence Against Women as a Human Rights
             Violation: International Institutional Responses   481
             Johanna Bond and Robin Phillips

Author Index   501

Subject Index   518

About the Authors   531

Foreword

Ten years ago, we began a journey. With the guidance of researchers, educators, and advocates, we set out to learn everything we could about the violence against women that affects so many. We traveled around the country to hear the stories of battered women and their children, to see firsthand the operation of shelters and crisis centers, and, ultimately, to gather the tools needed to create effective public policy. We were fueled by a collective passion not only to pass legislation that would affect the lives of women living with violence but also to concurrently create a heightened awareness of this epidemic.

The grassroots efforts of women's organizations, college students, advocates, educators, policy makers, and courageous women who have survived this violence have caused a paradigm shift. In 1994, Congress passed the most comprehensive anti-violence legislation to date. The Violence Against Women Act (VAWA) of 1994 put a legislative frame around the whole of our efforts. Our work now continues in the spirit of expanding this law and its enforcement, increasing women's access to services, and providing tools for those community-based organizations to expand their research, collaborations, and services.

As we consulted the enormous amount of information available, we felt the lack of a comprehensive resource that would augment our experiences. We recognized that such a resource would serve as a valuable educational tool for the general public. We have now found a compilation of all of these resources in *Sourcebook on Violence Against Women*.

In the *Sourcebook*, we find a uniquely comprehensive resource on violence-against-women issues. Topics include types of violence, prevention and direct intervention strategies, and an informative essay on VAWA. Drs. Renzetti, Edleson, and Bergen have brought policy

makers, advocates, and researchers together to address these issues in striking
form, and the *Sourcebook* will serve as a
comprehensive tool for students and consumers across lines of gender, age, and
profession.

For the first time in one book, great
minds from three domains address the issue of violence against women in a more
effective and thus life-saving form. For
too long, researchers, advocates, and policy makers have engaged in separate efforts, and thus, their outcomes have
lacked full efficacy. Only when all three
entities work together can these issues be
addressed authentically to truly help those
who experience this violence. This shared
work of a concerted group of experts
promises to affect all of us by saving the
lives of women.

The *Sourcebook* encompasses multiple
aspects of violence against women including rape, female genital mutilation,
sexual assault, and domestic violence. It
addresses prevention and direct intervention by providing information on services,
shelters, and other intervention strategies
that will improve the way that violence
against women is addressed, prosecuted,
and prevented through education. In this
book, we find ideas that will be catalysts
to awareness, prevention, and intervention. The book will serve as a resource to
people of any class, gender, age, and profession and will help to instill in our society the values that will alleviate violence
against women.

Violence against women happens to
the women we love, the women with
whom we work and worship, our neighbors and our friends. Violence knows no
boundaries, not economic status, sexual
identity, rural or urban residence, race or
religious affiliation, age or gender. It is
startlingly common, and our efforts to
stop it must be relentless to be effective.

The *Sourcebook* will facilitate these efforts. It will affect our communities and
ourselves by providing ideas and awareness, which will lead to stronger prevention and intervention. Drs. Renzetti,
Edleson, and Bergen have combined
communities of thinkers in a concerted effort to challenge this convention of behavior and to change the lives of women
by alleviating fear and ending the cycle
of violence. It is a controversial and
forward-thinking piece of work, which
addresses topics that warrant attention
and have often been taboo. This unfiltered
look at the violence that permeates
women's lives will no doubt enrich our
understanding and expand our capacity to
affect social and legislative change.
Sourcebook on Violence Against Women
is a landmark in this journey.

PAUL D. WELLSTONE
United States Senator,
Minnesota

SHEILA WELLSTONE
National domestic violence advocate
St. Paul, Minnesota

Preface

The impetus for this book came from Charles (Terry) Hendrix, former editor of books on interpersonal violence for Sage. During a lunch meeting—which, with Terry, always involves delicious food and lots of good humor—he told us about the various handbooks and manuals Sage was publishing in areas where research was simply burgeoning. The goal was to provide a solid overview of the important topics and the latest research addressing them. He was surprised that no one had proposed such a book in the area of violence against women, so we set to work thinking about whom we could recruit to edit the volume. Somehow—we suspect sublimal prodding from Terry was at work—we struck on the idea of doing the book ourselves. Although the undertaking at first seemed daunting, it turned out to be a truly pleasant and rewarding task.

The book is composed of 24 chapters organized into four parts: theoretical and methodological issues in researching violence against women, types of violence against women, prevention and direct intervention, and continuing and emerging issues. Each part opens with a brief introduction that previews the forthcoming chapters. We did our best to be thorough in coverage, but it is likely impossible to include all the topics worthy of discussion in this rapidly growing field. We have included, however, many topics not typically covered in current violence-against-women texts, such as men who research violence against women, collaborative research efforts, female genital mutilation, disability pornography, religious issues, the media as tools of social change, the relationship between domestic violence and welfare-to-work transition, criminalization of pregnancy, sex tourism, and violence against women as a human rights violation. Within each part, we have included special topics that highlight important issues not covered by chapters in that part but related to them. Our goal is to encourage discussion of and debate about the material in the special topic sections.

The ordering of the editorship for the book is completely arbitrary; the labor was shared equally among the editors, and the end product represents genuine teamwork throughout the entire editing process. Like all teams, however, this one involves many more players than just the "first string," so we would like to take this opportunity to express our gratitude to those who helped bring the book to fruition. Of course, we are grateful to Terry Hendrix for planting the idea for the book in our heads and for encouraging us to pursue it. We also thank Nancy Hale, Terry's able successor as editor of interpersonal violence books at Sage, for guiding the book to completion and holding us to our deadline. Thanks as well to Heather Gotlieb, editorial assistant at Sage, who graciously handled the nitty-gritty details of production. We are grateful, too, to Denise Shaw, secretary extraordinaire of the Sociology Department at St. Joseph's University, for keeping files, lists, and correspondence organized when chaos

threatened. Most of all, we are grateful to the chapter authors, not only for their contributions to the book but also for their deep commitment to ending violence against women.

On a personal note, Claire Renzetti thanks her husband, Dan Curran, and sons, Sean and Aidan, for living as constant reminders of what loving, nonviolent intimate relationships are all about. Jeff Edleson wishes to thank his sons, Daniel and Eli, for their support and to acknowledge both the clients and staff of Domestic Abuse Project, Inc., in Minneapolis, Minnesota, and University of Minnesota's School of Social Work for their strong support of his research on domestic violence over the past 17 years. Raquel Bergen is grateful to her husband, Mike, and their children, Devon and Michael Ryan, for their patience and support.

PART I

Theoretical and Methodological Issues in Researching Violence Against Women

In only about three decades, research and writing about violence against women have mushroomed. As Walter S. DeKeseredy and Martin D. Schwartz point out in Chapter 2 of this volume, *Violence and Abuse Abstracts* currently summarizes more than 1,300 articles and chapters each year, many of which focus directly on some aspect of violence against women. Many of these articles appear in such journals as the *Journal of Interpersonal Violence, Violence and Victims,* and most recently, the *Journal of Religion and Abuse,* journals that specialize in work about intimate violence, in which, we know, the majority of victims are females. The international interdisciplinary journal *Violence Against Women* was first published in March 1995 as a quarterly publication. But even with an acceptance rate of only about 10%, the journal quickly built up a backlog of ac-

cepted manuscripts, many reporting on cutting-edge research or highly effective interventions. To accommodate contributors and to get this work into the hands of readers as quickly as possible, the journal went to bimonthly publication in 1997; in 1999, the journal began monthly publication.

With so much research being done, an important question to address is how do we know what we know. The chapters in this part of the *Sourcebook* speak to this question. In Chapter 1, Jana L. Jasinski introduces the major paradigms that violence-against-women researchers use to frame their work and help them explain their findings. A *paradigm* is a school of thought that guides a researcher in choosing the problems to be studied, in selecting methods for studying them, and in explaining what has been found. As Jasinski shows by summarizing the main assumptions of each paradigm, researchers who use a particular paradigm tend to focus on certain issues, but, at the same time, this paradigm blinds them to the significance of other issues and also colors their view of the social world. This is not to say that there is no objective reality to the problem of violence against women or that our research findings simply mean what our favorite paradigm tells us they mean. Rather, it cautions us that our scientific research has a dualistic character: It has both subjective and objective dimensions.

DeKeseredy and Schwartz's chapter also illustrates the dualistic nature of violence-against-women research by examining the debate surrounding how researchers should define such concepts as *abuse, violence, sexual assault,* and *rape.* By citing specific examples from various research studies, DeKeseredy and Schwartz demonstrate that the way we operationalize these central concepts in our studies has serious consequences on a number of interrelated levels. For example, defining abuse in different ways influences the rate of the behavior that is reported, which, in turn, can affect the extent to which policy makers see the problem as important, which, in turn, affects the amount of money they are willing to allocate to services. On a more personal level, a broad or narrow definition may influence whether or not a woman sees herself as abused or victimized, whether or not she seeks services, and, given the funding issue just raised, whether the services she needs are even available.

Of course, in research, definitional questions become questions of operationalization. Problems of operationalization are further addressed in Sujata Desai and Linda E. Saltzman's chapter on measurement issues in violence-against-women research. Desai and Saltzman first explore the question of how to best develop operational definitions of violence against women, and then they turn to a discussion of various measurement strategies, exploring the advantages and drawbacks of each approach. They also review the major features as well as the strengths and weaknesses of some of the most widely used research instruments in violence-against-women studies.

One of the issues that Desai and Saltzman raise in their review of particular research strategies is how characteristics of the researcher may bias or affect the research process. This topic is further explored by Neil Websdale in the Special Topic in this part. Websdale has been conducting quantitative and qualitative research on violence against women for many years now. In this box, he discusses some of the challenges male researchers specifically must address when they conduct in-person qualitative research with female victims of violence. He considers traditional patterns of communication between women and men and offers advice for male researchers on how to avoid the pitfalls of conversational styles that may seem "natural" but are sexist, harmful, and counterproductive to the research enterprise.

In Chapter 4, Jacquelyn C. Campbell and Jacqueline D. Dienemann turn our attention to ethical issues in research on violence against women. The authors discuss issues that many readers would expect to find in a chapter on ethical research practices: reducing the possibility of harm to participants, protecting participants' confidentiality, and working to ensure that research findings are used responsibly and appropriately. But Campbell and Dienemann expand these topics to raise points that most readers have probably not considered, such as treating gender as an ethical issue, ensuring the safety of participants *and* researchers, and maximizing the cultural competence of the research. In their thorough discussion, Campbell and Dienemann make clear that they personally prefer the emancipatory research paradigm, which includes critical theory, participatory action research, and feminist research traditions. They underline the point made by Jasinski in Chapter 1: that the paradigm one chooses to frame one's work leaves an indelible mark on the research process, for better or for worse.

Finally, in this part of the *Sourcebook,* Jeffrey L. Edleson and Andrea L. Bible discuss collaborative research between academics and practitioners. By interviewing academics and practitioners who have successfully collaborated on research projects, and through a careful review of the literature on collaborative efforts, Edleson and Bible identify three themes of successful collaboration, as

well as the difficulties and benefits of academic-practitioner collaboration. They discuss a number of best practices for collaboration but are realistic in their assessment of the challenges faced by both academics and practitioners who wish to undertake a collaborative research project. Readers who have participated in collaborative projects are likely to find the keys to their success or failure in this chapter, and those who are contemplating a collaborative project may use this chapter as a blueprint for improving their chances of success and minimizing problems for all involved.

In short, this first part of the *Sourcebook* examines some of the most pressing issues currently occupying researchers of violence against women. Novice researchers or seasoned veterans, readers will find useful information for designing and implementing research studies. What is more, the chapters in this part provide a foundation for understanding and evaluating the multitude of studies discussed by the contributors to Part II.

CHAPTER 1

Theoretical Explanations for Violence Against Women

Jana L. Jasinski

Violence against women began to draw attention as a serious social problem in the late 1960s and early 1970s. Since then, the term *violence against women* has been used to describe a variety of different behaviors, including emotional, sexual, and physical assault; murder; genital mutilation; stalking; sexual harassment; and prostitution (Crowell & Burgess, 1996). This review will focus specifically on the two forms of violence against women that have received the most theoretical development, intimate partner violence and rape. Early estimates of intimate partner violence suggested that violence against women occurred in one out of six couples (Straus & Gelles, 1990; Straus, Gelles, & Steinmetz, 1980). More recently, the National Violence Against Women Survey (Tjaden & Thoennes, 1997) found that, in the year prior to the survey, almost 2 million women were physically assaulted and more than 300,000 women experienced a completed or attempted rape. This same survey also estimated that, in their lifetime, more than 50 million women were physically assaulted and almost 20 million experienced an attempted or completed rape.

Despite these staggering numbers, no definitive solutions to the problem of violence against women currently exist. What these studies have allowed researchers to do, however, is work toward developing theoretical explanations that will aid in understanding the problem of violence against women. By understanding some of the risk factors or causes of violence against women, more effective prevention and intervention programs can be developed. At the same time, the development of theoretical frameworks for the study of violence against women has helped eliminate myths suggesting that women really want to be raped and that they ask for it by dressing and acting provocatively. Other myths surrounding intimate partner violence suggest that women do something to make their partner angry and that if the violence really was as bad as they claim, they would have left the relationship.

Explanations for violence against women have developed within a wide variety of disciplines, including sociology, psychology, criminal justice, public health, and social work. Consequently, there are a number of competing theories, each with different implications for policies aimed at eliminating the problem. Some have argued that these theoretical conflicts are due to the presence of two distinct forms of violence, common couple violence (a form of violence that is often detected by research using large samples) and patriarchal terrorism (more commonly seen in clinical or shelter samples) (Johnson, 1995). One consistent trend, however, is that theoretical explanations of violence against women have tended to focus predominately on characteristics of the perpetrator (Hotaling & Sugarman, 1986), although characteristics of the victim have been considered, as well.

Early theory development on the causes of violence against women identified 15 theories, organized into three broad categories: intra-individual theory, social psychological theory, and sociocultural theory (Gelles & Straus, 1979b). A distinction has also been made between micro- and macro-oriented theories (Barnett, Miller-Perrin, & Perrin, 1997). Today, more emphasis is being placed on the use of multidimensional models of violence against women. Combinations of theories originally developed within a specific discipline are being used to develop a more complete explanation of the problem of violence against women. The following review of the theoretical explanations of violence against women will first discuss the separate theories developed to explain violence against women and will

incorporate the frameworks suggested by Gelles and Straus (1978) and Barnett and associates (1997). Second, multidimensional theoretical explanations will be addressed.

Micro-oriented Theories: Intra-Individual and Social Psychological Explanations

Explanations of violence against women that rely on an examination of characteristics of individuals are using a micro-level or individual-level perspective (Burgess & Draper, 1989). Theoretical explanations that fall under the umbrella of the micro perspective include social learning theory, psychopathology, psychological and physiological explanations, resource theory, and exchange theory.

Social Learning

Social learning theory is one of the most popular explanatory frameworks for violence against women, suggesting that individuals learn how to behave through both experience of and exposure to violence. Early work looking at the behavior of the offender using this perspective focused on the concept of modeling (Bandura, 1973). When individuals observe or imitate behavior, they learn what those around them consider appropriate. Social learning theory also used the concepts of classical and operant conditioning from the discipline of psychology. Classical conditioning suggests that learning occurs because of the association of a stimulus with a response. Operant conditioning suggests that learning occurs when a behavior is reinforced (Skinner, 1953).

When applied to violence against women, this theory, more often termed *the intergenerational transmission of violence,* suggests that violence is learned in the context of socialization in the family, the primary agent of socialization (Kalmuss, 1984; O'Leary, 1988; Straus et al., 1980). In particular, individuals who experience or witness violence in their family of origin learn that violence is an appropriate tactic for getting what they want. Straus and associates (1980) have suggested that each generation learns to be violent by participating in a violent family. This role allows the individual to learn that violence is an acceptable means when other things have not worked. In addition, individuals who experience violence also learn that those who hit you are those who love you the most. In other words, the family becomes the training ground for violence. Bandura (1978) suggested that violence can be learned from three primary sources: family, culture and subculture, and the media. He argued that the role of the media was especially important because media desensitized viewers to violence through repeated acts, demonstrated rationalizations for committing violent acts, and taught actual methods of aggression. Rape, for example, is aggressive behavior toward women learned by imitating rape scenes and other acts of violence seen in the mass media; associating sexuality and violence (i.e., viewing sex and violence together); perpetuating rape myths; and desensitizing viewers to the pain, fear, and humiliation of sexual aggression (Ellis, 1989).

Critics of social learning theory argue that it does not explain much of the phenomenon of violence against women. They suggest that the theory is insufficient because not everyone who was abused as a child grows up to be violent.

One review found that the rate of intergenerational transmission of violence was only 30%, implying that two thirds of people who witness or experience violence do not go on to perpetrate violence (Kaufman & Ziegler, 1987). Others have found that only a small percentage of violent individuals have been exposed to violence as children (Arias & O'Leary, 1984, cited in OLeary, 1993). Proponents of the social learning perspective have countered this line of reasoning by suggesting that although their theory may not explain all violence, it remains an important risk factor, in that individuals who experience violence as children have an increased risk of engaging in violent behavior as adults (Straus, 1991). Other research has suggested that both victimization and witnessing of violence are among the most consistent risk markers for adult violence (Hotaling & Sugarman, 1986).

Social learning theory can also be used to examine how the interaction between the victim and the offender contributes to the continuance of violence. Walker (1984), for example, used the term *learned helplessness* to discuss why women found it difficult to leave an abusive relationship. Walker argued that women's attempts to control their abusive partners, together with the abusers' unpredictable pattern of behavior, result in feelings of learned helplessness. In other words, abusive events are perceived by women as occurring without their control and, consequently, result in depression and an inability to help themselves. This learned helplessness would then interfere with the women's ability to leave the relationship.

Although the intention of introducing the idea of learned helplessness was to understand more fully the dynamics of an abusive relationship, particularly battered women's entrapment in violent relationships, the concept backfired in some respects. The idea of a helpless, passive woman quickly became entwined with the commonly asked question, "Why does she stay?" The result was a picture of a masochistic woman who is completely to blame for her situation. Responding immediately, practitioners in the field, together with feminist scholars and activists, tried to shift the blame onto the patriarchal social structure instead of the individual woman. Other criticisms have suggested that learned helplessness cannot explain why so many women have been able to get away from their violent partners. The concept of learned helplessness also portrays women as passive rather than as active individuals seeking help (Bowker, 1993). In contrast, evidence suggests that what, on the surface, may appear as helplessness is really an attempt to find some strategy that is effective. In other words, women may try a particular strategy only once because it does not work. Furthermore, informal sources of help may prove to be more effective than more formal sources, such as the police. The theory of learned helplessness also ignores the multiple dimensions in the process of leaving, including, for example, the potential for even greater violence if attempts to escape are unsuccessful or for retaliatory violence against other family members and friends, as well as the shame associated with admitting victimization to others outside the family. Furthermore, evidence in support of learned helplessness consists primarily of assessments of personality characteristics of women after they have left an abusive relationship. Some have argued that what is interpreted as evidence in support of learned helplessness may, in fact, simply be an adjustment to active help-seeking (Gondolf & Fisher, 1988). Moreover, it has also been suggested that the preoccu-pation with learned helplessness is the direct result of patriarchal assumptions of individual pathology, the adoption of a medical model as the most appropriate for treatment, and the privatization of family life (Dobash & Dobash, 1992; Gondolf & Fisher, 1988).

In contrast to the learned helplessness model, Gondolf (1988) has developed a model of survivorship. This model suggests that women are active survivors who try to escape violent relationships but are often limited by the unavailability of resources. In other words, women respond to abuse by attempting to seek help that does not exist. Rather than blaming the victim, this model places blame on the social structure that prevents access to needed resources.

Personality Characteristics and Psychopathy

Increasingly, attention is being drawn to variations in psychological pathology among batterers (Dutton, Saunders, Starzomski, & Bartholemew, 1994; Gondolf, 1988; Holtzworth-Munroe & Stuart, 1994). A psychopathological explanation suggests that individuals who are violent toward women have some sort of personality disorder or mental illness that might get in the way of otherwise normal inhibitions about using violence. According to this theory, violence is a rare occurrence engaged in by sick individuals who are different from other people (Pagelow, 1984). Some researchers have also suggested that certain characteristics, such as borderline personality organization, may interact with learned behavior to produce intense anger and violence (Dutton & Starzomski, 1993).

The importance of including personality, neurological, and even physiological factors in models of violence against women has also been suggested (Miller, 1994). Profiles of violent men suggest that they have low self-esteem (Gondolf, 1988; Neidig, Friedman, & Collins, 1986; Pagelow, 1984), are extremely jealous (Bowker, 1983b; Holtzworth-Munroe, Stuart, & Hutchinson, 1997), have aggressive or hostile personality styles (Heyman, O'Leary, & Jouriles, 1995; Maiuro, Cahn, & Vitaliano, 1986), and use poor communication and social skills (Browning & Dutton, 1986; Holtzworth-Munroe, 1992; Murphy, Meyer, & O'Leary, 1994; Rounsaville, 1978). In addition, some research suggests that violent men have greater needs for power (Dutton & Strachan, 1987). Studies comparing wife assaulters with nonassaultive men, matched on demographic characteristics, found that assaultive men had great needs for power (Dutton & Strachan, 1987). One explanation for this phenomenon is that men who feel powerless because of low self-esteem, or who feel little control over others or the events in their lives, have great needs for power. Dutton and Strachan (1987) also hypothesized that men who view intimacy with women as dangerous, threatening, and uncontrollable can become highly anxious and angry. These feelings of psychological discomfort may then lead to behaviors such as violence to control their partners and to reduce their own anxiety and anger.

Elevated levels of depressive symptomatology have also been found among individuals who have assaulted their partners (Julian & McKenry, 1993; Vivian & Malone, 1997). Depression may be associated with feelings of helplessness, and violence may be one way to eliminate or reduce these feelings (Maiuro, Cahn, Vitaliano, Wagner, & Zegree, 1988; Tolman & Bennett, 1990). In contrast, other research has found that the relation-

ship between the frequency of aggression and depressive symptomatology appears to be accounted for by a third variable, self-reported anger (Feldbau-Kohn, Heyman, & O'Leary, 1998). Other research has found that abusive men have narcissistic personality styles (Beasley & Stoltenberg, 1992; Dutton, 1994a; Hamberger & Hastings, 1990), and they are more anxious about abandonment (Holtzworth-Munroe et al., 1997) than nonabusive men. Recent research has also found that aggressive men take a longer time to commit to a relationship and have greater feelings of dependency than men who are not aggressive (Ryan, 1995).

Focusing on personality characteristics of both victims and abusers satisfies most people's need to view violence as a behavior exhibited by someone who is different from themselves. Early efforts to identify defective personality characteristics of individuals engaged in violent relationships focused primarily on the victim. This resulted in a tendency to blame the victim, often suggesting that she had a masochistic personality. The lack of any real evidence for this, together with pressure by the women's movement, led to a new focus on personality characteristics of batterers (O'Leary, 1993). Although the evidence suggests that some abusive men may have an explosive or sadistic personality disorder, this does not apply to most abusive men (O'Leary, 1993). Others have suggested that only about 10% of abusive incidents are caused by mental illness (Straus, 1980b). One of the major criticisms of explanations of abusive behavior focusing exclusively on psychological factors is that they tend to decrease the abuser's responsibility for his actions and let him off the hook (Dutton, 1994b; O'Leary, 1993). This framework also tends to overlook or minimize the contributions of social structure.

One of the more practical applications of individual-level theories has been the development of typologies or classifications of male batterers. These typologies are important because they suggest that different prevention, intervention, and treatment efforts are necessary for different types of batterers. Certain interventions may work for one type of batterer but not for another. Personality characteristics are among the multiple dimensions used to create classification schemes. For example, Holtzworth-Munroe and Stuart's (1994) typology includes among its three categories two that are distinguished by personality characteristics. Other researchers have included individual physiological characteristics as a mechanism for developing batterer typologies (Gottman et al., 1995). Regardless of the criteria for classification, the implications of this type of research are the greatest for intervention and treatment. If differences in personality characteristics are a cause, a psychological approach involving counseling sessions and perhaps including prescribed medication is suggested, whereas if physiological differences are found, a medical model for treatment would be more likely. Ultimately, however, this type of classification scheme reduces the level of responsibility that can be assigned to the perpetrator.

Biological and Physiological Explanations

The evolutionary perspective suggests that violence against women is related to the process of natural selection. The ultimate goal for males is to reproduce as much as possible to increase the chance of passing on their genes. Rape, therefore, can be viewed as an extreme response to the natural selection pressure on men to reproduce, combined with attempts by females to control the identity of their mate. Men who have difficulty finding female partners with whom to reproduce are likely to use force in the form of rape. Among intimate partners, this theory suggests that male sexual jealousy, a common personality characteristic of male batterers, developed as a way of maximizing their reproductive prowess (Burgess & Draper, 1989).

The contribution of individual biological and neurological factors, such as childhood attention deficit disorders or head injuries (Elliott, 1988; Warnken, Rosenbaum, Fletcher, Hoge, & Adelman, 1994), as risk markers for relationship aggression is another focus of researchers working from the biological perspective. Other areas of interest to these researchers include the association between aggression and biochemical factors, such as testosterone and serotonin (Johnson, 1996). Recent research that considers the relationship between physiological factors and violence has suggested the importance of looking at head injuries. The relationship between head injury and violence may be a result of lowered impulse control as a consequence of damage to various parts of the brain. Rosenbaum and associates (1994) found that more than half of the batterers in their sample had experienced a closed head injury, compared to 25% of nonviolent men. Rosenbaum et al. found that men with head injuries were almost six times more likely to be batterers than men without head injuries. Furthermore, more than 90% of the men had experienced the head injury prior to the first instance of aggression. Head injury may also be related to an increased sensitivity to alcohol, so that an individual who has had a head injury becomes intoxicated at a faster rate than someone without the injury (MacFlynn, Montgomery, Fenton, & Rutherford, 1984, cited in Rosenbaum, 1991). What many of these studies do not address, however, is whether or not the aggression is directed specifically against women, or if it is directed against anyone. In addition, a focus based exclusively on a biological framework does not take into account the importance of the social structure and effectively eliminates responsibility on the part of the offender for his actions.

The Role of Alcohol in Violence Against Women

Alcohol is the drug most commonly associated with violent behavior (Fagan, 1990, 1993), and its use is consistently found in many of the profiles of abusive men. Estimates suggest that anywhere from 6% to 85% of intimate assaults involve alcohol. Alcohol-related family assaults have been explained in many ways, pointing to the importance of the association between social context and alcohol use (e.g., fights over a spouse's drunkenness that lead to violence). In addition, other research has revealed a significant association between a family history of violence and current alcohol use and the incidence of wife abuse (Kaufman Kantor, 1990, 1993). Alcohol use has also been linked to rape (Harney & Muehlenhard, 1991; Schwartz & DeKeseredy, 1997). Abbey (1991) suggests that the relationship between alcohol use and rape may be a result of a number of factors, including expectations about the effects of alcohol, misperceptions of sexual intent, justification for inappropriate behavior, and stereotypes about women who drink. A focus exclusively on alcohol as a causal factor for violence, however, tends to reduce the responsibility of the batterer and place the blame on the effects of drinking.

Exchange Theory

The basic premise behind exchange theory is that individuals engage in behavior either to earn rewards or to escape punishment (Homans, 1967). All behavior is driven by a calculated assessment of the risk versus the return on any particular action. Violence is a means by which individuals or groups can maintain or advance their interests. Violence against women by men, therefore, can be interpreted as a means for men to maintain their position in the social structure. It should occur when the costs of being violent do not outweigh the rewards. If we begin to think about the dynamics of violence against women and the social response to it, we can see that violence is an effective mechanism of control. Historically, violence in the home has been viewed as a private matter that should not involve government agencies, such as the police. In addition, the use of violence is often associated with the desired outcome, which serves as a reinforcer.

Resource Theory

Situated within the framework of exchange theory is resource theory. This theoretical perspective has been used principally as an explanation for violence that occurs within the family (Bersani & Chen, 1988). The primary organizing concept in resource theory is the idea of power. *Power* is defined as the ability of one individual to influence the other

(Blood & Wolfe, 1960). According to Goode (1971), the family is a power system, and violence may be used as the ultimate resource when other resources are lacking. In a relationship, the person who brings the greatest number of resources into the relationship is in possession of more power. The use of violence is further influenced by societal norms maintaining its appropriateness as a method of sustaining power. Children learn from an early age, for example, that the use of force is justified in certain situations, and even the mere threat of force is an effective means to achieve desired ends.

Macro-Oriented Theories: Sociocultural Explanations

In contrast to micro theories, macro or sociocultural theories focus on the social and cultural conditions that make violence a likely occurrence. A number of explanations can be counted in the macro perspective, including the cultural acceptance of violence, patriarchy or feminist perspectives, subculture of violence, and structural stress. Sociocultural theories focus on the influence of social location (social class, education, income) on violence against women and have attempted to integrate both social structural and family processes (Kaufman Kantor, Jasinski, & Aldarondo, 1994; Straus, 1973).

Feminist Theory

The feminist perspective focuses primarily on the concept of patriarchy (Dobash & Dobash, 1979) and the societal institutions that help maintain it. Feminist analyses of violence against women center on the structure of relationships in a male-dominated (patriarchal) culture, on power, and on gender (Bograd, 1988). The main factors that contribute to violence against women include the historically male-dominated social structure and socialization practices teaching men and women gender-specific roles (Pagelow, 1984; Smith, 1990; Yllö, 1984). According to some researchers, the traditional marriage is the mechanism by which patriarchy is maintained (Martin, 1976; Yllö & Straus, 1990). Feminist explanations of violence also focus on the relationship between this cultural ideology of male dominance and structural forces that limit women's access to resources. Violence against women, therefore, is a result of the subordinate position women occupy in the social structure, and this subordination is the cultural legacy of the traditional family. In other words, violence against women is one manifestation of a system of male dominance that has existed historically and across cultures (Yllö & Straus, 1990). Violence becomes a method by which to maintain social control and male power over women. Support for the relationship between male dominance and violence comes from cross-cultural research that has found less violence in more egalitarian societies (Levinson, 1989). Similarly, other researchers working from the feminist perspective suggest that marital violence stems from inequality in marriages and marriage-like relationships (Schlecter, 1988). Applied to rape, the feminist perspective would suggest that rape is a result of long-held traditions of male dominance. This male dominance is reinforced by prostitution and pornography, in which women are degraded and treated in subservient ways. In other words, rape is the male response to social inequality between men and women. Consequently, the feminist perspective would argue that sexual gratification is not the primary motive; rather, the objective of rape is control and domination (Ellis, 1989).

Feminist explanations for violence against women tend to focus on the concept of patriarchy as the primary factor responsible for violence against women. This narrow focus, however, has often been criticized (Gelles, 1993). Although feminists have argued that other theoretical frameworks ignore gender in their explanations, at the same time, they have been criticized for their exclusive focus on gender. Critics have argued, for example, that the single-variable approach is insufficient as an explanation. In addition, Dutton (1994b) argues that broad statements regarding male privilege and male dominance are too simplistic because they ignore differences among men. Moreover, Dutton (1994b) suggests that because feminist explanations argue that structural patriarchy causes violence, the explanatory power of this perspective is limited. This is because it is an ecological fallacy to assume that macro-structural factors can predict individual thoughts or actions. In addition, there is no empirical evidence suggesting a relationship between structural inequality and norms supporting violence against women (Dutton, 1994b). Other critics of the feminist perspective argue that this framework cannot account for violence *by* women. In both lesbian and heterosexual relationships, there is evidence to suggest that women are as violent or more violent than men (Straus & Gelles, 1990; Straus et al., 1980). This evidence has been heavily criticized by feminists, who argue that it contradicts the reality seen by shelter workers and courtroom personnel and fails to take the context of violent actions

into account (Dobash & Dobash, 1992; Yllö, 1993). What remains a problem for feminist explanations, however, is the question of why, in a culture dominated by patriarchy, only a small percentage of men use violence against women.

Family Violence Perspective

Most often criticized by the feminist perspective is the family violence perspective. The family violence perspective is more general than the feminist perspective and generally talks about either spouse abuse or family violence rather than solely violence against women. The implications of this perspective—that women can also be violent—are both clear and controversial. This approach argues that violence affects all family relationships and that the origin of the problem is in the nature of the family structure. Straus (1990c) suggests a number of characteristics unique to the family that make it prone to violence. For example, he argues that families legitimate violence by using corporal punishment and accepting violence as one solution to family conflict. In other words, the marriage license is a license to hit. Straus also suggests that families provide basic training in the use of violence through physical punishment, thus creating a link between love and violence. Finally, family membership is only semivoluntary. Both children and adults cannot easily—or, in the case of children, legally—leave a family, thereby necessitating some form of conflict resolution.

The tension that exists between those who support the family violence perspective and those who support the feminist perspective is not easily resolvable. One of the most divisive issues is that of violence by women. Proponents of the family violence perspective have found that women are as violent, if not more violent, than men (Stets & Straus, 1990; Straus et al., 1980). Much of the research indicating high levels of violence by women has used the Conflict Tactics Scales (Straus, 1979, 1990a, 1990b), a research instrument that has been criticized by many feminist researchers for its simplicity and lack of context (Desai & Saltzman, Chapter 2, this volume; Dobash & Dobash, 1979; Kurz, 1997). In contrast, feminist researchers argue that data taken from emergency rooms, victimization surveys, shelter interviews, and police arrests suggest that women are the victims in 90% to 95% of cases (Kurz, 1997). Feminists argue that proponents of the family violence perspective shift the focus away from women as victims and, as a consequence, may unintentionally assist in the reallocation of vital resources. At least one study has attempted to reconcile the two perspectives by testing hypotheses from both the family violence and feminist perspectives (Anderson, 1997). The results of this study suggest support for both perspectives.

Subculture of Violence

The subculture of violence perspective was originally developed to explain violent actions committed by young, lower-class, minority men (Wolfgang, 1958). This theoretical perspective suggests that certain groups in society may be more likely than other groups to accept the use of violence in specific situations. In these subcultures, violence is viewed as acceptable and is even encouraged. In particular, this framework argues that individuals who are part of the lower class are more likely to subscribe to the use of violence than are individuals from higher social classes, because violence is a way of life for them (Wolfgang & Ferracuti, 1982). Applied to violence against women, this perspective would suggest that some groups maintain values that justify wife beating. More recent work using this perspective suggests that violence against women is more likely to occur when male peer subgroups reinforce values that condone violent behavior (Bowker, 1983a). Schwartz and DeKeseredy's (1997) development of the male peer support-group model to explain rape (described in detail later in this chapter) is also based to some extent on this theoretical framework.

Cultural Acceptance of Violence

U.S. society features both a high level of actual violence and norms that glorify both aggression and violence. Violent movies make millions of dollars, and attendance at violent sporting events is high. There is also a continuing debate about the appropriate use of corporal punishment by parents (Straus, Larzelere, & Rosemond, 1994). Some researchers have argued that this cultural approval of violence may actually spill over into other areas of interpersonal interaction and contribute to the use of violence against women (Baron & Straus, 1989; Straus, 1977). Specifically, Baron and Straus (1989) argue that the more societies endorse the use of violence or physical force as a legitimate means to achieve desired ends, the more likely this approval will carry over into other areas, such as violence against women. Other evidence supporting the relationship between normative approval of violence and actual violent behavior has found that levels of approval have decreased at the same time that there is evidence of a decreasing amount of violence (Straus & Gelles, 1986; Straus, Kaufman Kantor, & Moore, 1997). This perspective, however, cannot explain why only some men use violence against women.

Stress

Stress has been viewed primarily as a significant risk factor for violence against women that occurs in the context of the family (Farrington, 1986; Gelles & Straus, 1979a; McCubbin et al., 1980; Straus, 1980a). Farrington (1980) has suggested that when individuals or groups are faced with stressors, they can either master or fail to master the stressors. If they fail to master the stressor, stress levels can increase and potentially lead to violence. According to Farrington (1980), structural variables such as social status and the organization of the family institution act as stressor stimuli, imposing demands on individuals and families. In fact, the family is an institution with particularly high levels of conflict and stress (Straus, 1990c). When the demands reach a level that is intolerable, violence may be used as an acceptable response to the stressful situation.

Multidimensional Theories

Well-developed, integrated explanations of violence against women might contain both social factors (such as race, class, gender, and culture) and individual characteristics or characteristics of the relationship (e.g., social support, relationship dynamics, alcohol or drug use, and personality characteristics). Several such models have been created, including Gelles's (1983) multidimensional explanation for violence against women using the principles of both exchange theory and social control theory.

Exchange theory assumes that all human interaction is guided by the pursuit of rewards and the avoidance of punishment. Control theory suggests that deviant or criminal behavior will occur in the absence of societal controls to sanction the behavior. Applying this multidimensional model to violence against women, Gelles (1983) argues that violence and abuse are higher when the rewards of this behavior exceed the costs (exchange theory). In addition, the private nature of some institutions, such as the family, as well as the reluctance of institutions to intervene (control theory), assists in reducing the costs of violence. Furthermore, cultural approval of the use of violence serves to increase the rewards for this behavior. In other words, men hit women because they can.

Gender and Violence

Another model, developed by Anderson (1997), combines elements of both feminist and family violence frameworks to explain domestic violence. Researchers using feminist theory and those using the family violence perspective have often been at odds with each other over the role of the patriarchal system in violence against women. According to Anderson (1997), this is primarily due to the use of different methodologies. The problem, as outlined by Anderson (1997), is that some domestic violence researchers do not include gender in their analysis, and some feminist researchers have not considered that factors other than gender may influence how power is constructed. The solution to this theoretical conflict may be to frame the analysis of violence against women in terms of gender theory. Gender theory suggests that men and women view violence differently and that violence is one means of constructing masculinity. Elements of the social system that serve to maintain a patriarchal system may increase the risk for violence against women because they influence the power structure within intimate relationships and support relationships in which males have a higher relative status than females.

Male Peer-Support Model

Male peer-support theory, developed by Schwartz and DeKeseredy (1997), combines both micro and macro factors into a model designed to explain violence, especially rape, against college women. This model suggests that a number of factors (a patriarchal social structure, male peer social support, membership in social groups, alcohol use, and a lack of deterrence) contribute to the increased likelihood of a rape occurring. For example, the patriarchal social structure (sometimes referred to as a "rape culture") influences the way men are socialized. In particular, men learn that it is acceptable to dominate and control women. Men also learn from these influences that women are to be objectified. Alcohol is also included in this model, as it is often a vital part of male peer groups and is sometimes used to render women unable to resist sexual aggression. Male peer-support groups serve to reinforce and maintain patriarchal values, including a narrow defi-

nition of masculinity. This definition suggests that real men are not controlled by women, they obtain sexual gratification when they desire it, and they do not accept attacks on their masculinity. Male peer-support groups also reinforce group solidarity through secrecy and serve to maintain the message that their actions are acceptable. Finally, the absence of deterrence in the form of negative societal sanctions also serves to increase the likelihood of rape. Date or acquaintance rape is difficult to prosecute and often is not even considered a crime. In other words, a combination of both social structural and individual factors contributes to the increased likelihood that men will rape women.

Social Etiological Model

Heron, Javier, McDonald-Gomez, and Adlerstein (1994) outline a multidimensional interactive model of violence and aggression that incorporates both structural and personal factors. At the societal level, they argue that violence is the result of structural inequality, which establishes a pattern of exploitation and domination of one group by another. According to this model, violence against women is the result of the inequalities inherent in the structure of the social system. In particular, the organization of the family contributes to the likelihood of violence occurring. At the personal level, individuals may use violence to resolve conflicts, particularly when they want to gain or regain control. Violent individuals also tend to have distortions of reality and morality. Abuse, for example, may be justified in the abuser's mind as a form of punishment. Furthermore, the abuser may feel that he has the right to administer the abuse. It is this combination of structural factors and personal characteristics that Heron et al. (1994) argue will provide a more complete explanation of violence.

Conclusion

The development of the research on violence against women has proceeded within a variety of specific disciplines rather than under the umbrella of one particular discipline. Although this resulted in a diversity of research designs, another consequence has been the emergence of multiple theoretical frameworks. Individually, each addresses only part of the issue. More recently, however, the trend has moved toward the development of multidimensional theories of violence that take into account social structural factors as well as individual characteristics. Theories on the causes of violence against women provide a framework for understanding and responding to this phenomenon. Thus, the more integrated and encompassing the theoretical model, the more valid the model will be for the purpose of predicting violence and aiding practitioners and policy makers. Acknowledging the existence of multiple risk factors is an important step in understanding the dynamics of violence against women. In addition, a greater awareness of the complexities of the patterns of violent relationships will also improve targeting by intervention programs and, thus, improve allocation of funding and other resources.

References

Abbey, A. (1991). Acquaintance rape and alcohol consumption on college campuses: How are they linked? *Journal of American College Health, 39,* 165-169.

Anderson, K. L. (1997). Gender, status, and domestic violence: An integration of feminist and family violence approaches. *Journal of Marriage and the Family, 59,* 655-669.

Arias, I., & O'Leary, K. D. (1984, November). *Factors moderating the intergenerational transmission of marital aggression.* Paper presented at the 18th Annual Meeting of the Association for the Advancement of Behavior Therapy, Philadelphia, PA.

Bandura, A. (1973). *Aggression: A social learning analysis.* Englewood Cliffs, NJ: Prentice Hall.

Bandura, A. (1978). *Social learning theory of aggression.* Englewood Cliffs, NJ: Prentice Hall.

Barnett, O. W., Miller-Perrin, C. L., & Perrin, R. D. (1997). *Family violence across the lifespan: An introduction.* Thousand Oaks, CA: Sage.

Baron, L., & Straus, M. A. (1989). *Four theories of rape in American society: A state-level analysis.* New Haven, CT: Yale University Press.

Beasley, R., & Stoltenberg, C. D. (1992). Personality characteristics of male spouse abusers. *Professional Psychology: Research and Practice, 23,* 310-317.

Bersani, C. A., & Chen, H. T. (1988). Sociological perspectives in family violence. In V. B. Van Hasselt, R. L. Morrison, A. S. Bellack, & M. Hersen (Eds.), *Handbook of family violence* (pp. 57-88). New York: Plenum.

Blood, R. O., & Wolfe, D. M. (1960). *Husbands and wives: The dynamics of married living.* Glencoe, IL: Free Press.

Bograd, M. (1988). Feminist perspectives on wife abuse: An introduction. In K. Yllö & M. Bograd (Eds.), *Feminist perspectives on wife abuse* (pp. 11-28). Newbury Park, CA: Sage.

Bowker, L. H. (1983a). *Beating wife beating.* Lexington, MA: Lexington Books.

Bowker, L. H. (1983b). Marital rape: A distinct syndrome? *Social Casework, 64,* 347-352.

Bowker, L. H. (1993). A battered woman's problems are social, not psychological. In R. J. Gelles & D. R. Loseke (Eds.), *Current controversies on family violence* (pp. 154-165). Newbury Park, CA: Sage.

Browning, J., & Dutton, D. (1986). Assessment of wife assault with the Conflict Tactics Scale: Using couple data to quantify the differential reporting effect. *Journal of Marriage and the Family, 48,* 375-379.

Burgess, R. L., & Draper, P. (1989). The explanation of family violence: The role of biological, behavioral, and cultural selection. In L. Ohlin & M. Tonry (Eds.), *Family violence* (Vol. 11, pp. 59-116). Chicago: University of Chicago Press.

Crowell, N. A., & Burgess, A. W. (1996). *Understanding violence against women.* Washington, DC: National Academy Press.

Dobash, R. E., & Dobash, R. P. (1979). *Violence against wives: A case against the patriarchy.* New York: Free Press.

Dobash, R. E., & Dobash, R. P. (1992). *Women, violence, and social change.* New York: Routledge.

Dutton, D. G. (1994a). The origin and structure of the abusive personality. *Journal of Personality Disorders, 8,* 181-191.

Dutton, D. G. (1994b). Patriarchy and wife assault: The ecological fallacy. *Violence and Victims, 9,* 167-182.

Dutton, D. G., Saunders, K., Starzomski, A., & Bartholemew, K. (1994). Intimacy-anger and insecure attachments as precursors of abuse in intimate relationships. *Journal of Applied Social Psychology, 24,* 1367-1386.

Dutton, D. G., & Starzomski, A. J. (1993). Borderline personality in perpetrators of psychological and physical abuse. *Violence and Victims, 8,* 327-337.

Dutton, D. G., & Strachan, C. E. (1987). Motivational needs for power and spouse-specific assertiveness in assaultive and nonassaultive men. *Violence and Victims, 2,* 145-156.

Elliott, F. A. (1988). Neurological factors. In V. B. Van Hasselt, R. L. Morrison, A. S. Bellack, & M. Hersen (Eds.), *Handbook of family violence* (pp. 359-382). New York: Plenum.

Ellis, L. (1989). *Theories of rape: Inquiries into the causes of sexual aggression.* New York: Hemisphere.

Fagan, J. (1990). Intoxication and aggression. In M. Tonry & J. Q. Wilson (Eds.), *Drugs and crime* (pp. 241-320). Chicago: University of Chicago Press.

Fagan, J. (1993). *Set and setting revisited: Influences of alcohol and illicit drugs on the social context of violent events.* Rockville, MD: National Institute on Alcohol Abuse and Alcoholism Research.

Farrington, K. (1980). Stress and family violence. In M. A. Straus & G. T. Hotaling (Eds.), *The social causes of husband-wife violence.* Minneapolis: University of Minnesota Press.

Farrington, K. (1986). The application of stress theory to the study of family violence: Principles, problems, and prospects. *Journal of Family Violence, 1,* 131-147.

Feldbau-Kohn, S., Heyman, R. E., & O'Leary, K. D. (1998). Major depressive disorder and depressive symptomatology as predictors of husband to wife physical aggression. *Violence and Victims, 13,* 347-360.

Gelles, R. J. (1983). An exchange/social control theory. In D. Finkelhor, R. J. Gelles, G. T. Hotaling, & M. A. Straus (Eds.), *The dark side of families: Current family violence research* (pp. 151-165). Beverly Hills, CA: Sage.

Gelles, R. J. (1993). Through a sociological lens: Social structure and family violence. In R. J. Gelles & D. R. Loseke (Eds.), *Current controversies on family violence* (pp. 31-46). Newbury Park, CA: Sage.

Gelles, R. J., & Straus, M. A. (1979a). Determinants of violence in the family: Toward a theoretical integration. In W. R. Burr, R. Hill, F. I. Nye, & I. L. Reiss (Eds.), *Contemporary theories about the family* (Vol. 1). New York: Free Press.

Gelles, R. J., & Straus, M. A. (1979b). Violence in the American family. *Journal of Social Issues, 35,* 15-39.

Gondolf, E. W. (1988). Who are those guys? Toward a behavioral typology of batterers. *Violence and Victims, 3,* 187-203.

Gondolf, E. W., & Fisher, E. R. (1988). *Battered women as survivors: An alternative to treating learned helplessness.* Lexington, MA: Lexington Books.

Goode, W. J. (1971). Force and violence in the family. *Journal of Marriage and the Family, 33,* 624-636.

Gottman, J. M., Jacobson, N. S., Rushe, R. H., Shortt, J. W., Babcock, J., La Taillade, J. J., & Waltz, J. (1995). The relationship between heart rate reactivity, emotionally aggressive behavior, and general violence in batterers. *Journal of Family Psychology, 9,* 227-248.

Hamberger, L. K., & Hastings, J. E. (1990). Recidivism following spouse abuse abatement counseling: Treatment implications. *Violence and Victims, 5,* 157-170.

Harney, P. A., & Muehlenhard, C. L. (1991). Factors that increase the likelihood of victimization. In A. Parrot & L. Bechhofer (Eds.), *Acquaintance rape: The hidden crime* (pp. 159-175). New York: John Wiley.

Heron, W. G., Javier, R. A., McDonald-Gomez, M., & Adlerstein, L. K. (1994). Sources of family violence. *Journal of Social Distress and the Homeless, 3,* 213-228.

Heyman, R. E., O'Leary, K. D., & Jouriles, E. N. (1995). Alcohol and aggressive personality styles: Potentiators of serious physical aggression against wives? *Journal of Family Psychology, 9,* 44-57.

Holtzworth-Munroe, A. (1992). Social skill deficits in maritally violent men: Interpreting the data using a social information processing model. *Clinical Psychology Review, 12,* 605-617.

Holtzworth-Munroe, A., & Stuart, G. L. (1994). Typologies of male batterers: Three subtypes and the differences among them. *Psychological Bulletin, 116,* 476-497.

Holtzworth-Munroe, A., Stuart, G. L., & Hutchinson, G. (1997). Violent versus nonviolent husbands: Differences in attachment patterns, dependency, and jealousy. *Journal of Family Psychology, 11,* 314-331.

Homans, G. C. (1967). Fundamental social processes. In N. Smelser (Ed.), *Sociology* (pp. 549-593). New York: John Wiley.

Hotaling, G. T., & Sugarman, D. B. (1986). An analysis of risk markers in husband to wife violence: The current state of knowledge. *Violence and Victims, 1,* 101-124.

Johnson, H. C. (1996). Violence and biology: A review of the literature. *Families in Society: The Journal of Contemporary Human Services, 77,* 3-18.

Johnson, M. P. (1995). Patriarchal terrorism and common couple violence: Two forms of violence against women. *Journal of Marriage and the Family, 57,* 283-294.

Julian, T. W., & McKenry, P. C. (1993). Mediators of male violence toward female intimates. *Journal of Family Violence, 8,* 39-56.

Kalmuss, D. (1984). The intergenerational transmission of marital aggression. *Journal of Marriage and the Family, 46,* 11-19.

Kaufman, J., & Ziegler, E. (1987). Do abused children become abusive parents? *American Journal of Orthopsychiatry, 57,* 186-192.

Kaufman, G. Kantor. (1990, November). *Ethnicity, alcohol, and family violence: A structural and cultural interpretation.* Paper presented at the annual meeting of the American Society of Criminology, Baltimore, MD.

Kaufman, G. Kantor. (1993). Refining the brushstrokes in portraits of alcohol and wife assaults. In *Alcohol and interpersonal violence: Fostering multidisciplinary perspectives* (NIH Research Monograph No. 24, pp. 281-290). Rockville, MD: U.S. Department of Health and Human Services.

Kaufman, G. Kantor, Jasinski, J. L., & Aldarondo, E. (1994). Sociocultural status and incidence of marital violence in Hispanic families. *Violence and Victims, 9,* 207-222.

Kurz, D. (1997). Violence against women or family violence? Current debates and future directions. In L. L. O'Toole & J. Schiffman (Eds.), *Gender violence: Interdisciplinary perspectives* (pp. 443-453). New York: New York University Press.

Levinson, D. (1989). *Family violence in cross-cultural perspective* (Vol. 1). Newbury Park, CA: Sage.

MacFlynn, G., Montgomery, E. A., Fenton, G. W., & Rutherford, W. H. (1984). Measurement of reaction time following minor head injury. *Journal of Neurology, Neurosurgery, and Psychiatry, 47,* 1326-1331.

Maiuro, R. D., Cahn, T. S., & Vitaliano, P. P. (1986). Assertiveness deficits and hostility in domestically violent men. *Violence and Victims, 1,* 279-289.

Maiuro, R. D., Cahn, T. S., Vitaliano, P. P., Wagner, B. C., & Zegree, J. B. (1988). Anger, hostility, and depression in domestically violent versus generally assaultive men and nonviolent control subjects. *Journal of Consulting and Clinical Psychology, 56,* 17-23.

Martin, D. (1976). *Battered wives.* New York: Praeger.

McCubbin, H. I., Joy, C. B., Cauble, A. E., Comeau, J. K., Patterson, J. M., & Needle, R. H. (1980). Family stress and coping: A decade review. *Journal of Marriage and the Family, 42,* 855-871.

Miller, S. L. (1994). Expanding the boundaries: Toward a more inclusive and integrated study of intimate violence. *Violence and Victims, 9,* 183-194.

Murphy, C. M., Meyer, S. L., & O'Leary, K. D. (1994). Dependency characteristics of partner assaultive men. *Journal of Abnormal Psychology, 103,* 729-735.

Neidig, P. H., Friedman, D. H., & Collins, B. S. (1986). Attitudinal characteristics of males who have engaged in spouse abuse. *Journal of Family Violence, 1,* 223-233.

OLeary, D. (1993). Through a psychological lens: Personality traits, personality disorders, and levels of violence. In R. Gelles & D. Loseke (Eds.), *Current controversies on family violence* (pp. 7-30). Newbury Park, CA: Sage.

O'Leary, K. D. (1988). Physical aggression between spouses: A social learning theory perspective. In V. B. Van Hasselt, R. L. Morrison, A. S. Bellack, & M. Hersen (Eds.), *Handbook of family violence* (pp. 31-56). New York: Plenum.

Pagelow, M. D. (1984). *Family violence.* New York: Praeger.

Rosenbaum, A. (1991). The neuropsychology of marital aggression. In J. S. Milner (Ed.), *Neuropsychology of aggression* (pp. 167-179). Boston: Kluwer Academic Publishers.

Rosenbaum, A., Hoge, S. K., Adelman, S. A., Warnken, W. J., Fletcher, K. E., & Kane, R. L. (1994). Head injury in partner-abusive men. *Journal of Consulting and Clinical Psychology, 62,* 1187-1193.

Rounsaville, B. (1978). Theories in marital violence: Evidence from a study of battered women. *Victimology, 3,* 11-31.

Ryan, K. (1995). Do courtship-violent men have characteristics associated with a "battering personality"? *Journal of Family Violence, 10,* 99-120.

Schechter, S. (1988). Building bridges between activists, professionals, and researchers. In K. Yllö & M. Bograd (Eds.), *Feminist perspectives on wife abuse* (pp. 299-312). Newbury Park, CA: Sage.

Schwartz, M. D., & DeKeseredy, W. S. (1997). *Sexual assault on the college campus: The role of male peer support.* Thousand Oaks, CA: Sage.

Skinner, B. F. (1953). *Science and human behavior.* New York: Macmillan.

Smith, M. D. (1990). Patriarchal ideology and wife beating: A test of a feminist hypothesis. *Violence and Victims, 5,* 257-273.

Stets, J. E., & Straus, M. A. (1990). Gender differences in reporting of marital violence and its medical and psychological consequences. In M. A. Straus & R. J. Gelles (Eds.), *Physical violence in American families: Risk factors and adaptations to violence in 8,145 families* (pp. 151-165). New Brunswick, NJ: Transaction.

Straus, M. A. (1973). A general systems theory approach to a theory of violence between family members. *Social Science Information, 12,* 105.

Straus, M. A. (1977). Wife beating: How common and why? *Victimology, 1,* 54-76.

Straus, M. A. (1979). Measuring intrafamily conflict and violence: The Conflict Tactics (CTS) Scales. *Journal of Marriage and the Family, 41,* 75-88.

Straus, M. A. (1980a). Social stress and marital violence in a national sample of American families. In F. Wright, C. Bahn, & R. W. Rieber (Eds.), *Forensic psychology and psychiatry* (Vol. 347, pp. 229-250). New York Academy of Sciences.

Straus, M. A. (1980b). A sociological perspective on the causes of family violence. In M. G. Green (Ed.), *Violence and the family* (pp. 7-31). Boulder, CO: Westview.

Straus, M. A. (1990a). The Conflict Tactics Scales and its critics: An evaluation and new data on validity and reliability. In M. A. Straus & R. J. Gelles (Eds.), *Physical violence in American families: Risk factors and adaptations to violence in 8,145 families* (pp. 49-73). New Brunswick, NJ: Transaction.

Straus, M. A. (1990b). New scoring methods for violence and new norms for the Conflict Tactics Scales. In M. A. Straus & R. J. Gelles (Eds.), *Physical violence in American families: Risk factors and adaptations to violence in 8,145 families* (pp. 341-367). New Brunswick, NJ: Transaction.

Straus, M. A. (1990c). Social stress and marital violence in a national sample of American families. In M. A. Straus & R. J. Gelles (Eds.), *Physical violence in American families: Risk factors and adaptations to violence in 8,145 families* (pp. 181-201). New Brunswick, NJ: Transaction.

Straus, M. A. (1991). New theory and old canards about family violence research. *Social Problems, 38,* 180-197.

Straus, M. A., & Gelles, R. J. (1986). Societal change and change in family violence from 1975 to 1985 as revealed by two national surveys. *Journal of Marriage and the Family, 48,* 465-479.

Straus, M. A., & Gelles, R. J. (Eds.). (1990). *Physical violence in American families: Risk factors and adaptations to violence in 8,145 families.* New Brunswick, NJ: Transaction.

Straus, M. A., Gelles, R. J., & Steinmetz, S. (1980). *Behind closed doors: Violence in the American family.* Garden City, NJ: Anchor Press.

Straus, M. A., Kaufman Kantor, G., & Moore, D. W. (1997). Change in cultural norms approving marital violence from 1968 to 1994. In G. Kaufman Kantor & J. L. Jasinski (Eds.), *Out of the darkness: Contemporary perspectives on family violence* (pp. 3-16). Thousand Oaks, CA: Sage.

Straus, M. A., Larzelere, R. E., & Rosemond, J. K. (1994). Should the use of corporal punishment by parents be considered child abuse? In M. A. Mason & E. Gambrill (Eds.), *Debating children's lives: Current controversies on children and adolescents* (pp. 196-222). Thousand Oaks, CA: Sage.

Tjaden, P., & Thoennes, N. (1997). *The prevalence and consequences of partner violence: Findings from the National Violence Against Women Survey.* Unpublished manuscript, Center for Policy Research, Denver, CO.

Tolman, R. M., & Bennett, L. W. (1990). A review of quantitative research on men who batter. *Journal of Interpersonal Violence, 5,* 87-118.

Vivian, D., & Malone, J. (1997). Relationship factors and depressive symptomatology associated with mild and severe husband-to-wife physical aggression. *Violence and Victims, 12,* 3-18.

Walker, L. E. (1984). *The battered woman syndrome.* New York: Springer.

Warnken, W. J., Rosenbaum, A., Fletcher, K. E., Hoge, S. K., & Adelman, S. A. (1994). Head injured males: A population at risk for relationship aggression. *Violence and Victims, 9,* 153-166.

Wolfgang, M., & Ferracuti, F. (1982). *The subculture of violence* (2nd ed.). London: Tavistock.

Wolfgang, M. E. (1958). *Patterns in criminal homicide.* Philadelphia: University of Pennsylvania Press.

Yllö, K. (1984). The status of women, martial equality, and violence against wives. *Journal of Family Issues, 5,* 307-320.

Yllö, K. (1993). Through a feminist lens: Gender, power, and violence. In R. J. Gelles & D. R. Loseke (Eds.), *Current controversies on family violence* (pp. 47-62). Newbury Park, CA: Sage.

Yllö, K., & Straus, M. A. (1990). Patriarchy and violence against wives: The impact of structural and normative factors. In M. A. Straus & R. J. Gelles (Eds.), *Physical violence in American families: Risk factors and adaptations to violence in 8,145 families* (pp. 383-399). New Brunswick, NJ: Transaction.

CHAPTER 2

Definitional Issues

Walter S. DeKeseredy
Martin D. Schwartz

From a start that might best be called slow, the number of studies on violence against women has increased dramatically in recent years. For many years, *violence* was just one category in the various abstracting services of different disciplines, but now, an interdisciplinary set of abstracts just in this one field is warranted. *Violence & Abuse Abstracts: Current Literature in Interpersonal Violence* summarizes more than 1,300 articles and chapters in the professional literature each year.

Still, reading these articles makes it clear that we have not yet dealt particularly well with some of the most basic questions. Is it really possible to have all of these many researchers studying "family violence" when we do not have an agreed on definition of *family* and are not even close to determining the definition of *violence*? The answer must be yes, because we do have thousands of such studies, but the lack of any such agreement

means that their utility and validity remain in some doubt.

These issues are not idle, as they affect every aspect of the research process. As a start, "specific definitions of sexual violence constitute arenas of political struggle and underpin much professional and public debate" (Kelly & Radford, 1998, p. 56). Such definitions affect the wording of questions, the specific people whom researchers interview, and the way in which researchers define the subjects they choose to study. Key among these debates, as we shall see throughout this chapter, is whether the definitions should be broad or narrow. However, there are many other potential dimensions of this debate. Just one of these, Kelly and Radford (1998) point out, is that, in many times and places, the question that informs the research process is who or what is being violated—the individual woman, the family, the patriarchal father or husband, or even national honor.

To choose one illustration, let us presume that a researcher wants to know how many women in a particular group have been raped—how common is rape on a campus, in a community, in a certain age group, or whatever. We will assume that the question is one of measuring the individual woman as the victim and that we are not conceptualizing the issue as one of a group of outside invaders attacking another group using rape as an instrument of terror or revenge.

How do you ask a woman if she has been raped or sexually assaulted? One method, not often adopted because of methodological difficulties, is to empower the research subject by asking her about her experiences and then using the woman's own definition (Kelly, 1988). The methodological difficulty is in knowing just what the research subject is thinking: Are these women using the idea of sexual assault in the same way as the researchers, the readers, and the women to whom the findings might be generalized?

North American researchers have tended to ask behaviorally specific questions. Mary Koss and many others have shown that when women are asked if they have been "raped," not many say yes. However, if the researcher describes rape and asks if this has happened to the subject, many more women say that they have had this experience. The women answering differently are not being difficult or obtuse. Rather, as feminist critics have often pointed out, in a male-dominated society, the experiences or perspectives of men are often used to develop terms that are then supposed to reflect the experiences of women (Muehlenhard, Powch, Phelps, & Giusti, 1992).

For example, throughout most of history, police, prosecutors, courts, or society at large did not accept as rape events that today are considered felony rape. Unsurprisingly, many people still hold to that older view. Many authorities personally accept rape as a crime only when the woman fights to the point of death before being overcome. If a woman grew up with that definition, but in her rape victimization, she stopped resisting before any bones were broken, she might have trouble defining what happened to her as rape—even to herself. She'll certainly know that something very bad happened, but she might not realize that the word *rape* applies. Until about 20 years ago, it was commonplace for states to have definitions that required proof of active victim resistance to maintain a charge of rape. Thus, it was a great shock to many to learn (Amir, 1971) that most victims do not use physical resistance as a tactic. Faced with a superior force such as a weapon or a much stronger adversary, they avoid death or injury by not resisting. It should be pointed out that Amir studied police files, not women who did not report an occurrence to the police because they had learned that an unresisted rape was not defined by society as a rape.

Thus far, we have dealt with the problem that research subjects might define rape differently than the researchers. Another problem is that researchers themselves may differ on what they term sexual assault or rape. It can be defined by the behavior of the victim, such as fighting and screaming (Alder, 1985; Kanin, 1967). Or it can be defined in terms of sexual intercourse that took place "when you didn't want it to" (e.g., Koss, Gidycz, & Wisniewski, 1987; Schwartz & Pitts, 1995). Sanday (1996) would like to see a definition that emphasizes a male's failure to obtain an affirmative "yes" before proceeding with sex. Most studies do not even take on these issues, but there are still questions about exactly what acts are counted. Typically, studies limit rape to penile-vaginal intercourse (Muelhenhard et al., 1992), although a number include oral and anal attacks, as well as rape by instrumentation (e.g., Schwartz & Leggett, 1999).

These are not petty points. The most powerful and repeated attacks on violence-against-women data (but the absolutely least studied area empirically) have been over specific words and short phrases that are key to many studies, such as "force," "held down," "gave you alcohol," and "you could not give consent." DeKeseredy and Schwartz (1998b) argue, for example, that in interpersonal violence, words such as *retaliation* and *self-defense* may not mean the same things to all women. Major political decisions, however, are being made on questions such as how much of women's violence against men are acts of self-defense. The most popular scale used to measure relationship violence is the Conflict Tactics Scale (DeKeseredy & Schwartz, 1998a; see also Desai & Saltzman, Chapter 3, this volume), which almost invariably shows that women and men use various forms of violence as a tactic roughly equally. Some politicians and men's rights advocates read these data as saying that women are, therefore, as violent as men and do not act in self-defense. This has been turned into arguments against spending money on shelters, services, or police involvement for women victimized by intimate violence, or even arguments for taking money away from victimized women in an attempt to locate "equality" by funding services for victimized men.

The way that definitions are drawn up, questions are asked, and data are analyzed, then, can have a major effect on the lives of many people. For the most part, North Americans are only interested in charity for the deserving poor, and violent women are not seen as deserving (Loseke, 1992). On the other hand, if women are not as violent as men, and violent women are mostly acting in self-defense against terrorizing mates (DeKeseredy & Schwartz, 1998b; Saunders, 1988), then much more sympathy is in order, most of us feel. Thus, the questions we ask (do we ask about self-defense at all?) and the way in which we ask them (what is self-defense?) can have dramatic effects on the political landscape.

Broad Versus Narrow Definitions

Of course, any attempt to simplify the debates in this field of methodological problems will only do injustice to the great complexities recognized by the better researchers, students, and workers in the field. Still, there is some value, for discussion purposes, in attempting to develop a scheme that enables us to understand some of the broad contours of the ongoing debates. A debate that will inform much of our discussion here is the one between broad and narrow definitions of violence.

The question is what should be included in a definition of violence. Typically, researchers look at physical abuse, sexual abuse, or both. Generally, few researchers look at psychological, verbal, or economic abuse, arguing (if they discuss it at all) that so many categories of abuse studied simultaneously would just cause confusion. Of course, researchers who thus argue against a broad definition of abuse tend to believe that there is a qualitative and quantitative difference between physical abuse and psychological abuse.

Typically, attacks on broad definitions have come from political conservatives, who argue that violence-against-women studies are often ideologically driven (Fekete, 1994) and are designed to artificially inflate the rates of sexual abuse to make feminist political points (Gilbert, 1994). Still, similar attacks also come from feminist quarters. Fox (1993), for example, states that "by combining what is debatably abusive with what everyone agrees to be seriously abusive" (p. 322), the latter becomes trivialized. There are also feminists who define psychological assaults as "early warning signs" of physical and sexual attacks, rather than as abusive in and of themselves (e.g., Kelly, 1994).

Those who favor a broad definition of abuse contend that violence against women is multidimensional in nature and argue that many women's lives rest on a "continuum of unsafety" (Stanko, 1990) or a "continuum of violent actions" (National Institute of Justice & Bureau of Justice Statistics, 1996). They argue that psychological or emotional abuse can be more painful than physical and sexual violence and that some women simultaneously experience different types of abuse (Okun, 1986; Saltzman, Fanslow, McMahon, & Shelley, 1999).

Narrow Definitions

Many North American crime surveys define sexual and physical violence in narrow legalistic terms. This is especially true for surveys done by government agencies. For example, the 1982 Cana-dian Urban Victimization Survey (Research and Statistics Group, 1984) and the third cycle of the General Social Survey (Sacco & Johnson, 1990) uncovered very low incidence rates of wife abuse (less than 1% and 1.5%, respectively). In this context, incidence rates refer to the percentage of women who said they were physically abused by their partners in the previous 12 months. However, most large-scale representative sample surveys that have used a modified version of Straus's (1979) much broader Conflict Tactics Scale (CTS) have elicited much higher rates (see, e.g., Ellis & DeKeseredy, 1996). As a general statement, these studies show that at least 11% of North American women in marital/cohabiting relationships are physically abused by their male partners in any 12-month time period.

In other words, if we limit our operational definitions of intimate male-to-female violence to the limited realm of the criminal law, then we will uncover relatively less violence in the family. If we use broader definitions of conflict and violence, the amount of violence uncovered is many times higher.

Similar findings can be found in studies of dating violence. For example, Statistics Canada's (1993) Violence Against Women Survey used narrow, legalistic questions to measure dating violence, questions derived from the Canadian Criminal Code (Johnson, 1996). Not surprisingly, prevalence (since age 16) rates for all women in the sample 18 years and over are not high: 12% for sexual assault and 7% for physical violence. A comparison can be made to the Canadian National Survey, a national representative sample survey of college students that used broader questions about experiences (DeKeseredy & Schwartz, 1998b). Here, the prevalence (assaults that occurred since leaving high school) rates for women were 45% for sexual assault and 35% for physical assault.

There are a number of reasons why advocates worry about low rates uncovered by some surveys. Perhaps most important is that many policy makers tend to listen only to large numbers, which has led to a tendency to prefer definitions that yield larger results (Best, 1999). When narrow definitions are used, some government officials offer these findings as a rationale for withholding funding to deal with the problem (Smith, 1994).

Another common worry over narrow definitions is that many people tend to equate true seriousness with the way in which the criminal law structures its penalty system. Such a viewpoint suggests that abuse is not worthy of attention if it is not a major criminal act. This can be a rather serious problem for victims, who often cannot tidily contain their suffering only to those areas where the legislature has mustered a majority to legitimate their abuse. For example, in many countries, a man cannot be convicted of raping his wife. In a majority of American states, a husband is still exempt from prosecution for marital rape in at least some situations (Bergen, 1996). An extraordinarily low number of successful prosecutions suggests that even where marital rape is technically illegal, it is effectively allowed. This societal tolerance does not mean that marital rape is free from major pain and suffering. Consider what happened to Lorraine, a woman who was frequently sadistically raped by her husband. In an interview with Bergen (1996), she remembered

> just waking up and being tied to the bed by my arms and legs, and the thing that woke me up was him touching me [vag-

inally] with a feather and me waking up in shock. And he had this thing about taking pictures of it all and trying to open me up [vaginally]. So he would use his fist and other objects and then make me do exercises on the toilet to tighten [my vagina] up again. (p. 18)

Narrow definitions not only trivialize many abused women's subjective experiences, they also restrain them from seeking social support. For example, if a husband's brutal conduct does not coincide with what researchers, criminal justice officials, politicians, or the general public refer to as abuse or violence, the survivor may be left in a twilight zone where she knows that she has been abused but cannot define or categorize it in a way that would help her (Duffy & Momirov, 1997).

Finally, there is an issue that should be of great worry to quantitative methodologists. We have seen that narrow questions elicit fewer responses. Are the women who do respond in fact representative of all women in the sample, or has the scientific credibility of the entire study been compromised (Smith, 1994)?

Broad Definitions

A central argument of this chapter has been that how one defines violence against women is one of the most important research decisions that a methodologist will make (Ellis, 1987). This has been particularly debated in the areas of psychological and emotional abuse. Researchers have argued that, although they do not intend to trivialize physical abuse, many women (as seen in many studies) find pressure to have sex and verbal aggression to be just as or more threatening to their well-being as physically and/or sexually violent acts (Currie, 1998; Duffy & Momirov, 1997; Kirkwood, 1993; Straus & Sweet, 1992; Walker, 1979). Many of these researchers do not deny the value of narrow definitions of violence, but they see limitations of such an approach at the same time. Dobash and Dobash (1998), for example, argue that

> A more "narrow" or circumscribed definition of violence, with each type examined in its own right and statistics gathered accordingly, may sometimes have the advantage of increasing clarity about the nature and context of a specific form of violence, but may simultaneously lose the prospect of generalizing across a much wider spectrum of violence(s). (p. 4)

Similarly, Kelly and Radford (1998) argue that an attempt to isolate certain specific illegal acts of abuse may, in fact, be useful and important for certain analytical tasks. Yet, it is essential to keep in mind the difference between analytical and experiential boundaries. For example, a researcher might choose to ignore rape for the time being and to instead devote attention to studying spousal violence, sexual harassment, prostitution, or sexual trafficking, such as sex tourism. However, it is impossible to make an experiential differentiation along the same lines, as forcible rape is an integral component in many episodes of each of these latter forms of violence.

Of course, we do not have, as yet, any single accepted broad definition of violence against women that is universally accepted. One definition that has been suggested is:

> Woman abuse is the misuse of power by a husband, intimate partner (whether male or female), ex-husband, or ex-partner against a woman, resulting in a loss of dignity, control, and safety as well as a feeling of powerlessness and entrapment experienced by the woman who is the direct victim of ongoing or repeated physical, psychological, economic, sexual, verbal, and/or spiritual abuse. Woman abuse also includes persistent threats or forcing women to witness violence against their children, other relatives, friends, pets, and/or cherished possessions by their husbands, partners, ex-husbands, or ex-partners. (DeKeseredy & MacLeod, 1997, p. 5)

There are, of course, many critics of such a broad approach, starting with Turk's (1975) critiques of broad radical or critical criminological definitions of crime that include violations of human rights. Many researchers (e.g., Gelles & Cornell, 1985), policy analysts, and members of the general public contend that definitions such as the one by DeKeseredy and MacLeod (1997) are problematic because they include "everything but the kitchen sink." For these critics, such definitions are so broad that almost every North American woman seems to have been victimized. Furthermore, some critics, such as Fekete (1994), claim that many of the behaviors included in such definitions are simply "unwanted interactions" that researchers have added to their "corrupt continuum of abuse."

Of course, including too many behaviors under the rubric of violence may result in a breakdown of social exchanges between people, as they label each other's behaviors abusive or violent (Duffy &

Momirov, 1997). Moreover, it is much more difficult to study 50 behaviors at once than to study one or two. Nevertheless, qualitative studies show that abused women reject the notion that "sticks and stones may break my bones but words will never hurt me." In fact, women who have experienced male violence often say that it is the psychological, verbal, and spiritual abuse that hurts the most and longest. Fitzpatrick and Halliday's (1992) respondents would often tell them that "they would much rather be hit than endure the constant put-downs and mind games inflicted on them by their abusive partners" (p. 76). In the long run, it is the damage to their self-esteem and their ability to relate to others that most bothers many women. One has argued,

> I was raped by my uncle when I was 12 and my husband has beat me for years. For my whole life, when I have gone to a doctor, to my priest, or to a friend to have my wounds patched up, or for a shoulder to cry on, they dwell on my bruises, my cuts, my broken bones. My body has some scars . . . that's for sure . . . I don't look like anything like I did 15 years ago, but it's not my body that I really wish could get fixed. The abuse in my life has taken away my trust in people and in life. It's taken away the laughter in my life. I still laugh, but not without bitterness behind the laughter. It's taken away my faith in God, my faith in goodness winning out in the end, and maybe worst of all, it's taken away my trust in myself. I don't trust myself to be able to take care of my kids, to take care of myself, to do anything to make a difference in my own life or anyone else's. That's the hurt I would like to fix. I can live with my physical scars. It's these emotional

scars that drive me near suicide sometimes. (DeKeseredy & MacLeod, 1997, p. 5)

In sum, many nonviolent, highly injurious behaviors are just as worthy of in-depth empirical, theoretical, and political attention as those that cause physical harm. Furthermore, physical abuse, sexual abuse, and psychological abuse are not mutually exclusive. For example, psychological abuse almost always accompanies physical assaults in intimate relationships (Gelles & Straus, 1988; Okun, 1986).

A Search for Clarity and Consensus

Defining violence against women has been a catalyst for bringing people together, including survey researchers. Unfortunately, it has also created bitter divisions between social scientists and others involved in the struggle to make intimate, heterosexual relationships safer. How do we minimize or overcome these divisions? How can we achieve consensus in defining violence against women? There are no simple answers to these questions, and perhaps there will never be a consensus. Like the study of poverty, unemployment, education, and other social problems, violence against women is a highly politicized area of social inquiry, and thus, many more new conflicting definitions are likely to be developed in the near future (Dobash & Dobash, 1998).

Still, a growing number of researchers are recognizing the merits of broad definitions. Consider the National Violence Against Women Survey (Tjaden & Thoennes, 1998a, 1998b). This study included measures of stalking, physical violence, sexual assault, and emotionally abusive or controlling behaviors. Stalking measures are important, because victims of stalking experience a substantial amount of psychological pain and suffering, and male intimates who stalk their female partners may also physically assault them. For example, the survey found that 81% of female respondents who were stalked by a current or former husband or cohabiting partner were also physically abused by the same partner. Furthermore, 31% of the women stalked by a current or former male intimate partner were sexually assaulted by the same partner. Stalking is also strongly related to psychologically or emotionally abusive behavior (Tjaden & Thoennes, 1998b).

Another leader in the move toward broad definitions is the Centers for Disease Control and Prevention (CDC). For example, the Family and Intimate Violence Prevention Team, National Center for the Injury Prevention and Control, CDC, held a series of meetings and workshops to create a set of uniform definitions and a set of Recommended Data Elements for the surveillance of intimate partner violence. In epidemiological terms, *surveillance* refers to the systematic collection, analysis, and interpretation of data and the general monitoring of a health event. The uniform definitions and Recommended Data Elements are broad in scope and focus on psychological and emotional abuse, as well as sexual and physical violence. Methods of statewide surveillance of violence against women are being pilot-tested by state health departments in Massachusetts, Michigan, and Rhode Island. These projects, funded by the CDC, are using the uniform definitions and Recommended Data Elements. These pilot-tests will likely enhance a social scientific understanding of violence against women and have the potential to influence many states to develop effective surveillance activities.

There is no question but that studies that broadly operationalize violence against women uncover more victimization and arguably provide more accurate estimates of brutal assaults on females. Interestingly, we are currently witnessing a progressive rapprochement between feminist and mainstream empirical approaches to violence-against-women research. For example, feminists have long argued that studies of domestic violence have ignored sexual violence; the Conflict Tactics Scales, the most widely used mainstream instrument in this area, has now been changed to include questions on sexual assault (Straus, Hamby, Boney-McCoy, & Sugarman, 1995).

However, a major problem still remains. Despite the trend toward using broad definitions, we still see variance in incidence and prevalence rates across studies, even when they use similar measures. This problem is due to sampling differences, different data-gathering techniques (telephone vs. face-to-face interviews), and other methodological factors. Obviously, definitional consensus does not necessarily translate into scientific consistency. Unfortunately, methodological differences are difficult, if not impossible, to overcome. After all, there is no way to make every survey researcher use the same methods. For example, as Saltzman et al. (1999) point out, no single agency is likely to collect all of the CDC's Recommended Data Elements. This is not to say, however, that some techniques are not better than others. For example, despite their pitfalls, the CTS and CTS-2 are superior to measures used in crime surveys such as the third cycle of the General

Social Survey (Sacco & Johnson, 1990). At the same time, these measures themselves have a series of built-in flaws (DeKeseredy & Schwartz, 1998a).

Let's suppose that we reach a point where all survey researchers use exactly the same measures and administer them to very similar samples. It is fair to assume that these scholars will generate similar incidence and prevalence rates; nevertheless, they will still have to deal with underreporting. It is commonly argued, for example, that many respondents are reluctant to disclose abusive experiences because of embarrassment, memory error, fear of reprisal, reluctance to recall traumatic memories, and a host of other factors (Kennedy & Dutton, 1989; National Institute of Justice & Bureau of Justice Statistics, 1996; Smith, 1994). Kupek (1998), however, argues that recall accuracy is still a larger problem than the sensitivity of the topic, so this remains an important area for future research.

Still, little attention has been paid in the literature to various validity problems. Do women feel that the wording in various questions and screening questions accurately reflects their lived experiences? If they do not feel that the questions apply to them, they will not disclose. Unfortunately, some people "hear" words differently than others. Still more will not discuss their experiences until a measure of trust is developed with the interviewer. This means that one or two blunt screening questions in a survey are unlikely to elicit high prevalence rates (Koss, 1993).

Do the questions we ask reveal the information we seek? Perhaps the most important need in newer surveys today is for measures of context, meaning, and motive. The CTS-2 has begun to introduce some measures of context, for example, differentiating between a slight slap and one that sends a person to the hospital. However, meaning and motive measures would, for example, see if some equal-looking blows were meant in self-defense or retaliation, whereas others were meant to dominate, control, or harm. Most surveys on battering ask only about violence in the context of family conflict or "spats" and not about violence that is aimed at control.

There are many other problems with surveys. One more recently discovered problem is that because so many people do not view marital violence as criminal, when women are asked in the context of crime surveys if they have been victimized, they will say that they have not (Straus, 1999), even if the behavior is clearly a violation of state criminal law. If the context of the questioning is family difficulty, there is a dramatic increase in disclosure (Mihalic & Elliot, 1997).

Another area where there has been very little study has been the influence of gender (Bograd, 1999). Although there is no question that men and women answer some surveys differently, there has been little work on the question of how often this comes from gender differences in processing the questions. People who tend to use the CTS have presumed that differences in answers reveal true differences, whereas other researchers have presumed that differences show that men do not store information about their past behaviors in the same way that women do—that men trivialize their own violent behaviors (Dobash & Dobash, 1998).

There are a number of solutions suggested in the methodological literature for some of these problems, but one that seems particularly important is the use of multiple measures of violence. Most survey researchers in this area only use one measure, such as the CTS. Thus, respondents are not given additional opportunities to disclose violent experiences. At the outset, people may not report incidents for reasons such as embarrassment. However, if respondents are probed later by an interviewer or asked to complete self-report, supplementary, or open- and closed-ended questions, some silent or forgetful participants will reveal having been attacked or abusive (Smith, 1994). For example, Smith (1987) found that some reluctant or forgetful female victims ($N = 60$) changed their answers when asked again in different words by a telephone interviewer. Belated responses increased the overall violence prevalence rate by about 10%, and 21 belated disclosures increased the severe violence prevalence rate. In addition to giving respondents more opportunities to reveal events, supplementary open-ended questions build researcher-respondent rapport (Smith, 1994).

Another commonly ignored problem is that definitional consistency, standard measures, similar samples, and multiple questions will not make much of a difference if respondents cannot understand the survey. Many immigrants and refugees do not read or speak English, and thus, it is pointless to ask them to complete a survey unless it is translated into their native language, an approach that is expensive, albeit empirically fruitful, because it results in improved response rates (Smith, 1987). Administering surveys to ethnic minority "booster samples" can generate a sufficient number of minorities to allow for complex, multivariate analyses of patterns of violence against women.

Another problem that must be considered in working with many samples is the dramatically high rate of functional illiteracy in the United States. For example, some have estimated that more than 10% of American youths are effectively illiter-

ate (Glassner, 1999). This limits dramatically the techniques that can be used, such as the development of new computer-based survey questionnaires. Even when questions are provided through computer audio, less educated youth seem to have problems (Bloom, 1998).

Conclusions

Definitions of violence against women in intimate relationships are important "because of the power conveyed by 'scientific authority'"; thus, a critical examination of these formulations is necessary (Muehlenhard et al., 1992, p. 49). This chapter shows that there is sharp disagreement over what constitutes violence against women. However, a growing number of survey researchers and some government agencies are developing broader conceptions. Nevertheless, there is great variation in how these definitions are operationalized, which in turn results in inconsistent incidence and prevalence rates. Perhaps, using standard measures and similar samples will reduce this problem. However, these techniques do little, if anything, to address the problem of underreporting. At minimum, multiple measures, translated questionnaires, and ethnic minority booster samples are necessary.

For many women, especially those who are battered, psychologically abused, or sexually assaulted, a key point to consider here is whether researchers' definitions are sensitive to their subjective experiences. Therefore, surveys that adequately address the complexities of violence against women in a variety of contexts and social settings need to begin with a qualitative component. This might include in-depth interviews with women and men, researchers, friends, family members, criminal justice officials, and shelter workers. Such information is rich and sensitizes research teams to the importance of using several supplementary open- and closed-ended questions that reflect women's subjective experiences. This preparatory research contributes to the development of broad definitions of woman abuse. Just "ask any woman" about her experiences with violence and other types of intimate abuse, and you will undoubtedly discover that she will call for a definition that includes many harmful nonphysical and nonsexual behaviors (Hall, 1985).

References

Alder, C. (1985). An exploration of self-reported sexually aggressive behavior. *Crime and Delinquency, 31,* 306-331.

Amir, M. (1971). *Patterns in forcible rape.* Chicago: University of Chicago Press.

Bergen, R. K. (1996). *Wife rape: Understanding the response of survivors and service providers.* Thousand Oaks, CA: Sage.

Best, J. (1999). *Random violence: How we talk about new crimes and new victims.* Berkeley: University of California Press.

Bloom, D. E. (1998). Technology, experimentation, and the quality of survey data. *Science, 280,* 847-848.

Bograd, M. (1999). Strengthening domestic violence theories. *Journal of Marital and Family Therapy, 25,* 275-289.

Currie, D. H. (1998). Violent men or violent women? Whose definition counts? In R. K. Bergen (Ed.), *Issues in intimate violence* (pp. 97-111). Thousand Oaks, CA: Sage.

DeKeseredy, W. S., & MacLeod, L. (1997). *Woman abuse: A sociological story.* Toronto: Harcourt Brace.

DeKeseredy, W. S., & Schwartz, M. D. (1998a). *Measuring the extent of woman abuse in intimate heterosexual relationships: A critique of the Conflict Tactics Scales* [On-line]. Available: www.vaw.umn.edu/research.asp

DeKeseredy, W. S., & Schwartz, M. D. (1998b). *Woman abuse on campus: Results from the Ca-*

nadian national survey. Thousand Oaks, CA: Sage.

Dobash, R. E., & Dobash, R. P. (1998). Cross-border encounters: Challenges and opportunities. In R. E. Dobash & R. P. Dobash (Eds.), *Rethinking violence against women* (pp. 1-22). Thousand Oaks, CA: Sage.

Duffy, A., & Momirov, J. (1997). *Family violence: A Canadian introduction.* Toronto: Lorimer.

Ellis, D. (1987). *The wrong stuff: An introduction to the sociological study of deviance.* Toronto: Macmillan.

Ellis, D., & DeKeseredy, W. S. (1996). *The wrong stuff: An introduction to the sociological study of deviance* (2nd ed.). Toronto: Allyn & Bacon.

Fekete, J. (1994). *Moral panic: Biopolitics rising.* Montreal: Robert Davies.

Fitzpatrick, D., & Halliday, C. (1992). *Not the way to love: Violence against young women in dating relationships.* Amherst, Nova Scotia: Cumberland County Transition House Association.

Fox, B. J. (1993). On violent men and female victims: A comment on DeKeseredy and Kelly. *Canadian Journal of Sociology, 18,* 320-324.

Gelles, R. J., & Cornell, C. P. (1985). *Intimate violence in families.* Beverly Hills, CA: Sage.

Gelles, R. J., & Straus, M. A. (1988). *Intimate violence: The causes and consequences of abuse in the American family.* New York: Simon & Schuster.

Gilbert, N. (1994). Miscounting social ills. *Society, 31,* 18-26.

Glassner, B. (1999). *The culture of fear: Why Americans are afraid of the wrong things.* New York: Basic Books.

Hall, R. (1985). *Ask any woman: A London inquiry into rape and sexual assault.* London: Falling Wall Press.

Johnson, H. (1996). *Dangerous domains: Violence against women in Canada.* Toronto: Nelson.

Kanin, E. (1967). An examination of sexual aggression as a response to sexual frustration. *Journal of Marriage and the Family, 29,* 428-433.

Kelly, K. D. (1994). The politics of data. *Canadian Journal of Sociology, 19,* 81-85.

Kelly, L. (1988). *Surviving sexual violence.* Minneapolis: University of Minnesota Press.

Kelly, L., & Radford, J. (1998). Sexual violence against women and girls: An approach to an international overview. In R. E. Dobash & R. P. Dobash (Eds.) *Rethinking violence against women* (pp. 53-76). Thousand Oaks, CA: Sage.

Kennedy, L., & Dutton, D. G. (1989). The incidence of wife assault in Alberta. *Canadian Journal of Behavioral Science, 21,* 40-54.

Kirkwood, C. (1993). *Leaving abusive partners.* Newbury Park, CA: Sage.

Koss, M. P. (1993). Detecting the scope of rape: A review of prevalence research methods. *Journal of Interpersonal Violence, 8,* 198-222.

Koss, M. P., Gidycz, C. A., & Wisniewski, W. (1987). The scope of rape: Incidence and prevalence of sexual aggression and victimization in a national sample of higher education students. *Journal of Consulting and Clinical Psychology, 55,* 162-170.

Kupek, E. (1998). Determinants of item nonresponse in a large national sex survey. *Archives of Sexual Behavior, 27,* 581-594.

Loseke, D. R. (1992). *The battered woman and shelters: The social construction of wife abuse.* Albany: State University of New York Press.

Mihalic, S. W., & Elliot, D. (1997). If violence is domestic, does it really count? *Journal of Family Violence, 12,* 293-311.

Muehlenhard, C. L, Powch, I. G., Phelps, J. L., & Giusti, L. M. (1992). Definitions of rape: Scientific and political implications. *Journal of Social Issues, 48,* 23-44.

National Institute of Justice and Bureau of Justice Statistics. (1996). *Domestic and sexual violence data collection.* Washington, DC: Government Printing Office.

Okun, L. (1986). *Woman abuse: Facts replacing myths.* Albany: State University of New York Press.

Research and Statistics Group. (1984). *Canadian Urban Victimization Survey, summary report.* Ottawa: Ministry of the Solicitor General.

Sacco, V. F., & Johnson, H. (1990). *Patterns of criminal victimization in Canada.* Ottawa: Statistics Canada.

Saltzman, L. E., Fanslow, J. L., McMahon, P. M., & Shelley, G. A. (1999). *Uniform definitions and recommended data elements for intimate partner violence surveillance.* Atlanta, GA: Centers for Disease Control and Prevention, National Center for Injury Prevention and Control.

Sanday, P. R. (1996). *A woman scorned: Acquaintance rape on trial.* New York: Doubleday.

Saunders, D. (1988). Wife abuse, husband abuse, or mutual combat: A feminist perspective on the empirical findings. In K. Yllö & Bograd, M. (Eds.), *Feminist perspectives on wife abuse* (pp. 90-113). Newbury Park, CA: Sage.

Schwartz, M. D., & Leggett, M. S. (1999). Bad dates or emotional trauma? The aftermath of campus sexual assault. *Violence Against Women, 5,* 251-271.

Schwartz, M. D., & Pitts, V. L. (1995). Toward a feminist routine activities theory on campus sexual assault. *Justice Quarterly, 12,* 9-31.

Smith, M. D. (1987). The incidence and prevalence of woman abuse in Toronto. *Violence and Victims, 2,* 33-47.

Smith, M. D. (1994). Enhancing the quality of survey data on violence against women: A feminist approach. *Gender & Society, 8,* 109-127.

Stanko, E. A. (1990). *Everyday violence: How women and men experience sexual and physical danger.* London: Pandora.

Statistics Canada. (1993). *Violence against women survey.* Ottawa, Canada: Author.

Straus, M. A. (1979). Measuring intrafamily conflict and violence: The Conflict Tactics (CT) Scales. *Journal of Marriage and the Family, 41,* 75-88.

Straus, M. A. (1999). The controversy over domestic violence by women. In X. Arriaga & S. Oskamp (Eds.), *Violence in intimate relationships.* Thousand Oaks, CA: Sage.

Straus, M. A., Hamby, S. L., Boney-McCoy, S., & Sugarman, D. B. (1995). *The revised Conflict Tactics Scales (CTS2-Form A).* Durham: University of New Hampshire, Family Research Laboratory.

Straus, M. A., & Sweet, S. (1992). Verbal/symbolic aggression in couples: Incidence rates and relationships to personal characteristics. *Journal of Marriage and the Family, 54,* 346-357.

Tjaden, P., & Thoennes, N. (1998a). *Prevalence, incidence, and consequences of violence against women: Findings from the National Violence Against Women Survey* (NCJ 172837). Washington, DC: U.S. Department of Justice, National Institute of Justice.

Tjaden, P., & Thoennes, N. (1998b). *Stalking in America: Findings from the National Violence Against Women Survey* (NCJ 169592). Washington, DC: U.S. Department of Justice, National Institute of Justice.

Turk, A. T. (1975). Prospects and pitfalls for radical criminology: A critical response to Platt. *Crime and Social Justice, 4,* 41-42.

Walker, L. E. (1979). *The battered woman.* New York: Harper & Row.

CHAPTER 3

Measurement Issues for Violence Against Women

Sujata Desai
Linda E. Saltzman

Violence against women is widely studied in fields such as anthropology, criminology, epidemiology, psychology, and sociology. Various disciplines define the subject differently, often making it difficult to determine accurately the nature and magnitude of violence against women. Differences in how violence against women is defined or measured result in varying estimates, which in turn makes it difficult to point to the "real" nature and magnitude. Accurate assessment is essential, however, if we are to identify high-risk populations, track changes in incidence and prevalence, monitor the effectiveness of programs, identify and understand the consequences of victimization, allocate resources, and make policy decisions effectively to reduce violence (National Research Council, 1996). Only with accurate measurement can we determine whether resource allocations, programs, and policy decisions are having a beneficial effect on victims and reducing the magnitude of the problem.

The measurement of violence against women has many facets. The most basic issue in measuring any phenomenon is how we define it. We begin by discussing the ways researchers have defined violence against women, and then, we discuss the implications of the various definitions for understanding violence against women. Once a definition is determined (e.g., violence against women includes physical and sexual abuse resulting in physical injury), a measurement strategy (e.g., surveys versus hospital record reviews) most appropriate to the final use of the data should be selected. Each measurement strategy has its strengths and limitations, and each strategy can provide different types of information about violence against women.

In this chapter, we identify critical issues involved in measuring violence against women (we include intimate partner violence and sexual violence by any perpetrator when we refer to violence against women), and we provide a basic introduction to different measurement strategies used to collect data about violence against women. We provide descriptions of various survey instruments used to collect data, and we discuss the selection of measurement strategies. We also consider implications for practice and policy, suggesting future directions in the field of violence against women.

Definitions of Violence Against Women

Components of Definitions of Violence Against Women

Most researchers agree that there are four major components of violence against women: emotional, physical, sexual, and verbal violence. The decision to include one, some, or all of these components in definitions of violence against women can differ from researcher to researcher and from discipline to discipline (Gordon, 2000). Different definitions of violence against women can result in different estimates of incidence and prevalence. For example, if we include physical and sexual violence only, the rate of violence against women will differ from a rate that includes all four components. Some conceptual or operational definitions of violence against women include the threat of violence, but other definitions require specific consequences, such as physical injury. Other definitions may or may not require psychological consequences, such as posttraumatic stress

disorder (PTSD), eating disorders, or suicidal ideation, to meet definitional criteria. Thus, rates can differ according to the components of violence considered or criteria used to define violence against women.

Differences in Definitions of Violence Against Women

Definition Differences Due to Disciplines

Scientists may define violence against women in ways specific to their discipline's methods of research. In addition, research questions among these different disciplines often differ, so researchers may define violence against women according to their potential uses of the data. Different disciplines have different goals and objectives. Within a public health approach, measurement of violence against women may focus on factors that affect physical well-being, such as morbidity (injuries) and mortality (deaths). The focus within public health is to reduce the burden of injuries on the public and the health care system and to prevent future occurrences of injuries and deaths due to violence. Traditional behavioral sciences such as psychology and sociology may focus more on risk and protective factors, consequences of being violently victimized, and treatment, because the goal is to understand human behavior and interaction. In these disciplines, researchers sometimes focus more on the victim because it is critical to identify what factors may put a woman at risk, what factors can protect her from victimization, and what can be done to treat and rehabilitate batterers. In contrast, within the criminal justice system, measurement of violence against women may be based on cases defined by state laws and may focus on perpetrators. The criminal justice system focuses more on identifying and apprehending perpetrators. Thus, rates of violence against women obtained through the criminal justice system may come from number of perpetrators and possibly from number of violent incidents. However, the number of women victimized may not be counted. Information about types of injuries and consequences may not be available. Even within the criminal justice system, definitions of intimate partner, family, and sexual violence often differ from state to state. In addition, criminologists may not use the same definitions that people employed in the criminal justice system (e.g., law enforcement, courts) use. Criminologists may focus more on the behavior of perpetrators. Thus, measured rates can differ across and even within disciplines according to criteria selected. Different criteria make it difficult to assess the scope of the problem.

Definition Differences Due to Violence Component Being Measured

Rates may also differ according to which component of violence against women is being measured. For example, if violence is defined only as physical violence, rates are different than they are when sexual, verbal, and emotional violence are also included. If violence is defined in terms of consequences, such as injury due to physical violence, rates may also be different than when physical violence, regardless of injury, is used as the definition. Rates can be different if both the threat of violence and actual acts of violence are included in the definition.

Specifying the requisite relationship between the victim and perpetrator is also part of defining specific types of violence. The definition of violence has a direct impact on the rates measured. For example, if we restrict violence against women to married women abused by their husbands, then incidence rates may be less than those found when we define violence against women as abuse by any current or former intimate partner. Therefore, it is critical to be explicit about the types of violence included in the definition or criteria being used to measure violence against women.

Uniform Definitions and Recommended Data Elements: Intimate Partner Violence

The Centers for Disease Control and Prevention (CDC) initiated a process to address the need to improve the quality of data about violence against women. The decision was made to concentrate on developing definitions and data elements (variables) for public health surveillance (the ongoing and systematic collection, analysis, and interpretation of health data in the process of describing and monitoring a health event [CDC, 1988]) of one subset of violence: intimate partner violence. A consultative process was initiated to address scientific issues related to definitions and potential data elements that might be appropriate to collect as part of surveillance activities. The result of this work, *Intimate Partner Violence Surveillance: Uniform Definitions and Recommended Data Elements,* Version 1.0, has recently been published (Saltzman, Fanslow, McMahon, & Shelley, 1999). Types of intimate partner relationships used in the uniform definitions are presented in Table 3.1. Categories of vio-

TABLE 3.1 Types of Intimate Partners in the Uniform Definitions

Current spouses (including common-law spouses)
Current nonmarital partners
Dating partners, including first date[a] (heterosexual or same-sex)
Boyfriends/girlfriends (heterosexual or same-sex)
Former marital partners
Divorced spouses
Former common-law spouses
Separated spouses
Former nonmarital partners
Former dates (heterosexual or same-sex)
Former boyfriends/girlfriends (heterosexual or same-sex)

a. The panel of experts who developed the uniform definitions determined that it was difficult to identify when a relationship begins, so the decision to include first dates was an attempt to provide a more inclusive definition.

TABLE 3.2 Categories of Violence in the Uniform Definitions

Physical violence
Sexual violence
Threat of physical or sexual violence
Psychological/emotional abuse (including coercive tactics) when there has also been prior physical or sexual violence or prior threat of physical or sexual violence

lence in the uniform definitions are presented in Table 3.2.

What Is the Research Question

Because rates are likely to be different according to the definition selected (i.e., broader definitions will produce higher rates than narrow definitions will), it is useful to understand what is being counted, for whom, and with what purpose (DeKeseredy, 2000). Within a public health domain, if knowing the number of incidents of violence-related injuries treated in an emergency department is of interest for prevention purposes, it is necessary to count discrete victimizations rather than the number of victims. However, if emergency department data are being used to determine how many women are affected by violence, counting the number of female victims may be more appropriate. Counting the number of injury incidents will result in different rates of violence against women than counting the number of women victim-

ized. Counting the number of perpetrators (e.g., within a criminal justice context) will also result in different rates than will counting the number of female victims because a perpetrator may have victimized more than one woman or may have victimized a given woman more than one time. If rates are being calculated to determine allocation of resources for female victims of violence, counting the number of victims may be more relevant than counting the number of victimizations. The number of perpetrators is more relevant than the number of victims or victimizations, for example, when determining allocation of resources for batterer intervention programs. Therefore, it is important to know what information is being counted and for what purpose.

Measurement Strategies

Various strategies are used to measure violence against women. It is important to understand that no single strategy can address every issue relevant to understanding the magnitude of violence against women. Also, each strategy has its strengths and limitations. Information regarding violence against women can be obtained through direct contact with both victims and perpetrators, and it can also be obtained indirectly by reviewing records such as police or hospital files.

Information Collected From Individuals

Whenever data about violence against women are being collected from individuals, the safety of victims should be the foremost priority. Whether data are being collected through surveys, interviews, or peer reports, participants should always be informed that they can stop participating at any time, especially if they feel they are jeopardizing their own or someone else's safety. Information about hot lines, shelters, and police services should be provided to the participants.

Information about victimization and perpetration can be obtained directly from victims, perpetrators, family members (e.g., siblings, children, parents), friends, and coworkers, but information obtained from individuals can be affected by social desirability bias. That is, individuals are sometimes reluctant to disclose information regarding victimization or perpetration because of the stigma associated with being either a victim or a perpetrator (Ammerman & Hersen, 1992; Rosenbaum, 1988). Intentional misrepresentation leads to deflated rates of victimization and perpetration. In addition, what we may sometimes assume is underreporting of victimization or even perpetration due to social desirability could, in fact, result from accidental mistakes in recall (Krosnick, 1999).

Retrospective or recall bias can also lead to deflated rates of victimization and perpetration. Respondents may or may not have difficulty recalling events that occurred during the past 6 months or year, but it can certainly be challenging for respondents to recall details about specific events or behaviors from 4 or 5 years ago or from any time in their lifetime. It can also be challenging for respondents to remember the number of times certain events occurred in the past. Recalling past events or behaviors can also pose a challenge to family members and friends. Thus, the effect of retrospective bias may result in inaccurate estimates of victimization and perpetration experiences.

The difference between intentional and unintentional misrepresentation is often difficult to distinguish, but both increase measurement error. Social desirability scales can be administered in conjunction with victimization or perpetration surveys, but doing so will increase the overall length of the interview. In addition, numerous researchers (Arias & Beach, 1987; Dutton & Hemphill, 1992; Saunders, 1991) have found that including social desirability scales did not improve the likelihood of accurate representation, especially regarding perpetration, when they were administered in conjunction with the Conflict Tactics Scales (CTS) (Straus, 1979).

Definitions and context also affect responses. Within a marital relationship, a victim may not consider forced sex to be a crime or even violence. Friends or family members may not consider violence that occurs in a family to be a crime. Information received from spouses and family members, therefore, can result in inaccurate estimates of victimization and perpetration rates.

Although representative numbers can be obtained through direct contact with individuals, the rates may be artificially underestimated due to social desirability or retrospective bias. However, if data are collected on an ongoing, annual basis, the effects of these types of biases should remain constant over time. Therefore, even though retrospective and social desirability biases do lead to an overall underestimate of violence against women rates, any significant fluctuations in the rates would not be due to these biases.

There are a number of methods for obtaining information regarding violence against women directly from victims and perpetrators. Surveys (e.g., self-administered questionnaires, interviews) are the most common. It is also possible to get information about victims and perpetrators through observation and peer reports.

Observation and Peer Reports

Information needed to measure violence against women is difficult for a researcher to obtain by observation, and due to the private nature of settings, it is rare for partner violence or sexual violence to be observed by family members or friends, with the possible exception of children living in the same household. Family members living in the same household may observe or hear the violence, but they are often reluctant to confront or report the perpetrator. It is even less likely that peers or friends will witness violence. Thus, not only is partner violence hard to observe, it may not be disclosed even when it is observed. Similarly, sexual violence can take place in isolated settings where there may not be any witnesses. If there are witnesses, they may be reluctant to disclose information because they are scared or unwilling to become involved.

Peer reports of violence against women are also rare. Peers may not be aware of the abusive situation and may not observe violence that occurs in a private setting. In addition, even if a peer has observed violence, peer reports can be affected by retrospective bias as well as by the peer's desire to protect either the victim or perpetrator. Thus, a more effective way to gather information from individuals regarding violence against women is to obtain it directly from the victims and perpetrators. Survey research (e.g., self-administered questionnaires, interviews) is the most common method used to obtain this information.

Surveys

Surveys are questionnaires that can be administered in a number of ways. They can be self-administered (e.g., paper-and-pencil format in person or through the mail; on a computer) or administered by an interviewer (e.g., telephone or face-to-face interviews). Interviewers can record responses on paper or use computer-assisted telephone interviewing (CATI). Victims, perpetrators, friends, or family members may complete surveys and interviews. In certain cases (e.g., suicides), surveys and interviews obviously need to be completed by someone other than the victim, perhaps family members or friends. These "psychological autopsies" are reliable methods for gathering information about victims and their history of previous violent victimization (Beskow, Runeson, & Asgard, 1990).

Gordon (2000) posits that to locate victims of more severe abuse, data should be collected at sites where higher proportions of more serious abuse (e.g., police reports, emergency department records) tend to be reported, rather than among the general population. Although most surveys measure only frequency, a few measure both severity and frequency of violent behaviors experienced and perpetrated, so it is possible to obtain some data from surveys regarding severity of abuse experienced.

Frequency of violent behaviors experienced or perpetrated can be recorded in two different ways: Victims can be asked to indicate the number of times they have experienced a violent behavior, or they can respond on a continuum (e.g., *never* or *rarely* to *frequently* or *all the time*).

Although filling in the number of times a particular behavior has occurred can provide a precise estimate of the magnitude of violence against women, this particular strategy can be affected by retrospective bias. It is difficult for respondents to recall the exact number of times they have been victimized a particular way, especially if the frequency is high. It is even more difficult to recall violent behaviors that may have occurred years ago, as respondents are asked to do when we try to measure lifetime prevalence. This particular strategy can also be affected by social desirability bias, especially if the frequency or severity of a particular violent behavior is very high. These biases may also occur with respondents asked to fill in the number of times they have perpetrated a particular violent behavior, also affecting rates of perpetration.

The Likert scale format, commonly used to measure frequency, provides a range (e.g., *never, rarely, sometimes, always*) from which respondents can choose. This strategy can also be affected by retrospective bias but less so than strategies asking respondents for an exact number. Measuring frequency on a continuum, however, provides a less precise estimate of the magnitude of violence against women. In addition, value labels and ranges on Likert scales are often selected arbitrarily. What means *rarely* to one respondent may mean *sometimes* to another. These labels can also have different meanings for different researchers. Differences in what these value labels mean or represent can be standardized when value labels are quantified (e.g., *never* = 0, *frequently* = 10-15). Numbers should always reinforce the meaning of the value labels (Krosnick, 1999). Although retrospective bias remains an issue of concern, carefully selected value labels can increase the validity of respondents' answers.

Surveys can produce inconsistent findings depending on the context in which a survey is administered (e.g., a survey about personal safety vs. one about crime) or the types of screening questions used to determine experiences with violence (Tjaden & Thoennes, 2000). Moreover, certain types of surveys (e.g., telephone surveys) can yield higher rates of disclosure than other types (e.g., mailed surveys). It is important to be cognizant of the fact that the context of survey questions, the type of survey methodology, or even the types of questions used to screen for victimization experiences can affect rates of violence against women.

Self-Administered Surveys

Self-administered surveys can be mailed to residences or administered in other settings, such as shelters or hospitals. Advantages of mailed surveys are that they cannot be affected by any type of interviewer bias, they have standardized instructions, and respondents have the opportunity to respond at their convenience. On the other hand, mailed surveys can result in low response rates, even when they are followed by mailed reminders. There is also the possibility that a mailed survey can jeopardize a woman's safety if she is currently in an abusive relationship. A perpetrator discovering such a survey in the household may mistakenly assume the victim contacted someone about the abuse. This mistaken assumption may then precipitate a violent incident.

Surveys completed in settings other than the respondent's home may elicit higher response rates than mailed surveys (Fowler, 1993). It is also possible that victims are safer when they complete surveys in settings other than their home. A possible disadvantage of paper-and-pencil surveys or surveys on computers that are administered in settings other than the home (e.g., shelters, batterer intervention programs) is that they can be biased by interviewer effects, such as differences in an interviewer's inflection or incomplete instructions. These interviewer effects may vary across groups, but they are likely to remain constant across large numbers of respondents. With self-administered surveys, either paper-and-pencil surveys or surveys on a computer, literacy of the respondents is also an issue. Surveys should be designed so that respondents with low reading levels can understand them. Respondents who cannot read will need to receive personal interviews.

Interviews

Interviews can be conducted by telephone or in person. Telephone interviews can produce low (less than 60%) response rates (Dillman, 1978). In addition, households without telephones are excluded from the sample. Women of low socioeconomic status may be at increased risk for violent victimization (Tjaden & Thoennes, 1998) and thus should be included in surveyed samples, but these women may not have phones. Survey methods other than telephone surveys may be more useful in reaching low SES women. Telephone interviews also run the risk of jeopardizing the safety of women who are currently in abusive relationships. As is the case with mailed surveys, perpetrators may assume their partners contacted someone about the abuse, and violent incidents can result. Instructions given to a participant prior to the start of a telephone interview should state that the participant can hang up at any time if she feels unsafe. Participants should also be provided with a toll-free telephone number to call if they would prefer to conduct the interview at another time.

Telephone interviews can be used to collect data from both victims and perpetrators at the same time, but again, such interviews may run the risk of jeopardizing the safety of women who are currently in abusive relationships. Telephone interviews can also be used to survey victims and perpetrators separately about the same or different incidents.

Face-to-face interviews can provide accurate information from both victims and perpetrators. Face-to-face interviews are usually longer than telephone interviews, and in a longer interview, it is possible to collect qualitative data, which can provide a wealth of information regarding violence against women. In addition, with training, interviewers can often develop a rapport with the participants; the establishment of rapport can increase the likelihood that participants not only will respond honestly but also will provide more extensive information.

If conducted outside the home in safe settings (e.g., shelters, treatment programs), face-to-face interviews probably do not jeopardize the safety of victims, but interviewer effects such as inflection or incomplete or inconsistent instructions can bias these interviews. Interviewers should be trained in how to establish rapport, provide consistent instructions, read items aloud, and answer questions participants might have. They should also be trained to make appropriate referrals for women reporting current violence.

A number of different measurement instruments are useful for collecting information directly from individuals. These instruments can be used in peer reports, self-administered surveys, and interviews. The following section provides brief descriptions of some survey instruments commonly used to measure violence against women. Reliability and validity evidence, when available, is also provided. Little research has been done to test the validity of most of these measures; in some cases, less stringent tests of validity have been conducted, whereas in others, more rigorous methods have been applied. Each of the following measures is useful in survey research, however, each one has its strengths and limitations. To prevent promotion or recommendation of any particular instrument, we discuss them in alphabetical order.

Selected Violence Against Women Measures

The Abusive Behavior Inventory

The Abusive Behavior Inventory (ABI) (Shepard & Campbell, 1992) incorporates both physical and psychological abuse items to which both batterers and their partners can respond. The ABI is based on feminist theory, which views physical abuse as a means of establishing power and control over a victim, rather than on the theory that regards conflicts in families along a continuum from heated discussions to physical violence. The ABI has been used only in self-administered surveys to date. It is a 30-item instrument measured on a 5-point Likert scale (*never, rarely, occasionally, frequently, very frequently*) that assesses the frequency of abusive behaviors experienced during a 6-month period. The ABI consists of two subscales. Twenty psychological abuse items measure emotional violence, isolation, intimidation, and threats. Ten physical abuse items assess assaultive behaviors, including forcing the victim to engage in sexual activity against her will. Three of these 10 physical abuse items assess sexual violence. Mean scale scores for both scales indicate the average frequency of physical and psychological abuse experienced.

The ABI was empirically tested on a sample of 178 physically abusive and nonabusive men and on their abused and nonabused female partners. Reliability coefficients for the psychological abuse subscale were .79 and .88 for the nonabusive men and abusive men, respectively. Reliability coefficients for the physical abuse subscale were .82 for both the nonabusive men and abusive men. Reliability coefficients for the psychological abuse subscale were .92 and .88 for the nonabused women and abused women, respectively. Reliability coefficients for the physical abuse subscale were .88 and .70 for the nonabused women and abused women, respectively. The authors present evidence of moderate criterion-related validity by comparing mean scores for the no-abuse and abuse groups. Construct validity was assessed by correlating subscales scores with similar (e.g., clinician's assessment, arrest records) and dissimilar (e.g., age, household size) variables.

Moderate levels of construct validity were obtained.

The Conflict Tactics Scales

The original Conflict Tactics Scale (CTS) (Straus, 1979) consists of 14 items (Form A, self-administered survey). The first items are low in coerciveness and increase in coerciveness with each successive item (a low-coerciveness item would be "discussing the issue calmly," whereas a high coerciveness item would be "slapping and hitting"). There are four items in the Reasoning scale, five in the Verbal Aggression scale, and five in the Violence scale. Form N, used with face-to-face interviews, consists of 18 items and focuses more on verbal aggression. One Reasoning scale item is excluded, two items are added to the Verbal Aggression scale, and three are added to the Violence scale. Neither Form A nor Form N includes any items that measure sexual violence. Participants indicate their responses on a 6-point scale ranging from 0 = *never* to 5 = *more than once a month*. The CTS was designed to assess conflict tactics within eight family role structures: wife to husband, husband to wife, father to child, mother to child, child to father, child to mother, child to sibling, and sibling to child. The same instrument can be used to assess any of the eight relationships by changing the key word (i.e., wife, husband, mother, sister) in relevant items. The CTS has been used in self-administered surveys as well as in face-to-face and telephone interviews.

Reliability of the CTS (husband-to-wife and wife-to-husband perpetration rates) was assessed by using item-total correlations. The item-total correlation for the Reasoning scale was .74 for men and .70 for women. The item-total correlation for the Verbal Aggression scale was .73 for men and .70 for women. The item-total correlation for the Violence scale was .87 for men and .88 for women. Concurrent validity of the CTS was assessed by administering it to college students, who were asked to indicate the number of times each of the tactics was used by their mother and their father. The correlations ranged from −.12 to .64, indicating low to moderate concurrent validity.

The Conflict Tactics Scale 2

The Conflict Tactics Scale 2 (CTS2) (Straus, Hamby, Boney-McCoy, & Sugarman, 1996) was developed to address some of the flaws in the original CTS (Straus, 1979). The CTS2 includes five subscales measuring negotiation, psychological aggression, physical assault, sexual coercion, and injury. The 78 items are designed to measure behaviors of both respondents and their partners. Respondents answer 39 questions about violent behaviors they have perpetrated and another 39 symmetrical questions about violent behaviors they have experienced. The CTS2 provides finer operationalization of the distinction between minor and severe acts for four scales (not for the Negotiation scale) than does the original CTS. Participants respond on a 6-point Likert scale ranging from 1 = *once in past year* to 6 = *more than 20 times in past year. Never happened* and *happened, but not in past year* options are also included. The CTS2 presents the items in random order as opposed to presenting them in order of increasing severity, as the original CTS does. The CTS2 includes seven items on sexual coercion and six on resulting injuries. Items measuring these two constructs are not included in the original CTS. The CTS2 uses the term *partner* rather than *he* or *she*. Items on the CTS2 read, "My partner tried to . . . "

rather than "he tried to . . . " for females answering the question or "she tried to . . ." for males answering the question. The term *partner* can be used globally for same-sex partners and can also be used for dating or cohabiting relationships in addition to marital relationships. The authors who developed the CTS2 have only used it in self-administered surveys.

Internal consistency reliability of the subscales for self-reports of perpetration, men and women combined, is .86 (negotiation), .79 (psychological aggression), .86 (physical assault), .87 (sexual coercion), and .95 (injury). There is only limited construct (moderate correlations among theoretically related scales) and discriminant (low correlations among unrelated scales) validity evidence.

The Index of Spouse Abuse

The Index of Spouse Abuse (ISA) (Hudson & McIntosh, 1981) is a 30-item scale measuring frequency of both physical and nonphysical abuse inflicted on a woman by her spouse. Responses are based on a 5-point Likert scale ranging from 1 = *never* to 5 = *very frequently.* Items are also weighted so severity scores can be calculated. The ISA has been used in both self-administered surveys and interviews.

The ISA was tested on two samples: women recruited from social agencies and protective shelters who were classified by therapists as abused or nonabused and graduate and undergraduate female students. Internal consistency reliability of the ISA was calculated using Cronbach's alpha. Reliability coefficients for the physical subscale were .90 and .94 in the clinical sample and student sample, respectively. Reliability coefficients for the nonphysical subscale were .91 and .97 in the clinical sample and student sample,

respectively. Strong discriminant validity, calculated by correlating ISA subscales with theoretically unrelated measures (e.g., quality of work, problems with friends, age, education), was indicated by low correlations. Some evidence of convergent validity (ISA subscale correlations with depression, marital problems, anxiety, fearfulness) was indicated by low to moderate correlations.

The Measure of Wife Abuse

The Measure of Wife Abuse (MWA) (Rodenburg & Fantuzzo, 1993) includes four subscales measuring physical, psychological, sexual, and verbal violence. Sixty items are included in parallel versions that can be administered to both a wife and a husband. The first set of items measures the frequency of perpetrating or experiencing the abusive behaviors (perpetrators fill in the number of times they have perpetrated the behavior in the past 6 months; victims fill in the number of times they have experienced the behavior in the past 6 months). A second set of 60 items measures emotional consequences to the victim. The MWA has been used in self-administered surveys only.

The MWA was tested on a sample of women who had been abused by their husbands. They were recruited from an outpatient clinic, a battered women's shelter, and radio and newspaper advertisements. Internal consistency reliability coefficients for the subscales were .81 (physical abuse), .73 (sexual abuse), .94 (psychological abuse), and .83 (verbal abuse). Internal consistency reliability was .93 for the total instrument. Some concurrent validity was shown by low correlations with the CTS (Straus, 1979) Verbal Aggression subscale and by low to moderate correlations with the CTS Violence subscale.

The Partner Abuse Scales

The Partner Abuse Scales (PAS) (Hudson, 1990) has two subscales, Physical and Non-Physical. Each subscale has 25 items. The Physical subscale includes items that measure both physical and sexual violence. Items are scored on a 7-point Likert scale ranging from 1 = *never* to 7 = *all the time*. The PAS is designed for use with either heterosexual or homosexual couples, as well as with dating, cohabiting, or married couples. The PAS has been used only as a self-administered survey.

In a separate study, data were collected from a group of abused women recruited from a crisis center (Attala, Hudson, & McSweeney, 1994). Data were also collected from a convenience control sample of nursing students. Reliabilities for the Physical and Non-Physical subscales in the clinical sample were .94 and .95, respectively. The authors also calculated internal consistency reliability for both samples combined. Reliabilities for the Physical and Non-Physical subscales in the combined sample were .97 and .98, respectively. Concurrent validity evidence was obtained by correlating the PAS subscales with measures of stress and contentment. Low to moderate correlations ranging from .36 to .64 were obtained, indicating moderate concurrent validity of the PAS.

The Severity of Violence Against Women Scales

The Severity of Violence Against Women Scales (SVAWS) (Marshall, 1992) measures both frequency and severity of abusive behaviors experienced by women. It has been used in both self-administered surveys and face-to-face interviews. The SVAWS includes 46 items rated on a 4-point Likert scale, ranging from 1 = *never* to 4 = *many times*. Physical, verbal, emotional, and sexual abuse are represented in the items.

Analyses were conducted on two samples: the first consisted of female college students, and the second sample was obtained by mailing the SVAWS to randomly selected women in the community. Analyses comparing results obtained from both groups were also conducted. Reliability was calculated in the student sample for each of nine factors identified in a factor analysis (symbolic violence, mild threats, moderate threats, serious threats, minor violence, mild violence, moderate violence, sexual violence, serious violence). These coefficients ranged from .92 to .96. Reliability coefficients for the community sample were not presented, although a similar factor structure was obtained. *T*-tests comparing factor scores between the student and community samples were conducted. These two groups differed only on the sexual violence score, with the community sample of women scoring significantly higher.

The Sexual Experiences Survey

The Sexual Experiences Survey (SES) (Koss & Oros, 1982) was developed to identify hidden occurrences of rape and to identify a dimensional view of sexual aggression and victimization (rape would represent an extreme behavior on a continuum with normal male behavior within a given culture). The SES has only been used as a self-administered survey. It includes 12 yes/no items that can be administered in parallel versions.

The Sexual Experiences Survey was tested on a college sample of both males and females. Reliability was .74 for females and .89 for males (Koss & Gidycz, 1985). Test-retest reliability (1-week time interval) was assessed on a smaller sample of 71 females and 67 males. The mean item agreement was .93.

The Women's Experience With Battering Scale

The Women's Experience with Battering Scale (WEB) (Smith, Earp, & DeVellis, 1995) was developed to operationalize the experiences of battered women rather than the discrete abusive behaviors they experience. In other words, a woman is asked to indicate on a 6-point Likert scale (*agree strongly* to *disagree strongly*) if her male partner makes her feel unsafe in her home, ashamed of the things he does to her, or like a prisoner, and if he can make her feel scared and controlled. Higher scores indicate higher levels of psychological vulnerability. There are 10 items in the scale. Items were originally developed through focus groups (Smith, Tessaro, & Earp, 1995) and then condensed through surveys given to battered and nonbattered women (Smith, Earp, et al., 1995). Forty items were identified through the surveys and subjected to a factor analysis. Ten items with the highest factor loadings and item-total correlations were selected to form the WEB scale.

Reliability and validity were calculated for the 10-item scale on the same sample used to develop the initial 40 items. Internal consistency reliability was calculated using Cronbach's alpha. Reliability coefficients were .93 for the battered women and .86 for the nonbattered women. Validity was tested by correlating the WEB Scale with the ISA and the CTS. After controlling for demographic factors on which the two samples differed, high cor-relations between the WEB Scale and the ISA and between the WEB Scale and the CTS were obtained, indicating strong convergent validity. High discriminant validity was shown through low correlations with a measure of social desirability.

Information Collected From Record Reviews

Information about violence against women can be obtained through reviewing records such as hospital or criminal justice databases. Data from these sources can provide information about the types and severity of violence, injuries sustained, types of services used by victims, and the number of victims using different services.

Record reviews are free of recall or social desirability bias at the time of the review, but there may be some recall and social desirability biases on the part of the recorder at the time the information about the violent incident is documented. In addition, information obtained through record reviews may represent a biased sample in that these cases represent incidents severe enough to require medical or legal intervention. However, it is important to consider that information obtained through record reviews is generally free of biases that are present when obtaining information from individuals. Collecting information directly from individuals, however, can provide information about less severe incidents as well as more severe ones.

Hospital Records

Data from emergency department, billing, and discharge records can provide information regarding an incident, the type and severity of injuries sustained, and prior history of injuries due to violence. To collect consistent and accurate data, however, health care providers may need training in screening, referrals, case definitions, and data extraction.

Data extraction based on uniform case definitions, with the cooperation of hospitals and medical care facilities in a target area, can be a difficult and lengthy process, and it is likely to be impractical. One alternative may be to identify a representative sample of hospitals and to derive estimates from the sample data.

Hospital records usually do not include any information regarding perpetrators and may not consistently provide information about incidents and prior history of victimization. Although the Joint Commission on Accreditation of Healthcare Organizations (JCAHO) standards require hospitals to screen for a variety of forms of abusive behavior, no documentation is required (CDC, 1993). The JCAHO standards also require that emergency-department patient care for victims of domestic abuse by spouses or partners must be guided by written policies and procedures; however, the standards do not offer much guidance for the content of hospital policies. Consistent with the national health objective for the year 2000, the JCAHO has recommended that accredited emergency departments have policies, procedures, and education in place to guide staff in the treatment of battered adults.

Data obtained from hospitals usually represent more serious incidents in which severe injuries are sustained. Incidents involving victims of emotional or physical violence that do not result in physical injury are less likely to be recorded in hospital files. Furthermore, information about victims who do not have access to hospitals (because they lack medical insurance or transportation, for instance) is unlikely to be captured in hospital records.

Civil and Criminal Justice Records

Civil and criminal justice records (e.g., police data, temporary protective orders) can provide information about perpetrators of violence against women, incidents of violence, and relationships between victims and perpetrators. Civil and criminal justice data may not provide information about the victim, such as injuries sustained, verbal or emotional violence, or prior history of victimization; however, these records are unique in that they may provide information regarding actions taken after the incident has occurred. From these records, it may also be possible to determine whether a perpetrator has been charged, whether a perpetrator has a prior history of abuse, and whether a perpetrator was referred to a treatment program.

Service Provision Records

Service provision records (e.g., social service data; crisis lines) can provide victim information regarding violence in the current relationship, relationship to perpetrator, types of violence, and prior history of violence. These records may also contain information about the perpetrator.

Service providers are careful about offering information to third parties (e.g., researchers, local health departments) that may put victims in danger. Because safety of the victims is often the main priority of service providers, it may be difficult for researchers to obtain records with

information that could potentially identify a victim or perpetrator. If the records
are accessible to researchers, however,
linking service provider records with
other types of records can provide more
detailed information.

Information Collected
From Hybrid Strategies

Using more than one data collection
strategy can provide more detailed information and stronger validity evidence
than using a single method can. For example, combining interviews and self-
administered surveys can provide quantitative responses as well as in-depth qualitative responses to interview questions.
Hybrid strategies provide unique information from each individual strategy as
well as overlapping information from
combining the strategies. Rates of violence against women can also be compared across data collection strategies.
Similar rates found by using different
methods within one sample indicate
higher validity than do similar rates found
by using identical methods (Campbell &
Fiske, 1959).

Moreover, using more than one data-
collection strategy enables researchers to
reach a larger population. For example,
by combining telephone surveys and hospital databases, it is possible to obtain
data from women who do not have telephones and those who do not have access
to hospital resources. While combining
strategies can increase the sample size, it
is not the perfect solution to the problem.
In this example, for instance, women who
do not have telephones and also do not
have access to hospital care will still be
missed. It is important to note that not all

data collection methods will be able to
reach all segments of the population, although combination or hybrid strategies
may reach more of them.

Hybrid strategies are generally more
expensive, and they require the elimination of duplicate counts of incidents, victims, or perpetrators to get accurate rates
of violence against women. Thus, data
linkage is necessary to avoid duplication
when counting victims, violent incidents,
and perpetrators.

Conclusion

Differences in the way violence against
women is interpreted or defined can affect
rates of victimization and perpetration.
The four major components of violence
against women include physical, sexual,
verbal, and emotional abuse; however, the
decision to include some or all of these
components can differ depending on the
researcher and respective discipline. Including only one or two of these may produce rates of violence against women that
are significantly lower than including all
four components. Similarly, if certain outcomes (e.g., physical injury, psychological trauma) are used to determine what
defines an incident of violence, measured
rates will differ. Counting incidents of violence versus number of victims versus
number of perpetrators will also affect
rates obtained. The lack of consensus
about the definition of violence against
women limits our ability to accurately
measure the magnitude of the problem,
track changes in incidence and prevalence, identify high-risk populations, and
evaluate the effectiveness of prevention
and intervention activities. The use of uniform or standardized definitions can in-

crease the accuracy of rates obtained, which can lead to an efficient allocation of resources.

Several measurement strategies are available to measure violence against women. Rates can be obtained through direct contact with individuals (e.g., surveys) and through record reviews (e.g., hospital records; police records). Survey research is generally the most widely used method to collect violence-against-women data. Despite limitations such as recall bias, social desirability bias, and often inadequate reliability and validity evidence, there are numerous strengths to survey research. Survey research is an inexpensive method for obtaining violence-against-women information from large samples. Surveys can be administered in different languages, and they can be used to obtain victimization and perpetration data; long-term consequences can be identified, and in some cases, results can be generalized to the population.

There are numerous violence-against-women measures with varying reliability and validity estimates. Some instruments measure only frequency (e.g., ABI, CTS, CTS2, PAS), whereas others also measure severity (e.g., ISA, SWAVS). Most instruments measure both victimization and perpetration. It is important to select an instrument with strong reliability and validity evidence, and that will be most appropriate to the potential uses of the data.

Record reviews can provide data such as injuries sustained, services used, and actions taken against the perpetrator. Although record reviews have some limitations (e.g., hospital records may represent a biased sample of women who have sustained severe injuries requiring medical attention; police may not be called to less severe incidents of violence), they have some strengths as well. Record reviews are generally free from biases such as re-

call or social desirability, and information about both victims and perpetrators can be obtained. There is also no threat posed to the victims or friends and family.

Using a combination of survey research and record reviews to obtain violence-against-women information may produce the most comprehensive and accurate data. Using more than one type of record review (i.e., using hospital and police records) may require the elimination of duplicate counts. Although this can be time-consuming and expensive, it will produce valid information. Survey research can also validate rates of violence against women obtained through record reviews.

Selecting a Measurement Strategy

Selecting a measurement strategy has important implications for programs, policy making, and data collection. It is important to understand the strengths and weaknesses of the different strategies. Although there is no best strategy, some strategies are more appropriate than others for certain tasks. For example, policy decisions about resource allocation for services such as batterer interventions or victim shelters might be made by using record reviews, whereas relevant research results used to determine program components might best be obtained through self-report data. Selection of a measurement strategy should always take into account the future use of the data and results.

Implications for Practice, Policy, and Research

Definitions and measurement strategies can strongly affect the types of results obtained in public health surveillance or research. The use of narrow or broad definitions and the selection of criteria can affect the rates of violence against women. It is critical to understand what rates are being calculated and how these numbers will be used. Again, the measurement strategy most relevant or appropriate to the final use of the data should be selected.

Future Directions

Widespread use of uniform definitions for violence against women will lead to more reliable and comparable results across research studies and will enable practitioners, policy makers, and researchers to understand the nature and scope of the problem. Even where definitions vary, however, explicit information about definitions or criteria used will allow us to understand the differences in research or surveillance findings.

CDC's Intimate Partner Violence Surveillance document (Saltzman et al., 1999) is intended for voluntary use to improve the consistency of surveillance. If the recommended data elements can be uniformly collected and recorded, then more accurate estimates of the incidence and prevalence of intimate partner violence can be obtained. An expert panel is currently developing uniform definitions and recommended data elements for sexual violence, using a similar process used to develop the intimate-partner-violence definitions and data elements.

More sophisticated research such as longitudinal designs can identify long-term consequences of being a victim, witnessing violence, and being a perpetrator. One way to address some of the flaws with survey research is to include qualitative data in conjunction with quantitative data.

Although it is still possible to obtain information on a wide range of topics related to violence against women by using only one measurement strategy such as surveys, combining measurement strategies, although expensive and time-consuming, can provide more information on a wider range of topics (e.g., types of injuries sustained, service use, long-term consequences of victimization) related to violence against women.

Finally, it is important to note that no single measurement strategy will provide the most accurate information (Gelles, 2000; Gordon, 2000). Rather, a combination of a number of different factors—standardization of definitions, use of reliable and valid survey instruments, and use of hybrid measurement strategies (e.g., combining self-report data with record reviews)—will provide the most comprehensive, accurate information and results needed by researchers, practitioners, and policy makers as they determine future surveillance and research activities, programmatic issues, and policy decisions about intervention in and prevention of violence against women.

References

Ammerman, R. T., & Hersen, M. (1992). Current issues in the assessment of family violence. In R. T. Ammerman & M. Hersen (Eds.), *Assessment of family violence: A clinical and legal sourcebook* (pp. 3-10). New York: John Wiley.

Arias, I., & Beach, S. R. (1987). Validity of self-reports of marital violence. *Journal of Family Violence, 2,* 139-149.

Attala, J. M., Hudson, W. W., & McSweeney, M. (1994). A partial validation of two short-form partner abuse scales. *Women and Health, 21,* 125-139.

Beskow, J., Runeson, B., & Asgard, U. (1990). Psychological autopsies: Methods and ethics.

Suicide and Life-Threatening Behavior, 20, 301-323.

Campbell, D. T., & Fiske, D. (1959). Convergent and discriminant validation by the multitrait-multimethod matrix. *Psychological Bulletin, 56,* 81-105.

Centers for Disease Control and Prevention. (1988). Guidelines for evaluating surveillance systems. *Morbidity and Mortality Weekly Report, 37*(S-5), 1-18.

Centers for Disease Control and Prevention. (1993). Emergency department response to domestic violence: California, 1992. *Morbidity and Mortality Weekly Report, 42,* 617-620.

DeKeseredy, W. S. (2000). Current controversies on defining nonlethal violence against women in intimate heterosexual relationships: Empirical implications. *Violence Against Women, 6,* 728-746.

Dillman, D. A. (1978). *Mail and telephone surveys: The total design method.* New York: John Wiley.

Dutton, D. G., & Hemphill, K. J. (1992). Patterns of socially desirable responding among perpetrators and victims of wife assault. *Violence and Victims, 7,* 29-39.

Fowler, F. J. (1993). *Survey research methods.* Newbury Park, CA: Sage.

Gelles, R. J. (2000). Estimating the incidence and prevalence of violence against women. *Violence Against Women, 6,* 784-804.

Gordon, M. (2000). Definitional issues in violence against women. *Violence Against Women, 6,* 747-783.

Hudson, W. W. (1990). *Partner abuse scale: Physical.* Tempe, AZ: Walmyr.

Hudson, W. W., & McIntosh, S. R. (1981). The assessment of spouse abuse: Two quantifiable dimensions. *Journal of Marriage and the Family, 43,* 873-885.

Koss, M. P., & Gidycz, C. A. (1985). Sexual experiences survey: Reliability and validity. *Journal of Consulting and Clinical Psychology, 53,* 422-423.

Koss, M. P., & Oros, C. J. (1982). Sexual experiences survey: A research instrument investigating sexual aggression and victimization. *Journal of Consulting and Clinical Psychology, 50,* 455-457.

Krosnick, J. A. (1999). Survey research. *Annual Review of Psychology, 50,* 537-567.

Marshall, L. L. (1992). Development of the severity of violence against women scales. *Journal of Family Violence, 7,* 103-123.

National Research Council. (1996). *Understanding violence against women.* Washington, DC: National Academy Press.

Rodenburg, F. A., & Fantuzzo, J. W. (1993). The measure of wife abuse: Steps toward the development of a comprehensive assessment technique. *Journal of Family Violence, 8,* 203-228.

Rosenbaum, A. (1988). Methodological issues in marital violence research. *Journal of Family Violence, 3,* 91-104.

Saltzman, L. E., Fanslow, J. L., McMahon, P. M., & Shelley, G. A. (1999). *Intimate partner violence surveillance: Uniform definitions and recommended data elements* (Version 1.0). Atlanta, GA: Centers for Disease Control and Prevention, National Center for Injury Prevention and Control.

Saunders, D. G. (1991). Procedures for adjusting self-reports of violence for social desirability bias. *Journal of Interpersonal Violence, 6,* 336-344.

Shepard, M. F., & Campbell, J. A. (1992). The abusive behavior inventory: A measure of psychological and physical abuse. *Journal of Interpersonal Violence, 7,* 291-305.

Smith, P. H., Earp, J., & DeVellis, R. (1995). Measuring battering: Development of the women's experience with battering (WEB) scale. *Women's Health: Research on Gender, Behavior, and Policy, 1,* 273-288.

Smith, P. H., Tessaro, I., & Earp, J. L. (1995). Women's experiences with battering: A conceptualization from qualitative research. *Women's Health Issues, 5,* 173-182.

Straus, M. A. (1979). Measuring intrafamily conflict and violence: The conflict tactics (CT) scales. *Journal of Marriage and the Family, 41,* 75-88.

Straus, M. A., Hamby, S. L., Boney-McCoy, S., & Sugarman, D. B. (1996). The revised conflict tactics scales (CTS2). *Journal of Family Issues, 17,* 283-316.

Tjaden, P., & Thoennes, N. (1998, November). *Prevalence, incidence, and consequences of violence against women: Findings from the National Violence Against Women Survey* (National Institute of Justice, Research in Brief, NCJ No. 172837). Washington, DC: Department of Justice.

Tjaden, P., & Thoennes, N. (2000, July). *Extent, nature, and consequences of intimate partner violence* (National Institute of Justice, Research Report, NCJ No. 181867), Washington, DC: Department of Justice.

MEN RESEARCHING VIOLENCE AGAINST WOMEN

Neil Websdale

There are many ways to conduct research on violence against women, as the chapters in Part I demonstrate. Statistical research often involves surveying a sample of people (e.g., victims, perpetrators, criminal justice personnel) using closed-ended questions to ascertain levels and forms of victimization. Another quantitative approach is to analyze crime statistics, such as arrests for assault, homicide data, and court convictions of batterers. Building a statistical data set on violence against women involves choosing what questions to ask, whom to ask them of, how to ask them, and how to code them. Analyzing such a data set involves a selective process of choosing what to study, what correlations to draw, and what findings to emphasize. All of these steps involve political choices. Both men and women have conducted this kind of research. Unfortunately, a significant amount of this research has ignored or downplayed the importance of women's own words, experiences, and voices regarding their victimization. These words, experiences, and voices are more subjective, varying greatly between individuals. As such, they are more difficult to code than answers to closed-ended questions.

Not many men have conducted qualitative research on violence against women. Some have interviewed mostly male prosecutors, judges, police officers, and other criminal justice system players to obtain multiple perspectives. Others have interviewed batterers to learn more about violence against women. Fewer have used personal, in-depth, open-ended, focused or unstructured interviews to ask survivors of violence about their experiences. In such a setting, interviewees are perhaps more likely to share personal information about their violent victimization if they perceive that the interviewer is receptive to their stories. Given that women are much more likely to suffer interpersonal victimization at the hands of men than at the hands of other women, it is perhaps understandable that some researchers have argued that women interviewers are more likely to uncover intimate details than their male peers. Female interviewers might be more likely to establish rapport with victims and share common understandings on the basis of gender; they might be more in tune with the language of feelings that provides a window into personal pain. If it is the case that female interviewers establish rapport more readily with female victims of violence, then does it also follow that male researchers are more likely to establish rapport with male batterers because of a certain deep gender congruence or to share political positions that transcend the individual behaviors of the men themselves? Similarly, given that the criminal justice system is peopled by many more men than women, is it likely that qualitative research conducted by men with system players will be more fruitful?

Notwithstanding these concerns, men have successfully interviewed female victims of violence. I feel that my own work with rural battered women successfully revealed many of the intimate details of these women's lives in a manner that increased our understanding of rural domestic violence (Websdale, 1998). In cases such as these, it appears men have been good listeners, established rapport around commonalities other than gender (e.g., social class), and have followed and developed leads provided by women. I established rapport with battered women through a number of techniques. My snowball sampling encouraged women to tell others in the shelter about our conversations and my purpose in highlighting the plight of rural battered women. These aspects of my approach encouraged other women to talk with me, thus establishing initial rapport at the level of helping prevent domestic violence in understudied and much ignored rural regions. From this common ground, I openly talked with women, made appropriate eye contact, listened intently, and started our conversations by asking biographical questions that displayed an interest in them as people, rather than as shelter residents, or battered women, or cogs in a system. This type of approach to interviewing usually reverses conversational interchanges between men and women, where men usually talk more, interrupt more, and have their ideas pursued more readily, whereas women typically ask more questions than men and do more to keep the conversation going. Again, in my own case, I approached interviews with rural battered women knowing some of the stereotypical dynamics of male-female exchanges, and I consciously reminded myself as the interview proceeded to modify those stereotypical dynamics if they appeared to me to be developing. In particular, I used silence as a means of creating deliberate conversational spaces for women to enter if they so chose. I was mindful not to interrupt, especially during the telling of what appeared to me to be painful episode. At other times, the rapport I established was more spontaneous, perhaps reproducing some of the more traditional/stereotypical male-female exchanges, perhaps not.

In my own research on violence against women, I talked with some battered women who actively sought out my opinions about their cases, almost as if I could somehow influence the outcomes, inform the process, and, perhaps, rescue them to some degree. I refer to this as viewing the male researcher as "knight in shining armor." I had to think carefully about this phenomenon and anticipate/negotiate emerging ethical problems, especially the possibility of using my apparent power to manipulate women. This does not mean that women will necessarily perceive men who interview them as being dominant in the way that those who victimized them were dominant.

I was assured by many advocates for battered women that these women wanted to tell their stories, regardless of the sex of the interviewer, because they had hitherto been silenced, both in their interpersonal relationships and, at times, by the criminal justice system. Nevertheless, male interviewers, and interviewers in general, need to be careful in interpreting the meanings of their conversations with female victims of violence. Men cannot assume that just because the information women share in an interview appears to the male interviewer to be private, sensitive, and confidential that it actually is perceived to be that way by women themselves. It may be that a woman will read the interviewer far more astutely than the interviewer will read her, and she will provide him with what he appears to need, while resisting and holding back on other pertinent details.

Violence against women is a complex phenomenon, and those researching it have to be cognizant of what this violence actually means to women themselves, how they contextualize it in terms of their biography and their social circumstances. Likewise, men who do research on violence against women are not all cut from the same cloth. Some men have been oppressed because of their social class or racial characteristics; other have been brutalized in their own families as they grew up. Still others may have abused women physically and emotionally. Male researchers need to take these differences into account in order to establish rapport with women harmed by violence.

Reference

Websdale, N. (1998). *Rural woman battering and the justice system: An ethnography.* Thousand Oaks, CA: Sage.

CHAPTER 4

Ethical Issues in Research on Violence Against Women

Jacquelyn C. Campbell
Jacqueline D. Dienemann

Conducting research in the area of violence against women presents particular ethical challenges. Women who have experienced or are currently experiencing violence are a vulnerable population in terms of their victimization status, their compromised physical and mental health status, the documented gender bias of the criminal justice system, and the stigmatization that society inflicts on them. They may also be in physical danger and at emotional risk from ongoing abuse, a risk that may be increased by research participation. Another aspect of vulnerability is the sensitive nature of the issue, so that any questioning related to it imposes the risk of creating emotional distress and is usually considered at least somewhat intrusive. In addition, a substantial number of female victims and survivors are of minority group status (ethnic or sexual orientation), which compounds their vulnerability. Research participants from vulnerable and minority populations are given specific safeguards by the Institu-

tional Review Board (IRB) process in the United States, but not all IRB members are thoroughly knowledgeable about the particular vulnerabilities of this population. It is a responsibility of the researcher to carefully consider these issues; funding review panels and faculty who are training future researchers must become experts in this area and teach others to be equally vigilant.

This chapter will discuss complex research ethics issues related to six topics, roughly organized by when they occur in the research process. The topics are research paradigm employed, cultural context and community involvement, safety, participation and informed consent, confidentiality, and dissemination. The topics will be framed within the ethical principles to which they are most pertinent. The lack of "right" answers to ethical dilemmas that arise when ethical principles or the needs of different participants in research are in conflict will be recognized. Resolution depends on reflexive contemplation of the context, ethical principles, and viewpoints of participants, as well as the experience and best judgment of the researcher. Acknowledging this process and citing it in dissemination is the responsibility of the ethical researcher.

Research Paradigm Employed

Many authors from various disciplines have discussed research paradigms in terms of theory, types of data used, the worldview from which one approaches research, research questions, and the basic purpose of the research study (Coyne, Immelt, Stashinko, & Campbell, 1999). The basic ethical principle of justice as applied to research states that the good from the results and the process of the study must outweigh any harm or risk of harm to the participants (National Commission, 1978; Nuremberg Code, 1949). In other words, it is not good enough to benefit the whole of humankind or even a subgroup (e.g., all battered women) with the results of a study if the participants in that study are substantively harmed or incur a substantive risk of harm. Therefore, the purpose of the research must be important, and the process of the research must pose minimal risk (or risks that are outweighed by the probable benefits) to the actual participants. Because women victimized by violence are a vulnerable population, the burden of responsibility becomes even greater.

In this vein, it becomes important for researchers to pay careful attention to the women who have been victimized by violence and the advocates who have worked with them. These are the experts about what research topics are truly important and what is likely to harm their

cause and/or participants. Dialogues between researchers, advocates, and victimized women are extremely important throughout the research process (Block, Engel, Naureckas, & Riordan, 1999; Gondolf, Yllö, & Campbell, 1997), but never more important than when decisions are being made about the research purpose and the paradigm from which it is to be conducted.

Research Paradigms and Ethical Issues

Coyne and colleagues (1999) have proposed three distinct current research paradigms: (a) prediction (post-positivist) or seeking to predict outcomes, with emphasis on generalizability and statistical analysis of quantitative data; (b) comprehension (naturalistic or constructivist), which uses primarily qualitative data to understand phenomena in depth; and (c) emancipation (critical theory, participatory action, and feminist research traditions), where qualitative and/or quantitative data are collected in a collaborative process for the basic purpose of improving conditions for the participants in the research process and the population they represent.

We have a bias toward the emancipation paradigm, because we feel it fits most closely with the ethical imperative of justice for women victimized by violence. The emancipation paradigm insists not only on the principle of justice for individual participants, as any research paradigm must, but also on the principle of beneficence: that the research results are used for the good, to improve systems for the group that the participants represent. Thus, emancipation researchers are concerned about extending their results to influence policy and practice. In contrast, more traditional researchers, especially those following the prediction paradigm, would insist that they are only concerned about the scientific rigor of their results and dissemination to other researchers and not about how the results are used thereafter. This tradition trains researchers that their research is "objective" and basically value-free. Researchers using this paradigm need to become sensitive about clearly stating the generalizability and predictive accuracy of their results, because they may be used for policy decision making. For instance, incidence and prevalence studies of violence against women are often used as standards to measure the societal importance of creating policies regarding this problem (Lidz, Mulvey, & Gardner, 1993). In addition, researchers must report who subjects are and how they were recruited and retained, in light of how this may increase or decrease the rates the researchers found (Koss, 1992).

Both the comprehension and emancipation paradigms help the researcher see that no research is totally value-free, that beliefs and attitudes shape the research process from purpose onward (Murphy & O'Leary, 1994). The emancipation paradigm adds the responsibility to follow the impact of results and work for them to be used in positive policy initiatives (Mastroianni, Faden, & Federman, 1994).

However, we also realize that research with any paradigm may benefit abused women more than it puts them at risk. Our point is that it is important for researchers to think about these issues and to be aware of the paradigm from which their research emanates. Simultaneously, it is equally important to realize that no one paradigm is inherently more ethical than another and that unethical research can be conducted from any paradigm (Murphy & O'Leary, 1994).

Codes of Ethics and Ethical Oversight

This realization led to the development not only of codes of ethics for professions that include ethical research guidelines (American Medical Association, 1996; American Psychological Association, 1981; Silva, 1995), but also of government regulations for the protection of human subjects (National Commission, 1978; Nuremberg Code, 1949; U.S. Department of Health and Human Services, 1981). These codes and regulations are intended to provide guidance for peer and governmental oversight to monitor the ethical behavior of all scientists, including those who do research on violence against women.

Gender as an Ethical Issue

Gender is an ever-present issue in violence-against-women research, one that the researcher needs to be aware of and to avoid either ignoring or overemphasizing. Ignoring gender is done under the rubric of viewing intimate relationships as being between two equal, consenting adults and ignoring gender differences. When ignoring gender, the male perspective is viewed as normative, and any deviation is seen as pathological. Consequently, the research may ignore women's socialization into cultural expectations, childhood experiences of abuse, smaller stature and physical strength, and ethical stance of caring and connection (Wyatt, 1994).

The other extreme, which can be just as unethical, is to emphasize the patriarchal nature of society and the victimization of women to the extent that their resourcefulness in coping, self-efficacy in problem solving, and ability to survive are not perceived (Campbell, 1998). There is increasing evidence that men and women often do change their relationships to control the violence that has been perpetrated against women, with or without intervention by professionals; more research is needed to identify the factors that promote this behavior change and the dynamics that stabilize safety (Campbell, Rose, Kub, & Nedd, 1998). Also, women are pluralistic in their backgrounds, responses to violence, personal strengths, and vulnerabilities. To summarize, scientists need to be open to their own and their participants' suppositions and to beliefs embedded in their work, so that they can use this knowledge to advance their work (Committee on Science, Engineering, and Public Policy, 1995).

Cultural Context and Community Involvement

Cultural competence in conducting research may also be thought of as an ethical responsibility for researchers. Competence goes beyond being sensitive to being knowledgeable about how cultural groups involved in the research differ from and concur with the researcher's culture (Orlandi, 1992). Access to this knowledge comes from personal cultural self-knowledge and an openness to learn from written reports, personal observations, and stories of key informants. All research in this field needs to be culturally

competent, but very little has been in the past.

Cultural competence needs to occur at all points in the research process. It is not required only in cross-cultural research. The essential factor is the explicit inclusion of culture within the design, implementation, and dissemination. This begins with the examination and critique of prior research for results specific to ethnicity and culture of participants, followed by the synthesis of relevant findings or noting the absence thereof. In the design, culturally relevant theory and cross-ethnic concepts, such as acculturation and ethnic identity, should be included. Measurement instruments need to be chosen in terms of their appropriateness to the cultural groups being studied. A pilot study with ethnically specific psychometric evaluation of instruments should be conducted, if this has never been reported (Porter & Villarruel, 1993). Translation is an important issue, but so are the validity and meaning of the concepts (Marin & Marin, 1991).

Community as Research Participant

Access to do research in many communities involves approaching and working with gatekeepers, such as political leaders, clergy, elders, community activists, or others. To assure cultural congruence and assist in building positive working relationships with the community, some researchers form an advisory committee or recruit local colleagues as co-investigators or hire key informants who are involved in the entire research design process. Other researchers hire and train community outreach workers to conduct interviews with community members.

These approaches are viable to increase community acceptance and cultural congruence, but they may also raise issues of confidentiality when community residents are involved in the research process.

Research not only may offer long-term benefits but also may incur costs for a community. Some communities negotiate for compensation, such as donation of equipment or databases used in the research. Costs at the end of a study, often not seen by researchers, are the loss of jobs for those hired, the sense of being used that residents may feel after sharing sensitive information, the loss of services that were part of the research protocol, worry that reports will not protect the confidentiality of the community and "give it a bad name," and the loss of supportive relationships with researchers, especially in longitudinal studies (Liss & Solomon, 1996).

Cultural Congruence

Choice of natural gathering places and approaches using culturally congruent techniques for sample recruitment are needed to assure that samples are appropriately heterogeneous within and across ethnic groups. Without such strategies and monitoring during recruitment, the danger is that the sample will not represent the wider body of women and is likely to include those who are most available for recruitment, such as women in shelters.

Nonhierarchical and culturally sensitive interview techniques must be used. The assumption that culturally matched, local interviewers are superior in researching sensitive topics has not been tested systematically in research. Although intuitively appealing, it may also introduce other problems, such as fear of lack of confidentiality within small communities. Also, the communication skills and sensitivity of the interviewers may be more important to cultural congruence than their ethnic heritage. When interviewers are of another ethnic heritage, care needs to be taken to establish trust across cultures and to determine local meanings of words and dialect pronunciations (Marin & Marin, 1991).

Cultural competence in data analysis is also extremely important, and it must go beyond making a simplistic analysis for differences or including ethnicity/race as a dichotomous predictor. Researchers must be sensitive to the danger that racism is shaping analysis when the white majority is used as the norm for comparison. At the least, race/ethnicity must be included with socioeconomic status (SES), so that the relative effects of the two closely entwined variables may be analyzed. The race/ethnicity classifications often used are too few and too broad to be sensitive to cultural influences on violence-related phenomena. Many ethnicities are not included at all (e.g., Arabs), and the categories used (e.g., Hispanic) are too broad to reflect the enormous cultural and acculturation differences within each category (Marin & Marin, 1991; Torres et al., in press). Sophisticated multivariate analysis techniques, including weighting, are available to control for income and education, explore for interactions between ethnicity and closely intertwined variables such as SES, address heterogeneity within ethnic groups, and include interactions with key neighborhood and individual characteristics (see, e.g., Sampson, Raudenbush, & Earls, 1997).

Finally, it is imperative that the results be interpreted within a culturally specific context that is not harmful to that group.

The terminology and media chosen may avoid or promote the development of negative stereotypes or harmful public policy. Whatever paradigm researchers use, the principles of justice and nonmaleficence should guide them in reporting results.

Safety

One of the major ethical challenges of conducting research on violence against women is protecting the safety of participants (Watts, Heise, & Ellsberg, 1998). In terms of participation, one issue is the potential conflict between attracting a representative sample and ensuring research participant safety. Concerns have been raised as to the validity of studies of violence due to lack of representativeness of samples and the reluctance of many to report violent acts accurately (Lidz et al., 1993). In fact, social beliefs labeling victims as to blame for abuse may have a substantial impact on the willingness of participants to report incidents, even to researchers (Koss, 1992). To comply with the principles of autonomy and nonmaleficence, researchers need to devise ways to respect both the perpetrator and the victim and to prevent harm to either during the research. This, in turn, may increase both safety and participation of potential participants and their significant others.

Autonomy and Mandatory Reporting

Victims and perpetrators have total autonomy about reporting violence, except when reporting to social service or the police is legally required or ethically mandated. Researchers need to be aware of local statutes and their time limitations regarding child abuse, domestic violence, rape, children's aggressive behaviors, potential harm to self or third parties, or ongoing criminal activity in regard to research (Urquiza, 1991). For instance, the Child Abuse and Prevention and Treatment Act of 1974 required all states to enact legislation defining child abuse and neglect and mandatory reporting. The definitions and scope of those people responsible to report varies widely from state to state. In addition, professional codes of ethics for specific professions may direct researchers to report. A third consideration is the welfare of participants and their families if the researcher does or does not report.

If researchers determine that the study may fall under a mandatory reporting statute or ethical mandate, they need to delineate how they will inform participants and what procedures they will use if a case is identified (Urquiza, 1991). If the participants are children or vulnerable adults, then procedures for informing the legal guardian and participant are necessary. Consultation with colleagues and professional associations is often helpful in clarifying requirements and frequently used strategies to meet them. One strategy is to inform participants of mandatory reporting requirements as a part of informed consent and then to remind them of this immediately preceding parts of the interview that ask directly about actions that must be reported. For instance, in Maryland, mandatory reporting of child abuse applies to adults who were abused as children, so we include a reminder in the section of the questionnaire that asks about childhood discipline. This may reduce the accuracy of self-report, but it allows for autonomous choice by participants. Another strategy is to adapt questions to avoid direct reports, such as asking for information that does not include description of actual instances or asking if child abuse has been reported in the past. Where reporting is not legally mandatory but researchers believe that ethics require them to report violence or danger, one strategy is to discuss their beliefs with the participants and seek their consent to report it or willingness to report the violence themselves. At minimum, researchers should inform the participant of their intention to report.

Danger Engendered by Research

When first approaching potential participants, researchers need to consider what danger they are creating. With mail surveys to the home, researchers do not know who might see the mail or open it without the consent of the addressee. This has led to sending a letter of invitation describing the study in general terms to the home address and asking for a return postcard indicating interest, with a telephone number or work address where further contact can be made. Informed consent is obtained in the next mail or telephone contact. This strategy also increases the cost of research. This raises the ethical issue of whether deception infringes on the autonomy of the participant to make an informed decision. Researchers must balance the need for candid information with the safety needs of participants. They must never allow their desires for a larger or more representative sample to justify deception.

Telephone surveys of the general population may introduce danger by asking questions whose replies may upset a perpetrator standing nearby or listening on an extension, causing subsequent violence. Even if the perpetrator is not pres-ent, caller-identification recording systems may inform the perpetrator of phone calls from survey researchers. Safety protocols need to be well developed and include thorough evaluation of how the length, content of questions, and possible answers may endanger participants. Interviewers need to be trained in how to use the protocol and how to recognize danger and intervene (e.g., by calling 911). For example, women may be asked if it is a good time to talk before the interview begins, told they may hang up at any time they do not feel safe, and given a toll-free number to call back at a better time. Excellent examples of protocols are given by Wilson, Johnson, and Daly (1995) and Tjaden and Thoennes (1998). When doing interviews using qualitative methods, researchers need to first consider that full disclosure of risks cannot be given to people at the time when they are deciding whether to participate. By definition, the questions and flow of information evolve during the research process. In choosing a location, researchers should be aware that the home may be more convenient for some participants but also more danger-ous, both by exposing participants to the perpetrator and by providing more information than the participant wishes to reveal. Home visits tell a researcher a great deal about the context of a person's life and may create a more intimate atmo-sphere, which reduces the participant's control over what to reveal. In any location, interviewers should always monitor the atmosphere being created and be careful not to interrogate or push the partici-pant to reveal information he or she may later regret (Parker & Ulrich, 1990). In a home visit, others, including the perpetra-tor, may see the researcher come in and out of the home, or the perpetrator may interrupt the interview, resulting in harm to the participant or the researcher. For example, when a teen rape victim is interviewed in her home, she may disclose that her father is the rapist. For these reasons, many researchers prefer to meet participants in a public place such as a park or café, a public building such as a hospital or school, or an office building.

Finally, the greatest challenge to ethical behavior by researchers comes in doing participant-observation fieldwork. Here, again, the issues of harming others through restriction of privacy, confidentiality, informed consent, and deception need to be balanced with social desirability changing behavior and severely reducing the validity of the research. For example, how can consent be obtained from everyone being observed on a playground for male-female aggressive behavior patterns among children? Perhaps, some measure of deception (such as posing as a baby-sitter at the playground) is acceptable where the benefits of knowledge outweigh the harms, which have been minimized by assuring anonymity of the children (by not asking their names) and confidentiality (by not revealing the site and dates in dissemination).

The issues become more problematic when the research involves illegal activity such as prostitution, substance abuse, assault and battery, or abuses of power, such as corrections guards' violent abuse of women prisoners. Some researchers argue that privacy, harm, and confidentiality are waived when an institution is seen as corrupt, but others adamantly disagree (Punch, 1994).

An additional safety issue not always contemplated is the danger that the victim may be suicidal (Monahan, Applebaum, Mulvey, Robbins, & Lidz, 1993). Female victims of violence are at higher risk for suicide than nonabused women (Stark &

Flitcraft, 1995). If a researcher recognizes depressive symptoms, the potential for suicide must be investigated, and if it is present, appropriate immediate referral must be made.

Participation and Informed Consent

In the aftermath of the Nuremberg trials, a movement to protect human subjects of research resulted in publication of a code of ethics (Nuremberg Code, 1949). This code excluded women participants from biomedical research due to risk during pregnancy. This exclusion was legislated in the United States in the mid-1970s. The watershed event signaling a shift from this protectionism was the Belmont Report in 1978, which identified three comprehensive ethical principles as an analytical framework to guide scientists regarding ethical issues inherent in research with human subjects. They are (a) respect for people as autonomous beings and protection of those with diminished capacity; (b) beneficence to maximize possible benefits and minimize possible harms; and (c) justice in selection of subjects, especially equity in gender, race, ethnicity, and socioeconomic status (National Commission, 1978). Protectionism had, in fact, harmed women: Although using a male norm, studies inferred that their results could be applied equally to all people and inadvertently camouflaged health problems unique to women. The National Institutes of Health (NIH) Revitalization Act of 1993 (P.L. 103-43) included several provisions for the inclusion of women and minorities, unless the researcher justified their absence (Monahan et al., 1993). This resulted in the publication of guidelines for the inclusion of women and minorities as subjects in clinical research (NIH, 1994). The implementation of these guidelines is reinforced by case and constitutional law that supports women's rights to equal protection, privacy, and liberty to choose, protection under antidiscrimination statutes, and tort liability for exclusion (Rothenberg, 1996). These guidelines become increasingly relevant as violence is becoming eligible for biomedical research funding as a result of the merger of NIH and the Alcohol, Drug Abuse, and Mental Health Administration (ADAMHA) (Touchette, 1993).

Violence Research and Public Policy

Many prevalence studies of violence against women have been criticized for not being representative or not including male victims (Jones et al., 1999). The first issue is valid; the differential effects of ethnicity/race, social status, and health outcomes remain under-researched and unresolved (Guralnik & Leveille, 1997). The second objection is based on findings using the Conflict Tactic Scales, showing similar frequency of women and men as perpetrators, but these studies also show that women are significantly more often injured and controlled in intimate relationships (Berk, Berk, Loseke, & Rauma, 1983; Schwartz, 1987).

Sensitive Nature of Inquiry

Another participation issue that needs to be addressed is the sensitive nature of the information that researchers on violence against women seek. Some issues have already been discussed relating to qualitative research methods that lead to disclosures later regretted. Two additional strategies to reduce this are reminding participants of their freedom to not answer questions when interviewers sense that sensitive information is being revealed and, at the end of the interview, asking if the participant wishes to review the transcript later, both for what data are relevant to include in analysis and for confirmation of interpretation by the scientist.

The sensitive nature of the information also may reduce participation. Scientists may see the research as significant and worth the costs of participation. They may also have included safeguards they think are sufficient. Potential participants may have a different set of values. Violence-against-women research always involves other people with whom the participants have or have had an intimate and, many times, a family relationship. To honor the ethical principle of caring, which emphasizes respect for the relational connections of subjects to others, researchers should be aware and respect that some women will refuse to participate out of concern for others they love.

Trauma From Participation

Domestic violence also usually involves a traumatic and, many times, chronic traumatic experience that has left the participant more vulnerable. Researchers have pointed out the added vulnerability caused by the many losses women experience from domestic violence. Researchers should be aware that these losses may include loss of her positive image of the relationship or previous lifestyle (Cook, 1995). In many ways, violence research using qualitative methods resembles therapy, in that it involves discussion of intimate, perhaps shameful details of one's life that are usually taboo.

There is controversy concerning whether additional trauma is caused by research interviews that talk about the trauma. Bergen (1993) reported an increase in distress caused by her interviews with women who had experienced marital rape. Pennebaker (1993) found writing about or talking about stressful life events resulted in positive gains in mood state and health, as well as reduced use of health services. Potential trauma from participation may be reduced when interviewers are alert and sensitive to cues to trauma. Debriefing sessions, support groups, hotline numbers, or other appropriate professional interventions may also help. Researchers find that regular debriefing and referrals are also needed for interviewers, because there is often substantial emotional impact to them from the process (Armstrong, 1996; Block et al., 1999).

Freedom to Not Participate or Withdraw

Another related consideration is the degree to which the potential participant feels free to choose to participate or withdraw during the research study. In some circumstances, peers, other participants, agency personnel, or family members may exert pressure on prospective participants because they think participation will "help" either the researcher or the participant. This is especially likely to happen in a situation where participants are recruited from a shelter, therapeutic day care center, prison or substance abuse program, or court or probation office. Special protection against coercion should be provided for recruits in such low-power positions. Recruitment of prisoners must include evidence of compliance with the Code of Federal Regulations (CFR) Part 46, Subpart C, describing actions necessary to protect the rights of prisoners involved in research (Mastroianni et al., 1994). To avoid having personnel coerce potential participants, it may be useful to have a letter of agreement with the agency that describes the confidentiality of participants, the data from the study, and the freedom of potential participants to refuse, join, or leave the study during its progress. During a session with staff who work with potential participants, the study should be explained, providing information on the role of personnel in recruiting subjects and stressing the freedom of potential participants to refuse to enter and, alternatively, to leave during the study.

Researchers may further ameliorate coercion by recruiting potential participants in private and stressing confidentiality of choice and the freedom to enter or leave the study at any time. Here are some strategies to avoid revealing to others in an agency who participants are: (a) having the same time period with the researcher for those who decline as for those who complete questionnaires, (b) having those participating return another day and go to what appears to be a usual activity, and (c) asking participants not to disclose their participation. An additional approach to consider is to include a participant advocate on the research team, someone who meets with participants to ensure they do not feel coerced.

Potential participants may erroneously believe that participation will be rewarded within the program or agency or that refusing to participate in or leaving the study may result in punishment. The informed consent process needs to include assurance that participation will not be reported to the agency and that the person's decision will not affect treatment, sentence, or any other activity at the institution where he or she was recruited. In other circumstances, the person may agree to participate only to please the researcher. This may especially be a problem with children who are trying to be obedient to adult requests, with the elderly, or with people from group-centered cultures where individuals are not supposed to disagree. With these potential participants, it may be essential to ask them to talk about their actual wishes and "test" their comprehension of the informed consent information. Researchers have found many potential subjects do not understand informed consent information, and verbal questioning and repetition of information often increase comprehension and understanding of freedom to not consent (Sorrell, 1991).

Incentives and Participation

Participation may also be influenced by compensation given to reimburse participants for their time and discomfort and to encourage retention in longitudinal studies. Compensation may include intangibles, such as a relationship that builds over time with the researcher, a newsletter or biannual report of study progress, a birthday card, a telephone call or postal reminder, or time spent listening and talking with participants. Compensation of tangible value may include mugs or pens, gift certificates, lottery tickets, telephone cards, compact discs, coupons, bus tokens, taxi script, services such as a health examination, or money. Money was found to be the preferred tangible gift by Rudy,

Estok, Kerr, and Menzel (1994). Wineman and Durand (1992) discussed how monetary incentives, especially for low-income participants, may be unethical coercion. Alternatively, payment at a minimum-wage level may be viewed as just compensation for their "work," demonstrating respect for the person's time; it may have the added value of increasing participant commitment to the study. Higher levels of payment may be offered when participation entails more effort or discomfort. Social justice should guide researchers to give the same initial level of compensation to control and intervention subjects as they each agreed to participate and the researcher assigned them to different time commitments. Offers of monetary compensation should always be included in cover letters or informed consent forms, emphasizing choice. If researchers decide to give a monetary reward by check, a protocol should be developed to assure participant confidentiality, especially if the researchers' institution requires a social security number to issue a check. The subject's name and social security number should be stored on separate lists from the study identification numbers. Payroll staff should not be aware that the checks are for research participation. Keep in mind that safety of participants in personal danger situations may preclude sending the checks to their home address; participants should be asked for a safe address to which the check can be sent.

Confidentiality

Confidentiality is not anonymity. It is the protection of the participant's right to privacy by prevention of identification of the participant by others during the study, as well as protection of data linked to the participant by those working on it and, afterward, in all dissemination media (Bayer, 1990). Participants include individuals, families, cooperating agencies, and the community where the study took place. The study protocol should plan for confidentiality and prepare for responses when breaches occur. These include intentional breaches, such as mandatory reporting and quality review by authorized third parties, and unintentional breaches. Times of vulnerability in a study are recruitment, coding, and dissemination. Recruitment was discussed under participation.

Coding Threats to Confidentiality

Those doing coding should be trained to separate study identification numbers and data from personal identification data to protect confidentiality. Some strategies include separating the person or place with the linking information from those doing interviews or analysis, for example, by sending data to a colleague from another institution or storing it in safe deposit boxes, out-of-state storage, or a locked cabinet out of the office of the principal investigator (Liss & Solomon, 1996). A second set of security procedures is needed in intervention studies so that researchers are working with participants while blind to the individual's assignment as a case or control.

Confidentiality may also be threatened by qualitative research, especially in families or longitudinal studies. Reports of research include use of pseudonyms for participants and scrutiny of quotations from the interviews for identifying informa-

tion. This is of greater importance if the study is conducted in a rural area or other community where all residents are known to each other. With family studies, individual interviews may contain material unknown to other family members or that the participant may not wish to disclose to them. Maintaining confidentiality requires extra diligence by investigators. In conjoint interviews, researchers need to understand the greater ethical risks, as family members have less control over what is said and may feel coerced to appear cooperative, saying things they later regret. Merely participating and reflecting may reveal to family members information they had been unaware of within their family, destroying confidentiality. Risks and benefits of disclosure should always be chosen to the participant's benefit (Ford & Reutter, 1990).

Certificates of Confidentiality

One danger to confidentiality is a subpoena from a court or lawyer, requesting data given by a participant in a study that is relevant to a pending case. These situations often involve allegations of domestic violence, abuse, and sexual assault in divorce, child custody, criminal, or civil suits. One protection from revealing data is a certificate of confidentiality (COC). The COC was created by the Health Omnibus Programs Extension of 1988 to the Public Health Service Act in subsection 301(d) (42 U.S.C. § 242a) (Public Health Service Act, 1988) for researchers doing biomedical, behavioral, clinical, or other research to protect the names and identifying characteristics of subjects. Researchers may not be compelled by subpoena from any federal, state, or local civil, criminal, administrative, legislative, or other proceedings to identify such individuals (Melton, 1990). The Office of Justice Assistance in the U.S. Department of Justice requires all grantees to have a COC as a requirement for funding (Gray & Melton, 1985). Violence researchers should seriously consider obtaining a COC from the Office of the Assistant Secretary of Health or an institute at the NIH or the Public Health Service to protect their participants. Many IRBs require a violence researcher to have a COC. However, keep in mind that COCs are limited to research of a sensitive nature, resulting in a case-by-case determination that significantly increases processing time.

The COC has not been tested in court. Thus, there is no precedent by which to judge the extent of protection or the definition of sensitive or whether the COC applies to all data or only identifying data (Liss & Solomon, 1996). The degree to which a COC would protect a researcher from mandatory reporting is also unknown.

Dissemination

In disseminating results, written reports need to include the context of a battering relationship and the realities that women face. Readers without their own experience with women who have experienced violence, and/or who do not collaborate with advocates, and/or who have not widely read the interdisciplinary research in the field may be naive about these complex realities. There is the danger that the research will be interpreted from a simplistic framework, such as victim blaming or emphasizing pathology.

Methodologies from the comprehension paradigm include mechanisms for returning to participants to check the validity of the results with them (Munhill, 1988). The emancipation paradigm also includes involvement to positively influence policy. This has also been described as "catalytic validity" by Lather (1991), or the ability of the results to be a catalyst for change. Program evaluations should begin with negotiation between researchers and program administrators about the processes to be followed in reporting the results, with consideration given to how negative results will be reported.

Researchers on violence against women have several resources available to assist them in being proactive about reporting the results of their research. One is to meet with advocates for the vulnerable population. Such advocates often have experience with the policy and legislative process on this issue and can advise researchers about pitfalls and opportunities. There are also organizations that have extensive experience and skill in providing advice to researchers about how to respond to questions from media and policy makers in ways that avoid harm to women victimized by violence and the organizations that provide services to them (see www.fvpf.org, the Web site for the Family Violence Prevention Fund, for more information).

Finally, ethically responsible researchers ensure that the results of the research return back to the participants themselves and to other women victimized by violence. Survivors and victims seldom read scholarly publications. Researchers can reach them through the popular media by providing copy to magazines, television, and the press. They can directly write newsletters for the community and send an abstract in lay language back to participants who are at a safe address. In the past, these activities have not been considered part of the research role. However, it is difficult for the research process to benefit those affected by violence if they are never able to learn the results.

References

American Medical Association. (1996). *Code of medical ethics: Current opinions with annotations.* Chicago: Author.

American Psychological Association. (1981). Ethical principles of psychologists. *American Psychologist, 36,* 633-638.

Armstrong, J. G. (1996). Emotional issues and ethical aspects of trauma research. In E. Carlson (Ed.), *Trauma research methodology* (pp. 174-187). Lutherville, MD: Sidran.

Bayer, R. (1990). Beyond the burdens of protection: AIDS and the ethics of research. *Evaluation Review, 14,* 443-446.

Bergen R. K. (1993). Interviewing survivors of marital rape: Doing feminist research on sensitive topics. In C. M. Renzetti & R. M. Lee (Eds.), *Researching sensitive topics.* Newbury Park, CA: Sage.

Berk, R., Berk, S., Loseke, D. R., & Rauma, D. (1983). Mutual combat and other family violence myths. In D. Finkelhor, R. J. Gelles, G. T. Hotaling, & M. A. Straus (Eds.), *The dark side of families* (pp. 191-212). Beverly Hills, CA: Sage.

Block C. R., Engel, B., Naureckas, S. M., & Riordan, K. A. (1999). The Chicago women's health risk study: Lessons in collaboration. *Violence Against Women, 5,* 1157-1176.

Campbell, J. (1998). Making the health care system an empowerment zone for battered women. In J. Campbell (Ed.), *Empowering survivors of abuse.* Thousand Oaks, CA: Sage.

Campbell, J., Rose, L., Kub, J., & Nedd, D. (1998). Voices of strength and resistance: A contextual and longitudinal analysis of women's responses to battering. *Journal of Interpersonal Violence, 14,* 743-762.

Committee on Science, Engineering, and Public Policy. (1995). *On being a scientist: Responsible conduct in research* (2nd ed.). Washington, DC: National Academy Press.

Cook, A. S. (1995). Ethical issues in bereavement research: An overview. *Death Studies, 19,* 103-122.

Coyne, K., Immelt, S., Stashinko, E., & Campbell, J. C. (1999). *Using the paradigm mosaic to build nursing knowledge* Unpublished manuscript, Johns Hopkins University, Baltimore, MD.

Ford, J. S., & Reutter, L. I. (1990). Ethical dilemmas associated with small samples. *Journal of Advanced Nursing, 15,* 187-191.

Gondolf, E. W., Yllö, K., & Campbell, J. C. (1997). Collaboration between researchers and advocates. In G. K. Kantor & J. L. Jasinski (Eds.), *Out of the darkness: contemporary perspectives on family violence* (pp. 255-267). Thousand Oaks, CA: Sage.

Gray, J. N., & Melton, G. B. (1985). The law and ethics of psychosocial research on AIDS. *Nebraska Law Review, 64,* 637-688.

Guralnik, J. M., & Leveille, S. G. (1997). Annotation: Race, ethnicity, and health outcomes—unraveling the mediating role of socioeconomic status. *American Journal of Public Health, 87,* 728-730.

Jones, A. S., Gielen, A. C., Campbell, J. C., Schollenberger, J., Dienemann, J., Kub, J., O'Campo, P. J., & Wynne, E. C. (1999). Annual and lifetime prevalence of partner abuse in a sample of female HMO enrollees. *Women's Health Issues, 9,* 295-305.

Koss, M. P. (1992). The underdetection of rape: Methodological choices influence incidence estimates. *Journal of Social Issues, 48,* 61-75.

Lather, P. (1991). *Getting smart: Feminist research and pedagogy within the postmodern.* New York: Routledge, Chapman & Hall.

Lidz, C., Mulvey, E., & Gardner, W. (1993). The accuracy of predictions of violence to others. *Journal of the American Medical Association, 269,* 1007-1011.

Liss, M., & Solomon, S. D. (1996). *Ethical considerations in violence related research.* Unpublished manuscript, National Institutes of Health, Office of Behavioral and Social Sciences Research.

Marin, G., & Marin, B. V. (1991). *Research with Hispanic populations.* Newbury Park, CA: Sage.

Mastroianni, A. C., Faden, R., & Federman, D. (Eds.). (1994). *Women and health research: Ethical and legal issues in including women in clinical studies* (Vol. 1). Washington, DC: National Academy Press.

Melton, G. B. (1990). Certificates of confidentiality under the public health service act: Strong protection is not enough. *Violence and Victims, 5,* 67-71.

Monahan, J., Applebaum, P. S., Mulvey, E. P., Robbins, P. C., & Lidz C. W. (1993). Ethical and legal duties in conducting research on violence. *Violence & Victims, 8,* 387-396.

Munhill, P. L. (1988). Ethical considerations in qualitative research. *Western Journal of Nursing Research, 10,* 150-62.

Murphy, C. M., & O'Leary, K. D. (1994). Research paradigms, values, and spouse abuse. *Journal of Interpersonal Violence, 9,* 207-223.

National Commission for the Protection of Human Subjects of Biomedical and Behavioral Research. (1978). *The Belmont report: Ethical principles and guidelines for the protection of human subjects of research* (DHEW Publication No. [OS] 78-0012). Washington, DC: Department of Health, Education, and Welfare.

National Institutes of Health. (1994). NIH guidelines on the inclusion of women and minorities as subjects in clinical research (RIN 0905-ZA18). *Federal Register, 59,* 59.

Nuremberg Code. (1949). *Trials of war criminals before the Nuremberg Military Tribunals under Control Council Law No. 10, 2 P181.* Washington, DC: Government Printing Office.

Orlandi, M. A. (1992). Defining cultural competence: An organizing framework. In *Cultural competence for evaluators* (OSAP Cultural Competence Series). Washington, DC: Public Health Service.

Parker, B., & Ulrich, Y. (1990). A protocol of safety: Research on abuse of women. *Nursing Research, 39,* 248-250.

Pennebaker, J. W. (1993). Putting stress into words: Health, linguistic, and therapeutic implications. *Behavior Research and Therapy, 31,* 539-548.

Porter, C., & Villarruel, A. (1993). Nursing research with African American and Hispanic people: Guidelines for action. *Nursing Outlook, 41,* 59-67.

Public Health Service Act, Health Omnibus Programs Extension of 1988, Subsection 301(d) (42 USC § 242a).

Punch, M. (1994). Politics and ethics in qualitative research. In N. Denzin & Y. Lincoln (Eds.), *Handbook of qualitative research* (pp. 83-97). Thousand Oaks, CA: Sage.

Rothenberg, K. H. (1996). Gender matters: Implications for clinical research and women's health care symposium. *Houston Law Review, 32,* 1201-1272.

Rudy, E. B., Estok, P. J., Kerr, M. E., & Menzel, L. (1994). Research incentives: Money versus gifts. *Nursing Research, 43,* 253-255.

Sampson, R. J., Raudenbush, S. W., & Earls, F. (1997). Neighborhoods and violent crime: A multi-level study of collective efficacy. *Science, 277,* 918-924.

Schwartz, M. D. (1987). Gender and injury in spousal assault. *Sociological Focus, 20,* 61-74.

Silva, M. (1995). *Ethical guidelines in the conduct, dissemination, and implementation of nursing research.* Washington, DC: American Nurses Publishing.

Sorrell, J. M. (1991). Effects of writing/speaking on comprehension of information for informed consent. *Western Journal of Nursing Research, 13,* 110-122.

Stark, E., & Flitcraft, A. (1995). Killing the beast within: Woman battering and female suicidality. *International Journal of Health Services, 25,* 43-63.

Tjaden, P., & Thoennes, N. (1998). *Prevalence, incidence, and consequences of violence against women: Findings from the national violence against women survey* (National Institute of Justice J28.24:V 81/6 [0718-A-031]). Washington, DC: Department of Justice.

Torres, S., Campbell, J. C., Campbell, D. W., King, C., Ryan, J., & Stallings, R. (in press). Prevalence of abuse during pregnancy in six ethnic groups. *Violence & Victims.*

Touchette, N. (1993). NIH panel sidesteps concerns about violence research. *Journal of NIH Research, 5,* 29-31.

Urquiza, A. J. (1991). Retrospective methodology in family violence research. *Journal of Interpersonal Violence, 6,* 119-126.

U.S. Department of Health and Human Services. (1981). Final regulations amending basic HHS policy for the protection of human research subjects. *Federal Register, 46,* 8366-8391 (codified as 45 C.F.R. pt. 46).

Watts, C., Heise, L., & Ellsberg, M. (1998). *Putting women's safety first: Ethical and safety recommendations for research on domestic violence against women.* Geneva: World Health Association.

Wilson, M., Johnson, H., & Daly, M. (1995). Lethal and nonlethal violence against wives. *Canadian Journal of Criminology, 37,* 331-362.

Wineman, N. M., & Durand, E. (1992). Incentives and rewards for subjects in nursing research. *Western Journal of Nursing Research, 14,* 526-531.

Wyatt, G. E. (1994). The sociocultural relevance of sex research. *American Psychologist, 49,* 748-754.

CHAPTER 5

Collaborating for Women's Safety

Partnerships Between Research and Practice

Jeffrey L. Edleson
Andrea L. Bible

Social scientists and practitioners alike know of the frantic search for letters of support as grant deadlines approach. From the community perspective, calls and letters from academicians seeking an agency's last-minute support for research funding, in amounts that often exceed their agency budgets, are met with a mixture of anger and fear. Practitioners are angry that they were not included in the design and development of the research questions or methods and fearful that these researchers will use tremendous staff resources to collect data and never be heard from again. They may also fear that the research will compromise the safety of battered women and their children with its published results. Many social scientists also resent the expectation that community organizations will be partners in a research endeavor. It is sometimes viewed as one extra hurdle required by funders with short deadlines. Such requirements are sometimes seen as compromising the independence of scientific inquiry or researchers' academic freedoms, and they are not often taken seriously by the scientific community. These tensions have led one advocate to reframe collaboration as "forced bonding."[1]

AUTHORS' NOTE: This chapter is drawn from a paper first presented at the National Institute of Justice Annual Conference on Criminal Justice Research and Evaluation: Viewing Crime and Justice from a Collaborative Perspective, Washington D.C., July 28, 1998. It was revised in September 1998 and updated for this book. The original paper was published in *Viewing Crime and Justice from a Collaborative Perspective: Plenary Papers of the 1998 Conference on Criminal Justice Research and Evaluation* (pp. 25-38). Washington, DC: National Institute of Justice. The authors wish to thank Drs. Claire Renzetti and Sandra Beeman for their helpful feedback on the first draft of this chapter.

The issues that arise when scientific and practice communities attempt to collaborate on research and evaluation projects have been the subject of discussion and publications for over 50 years. One of the earliest and most frequently cited is Lewin's (1946) article describing action research. Models expanding on these ideas have been proposed in a variety of disciplines over the intervening decades. The action research model has been expanded (Greenwood & Levin, 1998; Stringer, 1996), and other variations have been developed, including participatory research (Cancian, 1993; Park, Brydon-Miller, Hall, & Jackson, 1993), participatory action research (Kondrat & Juliá, 1997; Mies, 1996), collaborative inquiry (Torbert, 1981), cooperative inquiry (Reason, 1994), feminist research (Gergen, 1988; Reinharz, 1992), and multicultural research (Uehara et al., 1996). These models tend to share several characteristics that make them unique in scientific inquiry. For example, they generally contain an explicit assumption that research is value-based, not value-free. They also promote research that serves social transformation and avoids harming those studied. Those being studied are believed to have extensive knowledge that requires their participation in the design, data collection and analysis, and use of research. Finally, the role of the researcher is also transformed in these models from one of detached expert to a partner, educator, and facilitator who works closely with those being studied.

In research on woman battering, there have been similar calls for a movement toward a collaborative research model that serves battered women. A decade ago, Hart (1988) outlined strategies for collaboration between researchers and advocates. Eisikovits and Peled (1990) and Dobash and Dobash (1990) have called for greater use of qualitative methods, which often reflect a collaborative stance. More recently, Gondolf, Yllö, and Campbell (1997) described a collaborative model of advocacy research in domestic violence. The publication of an entire issue of the journal *Violence Against Women* (Riger, 1999a) devoted to exploring collaborative efforts between practitioners and researchers suggests that collaboration is becoming standard practice in research on violence against women.

In this chapter, we use the term *collaborative research* to describe investigative partnerships between advocates, practitioners, social scientists, community activists, and women who have been battered. These relationships are characterized by intensive consultation from beginning to end of the research endeavor. This includes collectively identifying research questions, designing data collection methods, constructing implementation strategies, interpreting findings, and writing and disseminating the results. The collaborative researchers we describe share control of the research process with their collaborators.

The following sections of the chapter identify potential challenges to research partnerships, challenges that partially explain the relative scarcity of these collaborative relationships. Following this, we explore four successful collaborations between practitioners and researchers who examine the impact of adult domestic violence and the effectiveness of services aimed at stopping it. We then highlight strategies for successfully navigating the challenges presented by collaborative partnerships and conclude by arguing that collaborative partnerships between researchers and practitioners (or advocates) strengthen, rather than weaken, the process of scientific inquiry and program development.

Advocates, practitioners, and researchers involved in four successful collaborative research and evaluation projects on woman battering were interviewed in preparation for writing this chapter.[2] We asked participants to describe the nature of their collaborative relationship and to discuss the basic guidelines or elements that they believed made these collaborations work (e.g., partners' behaviors, the project design, program elements). We also asked participants to identify some specific benefits resulting from their collaborations, as well as the challenges they encountered in collaborating and what strategies they used to effectively respond to these challenges. Throughout the chapter, we draw on the experiences of these four successful collaborations and from the published literature.

Challenges to Collaborative Research Partnerships

We begin by addressing the barriers that arise when attempting to conduct collaborative research, barriers that explain why such partnerships are relatively rare. A number of authors and individuals we interviewed identified several challenges, including those related to shared control of the research process, time and trust, differences between disciplines, and skills of researchers and practitioners or advocates.

Sharing Control of the Research Process

Perhaps the most prevalent framework supporting interventions to reduce or end woman battering is one that places power and control as the central driving force behind violent behavior (see Pence & Paymar, 1993). It is not surprising, therefore, that when researchers approach these battered women's programs with requests to engage in research, there is an expectation that control over the research process—from conceptualization to interpretation and dissemination—will be shared equally among researchers, practitioners, and in some cases, the research subjects themselves. Several have cited the effort to share power and control of the research process as "a major barrier to resolve" when engaging in collaborative research (Israel, Schurman, & Hugentobler, 1992; Levin, 1999; Riger, 1999b).

Researchers may be concerned that this degree of collaboration will compromise the integrity of research designs, if advocates and others do not understand the need for experimental controls or other conditions necessary to maintain scientific standards (Galinsky, Turnbull, Meglin, & Wilner, 1993; Gondolf et al., 1997). In some instances, such concerns are well founded, as Urban and Bennett (1999) discovered when they undertook a collaborative project involving garment factory employees, employers, foundation representatives, and advocates. Although Urban and Bennett attribute the diminished empirical rigor of the evaluation they conducted to complications in the collaborative research process, they also identify practices that, had they been implemented, might have mediated the effects of the conflicts on the collaboration and the data collection process. These mediating strategies mostly include earlier collaboration with those working in the intervention environment.

Similarly, some funding agencies have traditionally viewed close collaborative relationships unfavorably and question researchers' independence when they are actively and closely involved with the program being evaluated. Some funders and researchers believe that such a close relationship will compromise the detached objectivity of the scientist by putting pressure on her or him to alter or hide results, especially when the results show unexpected negative outcomes. At the same time, some practitioners hesitate to collaborate on research projects out of fear that potentially negative evaluation results will harm their program's funding or reputation (Ford, 1995; Gondolf et al., 1997; Myers & Daly, 1997; Riger, 1997).

The situation at funding agencies has begun to change in recent years, as the Centers for Disease Control and Prevention and the National Institute of Justice (NIJ), among other organizations, have encouraged collaborative research projects. For example, in a recent NIJ research solicitation, practitioner-researcher collaborations were actively encouraged (NIJ, 1998; Riger, 1999b).

Time and Trust

One of the most commonly cited challenges of collaborative research is the intensive time commitment required by all involved (Campbell, Dienemann, Kub, Wurmser, & Loy, 1999; E. Fisher & E. W. Gondolf, personal communication, June 17, 1998; Levin, 1999; Myers & Daly, 1997; Riger, 1997; C. Sullivan, personal communication, June 17, 1998; Uehara et al., 1996). Negotiating the research design, implementation procedures, interpretation, and publication of results is extremely time-consuming in general, and even more so when the process is shared among collaborators from different disciplines, who often have different values. Furthermore, differences in race, class, sexual orientation, gender, and profes-

sional experience mean more time is required to build trust in relationships (Hart, 1988; Renzetti, 1997). Time is a tension-filled issue, both for researchers employed in an academic setting and for program staff. Researchers generally have more time than practitioners to devote to a research project because such work is recognized and rewarded as part of their jobs. Despite this built-in time for research, many researchers are evaluated on their ability to produce multiple products from their studies and to publish them as sole or first author in academically respected journals. Yet, the added time required for collaborative research can negatively affect researchers' career trajectories, because they are viewed as less productive if they take more time to complete research and publish findings (Cancian, 1993; Israel et al., 1992; Riger, 1999b).

Practitioners are seldom offered rewards for participating in research or publishing manuscripts, and they usually fit work on a research project into their already full days (E. Fisher, personal communication, June 17, 1998; Miedema, 1996; Riger, 1997). Thus, time spent in the research endeavor often means time away from critical work (Campbell et al., 1999; Hondagneu-Sotelo, 1993; Israel et al., 1992). Furthermore, advocates are accustomed to functioning in a crisis-oriented culture where quick responses are required, whereas researchers may be more comfortable with the longer-term processes research demands (Riger, 1999b). Such different time orientations can be a source of additional tensions.

Beyond these time pressures, both practitioners and researchers may be distrustful of each other's motives. Many domestic violence program staff members have known (or heard stories about) researchers who came to programs to collect data and then never contacted the program again, once the data were in hand (A. Schwartz, personal communication, June 26, 1998). One researcher labels such practices "drive-by data collection" (Riger, 1999b, p. 1100). This results in program staff feeling they have been exploited (Riger, 1997). Practitioners' concerns about exploitation may also extend to the women or other family members studied. Advocates may worry that interview questions will unnecessarily reactivate emotional trauma about battering, blame victims by focusing on women's behavior, or compromise women's safety (Gondolf et al., 1997; Riger, 1997; A. Schwartz, personal communication, June 26, 1998). Practitioners may also fear that a research protocol will substantially alter services, to the detriment of clients (C. Arthur, personal communication, July 2, 1998; Galinsky et al., 1993). Practitioners may also be concerned that they will end up doing researchers' work for them (Hondagneu-Sotelo, 1993). As stated earlier, researchers may not trust the ability of practitioners to understand or be helpful in designing a sufficiently rigorous study.

Differences Between Disciplines

Practitioners and researchers bring different skills, training, and experience to the collaboration. As one group of collaborators notes, such diversity can be viewed as "either enriching or divisive. The consultation from such an array of experience may be simultaneously helpful and yet overwhelming and confusing" (Gilfus et al., 1999, p. 1206). Researchers, advocates, and battered women may have different views on the relative value of empirical and experiential knowledge (Avis, 1994; Hart, 1988). Different perspectives, terminology, methods, interpretations, and concerns may lead to misunderstanding, and feelings of fear and mistrust may be perpetuated among collaborative partners if they remain unexplored (Gondolf et al., 1997; Hart, 1988).

Furthermore, the differences in race, class, gender, and sexual orientation mentioned earlier may add to differences in professional credentials between researchers, practitioners, and battered women, reinforcing power inequalities in traditional ways (Hart, 1988; Israel et al., 1992). These differences may fuel mistrust and miscommunication between collaborative partners if unacknowledged.

Skills of Researchers and Practitioners

The challenges identified above may well destroy attempts at collaborative research if left unresolved or unanswered. Elden (1981), Riger (1997), Short, Hennessy, and Campbell (1998), Uehara et al. (1996), and others have all argued that truly collaborative research places many new demands on researchers. The collaborative researcher's role is much different than that of the detached expert who designs a project and supervises its implementation by other research or agency personnel. The interpersonal skills required to negotiate and maintain collaborative relationships are not commonly taught in graduate research programs. Many researchers have excellent command of scientific methods but fail miserably in their ability to be an effective part of an interpersonal and interagency network of relationships (Riger, 1999b). Researchers trained in positivist scientific methods that seek "objective truths" may be reluctant to embrace advocates' and other practitioners' forms of knowledge as valid (Avis, 1994).

Also, although practitioners as a group are becoming increasingly professionalized by obtaining advanced training and degrees, they nonetheless may not have specific knowledge of research design, implementation, or interpretation. Campbell et al. (1999) describe a situation in which program staff had no knowledge of program evaluation methods and required extensive training to orient them to the measurement of processes and outcomes. Lennett and Colten (1999) also describe the process undertaken to educate practitioners regarding what conclusions were and were not supported by preliminary data.

Four Case Studies in Research on Woman Battering

Challenges do exist in collaborative partnerships, but many advocates, practitioners, battered women, and researchers have been involved in highly successful research relationships. As stated earlier, we interviewed the researchers and practitioners associated with four successful collaborative research projects. To introduce them, we present brief summaries of each collaborative partnership immediately below. We will continue to draw from their experiences and those of other researchers to identify the underlying assumptions and research strategies that

appear to promote successful research collaborations.

The Community Advocacy Project: A Michigan Battered Women's Shelter and Cris Sullivan

The Community Advocacy Project was a multiyear study that examined the effectiveness of alternative interventions with women who were leaving abusive partners (Sullivan, 1991; Sullivan & Bybee, 1999). The project's co-principal investigator was Dr. Cris Sullivan, an associate professor of ecological psychology at Michigan State University. Abby Schwartz was the administrative coordinator at the women's shelter with which Sullivan collaborated. The study not only involved a close partnership with the shelter, but also actively engaged shelter residents as collaborating partners in the research design.

Sullivan initiated the collaborative relationship with the women's shelter as a volunteer with the shelter, where she facilitated support groups and came to know agency staff and other volunteers. She also later joined the Board of Directors and served as its chair. Sullivan informed the staff and volunteers that she was a researcher who was interested in designing and evaluating an intervention project that would examine what women needed after leaving the shelter to increase their safety. She received permission from the shelter administration to talk with shelter residents regarding her research plan.

Sullivan's discussions with battered women led to the development of a 10-week advocacy program designed to aid women leaving the shelter in accessing resources that would help increase their safety. The subsequent study randomly assigned battered women to experimental and control groups, with members of the experimental group working with trained paraprofessionals for 10 weeks to access the resources participants identified as those they needed after leaving the shelter (see Sullivan, 1991).

The Domestic Abuse Project: A Minnesota Multiservice Agency on Domestic Violence and Jeffrey Edleson

The Domestic Abuse Project was 4 years old when Dr. Jeffrey Edleson moved to Minnesota in 1983. Edleson, a professor of social work at the University of Minnesota, first volunteered at the agency, co-leading groups for men who batter and helping to organize collected data for reporting to funding agencies. These data were then analyzed by several staff at the agency and used as research projects to fulfill requirements for graduate degrees (Grusznski & Carrillo, 1988). At the same time, Edleson assisted the agency in documenting its work and analyzing other sets of data (Brygger & Edleson, 1987; Edleson & Brygger, 1986; Edleson & Grusznski, 1988; Grusznski, Brink, & Edleson, 1988). He has worked closely with Carol Arthur, the project's executive director, in his role as a long-serving member of the agency's administrative team.

As the relationship grew, the Domestic Abuse Project's management and staff set research priorities based on their personal and clinical experiences, with Edleson's facilitation. These priorities resulted in a decade-long research program that experimentally examined group treatment programs for men who batter (Edleson &

Syers, 1990, 1991), surveyed the impact of coordinated interventions on battered women and their perpetrators (Gamache, Edleson, & Schock, 1988; Syers & Edleson, 1992), and investigated services to children who have witnessed adult domestic violence (Peled & Edleson, 1992, 1995, 1998, 1999). The culmination of several projects was an extensive dissemination effort through an agency newsletter, *DAP Research & Training Update,* sent to about 9,000 individuals and organizations semi-annually, and the publication of several books (Edleson with Frick, 1997; Peled & Davis, 1995; Peled, Jaffe, & Edleson, 1995).

The African American Task Force on Violence Against Women and Beth Richie

The collaborative work of the African American Task Force on Violence Against Women is unique among the four case studies featured here because its collaborative research project was undertaken in support of a larger community-organizing initiative. The task force received funding from the Violence Against Women Grants Office to bring together different community stakeholders in Central Harlem, New York, for the purpose of developing strategies in response to violence against women in their community. The task force was composed of community residents and representatives from organizations working on behalf of children and families, job readiness programs, public assistance programs, Head Start, the Urban League, health care providers, religious organizations, law enforcement groups, and others. Gail Garfield, director of the Institute on Violence, Inc., in New York City, managed the task force. Dr. Beth Richie, formerly of Hunter College of the City University of New York and now a professor in the Departments of Criminal Justice and Women's Studies at the University of Illinois at Chicago, is a senior research consultant with the institute.

The goal of the task force was to develop a community-defined plan of action to address the complex issues of violence against women in the Central Harlem community of New York City. To accomplish this aim, a Community Involvement Model (CIM) developed by the Institute on Violence was implemented (Garfield, 1998). As part of this model, a multiphased needs assessment was conducted, which included a systematic survey of organizations in the community, the gathering of descriptive information and data from community organizations and governmental agencies, and a series of focus-group interviews with community residents and clients of services. To guide the implementation of the needs assessment, the task force established subcommittees composed of community members.

Richie worked closely with the focus group subcommittee, which designed the focus-group discussions. This included identifying the appropriate questions to be asked and identifying what different community populations would participate, as well as assisting Richie in facilitating the interviews. The subcommittee also helped analyze the findings and reported the results to the community in various forums. Overall, 11 focus-group interviews were conducted during a 3-month period in 1997. The data from the needs assessment helped to inform the decision-making process by community members in the actual development of a plan of action to respond to violence against women.

Battered Women as Survivors: Texas Battered Women's Shelters and Edward Gondolf

The collaboration regarding battered women in Texas shelters between Dr. Edward Gondolf, a professor of sociology at Indiana University of Pennsylvania, and Ellen Fisher, then director of a Texas battered women's shelter, began when the two met in Portugal at the Third International Institute on Victimology in 1985. Fisher approached Gondolf at the conference regarding data that the Texas Council on Family Violence and the Texas Department of Human Services had collected from battered women residing in shelters during the women's intake and exit interviews. Fisher invited Gondolf to analyze the interviews of over 6,000 women who had entered 50 shelters in Texas during an 18-month period in 1984 and 1985. Gondolf and Fisher's (1988) analysis of these data was eventually presented in their book, *Battered Women as Survivors: An Alternative to Treating Learned Helplessness*.

Best Practices in Successful Collaborations

A review of the strategies that researchers and practitioners have outlined as keys to the success of their collaborative ventures points to a set of underlying assumptions and best practices. Individually, the strategies identified may look rather ordinary. Uehara et al. (1996) suggest that research projects become truly collaborative when strategies such as these become organic to the entire research endeavor. When taken together, these assumptions and strategies create a very different experience for both social scientists and practitioners. The strategies are likely to significantly affect every aspect of scientific inquiry, from initial problem and question formulation to the way in which the results are presented and disseminated. Although we advocate that these strategies are best employed in tandem, we do not wish to suggest that there is only one model for collaborative research. We recognize that collaboration is an organic process that will unfold uniquely with each project undertaken (Block, Engel, Naureckas, & Riordan, 1999; Greenwood, Whyte, & Harkavy, 1993; Riger, 1999b).

In the sections that follow, we first outline three basic underlying assumptions that commonly appear in published accounts of collaborative research and were voiced by the individuals we interviewed. These include using woman-centered advocacy as a metaphor for the research process, viewing both researchers and those studied as equal partners in the research enterprise, and assuming that research is value-based. After reviewing these underlying assumptions, we then identify concrete actions that bring life to these assumptions in the research process.

Assumptions in Collaborative Research

Advocacy as a Metaphor for the Research Process

In their book, *Safety Planning With Battered Women: Complex Lives, Difficult Choices,* Davies, Lyon, and Monti-Catania (1998) define woman-centered advocacy as giving a woman "the opportunity to make decisions . . . to guide the direction and define the advocacy . . . that she is the decision maker, the one who knows best, the one with power" (pp. 3-4). In the literature on collaborative research and in our interviews with collaborators, a similar theme appeared. Successful collaborative researchers appear to be those who spend a great deal of time being involved with a program or community, who share decision-making power with others in the collaborative partnership, and who help shape battered women's and/or practitioners' questions into research projects.

For example, a key element that contributed to the success of the Community Advocacy Project collaboration, according to Sullivan and Schwartz in Michigan, was that Sullivan became actively involved in the life of the shelter and its residents by volunteering as a support-group facilitator and serving on the Board of Directors. According to Schwartz, the fact that Sullivan became an active member of the shelter community helped build trust because she was considered one of them. She spent a great deal of time listening to battered women, shaping a service response with them, and then evaluating it.

The skills of collaborative researchers involve many of those commonly outlined in the program evaluation literature (see, e.g., Posavac & Carey, 1997) and include listening to the needs of practitioners and battered women, providing adequate information about the research project so that collaborative partners can make informed decisions about their involvement, and going forward with what the community partners want. Collaborative researchers also enter into the partnerships with an expectation that they are there to learn from women who have been battered. Such researchers view the women, program staff and volunteers, and community members as equal partners in the collaboration (Hall, 1981; Kondrat & Juliá, 1997).

Blurring the Line Between Researcher and Those Studied

If researchers adopt a woman-centered or practitioner-centered approach to research, the traditional line between who is the researcher and who is the client, advocate, or practitioner is often blurred. As Elden (1981) suggests,

> In participatory research compared to other types of research the researcher is more dependent on those from whom data come, has less unilateral control over the research process, and has more pressure to work from other people's definitions of the situation. (p. 261)

The collaborative researchers interviewed for this chapter and many others in this area of study have, to varying degrees, practiced in a form close to what Elden describes. They have given up unilateral control over the research process (Block et al., 1999; Gilfus et al., 1999; Torbert, 1981) and might be characterized as "advocate-researchers," as described by Gondolf et al. (1997). They take the questions, ideas, and strategies of advocates, battered women, and community members and make them central to the research study. Furthermore, such researchers are immersed in the advocacy community and function as advocates as well as researchers, serving in volunteer or administrative positions, on boards of direc-

tors, or as activists within the larger community.

The active involvement of battered women, advocates, and community members greatly enhances the research project by bringing crucial knowledge based in practical and lived experience to the project, as well as critical analyses. Their contributions to research design, implementation, and analysis are vital. When a project is fully collaborative, all involved function as "coresearchers" (Kondrat & Juliá, 1997; Reason, 1994). Underlying the sense of participants as coresearchers is the notion of reciprocal learning. The researchers, advocates, and battered women involved in the study both teach and learn from each other, with each partner bringing complementary and necessary skills to the project (Block et al., 1999; Campbell et al., 1999; Gilfus et al., 1999; Maguire, 1987; Renzetti, 1997). When a truly collaborative relationship is established, everyone's expertise and contributions are valued equally.

Fisher and Gondolf report that whereas Gondolf was responsible for analyzing the data, they interpreted the analyses together. Fisher would provide feedback on the written response, suggesting additions of summary charts or other tools to make the text more accessible to practitioners. Working in separate states, the two visited each other as often as limited funds allowed to devote uninterrupted time to the analysis. Their mutual commitment of time and energy to the process suggests that Fisher clearly functioned as a co-researcher on the project.

A Value-Based Science in Service to Social Change

Many authors promoting models of collaborative research reject the traditional notion that research is value-free.

Rather, they argue that *all* researchers bring a specific set of values to the enterprise (Kondrat & Juliá, 1997; Mies, 1996). As Urban and Bennett (1999) assert, attempting to achieve objectivity is "a political exercise involving power, control, and hierarchy" (p. 1180). The values motivating collaborative researchers are viewed as playing a major role in every stage of the research process, affecting the selection of a problem and research question, design of the study, definition and measurement of variables, and interpretation and dissemination of the results (Dobash & Dobash, 1990; Eisikovits & Peled, 1990). Collaborative research models call on researchers to make explicit their value orientation rather than asserting they are value-free (Levin, 1999; Riger, 1999b; Small, 1995; Urban & Bennett, 1999).

Uehara et al. (1996) argue that research "objectives should be linked to community empowerment, social justice, and social transformation goals" (p. 614). Advocacy research is intended to support the development of programs and public policies that improve the lives of battered women and their children (Gondolf et al., 1997). As Small (1995) states, "If our research is to be more than an intellectual exercise, we need to seriously consider who we hope will benefit as well as who may be harmed by our work" (p. 952).

The collaborative research partners we interviewed spoke to these values. Carol Arthur of the Domestic Abuse Project described one of the benefits of doing collaborative research as "creating a culture where we're constantly asking if what we're doing is effective" (C. Arthur, personal communication, July 2, 1998). In response to needs expressed by former clients in follow-up interviews, the agency developed an after-care program for women and men who had completed its

groups. In addition to improving agency services, the research supports the organization's efforts for social change by providing it with data on the effectiveness of the criminal justice system's response to victims and perpetrators of domestic violence.

Strategies for Successful Collaboration

The three key assumptions we have outlined above support several concrete strategies for collaboration. These strategies include providing equal access to funding, involving survivors of woman battering and their advocates in research projects from the beginning, identifying incentives for all parties involved, and establishing communication between research partners, which includes agreeing on basic standards for research and practice before engaging in the research endeavor, understanding roles of partners, being flexible regarding problem solving, and spending time in each others' domains and in neutral settings.

Provide Equal Access to Funding

Community agencies must be recognized as equal partners in collaborative research projects by both researchers and funders. The organization that controls the budget often also wields the greatest power in the relationship. Practitioners and their agencies should be fairly compensated for their contributions to research (E. Fisher & E.W. Gondolf, personal communication, June 17, 1998; Miedema, 1996). Block et al. (1999) suggest that the funding agency's staff also become part of the collaborative team. Collaborating partners should develop agreements in advance regarding funding allocations for operations and indirect costs, as well as strategies for fund raising (Gondolf et al., 1997).

Involve Survivors and Practitioners From the Beginning

Research that actively involves battered women in the conceptualization process will likely be enriched (Avis, 1994; Short et al., 1998). Involving battered women and their advocates in the research process will increase the likelihood that the research questions asked are relevant to the lives of battered women and the interventions designed to help them. Survivors and practitioners can help identify potential safety risks in the research design and implementation, create effective strategies for improving response rates and minimizing attrition, identify outcome variables, and validate the interpretation of results (Block et al., 1999; Gondolf et al., 1997; Lennett & Colten, 1999; Short et al., 1998). Battered women and their advocates can also help identify issues that are salient to survivors but that may not be initially viewed as scientifically relevant to researchers (Renzetti, 1997).

Furthermore, when collaborations do not actively involve all participants in the research process from the outset, the project is likely to encounter problems at the implementation stage. Levin (1999) recounts problems that emerged with project implementation when line staff in the welfare department were not a part of the research design from the outset. Campbell et al. (1999) encountered similar problems. Such complications can be minimized by ensuring that the skills and input of all collaborators are solicited

from the beginning (Block et al., 1999). This may involve conducting cross-disciplinary training in research and advocacy issues so that the entire research team has enough information to make informed contributions (Block et al., 1999; Campbell et al., 1999; Lennett & Colten, 1999).

In the Texas collaboration, Gondolf and his colleagues ran initial statistical analyses of the data and reached tentative conclusions, which shelter staff would then test with women in the shelter. In one case, this led the collaborators to modify the severity ranking of different kinds of threats. The researchers initially ranked threats to children as a moderately low-level threat, whereas shelter residents asserted that threats to children were the greatest threat to women.

In the Community Advocacy Project, Sullivan spent a considerable amount of time talking with shelter residents informally to gather information to aid in the development of an experimental advocacy program and evaluation project, with significant benefits to the project. As Sullivan recounts,

> I think I would never have designed an effective intervention if I hadn't listened to the women themselves, because everything I was reading at that point, the literature in the journals, would have led me in a completely different direction.

Sullivan's experience demonstrates the value of involving women who have been battered as equal partners in research on domestic violence. This example also illustrates the benefits resulting from investing significantly more time in consultation with battered women, advocates, and community members.

Offer Incentives for All Parties

Collaborative research on domestic violence should offer tangible benefits to all project participants (McGee, 1997). This helps to ensure the commitment of community programs and dispel feelings of mistrust or fear of exploitation. Examples of benefits to domestic violence programs are scientifically sound data to use in grant applications or policy recommendations (Lennett & Colten, 1999; Riger, 1999b), evaluation of programs to help improve services (Campbell et al., 1999), the creation of new more comprehensive services to battered women and their children (Campbell et al., 1999), the sharing and interpretation of new research information from published journals and conference papers, services and materials donated to the program, and a greater understanding of the experiences of battered women and their children.

Both Fisher in Texas and Arthur in Minnesota described having a vested interest in having program data analyzed so that their programs could demonstrate to funders the need for additional financial support. Gondolf and Edleson each had a professional interest in publishing quality research. Furthermore, all of the collaborators were motivated by the desire to learn more about the needs of battered women. According to Fisher, these incentives ensured that she remained responsive to requests from Gondolf.

The Community Advocacy Project collaboration in Michigan provided incentives to the shelter in several ways. First, residents assigned to the experimental group were provided advocacy services on leaving the shelter that the program was otherwise unable to provide. In addition, advocates solicited donations for the shelter as part of their training to become familiar with community resources. Research participants were also well paid for their time and their expertise. Finally, Sullivan was able to use the positive research findings to help the shelter write a grant for funding of an advocacy coordinator position. This position has received ongoing funding and is now viewed as an integral part of the shelter program.

Establish Ongoing Communication

Effective and culturally relevant communication is possibly the most essential and complex element of successful collaborations. Effective communication begins with all parties exploring their objectives, assumptions, roles, limits, and concerns. The participants in the 1996 Conference on Creating Collaborations, held in Detroit, Michigan, have created a helpful list of questions to guide dialogue among those considering collaboration (Creating Collaborations, 1996). Honest dialogue from the outset lays the foundation for establishing trust and alleviating fears cited earlier.

As the research process begins and evolves, collaborators must continue to create regular opportunities to discuss the research process and express concerns. Turnover in personnel at nonprofit agencies is often frequent enough that even the clearest communication must be repeated many times, with the aim of ensuring that all collaborators continue to be adequately informed. Regular and repeated communication will also help ensure that interventions or data collection methods are implemented as intended (Galinsky et al., 1993; Urban & Bennett, 1999). Schwartz, a staff member of the shelter in Michigan that collaborated with

Sullivan, cited such ongoing communication as one essential element that contributed to the success of the collaboration, as did Arthur in Minnesota, who collaborated with Edleson.

The content of ongoing communication will depend on the particular setting in which a research project is conducted. The collaborators interviewed raised a number of communication issues, including agreeing on basic standards for research and practice, clarifying role responsibilities, developing approaches to problem solving, and spending time together in each others' domains and in neutral settings.

Agree on Basic Standards
for Research and Practice Before
Engaging in the Research Endeavor

A number of research teams discuss the rewards of creating a set of basic standards or principles to help guide team members when engaging in research (Block et al., 1999; Gilfus et al., 1999; Israel et al., 1992; Urban & Bennett, 1999). When conflicts arise, group members can return to these principles to help determine the best resolution. For example, Gilfus et al. (1999) operate their discussion group, which is designed to promote collaborative research from a survivor-centered stance, according to six principles: the group is multidisciplinary; the group and its work sustain a multicultural focus; it is a collaborative process; the group is guided by profeminist perspectives on violence against women; members are concerned about ethics, methods, and responsible uses of research; and members value the expertise

and voices of survivors, advocates, researchers, and others (p. 1196).

Be Purposeful About Roles
in the Research Process

Several of the successful collaborators cited the benefit of clarifying the roles and responsibilities of each partner before engaging in research, including Gondolf and Fisher as well as Arthur and Edleson. These collaborators identified the need to establish decision-making strategies, lines of authority, authorship and publication, and timelines for completion of tasks (Galinksy et al., 1993; Gondolf et al., 1997; Riger, 1997; Urban & Bennett, 1999). Collaborators also must decide whose interpretation of the data will be upheld when researchers, advocates, or battered women disagree (E. Gondolf, personal communication, June 17, 1998; Riger, 1997). Gondolf and Fisher explained that, in their collaborative project, agreeing on an efficient division of labor, establishing practical steps and check-in points, clearly identifying goals, and setting a timeline were all factors that assisted them in completing the tasks associated with their collaboration.

In other cases, however, collaborations may benefit from allowing roles and responsibilities to overlap and to develop organically (Block et al., 1999; Lennett & Colten, 1999). Richie said that letting roles remain undefined was a key element in the success of the Harlem initiative. Because Richie and Garfield were perceived as members of the community and not as outside researchers, the boundaries between researcher and community were blurred. This facilitated feelings of trust among collaborators. Similarly, the collaborators involved in the Chicago Women's Health Risk Survey enjoyed permeable roles: Researchers engaged in site-related activities, such as developing site protocols for screening, and advocates engaged in research activities, such as developing and testing an instrument measuring social support. Thus, both the Harlem initiative and the Chicago survey created cultures in which participants were not restricted to their previously defined roles as advocates or researchers. In fact, such a blurring of roles is one of the hallmarks of collaborative research.

Be Flexible in Problem Solving

Regardless of whether or not collaborators find it useful to create agreements regarding roles and responsibilities, partners must be willing to problem-solve together regarding how to address conflicts; they must be prepared to renegotiate agreements as necessary (Block et al., 1999; Lennett & Colten, 1999; Riger, 1999b; Urban & Bennett, 1999). Fisher, Sullivan, and Schwartz each described the tendency for outside researchers to label program staff "uncooperative" and cited this tendency as an indication that the researchers were not willing to work together with program staff to solve problems.

Schwartz recounted the Michigan shelter's experience with a research team other than Sullivan's, which wanted to survey shelter residents using a written survey instrument. The vocabulary of the instrument was for college graduates. When shelter staff tried to explain that the language was not appropriate for shelter residents, the researchers were not receptive to their feedback and did not change the instrument. Furthermore, the research

team did not pay women for the considerable time it would take to fill out the survey. When shelter staff warned the researchers that they were unlikely to get a good response rate, the researchers acted as if the shelter staff were not being cooperative. As Schwartz (personal communication, June 26, 1998) recalls,

> It was like they thought, "If you were really helpful, you'd talk them [shelter residents] into it." But it wouldn't help us, it could in fact hinder us in doing our work, because women might be put off by it, and we have to spend a lot of time building trust, so there was no give and take.

The shelter's experience demonstrates not only the necessity of assuming an attitude of joint problem solving but also the benefits of recognizing the expertise of program staff.

Spend Time Together in Each Other's Domain and in Neutral Ones

Advocates and researchers often work in different environments. Some collaborators find that exposure to each other's workplaces can facilitate understanding of the demands placed on collaborators' time and attention (Block et al., 1999). Researchers may wish to consider attending regularly scheduled staff meetings at community agencies to give and receive reports about the research project or to collect feedback from staff (Campbell et al., 1999; Riger, 1997; A. Schwartz, personal communication, June 26, 1998). Using this time may be more efficient than scheduling additional meetings to discuss the research (Riger, 1997). Collaborators may want to schedule some meetings at the research team's offices, so community partners can familiarize themselves with researchers' environments as well.

Conversely, advocates and researchers often find it helpful to schedule time away from their respective offices to devote their undivided attention to the research project. This could be called "the kitchen table factor," as several collaborators identified the kitchen table as the location where the best work was accomplished. Fisher, in particular, stressed the benefit for practitioners of taking time away from the office to work on the project to ensure that required tasks are completed without the imposition of competing demands.

Make Research Products Useful

Small (1995) argues that research products must be made available to and useful for research partners if we are to truly fulfill the mission of collaborative research. In Massachusetts, the outcome of the AFDC Working Group collaborators was two scientifically grounded reports presented to the Governor's Commission on Domestic Violence to affect the direction of welfare reform policy (Lennett & Colten, 1999). The African American Task Force on Violence Against Women in New York used its research to support the development of community-generated strategies for responding to violence against women in Central Harlem. According to Gail Garfield, the task force collaboration also began to "lay a foundation for the community—however defined—to begin to take ownership of the issue" (G. Garfield, personal communication, July 6, 1998).

Disseminating research results in multiple formats was a strategy used by the Domestic Abuse Project in Minnesota when seeking to make information more useful. Study results were used to shape the redesign of agency programs and are integrated into training manuals that assist other programs in implementing and refining services. Results were also distributed widely in brief newsletter stories and press releases, through community presentations, and in a variety of longer publications and books. Although the results were not always to the staff's liking, funders, policy makers, and other practitioners have tended to appreciate the agency's willingness to expose itself to evaluation and then widely disseminate the findings, even when the study results point in a different direction than the agency's current program.

How Is Research Enhanced Through Collaboration With Practice?

Throughout this chapter, we have explicitly and implicitly argued that collaboration on research is beneficial. Although there is no guarantee that collaboration will generate the benefits we describe next, we believe that more meaningful and useful research is generated by holding to the assumptions and strategies we have outlined. A number of benefits that result from conducting research in partnership between researchers and practitioners have been identified in the literature and through our interviews. These include improvements to research questions, enhancements in research implementation, gains from complementary talents, increased legitimacy and utilization of research, enhanced accountability to battered women and their advocates, and a connection to a larger social movement.

Improved Research Questions

One of the most significant benefits of collaborating on domestic violence research is that the inquiry is often far more relevant to the lives of battered women. Numerous researchers have testified that working with battered women and their advocates led to the formation of research questions that researchers would not have created on their own—questions that were grounded in the experiences of battered women (Block et al., 1999; Lennett & Colten, 1999; Urban & Bennett, 1999). Gondolf asserts that, "Without Ellen's involvement . . . I probably would have asked the wrong questions, because there are a lot of cases where when you have all of this information in a database, you can start asking crazy questions" (E. Gondolf, personal communication, June 17, 1998).

Adopting research questions that are generated from battered women and their advocates also sets a precedent of valuing the expertise that these collaborators bring to a research project, which helps balance other possible power differentials. Furthermore, collaboration is more likely to generate multiple outcome measures, which more accurately reflect the complexity of battered women's lives (Gondolf et al., 1997). Richie (personal communication, July 3, 1998) recounted how community members helped her to view violence against African American women in relation to larger issues facing the community, stating,

It was very hard to stay on domestic violence in the narrowest sense. So while I was tempted scientifically to bring the group back, I didn't because I think it would have skewed what people were comfortable saying and would've made them focus on something that wasn't a discrete concept to them.

Enhanced Research Implementation

Research projects designed collaboratively, particularly those that include battered women in the design, often find that data collection methods are improved. Collaborative projects are more likely to collect information in ways that do not compromise the safety or confidentiality of participants, by paying attention to the timing, format, and location of interviews and surveys (Block et al., 1999; Gondolf et al., 1997). Battered women, advocates, and community members can help develop survey instruments that use language appropriate to and inclusive of its audience (Renzetti, 1997). Describing the collaboration behind the Massachusetts Mothers Survey to document the prevalence and effects of domestic violence among welfare recipients, Lennett and Colten (1999) state, "it took the best thinking of both experts in survey research and advocates with expertise in domestic violence and poor peoples' issues to work out a methodology that would succeed" (p. 1153). This methodology included the innovative use of tape recorders to protect survey respondents' privacy and to address the issue of the limited literacy of many of the women (Lennett & Colten, 1999).

Collaborative projects may also lead to the creation of more effective retention strategies for longitudinal studies by consulting with battered women regarding what incentives and contact methods are most likely to work. The Community Advocacy Project staff interviewed women in the control and experimental groups every 6 months for 2 years. Based on conversations with and feedback from women residing at the shelter, Sullivan and others on the research team designed a three-phase retention protocol that involved paying women progressively larger amounts of money for their participation over time and using women's social networks and community contacts to locate them if they relocated. This retention strategy enabled the study to maintain a 97% retention rate at the 24-month follow-up interviews (Sullivan, Rumptz, Campbell, Eby, & Davidson, 1996).

Benefit of Complementary Talents

When professionals with different training and experience collectively direct their energies toward the same outcome, the process is often synergetic. Collaborators repeatedly describe the results of the processes as achievements neither researchers nor practitioners could have accomplished alone (Block et al., 1999; Campbell et al., 1999; Lennett & Colten, 1999). Battered women and advocates are experts in interpreting responses to abuse. They are, therefore, valuable interpreters and validators of research results. Battered women and advocates may also be more aware of the effects of culture and ethnicity on those responses, and they can provide valuable insight regarding how to modify research instruments for various populations (Riger, 1997). Researchers

are trained in scientific methods and data analysis and can help link the experiences of battered women explored in a specific project to the theoretical contributions of existing research on violence against women. Also, as previously described, collaborative research enables practitioners and researchers to take on new roles and learn new skills (Block et al., 1999; Gilfus et al., 1999). As Block et al. (1999, p. 1169) describe it, "This flexibility [in roles] encouraged unforeseen and valuable cross-fertilizations" that enhanced the research endeavor.

When researchers, practitioners, and battered women apply their complementary talents in tandem, their collective efforts can often reach underserved populations in more effective ways than if they had worked independently. The diverse talents included in the African American Task Force on Violence Against Women initiative ensured that the data collected and the community intervention strategies developed were relevant to and inclusive of the Central Harlem community in which it was based.

Enhanced Legitimacy and Utilization of Research

Entering into a collaborative relationship with practitioners and their associated programs often provides enhanced legitimacy for researchers. Associations with domestic violence programs often provide researchers with data to which they would not otherwise have access. After agreeing to collaborate, Fisher and Gondolf met with the Texas Department of Human Services to secure access to the data. Gondolf recalled that the shelter's involvement in the project was a major source of legitimacy; without the shelter's involvement, Gondolf would have been less likely to get access to the data.

Practitioners may also benefit from the credibility that researchers contribute to a project through researchers' careful attention to the scientific rigor of the research design, data collection, and interpretation (Lennett & Colten, 1999). Fisher, Gondolf, Sullivan, and Arthur all identified the benefit of using scientifically sound data that expresses clients' needs, demonstrates the effectiveness of an intervention, or supports the assertions of battered women and their advocates.

Enhanced Accountability to Battered Women and Their Advocates

Truly collaborative research that involves advocates and battered women in the design, implementation, and interpretation of research increases the accountability of the research to battered women and their advocates (Avis, 1994; Gilfus et al., 1999). It is also more likely to enhance their ongoing efforts to create social change that ends violence against women (Hart, 1988). When collaborators share power in the research process, it may reflect a commitment to social change. The results of research are more likely to be trusted and used by advocates and other practitioners to improve services focused on enhancing the safety of battered women and holding perpetrators accountable.

Such enhanced accountability to battered women and their advocates includes increased responsibility to battered women in communities of color and other marginalized communities. As Gilfus et al. (1999) suggest, "researchers risk possible harm to participants and their communities in cross-cultural studies of family violence unless they enlist the expertise of those participants and their communities. Collaboration becomes a necessity to meet these challenges" (p. 1207).

Researchers who are active in advocacy or the larger community see collaboration as an added incentive to ensure that the research will make a difference in the lives of battered women and other community members. As Richie reports,

> I was a part of the community, not an outsider. And I didn't want to feel that I couldn't go back to a community meeting and have people say, "Whatever happened to that project that you did?" I didn't want to be faced with that. (B. Richie, personal communication, July 3, 1998)

Connection to a Larger Social Movement

Practitioners may find that collaborating on a research project can lead to increased exposure to the national battered women's movement and can expand advocates' understanding of issues concerning battered women and their children. Fisher described working with Gondolf as a "life-transforming experience" that broadened her thinking and analysis beyond the local or state level to a national analysis of how to make a difference in the lives of battered women. Deborah Cohan, a facilitator of groups for men who batter in Massachusetts and an educator on violence against women, asserts,

> One may intuitively know that others feel similarly or are working on research that is shaped by values and politics similar to their [sic] own, but it is

quite another thing to seek each other out and purposefully convene to engage in dialogue. (Gilfus et al., 1999, pp. 1208-1209)

Cohan identifies collaborative research as one mechanism that assuages the isolation those working to end violence against women often feel.

Researchers may also benefit from being connected to the larger movement to end violence against women as a result of collaborating with advocates and battered women. Gondolf asserted that his collaboration with Fisher grounded him in the political issues surrounding the field and pointed him toward research that affected public policy issues. Furthermore, the dialogue with Fisher and others matured his understanding of the field because real-life issues were involved.

Conclusion

We have attempted to describe elements of models of collaborative research that is grounded in the experiences of researchers, practitioners, and battered women. Many research partnerships and program evaluations currently use elements of these models, but given the challenges outlined, it is rare that most or all of these elements are applied in a single project.

Taken together, the assumptions and strategies of collaborative partnerships create a research environment with a very different culture than the one found in more traditional research projects. Research conducted in collaboration has the potential to transform both researchers and community partners when control of the research process is shared. Researchers may learn to shape studies around the questions of those in the field,

gaining tremendously from the input of practitioners and battered women with direct experience. Practitioners may increasingly value the opportunity to have their specific questions answered, becoming more motivated to use research information to shape practice and to participate in future studies. Collaborative research partnerships offer a potential path for helping to create more useful research and improved services for battered women, their families, and their communities.

Notes

1. Thanks to Sarah O'Shea, executive director of the Nebraska Coalition Against Domestic Violence, for her humorous contributions at many meetings, including coining the term *forced bonding.*

2. The authors would like to thank the following individuals for their willingness to be interviewed for this chapter: Carol Arthur, Ellen Fisher, Bob Foster, Gail Garfield, Edward Gondolf, Beth Richie, Abby Schwartz, and Cris Sullivan.

References

Avis, J. M. (1994). Advocates versus researchers—A false dichotomy? A feminist, social constructionist response to Jacobson [Commentary]. *Family Process, 33,* 87-91.

Block, C. R., Engel, B., Naureckas, S. M., & Riordan, K. A. (1999). The Chicago Women's Health Survey: Lessons in collaboration. *Violence Against Women, 5,* 1158-1177.

Brygger, M. P., & Edleson, J. L. (1987). The Domestic Abuse Project: A multi-systems intervention in woman battering. *Journal of Interpersonal Violence, 2,* 324-336.

Campbell, J. C., Dienemann, J., Kub, J., Wurmser, T., & Loy, E. (1999). Collaboration as partnership. *Violence Against Women, 5,* 1140-1157.

Cancian, F. M. (1993). Conflicts between activist research and academic success: Participatory research and alternative strategies. *The American Sociologist, 24,* 92-106.

Creating Collaborations. (1996). *Guidelines for creating collaborations between researchers and community organizations for research* [On-line]. Available: www.umich.edu/~socwk/trapped/irwg.html

Davies, J., Lyon, E., & Monti-Catania, D. (1998). *Safety planning with battered women: Complex lives, difficult choices.* Thousand Oaks, CA: Sage.

Dobash, R. P., & Dobash, R. E. (1990). How research makes a difference to policy and practice. In D. J. Besharov (Ed.), *Family violence: Research and public policy issues.* Washington, DC: AEI Press.

Edleson, J. L., & Brygger, M. P. (1986). Gender differences in self-reporting of battering incidents: The impact of treatment upon report reliability one year later. *Family Relations, 35,* 377-382.

Edleson, J. L., with Frick, C. (1997). *Evaluating domestic violence programs.* Minneapolis, MN: Domestic Abuse Project.

Edleson, J. L., & Grusznski, R. (1988). Treating men who batter: Four years of outcome data from the Domestic Abuse Project. *Journal of Social Service Research, 12,* 3-22.

Edleson, J. L., & Syers, M. (1990). The relative effectiveness of group treatments for men who batter. *Social Work Research & Abstracts, 26,* 10-17.

Edleson, J. L., & Syers, M. (1991). The effects of group treatment for men who batter: An 18-month follow-up study. *Research in Social Work Practice, 1,* 227-243.

Eisikovits, Z., & Peled, E. (1990). Qualitative research on spouse abuse. In D. J. Besharov (Ed.), *Family violence: Research and public policy issues* (pp. 1-12). Washington, DC: AEI Press.

Elden, M. (1981). Sharing the research work: Participative research and its role demands. In P. Reason & J. Rowan (Eds.), *Human inquiry* (pp. 253-266). New York: John Wiley.

Ford, D. A. (1995, March). *Conducting family violence research: Thoughts on guiding principles.* Paper presented at the Violence Against Women Research Strategic Planning Workshop sponsored by the National Institute of Justice and the U.S. Department of Health and Human Services, Washington, DC.

Galinsky, M. J., Turnbull, J. E., Meglin, D. E., & Wilner, M. E. (1993). Confronting the reality of collaborative practice research: Issues of practice, design, measurement, and team development. *Social Work, 38,* 440-449.

Gamache, D. J., Edleson, J. L., & Schock, M. D. (1988). Coordinated police, judicial, and social service response to woman battering: A multiple-baseline evaluation across three communities. In G. T. Hotaling, D. Finkelhor, J. T. Kirkpatrick, & M. A. Straus (Eds.) *Coping with family violence: Research and policy perspectives* (pp. 193-209). Newbury Park, CA: Sage.

Garfield, G. (1998). *A community-involvement model: A response to violence against women in Central Harlem.* New York: African American Task Force on Violence Against Women.

Gergen, M. M. (1988). Toward a feminist metatheory and methodology in the social sciences. In M. M. Gergen (Ed.), *Feminist thought and the structure of knowledge* (pp. 87-104). New York: New York University Press.

Gilfus, M. E., Fineran, S., Cohan, D. J., Jensen, S. A., Hartwick, L., & Spath, R. (1999). Research on violence against women: Creating survivor-informed collaborations. *Violence Against Women, 5,* 1194-1212.

Gondolf, E. W., & Fisher, E. (1988). *Battered women as survivors: An alternative to treating learned helplessness.* New York: Lexington Books.

Gondolf, E. W., Yllö, K., & Campbell, J. (1997). Collaboration between researchers and advocates. In G. Kaufman Kantor & J. L. Jasinski (Eds.), *Out of the darkness: Contemporary perspectives on family violence* (pp. 255-267). Thousand Oaks, CA: Sage.

Greenwood, D. J., & Levin, M. (1998). *Introduction to action research.* Thousand Oaks, CA: Sage.

Greenwood, D. J., Whyte, W. F., & Harkavy, I. (1993). Participatory action research as a process and as a goal. *Human Relations, 46,* 175-192.

Grusznski, R. J., Brink, J. C., & Edleson, J. L. (1988). Education and support groups for children of battered women. *Child Welfare, 67,* 431-444.

Grusznski, R. J., & Carrillo, T. P. (1988). Who completes batterers' treatment groups? An empirical investigation. *Journal of Family Violence, 3,* 141-150.

Hall, B. L. (1981). Participatory research, popular knowledge, and power: A personal reflection. *Convergence, 14,* 6-17.

Hart, B. (1988, March). *Collaboration for change.* Paper presented at a seminar of the American Enterprise Institute for Public Policy Research, Washington, DC.

Hondagneu-Sotelo, P. (1993). Why advocacy research? Reflections on research and activism with immigrant women. *The American Sociologist, 24,* 56-68.

Israel, B. A., Schurman, S. J., & Hugentobler, M. K. (1992). Conducting action research: Relationships between organization members and researchers. *Journal of Applied Behavioral Science, 28,* 74-101.

Kondrat, M. E., & Juliá, M. (1997). Participatory action research: Self-reliant research strategies for human social development. *Social Development Issues, 19,* 32-49.

Lennett, J., & Colten, M. E. (1999). A winning alliance: Collaboration of advocates and researchers on the Massachusetts Mothers Survey. *Violence Against Women, 5,* 1118-1139.

Levin, R. (1999). Participatory evaluation: Researchers and service providers as collaborators versus adversaries. *Violence Against Women, 5,* 1213-1227.

Lewin, K. (1946). Action research and minority problems. *Journal of Social Issues, 2,* 34-46.

Maguire, P. (1987). *Doing participatory research: A feminist approach.* Amherst: University of Massachusetts at Amherst, Center for International Education.

McGee, S. (1997). *Commentary on domestic violence research* [On-line]. Available: www.umich.edu/~socwk/trapped/commentary.html

Miedema, B. (1996). Building a research team: The struggle to link the community and the academy. *Atlantis, 21,* 89-93.

Mies, M. (1996). Liberating women, liberating knowledge: Reflections on two decades of feminist action research. *Atlantis, 21,* 10-24.

Myers, T., & Daly, J. (1997, June). *View and commentary from the trenches: A battering intervention project's reaction to participation as a site in program evaluation.* Paper presented at the Fifth International Family Violence Research Conference, University of New Hampshire, Durham.

National Institute of Justice. (1998). *Research and evaluation on violence against women.* Washington, DC: Author.

Park, P., Brydon-Miller, M., Hall, B., & Jackson, T. (Eds.). (1993). *Voices of change: Participatory research in the United States and Canada.* Westport, CT: Bergin & Garvey.

Peled, E., & Davis, D. (1995). *Groupwork with children of battered women.* Thousand Oaks, CA: Sage.

Peled, E., & Edleson, J. L. (1992). Multiple perspectives on groupwork with children of battered women. *Violence & Victims, 7,* 327-346.

Peled, E., & Edleson, J. L. (1995). Process and outcome in small groups for children of battered women. In E. Peled, P. G. Jaffe, & J. L. Edleson (Eds.), *Ending the cycle of violence: Community responses to children of battered women* (pp. 77-96). Newbury Park, CA: Sage.

Peled, E., & Edleson, J. L. (1998). Predicting children's domestic violence service participation and completion. *Research in Social Work Practice, 8*(6), 698-712.

Peled, E., & Edleson, J. L. (1999). Barriers to children's domestic violence counseling: A qualitative study. *Families in Society, 80,* 578-586.

Peled, E., Jaffe, P. G., & Edleson, J. L. (Eds.). (1995). *Ending the cycle of violence: Community responses to children of battered women.* Newbury Park, CA: Sage.

Pence, E., & Paymar, M. (1993). *Education groups for men who batter: The Duluth model.* New York: Springer.

Posavac, E. J., & Carey, R. G. (1997). *Program evaluation: Methods and case studies* (5th ed.). Englewood Cliffs, NJ: Prentice Hall.

Reason, P. (1994). Three approaches to participative inquiry. In N. K. Denzin & Y. S. Lincoln (Eds.), *Handbook of qualitative research* (pp. 324-339). Thousand Oaks, CA: Sage.

Reinharz, S. (1992). *Feminist methods in social research.* New York: Oxford University Press.

Renzetti, C. (1997). Confessions of a reformed positivist: Feminist participatory research as good social science. In M. D. Schwartz (Ed.), *Researching sexual violence against women: Methodological and personal perspectives* (pp. 131-143). Thousand Oaks, CA: Sage.

Riger, S. (1997, March). *Challenges in collaborative research: Trust, time, and talent.* Paper presented at the Conference on Collaboration Between Researchers and Activists on Domestic Violence and Sexual Assault, University of Illinois at Chicago.

Riger, S. (Ed.). (1999a). Collaboration in research on violence against women [Special issue]. *Violence Against Women, 5*(10).

Riger, S. (1999b). Working together: Collaborative research on violence against women [Guest editor's introduction]. *Violence Against Women, 5,* 1099-1117.

Short, L., Hennessy, M., & Campbell, J. (1998). Tracking the work. In M. Witwer (Ed.), *Family violence: Building a coordinated community response* (pp. 59-72). Chicago: American Medical Association.

Small, S. A. (1995). Action-oriented research: Models and methods. *Journal of Marriage and the Family, 57,* 941-955.

Stringer, E. T. (1996). *Action research.* Thousand Oaks, CA: Sage.

Sullivan, C. M. (1991). The provision of advocacy services to women leaving abusive partners: An exploratory study. *Journal of Interpersonal Violence, 6,* 41-54.

Sullivan, C. M., & Bybee, D. I. (1999). Reducing violence using community-based advocacy for women with abusive partners. *Journal of Consulting & Clinical Psychology, 67,* 43-53.

Sullivan, C. M., Rumptz, M. H., Campbell, R., Eby, K. K., & Davidson, W. S. (1996). Retaining participants in longitudinal community research: A comprehensive protocol. *Journal of Applied Behavioral Science, 32,* 262-276.

Syers, M., & Edleson, J. L. (1992). The combined effects of coordinated intervention in woman abuse. *Journal of Interpersonal Violence, 7,* 490-502.

Torbert, W. R. (1981). Why educational research has been so uneducational: The case for a new model of social sicence based on collaborative inquiry. In P. Reason & J. Rowan (Eds.), *Human inquiry* (pp. 141-151). New York: John Wiley.

Uehara, E. S., Sohng, S. S. L., Bending, R. L., Seygried, S., Richey, C. A., Morelli, P., Spencer, M., Ortega, D., Keenan, L., & Kanuha, V. (1996). Toward a values-based approach to multicultural social work research. *Social Work, 41,* 613-621.

Urban, B. Y., & Bennett, L. W. (1999). When the community punches a time clock: Evaluating a collaborative workplace domestic abuse prevention program. *Violence Against Women, 5,* 1178-1193.

PART II

Types of Violence Against Women

As the chapters in Part II indicate, women experience a multitude of forms of violence. From female infanticide to dating violence to the abuse of elder women, we see that women are victims of violence at every stage in their life course, and violence crosses racial, ethnic, and socioeconomic boundaries.

Historically, it was assumed that the family was a safe haven and that any acts of violence against women happened at the hands of strangers. Within the past 40 years, it has become apparent that the home is not a safe haven and in fact is a dangerous place for women and children. In 1962, the public's attention was first drawn to violence within the family when C. Henry Kempe and his colleagues published their findings about the "battered child syndrome" in the *Journal of the American Medical Association* (Johnson, 1995). The maltreatment of children became a serious concern for practitioners and the public in the early 1960s and re-sulted not only in the passage of child abuse legislation but also in a growing awareness of the need to critically examine power inequities and violence between intimates. This awareness was heightened by the growth of the women's movement in the early 1970s and a focus on wife battering and the creation of battered women's shelters.

Another concern of the women's movement was the problem of rape. In 1971, when Susan Griffin wrote, " 'I have never been free of the fear of rape,' she touched a responsive cord in most women" (Herman, 1989, p. 20). As women gave voice to their experiences, it became clear that they were raped not only by strangers but also more frequently by acquaintances, dates, family members, and husbands. Recent research on sexual violence indicates that sexual violence against women is extremely pervasive, although largely underreported (Koss & Cook, 1993; Tjaden & Thoennes, 1998).

Over the past two decades, several other types of violence against women have been "discovered" by researchers and the public. Violence against elder women, sexual harassment, and lesbian violence emerged as problems in the 1980s; however, there is still a dearth of information on the prevalence and effects of these types of violence. Two final forms of violence against women that have yet to be widely addressed in scholarly or popular literature are female genital mutilation (see Special Topic by Tamar Diana Wilson) and violence against women with disabilities.

The chapters in this part discuss not only the well-documented and popularly known types of violence against women, such as date rape and wife battering, but also lesser-known types, including wife rape, violence in lesbian relationships, and female infanticide. The goal of this part is to provide readers with an understanding of the myriad types of violence that women experience in their lives and their consequences.

In Chapter 6, Kathleen A. Kendall-Tackett addresses the victimization of female children from a cross-cultural perspective. Although there is a large body of research on maltreatment of children in general, Kendall-Tackett's focus is on the gendered nature of this violence. In particular, she focuses on the sexual abuse of young girls in the United States and the risk factors and effects of sexual violence. Kendall-Tackett argues that the victimization of female children worldwide is pervasive and explores the problem of female infanticide in China and India.

In Chapter 7, Karen Bachar and Mary P. Koss provide a comprehensive discussion of rape, with a focus on sexual violence against college-age women. In reviewing current research on sexual violence, they address vulnerability factors, including alcohol and previous victimization, and discuss a multifactored approach to understanding the causes of sexual violence. Most important, Bachar and Koss address college-based prevention programs from a critical perspective. Although there is a growing body of research on the prevalence and causes of various forms of sexual violence, there is little information about the effectiveness of prevention programs.

As Patricia Mahoney, Linda M. Williams, and Carolyn M. West argue in Chapter 8, women are more likely to be raped, beaten, and killed by intimate partners than by strangers. In this chapter, the authors provide a broad overview of various forms of violence against women that occur in intimate relationships, including battering, sexual violence, psychological abuse, stalking, and homicide. They argue that there is a continuum of violence against women from "common couple violence" to "patriarchal terrorism," and they explore some of the risk factors for women who are victimized in intimate relationships and their abusers. They address women's diverse experiences of intimate relationship violence, with a focus on certain populations of women who have received little scholarly attention; namely, women of color, immigrant women, and lesbians.

A specific population of women who are frequently overlooked as victims of violence—the elderly, is addressed by Linda Vinton in Chapter 9. Vinton argues that ageism, sexism, beautyism, and sometimes racism and classism have rendered the problem of violence against elder women largely invisible. Even among advocates for battered women and elder abuse researchers, specific attention has historically not been focused on elder women's experiences of violence with intimates. Vinton discusses the limited research on this subject and focuses on the programs (and lack thereof) available to elder women. Given the increasing number of elder women in society, Vinton addresses future directions for meeting the needs of this population.

In Chapter 10, R. Amy Elman provides an analysis of disability pornography and its relationship to sexual violence against women. She argues that women with disabilities are particularly vulnerable to sexual abuse (often at the hands of the men who are their caregivers) and that these women are unlikely to report their experiences of violence. Sexual abuse of women with disabilities is exacerbated by the genre of pornography known as "disability pornography." Such pornography "fetish-izes" certain disabilities, such as amputations, and commonly portrays women as sex objects through the role of either dominatrix or sexual masochist. Drawing on research from the United States, Sweden, and Great Britain, Elman explores how disability pornography has been mainstreamed and the political implications of this form of violence against women.

In the final chapter in this section, Phoebe Morgan defines the problem of sexual harassment and explores the complexity of this form of violence against women. Morgan argues that about 44% to 85% of women in the United States will experience some form of sexual harassment (National Council for Research on Women, 1992) and that some women are at higher risk for being victimized. For example, women who work in male-dominated occupations and sexualized workplaces, as well as those who depend on men for their employment, are more vulnerable to this form of violence against women. Morgan focuses on the multitude of effects that this violence against women in the workplace has on the personal and professional lives of women.

References

Griffin, S. (1971). Rape: The all American crime. *Ramparts, 10,* 26.

Herman, D. (1989). The rape culture. In J. Freeman (Ed.) *Women: A feminist perspective* (pp. 20-44). Mountain View, CA: Mayfield.

Johnson, J. M. (1995). Horror stories and the construction of child abuse. In J. Best (Ed.), *Images of issues: Typifying contemporary social problems.* Hawthorne, NY: Aldine.

Koss, M., & Cook, S. (1993). Facing the facts: Date and acquaintance rape are significant problems for women. In R. Gelles & D. Loseke (Eds.), *Current controversies in family violence* (pp. 104-119). Newbury Park, CA: Sage.

National Council for Research on Women. (1992). *Sexual harassment: Research and resources.* New York: Author.

Tjaden, P., & Thoennes, N. (1998). *Prevalence, incidence, and consequences of violence against women: Findings from the National Violence Against Women Survey* (Research in Brief, NCJ 172837). Washington, DC: U.S. Department of Justice.

CHAPTER 6

Victimization of Female Children

Kathleen A. Kendall-Tackett

In many regions of the world, it is dangerous to be a girl. Before birth, girls may succumb to sex-selective abortion. During infancy, they are vulnerable to female infanticide or selective neglect of female infants. Girlhood brings the risk of sexual abuse, child marriage, child prostitution and pornography, and female genital mutilation (see Special Topic by Tamar Diana Wilson, this volume). During adolescence and adulthood, females are vulnerable to dating violence, rape, forced prostitution, dowry murders, and partner abuse (World Health Organization, 1997).

Dating violence, child prostitution, and female circumcision are described elsewhere in this book. In this chapter, I describe two types of victimization of female children: sexual abuse and female infanticide. Sexual abuse of girls is described as it occurs in the United States, and it is compared to physical abuse and neglect. Although physical abuse and neglect are more common types of child maltreatment in the United States, they affect boys and girls in about equal numbers. Such is not the case in other parts of the world, where girls are more likely to be abused and neglected—sometimes fatally so. Fatal abuse and neglect are described in the final half of this chapter.

Sexual Abuse of Girls in the United States

The Third National Incidence Study of Child Abuse and Neglect (NIS-3) revealed that in the United States, girls' risk of abuse was 33% higher than that of boys. The difference was due to girls' increased risk of sexual abuse. Girls experienced sexual abuse at more than three times the rate that boys did (Sedlak & Broadhurst, 1996).

With girls being at higher risk, we might ask how often does sexual abuse occur? Incidence of sexual abuse varies depending on the definition of abuse and the population that is surveyed. In samples drawn from people seeking clinical mental health services, percentages are generally higher than in samples taken from the community at large. Current estimates across studies of contact abuse are that at least 20% of women (1 in 5) and 5% to 10% of men (1 in 10) have been sexually abused as children (Finkelhor, 1994; Gorey & Leslie, 1997). The peak age of vulnerability to sexual abuse is between 7 and 13 years of age (Finkelhor, 1994), but children older and much younger have been abused.

Why does this sex difference exist? Two possible explanations have been offered, but neither completely explains the sex differences. One explanation is male dominance of women. In this framework, men are described as the abusers of women and girls, especially within the family. Research has, in fact, demonstrated that perpetrators of sexual abuse are overwhelmingly male (Finkelhor, 1994), and the majority of victims are female. But this does not explain all sexual abuse. There are male victims and female perpetrators too, and male dominance of women does not explain these cases, indicating that this theory is not a complete explanation of why sexual abuse occurs (Sedlak & Broadhurst, 1996).

Access is another possible explanation for the sex difference in sexual abuse rates. Girls are most likely to be abused by family members, especially stepfathers, whereas boys are more likely to be abused outside the family (Finkelhor, 1994; Kendall-Tackett & Simon, 1992). Girls may be more vulnerable to sexual abuse because the people most likely to abuse them are right in their own homes. Analyzing data across several studies, Finkelhor (1994) found that for girls, 33% to 50% of perpetrators are family mem-

bers, whereas for boys, only 10% to 20% are. But girls abused outside the home and boys abused by family members do not fit within this framework. For example, in one clinical study, 10% of girls were abused by "friends of the family," and 33% of boys were also abused within the home (Kendall-Tackett & Simon, 1992). When looking at the entire data set from this study (males and females together), about 10% of abusers were brothers, and another 10% were uncles. Grandfathers were the abusers about 3% of the time, and strangers, about 1% (Kendall-Tackett & Simon, 1987). These perpetrators abused boys and girls in about equal numbers.

The Effects of Sexual Abuse

The effects of sexual abuse are probably its most highly studied aspect—and its most political. Some claim sexual abuse is always harmful. Yet, many children show no symptoms at all (Kendall-Tackett, Williams, & Finkelhor, 1993). Others maintain that some children actually benefit from these sexual experiences and that research is biased toward negative effects (Sandfort, 1984). The research reveals, however, the complexity of responses to sexual abuse. Some victims will show few, if any, effects. Others will have mild symptoms. Still others will be severely affected. Briere and Runtz (1987) estimate that 20% of adult survivors of sexual abuse (or 5% of the total population) will experience major long-term effects and show significant symptoms. Studies of the effects of sexual abuse are divided into short-term (the effects on children) and long-term (the effects on adults).

Short-Term Effects

Children experience a wide range of difficulties after they have been sexually abused. Some of the most common symptoms are nightmares, depression, withdrawn behavior, aggression, and regressive behavior. Some children are very symptomatic, whereas others show few symptoms. Sometimes, symptoms appear as delayed responses. In other cases, symptoms may get better over time.

Symptoms of posttraumatic stress disorder (PTSD) are common but not specific to sexual abuse (meaning that children who have experienced other traumatic events may also show symptoms of PTSD). PTSD, as the name implies, is a constellation of behaviors and reactions that occur in the wake of traumatic events. They were first noted among combat veterans, but more recently, this diagnosis has been used to describe the aftermath of other traumatic experiences, including child sexual abuse. These reactions may be manifested as hypervigilance, sleep disturbances, startle responses, and intrusive thoughts or flashbacks.

Perhaps the symptom that is most characteristic of children who have been sexually abused is sexualized behavior. Even this symptom does not occur in all sexually abused children, so its absence does not mean that sexual abuse has not occurred (Kendall-Tackett et al., 1993). Sexualized behavior is also one of the more disturbing symptoms, especially when noted in children who are 6 years old or younger. It includes public masturbation, sexual play with dolls, and invitations to other children and adults to participate in sexual activity. As children mature, these activities may be identified as promiscu-

TABLE 6.1 Effects of Sexual Abuse on Children: Most Commonly Occurring Reactions

Age	Most Common Symptom
Preschoolers	Anxiety
	Nightmares
	Inappropriate sexual behavior
School-age	Fear
	Mental illness
	Aggression
	Nightmares
	School problems
	Hyperactivity
	Regressive behavior
Adolescents	Depression
	Withdrawn, suicidal, or self-injurious behavior
	Physical complaints
	Illegal acts
	Running away
	Substance abuse

SOURCE: Kendall-Tackett, Williams, and Finkelhor (1993). Reprinted with permission of the American Psychological Association.

ity, or the children may be involved in prostitution or pornography.

The symptoms that children manifest also vary by age of the child. For example, preschool-age children are more likely to experience anxiety or sexual acting-out, whereas adolescents are more likely to manifest substance abuse or illegal behaviors. Table 6.1 gives an overview of symptoms that are most likely to occur within a given age group. Symptoms may also change over time. For example, a preschooler who is sexually acting out may become a teen who is highly promiscuous.

Long-Term Effects

Although not everyone who experiences sexual abuse shows symptoms, the effects of childhood abuse can also continue well into adulthood. These are known as long-term effects. Sometimes, children show functional coping behaviors in childhood (such as seeking the assistance of a supportive adult) and do not become symptomatic as adults. At other times, their coping abilities are less positive but still serve an important function during childhood. Symptoms adult survivors manifest are often logical extensions of dysfunctional coping mechanisms developed during childhood (Briere & Elliot, 1994). While these dysfunctional behaviors may have helped the child cope with ongoing abuse, they often have a negative impact on adult functions. Long-term effects can be divided into seven categories (Briere & Elliot, 1994; Kendall-Tackett & Marshall, 1998). These are described below.

Posttraumatic Stress Disorder (PTSD)

PTSD is a commonly occurring symptom among adult survivors of sexual abuse. According to Briere and Elliot (1994), 80% of abuse survivors have symptoms of PTSD, even if they do not meet the full diagnostic criteria. Again, these reactions may be manifested as hypervigilance, sleep disturbances, startle responses, and intrusive thoughts or flashbacks.

Cognitive Distortions

Sexual abuse survivors may develop a mental framework (or internal working model) in which they perceive the world as a dangerous place. Furthermore, they may feel helpless and unable to defend themselves. These cognitive distortions make them more vulnerable to both revictimization and depression because they perceive themselves to be powerless in their lives.

Emotional Distress

Emotional distress is perhaps the most common symptom that occurs among adult survivors. It includes depression, anxiety, and anger. Adult survivors of childhood sexual abuse have a lifetime risk of depression that is four times higher than that of their nonabused counterparts (Briere & Elliot, 1994). They may also experience anxiety ranging from mild to severe and may also be angry or experience rage on a regular basis.

Impaired Sense of Self

Survivors may have difficulty separating their emotional states from the reactions of others. In other words, their moods may often depend on the moods of others. For example, their partners are depressed or angry, so they are, too, without necessarily considering whether they really feel the same way. They may also have difficulties in self-protection, increasing their risk of revictimization.

Avoidance

Avoidance includes some of the more serious sequelae of past abuse. Survivors may experience dissociation, which includes alterations in body perception (including feelings of separation from their bodies), emotional numbing, amnesia for painful memories, and multiple personality disorder. Other types of avoidant be-

havior are substance abuse, suicidal ideation and attempts, and tension-reducing
activities including indiscriminate sexual
behavior, bingeing and purging, and self-
mutilation.

Interpersonal Difficulties

Adult survivors may have problems
with interpersonal relationships. They may
adopt an avoidant style, characterized by
low interdependency, self-disclosure, and
warmth. Or they may adopt an intrusive
style, characterized by extremely high
needs for closeness, excessive self-disclosure, and a demanding and controlling
style (Becker-Lausen & Mallon-Kraft,
1997). Both styles result in loneliness.

Physical Health Problems

Women who report a history of abuse
may have a variety of health problems.
Some of the symptoms that have been
noted in adult survivors of childhood
abuse include chronic pelvic pain, frequent feelings of fatigue, severe
premenstrual syndrome, irritable bowel
syndrome, frequent headaches, sleeping
disturbances, and frequent vaginal infections. Adult survivors also have overall
lower satisfaction with their physical
health than their nonabused counterparts
(Moeller, Bachman, & Moeller, 1993;
Walling et al., 1994).

Differences in Response to Sexual Abuse

As described earlier, children and adults
vary widely in their reactions to sexual
abuse. Some of the variation can be explained in terms of the child's overall coping abilities or the support available to the
child at the time of disclosure (assuming
that the abuse actually was disclosed).
But characteristics of the abuse itself can
also exert an influence. Some people are
more seriously affected by abuse because
their experiences were more severe. Characteristics that make an experience more
or less serious include the identity of the
perpetrator, the severity of the sexual acts,
the duration and frequency of the abuse,
and the use of force. Some ethnic group
differences in response to child sexual
abuse have also recently been observed.

Studying the characteristics of abuse
demonstrates the complexity of their effects. For almost any statement made, exceptions occur. To further complicate matters, many of these factors are related to
each other. For example, a perpetrator
who is a family member will have more
access to a child and for a longer time. So
identity of the perpetrator is often related
to duration of the abuse. Severity of the
sexual acts is often related to duration of
the abuse as well, with more severe acts
occurring over time. However, many one-
time assaults are rapes. In other words, instead of abuse that becomes gradually
more severe over time, the first contact includes penetration. Factors affecting
overall severity of the abuse experience
are described below.

In general, abuse will be more harmful
if the abuser is someone the child knows
and trusts and the abuse violates that
trust (Finkelhor, 1987). This is reflected
in the difference in the percentage of
abuse by parent figures in clinical versus
nonclinical samples. (Presumably, more
harmful abuse occurred among people
who are seeking treatment.) Abuse by
parent figures ranges from 16% in nonclinical samples to as high as 62% in clinical samples (Berliner & Elliot, 1996;
Kendall-Tackett & Simon, 1987). How-

ever, abuse by family members is not nec-essarily always more harmful. The child's emotional attachment to the perpetrator and sense of betrayal can be more impor-tant predictors of harm than strict familial relationship (Finkelhor, 1987).

Another important component related to symptoms is severity of the sexual acts. *Severity* tends to be defined by whether the abuse includes penetration (oral, vagi-nal, or anal). The percentage of subjects reporting penetration also varies by sam-ple. In nonclinical samples, the range is 4% to 25% (Conte & Berliner, 1988; Rus-sell, 1984), whereas in clinical samples, the range is from 43% to 48% (Kendall-Tackett & Simon, 1987; Pierce & Pierce, 1985).

Abuse that occurs often and lasts for years will typically be more harmful than abuse that happens only sporadically and over less time. The exception is the one-time violent assault (Kendall-Tackett et al., 1993). Not surprisingly, use of force has been shown to increase the severity of reaction to sexual abuse (Elwell & Ephross, 1987). Force may be more likely in stranger and/or one-time assaults, but this is not always true (Kendall-Tackett et al., 1993). Although all sexual abuse is, by definition, nonconsensual, sometimes, the abuser will use trickery or mental co-ercion, rather than force, to gain compli-ance. In other situations, the abuser will hit, assault, or physically restrain his vic-tim. Victims who experience this type of abuse are more likely to have symptoms.

There are also some ethnic group dif-ferences in both characteristics of abuse and in reactions to it. Asian children tend to be older at the onset of victimization than their non-Asian counterparts (Ber-liner & Elliot, 1996). African American victims have about the same rates of vic-timization as Caucasian children but are

more likely to experience penetration as part of their victimization experience (Wyatt, 1985). Moreover, Wyatt (1985) found a difference between the age of on-set for blacks and whites, but the age for both ethnic groups was prepubescent. Abuse of white girls was likely to start be-tween 6 and 8 years of age, whereas abuse of black girls was likely to start between 9 and 12 years of age (Berliner & Elliot, 1996).

The overall rates of sexual abuse are lowest for Asian women but high for His-panic women, when reported retrospec-tively (Russell, 1984). Mennen (1995) found no overall effect of ethnicity on the severity of symptoms manifested by Latina, African American, or white girls. Mennen (1995) did find that ethnicity and type of abuse together influence severity of symptoms. Latina girls who experi-enced penetration during their abuse had more anxiety and depression than did Af-rican American or white girls. The author feels that some of these findings could be due to the emphasis in Latin communities on purity and virginity. When virginity is lost, the trauma of sexual abuse is com-pounded because the Latina girls feel that they are no longer suitable marriage part-ners.

Comparisons With Other Types of Child Maltreatment

In the previous section, I focused on child sexual abuse because girls are much more likely than boys to experience this type of maltreatment. However, it is im-portant to realize that although there are no sex differences in other types of mal-treatment, many girls are physically abused or neglected (Sedlak & Broadhurst, 1996). For example, in the Third National Incidence Study of Child Abuse and Neglect cited earlier, the rate of sexual abuse per 1,000 children was 4.9 for females (1.6 for males). Yet, for physical abuse, the rate was 5.6 per 1,000 for females and 5.8 for males. For neglect, the rate is 12.9 per 1,000 for females and 13.3 for males. As you can see, girls are slightly less likely to be physically abused or neglected. Girls and boys have about the same rates of fatal injuries (.01/1,000 and .04/1,000 for females and males, respectively), and girls are more likely to have had moderate injuries as a result of their abuse than are boys (13.3/1,000 and 11.3/1,000), but this is not a significant difference (Sedlak & Broadhurst, 1996). Although there is no sex difference in these other types of child maltreatment, they do affect large numbers of girls and should also be of concern.

In conclusion, the experience of sexual abuse differs and reactions to it vary from person to person. The experiences of some survivors are relatively mild, whereas others experience severe abuse. Even when the experience is severe, however, there is hope for healing. In one study, survivors reported that good came from the tragedy of their abuse (McMillen, Zuravin, & Rideout, 1995). They described how their abusive pasts made them more sensitive to the needs of others. Many felt compelled to help others who had suffered similar experiences.

In describing the impact of past sexual abuse, we must also be mindful of the other types of child maltreatment that girls are likely to experience. In the United States, boys and girls experience physical abuse and neglect in about equal numbers. But this is not true in other countries. In the next section, I describe two cultures where life-and-death decisions are made on the basis of a baby's sex.

Female Infanticide in India and China

Killing baby girls, or allowing them to starve to death, is something most of us cannot imagine. But it occurs even today. As shocking and disturbing as this behavior is, however, we must look at it within its cultural context. According to Scheper-Hughes (1987), neglect or killing of children may reflect a survival strategy that the family adopts. Parents might decide to invest more heavily in their "best bets" and neglect the rest. In some cultures, the best bets are often male (Scheper-Hughes, 1987). Families in these cultures may decide to kill their female children either outright or passively, through abandonment or starvation, to increase the likelihood that their families might survive (Miller, 1987).

Most of us have no trouble labeling infanticide as wrong. A trickier issue is sex-selective abortion. Sex-selective abortion poses a genuine conundrum for those who support reproductive choice. On one hand, proponents of choice do not want to see a discussion of abortion in a chapter on victimization. On the other hand, many people who support reproductive choice are uncomfortable when it is applied selectively to females. Even the World Health Organization (1997) lists sex-selective abortion as one type of violence against women. I have witnessed some spirited and, at times, heated discussions of this issue among my colleagues at the University of New Hampshire. I have included sex-selective abortion in this chapter, but I acknowledge that not everyone agrees that it belongs here.

Below, I describe two cultures where both sex-selective abortion and female infanticide have been documented: China and India. Although infanticide occurs for different reasons, the cultures have similarities. In both cultures, the survival of the group is weighed more heavily than the survival of any individual. Both cultures also count on their sons to care for their aged. Daughters marry out and are no longer members of their families of origin. For this reason, daughters are considered more a liability than a blessing.

Many times, infanticide and sex selection in abortion are secretive and even illegal actions. Official reports may dramatically underestimate their incidence. On the other hand, many of the statistics and case reports provided by advocacy or relief organizations focus on more extreme cases. The true number is probably somewhere in between. To get an overall view of the problem, however, one statistic is helpful: the ratio of male to female births. In industrialized nations, the ratio is about 106 males to 100 females (U.S. Department of State, 1997). As we discuss India and China, I will provide numbers that you can compare to this ratio. This provides at least an estimate of the number of female infants and children who are not surviving, although we must be careful not to assume that all are victims of infanticide.

Birth Planning in China

In 1979, China implemented a highly intrusive policy to limit the number of births per family. Government workers monitor families for birth control usage and tell couples when they are authorized to conceive. Couples are pressured to ter-

minate unauthorized pregnancies, and this has occurred even in the eighth or ninth month of pregnancy (U.S. Department of State, 1997). The policy was implemented because of the enormous size of the Chinese population. The government predicted that it would be unable to meet the needs of this growing populace (Potter, 1987). The policy is more likely to be enforced in cities than out in the countryside, where families may be allowed to have more than one child because they need extra help on the farm (Potter, 1987).

The government's policy, however, runs counter to the family traditions of the Chinese people. In Chinese society, sons are the means of continuity, prosperity, and the only valid source of care and support. The happiness of aging relatives is thought to be secure when there are many sons who can help, thus the village expression: "the more sons, the more happiness." If a couple has only one child, and she is a girl, there will be no one to care for the parents as they age. It is a cause of great shame when aging parents must rely on the government for sustenance, and the amount provided by the government guarantees that the parents will end their days in poverty (Potter, 1987).

As you can see, there is a cultural incentive to have more than one child. To counter this, the government provides steep penalties to families who have unauthorized pregnancies. These include psychological coercion, loss of employment, heavy fines (up to twice annual earnings), and confiscation of property. The government does not authorize the use of force to compel people to submit to abortion or sterilization, but officials acknowledge that this does occur (U.S. Department of State, 1997).

Interestingly, the new Maternal and Child Health Care Law forbids the use of ultrasound to detect the sex of a fetus. Moreover, regulations forbid sex-selective abortions, even promising punishment of medical practitioners who violate this provision. However, population statistics at least suggest that these practices continue, nonetheless. The Chinese press has reported that the national ratio of male to female births is 114 to 100. One October 1994 survey of births in rural areas put the ratio as high as 117 male births to 100 female. However, these official statistics may actually underestimate the problem, in that they may exclude many female births, especially the second or third in a family. Such births are unreported so that the parents can keep trying to conceive a boy (U.S. Department of State, 1997). In some press accounts, the ratio is even higher. *The London Telegraph* reports that the sex ratio of China's population is 131 to 100 in favor of males. In Zhejiang province, there were 860,000 unmarried males age 22 and older, but only 360,000 unmarried females of the same age group. Among 20- to 25-year olds, the sex ratio was 167 to 100 in a rural county in Henan province. In a population of 25 million babies born in China each year, there were 750,000 more males than females (Hutchings, 1997).

Because China is a closed society, it is difficult to obtain accurate statistics. India, on the other hand, is more open and may provide a more candid view of female infanticide.

Female Infanticide in India

The root of female infanticide is different in India than it is in China. In both cultures, there is a preference for male children. However, unlike China, India has no government organization that limits the number of children a family can have. In India, the constraint is mostly economic—daughters will require a sizable financial dowry to marry. Because daughters leave their families of origin, they are often regarded as temporary members of their families and a drain on its wealth. There is an expression in India that "bringing up a daughter is like watering a neighbor's plant" (Anderson & Moore, 1993).

The dowry, theoretically illegal under the Dowry Prohibition Act of 1961, is a significant and pervasive theme. Although a law passed in September 1994 prohibits the use of amniocentesis and sonogram tests for sex determination, they are widely used for this purpose, and many female fetuses are terminated (U.S. Department of State, 1998). Advertisements in India for ultrasound clinics urge couples to spend "500 rupees today to save 50,000 rupees tomorrow" (World Vision, 1994, p.4). *Washington Post* reporters Anderson and Moore (1993) report that at one clinic in Bombay, of 8,000 abortions performed after amniocentesis, 7,999 were of female fetuses. This estimate was supported by a study of clinic records in a large city hospital in India. Seven hundred individuals sought prenatal sex determination. Of those, 250 fetuses were male. All of these pregnancies were brought to term. In contrast, of the 450 fetuses determined to be female, 430 were terminated (Ramanamma & Bambawale, 1980).

In rural areas, women do not have access to ultrasound or amniocentesis to make a prenatal determination of sex. When girls are born, they are still in danger, either through direct infanticide or through sex-selective neglect. Historically, there were tribes and castes that actually killed all their girls (Janssen-

Jurreit, 1992). The Bedees (a branch of the Sikhs) were known as *koree mar,* or "daughter butchers." Today, in India, the ratio of women to men has continued to decline from 972 females to 1,000 males in 1901, to 935 in 1981 (Venkatramani, 1992).

The English-language newspaper *The Hindu* reports that on an average, 105 female infants were killed every month in the Dharmapuri district throughout 1997. This was in spite of efforts to protect female children ("Female Infanticide," 1998). In another region, the Kallars (landless laborers in Tamil Nadu) view female infanticide as the only way out of the dowry problem. One mother interviewed in *India Today* said,

> I killed my child to save it from the life-long ignominy of being the daughter of a poor family that cannot afford to pay a decent dowry. But all the same, it was extremely difficult to steel myself for the act. A mother who has borne a child cannot bear to see it suffer even for a little while, let alone bring herself to kill it. But I had to do it, because my husband and I concluded that it was better to let our child suffer an hour or two and die than suffer throughout life. (Venkatramani, 1992, p. 127)

Officials estimate that about 6,000 female babies have been poisoned in Kallar villages in the past decade. The Usilampatti government hospital records nearly 600 female births among the Kallar every year. Five hundred and seventy are taken immediately from the hospital. About 450 (or 80%) are estimated to become victims of infanticide (Venkatramani, 1992). The Kallar also believe that if parents kill a girl child, their next baby will be a son.

Although some have assumed that poverty was the main motivation for female infanticide (de Lamo, 1997; "Female Infanticide," 1998), the reasons appear to be more complex. If social class were the sole determinant of infanticide risk, then we would expect to see lower rates of female infanticide in the upper classes. However, in the Punjab, India's richest state, Cowan and Dhanoa (1983) found even higher rates of female mortality. For example, females constituted 85% of deaths among infants age 7 to 36 months. Furthermore, Miller (1981, 1987) has argued that infanticide is more likely in the upper rather than lower castes. When the British colonial government outlawed female infanticide in 1870, it stated that the two chief causes were "pride and purse." "Purse" referred to the dowry. "Pride" referred to pride of the upper castes and tribes, which would rather murder female infants than give them to a rival group, even in marriage (Miller, 1987). This may at least partially explain why infanticide also occurs in middle-class and wealthy families.

Birth order appears to be a significant risk factor for girls, with second-, third-, or fourth- (or later) born girls at highest risk. Firstborn daughters are often allowed to live because they will help with the household chores (de Lamo, 1997). Perhaps this reflects a general negative attitude toward girls that goes beyond the need to provide a dowry.

Sex-selective neglect may also contribute to female mortality. Girls are breast-fed less frequently and for a shorter duration. To us, this may seem to be no big deal, but in the developing world, this puts them at significant risk. Furthermore, when girls get sick, the family is much less likely to seek medical assistance. One public health physician described this case:

> In one village, I went into the house to examine a young girl and I found that she had an advanced case of tuberculosis. I asked the mother why she hadn't done something sooner about the girl's condition because now, at this stage, the treatment would be very expensive. The mother replied, "then let her die. I have another daughter." At the time, the two daughters sat nearby listening, one with tears streaming down her face. (Miller, 1987, p. 95)

In one study of infants, toddlers, and preschoolers, 71% of females were malnourished compared to 28% of males. Boys are taken to the hospital twice as often (Venkatramani, 1992). Moreover, only 24% of girls in India are literate, compared to 47% of boys; and 84% of boys go to school, compared to 54% of girls. Furthermore, girls make up 85% of the child labor force. The work is often dangerous, putting them at further risk (Miller, 1987; World Vision, 1994).

Recent efforts to save baby girls in Tamil Nadu have not been particularly successful. Family honor is a barrier to these intervention efforts. Families don't want to allow a girl to live if she will go through life as an outcast, with no caste, identity, or family background. Also, families are concerned that the girl may one day return to dishonor the family or seek vengeance (de Lamo, 1997). For interventions to be successful, they must support parents and address their concerns about the future.

Conclusions

In this chapter, I have presented some grim examples of the victimization of female children. Many of these practices are so pervasive and embedded in the culture that it is hard to believe that they will ever change. As bad as things are, however, there is reason to hope. First, as world attention is drawn to the plight of girls, we can hope that the light of public scrutiny will bring changes to pass. Second, the victims themselves are beginning to act. In the United States, we have witnessed a dramatic increase in awareness of sexual abuse over the past 20 years because survivors of sexual abuse are speaking out. But there is still much to do. Girls are still being sexually abused, and our society still doesn't seem to be able to protect them. We also need to increase awareness of the other types of child maltreatment, which affect both boys and girls, and develop effective strategies to detect and prevent them.

We have also become much more aware of the neglect and abuse of girls in other countries. People wishing to change these practices, however, need to approach the cultures that permit them with sensitivity and knowledge about why they occur. Otherwise, their efforts will backfire. A similar caution is urged by the Director-General of the World Health Organization's Global Commission on Women's Health in a speech made April 12, 1994 (World Health Organization, 1996). In this speech, he was addressing the issue of female circumcision, but his remarks are relevant to infanticide as well.

> We must always work from the assumption that human behaviors and cultural values, however senseless or destructive they may look to us from our particular personal and cultural standpoints, have meaning and fulfill a function for those who practice them. People will change their behavior only when they themselves perceive the new practices proposed as meaningful and functional as the old ones. Therefore, what we must aim for is to convince people, including women, that they can give up a specific practice *without* giving up meaningful aspects of their own cultures. (pp. 2-3)

References

Anderson, J., & Moore, M. (1993, April 25). The burden of womanhood: Third world, second class. *Washington Post* [On-line]. Available: www.washingtonpost.com

Becker-Lausen, E., & Mallon-Kraft, S. (1997). Pandemic outcomes: The intimacy variable. In G. Kaufman Kantor & J. L. Jasinski (Eds.), *Out of darkness: Current perspectives on family violence* (pp. 49-57). Thousand Oaks, CA: Sage.

Berliner, L., & Elliot, D. (1996). Sexual abuse of children. In J. Briere, L. Berliner, J. A. Bulkley, C. Jenny, & T. Reid (Eds.), *The APSAC handbook on child maltreatment* (pp. 51-71). Thousand Oaks, CA: Sage.

Briere, J. N., & Elliot, D. M. (1994). Immediate and long-term impacts of child sexual abuse. *The Future of Children, 4,* 54-69.

Briere, J. N., & Runtz, M. (1987). Post sexual abuse trauma: Data and implications for clinical practice. *Journal of Interpersonal Violence, 2,* 367-379.

Conte, J. R., & Berliner, L. (1988). The impact of sexual abuse on children: Empirical findings. In L. E. Walker (Ed.), *Handbook on sexual abuse of children: Assessment and treatment issues* (pp. 72-93). New York: Springer.

Cowan, B., & Dhanoa, J. (1983). The prevention of toddler malnutrition by home-based nutrition education. In D. S. McLaren (Ed.), *Nutrition in the community: A critical look at nutrition policy, planning, and programmes* (pp. 339-356). New York: John Wiley.

de Lamo, C. (1997, March 12). India killing girls. *The London Times* [On-line]. Available: www.the-times.co.uk

Elwell, M. E., & Ephross, P. H. (1987). Initial reactions of sexually abused children. *Social Casework: The Journal of Contemporary Social Work, 68,* 109-116.

Female infanticide alarming in Dharmapuri. (1998, August 2). *The Hindu* [On-line]. Available: www.the-hindu.com

Finkelhor, D. (1987). The trauma of child sexual abuse: Two models. *Journal of Interpersonal Violence, 2,* 348-366.

Finkelhor, D. (1994). Current information on the scope and nature of child sexual abuse. *The Future of Children, 4,* 31-53.

Gorey, K. M., & Leslie, D. R. (1997). The prevalence of child sexual abuse: Integrative review adjustment for potential response and measurement biases. *Child Abuse & Neglect, 21,* 391-398.

Hutchings, G. (1997, April 11). Female infanticide will lead to an army of bachelors. *London Telegraph* [On-line]. Available: www.telegraph.co.uk

Janssen-Jurreit, M. (1992). Female genocide. In J. Radford & D. E. H. Russell (Eds.), *Femicide: The politics of woman killing* (pp. 67-76). New York: Twayne.

Kendall-Tackett, K. A., & Marshall, R. (1998). Sexual victimization of children: Incest and child sexual abuse. In R. K. Bergen (Ed.), *Issues in intimate violence* (pp. 47-63). Thousand Oaks, CA: Sage.

Kendall-Tackett, K. A., & Simon, A. F. (1987). Perpetrators and their acts: Data from 365 adults molested as children. *Child Abuse & Neglect, 11,* 237-245.

Kendall-Tackett, K. A., & Simon, A. F. (1992). A comparison of the abuse experiences of male and female adults molested as children. *Journal of Family Violence, 7,* 57-62.

Kendall-Tackett, K. A., Williams, L. M., & Finkelhor, D. (1993). The effects of sexual abuse on children: A review and synthesis of recent empirical studies. *Psychological Bulletin, 113,* 164-180.

McMillen, C., Zuravin, S., & Rideout, G. (1995). Perceived benefit from child sexual abuse. *Journal of Consulting and Clinical Psychology, 63,* 1037-1043.

Mennen, F. E. (1995). The relationship of race/ ethnicity to symptoms of childhood sexual abuse. *Child Abuse & Neglect, 19,* 115-124.

Miller, B. D. (1981). *The endangered sex: Neglect of female children in rural North India.* Ithaca, NY: Cornell University Press.

Miller, B. D. (1987). Female infanticide and child neglect in rural North India. In N. Scheper-Hughes (Ed.), *Child survival: Anthropological perspectives on the treatment and maltreatment of children* (pp. 95-112). Boston: D. Reidel.

Moeller, T. P., Bachman, G. A., & Moeller, J. R. (1993). The combined effects of physical, sexual, and emotional abuse during childhood: Long-term health consequences for women. *Child Abuse & Neglect, 17,* 623-640.

Pierce, R. L., & Pierce, L. H. (1985). Analysis of sexual abuse hotline reports. *Child Abuse & Neglect, 9,* 37-45.

Potter, S. H. (1987). Birth planning in rural China: A cultural account. In N. Scheper-Hughes (Ed.), *Child survival: Anthropological perspectives on the treatment and maltreatment of children* (pp. 33-58). Boston: D. Reidel.

Ramanamma, A., & Bambawale, U. (1980). The mania for sons: An analysis of social values in South Asia. *Social Science and Medicine, 14B,* 107-110.

Russell, D. E. H. (1984). The prevalence and seriousness of incestuous abuse: Stepfathers vs. biological fathers. *Child Abuse & Neglect, 8,* 15-22.

Sandfort, T. (1984). Sex in pedophiliac relationships: An empirical investigation among a nonrepresentative group of boys. *Journal of Sex Research, 20,* 123-142.

Scheper-Hughes, N. (1987). The cultural politics of child survival. In N. Scheper-Hughes (Ed.), *Child survival: Anthropological perspectives on the treatment and maltreatment of children* (pp. 1-32). Boston: D. Reidel.

Sedlak, A., & Broadhurst, D. D. (1996). *Third national incidence study of child abuse and neglect* (final report). Washington, DC: Department of Health and Human Services.

U.S. Department of State. (1997). *China country report on human rights practices for 1996.* Washington, DC: Bureau of Democracy, Human Rights, and Labor.

U.S. Department of State. (1998). *India country report on human rights practices for 1997.* Washington, DC: Bureau of Democracy, Human Rights, and Labor.

Venkatramani, S. H. (1992). Female infanticide: Born to die. In J. Radford & D. E. H. Russell (Eds.), *Femicide: The politics of woman killing* (pp. 125-132). New York: Twayne.

Walling, M. K., Reiter, R. C., O'Hara, M. W., Milburn, A. K., Lilly, G., & Vincent, S. D. (1994). Abuse history and chronic pain in women: I. Prevalence of sexual abuse and physical abuse. *Obstetrics & Gynecology, 84,* 193-199.

World Health Organization. (1996). *Female genital mutilation: Information pack.* Geneva, Switzerland: Author.

World Health Organization. (1997). *Violence against women information pack: A priority health concern.* Geneva, Switzerland: Author.

World Vision. (1994, Summer). Growing up a girl. *World Vision Childlife,* pp. 2-7.

Wyatt, G. E. (1985). The sexual abuse of Afro-American and white-American women in childhood. *Child Abuse & Neglect, 9,* 507-519.

FEMALE GENITAL MUTILATION

Tamar Diana Wilson

Some form of female genital mutilation (FGM) has affected an estimated 85 to 114 million African women residing in 26 countries. The practice is also found among African immigrants to North America, Europe, and Canada. It has been estimated that there are 2 million new cases of female circumcision each year (Toubia, 1993; see also Bunch, 1998). FGM can range from cutting away the clitoral prepuce, through removal of the clitoris and the labia minora, to excision of all external genitalia. The most extreme form of FGM, known as infibulation or Pharaonic circumcision, involves the removal of the clitoris, the labia minora, and parts of the labia majora, and the suturing together of the remaining pieces of the labia majora to form a pinhole opening over the hymen. This form of FGM is most widely practiced in the Sudan, parts of Somalia, and Egypt. Pharaonic circumcision has most recently spread to Uganda. Although practitioners of Pharaonic circumcision and other forms of FGM believe that they are acting in accordance with Islamic principles, the practice is absent in 80% of Islamic countries (Lightfoot-Klein, 1989).

Girls are usually infibulated between the ages of 4 and 8, although girls as young as 2 or 3 have been subjected to the surgery. Midwives get contracts to come into a village to circumcise a group of girls, usually without the benefit of anesthesia. In the cities, both midwives and doctors perform the operations. Among the immediate side effects of FGM are hemorrhaging (often leading to death), septicemia, tetanus, urinary tract and kidney infections, the development of anemia and pubic cysts or abscesses, extreme pain when passing menses, and keloid formation. Over the long term, sexual intercourse is often agonizing, and surgical scissors, a knife, or a razor often must be used to open the entry to the vagina when a girl marries (El Saadawi, 1980; French, 1992: Lightfoot-Klein, 1989). Complete penetration may often take more than a year after the wedding night to accomplish, despite invasive procedures to breach the pinhole-size opening. Giving birth is often a dangerous process that may result in trauma to the mother's bladder and in stillborn or brain-damaged babies.

It is believed that infibulation (as well as other forms of FGM) enhances the husband's sexual experience, an idea endorsed by some men but rejected, in the case of infibulation, by others, who do not see forcible entry as exciting (Lightfoot-Klein, 1989). Grandmothers are often the instigators in their granddaughters' circumcision. In the societies in which they live, women are expected to be virgins on marriage and faithful afterward. Both men and women believe that female sexuality is dangerous and that women are inclined toward promiscuity and capable of undermining the honor of the patrilineage through premarital or extramarital affairs, if not controlled by infibulation (Boddy, 1982; El Saadawi, 1980; Gruenbaum, 1997; Hayes, 1975). Uncircumcised girls are considered unmarriageable. Pharaonic circumcision has also been interpreted as a means to socialize women's sexuality for purely reproductive purposes by diminishing a woman's sexual desires— desires which people fear could lead to dishonorable conduct (Boddy, 1982; Gruenbaum, 1997: Lightfoot-Klein, 1989). All forms of female circumcision can be seen as symbolic rituals that ensure women's subordination to their husbands and the patrilineage into which they marry.

References

Boddy, J. (1982). Womb as oasis: The symbolic context of pharaonic circumcision in rural northern Sudan. *American Anthropologist, 9,* 682-698.

Bunch, C. (1998). Violence against women. In N. Stromquist (Ed.) *Women in the third world: An encyclopedia* (pp. 59-68). New York: Garland.

El Saadawi, N. (1980). *The hidden face of Eve: Women in the Arab world.* Boston: Beacon.

French, M. (1992). *The war against women.* New York: Ballantine.

Gruenbaum, E. (1997). The movement against clitoredectomy and infibulation in Sudan: Public health policy and the women's movement. In C. Brettel & C. Sargent (Eds.), *Gender in cross-cultural perspective* (pp. 441-452). Upper Saddle River, NJ: Prentice Hall.

Hayes, R. O. (1975). Female genital mutilation, fertility control, women's roles, and the patrilineage in modern Sudan: A functional analysis. *American Ethnologist, 2,* 617-633.

Lightfoot-Klein, H. (1989). *Prisoners of ritual: An odyssey into female genital mutilation in Africa.* Binghamton, NY: Harrington Park Press.

Toubia, N. (1993). *Female genital mutilation: A call for global action.* New York: Rainbo.

CHAPTER 7

From Prevalence to Prevention

Closing the Gap Between What We Know About Rape and What We Do

Karen Bachar
Mary P. Koss

In the mid 1970s, rape was commonly thought to be perpetrated by men at the fringe of society who sought social and economic control of women (Brownmiller, 1975). Thirty years later, we have a dramatically enlarged understanding. Researchers have documented that rape is one of the most underreported crimes in the United States, that perpetrators of sexual violence are found with varying frequency at all points along the social scale, and that the majority of rapes and attempted rapes are committed by someone known to the victim. Sexual violence has been acknowledged as a national problem in need of a governmental response. In 1994, President Clinton established the Office on Violence Against Women in the U.S. Department of Justice. Also, in 1994, Congress passed the Violence Against Women Act (VAWA), as part of the Violent Crime Control and Law Enforcement Act. As the result of a VAWA-funded mandate, the National Research Council established the Panel on Research on Violence Against Women in 1995. The panel's report *Understanding Violence Against Women* was in direct response to the council's request to "develop a research agenda to increase the understanding and control of violence against women" (Crowell & Burgess, 1996, p. 18). The panel made recommendations to increase research efforts on the context, scope, causes, and consequences of violence against women, and it advocated the use of theoretically based prevention efforts and conceptually clear evaluations with well-specified outcomes. It also recommended continued government involvement aimed at improving collaboration and research capacity. The panel concluded "that in order to significantly reduce the amount of violence against women in the United States, the focus must be on prevention" (Crowell & Burgess, 1996, pp. 2-3).

This chapter is an overview of the status of research on sexual violence against women with an emphasis on prevention. The consensus of current research on rape prevalence and incidence, vulnerability and risk factors, and the content and efficacy of college-based preventive interventions is described, and the chapter concludes with suggestions for improving studies of rape prevalence, prevention education, and evaluation efforts. Due to space limitations, it was necessary to exclude studies on treatment interventions (see Koss et al., 1994; Koss & Harvey 1991; for a summary of treatment interventions aimed at perpetrators, see Marques, 1999; Marx, Miranda, & Meyerson, 1999; for studies on the consequences of rape, see Crowell & Burgess, 1996; Foa, 1997; Goodman, Koss, & Russo, 1993; Jackson, 1996; Koss, 1993b, 1994; Koss & Harvey, 1991; Koss & Heslet, 1992; Koss, Koss, & Woodruff, 1991; Resick, 1993; for work on the effects on secondary victims and caregivers, see Davis, Taylor, & Bench, 1995; McCann & Pearlman, 1990; and for research on the impacts on society at large, see Cohen & Miller, 1998; Crowell & Burgess, 1996).

Prevalence

After murder, rape is the most serious crime against the person, and it is among the most challenging to count (Koss, 1993a; Koss, Gidycz, & Wisniewski,

1987; Tjaden & Thoennes, 1998). Historically, both the method used to measure rape and the representativeness of the sample have differed significantly between studies. Not surprisingly, the rates of rape detected have varied in relation to those differences, with recent estimates ranging from 2% (Gordon & Riger, 1989) to 56% (Goodman, 1991).

When looking at rape prevalence and incidence data, it is important to examine what they tell us. Incidence rates focus on acts and refer to the frequency of rape or attempted rape within a time-delimited period, typically 6 months or a year. According to this method, only people raped within this period are considered victims. The use of incidence rates in isolation may perpetuate the misimpression that "rape is clearly an infrequent crime" (Kallish, 1974, p. 12). Prevalence rates focus on people and consider the number of women whose lives are affected by rape or sexual assault over a more broadly defined period of time, up to and including their entire life span (Koss, 1993a).

Russell and Howell (1983) studied a random sample of 930 women in San Francisco. Based on their findings, they estimated that there was a 46% probability that a woman would be a victim of an attempted or completed rape and a 26% chance of a completed rape at some point in her life. In 1987, researchers reported that one in four women had experienced rape or attempted rape in their lifetimes and that 84% of these women knew their attacker (Koss et al., 1987). In recent years, national, methodologically solid studies have replicated that finding, substantiating rates first reported more than a decade earlier (Brener, McMahon, Warren, & Douglas, 1999; Koss, Woodruff, &

Koss, 1991; Muehlenhard & Linton, 1987; National Victim Center, 1992).

The remainder of this section focuses on contemporary national and college-based studies that use large-scale representative sampling strategies. Other important studies not reviewed in detail have focused on rape prevalence in various populations, such as children (Saunders, Kilpatrick, Hanson, Resnick, & Walker, 1999), men and adolescent boys (Moore, Nord, & Peterson, 1989), gay and lesbian populations (Coxell & King 1996; Garnets, Herek, & Levy, 1990; Pilkington & D'Augelli, 1995), the homeless (Goodman, 1991; Goodman, Dutton, & Harris, 1995), the mentally ill (Jacobson & Richardson, 1987), and patients seen in health care settings (Beebe, Gulledge, Lee, & Replogle, 1994; Coyle, Wolan, & Van Horn, 1996; Koss, Woodruff, et al., 1991; Walker, Gelfand, Gelfand, Koss, & Katon, 1995; Walker et al., 1997; Walker, Torkelson, Katon, & Koss, 1993).

The Violence Against Women Survey

The National Institute of Justice and the Centers for Disease Control and Prevention (CDC) recently funded the Center for Policy Research to conduct the Violence Against Women Survey (Tjaden & Thoennes, 1998). The study, a nationally representative telephone poll conducted between 1995 and 1996, questioned 16,000 women and men about their experiences with stalking, physical violence, and rape. Five questions were used to screen for rape victimization. Results indicated that 14.8% of women and 2.1 % of men reported completed rape at some point in their lives, with 54% of all rapes

occurring before the age of 18. The survey also reported that women raped prior to age 18 were "significantly more likely to be raped as adults" (Tjaden & Thoennes, 1998, p. 11) and noted ethnic differences in the risk of rape. The study, although important, is not without limitations. These limitations include failure to operationalize through screening questions for rapes that occurred when the victim was incapable of giving consent and failure to reach populations without phones.

The National College Health Risk Behavior Survey

The 1995 National College Health Risk Behavior Survey, funded by the CDC (Brener et al., 1999), examined the prevalence of forced sexual intercourse and health-risk behaviors among a national sample of 4,609 female college students. The study used a single question to screen for rape prevalence: "During your life, have you ever been forced to have sexual intercourse against your will?" (Brener et al., 1999, p. 253). In addition, the questionnaire included a variety of items related to risk-taking behaviors, including physical fighting, cigarette smoking, marijuana use, episodic heavy drinking, driving under the influence of alcohol, and suicidal ideation. In all, 20% of those surveyed disclosed that they had been the victim of a completed rape at some point in their life. When the estimate was restricted to women who had been raped since the age of 15, the authors found a prevalence rate of 15%. This figure is virtually identical to that reported by Koss et al. (1987). The data also confirmed previously reported links between victimization and risky health behaviors including drinking, smoking, drug use, and lack of condom use. The major limitations of this study are that only one question was used to screen for forced sexual intercourse and that no information was collected regarding the nature or number of forced sexual experiences. Nor did the survey ask about attempts that are part of the legal definition of the crime of rape.

Crime in the Ivory Tower

Another college-based study, Crime in the Ivory Tower (Fisher, Sloan, Cullen, & Lu, 1998), used the screening questions from the revised National Crime Victimization Survey (NCVS) with a nationally representative sample of 3,472 college students. The study reported a rape incidence rate of 4% for off-campus students and 4.3% for on-campus students for a period limited to the current school year (the past 6-9 months). The reference period for this study was much shorter than the standard practice in the field. Yet, even with this difference, the rates were more than three times higher than those reported by the NCVS. It is likely that the imprecision of the NCVS questions on rape led to some underidentification of rape in Fisher et al.'s study. Although revised, the NCVS questions do not include a definition for rape or sexual assault. In addition, the questions are overly broad in scope, and as a result, they may fail to trigger recall of a specific event on the part of survey respondents and/or make respondents hesitant to label their experiences as rape (Koss, 1996; Perkins, Klaus, Bastian, & Cohen, 1996).

The U.S. Naval Recruit Health Study

It is important to point out that college students may not be the group at highest risk for rape. The U.S. Naval Recruit Health Study (Merrill et al., 1998) collected data from a representative sample of 3,776 male and female recruits. Five questions from the female version of the Sexual Experiences Survey were used to screen respondents for rape victimization. Recruits filled out questionnaires at the start of basic training. Results indicated that 36.1% of female recruits had been raped prior to their enlistment. In addition, 14.8% of the men surveyed reported perpetrating attempted or completed rape prior to military service. Critics have implied that college student populations may be oversensitive to issues of victimization and that prevalence estimates obtained from this group may be inflated. Naval recruits come from ethnically and economically diverse backgrounds, and they are in the same age group as youth attending college. Female naval recruits report victimization at rates 2.4 times higher than college women, and male sailors report rates of perpetration that are 3.3 times higher than those of college men.

The Harvard School of Public Health College Alcohol Study

Although the primary focus of the Harvard School of Public Health College Alcohol Study was on binge drinking behaviors and subsequent health risk behaviors, it also examined the prevalence of sexual assault as a secondhand effect of others' binge drinking. The study collected information concerning changes in binge-drinking behaviors between 1993 and 1997 from a nationally representative sample of 14,521 college students at 130 colleges. Among female students who self-reported as non-binge drinkers, 23.3% said they had experienced unwanted sexual advances, and 2.2% reported being the victim of sexual assault or date rape. In reviewing these statistics, it is important to point out the limitations inherent in their collection. First, the rates reported are for a 6- to 9-month period, which may be an adequate time period to assess drinking behaviors but not to assess sexual assault prevalence. Second, the screening question that refers to unwanted sexual advances is conceptually ambiguous and may include behaviors ranging from unwanted flirtation to attempted rape. The single question asking about sexual assault or date rape is suboptimal. Many respondents do not wish to categorize their experience as rape because of the stigma attached to being labeled a rape victim. The stigma and other social factors contribute to victim silencing and may affect the prevalence rates obtained (Lira, Koss, & Russo, 1999; Pino & Meier, 1999). Finally, the authors failed to ask those women who self-reported as occasional or frequent binge drinking whether they had experienced unwanted sexual advances, sexual assault, or rape, limiting their focus to sexual acts that were a secondhand effect of others' binge drinking (Wechsler, Dowdall, Maenner, Gledhill-Hoyt, & Lee, 1998).

Although the research is continually improving, the level of rape and attempted rape identified depends on the methodological features of a study. Features such as definitional constraints, question context, question specificity, inclusion/exclusion criteria, and multiple counting form a context in which the numbers must be presented and interpreted (Brookover-Bourque, 1989; Crowell & Burgess, 1996; Koss, 1993a).

Some studies that attempt to assess rape prevalence do not define rape (Brener et al., 1999; Wechsler et al., 1998). However, the majority of recent studies define rape based on legal statutes in which forms of penetration other than penile-vaginal are included (Fisher et al., 1998; Koss et al., 1987; Koss, Woodruff, et al., 1991; Saunders et al., 1999; Tjaden & Thoennes, 1998). Although these latter studies use definitions that demonstrate considerable consistency, there are still many methodological variations, including the representativeness of the sampling frame, the context of questioning (estimates are frequently assessed in the context of crime, health, or sexuality surveys), the number and type of screening questions used to stimulate recall, the inclusion/exclusion of nonforcible rape, the use for prevalence periods of different lower age boundaries ranging from 12 (Perkins et al., 1996) to 18 (Wyatt, 1992), and the use of the terms "sexual assault" and "sexual experiences" as an alternative to "rape." These discrepancies may affect how respondents recall and/or classify their experiences and ultimately affect who is counted and who is excluded in studies of rape prevalence (Koss, 1992, 1993a, 1996; Koss et al., 1987).

Vulnerability

Research on risk factors examines the complex relationship of social, cultural, situational, interpersonal, and intrapersonal forces that perpetuate sexual violence (Berkowitz, 1992; Boswell & Spade, 1996; Buss & Schmitt, 1993; Cleveland, Koss, & Lyons, 1999; Dean & Malamuth, 1997; Koss & Cleveland, 1997; Lalumiere, Chalmers, Quinsey, & Seto, 1996; Ouimette, 1997). However, some researchers have tried to determine whether particular women are more vulnerable to rape and attempted rape. In general, vulnerability factors are not highly predictive of sexual assault, and when reviewing this line of research, it is important to make a distinction between vulnerability and victim blame. Vulnerability research describes factors that may increase a woman's risk for victimization without specifying responsibility, whereas victim blame assigns the responsibility for sexual victimization to women.

Research on vulnerability examines factors that can be categorized according to three major focuses (Koss & Dinero, 1989). The vulnerability-creating traumatic experiences model suggests that factors related to personal history, such as violence in the family of origin, sexual abuse, family instability, and socioeconomic status, place women at elevated risk for sexual assault in adulthood (Collins, 1998; Gidycz, Coble, Latham, & Layman, 1993; Gidycz, Hanson, & Layman, 1995; Mayall & Gold, 1995; Messman & Long 1996). The social-psychological characteristics model focuses on personality and attitudinal schema, such as adversarial beliefs, communication, difficulties in threat perception, hostility, locus of control, passivity, rape myths, self-esteem, sexual attitudes, and sexual conservatism (Abbey & Harnish, 1995; Breitenbecher, 1999; Burt, 1998; Lonsway & Fitzgerald, 1994; Messman & Long, 1996). The vulnerability-enhancing situation model focuses on the relation-

ship between sexual behaviors, current use of alcohol and/or drugs, and sexual assault (Abbey, Ross, McDuffie, & McAuslan, 1996; Gidycz et al., 1995; Himelein, 1995; Kilpatrick, Acierno, Resnick, Saunders, & Best, 1997; Kopper, 1996; Parks & Miller, 1997; Scott, Lefley, & Hicks, 1993).

Past Victimization

Both retrospective and prospective studies have suggested a relationship between victimization in childhood or early adolescence and adult revictimization. Research further suggests that this relationship does not appear to be direct (Gidycz et al., 1995; Koss & Dinero, 1989; Wyatt, Guthrie, & Notgrass, 1992). Earlier victimization was found to be related to psychological maladjustment and a variety of health risks, including an increased number of consensual sexual partners and substance abuse, which may in turn increase revictimization risk (Abbey et al., 1996; Gidycz et al., 1995; Kilpatrick et al., 1997; Norris, Nurius, & Dimeff, 1996). Alternatively, it has been demonstrated that sexual victimization may lead to increased use of alcohol and other substances among victimized women who had no prior substance abuse history (Kilpatrick et al., 1997).

Multiple Sexual Partners

Studies examining the link between sexual activity and rape vulnerability report that the frequency with which women date, the number of sexual partners they have, and the frequency with which they engage in consensual sex were all associated with having been raped (Abbey et al., 1996; Testa & Dermen,

1999; Wyatt, Newcomb, & Riederle, 1993). A proposed mechanism for this finding centers on the increased opportunity for victimization that sexual frequency engenders. It has also been shown that men may perceive that certain types of women, those perceived as having loose reputations, are fair targets for sexual aggression (Abbey et al., 1996; Himelein, Vogel, & Wachowiak, 1994; Koss & Dinero, 1989; Testa & Dermen, 1999; Wyatt et al., 1993).

Sexual Values

A related line of scholarship examines women's sex-role values and their experiences with sexual violence in childhood, adolescence, and adulthood. These researchers report that victims of sexual assault were more likely to believe that relationships are adversarial, to endorse nontraditional sex-role attitudes, and to accept interpersonal violence, as compared to women with no history of sexual victimization. However, it is not possible to tell whether victims of sexual assault endorsed these attitudes prior to being assaulted (Gidycz et al., 1995; Himelein, 1995; Muehlenhard & Linton 1987). In addition, gender differences in beliefs about dating and sexuality increase the likelihood that social interactions may involve misperceptions of sexual cues that ultimately lead to sexual assault (Abbey et al., 1996).

Koss and Dinero (1989) found that it was possible to classify just 23% of rape survivors by examining a full set of 13 vulnerability items, such as personality traits, sexual values, sexual behavior, and alcohol use, 19% by knowing just about previous sexual abuse, and 15% by chance. The authors concluded that although these findings indicate empirical

significance, they lack practical significance. The authors interpreted the results to indicate that "rape vulnerability was either linked to earlier experiences beyond a victim's control or was not predictable" (p. 249) and that most victims were different from women who had not been victimized primarily because they had encountered a sexually aggressive man.

Alcohol

Alcohol and sexual assault are frequently linked in the literature; however, the nature of the association and the strength of the relationship remain unclear (Abbey & Harnish, 1995; Abbey et al., 1996; Frintner & Rubinson, 1993; Norris et al., 1996; Parks & Miller, 1997; Stormo, Lang, & Stritzke, 1997; Testa & Dermen, 1999). Researchers report that drinking in general and victim's and perpetrator's alcohol consumption prior to an attack are associated with more severe levels of sexual victimization among college populations (Testa & Parks, 1996; Ullman, Karabatsos, & Koss, 1999). Given these findings, three possibilities emerge. Alcohol consumption may be directly associated with increased rape vulnerability. It is possible that alcohol consumption is indirectly related to rape vulnerability; for example, alcohol may interact with other situational risk factors to contribute to sexual violence. Alternatively, it is possible that certain intrapersonal traits may contribute to both alcohol consumption and sexual assault for both victims and perpetrators.

Most studies examining the relationship between alcohol and rape have used retrospective data gathered from college students. A recent nationally representative telephone survey questioned 3,006 women at multiple points over a 3-year period to document the relationship between alcohol/illicit drug use and rape vulnerability. The study design allowed for prospective analysis of new substance abuse and new sexual assault while controlling for past assault experiences and substance use. Results indicate that Wave 1 use of drugs, but not alcohol, increased odds of a new sexual assault between Waves 1 and 3. Results also indicate that a new sexual assault occurring between Waves 1 and 3 increased the risk of both alcohol and drug use at Wave 3, even when there was no alcohol or substance use history prior to the assault (Kilpatrick et al., 1997).

In general, drinking is a social activity, and bars are popular settings for both drinking and social interaction. Bars are also environments where a substantial amount of violence occur. A study of women who regularly drank in bars indicated that nearly one third (32.6%) experienced attempted or completed rape as a result (Parks & Miller, 1997). Other studies have shown that younger age, prior victimization, offender alcohol use, and more frequent drinking in bars were predictive of bar-related victimization (Parks & Zetes-Zanatta, 1999; Ullman et al., 1999). Women who drink alcohol in bar settings are frequently perceived as being the type of women who are willing to engage in sex. Some men may target these women because they realize that alcohol has impaired their critical judgment (making them an easier target). The assumption that a woman is sexually available when she is drinking may lead to increased pressure for sex and less inhibition about the use of force to have sex (Abbey & Harnish, 1995; Himelein, 1995; Koss & Dinero, 1989). In addition, a woman who drinks in social situations

might not call attention to a man's unwanted sexual pressures as readily as nondrinking woman because of embarrassment about her alcohol consumption or self-blame based on the belief that drinking alcohol means that she invited sexual advances. College women realize that alcohol consumption makes it more difficult to escape a potential rape and that the use of alcohol reduces the likelihood that a rape complaint will be taken seriously. Yet, these same women also believe that they do not have to modify their alcohol consumption because they are too intelligent to be raped (Norris et al., 1996).

Although a statistically significant increase has been attributed to past victimization, multiple sexual partners, sexual values, and drug consumption, the level of prediction accorded to these variables fails to present a practical improvement over using random chance to effect victimization. Furthermore, recent studies found no evidence to support a link between sexual assault and attitudinal or personality characteristics that supposedly make women more likely to be raped (Koss & Dinero, 1989; Pittman & Taylor, 1992; Testa & Dermen, 1999). Therefore, gender linkage of sexual violence remains the single best predictor of sexual assault. Rape is predominantly a crime against women that is perpetrated by men (Koss et al., 1994). We now turn our attention to the larger question: Why do men rape?

Risk/Causal Factors

No matter what researchers discover about vulnerability, and in spite of how well potential victims are trained in avoidance techniques, women will still be susceptible to rape and sexual assault to the extent that men commit these acts of sexual violence (Schewe & O'Donohue, 1996). Therefore, it is important to examine factors that influence the behavior of perpetrators so that these can inform prevention efforts. Traditionally, risk factors for sexual violence have been examined as single factors at individual, dyadic, institutional, and societal levels. Feminist theories of rape have also received much attention in the literature. More recently, multifactor models that incorporate various classes of influence have been developed (Crowell & Burgess, 1996).

Researchers who study individual level determinants attempt to understand how factors such as heredity, physiology, neurophysiology, social learning, traditional gender schemas, personality traits, attitudes regarding rape myths, sex and power motives, and alcohol use (specifically how alcohol interacts with other determinants) may function to make some men more likely to commit acts of sexual aggression. Scholarship at the dyadic level examines the contextual nature of relationships, focusing on variables such as communication styles, type and stage of relationship, and characteristics of the woman (vulnerability). Researchers who study how institutional factors contribute to rape focus on early socialization and examine how groups such as the family, school, athletic teams, religion, and the media may promote sex-role stereotypes by teaching or reinforcing female and male role imbalances, values favoring impersonal sex, and attitudes that downplay sexual aggression against women, as well as by failing to present alternatives to general or sexual aggression. Influences that have been studied at the societal level include cultural practices such as child

rearing, sexual initiation, dating, and marriage, as well as the society-wide propensity to value male toughness and aggression. For recent reviews of single-factor theories, see (Crowell & Burgess, 1996; Koss et al., 1994; White & Kowalski, 1998).

Single-factor theories have been criticized as limited because although they add to our understanding of rape and sexual assault, they focus on "identifying correlates of these behaviors rather than on developing or testing causal models" (Malamuth, Sockloskie, Koss, & Tanaka, 1991, p. 670). In response to the limitations of single-factor theories, researchers have developed theories that integrate classes of influence from the individual to the societal level (Crowell & Burgess, 1996). These multifactor theories either examine multiple causes of a single type of violence (Berkowitz, 1992; McKenry, Julian, & Gavazzi, 1995) or examine a confluence of factors believed to relate to multiple types of violence against women (Malamuth, Linz, Heavey, Barnes, & Acker, 1995; Malamuth et al., 1991; Shotland & Goodstein, 1992). These multifactor theories rely on data analytic methods such as structural equation modeling to represent relationships between variables and to predict sexual and nonsexual aggression directed against women (White & Kowalski, 1998).

The Confluence Model

Malamuth and colleagues (Malamuth et al., 1991, 1995; Malamuth & Thornhill, 1994) have developed and tested a multifactor theory known as the *confluence model,* which explains both sexual and nonsexual aggression. The model is based on the understanding that it is important to look at inherent differences in the male mind to understand the universality of male rape of women. The model posits that psychological mechanisms consistent with the expression of divergent and convergent interest strategies have evolved. An example of a convergent strategy would involve increased capacity for empathy in interpersonal interactions. A divergent strategy would result in the expression of anger in interpersonal interactions, which may lead to the expression of aggression and sexual arousal from the use of force. The use of sexual aggression, in turn, may lead to positive cognitions associated with imposing one's will on others to obtain sex. Nurturance versus dominance refers to the personality dimensions that describe the extent to which people solve problems by focusing on the interests of others versus their own interests. When dominance is high relative to nurturance, a divergent strategy is more likely. Harsh and unstable early social environments at home and among peers set the stage for the development of similar divergent mechanisms affecting future interactions with women. Whether a man uses aggressive/coercive tactics to gain sexual access depends on a wide range of intrapersonal characteristics including impulsivity, emotions (hostility toward women), and attitudes (the acceptance of violence against women, and/or the belief that women ask to be raped when they engage in certain behaviors).

Malamuth et al. (1991) report the results of a retrospective, cross-sectional study conducted with a nationally representative sample of 2,652 male college students. The study used a model that encompassed developmental factors and features existing at the time of aggressive

actions. Results indicated that hostile childhood events influence delinquent actions, leading to sexually aggressive behavior via two pathways described as hostile masculinity and promiscuous-impersonal sex. Nonsexual aggression was largely explained by the hostile masculinity pathway and a latent factor (social isolation). Hostile masculinity is defined as a personality profile including two related components: (a) a defensive, hypersensitive, insecure, distrustful, and hostile orientation to women combined with (b) gratification from using sex to dominate women and control their actions. Promiscuous-impersonal sex is characterized as an unrestricted, game-playing orientation to sex that is lacking affection and bonding.

Malamuth et al. (1995) extended previous work by examining sexual and nonsexual aggression in a prospective, cross-sectional, and longitudinal manner and by expanding the operationalization of hostile masculinity to include stress resulting from perceived threats to an individual's masculinity and proneness to general hostility. A baseline study was conducted, and a sample of young men were followed for 10 years with a goal of predicting who would be generally and sexually aggressive. It was hypothesized that sexual aggression and nonsexual aggression in later adulthood would be more accurately predicted by measuring both sexual aggression occurring in young adulthood and the two-path model (hostile masculinity and promiscuous-impersonal sex) than by either single assessment. This study replicated Malamuth et al.'s (1991) model with a somewhat expanded construct operationalization and strongly supported the predictive validity of the confluence model as a guide in identifying the variables that may contribute to both sexual aggression and nonsexual aggression.

Although no model can fully capture the variability of perpetrators, multifactor models are miles ahead of earlier research based on single-factor models. Multifactor models address factors from the societal to the individual level and use a longitudinal perspective that focuses on the development of a man's sexual and nonsexual aggression. Finally, the confluence model is described as a cumulative conditional probability model, meaning that (a) the probability that a factor will occur is affected by whether other antecedent factors have occurred, and (b) when certain antecedent factors occur in succession, the likelihood of a particular outcome is greater than when only some antecedent factors exist (Malamuth, 1998).

Although the scholarship on factors related to rape risk has improved, many of the theoretical advances in this area have yet to be used when planning preventive interventions. Prevention education programs continue to operate from overly narrow theoretical orientations, limiting both the creativity and the effectiveness of current preventive interventions.

Preventive Interventions

In 1994, the National Association of Student Personnel Administrators mandated rape-prevention education on campuses receiving federal funding (as reported in Heppner, Humphrey, Hillenbrand-Gunn, & DeBord, 1995). Because of this mandate, and in response to research delineating the nature and scope of sexual violence on college campuses (Brener et al., 1999; Gidycz et al., 1995; Hickman & Muehlenhard, 1997; Himelein et al., 1994; Koss & Dinero, 1989; Koss et al.,

1987), many universities established prevention-education programs (Berg, Lonsway, & Fitzgerald, 1999; Lonsway, 1996). It is not possible to tell the number of existing programs, their theoretical underpinnings, or to whom they are offered (Crowell & Burgess, 1996). Furthermore, the majority of programs are conducted without an empirical evaluation component (Schewe & O'Donohue, 1993). A search of databases in psychology and allied fields (primarily education and public health) since 1994 yielded 15 published university-based rape prevention-education programs with empirical evaluation components (for a review of earlier rape prevention education programs, see Lonsway, 1996).

Mixed-Sex Interventions

The majority of prevention education programs (8) reviewed in Table 7.1 were administered to mixed-sex audiences. These interventions ranged from a single 60-minute session intended to decrease rape supportive attitudes (Rosenthal, Heesacker, & Neimeyer, 1995) to a 90-minute, biweekly semester-length program designed to train college students to conduct rape prevention-education activities for campus peers (Lonsway et al., 1998). Most of these preventive interventions focused on challenging rape-myth acceptance, decreasing rape-supportive attitudes, and increasing knowledge (Anderson et al., 1998; Frazier, Valtinson, & Candell, 1994; Heppner et al., 1995; Lanier, Elliot, Martin, & Kapadia, 1998; Lonsway et al., 1998; Pinzone-Glover, Gidycz, & Jacobs, 1998; Rosenthal et al., 1995). Less frequent programmatic themes included communication assertiveness (Lanier et al., 1998; Lonsway

(text continued on page 133)

TABLE 7.1 Examination of University-Based Preventive Interventions Conducted Between 1994 and 1999

Study	Sample	Intervention Content	Study Design	Outcome Variables	Results
Anderson, Stoelb, Duggan, Hieger, Kling, & Payne, 1998	Mixed $N = 215$	Interactive talk show and structured video formats, both designed to decrease rape-supportive attitudes and rape-myth adherence	Random assignment to talk, video, or control group; pretest-posttest design and additional follow-up 7 weeks postintervention	Rape myths and rape-supportive attitudes	Both interventions resulted in attitude change compared to the control group. There was no difference between intervention type. Scores for both treatment groups rebounded to that of controls at Week 7.
Berg, Lonsway, & Fitzgerald, 1999	Males $N = 54$	Two 50-minute tapes presenting either a male or female describing acquaintance rape. Both tapes were designed to be as similar as possible. One 25-minute information-based presentation.	Prescreening to collect history, personality, and demographic data. Ten days later, men were assigned to one of the two treatment groups or the comparison group. Posttests were conducted 2 weeks later.	Behavioral intention rape attitudes and empathy, general empathy	No between-group differences were reported for rape attitudes and empathy or general empathy variables. The group assigned to listen to the female account of an acquaintance rape self-reported a greater likelihood of committing rape or engaging in rape-supportive behavior.
Breitenbecher & Gidycz, 1998	Females $N = 406$	Risk reduction program was designed to increase awareness and knowledge about sexual assault, the relationship between past and future victimization risk, rape myths, and prevention strategies.	Participants were randomized to the program or a no-treatment control group at the start of an academic quarter and pretested on materials included in the program. Posttests were conducted at the end of the quarter.	Incidence of sexual assault (between Time 1 and Time 2), dating behavior, knowledge, and sexual communication	Pretest data were collected to classify participants according to their sexual assault history. The program did not reduce sexual assault incidence among participants and was not significant in changing dating behavior, sexual communication, or sexual assault knowledge. These results were not related to sexual victimization history.

Study	Sample	Intervention	Design	Measures	Results
Breitenbecher & Scarce, 1999	Females $N = 224$	A 1-hour sexual assault education program designed to educate participants about prevalence, myths, sex role socialization, and the redefinition of rape	Participants were randomized to treatment or no-treatment control groups at the beginning of an academic year and pretested. The treatment group received the intervention. Both groups were posttested at the end of the academic year 7 months later.	Incidence of sexual assault (between Time 1 and Time 2) and knowledge	Pretest data were collected that classified participants according to their sexual assault history. The results indicate that the program increased knowledge about sexual assault but did not decrease sexual assault incidence. Specifically, 15% of women with no history of sexual victimization had been victimized at follow-up, and 39% of women with histories of sexual victimization had been revictimized at follow-up.
Foubert & McEwen, 1998	Fraternity males $N = 155$	Video and lecture format with focus on how to help a sexual assault survivor	Pretest-posttest and posttest-only with no treatment control group. Posttest conducted immediately postintervention	Behavioral intention and rape-myth acceptance	Pretest-posttest and posttest-only groups reported decreases in rape-myth acceptance and behavioral intent to rape a woman as compared to the control group immediately postintervention.
Frazier, Valtinson, & Candell, 1994	Mixed fraternity and sorority members $N = 192$	A 2-hour interactive theater intervention consisting of a drama that depicts a rape, solicits audience feedback, and reenacts the scene using audience suggestions to avoid the rape	Participants were assigned to treatment and no-treatment control conditions in sorority/fraternity units. Pretest administered 1 week prior to the intervention. Posttests immediately postintervention. Follow-up given 1-month later	Attitudes toward dating and sexual behavior, gender role beliefs, and subjective evaluations assessing self-reported learning and enjoyment	Immediately postintervention, participants reported a decrease in rape-supportive beliefs and gender stereotypes. Scores for the treatment group rebounded at the 1 month follow-up. Participants reported positive subjective evaluations.

(continued)

TABLE 7.1 Examination of University-Based Preventive Interventions Conducted Between 1994 and 1999 *(Continued)*

Study	Sample	Intervention Content	Study Design	Outcome Variables	Results
Heppner, Humphrey, Hillenbrand-Gunn, & DeBord, 1995	Mixed $N = 258$	Two 90-minute interventions: a theater-based interactional drama (see Frazier et al. above) and a didactic video that used standard psychoeducational materials. The control group consisted of a stress management workshop.	Random assignment to one of the three conditions. Data were collected at five time periods ranging from pretest to a posttest 5 months later. Data collected via phone call and thought listing	Rape myths, Elaboration Likelihood Model rating, recognition of sexual coercion and sexual consent, social desirability, speaker rating, and behavioral indicators	Participants in the interactive theater condition reported deeper levels of information processing as measured by the Elaboration Likelihood Model Questionnaire, were able to differentiate between coercion and consent, and responded in a more desirable direction on an array of behavior indices. Acceptance of rape myths was unchanged.
Heppner, Neville, Smith, Kivlighan, & Gershuny, 1999	Males $N = 119$	Two interventions, each consisting of three 90-minute modules designed to access cognitive, affective, and behavioral routes to attitude change. In addition, one group included culturally relevant information in each module	Random assignment. Data were collected at six time periods: at pretest, after each intervention module, immediately following the intervention, and 5 months after the intervention.	Rape-supportive attitudes, rape-myth acceptance, sexual experiences, behavioral change	Results indicated three general patterns of treatment response: rebounding, deteriorating, and improving. Black males found the culturally specific intervention to be more relevant to them.
Himelein, 1999	Females $N = 7$	Women identified as high risk participated in a five-session didactic and interactive group on rape myths/facts, alcohol, aggressive men, risky dating behaviors, gender, self-esteem, differences, assertiveness, self-defense techniques, and rape impact.	The 217 participants completed a risk-assessment questionnaire; 42 were classified as high risk and invited to participate. Schedule conflicts reduced the number to 7. Pretest at Session 1. Posttest 1 month after final group	Dating behaviors and sexual assault knowledge	At the last group session, members provided verbal feedback regarding utility of the intervention. At posttest, women reported increased knowledge and increased frequency in using precautionary dating behaviors.

Author	Sample	Intervention	Design	Measures	Results
Lanier, Elliot, Martin, & Kapadia 1998	Mixed N = 436	Participants watched an intervention or control play. Intervention play covered rape empathy, alcohol, communication, consent, and male concern about rape. Control play covered multicultural issues.	Stratified random assignment to treatment or conditions. Pretest immediately before and posttest immediately after the intervention	Date rape attitudes	Results indicate a reduction in rape-tolerant attitudes, particularly among those identified as being more tolerant of rape.
Lenihan & Rawlins, 1994	Mixed sorority and fraternity members N = 636	Mandatory group lecture on rape myths, date-rape realities, positive leadership, and alcohol abuse. Smaller, mixed gender discussion	Pretest-posttest with non-Greek control group, 6 weeks postintervention	Rape-supportive attitudes	At pretest, Greek students reported lower scores on measures of rape-supportive attitudes, but the intervention did not produce any change from the pretest.
Lonsway, Klaw, Berg, Waldo, Kothari, Mazurek, & Hegeman, 1998	Mixed N = 74	Campus Acquaintance Rape Education (CARE) program, a practicum course that trained college students to conduct rape education for peers in campus settings. Participants were offered three units of credit to participate and met twice a week for 90 minutes.	Pretest-posttest with comparison group from a human sexuality course. Two-year follow-up	Rape-myth acceptance, adversarial heterosexual beliefs, attitudes toward feminism, sexual communication	Quantitative: moderate decrease in rape-myth acceptance, small reduction in adversarial sexual beliefs, and more support for feminism. Qualitative: At posttest, women reported increased willingness to be more directive and assertive in their sexual communication. At 2-year follow-up, students in CARE were less accepting of rape myths.
Pinzone-Glover, Gidycz, & Jacobs, 1998	Mixed N = 152	Intervention group received prevalence statistics, rape myths/facts, behavior of rapists, personal safety, resource availability, and acquaintance rape scenarios. Comparison group received information on sexually transmitted diseases.	Random assignment to mixed-gender intervention or control groups. Pretest immediately before and posttest immediately after the intervention	Rape myths, rape empathy, attitudes toward women, attributions of rape responsibility	At posttest, the intervention group reported increases in empathy, and men in the intervention group expressed less traditional attitudes toward women and were significantly more likely to correctly identify date-rape scenarios. No difference in rape-myth acceptance reported at follow-up.

(continued)

TABLE 7.1 Examination of University-Based Preventive Interventions Conducted Between 1994 and 1999   *(Continued)*

Study	Sample	Intervention Content	Study Design	Outcome Variables	Results
Rosenthal, Heesacker, & Neimeyer, 1995	Mixed *N* = 245	A 60-minute didactic and role-play psycho-educational intervention designed to reduce rape-supportive attitudes	Assignment to treatment or no-treatment control group. Pretest 8 weeks prior to the intervention, posttest directly after. At 1 month, phone appeal for women's safety project volunteers	Acceptance of rape myths, sex-role stereotypes, rape-supportive attitudes	Intervention group reported decreases in rape-supportive attitudes and rape-myth acceptance at follow-up. Members of the intervention group were more likely to volunteer for the proposed women's safety projects but were not more likely to make positive comments or listen longer to the message.
Schewe & O'Donohue, 1996	Males *N* = 74	The VE/OE group consisted of a 50-minute video designed to increase empathy and awareness of negative consequences. Personal consequences and outcome expectancies were reviewed. RSC group watched a 50-minute video on the role of rape-supportive cognitions.	Participants identified as high risk during Phase 1 were randomly assigned to VE/OE, RSC, or no-treatment control group. Pretest immediately before and posttest immediately after the intervention	Sexual aggression and beliefs, acceptance of rape myths and sexual violence, social desirability, rape conformity	The VE/OE and RSC groups reported lower scores on the attraction to aggression scale. In addition, the RSC group reported decreases in rape-myth acceptance and adversarial sexual beliefs.

et al., 1998), information on alcohol use and abuse (Lanier et al., 1998; Lenihan & Rawlins, 1994), rape empathy (Lanier et al., 1998; Pinzone-Glover et al., 1998), and rape avoidance (Frazier et al., 1994).

Evaluations of these interventions show mixed results. A rape-prevention program that took the format of a semester-long course demonstrated lasting attitude change and increased assertiveness of communication about needs as compared to a human sexuality course comparison group (Lonsway et al., 1998). Fraternity and sorority students at a Midwest university attended a two-phase rape prevention-education program that consisted of a lecture and smaller mixed-sex discussion groups. Results indicated that although students reported lower scores (compared to students who were not fraternity or sorority members) on measures of rape-supportive attitudes prior to the intervention, their attitudes did not change as a result of the intervention (Lenihan & Rawlins, 1994). Participants in an acquaintance rape-prevention program conducted at two Midwestern universities reported increased empathy toward rape victims. Men were more certain of their definitions of rape after the intervention, but their acceptance of rape myths did not change (Pinzone-Glover et al., 1998). Some programs demonstrated reductions in rape myths and rape-supportive attitudes immediately after intervention and for short periods thereafter (Frazier et al., 1994; Lanier et al., 1998; Rosenthal et al., 1995). Other studies were able to demonstrate changes in rape-myth acceptance and rape-supportive attitudes after intervention, but the changes disappeared over time (Anderson et al., 1998; Heppner, Neville, Smith, Kivlighan, & Gershuny, 1999).

Interventions With Men

Although rape prevention is by definition a men's issue (Berkowitz, 1992), only 4 of 15 prevention-education interventions reviewed in Table 7.1 targeted males. These programs compared interventions designed to affect rape-supportive cognitions and victim empathy (Schewe & O'Donohue, 1996), examined whether listening to a male or a female describing an acquaintance rape would increase empathy and decrease rape-supportive behaviors (Berg et al., 1999), assessed traditional and culturally relevant interventions designed to evaluate the effect of peripheral and central route processing of rape-prevention messages on rape-supportive attitudes (Heppner et al., 1999), and educated participants with regards to assisting sexual assault survivors (Foubert & McEwen, 1998). The programs reported mixed success in addressing rape-supportive attitudes, rape-myth acceptance, rape empathy, rape-supportive behaviors, and other outcomes. A study by Foubert and McEwen (1998) reported declines in behavioral intention to rape and rape-myth acceptance as measured immediately postintervention. Schewe and O'Donohue (1996) found that interventions designed to change rape-supportive cognitions and victim empathy lowered participants' scores on measures assessing acceptance of interpersonal violence and attraction to sexual aggression; however, only the rape-supportive cognitions condition lowered participants' scores on scales measuring adversarial sexual cognitions and rape-myth acceptance. Heppner et al. (1999) measured postintervention decreases in rape-supportive attitudes over a 5-month period and were unable to discover why some men scored lower on such attitudes whereas others rebounded to the pre-intervention level. Finally, Berg and colleagues (1999) reported no postintervention differences on empathy or rape attitudes. They also reported that participants in the female audiotape condition (those who heard women describing an acquaintance rape) self-reported greater likelihood of committing a rape or engaging in rape-supportive behaviors. The authors advise caution when using similar empathy-inducing techniques (Berg et al., 1999).

Interventions With Women

Three rape prevention-education programs reviewed in Table 7.1 are directed at women. These programs sought to increase participant knowledge about rape and sexual assault-risk reduction (Breitenbecher & Gidycz, 1998; Breitenbecher & Scarce, 1999; Himelein, 1999), to examine the connection between risk-reduction education and rape incidence for women with and without sexual assault histories (Breitenbecher & Gidycz, 1998; Breitenbecher & Scarce, 1999), and to explore the relationship between knowledge change and precautionary dating behaviors for women described as being at high risk for victimization (Himelein, 1999). The results of the evaluations were mixed. One study targeted women identified as high risk who participated in a five-session rape-risk-reduction program. Participants responding to a questionnaire mailed 1 month after the intervention reported increased knowledge about sexual assault and more frequent use of precautionary dating behaviors (Himelein, 1999). Breitenbecher and Gidycz (1998) sought to expand on an earlier investigation, which found a risk-reduction program effectively reduced the incidence of sexual assault among women with no prior history of victimization but was not effective for women with prior sexual assault histories (Hanson & Gidycz, 1993). Breitenbecher and Gidycz (1998) modified the earlier program by adding content hypothesized to mediate revictimization. The revised program did not affect knowledge about sexual assault, sexual communication, or dating behaviors, nor did it reduce the incidence of sexual victimization for either group. A study by Breitenbecher and Scarce (1999) examined the relationship between a sexual assault education program and sexual assault incidence. Two hundred twenty-four women were randomly assigned to either treatment or no-treatment control groups. Members of the treatment group participated in a 60-minute education program. Both groups were followed up 7 months later. Whereas the intervention improved knowledge of sexual assault when compared to the control group, both groups had the same rate of rape and attempted rape at the 7-month follow-up, regardless of previous sexual assault history, and women with histories of sexual victimization were more than twice as likely to be assaulted during the follow-up period.

George McCall (1993) characterized rape-prevention efforts as "confused, scattered, and sporadic with little scientific underpinning" (p. 277), and this comment is still applicable today. The problems lie with the content and utility of preventive interventions and, to a lesser extent, with the quality of evaluative efforts. Most prevention-education programs lack theoretical grounding, overemphasize content that is out of date given current scholarship, and fail to target high-risk groups. The term *prevention* is used to describe programs aimed at mixed-sex audiences, potential perpetrators, and—all too frequently—victims or potential victims. Interventions targeting women are more accurately described as avoidance, deterrence, or risk-reduction programs.

Existing scholarship on the effectiveness of sexual assault education provides a somewhat confusing picture (Breitenbecher & Scarce, 1999). Test-retest intervals are short, with a number of posttests conducted immediately after an intervention (Foubert & McEwen, 1998; Lanier et al, 1998; Pinzone-Glover et al., 1998; Schewe & O'Donohue, 1996). These short-term changes in knowledge, rape-supportive attitudes, behavioral intentions, or rape-myth acceptance are generally accepted as evaluation. The results obtained are highly suggestive of experimental demand effects. Three of the 15 interventions had test-retest intervals of 5 months or longer (Breitenbecher & Scarce, 1999; Heppner et al., 1999; Lonsway et al., 1998); however only, one examined the effect of the intervention on preventing rape (Breitenbecher & Scarce, 1999). Most programs measure changes in variables such as knowledge, rape-myth acceptance, behavioral intention, and levels of empathy, which are proximal outcomes, and expect (in most cases tacitly) that changes in these variables will somehow decrease the incidence/prevalence of rape, which is the ultimate goal of prevention education. Furthermore, of the 15 studies reviewed, only one went beyond the standard measures of statistical significance to report measures of practical significance: that is, effect sizes (Lonsway et al., 1998). Most interventions take a shotgun approach to pre-

vention, and if they report significant results, they are unable to determine which program module was responsible for the effect. The large number of students in some studies makes it possible to use statistical techniques such as structural equations modeling to examine the differential effect of intervention components.

Programs that target mixed-sex audiences may be developed as a means of encouraging men and women to interact and learn from each other (Frazier et al., 1994). Alternatively, interventions for mixed-sex audiences may be preferred because of the erroneous assumption that men and women share the responsibility for preventing rape. These programs lessen the focus on potential perpetrators and may promote victim-blaming ideologies. Whatever the reason for mixed-sex interventions, they may not have the desired effect (Berg et al., 1999; Lenihan & Rawlins, 1994). As a female participant in a mixed-sex rape prevention-education discussion group stated, "as soon as we began to complain about how some of us have been treated sexually, they started booing and hollering back—and then they all got up and walked out; they didn't want to hear it" (Lenihan & Rawlins, 1994, p. 453).

Risk-reduction programs can teach women to take certain precautions, but deterrence and avoidance strategies cannot accomplish the goals of rape-prevention education. Prevention programming must target the real and potential perpetrators and address the primary cause of rape, namely, men's motivation to rape (Lonsway, 1996; Schewe & O'Donohue, 1996). As Berkowitz (1992) stated, "Rape prevention is clearly a men's issue, and we need prevention programs that draw on relevant research to help men begin a process of self-examination and change" (p. 180). It has been suggested that the low frequency of rape prevention-education programs directed at men may be due in part to the dearth of studies demonstrating the effectiveness of such programs (Schewe & O'Donohue, 1993). However, because the majority of prevention-education programs remain unevaluated, this is not especially likely (Crowell & Burgess, 1996). It is more probable that the lack of programs adequately targeting males and females results from the gap between theory development and prevention practice; closing this gap is one of the biggest challenges the field of research on rape prevention faces.

Conclusions and Recommendations

The foregoing review has examined research on prevalence, vulnerability, and risk in an attempt to discern what we know, and it has focused on recent college-based preventive interventions to discover whether gains realized in the previously mentioned areas have been used. The data presented here yield several conclusions.

First, we now have enough recent, nationally representative studies to support the validity of earlier rape prevalence estimates (Koss et al., 1987). Although there remain flaws in these study designs, including the use of single screening questions for forced sexual intercourse and the failure to collect information regarding the nature of forced sexual experiences, there is no evidence that the prevalence of rape is changing (Brener et al., 1999; Koss et al., 1987). The question remains: When will our numbers be good enough?

Given the limited funds directed at sexual violence, it would be better to focus on variation in rape prevalence by ethnicity and class, as well as on the links of various forms of violence against women across the life span, paying particular attention to the cumulative societal costs of the brutalization and coercion of women. Next, a number of studies have examined whether some women have heightened vulnerability to sexual violence. To date, the best predictor of future victimization is past victimization (Gidycz et al., 1995; Himelein, 1995). That it is not possible to predict a woman's vulnerability to rape with any certainty should come as no surprise. This finding reflects the reality that women's traits are not causally related to rape victimization. It has been demonstrated, however, that there is substantial predictability in terms of which men will and will not be likely to engage in rape (Malamuth, 1998; Malamuth et al., 1991, 1995). Future research needs to focus on the confluence of factors that predispose perpetration as opposed to continuing to examine factors indirectly or spuriously related to victimization.

The final and perhaps most notable conclusion is that despite the progress in risk-factor research, the field of prevention lags behind. We must increase the number of preventive interventions directed at men and incorporate content informed by theories that actually predict rape behavior. The majority of preventive interventions are directed at mixed-sex audiences or women. We need to move away from mixed-sex interventions because despite numerous evaluations, it has not been empirically established that these programs can accomplish the mutually exclusive goals of rape prevention and rape avoidance/resistance education in a way that is effective and that does not polarize program participants. If we continue to direct programs at women, we must consider different curricula. Research suggests that current programs have little impact on rape prevalence (Breitenbecher & Gidycz, 1998; Breitenbecher & Scarce, 1999). This is to be expected because women do not cause rape. Programs for women (both with and without previous histories of victimization) must reflect current theory. Preventive efforts targeting women have yet to incorporate rape-resistance training despite consistent scholarship that suggests resistance strategies increase women's ability to avoid rape without increasing their chance of being injured (Ullman, 1997, 1998; Ullman & Knight, 1995). We need to establish new educational partnerships and present rape prevention and avoidance training in new contexts. It is important to develop partnerships in areas that have been avoided or underserved, such as the juvenile justice system, alternative high schools, job training programs, junior colleges, and programs for teen mothers. New contexts for prevention programming that link drug and alcohol programs with rape-prevention education must also be established.

Creativity and flexibility need to be encouraged, both in terms of developing educational partnerships and in terms of revising prevention curriculum. This is no easy task, however, because federal and state funding initiatives mandate evaluation of program effectiveness, increasing the likelihood that variables highly susceptible to experimental demand will be targeted as indicators of change. Federal and state mandates also engender a hesitancy to modify existing curriculums, resulting in premature program solidification. The importance of well-conceptualized evaluation has been demonstrated by re-

cent studies. These studies indicate that current preventive interventions are largely ineffective. Now that we know what *doesn't* work, we need to rethink how we approach rape-prevention education. Because of recent scholarship on rape-risk behavior, we now have a greatly expanded foundation to stimulate the next wave of prevention-education efforts.

References

Abbey, A., & Harnish, R. J. (1995). Perception of sexual intent: The role of gender, alcohol consumption, and rape supportive attitudes. *Sex Roles, 32*(5-6), 297-313.

Abbey, A., Ross, L. T., McDuffie, D., & McAuslan, P. (1996). Alcohol and dating risk factors for sexual assault among college women. *Psychology of Women Quarterly, 20,* 147-169.

Anderson, L., Stoelb, M. P., Duggan, P., Hieger, B., Kling, K. H., & Payne, J. P. (1998). The effectiveness of two types of rape prevention programs in changing the rape-supportive attitudes of college students. *Journal of College Student Development, 39,* 131-142.

Beebe, D. K., Gulledge, K. M., Lee, C. M., & Replogle, W. (1994). Prevalence of sexual assault among women patients seen in family practice clinics. *Family Practice Research Journal, 14,* 223-228.

Berg, D. R., Lonsway, K. A., & Fitzgerald, L. F. (1999). Rape prevention education for men: The effectiveness of empathy-induction techniques. *Journal of College Student Development, 40*(3), 219-234.

Berkowitz, A. (1992). College men as perpetrators of acquaintance rape and sexual assault: A review of recent research. *Journal of American College Health, 40,* 175-181.

Boswell, A. A., & Spade, J. Z. (1996). Fraternities and collegiate rape culture: Why are some fraternities more dangerous places for women? *Gender &Society, 10,* 133-147.

Breitenbecher, K. H. (1999). The association between the perception of threat in a dating situation and sexual victimization. *Violence and Victims, 14*(2), 135-146.

Breitenbecher, K. H., & Gidycz, C. A. (1998). An empirical evaluation of a program designed to reduce the risk of multiple sexual victimization. *Journal of Interpersonal Violence, 13*(4), 472-488.

Breitenbecher, K. H., & Scarce, M. (1999). A longitudinal evaluation of the effectiveness of a sexual assault education program. *Journal of Interpersonal Violence, 14*(5), 459-478.

Brener, N. D., McMahon, P. M., Warren, C. W., & Douglas, K. A. (1999). Forced sexual intercourse and associated health-risk behaviors among female college students in the United States. *Journal of Consulting and Clinical Psychology, 67*(2), 252-259.

Brookover-Bourque, L. (1989). *Defining rape.* Durham, NC: Duke University Press.

Brownmiller, S. (1975). *Against our will: Men, women, and rape.* New York: Bantam.

Burt, M. R. (1998). Rape myths. In M. E. Odem (Ed.), *Confronting rape and sexual assault: Worlds of women* (pp. 129-144). Wilmington, DE: Scholarly Resources.

Buss, D. M., & Schmitt, D. P. (1993). Sexual strategies theory: An evolutionary perspective on human mating. *Psychological Review, 100*(2), 204-232.

Cleveland, H. H., Koss, M. P., & Lyons, J. (1999). Rape tactics from the survivors' perspective. *Journal of Interpersonal Violence, 14*(5), 532-547.

Cohen, M. A., & Miller, T. R. (1998). The cost of mental health care for victims of crime. *Journal of Interpersonal Violence, 13*(1), 93-110.

Collins, M. E. (1998). Factors influencing sexual victimization and revictimization in a sample of adolescent mothers. *Journal of Interpersonal Violence, 13*(1), 3-24.

Coxell, A. W., & King, M. B. (1996). Male victims of rape and sexual abuse. *Sexual & Marital Therapy, 11,* 297-308.

Coyle, B. S., Wolan, D. L., & Van Horn, A. S. (1996). The prevalence of physical and sexual abuse in women veterans seeking care at a veterans affairs medical center. *Military Medicine, 161,* 588-593.

Crowell, N. A., & Burgess, A. W. (Eds.). (1996). *Understanding violence against women.* Washington, DC: National Academy Press.

Davis, R., Taylor, B., & Bench, S. (1995). Impact of sexual and nonsexual assault on secondary victims. *Violence and Victims, 10*(1), 73-84.

Dean, K. E., & Malamuth, N. M. (1997). Characteristics of men who aggress sexually and of men who imagine aggressing: Risk and moderating variables. *Journal of Personality & Social Psychology, 72,* 449-455.

Fisher, B. S., Sloan, J. J., Cullen, F. T., & Lu, C. (1998). Crime in the ivory tower: The level and sources of student victimization. *Criminology, 36*(3), 671-710.

Foa, E. B. (1997). Trauma and women: Course, predictors, and treatment. *Journal of Clinical Psychiatry, 58,* 25-28.

Foubert, J. D., & McEwen, M. K. (1998). An all-male rape prevention peer education program: Decreasing fraternity men's behavioral intent to rape. *Journal of College Student Development, 39*(6), 548-556.

Frazier, P., Valtinson, G., & Candell, S. (1994). Evaluation of a coeducational interactive rape prevention program. *Journal of Counseling & Development, 73,* 153-158.

Frintner, M. P., & Rubinson, L. (1993). Acquaintance rape: The influence of alcohol, fraternity membership, and sports team membership. *Journal of Sex Education & Therapy, 19,* 272-284.

Garnets, L., Herek, G. M., & Levy, B. (1990). Violence and victimization of lesbians and gay men: Mental health consequences. *Journal of Interpersonal Violence, 5,* 366-383.

Gidycz, C. A., Coble, C. N., Latham, L., & Layman, M. J. (1993). Sexual assault experience in adulthood and prior victimization experiences: A prospective analysis. *Psychology of Women Quarterly, 17,* 151-168.

Gidycz, C. A., Hanson, K., & Layman, M. J. (1995). A prospective analysis of the relationships among sexual assault experiences. An extension of previous findings. *Psychology of Women Quarterly, 19,* 5-29.

Goodman, L. A. (1991). The prevalence of abuse among homeless and housed poor mothers: A comparison study. *American Journal of Orthopsychiatry, 61,* 163-169.

Goodman, L. A., Dutton, M. A., & Harris, M. (1995). Episodically homeless women with serious mental illness: Prevalence of physical and sexual assault. *American Journal of Orthopsychiatry, 65,* 468-478.

Goodman, L. A., Koss, M. P., & Russo, N. F. (1993). Violence against women: Physical and mental health effects: Part II. Research findings. *Applied & Preventive Psychology, 2,* 79-89.

Gordon, M. T., & Riger, S. (1989). *The female fear.* New York: Macmillan.

Hanson, K. A., & Gidycz, C. A. (1993). Evaluation of a sexual assault prevention program. *Journal of Consulting & Clinical Psychology, 61,* 1046-1052.

Heppner, M. J., Humphrey, C. F., Hillenbrand-Gunn, T. L., & DeBord, K. A. (1995). The differential effects of rape prevention programming on attitudes, behavior, and knowledge. *Journal of Counseling Psychology, 42,* 508-518.

Heppner, M. J., Neville, H. A., Smith, K., Kivlighan, D. M., & Gershuny, B. S. (1999). Examining immediate and long-term efficacy of rape prevention programming with racially diverse college men. *Journal of Counseling Psychology, 46*(1), 16-26.

Hickman, S. E., & Muehlenhard, C. L. (1997). College women's fears and precautionary behaviors to acquaintance rape and stranger. *Psychology of Women Quarterly, 21,* 527-547.

Himelein, M. J. (1995). Risk factors for sexual victimization in dating: A longitudinal study of college women. *Psychology of Women Quarterly, 19,* 31-48.

Himelein, M. J. (1999). Acquaintance rape prevention with high-risk women: Identification and inoculation. *Journal of College Student Development, 40*(1), 93-96.

Himelein, M. J., Vogel, R. E., & Wachowiak, D. G. (1994). Nonconsensual sexual experiences in precollege women: Prevalence and risk factors. *Journal of Counseling & Development, 42,* 411-415.

Jackson, T. L. (Ed.). (1996). *Acquaintance rape: Assessment, treatment, and prevention.* Sarasota, FL: Professional Resource Press.

Jacobson, A., & Richardson, B. (1987). Assault experiences of 100 psychiatric inpatients: Evidence of the need for routine inquiry. *American Journal of Psychiatry, 144,* 908-913.

Kallish, C. B. (1974). *Crimes and victims: A report on the Dayton-San Jose pilot study of victimization.* Washington, DC: National Criminal Justice Information and Statistics Service.

Kilpatrick, D. G., Acierno, R., Resnick, H. S., Saunders, B. E., & Best, C. L. (1997). A 2-year longitudinal study of the relationships between violent assault and substance use in women.

Journal of Consulting and Clinical Psychology, 65(5), 834-847.

Kopper, B. A. (1996). Gender, gender identity, rape myth acceptance, and time of initial resistance on the perception of acquaintance rape blame and avoidability. *Sex Roles, 34,* 81-93.

Koss, M. P. (1992). The underdetection of rape: A critical assessment of incidence data. *Journal of Social Issues, 48,* 61-76.

Koss, M. P. (1993a). Detecting the scope of rape: A review of prevalence research methods. *Journal of Interpersonal Violence, 8*(2), 198-222.

Koss, M. P. (1993b). The impact of crime victimization on women's medical use. *Journal of Women's Health, 2*(1), 67-72.

Koss, M. P. (1994). The negative impact of crime victimization on women's health and medical use. In A. J. Dan (Ed.), *Reframing women's health: Multidisciplinary research and practice* (pp. 189-200). Thousand Oaks, CA: Sage.

Koss, M. P. (1996). The measurement of rape victimization in crime surveys. *Criminal Justice & Behavior, 23*(1), 55-69.

Koss, M. P., & Cleveland, H. H. (1997). Stepping on toes: Social roots of date rape lead to intractability and politicization. In M. D. Schwartz (Ed.), *Researching sexual violence against women: Methodological and personal perspectives* (pp. 4-21). Thousand Oaks, CA: Sage.

Koss, M. P., & Dinero, T. E. (1989). Discriminate analysis of risk factors for sexual victimization among a national sample of college women. *Journal of Consulting & Clinical Psychology, 57,* 242-250.

Koss, M. P., Gidycz, C. A., & Wisniewski, N. (1987). The scope of rape: Incidence and prevalence of sexual aggression and victimization in a national sample of higher education students. *Journal of Consulting and Clinical Psychology, 55*(2), 162-170.

Koss, M. P., Goodman, L. A., Browne, A., Fitzgerald, L. F., Keita, G. P., & Russo, N. F. (1994). *No safe haven: Male violence against women at home, at work, and in the community.* Washington, DC: American Psychological Association.

Koss, M. P., & Harvey, M. R. (1991). *The rape victim: Clinical and community interventions* (2nd ed.). Newbury Park, CA: Sage.

Koss, M. P., & Heslet, L. (1992). Somatic consequences of violence against women. *Archives of Family Medicine, 1,* 53-59.

Koss, M. P., Koss, P. G., & Woodruff, W. J. (1991). Deleterious effects of criminal victimization on women's health and medical utilization. *Archives of Internal Medicine, 151,* 342-357.

Koss, M. P., Woodruff, W. J., & Koss, P. G. (1991). Criminal victimization among primary care medical patients: Prevalence, incidence, and physician usage. *Behavioral Sciences and the Law, 9,* 85-96.

Lalumiere, M. L., Chalmers, L. J., Quinsey, V. L., & Seto, M. C. (1996). A test of the mate deprivation hypothesis of sexual coercion. *Ethology & Sociobiology, 17*(5), 219-318.

Lanier, C. A., Elliot, M. N., Martin, D. W., & Kapadia, A. (1998). Evaluation of an intervention to change attitudes toward date rape. *College Health, 46,* 177-180.

Lenihan, G. O., & Rawlins, M. E. (1994). Rape supportive attitudes among Greek students before and after a date rape prevention program. *Journal of College Student Development, 35,* 450-455.

Lira, L. R., Koss, M. P., & Russo, N. F. (1999). Mexican American women's definitions of rape and sexual abuse. *Hispanic Journal of Behavioral Sciences, 21,* 236-265.

Lonsway, K. A. (1996). Preventing acquaintance rape through education: What do we know? *Psychology of Women Quarterly, 20,* 229-265.

Lonsway, K. A., & Fitzgerald, L. F. (1994). Rape myths. *Psychology of Women Quarterly, 18,* 133-164.

Lonsway, K. A., Klaw, E. L., Berg, D. R., Waldo, C. R., Kothari, C., Mazurek, C. J., & Hegeman, K. E. (1998). Beyond no means no. *Journal of Interpersonal Violence, 13*(1), 73-92.

Malamuth, N. M. (1998). The confluence model as an organizing framework for research on sexually aggressive men: Risk moderators, imagined aggression, and pornography consumption. In R. G. Geen & E. Donnerstein (Eds.), *Human aggression: Theories, research, and implications for social policy* (pp. 229-245). San Diego, CA: Academic Press.

Malamuth, N. M., Linz, D., Heavey, C. L., Barnes, G., & Acker, M. (1995). Using the confluence model of sexual aggression to predict men's conflict with women: A 10-year follow-up study. *Journal of Personality & Social Psychology, 69*(2), 353-369.

Malamuth, N. M., Sockloskie, R. J., Koss, M. P., & Tanaka, J. S. (1991). Characteristics of aggressors against women: Testing a model using a national sample of college students. *Journal of Consulting & Clinical Psychology, 59*(5), 670-681.

Malamuth, N. M., & Thornhill, N. W. (1994). Hostile masculinity, sexual aggression, and gender-biased domineeringness in conversations. *Aggressive Behavior, 20,* 185-193.

Marques, J. K. (1999). How to answer the question "Does sex offender treatment work?" *Journal of Interpersonal Violence, 14*(4), 437-451.

Marx, B. P., Miranda, R., & Meyerson, L. A. (1999). Cognitive-behavioral treatment for rapists: Can we do better? *Clinical Psychology Review, 19*(7), 875-894.

Mayall, A., & Gold, S. R. (1995). Definitional issues and mediating variables in the sexual revictimization of women sexually abused as children. *Journal of Interpersonal Violence, 10*(1), 26-42.

McCall, G. J. (1993). Risk factors and sexual assault prevention. *Journal of Interpersonal Violence, 8*(2), 277-295.

McCann, I. L., & Pearlman, L. A. (1990). *Psychological trauma and the adult survivor: Theory, therapy, and transformation.* New York: Brunner/ Mazel.

McKenry, P. C., Julian, T. W., & Gavazzi, S. M. (1995). Toward a biopsychosocial model of domestic violence. *Journal of Marriage & the Family, 57,* 307-320.

Merrill, L. L., Newell, C. E., Milner, J. S., Koss, M. P., Hervig, L. K., Gold, S. R., Rosswork, S. G., & Thornton, S. R. (1998). Prevalence of premilitary adult sexual victimization and aggression in a Navy recruit sample. *Military Medicine, 163,* 209-212.

Messman, T. L., & Long, P. J. (1996). Child sexual abuse and its relationship to revictimization in adult women: A review. *Clinical Psychology Review, 16*(5), 307-420.

Moore, K. A., Nord. C. W., & Peterson, J. L. (1989). Nonvoluntary sexual activity among adolescents. *Family Planning Perspectives, 21,* 110-114.

Muehlenhard, C. L., & Linton, M. A. (1987). Date rape and sexual aggression in dating situations: Incidence and risk factors. *Journal of Counseling Psychology, 34,* 186-196.

National Victims Center. (1992, April 23). *Rape in America: A report to the nation.* Arlington, VA: Author.

Norris, J., Nurius, P. S., & Dimeff, L. A. (1996). Through her eyes: Factors affecting women's perception of and resistance to acquaintance sexual aggression threat. *Psychology of Women Quarterly, 20,* 123-146.

Ouimette, P. C. (1997). Psychopathology and sexual aggression in nonincarcerated men. *Violence and Victims, 12*(4), 389-395.

Parks, K. A., & Miller, B. A. (1997). Bar victimization of women. *Psychology of Women Quarterly, 21,* 509-525.

Parks, K. A., & Zetes-Zanatta, L. M. (1999). Women's bar-related victimization: Refining and testing a conceptual model. *Aggressive Behavior, 25,* 349-364.

Perkins, C. A., Klaus, P. A., Bastian, L. D., & Cohen, R. L. (1996). *Criminal victimization in the United States, 1993* (NCJ 151657). Washington, DC: U.S. Department of Justice, National Institute of Justice.

Pilkington, N. W., & D'Augelli, A. R. (1995). Victimization of lesbian, gay, and bisexual youth in community settings. *Journal of Community Psychology, 23,* 34-56.

Pino, N. W., & Meier, R. F. (1999). Gender differences in rape reporting. *Sex Roles, 40,* 979-990.

Pinzone-Glover, H. A., Gidycz, C. A., & Jacobs, C. D. (1998). An acquaintance rape prevention program: Effects on attitudes toward women, rape-related attitudes, and perceptions of rape scenarios. *Psychology of Women Quarterly, 22,* 605-621.

Pittman, N. E., & Taylor, R. G. (1992). MMPI profiles of partners of incestuous offenders and partners of alcoholics. *Family Dynamics of Addiction Quarterly, 2,* 52-59.

Resick, P. A. (1993). The psychological impact of rape. *Journal of Interpersonal Violence, 8*(2), 223-255.

Rosenthal, E. H., Heesacker, M., & Neimeyer, G. J. (1995). Changing the rape-supportive attitudes of traditional and nontraditional male and female college students. *Journal of Counseling Psychology, 42*(2), 171-177.

Russell, D. E., & Howell, N. (1983). The prevalence of rape in the United Stated revisited. *Signs, 8*(4), 688-695.

Saunders, B. E., Kilpatrick, D. G., Hanson, R. F., Resnick, H. S., & Walker, M. E. (1999). Prevalence, case characteristics, and long-term psychological correlates of child rape among women: A national survey. *Child Maltreatment, 4,* 187-200.

Schewe, P. A., & O'Donohue, W. (1993). Rape prevention: Methodological problems and new directions. *Clinical Psychology Review, 13,* 667-682.

Schewe, P. A., & O'Donohue, W. (1996). Rape prevention with high-risk males: Short-term outcome of two interventions. *Archives of Sexual Behavior, 25,* 455-471.

Scott, C. S., Lefley, H. P., & Hicks, D. (1993). Potential risk factors for rape in three ethnic groups. *Community Mental Health Journal, 29,* 133-141.

Shotland, R. L., & Goodstein, L. (1992). Sexual precedence reduces the perceived legitimacy of sexual refusal: An examination of attributions concerning date rape and consensual sex. *Personality and Social Psychology Bulletin, 18,* 756-764.

Stormo, K. J., Lang, A. R., & Stritzke, W. G. (1997). Attributions about acquaintance rape: The role of alcohol and individual differences. *Journal of Applied Social Psychology, 27,* 279-305.

Testa, M., & Dermen, K. H. (1999). The differential correlates of sexual coercion and rape. *Journal of Interpersonal Violence, 14*(5), 548-561.

Testa, M., & Parks, K. A. (1996). The role of women's alcohol consumption in sexual victimization. *Aggression and Violent Behavior, 1,* 217-234.

Tjaden, P., & Thoennes, N. (1998). *Prevalence, incidence, and consequences of violence against women: Findings from the national violence against women survey* (NCJ 172837). Washington, DC: U.S. Department of Justice, National Institute of Justice.

Ullman, S. E. (1997). Review and critique of empirical studies of rape avoidance. *Criminal Justice and Behavior, 24*(2), 177-204.

Ullman, S. E. (1998). Does offender violence escalate when women fight back? *Journal of Interpersonal Violence, 13,* 179-192.

Ullman, S. E., Karabatsos, G., & Koss, M. P. (1999). Alcohol and sexual assault in a national sample of college women. *Journal of Interpersonal Violence, 14*(6), 603-625.

Ullman, S. E., & Knight, R. A. (1995). Women's resistance to different rapist types. *Criminal Justice & Behavior, 22,* 263-283.

Walker, E. A., Gelfand, A. N., Gelfand, M. D., Koss, M. P., & Katon, W. J. (1995). Medical and psychiatric symptoms in female gastroenterology clinic patients with histories of sexual victimization. *General Hospital Psychiatry, 17,* 85-92.

Walker, E. A., Keegan, D., Gardner, G., Sullivan, M., Bernstein, D., & Katon, W. J. (1997). Psychosocial factors in fibromyalgia compared with rheumatoid arthritis: Part II. Sexual, physical, and emotional abuse and neglect. *Psychosomatic Medicine, 59*(6), 572-577.

Walker, E. A., Torkelson, N., Katon, W. J., & Koss, M. P. (1993). The prevalence of sexual abuse in a primary care clinic. *Journal of the American Board of Family Practice, 6,* 465-471.

Wechsler, H., Dowdall, G. W., Maenner, G., Gledhill-Hoyt, J., & Lee, H. (1998). Changes in binge drinking and related problems among American college students between 1993 and 1997: Results of the Harvard School of Public Health. *College Health, 47,* 57-68.

White, J. W., & Kowalski, R. M. (1998). Male violence toward women: An integrated perspective. In R. G. Geen & E. Donnerstein (Eds.), *Human aggression: Theories, research, and implications for social policy* (pp. 203-228). San Diego, CA: Academic Press.

Wyatt, G. E. (1992). The sociocultural context of African American and White American women's rape. *Journal of Social Issues, 48,* 77-92.

Wyatt, G. E., Guthrie, D., & Notgrass, C. (1992). Differential effects of women's child sexual abuse and subsequent sexual revictimization. *Journal of Consulting and Clinical Psychology, 60,* 167-173.

Wyatt, G. A., Newcomb, M. D., & Riederle, M. H. (1993). *Sexual abuse and consensual sex: Women's developmental patterns and outcomes.* Newbury Park, CA: Sage.

CHAPTER 8

Violence Against Women by Intimate Relationship Partners

Patricia Mahoney
Linda M. Williams
Carolyn M. West

Although strangers and acquaintances are responsible for the majority of crimes and assaults against men, women are more likely to be raped, beaten, stalked, or killed by their intimate/romantic relationship partners than by strangers or any other type of assailant (Bachman & Saltzman, 1995; Finkelhor & Yllö, 1987; Russell, 1990; Tjaden & Thoennes, 1998a). At least 1.8 million women are severely beaten by their intimate partners every year in the United States; about one quarter of all women are estimated to experience intimate violence at some time in their lives (Stark & Flitcraft, 1988; Straus & Gelles, 1990; Tjaden & Thoennes, 1998a). When women in the United States are murdered, it is by an intimate partner in at least one third of all cases (Bachman & Saltzman, 1995; Greenfeld et al., 1998). Intimate violence leads to more physical injury to women than violence by strangers, and it has also been identified as a causal factor in the development of mental health problems in women, including depression, alcoholism, and suicidality (Bachman & Saltzman, 1995; Campbell, Kub, Belknap, & Templin, 1997; Goodman, Koss, & Russo, 1993; Stark & Flitcraft, 1995). Intimate violence has been cited as a major contributor to homelessness for women and children (Crowell & Burgess, 1996; Zorza, 1991). Even after 25 years of research and advocacy, intimate violence against women remains at epidemic proportions, affecting women of all age groups and all walks of life: from preteen girls to elder women, and women of all races, cultures, sexual orientations, and physical abilities.

There is a great deal of diversity of experience subsumed under the category of intimate violence. We try to cover as much of this diversity as is possible in this chapter. The chapter begins with an introduction to the challenge of defining what constitutes intimate violence, followed by a review of available statistics on incidence and prevalence rates. We then review research on the perpetrators and victims of intimate violence, as well as on the way violence and its impact differs depending on factors such as relationship stage, ethnic background, and sexual orientation. We briefly review the costs and consequences of intimate violence against women and end the chapter with a focus on new directions in research on intimate violence.

Defining Intimate Violence

Because we are focusing on intimate violence against women, the perpetrators of this type of violence can include current and former husbands, current and former boyfriends, and current and former girlfriends (i.e., lesbian relationship partners).[1] It includes people who are dating while living apart as well as those who are cohabiting or married; people who share children, as well as those who do not; young people dating for the first time and older people who are divorced. Although violence can happen in any of these types of relationships, the focus of this chapter is primarily on studies of violence in adult intimate relationships.

Defining what constitutes violence within a relationship is not a simple task. At issue is where we put our focus: on the violent acts themselves, the intent of the perpetrator, the experience of the victim, or the resultant injury; on discrete acts of violence, episodes of violence (which may include many different acts), patterns of violent episodes, or the overall climate of the relationship. Each of these aspects alone reveals a different piece of a complex picture, and our choice of approach to define intimate violence has wide-reaching repercussions: It determines who will be considered a victim or perpe-

trator and how we approach everything from offering services to making laws to planning prevention.

The majority of research conducted on intimate violence has approached definition and measurement by focusing on discrete acts of physical assault; that is, determining whether a person has slapped, punched, or otherwise committed an act of assault against an intimate partner. Such research often distinguishes between "minor" and "severe" abuse, although determining which experiences are minor or severe has been approached differently by different researchers. Some have classified certain acts as minor or severe based on their potential for physical injury—for example, shoves and slaps are considered minor, whereas a punch with a fist or assault with a weapon are considered severe. The chronicity of the abuse (i.e., how frequently such behaviors happen) may or may not be factored in when determining the overall severity of violence that a person has experienced or perpetrated (e.g., Hudson & McIntosh, 1981; Straus & Gelles, 1990). One problem with such an approach is that not all acts (for example, not all slaps) are equal. One slap may be light and barely cause a sting, whereas another might knock out a tooth, yet by some definitions, both would be considered minor. Furthermore, the emotional impact of such acts will vary depending on a complex set of factors (including past abuse and the context in which the behavior occurred, among other factors).

Weis (1989) suggested that definitions of violence include "actual, attempted, or threatened behavior that is intended to cause physical injury or create the fear of injury (particularly, to force someone to do something), and that actually does or is likely to cause injury or pain" (p. 126). Although the behavior is primary in this definition, there is also a focus on intent of the perpetrator as well as actual or potential injury or pain. Some have suggested a definition that includes "intention or perceived intention of causing pain or injury," thus considering the subjective experience of the victim (e.g., Burke, Stets, & Pirog-Good, 1989).

Some researchers and advocates have argued that measuring discrete acts of violence is a misguided approach to the measurement of intimate violence, and that such an approach is likely to misclassify people and their experiences (e.g., Currie, 1998; Smith & Earp, 1995; Yllö, 1993). Acts such as slaps or hits are not well represented by labels, distilled from the context in which they occur, including the context of the violent episode (e.g., an argument about dinner, a sexual encounter) as well as the overarching context of the relationship (e.g., past abuse, power imbalances). Each act of assault, although important, is likely to be merely a temporary physical manifestation (or what Smith & Smith, 1995, referred to as an "acute flare-up") of a larger problem: the ongoing abuse and control of a woman by her relationship partner, often referred to as *battering*.

Battering is a term used to describe a pattern of behaviors through which one person continually reinforces a power imbalance over another in an intimate/romantic relationship context. Typically, a batterer uses both assaultive and non-assaultive behaviors, which, over time, have the effect of dominating, controlling, and inducing fear and/or subservience in the relationship partner. This complex array of behaviors, often referred to collectively as *coercive control,* can include physical violence, sexual violence, threats of violence against the woman and children or other loved ones, emotional/psychological abuse, economic exploita-

tion, confinement and/or control over activities outside the home (e.g., social life, working), stalking, property destruction, burglary, theft, and homicide. Coercive control may be expressed in different ways during different stages of the relationship (e.g., dating, first year of marriage) and is typically expressed in multiple ways at one time (e.g., verbal degradation during a physical assault, within an economically exploitative relationship). It is important to note that the abusive climate of a battering relationship exists "outside and between" physically assaultive acts (Smith & Smith, 1995), meaning that the context of the relationship provides important information about the acts of violence and how violence in a given intimate relationship is likely to be experienced by the perpetrator and the victim.

One way to identify victims of battering using such an approach is suggested by Smith and Earp (1995), who developed a scale of psychological vulnerability that measures "women's continuous perceptions of susceptibility to physical and psychological danger, disempowerment, and loss of control in a relationship with a male partner" (p. 3). Using such a scale, they argue, would lead to a more accurate and meaningful identification of victims than the use of measures based on discrete acts. Furthermore, the use of discrete-acts measures lends itself to a conceptualization of intimate violence as a conflict-resolution problem (i.e., something that happens when people can't resolve their differences), while approaching intimate violence as a problem of battering more accurately frames the issue as one of domination and control.

Feminist researchers have also called our attention to the importance of situating any definition of battering within a sociocultural framework of gender inequality (i.e., patriarchy) (e.g., Currie, 1998; Johnson, 1995; Stark & Flitcraft, 1996; Yllö, 1993). They argue that although intimate violence by women against men has been documented (e.g., Straus & Gelles, 1990), there is no evidence that such violence leads to the type and extent of suffering caused by intimate violence against women, nor is there any evidence that men become entrapped in abusive relationships in the manner that has been observed in the lives of battered women. The level of physical and psychological trauma that results from woman battering requires an explanation and thus a conceptualization of battering that goes beyond the physical acts of violence and focuses on the ways in which our beliefs and social systems contribute to women's psychological trauma and entrapment in abusive relationships.

Some feminist researchers use the term *patriarchal terrorism* to refer to the systematic use of violence as well as economic subordination, threats, isolation, and other control tactics against a relationship partner, as this form of violence is the product of the patriarchal tradition of a man's right to control "his" woman (Johnson, 1995). The term patriarchal terrorism has the advantage of keeping our attention on the systematic, intentional nature of this form of violence, reminding us to attend routinely to the historical and cultural roots of intimate violence against women.

Characteristics of Intimate Violence Against Women

Although there may be some disagreement on how to best define and measure intimate violence, there is widespread agreement that intimate violence against women is distinct from other forms of interpersonal violence in important ways, as reviewed below.

Ongoing, Multidimensional, and Changing Nature of Violence

Although some people may experience a variety of violent acts perpetrated by different strangers or acquaintances throughout their lives, in the case of battering, a woman experiences repeated (or serial) victimization. Thus, to understand the scope of the negative physical and mental consequences of intimate violence, we must take into account the impact of chronic injury and/or trauma. Intimate violence victims experience this multiple victimization *by the same perpetrator* over time, and the perpetrator is likely to employ a variety of types of violence. For example, the person who threatens a woman with a knife is the same person who has beaten her in the past. Each violent episode builds on past violent episodes and threats.

Over time, the perpetrator may go through periods in which he is less violent and other periods when he is more violent. The violence may take a cyclical pattern, increase in severity over time, or follow no pattern at all. Although overlap of abuse types is common, some perpetrators may employ certain types of violence (e.g., sexual violence) regularly while not employing other types of violence (e.g., beating up) at all. Expression of physical violence may or may not mirror the intensity with which the perpetrator employs other forms of abuse (e.g., psychological abuse, isolation). Violence within a battering relationship is woven through "normal" interactions in a way that may make it difficult for a woman to clearly identify the beginning and end of a violent episode.

Intimate violence against women is, thus, a multidimensional and dynamic behavior, making the study of this type of violence quite complicated. We cannot expect to study only those violent events that took place within the past year, or only physically abusive acts in isolation from other types of abuses, and believe that we are accurately representing the experience of intimate violence. Nevertheless, these two approaches have commonly been used to identify victims and perpetrators in research.

Ongoing Relationship

To varying degrees, battering relationships share many similarities with nonbattering relationships. Although the perpetrator and victim share a history of abuse, they also share a history of hopes and dreams of a better future—a history of a first date, of mutual excitement and enjoyment. Because of this shared intimacy and affection, the situation a victim of intimate violence faces is clearly different from that confronted by a woman who is attacked by a stranger or casual acquaintance with whom she shares no history or expectation of future relationship. Despite serious abuse, a woman may have feelings of love for the perpetrator and thus may desire to protect him from harm. Given the high value placed on relationship stability, loyalty, and commitment to working through relationship problems, it is not surprising that many women stay with and stand by an abusive partner, at least for some time, while trying to find a way to salvage the relationship but get rid of the abuse.

Shared Lives

When a woman lives with her perpetrator, one of the ways her situation is different from the woman attacked by a stranger is that she has no safe haven, no place where she can feel safe and secure from another attack. Even women who do not live with their intimate partners may not feel safe, as dates and ex-partners often know how best to break into a woman's home; they know which doors and windows have no locks and when a woman may be most vulnerable.

In addition to a lack of safety, there are many other implications of living with one's attacker. In particular, a woman's opportunities to leave an abusive relationship can be affected in a variety of ways by sharing her life with her perpetrator. For example, the perpetrator may control all aspects of family finances; this can keep a woman from having enough financial resources to leave, but it may also serve to keep her ignorant of the skills she would need to support herself on her own (e.g., how to get a bank account). There are many other ways in which a woman may be dependent on or interdependent with her partner, in the same manner women and men in nonabusive relationships have interdependent lives. For example, a woman may be deeply connected to her partner's family. She may rely on them for emotional or financial support or for child care assistance. Such familial support may be especially important to women who live far away from their own families. A woman may also share the same circle of friends as her partner. Leaving her partner may mean leaving her entire network of friends and family. It might mean losing her source of child care, making her unable to work to support her children. If a woman and the perpetrator share children, this is another aspect of their lives that can complicate a woman's choice to leave an abusive partner. She may feel the children need the emotional (if not financial) support of their father or his family, or she may fear losing custody of her children.

Beliefs About Victim Responsibility for the Violence

The ways in which battered women are blamed for their own victimization include suggestions that the woman provoked the violence through her behavior and/or that she could avoid the violence if she would only change her behavior (e.g., do the dishes before he gets home, keep the children quiet). The woman is perceived as being responsible for the problem and the solution. Women are often blamed for staying with or returning to an abusive partner, suggesting that because she has chosen to be with an abuser, she is responsible for the abuse (e.g., "what does she expect?"). This simplistic and unsympathetic view leaves no room for the woman who is committed to working through relationship difficulties even in the face of personal hardship, the woman who believes that marriage vows are permanent, or the woman who is struggling to figure out how to respond to the violence while managing other important life decisions.

Ann Jones (1994) explores the public preoccupation with victim responsibility, noting how public discussion moves from "Why doesn't she leave him" (asked about women who stay with abusers) to "Why doesn't she leave town/leave the state/leave the country?" (asked about women who do leave their partners, yet continue to be abused by them). Notably absent from public discourse is equal at-

tention to the questions of why people batter and why some people hunt down and kill their partners and ex-partners. Jones (1994) writes,

> This question [why doesn't she leave] . . . is not a *real* question. It doesn't call for an answer, it makes a judgement. . . . It transforms an immense social problem into a personal transaction, and at the same time pins responsibility squarely on the victim. (p. 131)

Victim-blaming attitudes have been documented among police, lawyers, judges, spiritual leaders, medical professionals, and even social service workers (Hansen, Harway, & Cervantes, 1991; Kurz, 1990; McKeel & Sporakowski, 1993). In a 1991 Kentucky survey of service providers (mental health, social services, corrections, shelters, law enforcement courts, prosecution, and coroners), 13.9% agreed to strongly agreed with the statement "Victims 'ask' for it" (Wilson & Wilson, 1991). Such attitudes contribute to a woman's entrapment in an abusive relationship; if she is the cause of the abuse, then she should be able to change the abuse. Such attitudes also prevent professionals from giving appropriate support and assistance to victims who do seek help. Stark and Flitcraft (1988) suggest that it is the combined experience of being abused by an intimate partner and being blamed and/or neglected by social supports and institutions that leads to the negative psychological outcomes observed among many battered women.

Types of Abuse: Trends and Statistics

When we discuss rates of intimate violence against women, two rates are of interest: annual incidence (i.e., how many women are estimated to experience intimate violence every year) and lifetime prevalence rates (i.e., how many women are estimated to experience intimate violence at some point in their lives). Studies using probability sampling techniques are also able to provide estimates for the actual number of women expected to be victims, based on the percentage of the sample who were victims. Available research on rates of intimate violence is limited in many respects. Much of the literature has focused exclusively on physical abuse (to the exclusion of sexual and emotional abuse) as well as on discrete acts of abuse within a fixed time period, limiting what we are able to learn about the array of abuses women experience and how abuse types may change or overlap over the course of a relationship. Variations in definitions and methodology contribute to rather large differences in rates across studies. Clearly, the more types of abuse a study measures (physical, sexual, emotional; threats, attempts, completed acts), the higher the resulting rates. Other important methodological variations include how the sample is selected (e.g., random sample or convenience sample), how the information is gathered and from whom (e.g., face-to-face interviews or phone interviews with women, men or both), how many questions there are and how they are worded, and whether and how privacy and anonymity are guaranteed. It is widely agreed that even well-designed studies will not produce a true estimate of intimate violence due to the problem of underreporting. (For a more thorough review of methodological issues, see Chapter 3 in this volume. For a review of studies, see Plichta, 1992; Straus & Gelles, 1990).

Despite these limitations, there is ample evidence that intimate violence against women occurs at an alarming rate. Consistent with the available literature, we first review statistics and trends by abuse type. Although intimate violence has been documented in all countries across the globe, the statistics presented in this section are based on samples from the United States and Canada. This section concludes with a discussion of overlap, chronicity, and patterns of intimate violence.

Physical Abuse

Physical abuse in relationships has been defined as experiencing any act of physical aggression, including minor acts such as slaps and severe acts such as assault with a deadly weapon (as discussed above, the labels minor and severe may not accurately represent the impact of the behavior). Threats of physical abuse may be measured in studies of physical abuse, although some have argued that threats of violence are distinct from actual acts in important ways and should be considered a distinct type of abuse (Marshall, 1996). Some have suggested that only more severe physical acts should be considered violence. Typically, sexual abuse is not measured as part of physical abuse.

The best estimates of the rate of physical abuse in relationships come from a variety of studies. The National Family Violence Resurvey of 1985 produced estimates that 6.2 million women experience "any" physical violence by their marital or cohabiting partner, with 1.8 reporting "severe" violence, every year (Straus & Gelles, 1990). A recent study of over 8,000 women projected that 1.3 million women experience any intimate violence every year, with 22 million women experiencing any intimate violence in their lifetime (Tjaden & Thoennes, 1998a). It is important to note that these rates are based on physical violence only (i.e., incidents of sexual violence are not included).

Plichta (1992) reviewed 22 studies of physical assaults against wives in the United States from 1979 to 1990 and found between 9% and 53% of samples reporting any physical violence in the survey year, with 3% to 11% reporting severe physical violence. Stark and Flitcraft (1988), in their review of studies, conclude "we can safely estimate that between 20% to 25% of the adult women in the U.S. have been physically abused at least once by a male intimate: that is between 12 and 15 million women" (p. 300).

Sexual Abuse

Sexual abuse can take the form of any sexual act that a woman submits to against her will due to force, threat of force, or coercion. In addition, it can include sexual exploitation involving sexual contact with others against a woman's will. Abraham (1999) suggests a more inclusive definition of sexual abuse than is typically found in the research literature:

> It includes sex without consent, sexual assault, rape, sexual control of reproductive rights, and all forms of sexual manipulation carried out by the perpetrator with the intention or perceived intention to cause emotional, sexual, and physical degradation to another person. (p. 592)

This definition includes control over reproductive freedom, an issue that has received little attention in the United States. Control over reproductive freedom may include control over decisions about if and when to have children (including forced impregnation or forced abortion) and choice of and access to contraceptives or other family planning services.

Abraham's (1999) definition is theoretically valid, yet our understanding of the prevalence of intimate partner sexual abuse is compromised by considerable difficulties in how to define and measure this type of abuse. At the heart of any definition of sexual abuse are the two concepts of consent and force, yet determining what constitutes consent or force within the context of a relationship is a complicated task for victim and researcher alike. Force could take the form of violence or the threat of violence yet is often much less clear. For example, many women are pressured to engage in sex directly after being beaten, to "make up." A woman who has been physically assaulted by her partner in the past—particularly when that assault has occurred in the context of a sexual act—may choose to submit to unwanted sex acts out of fear, hopelessness, exhaustion, the desire to minimize injury to herself or others, or simply the hope that doing so will end the whole episode. Many women who experience such abuse are not likely to label such experiences "rape" or "sexual abuse," even when they are certain that the sex was unwanted, against their protests, and/or involved injury or pain (Basile, 1999; Bergen, 1996; Finkelhor & Yllö, 1985; Russell, 1990). For these and other reasons, many victims of intimate partner sexual abuse remain hidden from research efforts (see Mahoney & Williams, 1998; Russell, 1990).

The best available estimates of the rate of sexual assault in relationships indicate that 10% to 14% of ever-married or cohabited women experience this form of intimate violence in their lifetime (Finkelhor & Yllö, 1985; Russell, 1990).

Tjaden and Thoennes (1998a) found that 7.7% of women (based on all women, including some who had never cohabited) have been raped by an intimate partner, leading to the estimate that 7.7 million women in the United States have been raped by an intimate partner in their lifetime.[2] A number of studies that have examined rape by intimates as a percentage of the total number of rapes reported per year have found that rape by intimate partners accounts for over one quarter of all rapes (George, Winfeld, & Blazer, 1992; Randall & Haskall, 1995; Ullman & Siegel, 1993).

Across four studies of marital rape, the majority of women reported experiencing forced vaginal intercourse, and from one quarter to one third reported forced anal or oral intercourse (Bergen, 1996; Campbell & Alford, 1989; Finkelhor & Yllö, 1985; Russell, 1990). The victim may be forced to have sex in situations that are personally unacceptable or cause distress—for example, in front of other people (including her children), in groups, or with other people (including forced prostitution)—or to pose for pornographic photos or video. Campbell and Alford's (1989) study of 115 marital rape victims found that children witnessed the sexual assault in 18% of cases, half of the victims were forced to have sex when ill, and nearly half were forced immediately after discharge from the hospital, most often after childbirth. About half of marital rape victims report being beaten immediately preceding or during sexual contact (Bergen, 1996; Finkelhor & Yllö, 1985; Russell, 1990). A perpetrator may, through force or intimidation, pressure a woman to engage in sexual activity without the use of a condom and/or other forms of birth control against her will, putting her at risk of unwanted pregnancy

or sexually transmitted diseases, including HIV (Molina & Basinait-Smith, 1998; Wingood & DiClemente, 1997). The perpetrator may have sex with her without her consent when she is asleep, under heavy medication, or knocked unconscious. The experiences of women who have suffered this type of abuse make clear that intimate partner sexual abuse, like intimate physical abuse, is an expression of power, domination, and control.

Psychological Abuse

Researchers have been rather slow to turn their attention to psychological abuse, primarily because physical violence has been viewed as a more immediate concern and far more detrimental than psychological aggression. The growing body of research in this area suggests that psychological abuse can have severe consequences, even after controlling for the effects of physical abuse (Arias & Pape, 1999; Marshall, 1996). In fact, many battered women rate the impact of emotional abuse as worse than the impact of physical abuse in their lives (Follingstad, Rutledge, Berg, Hause, & Polek, 1990). It is believed that the type and severity of psychological abuse plays an important role in determining the extent of the negative consequences of physical and sexual abuse. Marshall's (1996) study of over 500 women revealed six distinct patterns of relationship abuse. She found that scores for psychological abuse, threats of violence, acts of violence, and sexual aggression made different contributions to women's health, help-seeking, and relationship perceptions, depending on the pattern of abuse they sustained, and she concluded that the effects of intimate violence will differ "depending on the particular pattern of psychologically abusive acts women endure" (p. 401). Psychological aggression has also been identified as a predictor of physical aggression in early marriage (Murphy & O'Leary, 1989).

Defining and measuring psychological abuse is a serious challenge, as this type of abuse can be expressed in so many different—and at times subtle—ways. Psychological abuse can take the form of a behavior designed to instill fear or otherwise undermine a woman's sense of self (e.g., stalking behaviors), or it may be expressed verbally (e.g., denigration, ridicule). Negative content may be expressed by a tone of voice, a facial expression, or gesture, making this type of abuse difficult to describe and name (Marshall, 1996). After an extensive review of the research, O'Leary (1999) defined psychological abuse as

> acts of recurring criticism and/or verbal aggression toward a partner, and/or acts of isolation and domination of a partner. Generally, such actions cause the partner to be fearful of the other or lead the partner to have very low self-esteem. (p. 19)

Researchers have approached the categorization of types of psychological abuse from different perspectives. Murphy and Hoover (1999) identified hostile withdrawal (e.g., acting cold or distant when angry), domination/intimidation (e.g., intentionally destroying belongings of the victim), denigration (e.g., calling partner names like failure or worthless), and restrictive engulfment (e.g., isolation from friends). Follingstad et al. (1990) described threats of abuse, ridicule, jealousy, threats of divorce, restriction, and damage to property. Some types of psy-

chological abuse, such as ridicule, have been rated as more severe than other types (Follingstad et al., 1990; Sackett & Saunders, 1999).

Marshall (1996) has argued for a conceptualization of psychological abuse that goes beyond a dominance/control model, noting that some forms of psychological abuse may be expressed in a "helpful" or even "loving" style (e.g., "I love you so much I just can't stand to see you talking to another man.") She suggests that different styles of expression of abuse are likely to result in different effects on the victim.

Psychological abuse is much more common than physical or sexual abuse in intimate relationships. Among samples of university women, 77% to 87% reported being psychologically abused in the year prior to the survey (DeKeseredy & Kelly, 1993; Neufeld, McNamara, & Ertl, 1999; White & Koss, 1991). This form of abuse appears to be prevalent and chronic in battering relationships. For example, more than half of a community sample of physically abused women reported a high frequency (i.e., once a week or more) of three types of emotional abuse, including restriction, jealousy, and ridicule (Follingstad et al., 1990).

Stalking

Many of the behaviors that have received attention in the battered women's literature are those that are now known as stalking. These include behaviors that are harassing or threatening, perhaps involving threats of serious harm, which are engaged in repeatedly. Common domestic violence stalking behaviors include surveillance activities (e.g., monitoring a woman's phone calls, reading her mail, following her outside the home), vandalism (e.g., breaking into a woman's home, stealing her belongings), and harassment (e.g., calling her repeatedly at home or work).

Many stalking behaviors may be difficult to recognize as abuse, even for the victim, because these behaviors could be considered normal under different circumstances (Walker & Meloy, 1998). For example, behaviors such as showing up at her workplace unexpectedly or leaving gifts on her doorstep are welcome when both parties are interested in starting or continuing a relationship; such acts have a very different meaning, however, if the woman has repeatedly expressed her desire to end the relationship and/or if the perpetrator has engaged in other controlling or stalking behaviors. Most definitions of stalking require that behaviors are repeated and produce a high level of fear in the victim (e.g., Tjaden & Thoennes, 1998b).

One study produced estimates that at least 1 million women are stalked annually. In 59% of cases reported by the women in the study, the stalker was a current or former intimate partner. Contrary to popular opinion, when a woman was stalked by her intimate partner, the stalking behavior was more likely to begin while the relationship was intact, rather than after the relationship had ended (Tjaden & Thoennes, 1998b).

Homicide

As with the other types of violence against women reviewed thus far, the perpetrator in cases of homicides of women (also known as *femicide*) is most often a current or former intimate partner. Statistics on the exact percentage of femicide victims who are killed by an intimate vary

greatly. This variance is due in large part to the problem of reliance on police reports and/or federal statistics for information on the relationship between the victim and perpetrator. Such information is often missing for a large percentage of cases (from 30% to 50% in many reports), and even when it is provided, it may be incorrect. Campbell (1992) notes that prior sexual partners are often identified as "acquaintance" or "friend" in such reports.

A review of available statistics indicates that 30% to 64% of femicide cases are a result of intimate violence (Campbell, 1992; Greenfeld et al., 1998; Hallinan, 1996; Wilt, Illman, & BrodyField, 1996). Although femicide occurs less frequently than many other forms of intimate violence, in 1997 alone, at least 1,217 women were killed by intimate partners in the United States (Fox & Zawitz, 2000).

Chronicity and Overlap of Types of Violence

It is important to acknowledge that for some women, intimate violence is a relatively isolated experience. For example, in Kurz's (1996) study of 129 divorced women, 16% reported only one act of violence.[3] This violence was typically minor and did not affect the woman's life in any major way. Stark and Flitcraft (1988) speculate that less than one third of women reporting violence typically fall into this category. It is possible that this type of violence does not have a significant impact on the lives of victims. In fact, those who experience isolated acts of intimate violence may not see themselves as victims at all.

These experiences may be part of a type of intimate violence referred to as "common couple violence" (Johnson, 1995). This type of intimate violence occurs when day-to-day conflicts occasionally get "out of hand," usually leading to minor forms of violence. Common couple violence is less a product of patriarchy and more a product of conflict resolution. This violence is no more likely to be enacted by men than by women, and violent incidents are initiated as often by women as by men. There appears to be little likelihood of escalation of the level of violence over time in common couple violence.

It is important to distinguish between such atypical and minor intimate violence and that which is a regular occurrence in a woman's life, as we can expect the latter type of intimate violence to be most disruptive and harmful to victims and society. As Plichta (1992) reports in her review of studies on intimate violence, 25% to 30% of physically abused wives experience physical violence on a regular basis. Such women experience abuse so regularly that numerical representations of the frequency of their abuse are difficult to establish. Many studies have used "20 or more times" as their highest frequency category, which has not allowed us to learn how many women would estimate their experiences of abuse to be in the hundreds or thousands. Bowker and Maurer (1987, cited in Plichta, 1992) found 46% of 1,000 battered women reporting 20 or more beatings throughout their relationship. Similarly, studies of marital rape have found high percentages of women reporting repeat assaults. Between 69% and 83% of wife rape survivors report being raped more than once, with one third to one half reporting 20 or more rapes over the course of the relationship (Bergen, 1996; Finkelhor & Yllö, 1985; Russell, 1990).

In addition to measuring chronicity, another way to examine the extent of intimate violence is to look at overlap of abuse types. For example, most studies of battered women have found that about half, but as many as 70%, have experienced both physical and sexual abuse by their partner (for a review of studies, see Hanneke, Shields, & McCall, 1986; Mahoney & Williams, 1998; Pagelow, 1988). Of women in one study who were stalked by an intimate partner, 81% reported physical assaults, and 31% reported sexual assaults by the same partner (Tjaden, 1997).

We must keep in mind when we consider the overlap of abuse types that some types of abuse that women experience in relationships do not fit well into the categories outlined in this chapter. For example, violence or threats of violence toward a woman's loved ones or pets, property destruction, and breaking and entering are not acts of violence against the woman victim, per se, yet such acts would clearly contribute to the overall climate of the relationship and the experience of the victim.

The most profound example of the importance of measuring chronicity and overlap of abuse types is in the case of intimate homicide. Those studying the killing of battered women by their husbands and the killing of battering husbands by their wives have identified overlapping and frequent abuse as a predictor of high homicide risk. Aldarondo and Straus (1994) found the following factors to be associated with life-threatening intimate violence: high frequency of violence, injury-producing violence, sexual violence, threats to kill partner, the killing or abuse of pets, and controlling and psychological maltreatment. Clearly, homicide by an intimate partner is rarely an isolated act of violence (Stout, 1993). About two thirds of women killed by intimate partners or ex-partners had been physically abused before they were killed (Campbell, 1981, 1992, as cited in Campbell, 1995). In one study, more than three quarters of battered women who killed their partners had been raped by their partner, with 40% saying they had been raped "often" (Browne, 1987).

Patterns of Intimate Violence

In the late 1970s, Walker (1979) identified a pattern of abuse in relationships that she referred to as the "cycle of violence." In this pattern, a period of tension building leads up to a battering incident. After the battering incident, the perpetrator attempts to "make up," expressing remorse for his behavior. After a while, the honeymoon period leads into another tension-building stage, beginning the cycle again. As the cycle of violence progresses throughout the course of a relationship, the honeymoon periods get shorter and may become nonexistent, while the violence increases in severity and frequency.

This is, however, only one possible pattern of intimate violence. As mentioned earlier, at least some women are expected to experience intimate violence on one or two occasions only. For women at the opposite end of the chronicity continuum, violence may be a daily occurrence, with no honeymoon period at all. Violence that occurs frequently, leads to injury, and is multidimensional in nature has been identified as a particularly damaging pattern. However, we have much to learn regarding how this pattern develops over time, how to identify which perpetrators are on the path to becoming "relentless" abusers, and how best to intervene with victims

and perpetrators, depending on current and past patterns of abuse in the relationship.

The Batterers

Our understanding of the characteristics of those who perpetrate violence against their female intimate partners suffers all of the limitations of the research discussed above. It is also constricted by limitations in prior conceptualizations of the problem of violence in relationships. Much of the research describes the batterers in terms of "only" one type of violent behavior, usually physical violence, homicide, or stalking. Although there has been some attention to the overlap of marital rape and battering, in general, there has been little attention paid to documenting the extent of a perpetrator's violence and to understanding the development of different patterns of battering. Even less attention has been given to the commission of violent behaviors with another partner. Indeed, we have a very limited understanding of the pattern of violent perpetration over the life course and how it is linked to developmental milestones, relationship stages, or other life events.

Typologies of Batterers

One way researchers have approached the study of batterers is through the development of typologies designed to categorize batterers in ways that may be meaningful for treatment or prevention strategies. Several dimensions are typically examined, such as severity of violence, generality of violence (e.g., whether he is violent both within and outside the home), and batterer psychopathology.

After a thorough review of the literature, Holtzworth-Munroe and Stuart (1994) proposed a typology consisting of three subtypes of batterers. The *family-only batterer* is described as less deviant or deficient on some indicators, including impulsivity, alcohol and drug abuse, and criminal behavior. He is hypothesized to have poor communication and social skills, a history of exposure to aggression in the family of origin, and high levels of dependency on partner(s). The *dysphoric/borderline batterer* is described as having a history of parental rejection, child abuse, high dependency on partner, poor communication and social skills, hostility toward women, and low levels of remorse for violence perpetrated. The generally violent *antisocial batterer* is described as having suffered family-of-origin violence, having a history of delinquency, having deficits in communication and social skills, and viewing violence as an appropriate response to provocation.

In another approach, Jacobson and Gottman (1998) studied severely violent batterers and examined their emotions in nonviolent arguments. Their data suggest that for this group of severe batterers, there are two emotional types: the "pit bulls" and the "cobras." The pit bulls are described as men whose emotions are quick to boil over. They were found to be driven by deep insecurities and dependence on their partners. The cobras were cool and methodical, systematic, controlling, and often sadistic in their behaviors toward their partners. Cobras showed evidence of severe antisocial and criminal-like traits.

These and other typologies of batterers need empirical testing to assess their va-

lidity, applicability, and usefulness. The typologies also need to be broadened to consider not only physical violence but also its persistence, desistence, and co-occurrence with other types of violence and abuse across the life span and with a series of partners.

Risk Markers and Identifying Characteristics of Men Who Commit Violence Against Their Partners

Research into risk factors for becoming involved in a violent relationship have concluded that it is characteristics of the aggressor that predict violence, rather than characteristics of the victim (Hotaling & Sugarman, 1986). Hotaling and Sugarman (1986), in their review of this literature, found that witness to parental violence, working-class occupational status, excessive alcohol usage, low income, low assertiveness, and low educational level were associated with battering behaviors. It is clear, however, that batterers are not a homogeneous group and different types of batterers may possess different characteristics and risk markers. A few of the risk factors most commonly studied are described below.

Alcoholism and Drug Use

Alcohol abuse and binge drinking have been consistently associated with partner violence incidents (Kaufman Kantor & Jasinski, 1998). It may be that alcohol abuse is associated with violence against female partners when it increases levels of impulsivity. Kaufman Kantor and Straus (1989) have emphasized alcohol's role as a disinhibitor and drunkenness as an excuse for violence against female partners.

Alcohol appears to have direct and indirect effects on aggression, mediated by beliefs about alcohol's impact on behavior. Alcohol provides a social context for violence, and alcohol abuse is most likely to be associated with the generally violent subtype—that is, men who are violent both within and outside the home (Holtzworth-Munroe & Stuart, 1994). Use of drugs such as barbiturates, amphetamines, opiates, cocaine, and alcohol/cocaine combinations have been associated with violence as well (Fagan, 1990; Goldstein, Belluci, Spunt, & Miller, 1989).

Personality Disorder and Characteristics

No single personality profile appears to characterize men who physically abuse their female partners. In fact, many batterers are not distinguishable from nonbatterers on a variety of measures. Hamberger and Hastings (1986) found that batterers had three major profiles: narcissistic/antisocial, schizoidal/borderline, and dependent/compulsive. In a study of a larger sample of 833 men in batterer treatment, three main groups of men were identified: Nonpathological men composed the bulk of the sample (335), with 212 considered to be antisocial and 148 passive-aggressive-dependent (Hamberger, Lohr, Bonge, & Tolin, 1996). O'Leary reported that personality disorders characterize men in severely abusive relationships and that aggressive and defensive personality style predicted later physical aggression (O'Leary, 1993; O'Leary, Malone, & Tyree, 1994). The most fruitful work in this area is exploring how various personality dimensions may interact to produce impulsive, aggressive,

or antisocial behavior (Holtzworth-Munroe & Stuart, 1994).

Cognitive Processes

Research on the role of cognitive processes in violence against women suggests that faulty attributions about a female partner's behaviors may be associated with increased risk for violent behaviors. Holtzworth-Munroe and Hutchinson (1993) found that violent husbands are more likely than nonviolent husbands to attribute hostile intent to the wife. Violent husbands are particularly likely to generate incompetent behavioral responses to situations portraying the wife's abandonment or rejection of the husband.

Early Childhood and Family Experiences

Many research studies have found that witnessing parental violence and experiencing abuse as a child are associated with violence against an intimate partner (Hotaling & Sugarman, 1986). The mechanism for these connections has not been clearly demonstrated. Such childhood experiences may lead to problems with attachment, difficulties in forming adolescent and adult relationships, an expectation that violence will be used when conflict is encountered, faulty cognitions, or substance abuse problems, all of which may lead to violence against female partners. Dutton (1999) suggests that a combination of early childhood experiences may lead to becoming a batterer; specifically, being abused or witnessing abuse as a child in conjunction with being shamed as a child and having a lack of secure attachments.

Holtzworth-Munroe and Stuart (1994) suggest a developmental model for understanding risk factors and propose distal/historical and proximal correlates of marital violence. Distal or historical correlates include genetic or prenatal influence, childhood family experiences, and peer experiences. Proximal correlates include attachment (dependency or empathy toward others), impulsivity, social skills, and attitudes toward women and violence.

Stability of Abuser Violence

In longitudinal studies of early marriage, O'Leary et al. (1989) observed considerable stability of aggression, finding that 90% of men who were not physically aggressive toward their partners prior to marriage remained nonaggressive after marriage, at 6- to 18-month and 18- to 30-month follow-ups. Of those men who were aggressive prior to marriage, a slight majority remained aggressive at follow-up. Other studies have found similar patterns of stability, with 76% of aggressors in the first year of marriage continuing this behavior in the next 2 years (Quigley, Leonard, & Senchak, 1996). One study of severely aggressive men suggests that the stability of their violence is even greater—of 27 untreated batterers followed up for 2 years, 93% were still aggressive (Jacobson, Gottman, Gortner, Berns, & Shortt, 1996).

Although these small, clinically based studies support the stability of abuser violence, larger cross-sectional and nonclinical studies indicate that intimate violence may decrease over the life course (Feld & Straus, 1990). Currently, there is not adequate longitudinal data to draw firm conclusions about this discrepancy. In addition, we know little about the actual nature of the physical violence and its co-occurrence with sexual violence, emotional abuse, or threats. Nor do we know whether men who stop abusing their partners physically continue to abuse them psychologically.

It seems likely that differences in stability of violence are related to different patterns of violence by perpetrators. For example, there may be a large number of men who commit minor violence infrequently against a partner and then desist, whereas there is a relatively smaller number of men who commit regular, more severe abuse against their partners and whose violence is stable or increases over time.

In summary, batterers appear to be a diverse group of people, many of whom may not be distinguishable from nonbatterers on a variety of measures, including life history and personality characteristics. The batterers committing the most severe abuse are those most likely to evidence personality disorders, and members of this group appear most resistant to change. It should be kept in mind, however, that the bulk of the research conducted with batterers is limited due to problems identifying and gaining access to batterers outside of treatment settings. In addition, the research literature on batterers has focused almost exclusively on physical assault. Studies have failed to adequately assess overlapping abuse types and chronicity of abuse, in addition to the perpetration of violence against a variety of partners over the life course. No known studies containing more than a handful of subjects have been conducted with men identified as sexually abusing their wives. Thus, we know little about whether treatment for such men should follow the treatment protocols established for batterers or those established for sex offenders, or if some combination would be more appropriate (Mahoney, Williams,

& Saunders, 1998). Information on overlap of abuse types and perpetration history with other partners would greatly inform our understanding of typologies and risk markers for batterers. Longitudinal studies that could identify precursors to intimate violence would greatly enhance our understanding of the causes of battering.

The Woman Survivor of Intimate Violence

Two central lines of inquiry regarding women who are survivors of intimate violence have been how women become involved in battering relationships and why women stay in battering relationships. Although some important information has resulted from studies that have focused on these issues, such studies have also been criticized for taking a victim-blaming approach to woman battering. For example, a focus on the victim's characteristics lends itself to a conceptualization of intimate violence as victim provoked. That is, it suggests that a particular woman's personality or behavior brought out the violence in a batterer, whereas a different woman partner would not have caused the battering. Reviews of the literature on risk markers clearly refute any claims that personality characteristics of the victim provoke intimate violence. In fact, mental health problems associated with battered women, such as alcoholism and depression, have been shown to be a result rather than a cause of battering (see Plictha, 1992; Stark & Flitcraft, 1988). Battering, like any other criminal behavior, is better understood by looking at the characteristics of the perpetrator rather than those of the victim (Hotaling & Sugarman, 1986).

Asking the question of why women stay in abusive relationships is important for learning how best to provide the proper supports for women trying to leave such relationships. All too often, however, this question frames the woman as complicit in her abuse. When one suggests that "if only she would leave the relationship, then the abuse would end," this question is not only victim-blaming (in that it suggests she allows the abuse to continue by staying), it also rests on the false assumption that when women leave, the perpetrator will stop the abuse (see the section on separation, page 163). Underlying this question are other false assumptions: that women who stay with their batterers are passive and accepting of the abuse; that it should be obvious to a woman that her partner will not change; and that leaving a relationship is easy and/ or always best for a woman and her family.

The battered women in Bowker's (1993) study provided evidence that "there are worse things than battering," including worse battering; retaliation against children, friends, or family members; starvation and homelessness; and loss of one's entire way of life. Bowker (1993) details the wide variety of strategies employed by 1,000 battered women in an attempt to end the abuse in their lives. These strategies included passive strategies, such as a woman's covering her body to shield herself from abuse (attempted at least once by 855 women), as well as active strategies, such as running away (651 women) or threatening to call police or file for divorce (758 women). Many used these strategies in conjunction with seeking help from family, friends, and social service agencies. Gondolf (1988) similarly documents the active strategies of battered women. His research indicates that prior to going to a shelter, women average six help-seeking behaviors.

Whereas some have suggested that the tendency for battered women to return to their abusers numerous times prior to permanently leaving is evidence of weakness or passivity, others have argued that this indicates the women's willingness to work through relationship problems, as well as their persistence and strength. Campbell, Rose, Kub, and Nedd (1998) term this phase of the relationship the "in/out" period and document how most battered women move through this phase on their way to permanent separation. As Stark and Flitcraft (1996) eloquently wrote, "linking the decision to stay in an abusive relationship with characterological dependency blames victims for problems they are desperately trying to resolve" (p. 164). Some research indicates that eventually, most battered women do leave their relationship partners permanently (Campbell et al., 1998; Strube & Barbour, 1984).

Intimate Violence and Relationship Stage

We know that for individuals, the experience of intimate violence changes throughout the course of a relationship. At some point in a relationship, the first act of physical violence occurs. As the relationship progresses, violence and other abusive behaviors change in frequency, intensity, and impact. Some studies have examined whether there are certain periods in relationships during which violence begins, escalates, or has a particular impact on the victim (e.g., Gazmararian et al., 1996; Kurz, 1996; Sugarman & Hotaling, 1991). Three relationship stages that have received considerable attention are dating, pregnancy, and separation.

Dating

The majority of the research on dating violence (also referred to as *courtship violence*) has been conducted with young people, typically high school or college students. This research has followed a similar path as the research on adult intimate violence, and for that reason, it contains many of the same limitations. Studies tend to rely on measures of physically violent acts and do not tend to measure sexual or psychological abuse, the overlap of abuse types, or the context of abuse. A notable difference between the research on this age group, however, is that there is a separate and rather strong body of research on date rape (this is in contrast to the relatively small amount of research on sexual abuse in marital and cohabiting relationships). For a thorough review of the literature on date rape, see Chapter 7 of this volume.

Violence against women in dating relationships has been shown to be at least as common as violence against women in marital relationships. In their review of 20 studies on dating violence, Sugarman and Hotaling (1991) concluded that about 28% of both males and females are involved in dating violence at some point in their lives. One finding that has received considerable attention in the dating violence literature is that females use violence against their partners at rates similar to or higher than the rates for males. Although this is also true for some studies of adults (e.g., Straus & Gelles, 1990), the support for female-to-male intimate violence is much stronger within the dating context. There are two important caveats to these findings. First, none of the studies that find comparable rates of violence have included the perpetration of sexual violence. Considering that males are overwhelmingly the perpetrators of sexual violence, this is an important missing piece of information (Murphy, 1988; Waldner-Haugrud & Magruder, 1995). For example, Murphy (1988) found similar rates for male-to-female and female-to-male physical violence in a study of university students. However, women were much more likely to experience sexual violence when compared to men, with 9.5% of females and 0.6% of males reporting being raped by a dating partner. A review of the literature on male perpetration of sexual violence in dating relationships indicates that 25% to 60% of males are sexually assaultive/coercive in a dating context (Berkowitz, Burkhart, & Bourg, 1994).

Furthermore, Currie (1998) found that acts of violence by females were qualitatively different than acts of violence by males reported in her study. She noticed a trend for males to upgrade female violence, whereas females downplayed male violence. For example, in contrast to female reports of more serious abuse, some of the males reported acts such as having a teddy bear thrown at them during teasing. This is not to suggest that males willfully attempt to distort the truth. Indeed, they were asked if a partner "threw something at you." Her findings highlight the importance of addressing context, meaning, and the impact of violence in such surveys. Future research on this issue must assess for sexual violence perpetration and find a means of qualitatively distinguishing between acts of violence reported.

With regard to the causes of teen dating violence, some researchers point to the strong influence of peer pressure and gender role expectations in this age group (Souza, 1999). Among college students, male peer support has been associated with higher levels of abuse, indicating that an important way men learn to abuse their partners and justify continued abuse of their partners is through the support of their male friends (DeKeseredy, 1990). Such research has led to an increased focus on encouraging nonabusive males to speak out against abuse among their peers (e.g., MVP, 1994) and on providing abuse prevention programs aimed at men (e.g., Berkowitz, 1994).

One of the challenges—and a potential strength—of the dating violence literature is that it includes such a wide range of relationships. A "date" could be a person with whom one has shared little life experience (e.g., a "blind" date), or a person who has been an integral part of one's life for many years. Some studies include unmarried cohabitors, whereas others might narrow the scope of relationships by including only those which fit certain criteria; for example, noncohabiting only, or relationships of at least 1 month duration. Because there is so much variety in relationship length, level of commitment, and other factors, some researchers have explored the relationship of these factors to the perpetration of intimate violence.

The research on level of commitment and perpetration of intimate violence within dating relationships indicates that higher levels of commitment are correlated with abuse. Sugarman and Hotaling (1991) found that violence was more likely within long-term and cohabiting dating relationships. Stets and Straus (1990) found that cohabitors had twice the level of intimate violence as noncohabiting dates. Interestingly, when examined in relation to rates of intimate violence among married couples, they found noncohabiting dates and married couples had similar levels of intimate violence, with cohabiting couples having the highest rate.[4] Clearly, more work is needed in this area to more accurately describe commitment and its impact on intimate violence.

Although teen relationships are a training ground for later relationships, it is unclear whether or not those teens involved in violent relationships are necessarily those destined for violent adult relationships. Many dating violence studies find that most victims remain with an abusive partner after the abuse incident reported (e.g., Bergman, 1992), but such studies have not adequately documented the pattern and overlap of abuse types and the relationship of all of these factors as well as others (e.g., commitment, peer pressure) to leaving an abusive partner. Furthermore, little is known about patterns of intimate violence across many dating partners, in the realm either of victimization or perpetration.

Pregnancy

Research investigating whether or not violence is likely to begin or increase in severity during a pregnancy has produced inconsistent findings (see Ballard et al., 1998; Gazmararian et al., 1996; Gelles, 1988). It is, nevertheless, clear that intimate violence during pregnancy is a common problem that poses serious health risks for both the mother and the developing fetus. Rates of intimate violence during pregnancy in the general population typically range from 3.8% to 8.3% (Gazmararian et al., 1995, 1996).[5] Such rates indicate that intimate violence is one of the most common problems of pregnancy, more common than other routine pregnancy problems, such as placenta previa, preeclampsia, or gestational diabetes (Campbell, 1998).

When a woman suffers physical or sexual violence while pregnant, the consequences affect both her and the developing fetus. Potential consequences from physical attacks on the abdominal area include fetal fractures, rupture of the mother's uterus, premature rupture of membranes leading to premature delivery, and miscarriage (Newberger et al., 1992). Other complications possible from sexual violence include contraction of an infection or sexually transmitted disease, including HIV. Other injuries to the mother could also lead to adverse consequences for a developing fetus due to various factors such as medical interventions or to resultant poor health.

The psychological consequences of intimate violence also affect the fetus in important ways. Maternal stress and depression have been shown to have both direct and indirect effects on the health of a fetus. Direct effects include exacerbation of illnesses such as hypertension, diabetes, or asthma. Stress and depression may lead to drug and alcohol use, cigarette use, and poor nutrition, all of which have been linked to negative birth outcomes (Newberger et al., 1992). Studies have shown that women experiencing intimate violence are more likely to delay entry into prenatal care, which is also related to negative birth outcomes (McFarlane, Parker, Soeken, & Bullock, 1992). This may be a result of depression or shame, or a woman's partner may limit her access to prenatal care by not providing her with a means of transportation or by forbidding her to visit a doctor.

There is some evidence that intimate violence against a woman may be greater during the postpartum period than during pregnancy (Gielen, O'Campo, Faden, Kass, & Xue, 1994). Postpartum is an important period for the mother to regain her physical health, and abuse during this time affects a woman's ability to heal herself as well as care for her new infant. Campbell (1998) suggests that coercive control by a partner may include forbidding a woman to breast-feed, despite the fact that breast-feeding is now known to be best for infants in their first 6 months of life (American Academy of Pediatrics, 1997).

Separation

Although violence may lead to separation, it may also begin, continue, or increase in severity following separation. Especially among women who are battered when the relationship is intact, separation has been identified as a high-risk period for physical and sexual assaults as well as homicide (Finkelhor & Yllö, 1985; Wilson, Daly, & Wright, 1993). For example, case studies indicate an increased risk for sexual assault just preceding, during, or after a separation or divorce. Bergen (1996) found that 20% of the women in her sample were sexually assaulted during this time period; Finkelhor and Yllö (1985) found that two thirds of the women in their sample experienced sexual assaults in the waning days of the relationship (either before or after separation). Russell (1990) reported that 8% of wife rape survivors experienced sexual assault by their husbands while separated, and 7% were assaulted just prior to separation. The victims as well as the researchers speculate that during these times, the husband may use rape to express anger at the loss of his wife, to express some form of dominance and power over his wife, or to reflect that he "has nothing to lose."

Tan, Basta, Sullivan, and Davidson (1995) followed up 141 battered women who had sought shelter. They found that of the 66% of women no longer with their partners, 28% had been physically harmed and 35% had experienced psychological abuse in the 6 months after leaving. Campbell et al. (1998) found that leaving the relationship and ending the abuse appeared to be two independent processes. Of nine women in this study who were still severely abused by the same partner after 3 years, four of them had totally ended the relationship. Unfortunately, ending the relationship does not always make a woman's life safer or free from abuse.

Violence or the threat of violence during separation may affect a woman's choices and/or abilities to negotiate a fair settlement in divorce and custody proceedings (Kurz, 1996). About 30% of Kurz's (1996) sample of 129 women said they were fearful during negotiations for child support. In addition, those women who reported fear during negotiations were less likely (34%) to receive child support than women who did not feel fear (60%). Given that many women face considerable financial challenges on leaving a marriage, the impact of fear on a woman's ability to negotiate fair settlement deserves particular attention.

Diverse Peoples and Intimate Violence

After more than two decades of research, it is clear that intimate violence transcends race, ethnicity, sexual orientation, and physical ability. Although some aspects of intimate violence are likely to be the same for all victims/perpetrators (e.g., the ongoing nature of the violence), we can also expect important differences. We

briefly review what is known about prevalence for certain groups of women, as
well as special circumstances facing the
victims of these groups that may act as
barriers to help-seeking.

Racial Differences in Intimate Violence Against Women

Because intimate violence is so pervasive, some researchers have taken a "color
blind" approach by assuming that the
rates and dynamics in violent relationships are similar across ethnic groups. Alternatively, other researchers have considered intimate violence to be a problem
that plagues people of color, particularly
African Americans (West, 1998b). The
reality is that intimate violence in the lives
of women of color is both similar to and
sometimes vastly different from the violence experienced by their white counterparts (Crenshaw, 1994; Kanuha, 1996).

Prevalence and Incidence

The studies conducted to date present a
complex picture of racial differences in
intimate violence. Several investigators
have discovered that rates of intimate violence did not differ by race. For instance,
in a community sample, one third of
both African American and white women
were physically abused (Lockhart, 1987,
1991). Likewise, researchers found similar rates for African American and white
women across shelter, urban prenatal
clinic, high school, and undergraduate
samples (McFarlane, Parker, Soeken,
Silva, & Reed, 1999; O'Keefe, 1994;
Rouse, Breen, & Howell, 1988; Symons,
Croer, Kepler-Youngblood, & Slater,

1994). Researchers using community,
clinical, and shelter samples found no differences in rates of intimate violence between Mexican American and Anglo
women (Mirande & Perez, 1987; Neff,
Holamon, & Schluter, 1995; Torres, 1991).
The National Crime Victimization Survey
revealed no significant differences among
the three largest ethnic groups (African
American, Latino, and Anglo American)
in rates of serious violence committed by
intimates (Bachman, 1994).

However, many other studies have
found differences by race, with rates for
minority women typically being higher
than rates for white women. Intimate violence against African American women
was reported at four times the rate for
white women in the first National Family
Violence Survey; in the resurvey, the rate
for African American women was twice
the rate for white women (Cazenave &
Straus, 1979; Hampton & Gelles, 1994;
Straus, Gelles, & Steinmetz, 1980).
DeMaris (1990) found that African American women experienced more mild and
severe dating violence. Although rates of
homicide against African American
women have declined over the past 20
years, African American women are still
three times as likely as white women to be
killed by an intimate partner (Greenfeld et
al., 1998).

Some studies have found rates of intimate violence among Latina women to be
higher than those found among white
women (Straus & Smith, 1990), whereas
other studies have found intimate violence against Latina women to occur at
lower rates (Sorenson, Upchurch, &
Shen, 1996). One study, which ran analyses separately for different Latina ethnic
groups, found large group differences.
Whereas Puerto Rican husbands were

twice as likely as white husbands to assault their wives (20.4% vs. 9.9%), Cuban husbands had considerably lower rates (2.5%) (Kaufman Kantor, Jasinski, & Aldarondo, 1994).

A study that used focus groups estimated that 20% to 30% of Chinese husbands hit their wives (Ho, 1990). In a convenience sample of 150 Korean immigrant women, 60% had been battered (Song, 1986). These rates, however, must be viewed with caution, as the samples are not representative. No representative sample surveys have been used to generate incidence or prevalence rates of intimate violence against Asian women (Sorenson et al., 1996). One study indicated that the rate of intimate violence against Native American women was higher than the rate for white women; however, given the small number of Native Americans in the study and the failure to assess tribal affiliation, these findings also need to be viewed with caution (Bachman, 1992).

This brief discussion of incidence and prevalence rates points to an important problem in the study of intimate violence against ethnic minority women: To date, most studies that have used representative samples have grouped together women whose cultural heritage, country of origin, and/or native language may be completely different (e.g., the category "Asians" may include people of Chinese, Korean, Japanese, Thai, or other heritage). Until research using representative samples large enough to produce rates for meaningful subgroups is conducted (measuring the appropriate variables), we will remain in the dark regarding not only how prevalent intimate partner violence is in many communities but also how the causes and consequences of intimate violence differ by ethnic subgroup.

Ethnic Minorities and Increased Risk for Intimate Violence

It is important to note that families of color are not inherently more violent than their white counterparts. Rather, they are more likely than whites to be overrepresented in demographic categories that are at greater risk for physical violence. In many instances, racial differences in rates of intimate violence against women disappear when age, social class, and husband's occupational and employment status are taken into account (Straus et al., 1980). That is, youthfulness, poverty, blue-collar status, and unemployment are demographic factors that are associated with intimate violence. Unfortunately, people of color are overrepresented in these demographic categories, which accounts for their increased experience with intimate violence.

How Minority Status Affects the Experience of Intimate Violence

As reviewed earlier in this chapter, the experience of intimate violence is affected by a variety of life history, relationship, and situational variables. Although we have pointed out the wealth of diversity subsumed under the category "minority," racial and ethnic minority groups in the United States do share the fact that they are considered "nonwhite" in a culture rooted in white supremacist beliefs and practices, many of which can still be seen today. Racism may exacerbate a woman's experience of intimate violence in many different ways. For example, if a woman has experienced racist comments or actions against her in her community, she may not feel welcome seeking help from a local shelter. Although she wants help, she may be reluctant to get her partner involved in the legal system, as she knows the legal system is unfair in its treatment of minorities. She may feel pressure by her community not to report acts of violence, as such reports may add negative stigma to communities already struggling to gain mainstream acceptance (Richie & Kanuha, 1993; White, 1994).

Immigrant Women

Only recently has attention turned toward understanding the experience of intimate violence for immigrant women. As Dasgupta (1998) notes, these women face the tripartite discrimination of misogyny, racism, and xenophobia, all of which can contribute to their isolation and entrapment in abusive relationships and act as barriers to escaping the abuse. A particular challenge of considering the experiences of immigrant women is to take into account the influence of a woman's cultural background without allowing stereotypes to direct one's attitudes about that woman's beliefs or her need for (and right to) personal safety. In particular, some immigrant women are viewed as being "quietly accepting of male dominance and control" and thus unable or unwilling to challenge male dominance in their lives (Dasgupta, 1998, p. 210).

Because immigrant women—like most people—do value their heritage and culture, perpetrators of intimate violence against immigrant women may exploit cultural differences to shame and confuse their partners into accepting their victimization. For example, the aggressiveness of American women may be talked about negatively (e.g., referred to as unfeminine) to encourage passivity in a partner (Song, 1996). Alternatively, a woman in

one study who was sexually abused by her husband was told, "You must be bold like them [American women] and do what I ask you to do because if you can't please me, I'll probably have to look for it elsewhere" (Abraham, 1999, p. 601).

Another method of controlling a partner that is unique to the situation of immigrant women is a male's control of her immigration status, made possible through the Marriage Fraud Act, referred to as an "instrument of torture" by Dasgupta (1998). Due to this act, men (who are typically the Legal Permanent Resident) are considered the sponsors of their wives, giving them control over a woman's ability to remain in the United States. Perpetrators of intimate violence against immigrant women can and do threaten them with deportation and separation from their children. Perpetrators may keep immigrant women from learning English, maintaining nearly absolute control over what the woman is able to learn about her rights or sources of assistance.

Dasgupta (1998) outlines the barriers facing immigrant women who want to leave abusive relationships as personal (shame, fear, financial impoverishment, lack of support system, dearth of survival skills), institutional (Immigration and Naturalization Service and public benefit policies, cultural insensitivity, financial requirements, child custody issues, language barriers), and cultural ideology (meaning of marriage, keeping family intact, acceptability of fate, tolerance towards the abuser).

Same-Sex Relationships

Information on lesbian battering only began to emerge in the late 1980s (for a review, see Burke & Follingstad, 1999; Leventhal & Lundy, 1999; Renzetti, 1992;

West, 1998a). Much of what is known about lesbian battering comes from small, nonrepresentative samples. Even when data were gathered from large samples, nonrandom sampling methods were used; for example, participants had been recruited through lesbian publications, organizations, and activities. As a result, most surveyed lesbians are Caucasian, in their middle thirties, and college educated. Less is known about lesbians who are ethnic minorities, older, or working class. It will be difficult to obtain a representative sample of lesbians as long as homophobia and discrimination forces this population to remain invisible.

Based on our limited information, researchers have detected several similarities between battering experiences of lesbians and heterosexual women. Rates of intimate violence against lesbians appear to be similar to those found among heterosexual women. For example, Brand and Kidd (1986) found similar rates of intimate physical abuse reported by heterosexual (27%) and lesbian (25%) women in committed relationships. Other studies have found rates of intimate physical violence to be near 30% in lesbian samples, a rate similar to heterosexual samples (Lie & Gentlewarrier, 1991; Lie, Schilit, Bush, Montagne, & Reyes, 1991; Lockhart, White, Causby, & Isaac, 1994). Between 73% (Myers, 1989) and 90% (Lockhart et al., 1994) of lesbians sampled at a music festival reported being the recipients of verbal or psychological abuse. Overlap of abuse types also appears to be similar, with half of battered lesbians reporting both physical and sexual abuse and nearly 90% reporting both physical and psychological abuse (Renzetti, 1992). Lesbian battering is also likely to be chronic, with more than half of one sample reporting more than 10 incidents of abuse over the course of the relationship (Renzetti, 1992).

Despite some similarities, there are important differences in the abuse experiences of lesbians. Internalized homophobia is a potential stressor in same-sex relationships. It is defined as the acceptance of negative societal attitudes toward lesbians (Pharr, 1986). Although empirical research is limited, this form of oppression is believed to be a potential contributor to intimate violence in lesbian relationships via two different avenues. First, researchers argue that societal discrimination fosters internalized homophobia, which in turn may contribute to low self-esteem, feelings of powerlessness, denial of group membership, and difficulty establishing committed, trusting, intimate relationships. These negative feelings may then be acted out in the form of intimate violence (Hart, 1986). In addition, this form of oppression also poses a barrier to help-seeking among battered lesbians, who may be reluctant to let their families, coworkers, or community know that they are lesbian.

Lesbian batterers also have homophobic control as an additional form of abuse at their disposal. Hart (1986) defines this as

> threatening to tell family, friends, employer, police, church, community etc. that the victim is a lesbian. . . . ; telling the victim she deserves all that she gets because she is a lesbian; assuring her that no one would believe she has been violated because lesbians are not violent; reminding her that she has no options because the homophobic world will not help her. (p. 189)

This form of abuse appears to be quite common, with 21% of one sample of battered lesbians saying that her partner had "threatened to bring her out"—or to reveal her sexual orientation without permission (Renzetti, 1992).

Battered lesbians may not feel welcome at shelters for battered women, which is related to their concerns that they are not perceived as "legitimate victims" because "batterers are men" (Renzetti, 1992). Similar to the experiences of ethnic minority women, lesbians may also face pressure from within the lesbian community to keep their personal problems with violence hidden, for fear that doing so could reinforce negative views of lesbian relationships.

Other Groups of Women

There are other groups of women who are not covered in this chapter, whose life experiences, backgrounds, or living situations place them at risk for intimate violence or pose barriers to help-seeking. For example, women living in rural areas are more isolated from their neighbors, and this isolation means not only that neighbors are less likely to overhear and thus be able to intervene but that a woman may have trouble escaping an abusive episode (e.g., if the nearest home is 3 miles away) (Fletcher, Lunn, & Reith, 1996). Other women facing particular conditions not covered here include mentally disabled women (Carlson, 1997), physically disabled women (see Chapter 10, this volume), and elder women (see Chapter 9, this volume).

Costs and Consequences of Intimate Violence Against Women

A considerable amount of research has documented a wide array of negative consequences of intimate violence against women for the victim, her family, and society. A comprehensive review of these consequences is beyond the scope of this chapter. What follows is a brief review to acquaint the reader with the broad themes of this work (see Arias, 1999; Barnett, Miller-Perrin, & Perrin, 1997; Giles-Sims, 1998; Sharps & Campbell, 1999).

Consequences for the Victim

Not surprisingly, studies have shown that battered women are more likely than nonbattered women to visit emergency rooms and private physicians (McLeer & Anwar, 1987; Stark & Flitcraft, 1988). Whereas visits to emergency departments may be due to a physical injury incurred during an assault, research indicates that battered women also are more likely to have chronic health complaints, which are apparently unrelated to the abuse. Being battered has been identified as a correlate of smoking, alcoholism, and repeated injury, all of which are also likely to result in poorer health for the victim (e.g., see Plichta, 1992; Stark & Flitcraft, 1988).

Physical injury is one important consequence of intimate violence. Studies have shown that women are more likely to be injured by an intimate partner than by any other type of assailant. Two national studies revealed 41% to 52% of women victimized by intimates sustain injury (Bachman & Saltzman, 1995; Tjaden & Thoennes, 1998a). Just as experiences of abuse are varied, so, too, is the realm of resulting physical injuries. Injuries may be minor (e.g., small cuts and light bruises), or they may require medical attention and lead to permanent disability or disfigurement. Based on findings from the National Crime Victimization Survey, Bachman and Saltzman (1995) found that 41% of women injured by their intimate partners had injuries requiring medical care. Physical consequences of sexual assaults include the contraction of sexually transmitted diseases such as HIV. In a sample of battered women residing in shelters, 50% had been infected with at least one form of sexually transmitted disease, and multiple HIV-exposure risk was strongly correlated with "high to extreme" levels of physical, psychological, and sexual abuse (Molina & Basinait-Smith, 1998).

Living with battering puts a woman at risk for a variety of psychological problems, including depression, alcoholism, anxiety, and suicidality (Campbell et al., 1997; Plichta, 1992; Stark & Flitcraft, 1996; Stets & Straus, 1990). Stark (1984, as cited in Stark & Flitcraft 1996) compared battered to nonbattered women in a medical setting and found that battered women were 3 times as likely to be diagnosed as depressed or psychotic, 15 times as likely to abuse alcohol, 9 times as likely to abuse drugs, and 5 times as likely to attempt suicide. Nearly 20% of the battered women in this study had attempted suicide at least once. Studies find that negative symptoms associated with battering are likely to subside, at least partially, when the woman is no longer being abused (Stark & Flitcraft, 1988).

Battered Women's Syndrome (BWS) is a label that has been used to describe a pattern of negative psychological sequelae observed in many battered women (Walker, 1979). The major components of BWS include symptoms of posttraumatic stress disorder (PTSD) (including intrusive memories, flashbacks, fear, anxiety, sleep disturbances, avoidance, and hypervigilance) and "learned helplessness." Learned helplessness, or the belief that abuse is inescapable, may develop as the strategies a woman uses to attempt to end the abuse (e.g., threatening to leave, con-

tacting the police, getting a restraining order, etc.) prove ineffective. The label of BWS is useful insofar as it outlines a pattern of symptoms that may develop in normal women responding to repeated exposure to trauma (i.e., battering). Clearly, BWS affects different women in different ways, "depending upon a particular woman's previous exposure to other oppressors, mental health status, available support systems, frequency and severity of the abuse, and a quality best described as 'hardiness' of the individual woman" (Walker, 1993, p. 134). The factors associated with the development of BWS symptoms include the pattern of violent incidents, pathological jealousy, possessiveness, isolation, sexual assault, threats to kill, psychological torture, and violence against a woman's loved ones (Walker, 1988).

Similarly, Stark and Flitcraft (1988) identify "The Battering Syndrome" as characterized by "a history of injury (often including sexual assault), general medical complaints, psychosocial problems, and unsuccessful help seeking" (p. 301). They found that such a history is associated with higher risk of rape, miscarriage, abortion, alcohol and drug use, attempted suicide, child abuse, and mental illness. They point to the importance of the "dual trauma" of personal assault and institutional neglect, leading to isolation, entrapment in the abusive relationship, and negative outcomes.

There is ample evidence that battering leads to negative physical and mental health outcomes for the victim. These outcomes are likely to affect her life as a mother, friend, and community member. Intimate violence also affects labor force participation in a variety of ways. In one analysis, battering resulted in absenteeism from work in 55% of battered women, lateness or leaving early in 62%, job loss in 24%, and batterer harassment at work in 56%. In addition, 33% of the battered women in this sample reported being prohibited from working, 21% were prevented from finding work, 59% were discouraged from working, 24% were not allowed to attend school, and 50% were discouraged from attending school (Shepard & Pence, 1988). Such difficulties affect a woman's ability to provide food and shelter not only for herself but also for her children. Health insurance and retirement income are also tied to job security, and these benefits will also be denied the woman whose labor force participation is compromised by abuse.

Intimate violence leads to numerous other social and economic losses. Although there is no way to put a monetary figure on the emotional losses experienced by the children, family, and friends of the victim and perpetrator, it is possible to estimate some of the economic costs associated with intimate violence (for a review of the costs and consequences as they relate to children, see Arias, 1999; Wolak & Finkelhor, 1998). In the United States alone, costs associated with lost work productivity are estimated to be $5 billion to $10 billion (Crowell & Burgess, 1996). As noted above, battered women are more likely to require both emergency and routine medical care. The percentage of women visiting emergency rooms due to intimate violence ranges from 7% to 37% (Plichta, 1992; Rand & Strom, 1997). One estimate of the annual cost of intimate violence to the health care industry, estimated in 1980 dollars, included 21,000 hospitalizations, 99,800 days of hospitalization, 28,700 emergency room visits, and 39,900 physician visits, resulting in a projected cost of $44,393,700 (McLeer & Anwar, 1987).

The above calculation is quite conservative, using estimates for services based on NCVS data. Other studies have indicated that the use of services is actually much higher. For example, one study of people treated for injuries in emergency rooms found that 37% of over 550,000 women's visits were due to victimization by an intimate (Rand & Strom, 1997). This would result in over 200,000 *annual* emergency room visits. These high costs are estimated for the health consequences of intimate violence alone and do not take into account the large burden intimate violence places on the criminal justice system, including the time and efforts of police, lawyers, and judges (Zorza, 1994).

New Directions

Nearly three decades of research and advocacy have provided ample evidence that intimate violence against women is an important social problem, affecting women of all ages and backgrounds at various points in their lives—dating women, pregnant women, immigrant women, lesbian women, and even women who have ended the relationship with their abusers. We have identified two different types of intimate violence, which appear to lie at opposite ends of an intimate violence continuum: common couple or atypical violence, which has little to no impact on a woman's life, and patriarchal terrorism, intimate violence that is accompanied by various measures of coercive control, leading to physical and mental health problems for the victim and substantial social and economic losses to society.

Clearly, there are many other patterns of intimate violence that differ from these two types. We must continue the work of refining our understanding of patterns of intimate violence and the interaction of such patterns with situational factors (e.g., poverty, lack of battered women's support services) and personal factors (e.g., no job skills, preschool-age children, language barriers) that lead to negative outcomes.

We must continue research and advocacy on behalf of victims—by identifying how to break down barriers to receiving help for women of all backgrounds. At the same time, we must improve our efforts to stop abuse before it starts, and these efforts must be focused on the perpetrator. Although we have been able to identify many factors that put someone at risk for being abusive, there is currently little agreement about how these factors interrelate over the life course of the perpetrator and ultimately lead to intimate violence. Few rigorous evaluations of treatment or prevention programs have been conducted (Chalk & King, 1998), and there is little agreement about whether such programs have been effective, or even how we can measure success in such programs. Little is known about interventions with perpetrators of different racial and ethnic backgrounds, socioeconomic status, life stage, or sexual orientation.

Throughout this chapter, we have attempted to cover the wide range of experiences that constitute intimate violence. We have taken a close look at each type of abuse and at different types of perpetrators and victims. Ultimately, it is also necessary to try to make sense of the connections: between types of violence (physical, sexual, emotional), between violence during different stages of a relationship (e.g., dating, married) or at different life stages (e.g., during pregnancy), between different patterns of abuse (sporadic, cyclical), and between intimate violence by people of differing cultural backgrounds. Focusing on these connections will strengthen our understanding of the causes and consequences of intimate violence and help illuminate the path to appropriate intervention and prevention strategies.

Notes

1. For ease of presentation, throughout this chapter, perpetrators will be referred to as *he,* even though women can and do perpetrate intimate violence against women.

2. It should be noted that this sample included all women (even those who had never married, cohabited, or dated), which is likely to be partially responsible for the lower rate arrived at in the study. That is, women who have never had an intimate partner could not have the experience of being abused by an intimate partner. Including such women in the base sample would lead to a lower rate of abuse by intimate partners.

3. About 13% reported two or three acts of violence, and 37% reported three or more acts or one "serious" incident.

4. These findings are based on intimate violence in a relationship by a male, a female, or by both parties. Presentation of findings in the original article does not allow for an analysis of male violence against women by relationship status.

5. These figures are based on 2 of 13 studies reviewed by Gazmararian et al., 1996, which listed rates by intimate perpetrators only: Helton, 1987 (8.3%) and Campbell, 1992 (7.2%) (both as cited in Gazmararian et al., 1996), as well as the research by Gazmararian et al. (1995), which produced rates of intimate violence across four states as ranging from 3.8% to 6.9%.

References

Abraham, M. (1999). Sexual abuse in South Asian immigrant marriages. *Violence Against Women, 5,* 591-618.

Aldarondo, E., & Straus, M. A. (1994). Screening for physical violence in couple therapy: Methodological, practical, and ethical considerations. *Family Process, 33,* 425-439.

American Academy of Pediatrics. (1997, December). Policy statement: Breast-feeding and the use of human milk (RE9729). *American Academy of Pediatrics, 100*(6), 1035-1039.

Arias, I. (1999). Women's responses to physical and psychological abuse. In X. B. Arriaga & S. Oskamp (Eds.), *Violence in intimate relationships* (pp. 139-162) Thousand Oaks, CA: Sage.

Arias, I., & Pape, K. T. (1999). Psychological abuse: Implications for adjustment and commitment to leave violent partners. *Violence and Victims, 14*(1), 55-67.

Bachman, R. (1992). *Death and violence on the reservation: Homicide, family violence, and suicide in American Indian populations.* Wesport, CT: Auburn House.

Bachman, R. (1994). *Violence against women: A National Crime Victimization Survey report.* Washington, DC: Department of Justice.

Bachman, R., Paternoster, R., & Ward, S. (1992). The rationality of sexual offending: Testing a deterrence/rational choice conception of sexual assault. *Law & Society Review, 26,* 343-372.

Bachman, R., & Saltzman, L. E. (1995). *Violence against women: Estimates from the redesigned survey.* Washington DC: Department of Justice.

Ballard, T. J., Saltzman, L. E., Gazmararian, J. A., Spitz, A. M., Lazorick, S., & Marks, J. S. (1998). Violence during pregnancy: Measurement issues. *Public Health Briefs, 88,* 274-276.

Barnett, O. W., Miller-Perrin, C. L., & Perrin, R. D. (1997). *Family violence across the lifespan: An introduction.* Thousand Oaks, CA: Sage.

Basile, K. C. (1999). Rape by acquiescence: The ways in which women "give in" to unwanted sex with their husbands. *Violence Against Women, 5*(9), 1036-1058.

Bergen, R. K. (1996). *Wife rape: Understanding the response of survivors and service providers.* Thousand Oaks, CA: Sage.

Bergman, L. (1992). Dating violence among high school students. *Social Work, 37,* 21-27.

Berkowitz, A. D. (1994). A model acquaintance rape prevention program for men. In A. D. Berkowitz (Ed.), *Men and rape: Theory, research, and prevention programs in higher education* (pp. 35-42). San Francisco: Jossey-Bass.

Berkowitz, A. D., Burkhart, B. R., & Bourg, S. E. (1994). Research on college men and rape. In A. D. Berkowitz (Ed.), *Men and rape: Theory,*

research, and prevention programs in higher education (pp. 3-20). San Francisco: Jossey-Bass.

Bowker, L. H. (1993). A battered woman's problems are social, not psychological. In R. J. Gelles & D. R. Loseke (Eds.), *Current controversies on family violence* (pp. 154-165). Newbury Park, CA: Sage.

Bowker, L. H., & Maurer, L. (1987). The medical treatment of battered wives. *Women and Health, 12*(1), 25-45.

Brand, P. A., & Kidd, A. H. (1986). Frequency of physical aggression in heterosexual and female homosexual dyads. *Psychological Reports, 59,* 1307-1313.

Browne, A. (1987). *When battered women kill.* New York: Free Press.

Burke, L. K., & Follingstad, D. R. (1999). Violence in lesbian and gay relationships: Theory, prevalence, and correlational factors. *Clinical Psychology Review, 19*(5), 487-512.

Burke, P. J., Stets, J. E., & Pirog-Good, M. A. (1989). Gender identity, self-esteem, and physical abuse in dating relationships. *Social Psychology Quarterly, 51,* 272-285.

Campbell, J. C. (1992). "If I can't have you, no one can": Power and control in homicide of female partners. In J. Radford & D. Russell (Eds.), *Femicide: The politics of woman killing* (pp. 99-113). New York: Twayne.

Campbell, J. C. (1995). Prediction of homicide of and by battered women. In J. C. Campbell (Ed.), *Assessing dangerousness: Violence by sexual offenders, batterers, and child abusers* (pp. 96-113). Thousand Oaks, CA: Sage.

Campbell, J. C. (1998). Abuse during pregnancy: progress, policy, and potential. *American Journal of Public Health, 88,* 185-187.

Campbell, J. C., & Alford, P. (1989). The dark consequences of marital rape. *American Journal of Nursing, 89,* 946-949.

Campbell, J. C., Kub, J., Belknap, R. A., Templin, T. N. (1997). Predictors of depression in battered women. *Violence Against Women, 3,* 271-293.

Campbell, J. C., Rose, L., Kub, J., & Nedd, D. (1998). Voices of strength and resistance. A contextual and longitudinal analysis of women's responses to battering. *Journal of Interpersonal Violence, 13*(6), 743-762.

Carlson, B. E. (1997). Mental retardation and domestic violence: An ecological approach to intervention. *Social Work, 42*(1), 78-89.

Cazenave, N. A., & Straus, M. (1979). Race, class, network embeddedness, and family violence: A search for potent support system. *Journal of Comparative Family Studies, 10,* 280-300.

Chalk, R., & King, P. A. (1998). *Violence in families: Assessing prevention and treatment programs.* Washington, DC: National Academy Press.

Crenshaw, K. W. (1994). Mapping the margins: Intersectionality, identity politics, and violence against women of color. In M. A. Fineman & R. Mykitiuk (Eds.), *The public nature of private violence: The discovery of domestic abuse.* New York: Routledge.

Crowell, N. A., & Burgess, A. W. (Eds.). (1996). *Understanding violence against women.* Washington, DC: National Academy Press.

Currie, D. H. (1998). Violent men or violent women? Whose definition counts? In R. K. Bergen (Ed.), *Issues in intimate violence.* Thousand Oaks, CA: Sage.

Dasgupta, S. D. (1998). Women's realities: Defining violence against women by immigration, race, and class. In R. K. Bergen (Ed.), *Issues in intimate violence.* Thousand Oaks, CA: Sage.

DeKeseredy, W. S. (1990). Woman abuse in dating relationships: The contribution of male peer support. *Sociological Inquiry, 60*(3), 236-243.

DeKeseredy, W. S., & Kelly, K. (1993). The incidence and prevalence of woman abuse in Canadian university and college dating relationships. *International Migration Review, 26,* 137-159.

DeMaris, A. (1990). The dynamics of generational transfer in courtship violence: A biracial exploration. *Journal of Marriage and the Family, 52,* 219-231.

Dutton, D. G. (1999). Limitations of social learning models in explaining intimate aggression. In X. B. Arriaga & S. Oskamp (Eds.), *Violence in intimate relationships* (pp. 73-87). Thousand Oaks, CA: Sage.

Fagan, J. (1990). Intoxication and aggression. In M. Tonry & J. Q. Wilson (Eds.), *Drugs and crime* (pp. 241-320). Chicago: University of Chicago Press.

Feld, S. L., & Straus, M. A. (1990). Escalation and desistance from wife assault in marriage. In M. A. Straus & R. J. Gelles (Eds.), *Physical violence in American families: Risk factors and adaptations to violence in 8,145 families* (pp. 489-505). New Brunswick, NJ: Transaction.

Finkelhor, D., & Yllö, K. (1987). *License to rape: Sexual abuse of wives.* New York: Holt, Rinehart & Winston.

Fletcher, S., Lunn, D., & Reith, L. (1996). Fear on the farm: Rural women take action against domestic violence. *Women and Environments, 38,* 27-29.

Follingstad, D. R., Rutledge, L. L., Berg, B. J., Hause, E. S., & Polek, D. S. (1990). The role of emotional abuse in physically abusive relationships. *Journal of Family Violence, 5*(2), 107-120.

Fox, J. A., & Zawitz, M. W. (2000). *Homicide trends in the United States* (NCJ 179767). Washington, DC: Bureau of Justice Statistics.

Gazmararian, J. A., Adams, M. M., Saltzman, L. E., Johnson, C. H., Bruce, F. C., Marks, J. S., & Zahniser, S. C. (1995). The relationship between pregnancy intendedness and physical violence in mothers of newborns. *Obstetrics & Gynecology, 85*(6), 1031-1038.

Gazmararian, J. A., Lazorick, S., Spitz, A. M., Ballard, T. J., Saltzman, L. E., & Marks, L. S. (1996). Prevalence of violence against pregnant women. *Journal of the American Medical Association, 275,* 1915-1920.

Gelles, R. J. (1988). Violence and pregnancy: Are pregnant women at greater risk of abuse. *Journal of Marriage and the Family, 50,* 841-847.

George, L. K., Winfeld, I., & Blazer, D. G. (1992) Sociocultural factors in sexual assault: Comparison of two representative samples of women. *Journal of Social Issues, 48,* 105-125.

Gielen, A. C., O'Campo, P., Faden, R. R., Kass, N. E., & Xue, X. (1994). Interpersonal conflict and physical violence during the childbearing years. *Social Science Medicine, 39*(6), 781-787.

Giles-Sims, J. (1998). The aftermath of partner violence. In J. L. Jasinski & L. M. Williams (Eds.), *Partner violence: A comprehensive review of 20 years of research* (pp. 44-72). Thousand Oaks, CA: Sage

Goldstein, P. J., Belluci, P. A., Spunt, B. J., & Miller, T. (1989). *Frequency of cocaine use and violence: A comparison between women and men.* New York: Narcotic and Drug Research.

Gondolf, E. W. (1988). *Battered women as survivors: An alternative to treating learned helplessness.* Lexington, MA: Lexington.

Goodman, L. A., Koss, M. P., & Russo, F. N. (1993). Violence against women: physical and mental health affects. Part I: research findings. *Applied & Preventive Psychology, 2,* 79-89.

Greenfeld, L. A., Rand, M. R., Craven, D., Klaus, P. A., Ringel, C., Warchol, G., Maston, C., & Fox, J. A. (1998). *Violence by intimates: Analysis of data on crimes by current or former spouses, boyfriends, and girlfriends.* Washington, DC: Department of Justice.

Hallinan, T. (1996). *Domestic terror: Family and domestic violence homicide cases in San Francisco, 1993-1994.* San Francisco: San Francisco Family Violence Project.

Hamberger, L. K., & Hastings, J. E. (1986). Personality correlates of men who abuse their partners: A cross-validation study. *Journal of Family Violence, 1*(4), 323-341.

Hamberger, L. K., Lohr, J. M., Bonge, D., & Tolin, D. F. (1996). A large sample empirical typology of male spouse abusers and its relationship to dimensions of abuse. *Violence and Victims, 11,* 277-292.

Hampton, R. L., & Gelles, R. J. (1994). Violence toward black women in a nationally representative sample of black families. *Journal of Comparative Family Studies, 25*(1), 105-119.

Hanneke, C. R., Shields, N. M., & McCall, G. (1986). Assessing the prevalence of marital rape. *Journal of Interpersonal Violence, 1,* 350-362.

Hansen, M., Harway, M., & Cervantes, N. (1991). Therapists' perceptions of severity in cases of family violence. *Violence and Victims, 6,* 225-235.

Hart, B. (1986). Lesbian battering: An examination. In K. Lobel (Ed.), *Naming the violence* (pp. 173-189). Seattle, WA: Seal.

Ho, C. K. (1990). An analysis of domestic violence in Asian American communities: A multicultural approach to counseling. In L. S. Brown & M. P. P. Root (Eds.), *Diversity and complexity in feminist therapy* (pp. 129-150). Binghamton, NY: Harrington Park Press.

Holtzworth-Munroe, A., & Hutchinson, G. (1993). Attributing negative intent to wife behavior: The attributions of maritally violent versus non-violent men. *Journal of Abnormal Psychology, 102,* 206-211.

Holtzworth-Munroe, A., & Stuart, G. L. (1994). Typologies of male batterers: Three sub-types and the differences among them. *Psychological Bulletin, 116*(3), 476-497.

Hotaling, G. T., & Sugarman, D. B. (1986). An analysis of risk markers in husband-to-wife vi-olence: The current state of knowledge. *Violence and Victims, 1,* 101-124.

Hudson, W. W., & McIntosh, S. R. (1981). The assessment of spousal abuse: Two quantifiable dimensions. *Journal of Marriage and the Family, 43,* 873-885.

Hutchison, I. W. (1999). Alcohol, fear, and woman abuse. *Sex Roles, 40*(11/12), 893-920.

Jacobson, N. S., & Gottman, J. M. (1998). *When men batter women: New insights into ending abusive relationships.* New York: Simon & Schuster.

Jacobson, N. S., Gottman, J. M., Gortner, E., Berns, S., & Shortt, J. W. (1996). Psychological factors in the longitudinal course of battering: When do the couples split up? When does the abuse decrease? *Violence and Victims, 11,* 371-392.

Johnson, M. P. (1995). Patriarchal terrorism and common couple violence: Two forms of violence against women. *Journal of Marriage and the Family, 57,* 283-294.

Jones, A. (1994). *Next time, she'll be dead.* Boston: Beacon.

Kantor, G. Kaufman, Jasinski, J. L., & Aldarondo, E. (1994). Sociocultural status and incidence of marital violence in Hispanic families. *Violence and Victims, 9,* 207-222.

Kantor, G. Kaufman, & Jasinski, J. L. (1998). Dynamics and risk factors in partner violence. In J. L. Jasinski & L. M. Williams (Eds.), *Partner violence: A comprehensive review of 20 years of research* (pp. 1-43). Thousand Oaks, CA: Sage.

Kantor, G. Kaufman, & Straus, M. A. (1989). Substance abuse as a precipitant of wife abuse victimization. *American Journal of Drug and Alcohol Abuse, 15,* 173-189.

Kanuha, V. (1996). Domestic violence, racism, and the battered women's movement in the United States. In J. L. Edleson & Z. C. Eisikovits (Eds.), *Future interventions with battered women and their families* (pp. 34-50). Thousand Oaks, CA: Sage.

Kurz, D. (1990). Interventions with battered women in health care settings. *Violence and Victims, 5,* 243-256.

Kurz, D. (1996). Separation, divorce, and woman abuse. *Violence Against Women, 2*(1), 63-81.

Leventhal, B., & Lundy, S. E. (Eds.). (1999). *Same-sex domestic violence: Strategies for change.* Thousand Oaks, CA: Sage.

Lie, G. Y., & Gentlewarrier, S. (1991). Intimate violence in lesbian relationships: Discussion of survey findings and practice implications. *Journal of Social Service Research, 15,* 41-59.

Lie, G. Y., Schilit, R., Bush, J., Montagne, M., & Reyes, L. (1991). Lesbians in currently aggressive relationships: How frequently do they report aggressive past relationships? *Violence and Victims, 6,* 121-135.

Lockhart, L. L. (1987). A reexamination of the effects of race and social class on the incidence of marital violence: A search for reliable differences. *Journal of Marriage and the Family, 49,* 603-610.

Lockhart, L. L. (1991). Spousal violence: A cross-racial perspective. In R. L. Hampton (Ed.), *Black family violence: Current research and theory* (pp. 85-102). Lexington, MA: Lexington Books.

Lockhart, L. L., White, B. W., Causby, V., & Isaac, A. (1994). Letting out the secret: Violence in lesbian relationships. *Journal of Interpersonal Violence, 9,* 469-492.

Mahoney, P., & Williams, L. M. (1998). Sexual assault in marriage: Prevalence, consequences, and treatment of wife rape. In J. L. Jasinski & L. M. Williams (Eds.), *Partner violence: A comprehensive review of 20 years of research.* Thousand Oaks, CA: Sage.

Mahoney, P., Williams, L. M., & Saunders, B. E. (1998, October). *Characteristics of men who rape their wives: Implications for treatment.* Paper presented at the Association for the Treatment of Sexual Abusers Research and Treatment Conference, Vancouver, BC.

Marshall, L. L. (1996). Psychological abuse of women: Six distinct clusters. *Journal of Family Violence, 11,* 379-409.

McFarlane, J., Parker, B., Soeken, K., & Bullock, L. (1992). Assessing for abuse during pregnancy. *Journal of the American Medical Association, 267,* 3176-3178.

McFarlane, J., Parker, B., Soeken, K., Silva, C., & Reed, S. (1999). Severity of abuse before and during pregnancy for African American, Hispanic, and Anglo women. *Journal of Nurse Midwifery, 44*(2), 139-144.

McKeel, A. J., & Sporakowski, M. J. (1993). How shelter counselors' views about responsibility for wife abuse related to services they provide. *Journal of Family Violence, 8,* 101-112.

McLeer, S. V., & Anwar, R. A. H. (1987). The role of the emergency physician in the prevention of domestic violence. *Annals of Emergency Medicine, 16,*1155-1161.

Mirande, A., & Perez, P. (1987). *Ethnic and cultural differences in domestic violence: A test of conflicting models of the Chicano family.* Paper presented at the Research Conference on Violence and Homicide in the Hispanic Community, Los Angeles.

Molina, L. S., & Basinait-Smith, C. (1998). Revisiting the intersection between domestic abuse and HIV risk. *American Journal of Public Health, 88*(8), 1267-1268.

Murphy, C. M., & Hoover, S. A. (1999). Measuring emotional abuse in dating relationships as a multifactorial construct. *Violence and Victims, 14*(1), 39-53.

Murphy, C. M., & O'Leary, K. D. (1989). Psychological aggression predicts physical aggression in early marriage. *Journal of Consulting and Clinical Psychology, 57*(5), 579-582.

Murphy, J. E. (1988). Date abuse and forced intercourse among college students. In G. T. Hotaling, D. Finkelhor, J. T. Kirkpatrick, & M. A. Straus (Eds.), *Family abuse and its consequences.* Thousand Oaks, CA: Sage.

MVP: Mentors in Violence Project. (1994). *The MVP playbook.* Boston: The Center for the Study of Sport in Society.

Myers, B. (1989). *Lesbian battering: An analyses of power.* Unpublished doctoral dissertation, Indiana University of Pennsylvania, Indiana, PA.

Neff, J. A., Holamon, B., & Schluter, T. D. (1995). Spousal violence among Anglos, Blacks, and Mexican Americans: The role of demographic variables, psychosocial predictors, and alcohol consumption. *Journal of Family Violence, 10,* 1-21.

Neufeld, J., McNamara, J. R., & Ertl, M. (1999). Incidence and prevalence of dating partner abuse and its relationship to dating practices. *Journal of Interpersonal Violence, 14*(2), 125-137.

Newberger, E. H., Barkan, S. E., Lieberman, E. S., McCormick, M. C., Yllö, K., Gary, L. T., & Schechter, S. (1992). Abuse of pregnant women and adverse birth outcome: Current knowledge and implications for practice. *Journal of the American Medical Association, 267,* 2370-2372.

O'Keefe, M. (1994). Linking marital violence, mother-child/father-child aggression, and child behavior problems. *Journal of Family Violence 9,* 63-78.

O'Leary, K. D. (1993). Through a psychological lens. In R. Gelles & D. Loseke (Eds.), *Current controversies on family violence* (pp.7-30). Newbury Park, CA: Sage.

O'Leary, K. D. (1999). Psychological abuse: A variable deserving critical attention in domestic violence. *Violence and Victims, 14*(1), 3-23.

O'Leary, K. D., Barling, J., Arias, I., Rosenbaum, A., Malone, J., & Tyree, A. (1989). Prevalence and stability of marital aggression between spouses: A longitudinal analysis. *Journal of Consulting and Clinical Psychology, 57,* 263-268.

O'Leary, K. D., Malone, J., & Tyree, A. (1994). Physical aggression in early marriage: Prerelationship and relationship effects. *Journal of Consulting and Clinical Psychology, 62,* 594-602.

Pagelow, M. (1988). Marital rape. In V. Morrison, R. Hasselt, & A. Hersen-Bellack (Eds.), *Handbook of family violence* (pp. 207-232). New York: Plenum.

Pharr, S. (1986). Two workshops on homophobia. In K. Lobel (Ed.), *Naming the violence: Speaking out about lesbian battering* (pp. 202-222). Seattle, WA: Seal.

Plichta, S. (1992). The effects of woman abuse on health care utilization and health status: A literature review. *Women's Health Issues, 2,* 154-163.

Quigley, B. M., Leonard, K. E., & Senchak, M. (1996). Desistance from marital violence in the early years of marriage. *Violence and Victims, 11,* 355-370.

Rand, M. R., & Strom, K. (1997). *Violence-related injuries treated in hospital emergency Departments: Special report* (NCJ-156921). Washington, DC: Department of Justice.

Randall, M., & Haskall, L. (1995). Sexual violence in women's lives. *Violence Against Women, 1*(1), 6-31.

Renzetti, C. M. (1992). *Violent betrayal: Partner abuse in lesbian relationships.* Newbury Park, CA: Sage.

Richie, B. E., & Kanuha, V. (1993). Battered women of color in public health care systems: Racism, sexism, and violence. In B. Blair & S. E. Cayleff (Eds.), *Wings of gauze: Women of color and the experience of health and illness* (pp. 288-299). Detroit, MI: Wayne State University Press.

Rouse, L. P., Breen, R., & Howell, M. (1988). Abuse in intimate relationships: A comparison of married and dating college students. *Journal of Interpersonal Violence, 3*(4), 414-429.

Russell, D. E. H. (1990). *Rape in marriage.* Indianapolis: Indiana University Press.

Sackett, L. A., & Saunders, D. G. (1999). The impact of different forms of psychological abuse on battered women. *Violence and Victims, 14*(1), 105-117.

Sharps, P. W., & Campbell, J. (1999). Health consequences for victims of violence in intimate relationships. In X. B. Arriaga & S. Oskamp (Eds.), *Violence in intimate relationships* (pp. 163-180). Thousand Oaks, CA: Sage.

Shepard, M. E., & Pence, E. (1988). The effect of battering on the employment status of women. *Affilia, 3*(2), 55-61.

Smith, P. H., & Earp, J. A. (1995, July). *Measuring battering: Development of the Women's Experiences with Battering (WEB) scale.* Paper presented at the 4th International Family Violence Conference, University of New Hampshire.

Smith, P. H., & Smith, J. (1995, June). *The measurement trap: Conceptualizing woman battering.* Paper presented at the National Council for International Health Annual Conference, Durham, New Hampshire.

Song, Y. I. (1986). *Battered Korean women in urban America: The relationship of cultural conflict to wife abuse.* Unpublished doctoral dissertation, Ohio State University, Columbus.

Song, Y. I. (1996). *Battered women in Korean immigrant families: The silent scream.* New York: Garland.

Sorenson, S. B., Upchurch, D. M., & Shen, H. (1996). Violence and injury in marital arguments: Risk patterns and gender differences. *American Journal of Public Health, 86*(1), 35-40.

Souza, C. A. (1999). Teen dating violence: The hidden epidemic. *Family and Conciliation Courts Review, 37*(3), 356-374.

Stark, E., & Flitcraft, A. (1988). Violence among intimates: An epidemiological review. In V. B. Van Hasselt, R. L. Morrison, A. S. Bellack, & M. Hersen (Eds.), *Handbook of family violence* (pp. 293-316). New York: Plenum.

Stark, E., & Flitcraft, A. (1995). Killing the beast within: Woman battering and female suicidality. *International Journal of Health Services, 25*(1), 43-64.

Stark, E., & Flitcraft, A. (1996). *Women at risk: Domestic violence and women's health.* Thousand Oaks, CA: Sage.

Stets, J. E., & Straus, M. A. (1990). Gender differences in reporting marital violence and its medical and psychological consequences. In M. A. Straus & R. J. Gelles (Eds.), *Physical violence in American families: Risk factors and adaptations to violence in 8,145 families* (pp. 151-166). New Brunswick, NJ: Transaction.

Stout, K. D. (1993). Intimate femicide: A study of men who have killed their mates. *Journal of Offender Rehabilitation, 193*(4), 81-94.

Straus, M. A., & Gelles, R. J. (1990). *Physical violence in American families: Risk factors and adaptations to violence in 8,145 families.* New Brunswick, NJ: Transaction.

Straus, M. A., Gelles, R. J., & Steinmetz, S. (1980). *Behind closed doors: Violence in the American family.* Garden City, NJ: Anchor.

Straus, M. A., & Smith, C. (1990). Family patterns and child abuse. In M. A. Straus & R. J. Gelles (Eds.) *Physical violence in American families: Risk factors and adaptations to violence in 8,145 families* (pp. 245-262). New Brunswick, NJ: Transaction.

Strube, M. J., & Barbour, L. S. (1984). Factors related to the decision to leave an abusive relationship. *Journal of Marriage and the Family, 46,* 837-844.

Sugarman, D. B., & Hotaling, G. T. (1991). Dating violence: A review of contextual and risk factors. In B. Levy (Ed.), *Dating violence: Young women in danger.* Seattle, WA: Seal Press.

Symons, P. Y., Croer, M. W., Kepler-Youngblood, P., & Slater, V. (1994). Prevalence and predictors of adolescent dating violence. *Journal of Child and Adolescent Psychiatric Nursing, 7*(3), 14-23.

Tan, C., Basta, J., Sullivan C. M., & Davidson, W. S., II. (1995). The role of social support in the lives of women exiting domestic violence shelters: An experimental study. *Journal of Interpersonal Violence, 10*(4), 437-451.

Tjaden, P. (1997). *The crime of stalking: How big is the problem?* Washington, DC: Department of Justice.

Tjaden, P., & Thoennes, N. (1998a). *Prevalence, incidence, and consequences of violence against women: Findings from the National Violence Against Women Survey* (NCJ 172837). Washington, DC: U.S. Department of Justice.

Tjaden, P., & Thoennes, N. (1998b). *Stalking in America: Findings from the National Violence Against Women Survey* (NCJ 169592). Washington, DC: Department of Justice.

Torres, S. (1991). A comparison of wife abuse between two cultures: Perceptions, attitudes, nature, and extent. *Issues in Mental Health Nursing, 12,* 113-131.

Ullman, S. E., & Siegel, J. M. (1993). Victim-offender relationship and sexual assault. *Violence and Victims, 8,* 121-134.

Waldner-Haugrud, L. K., & Magruder, B. (1995). Male and female sexual victimization in dating relationships: Gender differences in coercion techniques and outcomes. *Violence and Victims, 10,* 203-215.

Walker, L. E. (1979). *The battered woman.* New York: Harper & Row.

Walker, L. E. (1988). The battered woman syndrome. In G. T. Hotaling, D. Finkelhor, J. T. Kirkpatrick, & M. A. Straus (Eds.), *Family abuse and its consequences.* Newbury Park, CA: Sage.

Walker, L. E. (1993). The battered woman syndrome is a psychological consequence of abuse. In R. J. Gelles & D. R. Loseke (Eds.), *Current controversies on family violence.* Newbury Park, CA: Sage.

Walker, L. E., & Meloy, R. J. (1998). Stalking and domestic violence. In J. R. Meloy (Ed.), *The psychology of stalking.* San Diego, CA: Academic Press.

Weis, J. (1989). Family violence research methodology and design. In L. Ohlin & M. Tonry (Eds.), *Family violence* (pp. 117-162). Chicago: University of Chicago Press.

West, C. M. (1998a). Leaving a second closet: Outing partner violence in same-sex couples. In J. L. Jasinski & L. M. Williams (Eds.), *Partner violence: A comprehensive review of 20 years of research* (pp. 163-183). Thousand Oaks, CA: Sage.

West, C. M. (1998b). Lifting the "political gag order": Breaking the silence around partner violence in ethnic minority families. In J. L. Jasinski & L. M. Williams (Eds.), *Partner violence: A comprehensive review of 20 years of research,* (pp. 184-209). Thousand Oaks, CA: Sage.

White, E. (1994). *Chain, chain, change: For black women dealing with physical and emotional abuse.* Seattle, WA: Seal Press.

White, J. W., & Koss, M. P. (1991). Courtship violence: Incidence in a national sample of higher education students. *Violence and Victims, 6,* 247-256.

Wilson, D. G., & Wilson, A. V. (1991). *Spousal abuse cases: Perceptions and attitudes of service providers* (Report prepared for the Attorney General's Task Force on Domestic Violence Crime). Louisville: Kentucky Criminal Justice Statistical Analysis Center.

Wilson, M., Daly, M., & Wright, C. (1993). Uxorcide in Canada: Demographic risk patterns. *Canadian Journal of Criminology 35,* 265-291.

Wilt, S. A., Illman, S. M. & BrodyField, M. (1996). *Female homicide victims in New York City, 1990-1994.* New York: City Department of Health Injury Prevention Program.

Wingood, G. M., & DiClemente, R. J. (1997). The effects of an abusive primary partner on the condom use and sexual negotiation practices of African-American women. *American Journal of Public Health, 87*(6), 1016-1018.

Wolak, J., & Finkelhor, D. (1998). Children exposed to partner violence. In J. L. Jasinski & L. M. Williams (Eds.), *Partner violence: A comprehensive review of 20 years of research.* Thousand Oaks, CA: Sage.

Yllö, K. (1993). Through a feminist lens: Gender, power and violence. In R. J. Gelles & D. R. Loseke (Eds.), *Current controversies on family violence* (pp. 47-62). Newbury Park, CA: Sage.

Zorza, J. (1991). Woman battering: A major cause of homelessness. *Clearinghouse Review, 61,* 421-429.

Zorza, J. (1994). Women battering: High costs and the state of the law [Special issue]. *Clearinghouse Review, 28,* 383-395.

CHAPTER 9

Violence Against Older Women

Linda Vinton

Violence against older women by intimates has garnered scant attention as
a women's issue. Older women's issues
have been generally overlooked by the
women's, battered women's, and elder
abuse movements. This chapter begins
with a brief look at how attitudes toward
elders, and toward older women in particular, have evolved in American society
and how they contribute to this oversight.
During the 1990s, we saw the reframing
of many cases of physical and emotional
violence against older women by family
members as domestic violence. The ways
in which society responds to older abused
women have changed accordingly, and
older women experiencing family violence have more options when seeking assistance than they did in the past.

Between 1900 and 2000, the proportion of people age 65 and over in the total
population increased from 4% to 13%.
This growth will continue until 2030,
when the number of elderly people is projected to be double (69 million) what it
was in the 1990s and 21% of the American population will be age 65 and over

(U.S. Bureau of the Census, 1993b).
Among the 65-to-74 age group, 56% are
women; for the age group 85 and over,
72% are women; and female centenarians
outnumber male centenarians three to one
(U.S. Bureau of the Census, 1993a). As
the number and proportion of older
women in U.S. society grows, it is possible that greater attention will be paid to
older women's issues. Whether their social status as a group will change over
time will depend on the ferocity of ageist
and sexist views.

Older Women in Contemporary American Society

In his book, *Growing Old in America,*
Fischer (1977) describes early American
history as a period in which old age was
generally exalted, and elders were treated
with honor, except for some older women,
such as poor widows, paupers, and slaves.
Positive perceptions about the worth of
old people as a group appear to have
shifted to negative ones around the turn of

the 19th century (Achenbaum, 1978, 1979; Fischer, 1977). Along with a changing economic structure, demographic changes such as the rise in the median age and innovations in medical practices were seen as forces behind the deconstruction of positive attitudes toward elders. Youth and productivity were seen as the American ideals and valued; old age and the loss of work roles were devalued.

Ageism has been defined as a prejudice against the old, resulting in stigmatization of older people and discrimination against individuals and the group (Butler, 1975). Cockerham (1997) states that abominations of the body, perceived mental disorders or weakness, and sociocultural biases with respect to gender, race, nationality, sexual preference, and religion are sources of stigma that cause society to negatively stereotype older people as unattractive, unintelligent, asexual, and unemployable.

Although some argue that the term *ageism* was coined for political reasons and lacks objective, scientific analysis (Crockett & Hummert, 1987; Kogan, 1979; Schonfield, 1982), the literature is replete with empirical studies that demonstrate ageist thinking (Palmore, 1982). Nuessel (1982) goes so far as to conclude that even the English language, with its "dearth of agreeable vocabulary" to describe elderly people, is "symptomatic of the deep-rooted nature of individual and institutional ageism in our society" (p. 273).

Negative stereotypic assumptions about aging and older people have been shown to influence the self-definition and behavior of elders (Green, 1981; Warren, 1998), attitudes of elders toward their peers (Harris & Associates, 1981; Merrill & Gunter, 1969; Schulz & Fritz, 1987), and

actions of helping professionals and policy makers when dealing with the older population (Jorgensen, 1989; Kurcharski, White, & Schratz, 1979; Kurtz, Johnson, & Rice, 1989; Ray, McKinney, & Ford, 1987).

In a 1970 publication, Bart observed, "This is not a good society in which to grow old or to be a woman, and the combination of the two makes for a poignant situation" (p. 2). Whereas older women were at the forefront of the antislavery and suffrage movements, the Women's Movement of the 1960s and 1970s focused primarily on issues concerning girls and young women. During these years, the status and rights of older women were largely overlooked (Brown, 1973; Lewis & Butler, 1972). Furthermore, although War on Poverty legislation such as the Older Americans Act and Social Security Amendments made resources available to many elderly women, these policies did not address gender and racial disparities.

The convergence of multiple forces of oppression—ageism and sexism or ageism, sexism, and racism—have largely made older women, and elderly minority women in particular, invisible. Ageist, sexist, and racist constructions about women past midlife have served to limit their social, economic, legal, and political opportunities (Aitken & Griffin, 1996; Rosenthal, 1990). Sontag (1975) suggests our society has a double standard of aging and argued that whereas the status accorded youth affects both women and men as they age, getting old is more profoundly negative for women.

The impiety toward older women, according to Sontag, derives from another form of oppression, "beautyism." Because women's status is often intertwined with physical attractiveness, socially constructed beauty ideals that are based on youthful norms for skin tone, body shape, and hair color serve to devalue women as they age. Women expend more time, money, and effort than men to appear physically young and avoid such stigma (Gerike, 1990). In an ethnographic study of beauty shop culture, Furman (1997) explored the experience of old age among 20 women age 55 to 86 by examining meanings attached to aging faces and bodies. Although she discovered an "unintentional community" among the women, Markson (1999) commented that the women were "brought together by the urge to look right" and shared "a common concern with appearance as a source of self-worth" (p. 496). Furman suggested that the failure to look attractive was equated with being out of control and inadequate and repugnant to one's spouse and family.

Itzin (1984) suggests that ageist and sexist forces give out the message that women have two functions, one domestic and the other sexual, each involving availability and services to men. According to this view, older women may face disqualification because they are past their childbearing and child-rearing years and are viewed as physically unappealing and therefore sexually unattractive. The domestic roles left to older women are those of kinkeeper and caregiver to her aged husband.

In a recent review of books on older women's issues titled, *Research on Older Women: Where Is Feminism?* Hooyman (1999) decries the absence of a feminist, structural framework in understanding older women's issues. She states that the concept of feminist gerontology has taken hold only recently. Reinharz (1986) has joined gerontological and feminist theory in her writings, and Lynott and Lynott (1996) and Ray (1996) have furthered this conceptualization. Gender-specific research in gerontology has also become more prominent (Markson, 1992).

Aitken and Griffin (1996) adopt a "materialist feminist stance" in their writings, which highlight the significance of gender in elder abuse (p. 1). Throughout their book, they discuss sociocultural and economic inequalities that affect elder abuse. These authors further suggest that the lack of political will to provide more extensive resources to prevent, educate about, and intervene in elder abuse is due to the fact that older women are a disenfranchised group.

Cazenave (1981) and Crystal (1987) have suggested that more race-specific research on elder abuse in minority populations is needed. The first wave of studies on elder abuse had small numbers of African American elders in the samples and failed to explore cultural differences when examining family violence, according to these authors. In an early study, Cazenave and Straus (1979) found a lower rate of abuse by family members for African American elders than for Caucasian elders, but Sengstock and Hwalek (1987) later found no significant difference. Griffin, Williams, and Reed (1998) conclude that research is needed to determine the prevalence and dynamics of elder abuse among African Americans, research that takes into account their unique racial experience and heritage. They stress that sociocultural influences may contribute to how elder abuse is defined and assessed and that such factors differ for minority and nonminority elders. Availability, access, and use of services and resources in response to family violence also need to be examined in minority communities.

Older Women and the Domestic Violence Movement

Barnett, Miller-Perrin, and Perrin (1997) say that it is important to realize that family violence was a social condition long before it was constructed as a social problem. The acknowledgment that child abuse was a prevalent social problem during the activist years of the 1960s, in conjunction with the women's movement, led to the discovery of partner abuse. During the late 1960s and early 1970s, the abuse of women gained attention in the literature, and the shelter movement began as a grassroots effort to protect women and their children from their abusers. The roots of the battered women's movement were "personal and political," thus, feminist in orientation (Epstein, Russell, & Silvern, 1988; Schechter, 1982, p. 29). Although early research indicated that women of all ages experienced abuse (Fields, 1976), and the term "granny bashing" was coined by the British press in the 1970s to describe the battering of older women, the literature on domestic violence prior to the 1990s only rarely mentioned older women (McKibben, 1988; Rathbone-McCuan, 1984).

Quinn and Tomita (1997) describe the first and second waves of research on elder maltreatment and state that the first public knowledge of the problem came when a researcher, Suzanne Steinmetz, appeared before a congressional committee and spoke of "battered parents" (described in Steinmetz, 1978, 1980). The work of other researchers during this same time period coincided with this testimony (Lau & Kosberg, 1978; Rathbone-

McCuan, 1980), and Representative Claude Pepper from Florida became a national spokesperson for the cause to protect elders. Several first-wave studies (Block & Sinnott, 1979; Douglass, Hickey, & Noel, 1980; O'Malley, Segars, Perez, Mitchell, & Knuepel, 1979) showed that the phenomenon was known to health and social services workers, law enforcement, and members of the clergy. These researchers focused on elder abuse, however, and did not draw parallels to domestic violence. They focused primarily on the abuse and neglect of older, dependent people by their caregivers.

The second wave of research addressed some of the methodological limitations of the first and included interviews with victims. A comparison group was used by Sengstock and Hwalek (1987) in their examinations of indicators of maltreatment, and theories of elder maltreatment began to be empirically tested (Phillips, 1983; Pillemer, 1985; Wolf, Godkin, & Pillemer, 1984). Yet a third wave of research began in the 1990s, which paid specific attention to the abuse of older women (Brandl & Raymond, 1997; Harris, 1996; Seaver, 1996; Vinton, 1991a, 1992, 1998; Vinton, Altholz, & Lobell Bosch, 1997).

Valentine and Cash (1986) report some agreement in naming the major categories of elder abuse (physical, sexual, psychological) but not on defining these various types of maltreatment; myriad legal definitions exist. *Maltreatment* can be defined as behaviors perpetrated by abusers or by effects on victims or both. *Physical abuse,* for example, can be defined as behaviors such as "hitting, slapping, punching, pushing, shaking, biting, pulling hair, force-feeding, and other willful acts" (Wiehe, 1998, p. 130). The effects, or resulting bodily harm, range from scratches, cuts, or bruises to paralysis or death

(Quinn & Tomita, 1997, p. 50). Sexual abuse can be defined as "any form of sexual contact or exposure without the other person's consent" (Baron & Welty, 1996, p. 36). The effects may include genital or urinary irritation, sexually transmitted diseases, injury or trauma, scarring, or intense fear in reaction to a particular individual or to medical procedures (Holt, 1993; Quinn & Tomita, 1997, p. 52). Psychological or emotional abuse includes "name-calling, derogatory comments, the use of insults, harassment, and threats, and speaking to elderly persons in an infantilizing manner" (Wiehe, 1998, p. 131), and it can result in a range of effects from ambivalence, deference, obsequiousness, and shame to breakdown and suicide (Quinn & Tomita, 1997).

The Wisconsin Coalition Against Domestic Violence (1997) has written about the dynamics of the abuse of older women. Across age groups, victims of domestic violence tend to blame themselves for the abuser's violent behavior and may fear retaliation for telling others. They may also be isolated and manipulated via threats and insults in addition to physical abuse. The potential loss of income and assets is also a barrier to living violence-free lives for women, although older women often receive a Social Security check in their own names. A difference seen in older abused women is that physical health more often affects decision making. Poor health or the need for assistance, when coupled with generational values or a social context that encourages older women to maintain the status quo, can immobilize older victims.

The extent of partner violence in households with elders remained unknown until the 1990s. The National Family Violence Surveys are nationally representative studies that examine marital violence as measured by the Conflict Tactics Scale. National Family Violence Survey data were used by Suitor, Pillemer, and Straus (1990) to examine marital violence across the life course. These authors found that the direction and strength of the relationship between marital violence and age were similar for the 1975 and 1985 National Family Violence Surveys. Both indicated a statistically significant decrease in the rate of marital violence reported by husbands and wives across age groups (18-29, 30-39, 40-49, 50-65).

Contributing to the lack of attention paid to elderly women experiencing violence is that these nationwide studies of family violence were limited by the lack of survey respondents over the age of 65 or 70. Although it might be suggested that older individuals would be more reluctant to label behaviors abusive, no relationship was found between age and attitudes for either women or men when respondents were asked in the National Family Violence Surveys about their attitudes toward marital violence (Straus, 1990).

Older Women and the Elder Abuse Movement

The American general public did not recognize elder abuse as a social problem until the late 1970s or early 1980s, when congressional testimony and subsequent media attention made it known that it was not a rare phenomenon. Although some states already had adult protective statutes in place, others responded by passing what was termed *elder abuse legislation.* Modeled after child abuse legislation, it mandated public welfare agencies (adult protective services) and some private social service agencies that provided aging services to respond to the problem by investigating and offering services and protection as needed. Despite the fact that commonly used definitions of domestic violence were embedded in legal definitions of elder abuse, the main response to elder maltreatment was organized within the context of social and medical care institutions (Finkelhor & Pillemer, 1988).

In the first large-scale, random-sample survey of elder abuse, Pillemer and Finkelhor (1988) conducted a telephone survey of 2,020 community-dwelling people age 65 and over. As in the National Family Violence Surveys, the Conflicts Tactics Scale was used to examine violence between family members. In this study, the rate of abuse for people age 65 and over who were living only with a spouse was estimated to be 41 per 1,000 couples. It surprised some that 58% of the perpetrators were spouses, as compared to 24% who were adult children of the victims. The authors point out that people are most likely to be abused by people with whom they live, and substantially more older people, especially men, live with their spouses. This may further explain why the rate of violence perpetrated by elderly wives against their husbands was as high as husband-perpetrated violence.

Straus and Gelles (1988) have pointed to the greater size, strength, and aggressiveness of abusive men versus women, and Greenblat (1983) surmised that the same act of aggression is likely to be different in terms of pain or injury if inflicted by a male partner. Based on interviews with 16 physically abused elderly men in their prevalency study, Pillemer and Finkelhor (1988) found this to be the case. They reported that only one man (6%) stated that he suffered injuries as a result of maltreatment, whereas 8 or 57%

of the 14 female victims for whom follow-up data were available said they had sustained injuries.

In 1991, adult protective services data were available for 30 states. The number of elder abuse incidents was reported to be 227,000, and 55% of these cases were considered confirmed or substantiated (Tatara, 1993). Of the substantiated reports, a slight majority involved self-neglect, and 45% included abuse by others. Among the latter cases, 19% reported physical abuse, 17% financial abuse, 14% psychological abuse, and 1% sexual abuse. The adult protective services records showed that 68% of the victims were female.

Data were analyzed for 18 states with respect to the relationship of the perpetrator to the victim. Tatara (1993) reported that family members were involved in two thirds of the cases that were not primarily listed as self-neglect incidents. More than twice as many adult children (33%) as spouses (14%) were perpetrators. The discrepancy between the random-sample survey conducted by Pillemer and Finkelhor (1988) and reported cases with respect to the proportion of spouse and adult children perpetrators may be explained by (a) the more hidden nature of marital versus parent abuse when it comes reporting it to the authorities, (b) the likelihood that daughters are frequently caregivers of their parents, and (c) the greater likelihood of neglect by a caregiving adult child being witnessed and reported.

Older Women as Victims of Domestic Violence

Research focusing specifically on older women who have experienced family violence has just begun. In response to Finkelhor's (1983) chapter on the common features of family abuse, and Finkelhor and Pillemer's (1988) suggestion that some cases of elder abuse are spouse abuse, the author of this chapter contrasted causal theories and effects of physical abuse on young and older women. Whereas elder abuse statutes and programs were formulated with child abuse laws and services in mind, the dynamics of family violence against older people appear to be more akin to partner abuse (Finkelhor & Pillemer, 1988; Vinton, 1991a).

Even in cases where an elder is physically or emotionally abused by an adult son or daughter, the dynamics of intimate violence can be seen, whereby power and control (and often, male privilege) are used to intimidate, demean, isolate, and blame (Brandl & Raymond, 1997). Victims tend to have internalized messages that they are to blame for the abuser's violence. Finkelhor (1983) called this "psychological manipulation" (p. 20) because more powerful abusers have told their victims they provoked and deserve the abuse. Victims may fear either physical or psychological retaliation by their abusers or other relatives and may be isolated from people they might tell about their abuse. It is common across age groups for victims to be threatened with the loss of income and assets as well as emotional support. Victims of family violence often feel trapped in terms of taking action because they cannot envision breaking their ties with their abusers or living outside their present family situation. Seaver (1996) states that "Older women often stay because of a 'care imperative,' the need to take care of others or to find care for themselves when they can no longer be

independent" (p. 6); whereas younger women may stay in an abusive relationship because of social pressure to be in an intimate relationship (Gordon, 1988).

Using data from the National Family Violence Resurvey in 1985, Harris (1996) extracted a sample of people age 19 years of age or older who were married or living as a couple, for a total of 5,168 cases. The subjects were divided into two groups based on age—people age 60 and over and people under age 60, to compare the groups with respect to risk factors and consequences of partner abuse. Seventeen independent variables were analyzed including 6 demographic variables and 11 sociopsychological factors (experienced violence in family of origin, perceived legitimacy of violence, marital conflict, verbal aggression, history of couple violence, alcohol use, drug use, physical health, perceived stress, depression, and reasoning as a conflict mediation strategy). Harris (1996) found significant differences between the younger and older couples with respect to the incidence of reporting physical aggression, with the younger respondents more likely to report aggression, conflict, stress, depression, alcohol, and drug abuse. There was no significant difference between the groups with respect to views on the legitimacy of violence (e.g., OK to slap spouse). Among those spouses reporting violence, however, differences disappeared for the percentage experiencing aggression, stress, conflict, and depression. As might be expected, the younger group experiencing spouse abuse reported higher incidence of alcohol and drug abuse, whereas the older group disproportionately rated physical health as fair to poor. A logit analysis to estimate the effect of the risk factors on elderly spousal violence yielded a final model that included verbal aggression, marital conflict, and perceived stress (Harris, 1996).

Programs and Services for Older Women

A survey was conducted of 53 statewide domestic abuse coalitions, 50 state offices on domestic violence, 54 state offices on aging, 56 offices of the attorney general, and 27 participants of a forum, Abused Elders or Older Battered Women, which was sponsored by the American Association for Retired Persons (AARP) Women's Initiative (AARP, 1994). The purpose was to ascertain if there were data on the number of older battered women receiving services, if specialized programming was available, and where that was so. Most frequently, the data were kept by state offices on domestic violence (12 of the 27 agencies that responded), followed by domestic violence coalitions and state offices on aging. Although the response rate warranted caution in interpreting the results, it was tentatively concluded that older battered women were an underserved population: Only 15 specialized programs for older abused women were discovered across the country.

Most of the research relating to the abuse of older women has used records of domestic violence shelters. For example, McKibben (1988) reported that in a survey of Wisconsin's 52 domestic abuse programs, fewer than 10 women age 60 and older had ever been served. Similarly, Vinton (1992) found that less than 1% of the women served by shelter respondents in Florida in 1990 were age 60 and over.

In a 5-year follow-up study of Florida's shelters, Vinton et al. (1997) compared the total number of residents age 60 and over served by the 25 shelter respondents in the 1990 survey (93% response rate) to the number served by 23 respondents in the 1995 survey (77% response rate). The average number of residents age 60 or older served per shelter decreased from 12 to 5, although the number of shelters with special programming for older abused women had increased. Whereas two shelters in the 1990 study (8%) had programs, five (22%) had them in 1995. In the later study, the percentage of older people represented among staff members, volunteers, and board members of domestic violence shelters had also increased.

In contrast to AARP's (1994) study of programming for older abused women, which found 15 specialized programs, Vinton's (1998) nationwide survey of domestic violence programs yielded 61 programming efforts. In that study, 1,219 domestic violence programs were contacted, and 476 returned questionnaires (48 responses were eliminated because the program did not include a shelter). The accessibility of shelters to disabled people was explored, and three fourths reported being accessible to the handicapped. Because older women are more likely to take medications than younger women, storage and distribution policies were examined. The majority of shelters agreed to store medications for residents, and about one fourth stored and dispensed medications at the proper times.

Almost one fourth (23%) of the shelters responding had not sheltered a woman age 60 or older during 1994; 45% served between 1 and 3 older women; 19% between 4 and 9; and only 14% of the facilities had sheltered 10 or more older residents. Slightly more than 40% of the respondents said they had at least one paid female staff member who was age 60 or over, and 69% had at least one board of directors member in that age group.

In terms of providing community education about domestic violence, the shelters did not tend to address groups primarily interested in aging issues, with the exception of making presentations to adult protective services staff. When asked how often the civic groups to which they provided education had audiences consisting of a majority of older people, 25% said on no occasion, and 22% reported on one occasion during the past year. On a 10-point scale with 10 being *extremely critical,* the respondents were asked to rate the importance of shelters providing outreach to abused older women. More than one fifth of the sample used the highest rating of 10, and more than half used ratings of 8, 9, or 10, thus indicating a belief that outreach to abused older women (for shelters, in general, as well as their own shelter) was important. In terms of actual outreach efforts, among the 235 respondents who answered the question, 77 specifically targeted older abused women in media campaigns.

Sixty-one respondents (14.8%) checked yes in terms of offering special programming for older abused women, and 56 responses were categorized into the following areas: (a) training, (b) facilities, (c) media, (d) educational materials, (e) outreach, (f) individual interventions, and (g) support groups. Staff and volunteer training was mentioned nine times and constituted 16% of the total number of responses. Only one respondent each noted having a specific facility that was geared toward sheltering older people and using

the media to highlight older battered women.

Ten shelters (18%) reported developing or using educational materials that dealt with abuse among older couples, such as a videotapes or brochures. One respondent stated that a special lending library on the subject of domestic violence in later life had been created. The greatest number of responses referred to outreach efforts (19 or 34%), such as speaking to community groups that consisted of older people (e.g., AARP) and interfacing with community groups that focused on aging issues (e.g., adult protective services units, housing authority).

Individual interventions (11 or 19%) that were cited included providing one-on-one counseling, using special telephone counseling techniques, meeting with an older woman before she came to the shelter, and helping older victims develop a mentoring relationship with other elderly women who had established independent lifestyles after experiencing a loss. Five (9%) of the responses referred to support groups as special programming for battered older women. One administrator stated that her or his shelter's support group was facilitated by an older woman to provide peer support. A number of respondents commented, even though they checked no when asked if their shelters offered special programming. Eight respondents, for instance, said they hoped to offer programming in the near future or had formed advisory groups or task forces to look into the possibility. Results of the bivariate analyses indicated an association between special programming and three other variables. Shelters that offered special programming were significantly more likely to have sheltered 10 or more women age 60 and over during 1994, and two types of community education were associated with having special programming: presentations at senior centers and at aging services agencies.

In a description of one particular program, Seaver (1996), the manager of the Older Abused Women's Program at the Milwaukee Women's Center, reported that her program provided a weekly support group, volunteer mentors, case management, and shelter and community education. Located in a domestic violence shelter, the program had served 132 women between the ages of 53 and 90 (83% were Caucasian, 15% African American, and 2% Hispanic). Of these women, 11 had major impairments, but only 5 of this group relied directly on their abusers for care. Instead, more of the women were caregivers themselves. In the total sample, 58% of the abusers were husbands, and 42% were adult children or other relatives. Of the 77 abusive husbands, 11 (14%) relied on their spouse for care, and 66% (35 of 55) of the abusive adult children were financially dependent on their victims. In terms of outcomes, 39% of the women who were part of the Older Abused Women's Program freed themselves of abuse, 56% remained in the relationship with the abusive relative, and 5% were reported to be working on the relationship.

Seaver (1996) stated that the most visible impact of the Milwaukee program was on the 45 women who attended their support group. Christie (1992) also found that a group for older female victims of spousal abuse appeared to be beneficial. Seven older women who had experienced domestic violence met for a 10-week period with a co-leader. Based on an increase in a group score on the Lubben So-

cial Network Scale and interviews with the women, the author concluded that the group enhanced self-confidence and self-worth.

Community efforts to support programming for older abused women have been supported at the federal and state level. Wisconsin's Bureau on Aging and the Wisconsin Coalition Against Domestic Violence (WCADV) have worked together since the 1980s to bring attention to the abuse of older women and provide programming. Federal funds from the U.S. Department of Justice and Administration on Aging have been used by WCADV to increase awareness of domestic violence in late life on a national level. Numerous educational materials, newsletters, forums, and technical assistance have been provided by the coalition throughout the 1990s, and recently, it started a clearinghouse on older abused women's issues and programming.

Six other projects that focused on the abuse of older women were funded by the Administration on Aging during the late 1990s. Results of these grants included collaborative efforts on the parts of the domestic violence, aging services, and other helping networks, community outreach, training and conferences, and direct services to women such as housing, health care, legal assistance, group support, and counseling.

Future Directions

There are several fronts on which work remains in terms of our knowledge about domestic violence and older women. Little research has been done using older women as subjects, and there is no consensus on the age of women who should be studied. Some domestic violence programs and studies have included women age 45 and over, and others have used age 50, 60, or 65 as a marker of late life. Just as 20- and 40-year-old women may have things in common when they have experienced family violence, so might 50- and 70-year-old women; however, the range of years included in late life can be longer than for other developmental periods, and factors such as the risk of disability increase with advancing age.

Other within-group comparisons need to be examined. Older women who are victimized by their adult children are more likely to come to the attention of investigators and service providers than older women abused by their partners. Are the dynamics different when the perpetrator is a son rather than a daughter? In examining characteristics of older victims and perpetrators to predict who would accept help after a report of elder abuse had been investigated with a finding, Vinton (1991b) found that older women whose perpetrators were their sons (who were more likely to have physically abused their mothers than daughters) were significantly less likely to accept help than women whose daughters perpetrated maltreatment. Vinton suggested that sons may have been the "caregivers of last resort," and therefore, older women may have been more hesitant to allow formal service providers into the home for fear of losing family care. Pillemer (1985) has also reported that among elders who were abused by nonspouses in his case control study, abuser deviance and dependence were the strongest predictors of abuse. Adult sons who live with a parent may be more likely to have substance abuse and psychiatric problems than daughters and, in turn, to be dependent on

the parent for housing, money, and emotional support.

A report from a forum on older abused women sponsored by AARP (1993) brought together the domestic violence, aging services, legal, law enforcement, and research communities. It listed numerous recommendations with respect to community-based services for abused older women. These included (a) ensuring that appropriate, accessible, safe shelters and other services were available that take into account the needs of older women; (b) sensitizing and educating all service providers, including the medical and legal professions, counselors, and religious leaders, about sexism, racism, and ageism; (c) instituting cross-training, coordination, and coalition-building between the elder abuse and domestic violence communities; (d) providing support and social services by creating a comprehensive, integrated support and intervention system; (e) reaching out to older women by disseminating information about domestic violence through senior centers and home services, health clinics and physicians, civic association, and public benefits officers; and (f) providing victim advocates and creating sister-to-sister "buddy" programs between recently battered and formerly battered women (pp. 23-24).

There is some evidence that programs specifically designed for older abused women are increasing, and in general, services and resources available to older women have expanded. Whether such programs and services are effective, notably from the perspective of victims of abuse, is important to know. Proportionately, the number of older women is increasing. If ageist and sexist attitudes can be diminished, older women's issues, including domestic violence, could move to the forefront of social concerns.

_____

References

Achenbaum, W. A. (1978). *Old age in the new land: The American experience since 1790.* Baltimore, MD: Johns Hopkins University Press.

Achenbaum, W. A. (1979). The obsolescence of old age. In J. Hendricks & C. D. Hendricks (Eds.), *Dimensions of aging: Readings* (pp. 21-38). Cambridge, MA: Winthrop.

Aitken, L., & Griffin, G. (1996). *Gender issues in elder abuse.* Thousand Oaks, CA: Sage.

American Association of Retired Persons. (1993). *Abused elders or older battererd women? Report on the AARP forum.* Washington, DC: Author.

American Association of Retired Persons. (1994). *Survey of services for older battered women: Final report.* Washington, DC: Author.

Barnett, O. W., Miller-Perrin, C. L., & Perrin, R. D. (1997). *Family violence across the life-span.* Thousand Oaks, CA: Sage.

Baron, S., & Welty, A. (1996). Elder abuse. *Journal of Gerontological Social Work, 25*(1/2), 33-57.

Bart, P. (1970, November/December). Depression in middle-aged women: Portnoy's mother's complaint. *Transactions,* pp. 1-5.

Block, M. R., & Sinnott, J. D. (Eds.). (1979). *The battered elder syndrome: An exploratory study.* College Park: University of Maryland Center on Aging.

Brandl, B., & Raymond, J. (1997). Unrecognized elder abuse victims: Older abused women. *Journal of Case Management, 6*(2), 62-68.

Brown, C. L. (1973). Ageism and the women's movement. In J. R. Leppaluoto, J. Acker, C. Naffziger, K. Brown, C. M. Porter, B. A. Mitchell, & R. Hanna (Eds.), *Women on the move: A feminist perspective* (pp. 225-227). Pittsburgh, PA: Know.

Butler, R. (1975). *Why survive? Growing old in America.* New York: Harper & Row.

Cazenave, N. A. (1981, October). *Elder abuse and black Americans: Incidence, correlates, treatment, and prevention.* Paper presented at the Annual Meeting of the National Council on Family Relations, Milwaukee, WI.

Cazenave, N. A., & Straus, M. (1979). Race, class, network embeddedness, and family violence: A search for potent support systems. *Journal of Comparative Family Studies, 10*(3), 281-300.

Christie, J. L. (1992). *Empowering older female victims of spousal abuse: A group work process.* Unpublished master's thesis, University of Manitoba, Canada.

Cockerham, W. C. (1997). *This aging society* (2nd ed.). Upper Saddle River, NJ: Prentice Hall.

Crockett, W. H., & Hummert, M. L. (1987). Perceptions of aging and the elderly. In K. W. Schaie (Ed.), *The annual review of gerontology and geriatrics* (Vol. 7, pp. 217-241). New York: Springer.

Crystal, S. (1987). Elder abuse: The latest "crisis." *Public Interest, 88,* 56-66.

Douglass, R. L., Hickey, T., & Noel, C. (1980). *A study of maltreatment of the elderly and other vulnerable adults.* Ann Arbor: University of Michigan, Institute of Gerontology.

Epstein, S. R., Russell, G., & Silvern, L. (1988). Structure and ideology of shelters for battered women. *American Journal of Community Psychology, 16*(3), 345-367.

Fields, M. D. (1976). Wife beating: The hidden offense. *New York Law Journal, 175*(83), 1-7.

Finkelhor, D. (1983). Common features of family abuse. In D. Finkelhor, R. J. Gelles, G. T. Hotaling, & M. S. Straus (Eds.), *The dark side of families: Current family violence research* (pp. 17-30). Beverly Hills, CA: Sage.

Finkelhor, D., & Pillemer, K. (1988). Elder abuse: Its relationship to other forms of domestic violence. In G. T. Totaling (Ed.), *Family abuse and its consequences* (pp. 244-254). Newbury Park, CA: Sage.

Fischer, D. H. (1977). *Growing old in America.* New York: Oxford University Press.

Furman, F. K. (1997). *Facing the mirror: Older women and beauty shop culture.* New York: Routledge.

Gerike, A. E. (1990). On gray hair and oppressed brains. In E. R. Rosenthal (Ed.), *Women, aging, and ageism* (pp. 35-46). Binghamton, NY: Harrington Park Press.

Gordon, L. (1988). *Heroes of their own lives: The politics and history of family violence. Boston 1880-1960.* New York: Viking.

Green, S. K. (1981). Attitudes and perceptions about the elderly: Current and future perspectives. *International Journal on Aging and Human Development, 13*(2), 99-119.

Greenblat, C. S. (1983). A hit is a hit is a hit . . . or is it? Approval and tolerance of the use of physical force by spouses. In D. Finkelhor, R. J. Gelles, G. T. Hotaling, & M. A. Straus (Eds.), *The dark side of families: Current family violence research* (pp. 235-260). Beverly Hills, CA: Sage.

Griffin, L. W., Williams, O. J., & Reed, J. G. (1998). Abuse of African American elders. In R. K. Bergen (Ed.), *Issues in intimate violence* (pp. 267-284). Thousand Oaks, CA: Sage.

Harris, L., & Associates. (1981). *Aging in the eighties: America in transition.* Washington, DC: National Council on Aging.

Harris, S. B. (1996). For better or for worse: Spouse abuse grown old. *Journal of Elder Abuse and Neglect, 8*(1), 1-33.

Holt, M. G. (1993). Elder sexual abuse in Britain: Preliminary findings. *Journal of Elder Abuse and Neglect, 5*(2), 64-71.

Hooyman, N. R. (1999). Research on older women: Where is feminism? *Gerontologist, 39*(1), 115-116.

Itzin, C. (1984). The double jeopardy of ageism and sexism: Medical images of women. In D. B. Bromley (Ed.), *Gerontology: Social and behavioural perspectives* (pp. 170-183). London: Croom Helm.

Jorgensen, L. B. (1989). Women and aging: Perspectives on public and social policy. In J. D. Garner & S. Mercer (Eds.), *Women as they age: Challenge, opportunity, and triumph* (pp. 291-315). New York: Haworth.

Kogan, N. (1979). Beliefs, attitudes, and stereotypes about old people: A new look at some old issues. *Research on Aging, 1*(1), 11-36.

Kurcharski, L. T., White, R. M., & Schratz, M. (1979). Age bias, referral for psychological assistance, and the private physician. *Journal of Gerontology, 34*(3), 423-428.

Kurtz, M. E., Johnson, S. M., & Rice, S. (1989). Students' clinical assessments: Are they affected by stereotyping? *Journal of Social Work Education, 25*(1), 3-12.

Lau, E. A., & Kosberg, J. I. (1978). Abuse of the elderly by informal care providers. *Aging,* 299-300, 10-15.

Lewis, M. I., & Butler, R. N. (1972). Why is women's lib ignoring old women? *Aging and Human Development, 3,* 223-231.

Lynott, R. J., & Lynott, P. P. (1996). Tracing the course of theoretical development in the sociology of aging. *Gerontologist, 36*(6), 749-760.

Markson, E. W. (1992). On behalf of older women: An apologia and review. *AGHE Exchange, 15*(3), 1-3.

Markson, E. W. (1999). Communities of resistance: Older women in a gendered world. *Gerontologist, 39*(4), 495-502.

McKibben, M. (1988). *Programming issues regarding older battered women.* Madison: Wisconsin Bureau on Aging.

Merrill, S. E., & Gunter, L. M. (1969, July). A study of patient attitudes toward older people. *Geriatrics,* pp. 107-112.

Nuessel, F. H. (1982). The language of ageism. *Gerontologist, 22*(2), 273-276.

O'Malley, H. C., Segars, H., Perez, R., Mitchell, V., & Knuepel, G. M. (1979). *Elder abuse in Massachusetts: A survey of professionals and paraprofessionals.* Boston: Legal Research and Services for the Elderly.

Palmore, E. B. (1982). Attitudes toward the aged: What we know and need to know. *Research on Aging, 4*(3), 333-348.

Phillips, L. R. (1983). Abuse and neglect of the frail elderly at home: An exploration of theoretical relationships. *Journal of Advanced Nursing, 3,* 379-392.

Pillemer, K. (1985). The dangers of dependency: New findings on domestic violence against the elderly. *Social Problems, 33*(2), 146-157.

Pillemer, K., & Finkelhor, D. (1988). The prevalence of elder abuse: A random sample survey. *Gerontologist, 28*(1), 51-57.

Quinn, M. J., & Tomita, S. K. (1997). *Elder abuse and neglect: Causes, diagnosis, and intervention strategies* (2nd ed.). New York: Springer.

Ramsey-Klawsnik, H. (1995). Investigating suspected elder maltreatment. *Journal of Elder Abuse and Neglect, 7*(1), 41-67.

Rathbone-McCuan, E. (1980). Elderly victims of family violence and neglect. *Social Casework, 61*(5), 296-304.

Rathbone-McCuan, E. (1984). The abused older woman: A discussion of abuses and rape. In G. Lesnoff-Caravaglia (Ed.), *The world of the older woman* (pp. 49-70). New York: Human Services.

Ray, D. C., McKinney, K. A., & Ford, C. V. (1987). Differences in psychologist's ratings of older and younger clients. *Gerontologist, 27*(1), 82-86.

Ray, R. E. (1996). A postmodern perspective on feminist gerontology. *Gerontologist, 36*(6), 674-680.

Reinharz, S. (1986). Friends or foes: Gerontological and feminist theory. *Women's Studies International Forum, 9*(5, 6), 222-241.

Rosenthal, E. R. (1990). Women and varieties of ageism. In E. R. Rosenthal (Ed.), *Women, aging, and ageism* (pp. 1-6). Binghamton, NY: Harrington Park Press.

Schechter, S. (1982). *Women and male violence: The visions and struggles of the battered women's movement.* Boston: South End Press.

Schonfield, D. (1982). Who is stereotyping whom and why? *Gerontologist, 22*(2), 267-272.

Schulz, R., & Fritz, S. (1987). Origins of stereotypes of the elderly: An experimental study of the self-other discrepancy. *Experimental Aging Research, 13*(4), 189-195.

Seaver, C. (1996). Muted lives: Older battered women. *Journal of Elder Abuse & Neglect, 8*(2), 3-21.

Sengstock, M. C., & Hwalek, M. (1987). A review and analysis of measures for the identification of elder abuse. *Journal of Gerontological Social Work, 10*(3/4), 21-36.

Sontag, S. (1975). The double standard of aging. In *No longer young: The older woman in America* (pp. 31-39). Ann Arbor, MI: Institute of Gerontology.

Steinmetz, S. K. (1978). Battered parents. *Society, 15*(15), 54-55.

Steinmetz, S. K. (1980). *Elder abuse: The hidden problem.* Statement prepared for a briefing by the Select Committee on Aging, U.S. House of Representatives, 96th Congress, June 23, 1979, Washington, DC.

Straus, M. A. (1990). The National Family Violence Surveys. In M. Straus & R. Gelles (Eds.), *Physical violence in American families* (pp. 3-16). New Brunswick, NJ: Transaction.

Straus, M. A., & Gelles, R. J. (1988). How violent are American families? Estimates from the National Family Violence Resurvey and other studies. In G. T. Hotaling (Ed.), *Family abuse and its consequences* (pp. 14-36). Newbury Park, CA: Sage.

Suitor, J. J., Pillemer, K., & Straus, M. (1990). The National Family Violence Surveys. In M. Straus & R. Gelles (Eds.), *Physical violence in American families* (pp. 305-317). New Brunswick, NJ: Transaction.

Tatara, T. (1993). Understanding the nature and scope of domestic elder abuse with the use of state aggregate data: Summaries of the key findings of a national survey of state APS and aging services. *Journal of Elder Abuse & Neglect, 5*(4), 35-57.

U.S. Bureau of the Census. (1993a). Population projects of the United States by age, sex, race, and Hispanic origin: 1993-2050. *Current population reports* (P-25-1104). Washington, DC: Government Printing Office.

U.S. Bureau of the Census. (1993b). Projections of the population of the United States by age, sex, and race: 1983-2080. *Current population reports* (P-25-1104). Washington, DC: Government Printing Office.

Valentine, D., & Cash, T. (1986). A definitional discussion of elder maltreatment. *Journal of Gerontological Social Work, 9*(1), 17-28.

Vinton, L. (1991a). Abused older women: Battered women or abused elders? *Journal of Women & Aging, 3*(3), 5-19.

Vinton, L. (1991b). Factors associated with refusing services among maltreated elderly. *Journal of Elder Abuse & Neglect, 3*(2), 89-103.

Vinton, L. (1992). Battered women's shelters and older women: The Florida experience. *Journal of Family Violence, 7*(1), 63-72.

Vinton, L. (1998). A nationwide survey of domestic violence shelter programming for older women. *Violence Against Women, 4*(5), 559-571.

Vinton, L., Altholz, J. A., & Lobell Bosch, T. (1997). A five-year follow-up study of domestic violence programming for battered older women. *Journal of Women & Aging, 9*(1/2), 3-15.

Warren, C. A. B. (1998). Aging and identity in premodern times. *Research on Aging, 20*(1), 11-35.

Wiehe, V. R. (1998). *Understanding family violence: Treating and preventing partner, child, sibling, and elder abuse.* Thousand Oaks, CA: Sage.

Wisconsin Coalition Against Domestic Violence. (1997). *Developing services for older abused women: A guide for domestic abuse programs.* Madison: Author.

Wolf, R. S., Godkin, M. A., & Pillemer, K. A. (1984). *Elder abuse and neglect: Final report from Three Model Projects.* Worcester: University of Massachusetts Medical Center, University Center on Aging.

CHAPTER 10

Mainstreaming Immobility

Disability Pornography and Its Challenge to Two Movements

R. Amy Elman

This chapter provides a critical exploration of various visual media that both sexualize and ridicule those women and girls whose health and relative immobility make them especially vulnerable to sexual abuse.[1] More specifically, the prominent focus will be on pornography made of disabled women and girls, a group whose sexual exploitation is often unexamined because it is commonly assumed that they are rarely portrayed as sexual beings (Deegan & Brooks, 1985; Meekosha & Dowse, 1997; Wendell, 1989). Indeed, it is often argued that because "women are already seen as vulnerable, passive and dependent, there is little

artistic interest in portraying disabled women, unless it is as tragic or saintly figures" (Barnes, Mercer, & Shakespeare, 1999, p. 196). This work challenges the prevailing wisdom on sexuality and disability by suggesting that because disabled women and girls inherit ascriptions of passivity and weakness, pornographers and others have sometimes selected to portray them as the ultimate, compliant sex objects (Fine & Asch, 1985, 1988). The chapter, although brief, has four parts, all of which are influenced by events and scholarship in North America, Britain, and Sweden. After an overview of recent developments within ordinary

AUTHOR'S NOTE: My appreciation extends to Catharine MacKinnon, Natalie Nenadic, Katinka Ström, and Melinda Vadas for their critical reading, support, and numerous suggestions pertaining to my earlier work on this project. Correspondence concerning this chapter should be addressed to the author: Department of Political Science, Kalamazoo College, Kalamazoo, MI 49006.

pornography, we focus on the disability genre. Then, we reflect on the ways in which fetishists of disability have assumed prominence in the mainstream, and we conclude with a critical exploration of the political implications of these developments.

The fact that pornography is seldom regarded as evidence of harm testifies to the success men have had in concealing sexual assault by photographing it. Stated simply, through pornography, sexual abuse is decontextualized as assaultive and reconstituted as art and/or entertainment. In addition, the subordination of women and girls is continuously sexualized, perpetrated, photographed, and promoted through the standard media. Susan Sontag (1977) asserts that photographic images anesthetize political consciousness and, therefore, deaden our capacity for social change. "Social change is replaced by a change of images" (p. 178), she says.[2] Social movements thus confuse political progress with increased visibility, regardless of the substance of such portrayals. The disability rights and feminist movements are no exception.

The disability rights movements within the United States, Britain, and Sweden have focused on the stigma of asexuality, so that considerably less attention has extended to its coercive aspects. In addition, their feminist movements have been slow to recognize and respond to the greater vulnerability to sexual abuse and violence of disabled women and girls.[3] In consequence, there has been a dearth of research pertaining to the sexual abuse and exploitation of the disabled, especially through pornography.[4] This is especially the case in Sweden, where more general discussions of sexual abuse are relatively recent and rarely feminist (see Elman, 1996). This chapter attempts to bridge the

insights of these movements by emphasizing that like all pornography, but in its own way, too, the disability genre actively contributes to the second-class safety and status of all women and girls, particularly those who are disabled.

Ordinary Antics?

About 15 years ago, the American *Playboy* had a woman pose with her legs spread. She was in a plaster leg cast. Some time later, another woman appeared in a wheel chair. It seemed to some that *Playboy* was pursuing an agenda at odds with its promotion of the pornographic stereotype, liberating disabled women from the stigma of asexuality and/or sexual unattractiveness. Yet, pornographers have never promoted sexual liberation *for women*. Their sexualization of women's passivity and immobility, its fetishization and marketing, shows that such representations are entirely consistent with the central values of pornography. They are just one version of sexualized vulnerability. Focusing on disability pornography provides a deeper analysis of this dimension in all pornography.

In November 1985, the U.S. *Penthouse Forum* published its monthly "Ms. Americana." In this instance, she is seated with her legs to the side and beneath her. A quick glance at the photo suggests that the woman is wearing a prosthesis from hip to knee. Only on careful scrutiny does one realize that the pornographer has used the woman's body as a slide screen. The side of the U.S. Capitol building casts its shadow on her hip and extends to her knee. The U.S. flag flies just beneath her nipple. The woman looks immobilized. The slide was cast meticulously onto the woman's body to provide her with an intentionally immobile look. Nothing in these slick pornographic magazines is co-incidental. *Playboy* and *Penthouse* epitomize multinational corporate pimping made photogenic.[5] Indeed, *Playboy* began its Swedish-language edition in 1998, the same year the state adopted its much-publicized anti-prostitution law (see Arbetsmarknadsdepartmentet, 1998). The industrialization of sexuality (which includes the proliferation of brothels, phone sex operators, and pornographic vendors) was made possible, in part, through the industrialization of photography. Since the closing decades of the 20th century, images of women's sexualized subordination are promoted through television, video, and, more recently, computers. The enhanced accessibility and acceptability of pornography increases the pervasiveness of the abuse that is its central subject. In turn, the occurrence of sexual abuse is normalized.

Pornographers capture women's immobility and ensuing vulnerability for sex, celebration, and even humor. Indeed, one of the most effective ways to promote and maintain misogyny is through amusement. In a monthly feature cartoon strip entitled "Chester the Molester," *Hustler* portrays a pedophile named Chester whose central objective is to trivialize the sexual assault of girls by turning his carefully planned attacks into humorous games. Years ago (April, 1984), Chester's victim was a blind girl in a short red dress who was accompanied by her seeing eye dog. Chester uses a steak on the end of a string to capture the dog's attention and eventually the little girl. His pants are already at his ankles in anticipation.

"Adolescent humor" magazines are for boys what "adult entertainment" magazines are for men. They sexualize women's and girls' inequality and socialize young boys

to regard women and girls with contempt. Considering the similar objectives of each enterprise, it is not surprising that some adolescent magazines are subsidiaries of the pornographic institutions that want to ensure a cross-generational market. *Slam,*[6] a subsidiary of *Penthouse International,* is one such magazine. It is specifically directed at the teenage male consumer.

In one issue of *Slam,* boys are told how to rape mentally retarded girls and advised that they will probably get away with it.

> If you're accused [of molesting a mentally retarded girl] she certainly won't be believed because retarded people are always claiming one preposterous thing or another, so one more allegation won't cause any stir. Simply say, "No I didn't do that" and you'll be cleared completely, assuming anyone would actually press an inquiry on the claims of a scrunch face.

While mentally fit women and girls are often disbelieved, even when pornography has not yet been made of their abuse (see Lees, 1997), the environment of incredulity is significantly worse for mentally retarded women and girls (Cole, 1986; Crossmaker, 1991; McCarthy & Thompson, 1996; Valenti-Hein & Schwartz, 1993). Research indicates that they are particularly reluctant to report their abuse. One study revealed that only 3% of sexual abuse incidents involving the developmentally disabled were reported to the authorities (Tharinger, Horton, & Millea, 1990). Moreover, reported allegations rarely result in charges, to say nothing of conviction. For example, a review of 162 reports of sexual abuse involving the developmentally disabled revealed that although the offender was known in 95% of the cases, only 22% of the perpetrators were charged with an offense, and only 8% (36% of those charged) were convicted (Sobsey & Doe, 1991). Pornographers intentionally exploit this fact, as the cartoon and text within the pages of *Slam* make abundantly clear. Their industry provides instruction to men and boys on ways to elude detection and/or escape prosecution for sexual abuse. Catharine A. MacKinnon (1993) thus argues that defending pornography "means protecting sexual abuse as speech" (p. 9).

Although public rights discourse may acknowledge that mentally retarded men are frequently suspected as perpetrating sexual abuse, significantly less attention has extended to the fact that mentally retarded and disabled women and girls are particularly sexually vulnerable to "normal" (e.g., able-bodied) men (Crossmaker, 1991; Waxman, 1991). This greater risk for sexual abuse is well established (see Sobsey, 1994, Chapter 3). Estimates of their sexual victimization range from between 39% to 83% for girls with developmental disabilities (in Rappaport, Burkhardt, & Rotatori, 1997, pp. 6-7), whereas women with a variety of disabilities were about one and a half times as likely to have been sexually abused as nondisabled women (Doucette, 1986). Indeed, Liz Stimpson and Margaret Best (1991) suggest that more than 70% of women with a wide variety of disabilities have been victims of violent sexual encounters at some time in their lives.

Disabled women and girls are particularly at risk for abuse by those individual men and boys on whom they often depend. For example, a Connecticut study of 149 sexually abused mentally retarded adults (72% of whom were women) re-

vealed that only 3% of the abusers were strangers (Furey, 1994). An earlier Seattle, Washington, study involving over 300 incidents of sexual abuse of women and children with disabilities over 2 ½ years found that under one third reported the abuse because nearly all of the offenders were men on whom they relied (in Lonsdale, 1990, p. 72). These data coincide with a recent summary of the scholarship on sexual abuse and disability, which suggests that about 90% of the perpetrators are male caretakers (Rappaport et al., 1997, p. 7), most of them either family members or paid service providers (Sobsey, 1994, p. 76, Table 2a). Sadly, little progress has been made since Jenny Morris (1996) observed that scant attention has been paid to disabled women's experience of physical and emotional abuse within "caring relationships."

Entrusted with the public's welfare, statesmen have customarily pursued alarming policies against disabled women and girls. Their contempt, although sometimes distant, has nonetheless had far-reaching consequences. For example, in Sweden, Social Democratic governments between 1935 and 1976 coerced some 60,000 women into being sterilized, once they were labeled genetically or racially inferior. The typical victims were poor and disabled, often from non-Nordic backgrounds ("Swedish Scandal," 1997). More recently, a Swedish court ruled that a mentally retarded woman who was also paralyzed was not raped because she could not dissent (Elman, 1996, p. 87). The history of American and British court rulings is also littered with findings that repeatedly inferred consent from mentally retarded and disabled women and girls. Writing from Britain, Nasa Begum (1992) explains, "The perception that a disabled woman may never have sexual relations has been used as a justification for rape"

(p. 81), an erroneous conclusion that serves to limit social outrage.

More recently, however, the courts have increasingly moved away from a position of inferred consent in matters sexual and reproductive (Valenti-Hein & Schwartz, 1993). For example, in 1985, U.S. Associate Justice Byron White decried the legal system's treatment of the mentally retarded. Four years later, the brutal gang rape of a 17-year-old mentally retarded woman in Glen Ridge, New Jersey, captured the nation's attention. The court was unwilling to dismiss the rape as "sexual play," and all four defendants were convicted in 1993. Although this case was seen as a milestone in the United States ("Verdict," 1993), the sexual abuse of mentally retarded and disabled women and girls persists. Moreover, because most victims are often wrongly regarded as incompetent to testify, few perpetrators are held responsible (Valenti-Hein & Schwartz, 1993).

Dimensions of the problem remain further concealed, in part, because in the United States, Great Britain, and Sweden, crime statistics have not been maintained for people with disabilities.[7] Moreover, the U.S. National Hate Crimes Statistics Act of 1990, which mandated the monitoring of hate crimes nationally, excluded crimes against women (Pendo, 1994) and failed to include the disability community as a group at risk (Waxman, 1991). Within this political climate, pornographers and their readership are able to sexually abuse mentally retarded and disabled women and girls with near impunity.

The Genre of Disability Pornography

Just as some pornography is dedicated solely to the brutalization of a particular racial or ethnic group, and some pornography (like that noted above) contains some emphasis on disability, there is pornography that exclusively focuses on women and girls with disabilities. The most popular disability pornography is often amputee pornography, because this particular disability is one of the most visible. Consequently, it is the easiest to explicitly fetishize. *Amputee Times* is one such fetish magazine; within it, there is a pen sketch.[8] Of all the women in the sketch, only one woman appears to have captured the attention of the singular man. She is without an arm and leg, although this, itself, does not distinguish her from the others. Her disability is, however, the reason that she alone is captured on paper in stereotypical pornographic attire.[9] Throughout *Amputee Times,* there are drawings of one-legged women on crutches, their one leg always in a dark stocking and stiletto-heeled shoe; the women are usually shown in lingerie.

The men who consume amputee pornography are known among themselves as "devotees" and "fetishists," although the sexologist John Money and his colleague Kent W. Simcoe (1984-1986) refer to these men as *acrotomophiles.* They explain, "An acrotomophile is erotically excited by the stump or stumps of the amputee partner, and is dependent on them for erotosexual arousal and the facilitation or attainment of orgasm" (p. 44). Richard Bruno (1997), a researcher with the Department of Physical Medicine and Rehabilitation in the New Jersey Medical School, details the "problematic behaviors" of "devotees." These range from obsessive and intrusive phone calls and other communication with the disabled to attending and sometimes organizing disability-related events, "lurking in public places to watch, take covert pictures of, talk to and touch disabled persons, and even predatory stalking" (pp. 244-245).[10] Rather than presenting these "devotees" as exotic, it may be helpful to recognize that neither their behavior nor their fetish is entirely uncommon. Understanding this may be accomplished, in part, by noting the similarities that the preferred pornography of "devotees" has to other pornographic genres.

Disability pornography, like other pornography, particularly that of black women, often portrays the women in it as castrating, dominant, and violent. By promoting this image, men are able to offer a justification for their abusive behavior. Like the pornography of black women, disability pornography turns a woman's relative vulnerability and/or social subordination into a dominatrix-style fantasy. In reality, disabled women are not sexual victimizers; they are, instead, especially vulnerable to sexual abuse. Pornography preys on their vulnerability and increases the danger that they will, in fact, be abused.

When not portraying the disabled dominatrix, the pornographer offers the disabled woman as the ultimate masochist. The disabled woman is shown as a sexual object that delights in her brutal subordination. Pornography asserts that women take pleasure in subordination, generally, and, in the case of disabled women, pleasure derives particularly from their disability. The following quote provides insight into the users and producers of disability pornography: "The fanaticist imagines in his fantasies that, like himself, the female amputee glories in her conditions and will be delighted to perform with her stump to carry out his fondest dreams" (*Amputee Times,* p. 5). Like all women, the disabled woman is presented as one whose primary if not sole desire is to satisfy the sexual fantasies of

men. Moreover, she is portrayed as one who derives sexual pleasure from her disability because it is a fetish for men.

Disability pornography instructs its users that women who are not disabled desire to be so. In a letter entitled "Blind Faith," the pornographer writes that "she" is "thrilled" to read the letters of others who wish they could have a leg amputated or "just be crippled in some way." "Her" specific desire, however, is to be completely blind: "All I know is I'll be very happy being a blind woman for the rest of my life. I can't wait for my life of total darkness" (*Fetish Letters,* p. 43).[11] Making pornography of blindness presents both the condition of blindness and the idea of blinding women as sexually exciting. It is a fact that men blinded Cantonese prostitutes because they believed that blindness made these women better sexual slaves. Women are supposed to achieve untold satisfaction in being somewhat if not completely vulnerable. By perpetuating the myth of women's desired vulnerability, pornography has an integral part in denying women's civil rights. After all, why should women be given equal rights with men if women are the ones who derive so much sexual pleasure from their pain, harassment, and second-class status?

Mainstreaming the Sexualization of Disability

The assertion that women crave male sexual desire at any cost is common to all pornography. It is also a frequent message in sexist advertising, entertainment, and art. Yet disability pornography is distinctive from art, other entertainment, and sexist advertising in its sexual explicitness and often utter brutality, as well as in its intended use as a masturbatory aid.

The pornographic perspective, nonetheless, infests even the most successful standard media. In the February 1995 issue of *Vogue,* the infamous Helmut Newton provides a series of fashion photos that clearly fetishize women's disabilities. For example, women are portrayed wearing high heels and sitting in wheel chairs. Still others, women with only one leg, are attired in shorts and miniskirts in a manner that closely parallels the drawings found in *Amputee Times.* Newton characterized these portraits as "a towering symbol of the new femininity"—a description that *The New York Times* was loathe to contradict. Indeed, the newspaper provided the following, favorable review:

> At least Mr. Newton displays a semblance of humor, however warped, by dressing women who can't walk in shoes they can't walk in. He also photographs a model in a skirt slit to the waist (that ought to get their attention) who has only one leg; the second one stands on its [sic] own beside her (which ought to get their attention, too). (Goldberg, 1995, p. 49)

The New York Times's review of Newton was not this paper's only contribution to mainstreaming the pornographic perspective. Consider also the salutary review that was extended to *The Piano,* the 1993 Cannes Film Festival winner, a movie that was claimed to be about the sexual reawakening of a mute woman. Advertisements in the paper consistently promoted *The Piano* as "one of the most enchanting love stories to be seen on the screen in years" (e.g., on p. 14, in *The New York Times,* January 1, 1994).

Briefly, the "enchanting" story is this. We are introduced to a Scottish woman named Ada who has not spoken since the age of 6. Her father betroths her to a man in New Zealand named Stewart. Stewart does not seem to mind that she cannot talk (something one suspects that many men would not mind).[12] She travels to New Zealand with her daughter Flora and her piano—her only voice. Once in New Zealand, Ada meets George, a friend of Ada's new husband. George gives land to Stewart in exchange for Ada's piano and alleged "lessons" from her. Clearly, the two men have bargained with her voice. George then prostitutes Ada: In exchange for sexual favors, he promises to give her piano back. In a synopsis review (January 10, 1994, p. 10), *New Yorker* film critic Anthony Lane portrayed these events as "an erotic agreement that gathers intensity and drives the film onward." The notion of an "erotic agreement" conceals the coerced sex that George obtains by first taking Ada's piano (i.e., her voice). The resulting silence makes explicit dissent difficult. The audience is to infer consent. More insidious than this construction of consent is the revelation that once Ada has her piano back, we learn that it is George whom she most desires. Husband Stewart learns of this because he has watched Ada and George having sex through the cracked wood of George's cabin. After this episode, Stewart has Ada promise that she will never meet George again. She does not keep her promise and is soon betrayed by her daughter, who informs her husband of this. In a fit of anger, Stewart chops Ada's finger off with an ax. Ada then leaves him. She returns—with her daughter and without her piano—to George to begin a new life. The audience is to be comforted by a final scene in which Ada paces with her head covered in a black cloth—attempting to regain her voice. In the closing scene, Ada's metal finger clunks across the keys of another piano.

In summary, a mute woman is prostituted for her only voice, falls in love with her trick, and is mutilated and further disabled as a result. Most critics have regarded this as the sexual reawakening of a mute woman. For whom is this movie so enchanting? Might the appeal of this movie be, in fact, largely rooted in the pornographic notion that disabled women are mysteriously sexual?

The Piano's depiction of a disabled woman as the ultimate, acquiescent sexual object is hardly unique. It was also the central theme in yet another film, *Boxing Helena*. The summary of this film, provided on the jacket of the video box, reads,

> Fantasy and desire are unleashed in this haunting, erotic tale of love, lust and obsession. Nick . . . is a brilliant surgeon who seems to have it all—money, looks, prestige—everything except Helena, a voluptuous cold-hearted seductress. After a one-night stand with Nick, she refuses his advances, but he continues to pursue her.
>
> When Helena is in a tragic accident in front of Nick's mansion, he takes her into his home, imprisons her and transforms her into his version of the mythic Venus. Gradually, they are both forced to confront their inner dreams in torrid scenes filled with passion, voyeurism, and psychosexual torment . . . all building to a shocking not-to-be-missed conclusion.

This summary fails to mention that Nick's version of the mythic Venus is a female quadriplegic. Once denied her mobility, Helena becomes the compliant lover of Nick's dreams. In an effort to diminish appropriate outrage, the audience is to be relieved by the film's conclusion; all of the events never really happened—they were merely Nick's "fantasy."[13]

The Theory of Flight offers a superficial cinematic alternative to the common depiction of the disabled woman as sexually submissive by presenting a heroine, Jane, who describes herself as "a hideously crippled woman" obsessed by sex because she has never had it. Jane is anything but submissive, and the film centers on her search for satisfaction. To this end, she unsuccessfully solicits her male caretaker, Richard, who reacts by attempting to channel her attention elsewhere. Together, they visit nightclubs and sex shops until, eventually, he solicits a male prostitute on her behalf before finally ending up in bed with her himself. Humor and sentimentality obscure the problematic character of Richard's shift from caretaker to sexual intimate. In the end, Jane dies from Amytrophic Lateral Sclerosis (ALS or Lou Gehrig's Disease), and Richard reflects lovingly on their encounters. In sum, Jane has two key characteristics that prove inextricable. The first is her disability; the second is the sexual obsessions that she has developed in response to it.

Although a woman's disability is itself often sexualized, so too are orthopedic aids. In *Fetish Letters* (another pornographic magazine), a man writes: "I am terrifically turned on by women wearing any kind of orthopedic support: stockings, bandages, and supports made of flesh-colored elastic, back and knee braces, even casts, and let's face it, most women wear braces on their breasts" (*Fetish Letters,* p. 36). In disability pornography, orthopedic bandages replace the leather and the rope of the most common sadomasochistic pornography. Women are tied to wheel chairs rather than slave-stocks or bedposts. Hospital beds are turned into sexual playgrounds.

Even in death, women are made into pornography, and their cadavers are used as sexual toys. The director of the morgue at Copenhagen's Institute for Forensic Medicine was suspended after it was discovered that he charged admission for "unauthorized people" to view, touch, and photograph the dead ("The Director," 1994, p. 2). More recently, London's *Time Out* featured a story on embalmers entitled, "Fatal Attraction" (Kerr, 1999). The story acknowledged that, because this particular profession holds sexual appeal to some, careful screening of these professionals does take place. In Sweden, some years earlier, a pathologist suspected of murder was released after the court decided that, although he was guilty of having carved up a prostitute and photographing this, it could not be proven that such acts caused her death (Elman, 1990).

The Political Implications

Like all pornography, disability pornography both documents and encourages an active readership. For example, the articles reveal the pleasures to be had from raping disabled women and disfiguring others. Feminist work on battered women has long revealed the sexual pleasure that men derive from bruised and bleeding women.[14] Amputee pornography occupies just one space on the pornographic continuum.

Pornographers also solicit photographs from their readers. They establish "consent" by stating that all contributors must have the "model's" signature on the back of the photos before they can be considered publishable. As for the authenticity of the signature, we can assume that—as happens with all forms of sexual abuse—consent to the abuse is established with power. Consent is illusory within the context of prostitution, including prostitution in its photo form. It is similarly fragile in the flesh. For example, although Money and Simcoe (1984-86) insist that fetishists establish "reciprocated" relationships with amputees, they acknowledge that consensuality does not always prevail. Nonetheless, their presumption of mutuality ignores the social and political structures that constrain women's consent while concealing the fetishists' desire to dominate (Dworkin, 1981).

Pornographers inspire political participation among their consumers. Here is one letter from the editor to his readers:

> We have got to do as others before us have done: admit we are fetishists of a sort, identify ourselves in a carefully private way, organize ourselves and co-operate in the pursuit of our hobby with a clearinghouse of information. Individually, we will keep pursuing the battles against the odds of a daily increase in . . . improved orthopedic procedures. (*Amputee Times*, p. 7)

Why must pornographers and their consumers work so adamantly to deny women and girls good orthopedic treatment if, as they insist, so many women and girls are so happy to be (or wish they were) disabled? Stated simply, improving orthopedic treatment would effectively create increased comfort and greater mobility for disabled women and girls. In addition, improved orthopedics renders the disabled less identifiable, something the fetishist frequently complains about in his pornography. Moreover, disabled women who are provided improved conditions are less reliant on those men whom they may not have suspected as having fetishized their disability.

Disability pornography also provides its audience with tips on where to meet disabled women. The ultimate desire of *Amputee Times* is to compile a "national (or international) register of attractive amputees. This means that readers must report their sightings and the names and addresses of women they know about" (*Amputee Times,* p. 8). The Internet provides fetishists with an additional venue for bulletin boards, Web sites, and chat rooms. Indeed, according to Bruno, *America Online* maintains a bulletin board called "Bunion Love." It requested "photos, videos, or correspondence dealing with gals [having] deformed/crippled feet, or toe/toes amputated . . . or who have severe bunions on their feet. The more severe, the better" (Bruno, 1997, p. 244).

The very places where a disabled woman would expect to find support (rehabilitation centers, hospitals, and orthopedic supply stores) are often the same places that disability fetishists frequent, a problem that has become increasingly evident among activists within the disability rights movement. Contact ads in Britain's monthly paper, *Disability Now,* were once a preferred way for many within the disability community to meet. There are now warnings about "the dangers of such advertisements" because "some people are seeking disabled partners for reasons which can only be described as exploitive" (Shakespeare, Gillespie-Sells, & Davies, 1996, p. 124).

One woman amputee with direct experience of such exploitation wrote a letter to *Disability Now* to specifically warn others about "hobbyists" (i.e., "devotees"). She explained, "I really thought he was interested in me, but the morning after, he was moody and seemed to regret the intimacy—once I even caught a look of distaste on his face." She also observed that another man carried an inappropriate photo of his other amputee girlfriend, and she commented, "When I caught him taking a similar photo of me, from behind, that was it for the relationship. I find men very devious in hiding their fetishes. We disabled women must be careful" (in Shakespeare et al., 1996, p. 125).

The authors of *The Sexual Politics of Disability* (Shakespeare et al., 1996) make a perceptive parallel between "hobbyists" in their sexual pursuit of disabled women and the popularity of sex tourism, where Western men go to Southeast Asia in search of submissive women for their sexual gratification (Shakespeare et al., 1996, p. 126). They note "similar inequities and similar levels of objectification," but they fail to recognize a striking difference in context between sex tourism and stalking hobbyists. Whereas the tricks of sex tourism are relatively identifiable, hobbyists often operate within covert contexts, occasionally placing themselves in highly professional settings (e.g., hospitals) where the women they seek to abuse unknowingly rely on them. Thus, as noted above, hobbyists are particularly devious. Indeed, one writes that he learned first aid "to obtain close contact with injured people" (*Fetish Letters,* p. 180).

We would be foolish to believe men in health care settings are altogether devoted to their clients and/or that they use pornography any less than other men. Indeed, to assume that male health care professionals are somehow different is politically naive, especially in view of what we know about the compromised treatment that they extend women and girls. Begum's (1996) more recent research reveals that physicians are not immune from bigoted attitudes toward the disabled in general and women and girls with disabilities in particular. In fact, some medical practitioners preferred to focus on their patients' impairments rather than attend to their presenting condition.[15] Begum's (1996) conclusions are similarly substantiated in research specifically focused on the reproductive health care experiences of women with physical disabilities (Becker, Stuifbergen, & Tinkle, 1997). Researchers found that health care providers sometimes appeared surprised that these patients were sexually active. Moreover, accessing reproductive health care services was often so difficult for these women that some avoided regular gynecological visits altogether.

Although disabled women and girls are more vulnerable to sexual abuse, male health practitioners in presumably safe settings also victimize others who are entrusted to their care. Indeed, data pertaining to the sexual abuse and assault of the disabled revealed that 44% of the perpetrators were paid service providers who committed their crimes in disability service settings (Sobsey & Doe, 1991). A number of recently reported rape cases underscore this finding. For example, Bruce Allen Young, a registered nurse, was found guilty of raping a sedated 15-year-old girl in a hospital recovery room ("Nurse Pleads Guilty," 1995). He stated that he had chosen her because she was "helpless and pretty" ("Scores of Florida Women," 1994). In another case, Charles Arthur Morales, an occupational therapy aide, was charged in the rape of a 26-year-old woman, who stated that she had been raped three times during her hospital stay

("Another Hospital Rape Case," 1994). More recently, an obstetrician carved his initials into the stomach of a patient after he delivered her first child (Wong, 2000).

Aside from sexual assault and battery, a study published in the *New England Journal of Medicine* (Lurie et al., 1993) suggests that women generally receive better care from women physicians than from men physicians. Women often feel trivialized, uncomfortable, and powerless in male physicians' offices. This makes sense, given the very real ways in which they are often treated. Several studies indicate that between 7% and 15% of physicians admitted having sexual contact with their patients, and about 8% of female patients reported being sexually harassed by their physicians (McPhedran, 1992).[16]

When one takes a critical glimpse into the standard pornography men read, it is not difficult to grasp the role it plays in fueling the compromised quality of care all women receive. In one pornographic cartoon, a naked woman, with the exaggerated proportions of the pornographic stereotype (e.g., large breasts, a minuscule waist, and a baffled expression) is posed "seductively" on an examining table. A physician is putting on a shirt and is dressed in boxer shorts. He is opening a door for other male physicians to enter; one is in boxer shorts, and another has his pants at his ankles. The physician who is about to let the others in states, "You look perfectly healthy to me, Ms. Johnson, but how would you like a free second or third opinion?" (*Gallery*, June 1985, p. 22). Such sexual abuse is reduced to an exchange: sex for a "medical opinion." Rape is thus portrayed as the means through which male physicians arrive at their medical opinions.

Although this chapter centered on conditions in the United States, Britain, and

Sweden, it is important to realize that throughout the world, women and girls are generally denied mobility. The sexually explicit lack of physical mobility is as celebrated in disability pornography as political mobility is condemned in all pornography. Amputee pornography is but one end of a continuum. It shares the spectrum with Oscar-winning movies that romanticize and accentuate women's vulnerabilities. It keeps company with corsets, stiletto heels, and the maiming that results from battering. Yet, regardless of the genre, pornography mirrors the conditions of women and girls as they daily endure them. It is the documentation of female sexual subordination and expendability. Lurking behind the diminishing willingness to pronounce the injurious nature of pornography and other forms of sexist entertainment are often those whose pleasure and power is maintained by it.

Notes

1. This focus on women *and* girls is intentional. Just as the term *people* often renders women invisible, the word *children* has similar political implications for girls. For example, discussions of child sexual abuse often conceal the fact that girls are more likely to be harassed and sexually exploited by boys than by adult men. Moreover, whereas boys may be considered small and powerless to adult men, they are neither little nor vulnerable to the girls whom they abuse. I am indebted to Katinka Ström for this insight.

2. Thus, just when political opposition is most necessary, feminists are obstructed through contrived, illusive depictions of female agency, which suggest that their efforts on behalf of women are not needed.

3. For example, after an informal survey of battered women's shelters in Houston, Texas, the Center for Research on Women with Disabilities at Baylor College of Medicine found that 64% of these shelters were inaccessible to women in wheelchairs (Nosek, 1996).

4. For a feminist overview of the literature of both the feminist and disability movements, see Tilley (1998). After completing over 40 interviews with disabled British men and women on sexuality, researchers were "shocked and appalled by the frequency of abuse in the lives of the disabled people." Nearly half of the respondents had mentioned abuse despite the absence of any prompting to do so (Shakespeare et al., 1996). Elsewhere, Tom Shakespeare (1996) concluded, "it is clear to me that research is urgently needed into disabled people's experience of sexual abuse and exploitation" (p. 212).

5. For a recent analysis of pornography as a multinational industry, see Dines (1998, Chapter 3). The author focuses specifically on *Playboy*.

6. *Slam* has not been published since 1978, and a spokesman for Larry Flynt Publications, which the Library of Congress identifies as its publisher, said the company maintains no archives. A page from the article in question, with *Slam* clearly identified, was among slides made available by Women Against Pornography. The slide was part of a show that Women Against Pornography presented at venues around the country. Scholars may obtain a copy by writing the organization at P. O. Box 845 Times Square Station, New York, NY 10036.

7. In *Women and Disability,* Susan Lonsdale (1990) argues that "the U.S. has a longer and more successful history of attempting to outlaw discrimination" than does Britain (p. 153). However, given the European Union's recent recognition of the need to confront bigotry based in disability (see the Amsterdam Treaty), matters *may* change in Sweden and Britain, both of which are member states.

8. *Amputee Times* is a publication that includes no volume number, date, name of publisher, or place of publication. This particular issue was acquired by the author at a shop in New York City in 1987. The same issue will be referred to elsewhere in this article, and copies of this material are on file with the author.

9. Her one leg is fitted with black stocking and stiletto heel. Her leg is positioned to allow full view of her undergarments. Unlike the other women, who wear white turtlenecks, she is in a black top that exaggerates her breast size. She is at

the center of the drawing, in full view, splayed for the user's stare.

10. Although this article is one of the only ones to document the harmful behaviors of "devotees," Bruno's methodology remains questionable. He provides no explanation for his selection of two case studies, both of which are women. Also, Money and Simcoe present only one case for their above-mentioned article. They explain that their case stems from Money having received an unsolicited letter from an enthusiastic admirer of his work.

11. *Fetish Letters* is a publication that includes no volume number, date, name of publisher, or place of publication. In 1987, at a shop in New York City, the author acquired this issue, referred to elsewhere in this article. It too is on file with the author.

12. Professor Basinger, head of the film studies Department at Wesleyan University in the United States, provides the following explanation for the Oscar awards: "Oscars go to actresses who play prostitutes, nuns, cripples or mutes—Hollywood loves women who don't speak" (Weinraub, 1996, Section 4, p. 4).

13. Few seem to have knowledge of this film; however, many have heard about how the U.S. actor Kim Basinger withdrew from her contract. It was the gruesome story line that prompted her to do so. Basinger had verbally agreed to take the lead role and later declined to the director Jennifer Lynch, daughter of David Lynch (of *Blue Velvet* fame). The result of her refusal was a successful multimillion-dollar lawsuit filed by Main Line Pictures. Basinger's refusal to be exploited both cost her extensive court-awarded damages ($8.9 million) and damaged her reputation as a reliable actor (Welkos, 1993). Sexual dissent is costly for women.

14. British researchers found that over half of all battering incidents occur in the bedroom, and much of it is precipitated by sexual jealousy (Dobash & Dobash, 1979, pp. 14-21). In interviewing numerous batterers, Eva Lundgren (1989), Sweden's expert on violence against women, notes that the men explicitly state that they get sexual satisfaction from battering their wives and girl friends.

15. An earlier study by Mullan and Cole (1991) would appear to contradict Begum's (1996) conclusion. Their "study found that health care professionals displayed considerable concern about the emotional state of patients with disability who might have been sexually exploited" (p. 237). Although encouraging, the chief limitation of this finding is its reliance on those whom they surveyed. That is, Mullan and Cole surveyed those interested in and committed to disabled people at risk for sexual exploitation. In direct surveys of the disabled about their experiences with health care professionals, a different picture emerges.

16. Such behavior contradicts the Hippocratic oath: "In every house where I come I will enter for the good of my patients, keeping myself far from all intentional ill-doing and all seduction, and especially free from the pleasure of love with women or with men." In addition, both the American Medical Association and the American Psychiatric Association expressly condemn sexual relations between physicians and their clients.

References

Another hospital rape case. (1994, October 14). *The New York Times,* p. A13.

Arbetsmarknadsdepartmentet [Sweden's Department of Labor]. (1998). *Kvinnofrid* [Women's peace] [On-line]. Available: www.kvinnofrid. gov.se.

Barnes, C., Mercer, G., & Shakespeare, T. (1999). *Exploring disability: A sociological introduction.* Cambridge, UK: Polity.

Becker, H., Stuifbergen, A., & Tinkle, M. (1997, December). Reproductive health care experiences with physical disabilities: A qualitative study. *Archives of Physical Medicine and Rehabilitation, 78,* S26-S33.

Begum, N. (1992). Disabled women and the feminist agenda. *Feminist Review, 40,* 70-84.

Begum, N. (1996). General practitioners' role in shaping disabled women's lives. In C. Barnes & G. Mercer (Eds.), *Exploring the divide* (pp. 157-172). Leeds, UK: Disability Press.

Bruno, R. L. (1997). Devotees, pretenders, and wannabes: Two cases of factitious disability disorder. *Sexuality and Disability, 15*(4), 243-260.

Cole, S. S. (1986). Facing the challenge of sexual abuse in persons with disabilities. *Sexuality and Disability, 7* (3-4), 71-88.

Crossmaker, M. (1991). Behind locked doors—Institutional sexual abuse. *Sexuality and Disability, 9*(3), 201-219.

Deegan, M. J., & Brooks, N. A. (1985). *Women and disability: The double handicap.* New Brunswick, NJ: Transaction.

Dines, G. (1998). Dirty business: *Playboy* magazine and the mainstreaming of pornography. In G. Dines, R. Jensen, & A. Russo (Eds.), *Pornography: The production and consumption of inequality.* New York: Routledge.

The director of the morgue at Copenhagen's Institute for Forensic Medicine. (1994, February 10). *International Herald Tribune,* p. 2.

Dobash, R., & Dobash, R. (1979). *Violence against wives: A case against patriarchy.* New York: Free Press.

Doucette, J. (1986). *Violent acts against disabled women.* Toronto: DAWN (Disabled Women's Network).

Dworkin, A. (1981). *Pornography: Men possessing women.* New York: G. P. Putnam.

Elman, R. A.. (1990, March). Swedish politics: Women's subordination in a gender neutral context. *off our backs,* pp. 4, 7.

Elman, R. A.. (1996). *Sexual subordination and state intervention: Comparing Sweden and the United States.* Oxford, UK: Berghahn.

Fine, M., & Asch, A. (1985). Disabled women: Sexism without the pedestal. In M. J. Deegan & N. A. Brooks (Eds.), *Women and disability: The double handicap* (pp. 6-22). New York: Transaction.

Fine, M., & Asch, A. (1988). *Women with disabilities: Essays in psychology, culture, and politics.* Philadelphia: Temple University Press.

Furey, E. M. (1994). Sexual abuse of adults with mental retardation. Who and where. *Mental Retardation 32,* 173-180.

Goldberg, V. (1995, February 5). Newton still in a heel period. *The New York Times,* p. 49.

Kerr, J. (1999, July 14-21). Fatal attraction. *Time Out,* pp. 14-15.

Lees, S. (1997). *Ruling passions: Sexual violence, reputation, and the law.* London: Open University Press.

Lonsdale, S. (1990). *Women and disability: The experience of physical disability among women.* London: Macmillan.

Lundgren, E. (1989). Våldets normaliseringsprocess: Två parter—Två strategier [Normalizing violence: Two parties—Two strategies]. In *Kvinnomisshandel* (Vol. 14, pp. 113-140). Stockholm, Sweden: Jämfo Rapport [Ministry for Equality].

Lurie, N., Slater, J., McGovern, P., Ekcstrum. J., Quam, L., & Margolis, K. (1993, August 12). Preventive care for women: Does the sex of the physician matter. *New England Journal of Medicine,* pp. 778-782.

MacKinnon, C. (1993). *Only words.* Cambridge, MA: Harvard University Press.

McCarthy, M., & Thompson, D. (1996). Sexual abuse by design: An examination of the issues in learning disability services. *Disability & Society, 11*(2), 205-217.

McPhedran, M. (1992). Investigating the sexual abuse of patients: The Ontario Experience. *Health Law Review, 1*(3), 3-15.

Meekosha, H., & Dowse, L. (1997, May). Distorting images, invisible images: Gender, disability, and the media. *Media International Australia, 84,* 91-101.

Money, J., & Simcoe, K. W. (1984-1986). Acrotomophilia, sex, and disability: New concepts and case report. *Sexuality and Disability, 7*(1-2), 43-50.

Morris, J. (1996). *Pride against prejudice: Transforming attitudes to disability.* London: Women's Press.

Mullan, P., & Cole, S. (1991). Health care providers' perceptions of persons with disabilities: Sociological frameworks and empirical analyses. *Sexuality and Disability, 9*(3), 221-241.

Nosek, M. A. (1996). Sexual abuse of women with physical disabilities. In D. Krotoski, M. Nosek, & M. Turk (Eds.), *Women with physical disabilities: Achieving and maintaining health and well-being* (pp. 153-173). London: Paul H. Brookes.

Nurse pleads guilty in rape of patients. (1995, February 5). *New York Times,* p. 25.

Pendo, E. (1994). Recognizing violence against women: Gender and the Hate Crimes Statistics Act. *Harvard Women's Law Journal, 17,* 157-183.

Rappaport, S. R., Burkhardt, S. A., & Rotatori, A. F. (1997). *Child sexual abuse curriculum for the developmentally disabled.* Springfield, IL: Charles C Thomas.

Scores of Florida women fear they were raped at hospital. (1994, October 14). *The New York Times,* p. A13.

Shakespeare, T. (1996). Power and prejudice: Issues of gender, sexuality, and disability. In L. Barton (Ed.), *Disability and society: Emerging insights* (pp. 191-214). New York: Longman.

Shakespeare, T., Gillespie-Sells, K., & Davies, D. (1996). *The sexual politics of disability.* New York: Cassell.

Slam [Slide]. Available from Women Against Pornography, P. O. Box 845, Times Square Station, New York, NY 10036.

Sobsey, D. (1994). *Violence and abuse in the loves of people with disabilities: The end of silent acceptance?* Baltimore, MD: Paul H. Brookes.

Sobsey, D., & Doe, T. (1991). Patterns of sexual abuse and assault. *Sexuality and Disability, 9*(3), 243-259.

Sontag, S. (1977). *On photography.* New York: Delta.

Stimpson, L., & Best, M. C. (1991). *Courage above all: Sexual assault against women with disabilities.* Toronto: DisAbled Women's Network (DAWN).

Swedish Scandal. (1997, August 30). *New York Times,* p. 18.

Tharinger, D., Horton, C. B., & Millea, S. (1990). Sexual abuse and exploitation of children and adults with mental retardation and other handicaps. *Child Abuse & Neglect, 14,* 301-312.

Tilley, C. (1998). Health care for women with physical disabilities: Literature review and theory. *Sexuality and Disability, 16*(2), 87-102.

Valenti-Hein, D. C., & Schwartz, L. (1993). Witness competency in people with mental retardation: Implications for prosecution of sexual abuse. *Sexuality and Disability, 11*(4), 287-294.

Verdict after a day of horror: A rape case tests the rights of the retarded. (1993, March 29). *Newsweek,* p. 27.

Waxman, B. F. (1991). Hatred: The unacknowledged dimension in violence against disabled people. *Sexuality and Disability, 9*(3), 185-199.

Weinraub, B. (1996, March 24). Hey, what's talent got to do with it. *The New York Times,* Section 4, p. 4.

Welkos, R. (1993, March 25). Basinger ordered to pay $8.9 million for jilting film. *Los Angeles Times,* pp. A1, A24.

Wendell, S. (1989). Toward a feminist theory of disability. *Hypatia, 4,* 104-124.

Womendez, C., & Schneiderman, K. (1991). Escaping from abuse: Unique issues for women with disabilities. *Sexuality and Disability, 9*(3), 273-279.

Wong, E. (2000, February 6). Gauging medical misadventure: First, commit no crime. *New York Times,* Section 4, p. 3.

CHAPTER 11

Sexual Harassment

Violence Against Women at Work

Phoebe Morgan

Nearly a century ago, Louisa Mae Alcott (1874) published a moving account of a brief career in waged domestic work. According to Alcott, although the physical demands of house care took their toll, it was the uninvited sexual attention of her employer, the Reverend Joseph, that made her job intolerable. Fortunately for her—and for consumers of great literature—Alcott found the means to leave the Reverend's employ, quit domestic service altogether, and become one of America's most prolific novelists. The other working women of her day, however, were not so lucky.

At the turn of the last century, women whose only means of support was waged labor had little choice but to take work where toleration of sexualized aggression was part of the job. Like Alcott, those who complained about it or who confronted their harassers were punished with either demotion or the assignment of exceptionally harsh duty. Sadly, those who succumbed to seduction were deemed no better than whores by their family and friends and treated accordingly. In either case—those who confronted their harassers, as well as those who capitulated—sexually harassed women were nearly always dismissed. Those who lost their jobs to sexual harassment lost their reputations both as workers and as virtuous women. Deemed unfit for either marriage or reputable work, many sexual harassment victims joined the ranks of the poor and destitute (Bularzik, 1978).

Today, 97% of all employing and educational institutions in the United States have policies that expressly prohibit sexual harassment, and 84% of those who work and learn in these places are aware of the consequences for violating the rules ("Sexual Harassment," 1999). Steady increases in the number of reports made to state and federal agencies since 1991 suggest that a growing number of women are no longer tolerating such behavior (Bureau of National Affairs, 1994; U.S. Equal Employment Opportunity Commission, 1999). Despite these changes, sexual harassment continues to be one of American society's most pernicious forms of violence against women (National Council for Research on Women, 1992).

This chapter takes a closer look at this particular form of violence against women and, in so doing, addresses some of the more commonly asked questions about it. What exactly is sexual harassment? Who is at risk of becoming a sexual harassment victim? How does this type of victimization affect those who endure it? The following pages pursue answers to these questions through a synthesis of legal theory, social science research, government data, and firsthand accounts of victims and complainants.

What Is Sexual Harassment?

Although sexual harassment has been practiced since the advent of waged labor, it has only been in recent years that women have had a name for their experiences of it. A name is no small thing, for without one, victims cannot take the next step—to assign blame for their plights— much less lay claim to redress (Felstiner, Abel, & Sarat, 1980-1981). So, until there was language for articulating their experiences in a way that allowed authorities to hear their pain and meaningfully act on it, victims of sexual harassment suffered in silence. In the early 1970s, the phrase *sexual harassment* was first used (Farley, 1978). Since that time, millions of women and men around the world have added it to their daily lexicon.

In the early 1980s, the Equal Employment Opportunity Commission (EEOC) and the Office of Civil Rights (OCR) put the sex discrimination theory to the test by adding sexual harassment to their list of discriminatory behaviors. The U.S. Supreme Court has consistently upheld and therefore legitimized the actionability of sexual harassment claims under Titles VII and IX. As a result of these actions, early sexual harassment claims laid the foundation for more recent attempts to conceptualize violence against women as a civil rights issue.

The EEOC defines sexual harassment as any form of uninvited sexual attention that either explicitly or implicitly becomes a condition of one's work (U.S. EEOC, 1999). Along the same lines, the OCR conceptualizes it as a form of unwanted sexual attention that becomes a condition of one's educational experience (U.S. Office of Civil Rights, 1999). The types of behaviors that fit EEOC and OCR definitions include but are not limited to unwanted talk about sex, jokes about sex or sexualized horseplay, uninvited physical contact, requests for sexual favors, pressures for dates or sex, sexual abuse, and sexual assault. A substantial body of case law now supports the labeling of such behaviors as illegal and organizes them into two types of discrimination claims: quid pro quo and hostile environment.

Some Sexual Harassment Is Sexual Blackmail

The Latin phrase *quid pro quo* refers to the trading of favors. With respect to sexual harassment, it references the exchange of sexual favors for special employment treatment. In a quid pro quo situation, going on a date, providing sexual services, or simply enduring sexual touching or talk is rewarded with a decision to hire, to promote, or to deliver job-related perks (i.e., better office space, a new computer, the mobilization of travel stipends, etc.). Those who appear to renege or fail to deliver sexual favors risk punishment in the form of demotion, dismissal, or the denial of basic necessities for doing their jobs. Thus, as was so vividly illustrated by the plot of the highly controversial movie, *Disclosure,* quid pro quo harassment operates as a form of on-the-job blackmail.

Only those individuals with sufficient organizational authority to affect the condition of another person's employment have the power to perpetrate this type of sexual harassment. For this reason, the vast majority of quid pro quo complaints involve harassment of a subordinate by a person with the power to hire, promote, or assign benefits (Benson & Thomson, 1982).

Most Sexual Harassment Is a Manifestation of Hostility

The first wave of sexual harassment litigation almost exclusively involved complaints of quid pro quo harassment, and in fact, until the late 1980s, only those cases involving the loss of employment were deemed worthy of legal action. But in 1985, the U.S. Supreme Court broke new conceptual ground by declaring actionable a claim in which there was no evidence of the exchange of favors, nor was there any suggestion that the victim was punished for her intolerance (see *Meritor Savings Bank v. Mechele Vinson,* 1985). Their opinion legitimated a second category of perpetration, now commonly referred to as "hostile environment" harassment. Hostile environment is a far more common form of harassment than sexual

blackmail. In a study of graduate women, for example, 80% of the respondents who experienced harassment reported hostile environment experiences. Since *Meritor vs. Vinson,* the number of sexual harassment claims filed has grown almost exponentially (Bureau of National Affairs, 1994).

Hostile environments are created when sexualized talk and behavior is experienced by some as demeaning or humiliating. They occur when acts of sexual harassment are both the products and the precipitators of sexist thinking and misogynistic attitudes (Cook & Stambaugh, 1997). Hostile climates are nurtured in any organization where values supporting gender inequality are legitimated and hostility against women is permitted. They thrive in workplaces and classrooms where masculinity is conflated with success and femininity is associated with failure (Messerschmidt, 1993). As a result, many hostile environment complaints have been filed by women attempting to work in occupations where masculinity is an implicit job requirement—oil rigging (Holcombe & Wellington, 1992), coal mining (Yount, 1991), policing (Martin, 1994), corrections (Jurik, 1985), automobile manufacturing (Gruber & Bjorn, 1982), and the military (U.S. Department of Defense, 1993)—to name only a few.

Sexual Harassment Is Part of the Larger Continuum Of Violence Against Women

In a number of important ways, sexual harassment is more like than different from other forms of violence against women (National Council for Research on Women, 1992). Sexual harassment is a form of woman control. As with rape, incest, and battering, the locus of control is sex (MacKinnon, 1979, 1995). Sexual harassment sustains male dominance and women's subordination by privileging the sexual desires of men over the needs of women.

As in other forms of violence against women, secrecy shrouds the face of sexual harassment victimization (Fitzgerald & Ormerod, 1991). Sexual harassment is practiced in public at many workplaces and inside classrooms. It is common; yet, talk of the experience is taboo. Women have been socialized to keep the details of their victimization private. Thus, the pain that sexual harassment brings often goes unnoticed, and the suffering of its victims is greatly underestimated.

Mythology about the "true" sexual natures of men and women mystifies the motivations of sexual harassers and the responses of the women they target. Too often, men who impose talk about sex or sexual behavior onto women are forgiven for "just being a guy" or "acting like a man." When a woman questions the naturalness of such impositions, it is her own credibility and reasonableness—not the actions of her harasser, nor those of the organization that permitted it—that are suspect (Estrich, 1991).

Sexual Harassment Is a Form of Sex Discrimination

Whereas 44% to 85% of American women will experience sexual harassment at some point in their lifetime (National Council for Research on Women, 1992), less than 19% of men report being sexually harassed (U.S. Merit Systems Protection Board, 1981, 1988). Thus, a disproportionate number of women contend with this type of behavior and, there-fore, are unfairly burdened by its effects (MacKinnon, 1979).

The practice of sexual harassment supports the institutionalization of gender inequality in all its forms. Even those women who manage to avoid firsthand experience with it are negatively affected by its practice (MacKinnon, 1979). Too often, the decision to hire or promote a woman depends on the degree to which she appears capable of provoking, resisting, or simply surviving sexual harassment. Because so many women have no other recourse but to handle their sexual harassment problems by quitting or changing jobs, sexual harassment is a significant factor in women's job turnover and slower career advancement; therefore, it sustains the gender gap in pay.

For a lot of women, the term *sexual harassment* effectively summarizes a core experience associated with work or school. But for many, the term is an inadequate reference for their violation. For example, for lesbians, there is no specialized term to articulate the added dimension that being homosexual adds to their experience of being sexually harassed by a man (Schneider, 1982). For women of color, the experience of being harassed by white men does not fit neatly into the rubrics of either sexism or racism (Defour, 1990). As a consequence, for these women, evoking the term can mystify rather than clarify the ways in which homophobia and racism carve unique contours into an otherwise common experience (Winston, 1991).

Who Is at Risk of Becoming a Victim of Sexual Harassment?

In a highly hierarchical society such as ours, women and men work and attend school within complex interlocking systems of oppression (Collins, 1990). As a consequence, risk of sexual harassment victimization varies within the social strata. Certainly, the greatest risk factor is being female, as 44% to 85% of American women will experience sexual harassment during their academic or working lives (National Council for Research on Women, 1992). Although the risk of victimization for men is significantly smaller (12% to 19%), they are not immune, and the proportion of men reporting sexual harassment appears to be growing over time (U.S. EEOC, 1999; U.S. Merit Systems Protection Board, 1992).

The amount of risk a woman assumes varies according to the type of environment in which she performs her work or attends school. Women who work in highly sexualized environments experience more harassment than those who do not (Loe, 1996). Those who work in male-dominated workplaces or who assume masculine occupations report more harassment than those who perform jobs associated with women's work (Gruber, 1998). Especially vulnerable are those who depend on men for job security or career advancement (Defour, 1990).

The Sexualization of Work Promotes Sexually Harassing Behavior

It is not possible, nor even desirable, for students, teachers, workers, and their supervisors to check their sexual desires at the classroom or office door. However, when talk about sex and sexual behavior is part of a work group's routine, sexual harassment is likely to be, as well. Some lines of work invite sexualization more than others do, and as a result, they carry a higher risk of sexual harassment as well. Sexualization of work relieves the stress

of danger and even boredom. Once sexual behavior becomes routine, it becomes difficult for workers to imagine doing their jobs without it.

For example, in her participant observational study of underground coal mining, Yount (1991) noticed that male miners reduce stress and build solidarity by sharing especially crude jokes and engaging in highly sexualized horseplay. Those who are unwilling or unable to play along become easy targets for derision. As a consequence, most of the women coal miners became the butts of their coworkers' jokes.

In addition, those who have jobs where sex is commodified, or where it is performed as a service, endure more sexual harassment than those who do not. Waitresses, for example, who are required to wear sexually seductive uniforms, or who have been trained to flirt with their customers as part of the job, encounter sexual harassment from their supervisors and customers (Loe, 1996). An occupational hazard of the sex trades is sexualized violence, and sexual harassment by customers is endemic (Pettiway, 1996). Even those sex trade workers who provide services deemed legal assume a much greater risk but receive less protection than other types of service workers (Ronai & Ellis, 1989).

Male Domination Is a Primary Risk Factor

The vast majority of sexual harassers are men. One study, for example, found that only 1% of the female and 35% of the male respondents experienced harassment by a woman (Dubois, Knapp, Farley, & Kustis, 1998). Thus, next to being a woman, working or learning in close proximity to men increases one's risk of sexual harassment victimization more than any other factor.

Few areas of employment are more male-dominated than the armed forces. The majority of military personnel are men. In addition, the majority of jobs in the military continue to be viewed as "men's work." As the number of women inside military academies and on bases has grown, so have the number of sexual harassment complaints made by them (Moss, 1997). In fact, one survey by *The New York Times* ("Two Out of Three," 1991) found that two out of every three military women experience at least one form of sexual harassment. Although male domination in the armed forces is more visible than in other areas of the workforce, there are other masculine domains where sexual harassment is common. For example, sexual harassment is equally pervasive in such male-dominated occupations as criminology (Stanko, 1992) and criminal justice work (Martin & Jurik, 1996).

Women Who Depend on Men for Employment Are Especially Vulnerable

Despite significant advances within the last two decades, a disproportionate number of women perform low prestige jobs where their work is organized and evaluated by men (Kelly, 1989). Women who depend on men for their job security or for career advancement are especially vulnerable to on-the-job sexual blackmail—or, quid pro quo harassment.

Some women are more dependent on men for employment and educational opportunities than others, and as a result, their risk is especially high (DeCoster, Estes, & Mueller, 1999). Women who depend solely on their own wages to support themselves and their families are unlikely to take risks at work. Their reluctance to either confront or complain makes them easy prey for sexual harassers (Stambaugh, 1997). Single mothers—especially those unable to obtain child support—are in greatest need of employment and therefore have the least leverage for a direct confrontation (Morgan, 1999). It is no wonder that victimization rates are significantly higher among young, single, and divorced women than among older married women (U.S. Merit Systems Protection Board, 1988).

In addition, women building careers in male-dominated workplaces and professions have little choice but to depend on men for their training and mentoring. Thus, in workplaces where interactions have become sexualized and harassment is common, a woman's ability to obtain her own organizational authority rests on her efforts to manage not only harassment by male coworkers and supervisors but also harassment by her male subordinates. Those who complain about sexualized hazing or who protest sexualized epithets risk being branded as unduly sensitive or too brusque and are then passed over for promotion. For this reason, ambitious women whose careers are on the rise are likely to encounter more sexual harassment than the complacent (DeCoster et al., 1999).

Far more women of color than white women depend on men for job security and career advancement. With the exception of Asian women, women of color earn significantly less than either white women or white men. Because unemployment among men of color is disproportionately high, women of color are more likely than their white counterparts to be the family's breadwinner (Collins, 1990).

For these reasons, a larger proportion of women of color support entire families on a single wage, depend on male superiors for job security, and therefore have fewer options for escaping by their harassers (e.g., transferring, quitting, changing jobs). At least among auto workers, black women endure more sexual harassment and experience more severe forms of it than their white counterparts (Gruber & Bjorn, 1982). Perhaps for these reasons, women of color filed a preponderance of the first wave of sexual harassment claims (Winston, 1991).

Few women are more dependent on men that those residing in U.S. prisons. As a consequence, those most vulnerable to sexual harassment in all its forms are incarcerated women who are supervised by male correctional officers ("Patriarchy in Prison," 1997). Lawsuits filed by incarcerated women assert that sexual blackmail is commonplace. In addition, they claim that male correctional officers routinely subject female inmates to unwarranted surveillance and gratuitous pat-downs (Finder, 1998).

Those Who Challenge Male Dominance Are at Greater Risk Than Those Who Comply

When routinely practiced, sexual harassment does more than gratify the few individuals who perpetrate it, it also serves to enforce the patriarchal status quo (Wise & Stanley, 1987). Within highly patriarchal institutions, those who question the superiority of a few men, or who resist dominance by them, are likely to be labeled traitors and then treated accordingly. Within the ranks of traitors can be found noncompliant women, unconventional men, and homosexuals.

Women who challenge the superiority of men by acquiring social, economic, or organizational power over them are visible targets for sexualized hostility. In fact, the findings from one study revealed that the more tenure and education a woman possesses, the greater her risk of sexual harassment victimization will be (DeCoster et al., 1999). Thus, the more power a woman acquires, the more she is perceived to be a threat to those in power and the greater her risk of being sexually harassed will be.

Within any patriarchal system, only a few men possess superordinate status. Sexual harassment is one of many tools used by the powerful elite for managing unruly men, as well. Powerful men routinely sexually harass other men as a means to intimidate them into subservience (Messerschmidt, 1993). Men who violate patriarchal norms by doing women's work, being feminine, or questioning the superiority of men are at a greater risk than are those who accept their place without question.

Because heterosexuality as it has been traditionally practiced serves to normalize male dominance and female subordination, the acceptance of homosexuality poses a formidable challenge to the patriarchal status quo. Thus, inside organizations where the heterosexual mandate is especially strong, lesbians and gays who are out (as well as heterosexuals who are erroneously labeled as such) can become the lightning rods of homophobic hostility. Such homophobia is often expressed in the form of sexual harassment (Brienza, 1996; Bull, 1997). Crude jokes about homosexual acts, homophobic slurs (dyke, queer, homo, for example), negative commentary about the gay lifestyle, and even malicious gossip about a person's sexual orientation are all forms of sexual harassment that serve to punish those who fail to conform to heterosexual norms. In the armed forces, for example, regardless of their true sexual orientation, women who resist sexual blackmail or who complain about sexualized hostilities are labeled lesbians, and their fitness to serve is called into question (Moss, 1997).

How Does Sexual Harassment Affect Those Who Experience It?

There is no singular sexual harassment experience. The effects of sexual harassment are as varied and complex as the women who endure it. A history of victimization is a significant factor in how a person interprets and responds to sexual harassment. Specifically, past experience of other forms of violence against women —rape, battering, abuse, and incest, for example—may heighten the feeling of being violated (Fitzgerald, 1993).

In addition, a person's values about gender, sex, work, and relationships can color the experience. Those with feminist orientations, for example, are more likely to define unwanted sexual attention as harassing (Ryan & Kenig, 1991). Specifically, women who value gender equality, who believe that women should have the right to pursue careers, and who believe that working women can be good mothers are more offended by unwanted sexual attention at work than those who hold more traditional views.

The nature of the relationship between a woman and her harasser is important as well. The greater the power disparity, the more distressing the experience is likely to be (Benson & Thomson, 1982). Feelings of violation are particularly

strong when women are harassed by authorities entrusted with their care. Sexual harassment is especially traumatic when coaches, mentors, therapists, doctors, or clergy commit it (Rutter, 1989).

As previously mentioned, both the sexual and racial identities of the harasser make a difference, as well. Harassment by someone of a different orientation or race is more offensive than if the harasser and victim are of the same background (Defour, 1990; Schneider, 1982).

Even though no two sexual harassment experiences are alike, analysis of women's talk about how sexual harassment feels and its effect on their lives has uncovered a few salient themes. For most, loss is a core experience. Coping with the negative effects of sexual harassment is emotionally distressing as well as physically exhausting. Those who manage to survive the experience gain strength and wisdom from their adversity (Stambaugh, 1997).

A Core Experience Among the Sexually Harassed Is Loss

It is difficult for the sexually harassed to talk about their experiences without mentioning a loss. When victims share their stories, talk of job loss and the fear of losing one's job often dominate the conversation (Morgan, 1999; Stambaugh, 1997). Such fears are not unfounded, as 60% to 70% of victims who contact government agencies for assistance are unemployed (Coles, 1982; New York Governor's Task Force on Sexual Harassment, 1993; Welsh & Gruber, 1999). In filing formal claims, victims usually seek monetary compensation for lost promotions, wages, and benefits. But, beneath these more tangible losses lie less obvious but no less traumatizing sacrifices. Regardless of the circumstances, recipients of unwanted sexual attention commonly feel a loss of personal dignity. Being sexually harassed is an embarrassing, if not humiliating experience. The pressure to exchange sexual favors for employment is demeaning, as is being the butt of a sexualized joke or gag. A consequence is the erosion of trust in others, especially men (Rutter, 1989). For example, in a recent study, 53% of the victims who experienced quid pro quo harassment lost confidence in themselves, 45% lost their confidence in others, and 44% experienced a loss of trust in men (Van Roosmalen & McDaniel, 1998).

The act of filing a report or complaint incurs additional loss of dignity and trust in others. Those who are accused often vilify those who blow the whistle on them or on institutions that harbor them; complainants are also ostracized by those who support sexual harassment (Dandekar, 1990). As a result, the cost of complaint can be the loss of one's reputation, along with collegiality and the support of coworkers.

For Most, Sexual Harassment Is a Distressing Experience

The *Diagnostic and Statistical Manual (DSM-IV)* (American Psychiatric Association, 1994) lists sexual harassment as a significant psychosocial stressor, and a growing number of clinicians rate its effects on their patients as severe to extreme (Charney & Russell, 1994). Nearly all (90%) of those who seek help report at least some degree of emotional distress (Crull, 1981). Because sexual harassment

is a humiliating experience, most victims experience intense anger. Without the means to fully express it, depression and self-destructive behavior can result. Ironically, the strategies most women employ to control their anger (e.g., escape and avoidance) lead to social isolation, which in turn exacerbates feelings of helplessness and hopelessness (Koss, 1993).

The stress of coping with sexual harassment victimization undermines physical health, as well. Nearly 63% of the women who sought assistance from the Working Women's Institute associated physical illness with being sexually harassed (Crull, 1981). Among them, nausea, headaches, and exhaustion were the most commonly reported forms of physical distress. In one study, a significant minority of victims reported sexual inhibition (Van Roosmalen & McDaniel, 1998)

In many cases, the emotional and physical distress of being sexually harassed lingers long after the violation ends. Without proper treatment, the physical manifestations of suppressed anger and feelings of loss can develop into chronic health conditions. For example, the experience of being sexually harassed can trigger the onset of eating disorders. Thus, in those cases where the harassment was severe, or when it was perpetrated over an extended period of time, it can take years to fully heal (Koss, 1993).

Finally, sexual harassment erodes feelings of satisfaction. Surveys of university and corporate employees document significant differences in job satisfaction between victims and nonvictims (Klein, 1988; Stambaugh, 1993). Those who manage to keep their jobs can become apathetic about work and disaffected with administration (Morgan, 1999). The experience for students is similar. Victims often cite a change in attitude toward school, and some experience a sharp decline in their ability to perform in class (Benson & Thomson, 1982; Van Roosmalen & McDaniel, 1998).

Reporting Is Rarely Satisfying and Can Be Traumatic

Despite the fact that mechanisms for reporting sexual harassment abound, the vast majority of those who could benefit from engaging them choose not to do so. Only about 24% of victims who participated in the last U.S. Merit Systems Protection Board (1992) told anyone of their plight, and less than 12% took formal action. Instead, sexually harassed women tend to handle their sexual harassment problems via escape or avoidance (Gruber, 1989). Students escape harassers by dropping courses or changing their programs of study. Workers often seek relief by transferring to a different office or shift, or by quitting altogether. When asked why they do not seek intervention, victims commonly cite fear of retaliation, of not being believed; they express the suspicion that reporting will "do no good" (Gutek, Groff, & Tsui, 1996).

There is evidence to indicate their fears are well founded. Complaints rarely go unpunished, and litigation is quickly becoming the weapon of choice. Increasingly, those accused of harassment punish their accusers and the institutions that stand by them by filing civil suits, the majority of which never go to trial (Conte, 1996). The victims of counterclaims experience the process of litigation as an additional or secondary harassment. In addition, in most cases, countersuits undermine the ability of an employer to deliver meaningful support to the victims who seek their aid, as they divide the attention and loyalty of complaint handlers and tap already limited resources for aid and resolution (Morgan, 1999).

The vast majority of those who seek legal assistance with their sexual harassment problems are turned away (Morgan, 1999). With respect to government agencies, the size of the budget has not kept pace with the rising caseload. As a result, the number of requests for investigation has outstripped agency resources for conducting them. In some states, the result has been a 1- to 2-year backlog in claim processing (Bureau of National Affairs, 1994). As a consequence, agencies prioritize claims, and only the most egregious, and those with ample documentation, are expeditiously processed. Too often, the remaining complaints are disposed of with personal advice and moral lectures before they can ever become cases (Morgan, 1999).

Likewise, because sexual harassment claims have a reputation for being high-risk cases with low returns on the investment, most attorneys practice caution in taking them. Less than 1% of all sexual harassment claims are heard in court, and only one third of the outcomes favor the plaintiff (Terpestra & Baker, 1988). As a consequence, most of those who seek legal aid fail to obtain it. Rejection by agencies and attorneys becomes one more in a long line of betrayals by those with the authority to intervene (Madigan & Gamble, 1991).

For those fortunate enough to garner government intervention or legal representation, the pursuit of justice takes its toll. Without the benefit of legal protections comparable to rape shield laws, the medical, work, and sexual histories of sexual harassment complainants are open to investigation. Credit histories, medical reports, even adoption papers have been probed for evidence of a complainant's unreasonableness. Along with counterclaims, attempts at discrediting them become a third—and for those who have lost their jobs, a fourth—victimization.

Surviving Sexual Harassment Can Be Empowering

The humiliation of being sexually harassed is indeed distressful. To be fired or demoted for confronting or complaining about harassment can be traumatizing. Being disbelieved by supervisors, lectured to by government agents, and then sued by one's harasser pours a significant amount of salt into an already gaping wound. Regardless of the outcome, those who successfully survive their ordeals report intense feelings of empowerment (Stambaugh, 1997). For some, the experience of surviving their harassment, complaint, or litigation experience results in a significant increase in personal pride and sense of self-worth.

In addition to pride, those who pursue formal redress find their knowledge of the law is enhanced. Many victims exit the complaint process with greater understanding of their rights at work, the legal system, and the enforcement of rules. Exercising this new expertise can restore self-confidence eroded by harassment. Survivors draw on their legal knowledge to research potential employers, to assess and respond to their work evaluations, and to negotiate better terms of employment (Morgan, 1999).

Finally, the experience of being sexually exploited and economically coerced can be politicizing. Many survivors put their shoulders to the communal wheel by forming peer support groups, writing or participating in media exposes, organizing protests, and lobbying for change.

Conclusions

Louisa Mae Alcott is not the only woman to write about her experience of sexual harassment. Since her account was first published, millions of women from around the world have shared similar accounts. Although the details of each story differ, the plot lines are painfully similar. With each telling, the silence regarding this endemic social problem is broken, and one of America's greatest shames is once again exposed.

Comparing the current level of public concern about the plight of sexual harassment victims with that of Alcott's day, it appears we have come quite a long way, indeed. In just a few short decades, a practice that was once considered to be the working man's prerogative has been recast as an unconscionable abuse of power. Today, women have a name for their experience, laws that prohibit its practice, and mechanisms for redress and justice. Yet the problem of sexual harassment appears to be exceptionally resistant to current efforts to eliminate it.

Since efforts were first made to document them, rates of victimization, at least in the United States and Canada, have remained remarkably stable. Nationwide, incidence hovers around 42%. Among those working and attending school in male-dominated sectors of society, the rates are much higher. Thus, sexual harassment continues to be a pervasive experience among women, and the number of men suffering from it appears to be in the rise.

Increasingly, clinical studies and survey data portray sexual harassment as an occupational health hazard, the risks of which are disproportionately borne by women. Despite widespread institutionalization of reporting mechanisms, most victims continue to endure the problem in silence.

Less than one quarter of the women who experience legally actionable forms of unwanted sexual attention tell anyone about their plight, and only a handful—12%—ever make the attempt to avail themselves of the opportunities for formal redress. Of those who do, most lose their jobs in the process, some are sued, and only a few exit the process feeling justified.

Today, it is almost impossible to talk of sex, work, rights, and law without evoking the term sexual harassment (Schultz, 1998). Yet there remains considerable confusion about the types of behaviors constituting legal action (Fisher, 1998). It is primarily case law that stakes out the boundary that divides a personal problem from a legally actionable one. With respect to sexual harassment, shifts in politics, ideology, and resources have caused the line to drift. Some of the consequences have been confusion and neglect at the institutional level, inadequate protection and intervention by government agencies, and insufficient advocacy among the legal profession. Given the response (or lack of response) that most victims receive from authorities, it is no wonder that most women prefer to resolve their sexual harassment problems via escape or avoidance.

All male violence against women is political; but few experiences so blatantly connect the personal with the political as that of being sexual harassed at work (Koss et al., 1994). Sexual harassment oc-curs at those places within the social strata where economic and sexual power overlap (Bularzik, 1978). When political, economic, and sexual power converge, the environment is especially ripe for abuse (Benson & Thomson, 1982). Thus, sexual harassment is a unique manifestation of the struggle between those who possess (and abuse) power and those who seek to reclaim it (Smart, 1987), and any response to the problem that fails to acknowledge that reality will fail to resolve it.

References

Alcott, L. M. (1874, June 4). How I went out to service. *The Independent* (New York).

American Psychiatric Association. (1994). *Diagnostic and statistical manual of mental disorders, 4th edition.* Washington, DC: Author.

Benson, D., & Thomson, G. (1982). Sexual harassment on a university campus: The confluence of authority relations, sexual interest, and gender stratification. *Social Problems, 29*(3), 236-251.

Brienza, J. (1996). No recourse for same-sex harassment. *Trial, 32*(3), 78-80.

Bularzik, M. (1978). *Sexual harassment at the workplace: Historical notes.* Somerville, MA: New England Free Press.

Bull, C. (1997, November 25). Same-sex harassment: Gay men and lesbians being harassed in the workplace are about to have their day in court. *The Advocate,* pp. 30-34.

Bureau of National Affairs. (1994). New charges, backlog rising. *Current Developments, 3,* 616.

Charney, D., & Russell, R. (1994). An overview of sexual harassment. *American Journal of Psychiatry, 151*(1), 10-17.

Coles, F. (1982). Forced to quit: Sexual harassment complaints and agency responses. *Sex Roles, 14*(1/2), 81-95.

Collins, P. (1990). *Black feminist thought.* Boston: Unman & Hyman.

Conte, A. (1996). When the tables are turned: Courts consider suits by alleged harassers. *Trial, 32*(3), 30-37.

Cook, K., & Stambaugh, P. (1997). Tuna memos and pissing contests: Doing gender and male dominance on the Internet. In C. Ronai, B. Zsembik, & J. Feagin (Ed.), *Everyday sexism in the third millennium* (pp. 63-83).New York: Routledge.

Crull, P. (1981). The stress effects of sexual harassment on the job. *American Journal of Orthopsychiatry, 52,* 539-544.

Dandekar, N. (1990). Contrasting consequences: Bringing charges of sexual harassment compared with other cases of whistleblowing. *Journal of Business Ethics, 9,* 151-158.

DeCoster, S., Estes, S. B., & Mueller, C. W. (1999). Routine activities and sexual harassment in the workplace. *Work and Occupations, 26*(1), 21-43.

Defour, D. (1990). The interface of racism and sexism on college campuses. In M. Paludi (Ed.), *The ivory tower: Sexual harassment on campus* (pp. 45-52). Albany: University of New York Press.

Dubois, C., Knapp, D., Farley, R., & Kustis, G. (1998). An empirical examination of same- and other-gender sexual harassment in the workplace. *Sex Roles, 39*(9-10), 731-746.

Estrich, S. (1991). Sex at work. *Stanford Law Review, 43,* 813-844.

Farley, C. (1978). *Sexual shakedown: The sexual harassment of women on the job.* New York: McGraw-Hill.

Felstiner, W., Abel, R., & Sarat, A. (1980-1981). The emergence and transformation of disputes: Naming, blaming, claiming. *Law and Society Review, 15*(3), 631-654.

Finder, A. (1998, November 10). Female inmates sue over "pat frisks" by men. *The New York Times,* p. B-5.

Fisher, A. (1998, January 12). After all this time, why don't people know what sexual harassment means? *Fortune,* pp. 156-157.

Fitzgerald, L. (1993). Violence against women in the workplace. *American Psychologist, 48,* 1070-1076.

Fitzgerald, L., & Ormerod, A. (1991). Perceptions of sexual harassment: The influence of gender and context. *Psychology of Women Quarterly, 15,* 281-294.

Gruber, J. (1989). How women handle sexual harassment. *Social Science Research, 74*(1), 3-7.

Gruber, J. (1998). The impact of male work environments and organizational policies on women's experiences of sexual harassment. *Gender & Society, 12*(3), 301-319.

Gruber, J., & Bjorn, L. (1982). Blue collar blues: The sexual harassment of women autoworkers. *Work and Occupations, 9*(3), 271-298.

Gutek, B., Groff, A., & Tsui, A. (1996). Reactions to perceived sex discrimination. *Human Relations, 49*(6), 791- 814.

Holcombe, B., & Wellington, C. (1992). *Search for justice.* Walpole, NH: Stillpoint.

Jurik, N. (1985). An officer and a lady: Organizational barriers to women working in men's prisons. *Social Problems, 32,* 375-388.

Kelly, R. (1989). *The gendered economy.* Newbury Park, CA: Sage.

Klein, F. (1988). *The 1988 working women sexual harassment survey executive report.* Cambridge, MA: Klein & Associates.

Koss, M. (1993). Changed lives. In M. Paludi (Ed.), *Ivory power* (pp. 73-92). New York: SUNY Press.

Koss, M., Goodman, L., Browne, A., Fitzgerald, L., Keita, G., & Russo, N. (1994). *Male violence against women at home, at work and in the community.* Washington, DC: American Psychological Association.

Loe, M. (1996). Working for men—at the intersection of power, gender, and sexuality. *Sociological Inquiry, 66*(4), 399-421.

MacKinnon, C. (1979). *The sexual harassment of working women.* New Haven, CT: Yale University Press.

MacKinnon, C. (1995). Sexual harassment: Its first decade in court. In B. Price & N. Sokoloff (Eds.), *The criminal justice system and women* (pp. 297-311). New York: McGraw-Hill.

Madigan, M., & Gamble, N. (1991). *The second rape: Society's continued betrayal of the victim.* New York: Lexington.

Martin, S. (1994). Outsider within the station house: The impact of race and gender on black women police. *Social Problems, 41,* 383-400.

Martin, S., & Jurik, N. (1996). *Doing justice, doing gender.* Thousand Oaks, CA: Sage.

Meritor Savings Bank v. Mechele Vinson, 477 U.S. 57.65 (1985).

Messerschmidt, J. (1993). *Masculinities and crime.* Lantham, MD: Rowman & Littlefield.

Morgan, P. (1999). Risking relationships: Understanding the litigation choices of sexually harassment women. *Law and Society Review, 33*(1), 67-92.

Moss, J. (1997, February 4). Lesbian baiting in the barracks. *The Advocate,* pp. 36-40.

National Council for Research on Women. (1992). *Sexual harassment: Research and resources.* New York: Author.

New York Governor's Task Force on Sexual Harassment. (1993). *Sexual harassment: Building a consensus for change.* New York: Office of the Governor.

Patriarchy in prison. (1997). *off our backs, 27*(2), 3-4.

Pettiway, L. (1996). *Honey, honey, miss thang: Being black and gay on the streets.* Philadelphia: Temple University Press.

Ronai, C., & Ellis, C. (1989). Turn-ons for money, interactional strategies of the table dancer. *Journal of Contemporary Ethnography, 18*(3), 271-298.

Rutter, P. (1989). *Sex in the forbidden zone: When men in power—therapists, doctors, clergy, teachers, and others—betray women's trust.* New York: Fawcett.

Ryan, J., & Kenig, S. (1991). Risk and ideology in sexual harassment. *Sociological Inquiry, 61*(2), 231-241.

Schneider, B. (1982). Consciousness about sexual harassment among heterosexual and lesbian women workers. *Journal of Social Issues, 38,* 75-97.

Schultz, V. (1998). Reconceptualizing sexual harassment. *Yale Law Journal, 107*(6), 1683-1805.

Sexual harassment charges (and dismissals) escalate. (1999). *HR Focus, 76*(4), 4-5.

Smart, C. (1987). *Feminism and the power of law.* London: Routledge.

Stambaugh, P. M. (1993). *Unwanted sexual attention at Arizona State University.* In the unpublished annual report of The ASU Commission on the Status of Women, Arizona State University, Tempe.

Stambaugh, P. M. (1997). The power of law and the sexual harassment complaints of women. *National Women's Studies Association Journal, 9*(2), 23-42.

Stanko, B. (1992). Sexual harassment in the criminological profession. *Criminologist, 17*(5), 1-3.

Terpestra, D., & Baker, D. (1988). Outcomes of sexual harassment charges. *Academy of Management Journal, 31*(1), 181-190.

Two out of three women in the military study report sexual harassment incidents. (1991, September 12). *New York Times,* p. A-22.

U.S. Department of Defense. (1993). *The Tailhook report.* New York: St. Martin's.

U.S. Equal Employment Opportunity Commission. (1998). *Sexual harassment* [On-line]. Available: www.access.gpo.gov/nara/cfr/waisidx/29cfr1604.html

U.S. Equal Employment Opportunity Commission. (1999). *Sexual harassment charges EEOC and FEPAS combined: FY 1992-FY 1998* [On-line]. Available: www.eeoc.gov/state/harass.html

U.S. Merit Systems Protection Board. (1981). *Sexual harassment in the federal government.* Washington, DC: Author.

U.S. Merit Systems Protection Board. (1988). *Sexual harassment in the federal government: An update.* Washington DC: Author.

U.S. Merit Systems Protection Board. (1992). *Sexual harassment in the federal government workplace.* Washington DC: Author.

U.S. Office of Civil Rights. (1999). *Sexual harassment* [On-line]. Available: www.doc.gov/ocr

Van Roosmalen, E., & McDaniel, S. (1998). Sexual harassment in academia: A hazard to women's health. *Women & Health, 28*(2), 33-55.

Welsh, S., & Gruber, J. (1999). Not taking it any more: Women who report or file complaints of sexual harassment. *Canadian Research Society Association, 4,* 559-583.

Winston, J. (1991). Mirror, mirror on the wall. Title VII, Section 1981, and the intersection of race, gender. and the Civil Rights Act of 1990. *California Law Review, 79,* 775-825.

Wise, S., & Stanley, L. (1987). *Georgie porgie: Sexual harassment in everyday life.* London: Pandora.

Yount, K. (1991). Ladies, flirts, and tomboys: Strategies for handling sexual harassment in an underground mine. *Journal of Contemporary Ethnography, 19*(4), 396-422.

PART III

Prevention and Direct Intervention

Intervention to stop and reduce violence against women began with small groups of women who opened their homes and volunteered their time to help victims of rape and battering. Slowly, over the past three decades, these interventions have evolved into a network of social services and advocacy programs. The infusion of federal and state tax dollars has led to the rapid expansion of these efforts and to a wide variety of interventions. These interventions include well-established crisis responses as well as projects that have expanded into new sections of society to identify victims, educate the public, and prevent violence from occurring. This part of the *Sourcebook* does not cover the entire array of current responses but, instead, conveys the rich variety of responses currently in place in our society.

The part starts with a focus on services to survivors of both sexual assault and battering. In Chapter 12, Rebecca Campbell and Patricia Yancey Martin provide an in-depth overview of how services to rape crisis centers have developed over the past several decades. They then describe the work that occurs in rape crisis centers and what we know about the effectiveness of these programs. They end with a discussion of broader community issues and involvement. A *Special Topic* by Linda E. Ledray describes the pioneering work of sexual assault nurse examiners and the role they play within a multidisciplinary intervention to support victims of sexual assault.

In Chapter 13, Cris M. Sullivan and Tameka Gillum address how shelters and other community-based services have developed for battered women over the past quarter century. They start by describing the evolution of shelters and then continue by showcasing the diversity of shelter-based programs that have been developed to assist women within particular communities. Following this, they examine the emergence of programs for children of battered women. They conclude by describing the expansion of women's services into nonresidential, community-based efforts.

Following these two chapters is Chapter 14, by Larry W. Bennett and Oliver J. Williams, on intervention programs for men who batter. Programs for men who batter have expanded rapidly in the past two decades. Bennett and Williams provide a brief history of batterer intervention programs and then describe in detail the way in which these programs are delivered. Their chapter ends with a discussion of major issues surrounding batterer intervention, such as state regulation and the cultural competence of such programs.

The next several chapters focus on the U.S. legal system and various efforts to enforce laws and influence the criminal justice system to be more sensitive to the needs of victims. In Chapter 15, Roberta L. Valente, Barbara J. Hart, Seema Zeya, and Mary Malefyt describe the U.S. Violence Against Women Act (VAWA) of 1994. They describe the basic tenets of VAWA and then show how particular sections of the Act provide relief to women victims in several areas of federal law.

Chapter 16, by LeeAnn Iovanni and Susan L. Miller, provides a detailed description of how the criminal justice system responds to violence against women. The authors review mandatory and presumptive arrest policies, which have been passed into law and adopted by many police departments, and the increased granting of civil restraining orders to victims of violence. They also examine "no-drop" policies, which require prosecutors to move forward with cases against perpetrators in a way that removes the burden of proof from the victim, as well as integrated or unified courts, which allow a single judge to hear criminal cases against a perpetrator while also possibly hearing

child custody or dependency cases involving the battered mother and her children. Each of these efforts is also examined for its effect, based on available research.

In Chapter 17, Ellen Pence describes the work of battered women's advocates with individual women and with entire communities. Pence is one of the developers of the Duluth Model, probably the most widely replicated system of advocacy and intervention on behalf of battered women and their families. Pence brings this deep experience to her description and discussion of the work of advocates.

The number of systems outside traditional, grassroots battered women's programs has greatly expanded in just the past 10 years. In the next several chapters, the authors cover the response of the health care system (Chapter 18 by Evan Stark), religious institutions (Chapter 19 by Marie M. Fortune), and school systems (Chapter 20 by Mary K. O'Brien). Stark's chapter on the health care response explains why violence against women should be considered a health issue for women. In the second section of his chapter, Stark focuses on the many ways in which individual health care professionals as well as entire health care systems have responded to this epidemic.

In Chapter 19, Fortune reviews the role of religion in the lives of women victims of violence. She reviews in depth how religious traditions have both encouraged violence against women and contributed to stopping it. She concludes with a discussion of how religious and secular institutions are now collaborating to stop violence against women.

Schools are one location within our social ecology where many of us have spent a large portion of our childhood. O'Brien takes us through the wonderful diversity of prevention education that is occurring in primary and secondary schools across North America. She provides us with detailed descriptions of dozens of school-based programs and with evaluations of their effectiveness.

Finally, in the last chapter in this section (Chapter 21), Marissa Ghez examines the important role of mass media in preventing violence. She presents several avenues to influence mass change and describes local and national efforts that have successfully used these methods. Ghez, who worked at the Family Violence Prevention Fund, has firsthand experience in implementing national prevention efforts and describes in rich detail how the fund has succeeded and where it has learned hard lessons.

We hope this section of the *Sourcebook* will provide you with insights into how many thousands of people in North America and elsewhere are organizing their work to help stop or reduce violence against women.

CHAPTER 12

Services for Sexual Assault Survivors

The Role of Rape Crisis Centers

Rebecca Campbell
Patricia Yancey Martin

Rape crisis centers (RCCs) are remarkable organizations. Characterized by Ferree and Martin (1995) as the harvest of second-wave feminism, RCCs are a consequential feature of contemporary U.S. society, we suggest. Many of these organizations, which were formed through grassroots organizing and volunteer labor, have survived for 20 or more years, and they continue "do[ing] the work of the movement" (Ferree & Martin, 1995, p. 3). This chapter reviews the circumstances that led to the creation and persistence of RCCs, the services provided for victims by these organizations, and the impact of RCCs on victims and society. With over 1,200 RCCs currently in operation in the United States, an average of 24 per state, services to survivors and to the legal, medical, and mental health systems that work with victims are

unlikely to disappear any time soon (see Martin, 1997, Martin & Powell, 1994). Indeed, our review suggests that the effects of RCCs on mainstream society are important not only to antirape activists but also to students of social movements and societal change. RCCs provide exemplars of how radical feminist ideology indoctrinates and survives within mainstream human service-delivery models.

To explore these issues, this chapter is organized into four sections. First, to set the stage for our discussions on the current work of RCCs, we briefly review the history of the antirape movement in the United States, with specific attention to the emergence of RCCs. Second, we turn our attention to contemporary issues in the antirape movement, focusing on the existing structures and functions of RCCs. The staff and volunteers of RCCs work with the legal, medical, and mental health systems to provide comprehensive services to victims of sexual assault and their families. In addition, these centers provide community education, sponsor rape-prevention programs, and engage in institutional advocacy to create systems-level changes. Third, we examine the effectiveness of these activities in facilitating victim recovery and raising community awareness about violence against women. Fourth, in light of the fact that RCCs have been effective in fostering beneficial individual and societal level outcomes, we delve into how these organizations are able to assist survivors and their communities. We review the specific mobilizing strategies and tactics that RCCs employ as women's movement, antirape organizations concerned with helping victims and with ending rape. We close with a discussion of prospects for the RCCs to continue to have a positive impact on victims and social institutions.

The History of the Antirape Movement

The Emergence of the First Rape Crisis Centers

The first U.S. RCCs emerged in the 1970s as part of the radical feminist women's movement. Although the academic study of RCCs tends to use phrases such as *antirape movement, isomorphic dynamics,* and *affiliational structures,* fundamentally, these centers emerged from the emotions and passions of feminist activists (Collins & Whalen, 1989; Schechter, 1982). Anger—at widespread violence against women. Fear—for the safety of all women and children. Hope—

for healing and social change. RCCs were formed to provide services to victims in crisis, to educate communities on violence against women, and to mobilize efforts for social change. Truly a grassroots effort, many of the first RCCs were run out of women's own homes with donated materials (e.g., telephones, furniture, printing for flyers) (O'Sullivan, 1978; Pride, 1981). The staff of these early centers were often community volunteers who did not have counseling or professional service backgrounds. Women joined these groups because they were committed to helping victims and to politicizing them to change society (Gornick, Burt, & Pittman, 1985; Matthews, 1994).

In sharp contrast to traditional social service agencies, many of these fledging centers were run as feminist collectives, where power and decision making were shared among all members of the organization (see Koss & Harvey, 1991). Early RCCs rejected hierarchical organizational practices, such as appointing an executive director or forming a board of directors (Koss & Harvey, 1991). Similarly, these organizations were free-standing agencies, completely autonomous and not affiliated with or dependent on a parent organization (e.g., a YWCA, hospital, mental health agency). In fact, many centers were suspicious of the underlying motives and support offered by mainstream organizations (Byington, Martin, DiNitto, & Maxwell, 1991; Martin, DiNitto, Byington, & Maxwell, 1992; Matthews, 1994; Schechter, 1982). Even without the support of established social service agencies and government funding, RCCs continued to grow in numbers throughout the United States.

Although each center has its unique organizational history, there was remarkable similarity across RCCs with respect to the services they offered rape victims (Gornick et al., 1985; Koss & Harvey, 1991; O'Sullivan, 1978). Most had 24-hour crisis hot lines to provide information, referrals, and crisis counseling. In addition, RCCs trained volunteers as legal and medical advocates to accompany victims to police departments and hospitals. These volunteers provided information to victims about their legal rights and advocated on their behalf. Influenced by the radical feminist women's movement, early RCCs actively supported a social action agenda by sponsoring public demonstrations, protests, and marches, as well as lobbying the state for stronger laws on violence against women (Koss & Harvey, 1991; Martin et al., 1992; O'Sullivan, 1978).

The Evolution of the Antirape Movement

As time passed, many of the original leaders of the antirape movement grew tired from years of struggle and over-commitment to the cause (Gornick et al., 1985; Matthews, 1994). As they left, new women came on board who valued a more conventional and apolitical approach. With this new diversity, varied visions emerged for the structure and function of RCCs (Gornick et al., 1985; Koss & Harvey, 1991; O'Sullivan, 1978). This shift from radical social change agencies to social service organizations happened in varying degrees over many years. By the mid-1970s, many centers began applying for and receiving funds from the Law Enforcement Assistance Administration (LEAA) and United Way (Gornick et al., 1985; Matthews, 1994; O'Sullivan, 1978; Pride, 1981). The arrival of government funding in RCCs brought about

three interrelated changes. First, many centers moved from collectives to hierarchical organizational structures, designating executive directors, program coordinators, and boards of directors with formal decision-making power over members, programs, and policies (Collins & Whalen, 1989; O'Sullivan, 1978; Pride, 1981). Second, with the move from collectives to traditional structures came a shift in staffing. Government funding sources began stressing the importance of professionally certified personnel. It was no longer enough for staff to be former rape victims committed to empowering women; they now had to be trained and certified as professionals or paraprofessionals (Collins & Whalen, 1989). Third, with the competition for public funding resources came the need for affiliation (Byington et al., 1991). To remain in operation, many formerly free-standing centers affiliated with or were absorbed by agencies such as YWCAs, community mental health centers, hospitals, and district attorney's offices (Gornick et al., 1985; Matthews, 1994; Pride, 1981; Schechter, 1982).

Whereas the antirape movement experienced a general shift toward professionalization, individual centers varied in how much they changed their structures and functions. For instance, not all centers changed to hierarchical structures with hired professionals, and many centers were successful in warding off co-optation within a mainstream organization. In one of the first studies on this professionalization shift, O'Sullivan (1978) surveyed 90 completely autonomous RCCs that had been founded prior to 1976. Even though these centers had started receiving substantial government fiscal support, only 43% had boards of directors. Most centers favored steering committees over boards of directors, as they saw this format as less hierarchical and more consistent with feminist collective ideology.

In the 1980s, Gornick et al. (1985) surveyed a sample of 50 nationally representative RCCs (see also Harvey, 1985). In the time since O'Sullivan's research, more variation had emerged with respect to organizational structures, staff composition, and funding sources. Gornick et al. (1985) identified four typologies of rape crisis centers: (a) programs resembling the original feminist collectives of the 1970s, (b) programs more mainstream and traditional in structure, (c) programs embedded in a social service or mental health agency, and (d) programs based in hospital emergency rooms. Furthermore, Gornick et al.'s results revealed that independent centers were more politically active than affiliated centers, and collectively run centers were more service-oriented than bureaucratic centers (see also Bordt, 1997). Matthews (1994) replicated many of these findings in her study of six RCCs in Los Angeles during 1988 and 1989. Matthews (1994) argued that rape crisis work had been influenced by a more conservative service-delivery approach because of the ongoing struggle between the antirape movement and the state. Centers that started out with different styles and perspectives soon became more similar, as RCCs developed consistent procedures and bureaucratic structures in response to government funding requirements (see DiMaggio & Powell, 1991).

In the 1990s, national work by Campbell, Baker, and Mazurek (1998) continued to find evidence of this shift toward homogenized professionalization. In a study of 168 RCCs throughout the country, Campbell et al. (1998) found a cohort effect that differentiated centers formed at the peak of the antirape movement, in 1978 or earlier, from those founded in a more conservative era in U.S. politics, 1979 or later. The older centers had larger budgets and more staff but were more likely to be free-standing collectives. Their internal communication style was more likely to stress participatory decision making, with all members of the organization, from the board of directors to the volunteers and clients, involved. Older centers were also more likely than younger centers to participate in social change activities, such as public demonstrations against violence against women and rape-prevention programming. The younger centers had comparatively smaller budgets and staffing levels and were more likely to be hierarchical organizations affiliated with larger social service agencies. Internal decisions in these agencies were made without the participation of the less powerful members of the organization (e.g., volunteers and clients). These younger centers were less likely to be engaged in public demonstrations or prevention work, but they were more likely than the older centers to be involved in lobbying elected politicians. The top-down approach of political lobbying may be more consistent with these younger organizations' philosophies than the grassroots tactics favored by older centers. These results suggest that RCCs have altered their structure and function since the beginnings of the antirape movement, but these changes may have been necessary to survive the different political climate of the 1980s and 1990s. The staff at many of these centers may have felt that deradicalizing was key to long-term organizational sustainability in an era of increasingly conservative state politics (see Spalter-Roth & Schreiber, 1995).

The Current Activities of Rape Crisis Centers

Services Provided by Rape Crisis Centers

Whereas the political activism of RCCs has tempered over time, the direct services these agencies provide to survivors have remained essentially the same throughout the history of the antirape movement. In fact, current funding sources (e.g., state Victims of Crime Act funds) often require agencies to offer three basic services: (a) 24-hour hot line, (b) counseling (individual, group, support groups), and (c) legal and medical advocacy. Crisis hot lines are typically staffed by volunteers who have completed an intensive training program in crisis intervention (Campbell et al., 1998). Counseling services are most commonly provided by licensed professionals (e.g., practitioners at the level of the master's in social work), although some centers still employ paraprofessionals for short-term counseling and support group facilitation (Campbell et al., 1998).

Yet, of these three basic services, legal and medical advocacy remain the most challenging tasks for center staff (Campbell, 1996; Martin, 1997). Rape victim advocates have the simultaneous job of assisting rape survivors in crisis and educating staff from other service systems (e.g., police officers, detectives, prosecutors, doctors, nurses). Throughout all aspects of their work, rape victim advocates

are trying to prevent "the second rape"— insensitive, victim-blaming treatment from community system personnel. In what is also termed *secondary victimization,* rape victims often experience negative treatment from society that mirrors and exacerbates the trauma of the rape (Campbell, 1998; Campbell & Bybee, 1997; Campbell et al., 1999; Frohmann, 1991; Madigan & Gamble, 1991; Martin & Powell, 1994; Matoesian, 1993; Williams, 1984). The job of rape victim advocates, therefore, is not only to provide direct services to survivors but also to prevent secondary victimization.

Medical/legal advocates are typically volunteers who have completed a comprehensive training program to assist victims in accessing emergency medical services and reporting the assault to the police. The process of reporting and prosecuting a rape can be a long and complicated affair, and in fact, most rape victims never report the assault to the criminal justice system (Campbell et al., 1999; Golding, Siegel, Sorenson, Burnam, & Stein, 1989; Ullman, 1996). For those who do report, their first contact is with police officers and detectives, who record victims' accounts of the assault and conduct a preliminary investigation. At this stage, some jurisdictions automatically forward the report or investigation to the local prosecutor, whereas others allow the police to decide whether to forward the report. The prosecutor then chooses whether to authorize an arrest and press charges. Not all cases are charged as rapes or sexual assaults, as some are charged at lesser offenses (e.g., simple assault, reckless endangerment). If the charges are not dropped, the accused rapist has the choice of pleading guilty to the original offense or, if a bargain has been struck, to a lesser offense, or of going to trial. If he is convicted at the trial, the judge or jury must decide whether probation or jail time will suffice as punishment.

With a system this complex, it is quite likely that some cases will slip through the cracks, and in fact, most rape survivors never get their day in court. Only 25% of reported rapes are accepted for prosecution, 12% of defendants are actually found guilty, and 7% of all cases result in a prison term (Frazier & Haney, 1996). In addition, Campbell (1998) found that even in cases where survivors had the assistance of a rape victim advocate, 67% of cases were dismissed, and over 80% of the time, this decision was made by legal personnel and contradicted the victims' wishes to prosecute. Thus, the effectiveness of RCCs advocates can be limited because widespread effective prosecution of rape remains elusive.

Besides providing legal advocacy, RCC staff also assist victims with their medical needs (see Martin & DiNitto, 1987; Martin, DiNitto, Harrison, & Maxwell, 1985). After a sexual assault, rape victims may need emergency medical care for several reasons. Victims are sometimes physically injured in the assault (e.g., cuts, bruises, vaginal or anal lacerations), so a medical exam is helpful to detect and treat these problems. In addition, forensic evidence such as semen, blood, and/or samples of hair, fiber, or skin can be collected from victims' bodies during this exam (often called the "rape kit"; see Martin et al., 1985). For many women, concerns about exposure to sexually transmitted diseases (STDs) and the risk of pregnancy are paramount, and hospital staff can provide information and preventive treatments (e.g., the morning-after pill to prevent pregnancy). In practice, seeking medical care can be a har-

rowing experience for rape survivors: disrobing in front of the hospital staff, turning over their clothes to police as evidence, enduring a lengthy pelvic exam (to check for injuries and obtain semen samples), and submitting to other evidence collection (combing pubic hair, scraping under fingernails). In the midst of these procedures, nurses come and go taking blood (for pregnancy tests, STD screening) and bringing medications (the morning-after pill, antibiotics). This medical care is typically provided in a hospital emergency room, a trauma-focused setting where the ambience can be quite frenetic (see Ahrens et al., in press). The job of the medical advocate is to explain these medical procedures and help victims by restoring their sense of control.

Despite these diverse medical needs, current research suggests that many survivors are not receiving adequate care. The National Victim Center's (1992) national survey of female survivors of sexual assault found that 60% of victims were not advised about how to obtain pregnancy testing or how to prevent pregnancy. Although 43% of the women who had been raped within the previous 5 years were very concerned about contracting HIV from the assault, 73% were not given information about testing for exposure to HIV. Another 40% were not given information about the risk of contracting other STDs. Yet, working with an RCC medical advocate appears to increase the likelihood of receiving needed medical services. Campbell and Bybee (1997) found that in a sample of rape survivors who had the assistance of an advocate, 67% of the victims who wanted information about STDs actually received such information from hospital staff. Similarly, 70% of the victims who wanted information about pregnancy obtained it, but only 38% of the victims who wanted the morning-after pill to prevent pregnancy actually received this medication, despite intensive efforts of the advocates. These results suggest that RCC medical advocates can be a useful presence in the hospital emergency room, as they may be able to obtain needed resources for rape victims.

The Work of Assisting Rape Survivors in Crisis

Working in an RCC can be quite stressful for staff and volunteers. In their jobs, hot-line staff, counselors, and advocates bear witness to the pain and devastation of rape over and over again. In addition, experiences with other community agencies, such as the legal and medical systems, can be frustrating as advocates try to prevent the secondary victimization of rape survivors. As a result of this close contact, the trauma of rape reaches far beyond the lives of its primary victims to also harm those close to survivors. Research in psychology, nursing, and social work has demonstrated that husbands/significant others, family, and friends of rape survivors are also detrimentally affected by sexual assault (see Ahrens & Campbell, 2000; Davis, Taylor, & Bench, 1995). Similarly, when rape survivors turn to community systems for assistance, service providers are also emotionally touched by this crime. The staff and volunteers of RCCs can experience a variety of distressing emotions (e.g., anger, fear, sadness) as a result of their work with rape survivors.

The traumatic effect of working with survivors of violence is most commonly referred to as *secondary traumatic stress* (Dutton & Rubinstein, 1995), *vicarious traumatization* (McCann & Pearlman,

1990), or *compassion fatigue* (Figley, 1995; Joinson, 1992). Figley (1995) noted "that people can be traumatized without actually being physically harmed or threatened with harm. That is, they can be traumatized simply by learning about the traumatic event" (p. 4). The key cause of compassion fatigue is rooted in the meaning of *compassion*: a feeling of deep sympathy and sorrow for another who is stricken by suffering or misfortune, accompanied by a strong desire to alleviate the pain or remove its cause. Empathy is a major resource for trauma workers, who must use it to assess victims' problems and develop intervention approaches. Repeated exposure to this pain and the need to empathize continually with survivors' suffering produces psychological distress reactions in trauma service providers. The compassion fatigue model maintains that such distress is not only a normal part of this work, it is essential. By its very nature, the role of trauma service provider requires empathic exploration of painful material.

Consistent with the compassion fatigue model, several researchers have documented that therapists, counselors, and rape victim advocates who work with rape survivors experience many of the same reactions as do victims: anxiety, fear, exaggerated startle response, difficulty sleeping, nightmares, and physical health problems (e.g., gastrointestinal distress, repeated headaches). For example, Schauben and Frazier (1995) studied 220 female counselors and learned that as the percentage of therapists' caseloads devoted to treating sexual assault victims increased, counselors reported more posttraumatic stress symptoms. Similarly, Tyra (1979) and Eberth (1989) found that volunteer rape crisis counselors also reported behavioral, somatic, and psychological reactions to their work. Yet, there is a functional role of these negative emotions. For instance, Wasco and Campbell (2000) noted that although rape victim advocates experience a variety of distressing emotions in their work (e.g., sadness, fear, anger), they also engage in a variety of adaptive coping strategies to respond to those stresses. Advocates used cathartic strategies to vent or release these feelings. In addition, advocates focused on the positive aspects of their work and the difference they were able to make in the lives of rape survivors. Similarly, Campbell (1996) found that rape victim advocates are able to withstand the stresses of this kind of work because of the personal satisfaction of assisting rape survivors. Wasco and Campbell (2000) argued that the emotions rape advocates feel as a result of their work are resources for strength and social change. Although these feelings can be distressing, most advocates find useful ways to cope with these emotions and use them as catalysts for their work.

Rape Crisis Centers' Effectiveness

Effects on Rape Survivors

Although RCCs have existed since the 1970s, few studies have explicitly examined if and how their services benefit survivors. In many respects, both researchers and antirape activists have assumed that RCCs help survivors precisely because the job of rape victim advocate is to intervene and prevent victim-blaming harm to survivors. RCC advocates appear to be successful in helping victims obtain needed resources from community sys-

tems (see Campbell, 1998; Campbell & Bybee, 1997). Yet, this evidence provides only indirect support for rape-crisis effectiveness, because neither study compared outcomes of victims who did and did not receive help from victim advocates. Thus, one approach to studying the effectiveness of RCC services would be to assess how victims benefit (or do not benefit) as a function of receiving advocacy services. Would the survivors who received RCC advocacy services be better off than those who did not?

As a first step in addressing this question, Campbell et al. (1999) interviewed 102 rape survivors in an urban metropolitan area about their post-rape experiences with various community agencies. This sample was carefully recruited through a variety of neighborhood contexts (e.g., public transportation, bookstores, coffee shops, beauty/nail salons, currency exchanges) to maximize racial/ethnic diversity as well as to ensure hearing from women who did and did not report the assault to community agencies, including RCCs. Consistent with prior studies, most victims in this study had not reported the assault to the criminal justice system, sought medical care, or obtained mental health services (only 39% had contact with the legal system, 43% sought medical care, and 39% obtained mental health services). Only one in five victims had worked with an RCC advocate. These varied reporting/contacting rates allow for direct comparisons between victims who did and did not receive RCC services. Campbell et al. (1999) replicated the results of other researchers (e.g., Madigan & Gamble, 1991; Ullman, 1996; Williams, 1984) who found that, overall, rape victims receive little help from the criminal justice system, and this victim-blaming contact tends to be quite distressing for survivors. This effect was far more pronounced for victims of non-stranger rape (i.e., acquaintance rape, date rape, marital rape), who were at particular risk for secondary victimization. Yet, working with an RCC advocate was associated with reduced victim distress (Wasco, Campbell, Barnes, & Ahrens, 1999). This same pattern of findings emerged for victims' experiences with the medical system. In other words, non-stranger rape victims were at considerable risk for poor treatment by legal and medical system personnel, but acquaintance, date, and marital rape victims who worked with RCC advocates experienced significantly less distress than those who did not have the assistance of an advocate. Taken together with the findings from Campbell (1998) and Campbell and Bybee (1997), this work suggests that RCC advocates are quite successful in helping victims obtain needed services and buffering victims from victim-blaming system personnel.

Effects on Society at Large

Throughout the 1980s and 1990s, RCCs have been challenged by federal, state, and local funders, some academic researchers, and other community service providers to "prove" that they are effective. On one hand, such challenges appear somewhat absurd: RCCs are helping rape victims; educating police, prosecutor, and hospital staff; making public service announcements about rape; encouraging victims to report rape; and lobbying legislatures to change rape laws. How can these efforts be viewed as less than effective? On the other hand, it is not uncommon for small, local social movement organizations, such as RCCs, to have trouble proving that they are effective

(Ferree & Martin, 1995; Katzenstein, 1987; Martin, 1990). Often small in size, dependent on volunteers for their labor power, and vulnerable in terms of human and material resources, RCCs have had little organizational time to devote to formal program evaluation (Byington et al., 1991; Campbell et al., 1998). Furthermore, their primary work is often behind the scenes and, given their political goals, RCCs are frequently unable to take credit for their achievements (Schmitt & Martin, 1999).

Evaluating how RCCs affect society at large is a far more complicated task than determining how the provision of services benefits individual survivors' recovery outcomes. Staggenborg (1995) provided a conceptual framework for understanding the society-level impact of social movement organizations, such as RCCs. Social movement effectiveness must take into account a movement's fluidity (that is, its changeability) and the fact that many movement organizations fail. However, the failure of a particular organization does not equate to a movement's failure. Movement organizations that fail can change their environments by leaving behind legacies, which make future mobilizing work possible. Thus, a particular RCC can fail and still in the end change its host community. Effectiveness must be evaluated over a substantial period of time, and researchers and policy makers must resist the impulse to declare a closed RCC a failure. Staggenborg (1995) argued that a movement's effectiveness should be gauged by its impact on its host society:

> Feminist organizations can be effective at the same time that they self-destruct as organizations and fail to achieve changes in public policy. Groups that are unsuccessful in terms of organiza-

tional maintenance and policy outcomes may be effective as the centers of movement communities and as the originators of cultural changes. Although the successes of many feminist organizations tend to be hidden, they are likely to have an impact on subsequent rounds of collective action. The women's movement is perpetuated not only by its movement organizations but also by its cultural achievements. (p. 353)

Most debates about effectiveness of social movements and movement organizations focus on whether a movement changed society in the ways it preferred. Gamson (1990, 1992) defined social movement success somewhat modestly as "acceptance of a challenging group as a legitimate representative of a constituency by the target of collective action . . . and new advantages won by a challenger" (cited by Staggenborg, 1995, p. 140). Mueller (1987) gauges a movement's effectiveness in terms of its influence on culture in the form of collective consciousness—the awareness and understanding of themes the movement promotes. She argued that the radical feminist women's movement successfully introduced new ideas, values, and practices into mainstream U.S. culture in ways that have made society's collective consciousness sympathetic to many feminist ideals.

Building on these and related discussions of social movement effectiveness, Staggenborg (1995) recommended viewing social movements as having multiple outcomes: (a) political and policy outcomes, (b) mobilization outcomes, and (c) cultural outcomes. First, *political and policy outcomes* refer to a movement's ability to bring about "substantive changes through the political system" (p. 341). That is, successful movements are able to influence political decision makers and implementers to adopt policies, laws, and/or regulations that the movement promotes. From this perspective, the U.S. antirape movement has been quite successful. Since the mid 1970s, all 50 states have dramatically reformed their rape statutes, removing many of the barriers victims used to face when attempting prosecution (e.g., defense attorneys are no longer allowed to extensively question victims about their prior sexual experiences) (Berger, Searles, & Neuman, 1988; Fischer, 1989). In addition, most jurisdictions now allow expert testimony in rape cases on Rape Trauma Syndrome (RTS) to explain to judges and juries how victims are harmed by sexual assault (Fischer, 1989). Much of the credit for these legal reforms goes to the grassroots organizing efforts of RCCs. For example, Schmitt and Martin's (1999) study of a Southern California RCC documents how the center successfully influenced state legislators to pass laws that eliminated a requirement for victims to prove that they physically resisted their attacker. Similarly, Martin et al. (1992) studied how one Florida RCC built relationships with 14 other organizations throughout the state to institute a variety of legal reforms that benefit victimized people.

Second, Staggenborg (1995) defined *mobilization outcomes* as an ability to carry out collective action (e.g., mobilize people and other resources to support movement aims). Again, there is ample evidence indicating that RCCs have been successful in fund-raising, letter-writing campaigning, and organization of community functions (the specific tactics for such mobilization are covered in a later section of this chapter). A key index of the antirape movement's mobilization efforts was the passage of the 1994 federal Violence Against Women Act (VAWA). Together with advocates for battered women and abused children, antirape activists secured millions of dollars in federal funding for services and prevention programs. Similarly, the number of RCCs in the United States and the budgets supporting those centers appear to be steadily increasing (see Martin, 1999), not decreasing as some have suggested (Harvey 1985; Jensen & Karpos, 1993). On a more local level, RCCs continue to be effective organizers for violence-against-women demonstrations, such as the Take Back the Night March and the Clothesline Project (see Campbell & Ahrens, 1998). Schmitt and Martin (1999) described how one RCC in California obtained vast material resources—money, talent, filmmaking equipment, and skills—from the Hollywood entertainment industry to launch a national campaign against acquaintance rapes on college and university campuses.

Finally, *cultural outcomes* refer to a social movement's capacity to change a host society's values. As Mueller (1987) described, these values include "social norms, behaviors, and ways of thinking among a public that extends beyond movement constituents or beneficiaries . . . [and the] creation of a collective consciousness among groups such as women" (p. 341). The antirape movement has raised public awareness about all forms of violence against women, but it has had particular success in gaining recognition for forms of non-stranger rape— acquaintance, date, and marital rape—as being serious crimes (see Koss, 1990, 1992, 1993). Perhaps one of the most ironic sources of support for the cultural

impact of RCCs comes from national data on the number of reported rapes in the United States. Jensen and Karpos (1993) paid a backhanded compliment when they claimed that RCCs have influenced women to increase—they say "inflate"— reports of acquaintance rape. Their evidence of inflated reports is quite weak, but nevertheless, there does appear to be a substantial increase in the number of reported non-stranger rapes throughout the past two decades. Orcutt and Faison (1988) argued that sex-role attitude changes and community education efforts of RCCs explain increased reporting to officials. Increased reporting reflects broader social awareness about sexual assault. Making rapes known to legal-justice officials takes rape out of the closet, acknowledges it as a crime, and directs attention to the prosecution of assailants. The cultural effectiveness of RCCs is reflected by more women and girls reporting more instances of rapes more often than they previously did.

Mobilizing Strategies and Tactics

The individual and societal level effectiveness of RCCs is achieved through extensive community organizing and mobilization strategies. Social movement mobilizing is the marshaling of human, material, and symbolic resources on behalf of a movement's aims (see Schmitt & Martin, 1999). Strategies are general approaches, such as favoring public protests or educating the public, whereas tactics refer to specific activities such as teaching high school health classes about rape or drafting rape legislation. In this section, we identify strategies and tactics used by RCCs to mobilize their home communities.

Assisting Mainstream Organizations

In contrast to the "stand outside and allocate blame" strategy used by many early (and most radical) RCCs (e.g., publicly condemning practices by mainstream organizations), today's RCCs use a strategy of "occupy and indoctrinate" (Martin, 1999; Schmitt & Martin, 1999). This strategy entails gaining entry to the legal-justice and medical-therapeutic networks of a community and making themselves useful by helping mainstream organizations with their work. RCCs provide assistance by training police recruits about rape, teaching health education courses in public schools, teaching prosecutors about how to question victims and assailants, and writing legislation for legislative staff (see also Campbell & Ahrens, 1998). As Schmitt and Martin (1999) concluded, training staff of mainstream organizations is an effective way to occupy and indoctrinate.

Conducting Educational Campaigns

To inform the public and specific target groups about rape, many RCCs develop and distribute, often free of charge, materials about rape to the media. The Southern California RCC studied by Schmitt and Martin (1999) developed a film, posters, and public service announcements (PSAs), which it made available to the public in its city, state, and the nation. They sold 6,000 copies of the film at cost (for $50) and gave away the posters and PSAs. Similarly, RCCs have developed rape awareness and prevention programs for public schools (see Lonsway, 1996). RCC's educational efforts are also evident in the expert advice and testimony that center staff provide to various community groups such as the media, government, and private sector, who turn to them for information on violence against women (Fischer, 1989).

Developing Community Connections

In the past 5 years, several new service programs have emerged in a handful of RCCs throughout the country because of extensive, long-term community connections between RCCs and other community agencies (see Campbell & Ahrens, 1998). For example, in some areas, rape crisis counseling is readily available at churches and substance abuse treatment centers (Campbell & Ahrens, 1998). In addition, more communities are offering victims an alternative to traditional emergency room-based medical care: Sexual Assault Nurse Examiner (SANE) [See *Special Topic* by Linda E. Ledray, this volume] programs provide post-rape health care by a specially trained nurse in a safe, comfortable environment (e.g., a community clinic or a separate area of the hosptial/emergency room) (Ahrens et al., 2000; Ledray, 1999). Similarly, Martin's (1999) research on five Florida communities suggests that RCCs are often a hub in their communities, bringing together other community groups to develop new programs or improve existing services. RCCs have created a niche for themselves, and they exercise considerable influence on mainstream organizations and systems in their communities.

Conclusions

RCCs appear to be a permanent or at least long-term manifestation of the radical feminist women's movement. The structure and function of RCCs have changed over time, and many no longer resemble the feminist collectives of the early antirape movement. Yet, the passions of center staff and volunteers to empower survivors and educate society to end violence against women remain steadfast. Our analysis of RCCs suggests that they have been remarkably flexible and innovative: They have withstood changing political climates and continue to improve services for victims. As a case in point, RCCs were a major force in the early 1980s for establishing standardized post-rape emergency room medical care for victims (i.e., the rape kit, see Martin & DiNitto, 1987; Martin et al., 1985). In the late 1990s, RCCs continued to lead the way in developing more personalized care for survivors, as they have organized alternative programs to emergency room-based care (i.e., SANE programs; see Ledray, 1999). The ability of RCCs to establish programs and continue to revise and improve on them—even if such improvements require radical alterations of their previous work—reflects ongoing commitment to help victims and change society's tolerance of rape. RCCs have been effective not only in healing survivors but also in challenging dominant social institutions—the legal, medical, and mental health systems—to address sexist practices. The enduring contribution of the antirape movement has been raising the collective consciousness of society to understand violence against women as a political issue in need of political action.

References

Ahrens, C. E., & Campbell, R. (in press). The effects of assisting victim recovery from rape. *Journal of Interpersonal Violence, 15,* 959-986.

Ahrens, C. E., Campbell, R., Wasco, S. M., Aponte, G., Grubstein, L., & Davidson, W. S. (2000). Sexual assault nurse examiner programs: An alternative approach to medical service delivery for rape victims. *Journal of Interpersonal Violence, 15,* 921-943.

Berger, R. J., Searles, P., & Neuman, W. L. (1988). The dimensions of rape reform legislation. *Law and Society Review, 22,* 329-357.

Bordt, R. (1997). *The structure of women's nonprofit organizations.* Bloomington: Indiana University Press.

Byington, D. B., Martin, P. Y., DiNitto, D. M., & Maxwell, M. S. (1991). Organizational affiliation and effectiveness: The case of rape crisis centers. *Administration in Social Work, 15,* 83-103.

Campbell, R. (1996). *The community response to rape: An ecological conception of victims' experiences.* Unpublished dissertation, Michigan State University, East Lansing.

Campbell, R. (1998). The community response to rape: Victims' experiences with the legal, medical, and mental health systems. *American Journal of Community Psychology, 26,* 355-379.

Campbell, R., & Ahrens, C. E. (1998). Innovative community services for rape victims: An application of multiple case study methodology. *American Journal of Community Psychology, 26,* 537-571.

Campbell, R., Baker, C. K., & Mazurek, T. (1998). Remaining radical? Organizational predictors of rape crisis centers' social change initiatives. *American Journal of Community Psychology, 26,* 465-491.

Campbell, R., & Bybee, D. (1997). Emergency medical services for rape victims: Detecting the cracks in service delivery. *Women's Health, 3,* 75-101.

Campbell, R., Sefl, T., Barnes, H. E., Ahrens, C. E., Wasco, S. M., & Zaragoza-Diesfeld, Y. (1999). Community services for rape survivors: Enhancing psychological well-being or increasing trauma? *Journal of Consulting and Clinical Psychology, 67,* 847-858.

Collins, B. G., & Whalen, M. B. (1989). The rape crisis movement: Radical or reformist? *Social Work, 34,* 61-63.

Davis, R., Taylor, B., & Bench, S. (1995). Impact of sexual and nonsexual assault on secondary victims. *Violence & Victims, 10,* 73-84.

DiMaggio, P. J., & Powell, W. W. (1991). Introduction. In W. W. Powell & P. J. DiMaggio (Eds.), *The new institutionalization in organizational analysis* (pp. 1-38). Chicago: University of Chicago Press.

Dutton, M. A., & Rubinstein, F. L. (1995). Working with people with PTSD: Research implications. In C. R. Figley (Ed.), *Compassion fatigue: Coping with secondary traumatic stress disorder in those who treat the traumatized* (pp. 82-100). New York: Brunner/Mazel.

Eberth, L. D. (1989). *The psychological impact of rape crisis counseling on volunteer counselors.* Unpublished dissertation, The Wright Institute.

Ferree, M. M., & Martin, P. Y. (1995). Introduction. In M. M. Ferree & P. Y. Martin (Eds.), *Feminist organizations: Harvest of the new women's movement.* Philadelphia: Temple University Press.

Figley, C. R. (1995). Compassion fatigue as secondary traumatic stress disorder: An overview. In C. R. Figley (Ed.), *Compassion fatigue: Coping with secondary traumatic stress disorder in those who treat the traumatized* (pp. 1-20). New York: Brunner/Mazel.

Fischer, K. (1989). Defining the boundaries of admissible expert testimony on rape trauma syndrome. *University of Illinois Law Review,* pp. 691-734.

Frazier, P. A., & Haney, B. (1996). Sexual assault cases in the legal system: Police, prosecutor, and victim perspectives. *Law and Human Behavior, 20,* 607-628.

Frohmann, L. (1991). Discrediting victims' allegations of sexual assault: Prosecutorial accounts of case rejections. *Social Problems, 38,* 213-226.

Gamson, W. A. (1990). *The strategy of social protest* (2nd ed.). Belmont, CA: Wadsworth.

Gamson, W. A. (1992). *Talking politics.* New York: Cambridge University Press.

Golding, J. M., Siegel, J. M., Sorenson, S. B., Burnam, M. A., & Stein, J. A. (1989). Social support sources following sexual assault. *Journal of Community Psychology, 17,* 92-107.

Gornick, J., Burt, M. R., & Pittman, K. J. (1985). Structure and activities of rape crisis centers in the early 1980s. *Crime & Delinquency, 31,* 247-268.

Harvey, M. (1985). *Exemplary rape crisis program: Cross-site analysis and case studies.* Washington, DC: National Center for the Prevention and Control of Rape.

Jensen, G. F., & Karpos, M. (1993). Managing rape: Exploratory research on the behavior of rape statistics. *Criminology, 31,* 363-385.

Joinson, C. (1992). Coping with compassion fatigue. *Nursing, 22,* 116-122.

Katzenstein, M. F. (1987). Comparing the feminist movements of the United States and Western Europe: An overview. In M. F. Katzenstein & C. M. Mueller (Eds.), *Women's movements of the United States and Western Europe: Consciousness, political opportunity, and public policy* (pp. 3-20). Philadelphia: Temple University Press.

Koss, M. P. (1990). The women's mental health research agenda: Violence against women. *American Psychologist, 43,* 374-380.

Koss, M. P. (1992). Defending date rape. *Journal of Interpersonal Violence, 7,* 122-126.

Koss, M. P. (1993). Rape: Scope, impact, interventions, and public policy responses. *American Psychologist, 48,* 1062-1069.

Koss, M. P., & Harvey, M. R. (1991). *The rape victim: Clinical and community interventions.* Newbury Park, CA: Sage.

Ledray, L. E. (1999). *Sexual assault nurse examiners (SANE): Development and operations guide.* Washington, DC: Department of Justice, Office for Victims of Crime.

Lonsway, K. A. (1996). Preventing acquaintance rape through education: What do we know? *Psychology of Women Quarterly, 20,* 229-265.

Madigan, L., & Gamble, N. (1991). *The second rape: Society's continued betrayal of the victim.* New York: Lexington.

Martin, P. Y. (1990). Rethinking feminist organizations. *Gender & Society, 4,* 182-206.

Martin, P. Y. (1997). Gender, accounts, and rape processing work. *Social Problems, 44,* 464-82.

Martin, P. Y. (1999).*Rape processing work in organization and community context.* Unpublished manuscript, Florida State University, Department of Sociology.

Martin, P. Y., & DiNitto, D. (1987). The rape exam: Beyond the hospital ER. *Women and Health, 12,* 5-28.

Martin, P. Y., DiNitto, D., Byington, D., & Maxwell, M. S. (1992). Organizational and community transformation: The case of a rape crisis center. *Administration in Social Work, 16,* 123-145.

Martin, P. Y., DiNitto, D., Harrison, D., & Maxwell, S. M. (1985). Controversies surrounding the rape kit exam in the 1980s: Issues and alternatives. *Crime and Delinquency, 31,* 223-246.

Martin, P. Y., & Powell, M. R. (1994). Accounting for the "second assault": Legal organizations' framing of rape victims. *Law and Social Inquiry, 19,* 853-890.

Matoesian, G. M. (1993). *Reproducing rape: Domination through talk in the courtroom.* Chicago: University of Chicago Press.

Matthews, N. A. (1994). *Confronting rape: The feminist anti-rape movement and the state.* New York: Routledge.

McCann, I. L., & Pearlman, L. A. (1990). Vicarious traumatization: A framework for understanding the psychological effects of working with victims. *Journal of Traumatic Stress, 3,* 131-149.

Mueller, C. M. (1987). Collective unconsciousness, identity transformation, and the rise of women in public office in the United States. In M. F. Katzenstein & C. M. Mueller (Eds.), *Women's movements of the United States and Western Europe: Consciousness, political opportunity, and public policy* (pp. 89-108). Philadelphia: Temple University Press.

National Victim Center. (1992). *Rape in America: A report to the nation.* Arlington, VA: Author.

Orcutt, J. D., & Faison, F. (1988). Sex-role change and reporting of rape victimization, 1973-1985. *The Sociological Quarterly, 29,* 589-604.

O'Sullivan, E. A. (1978). What has happened to rape crisis centers? A look at their structure, members, and funding. *Victimology, 3,* 45-62.

Pride, A. (1981). To respectability and back: A ten-year view of the anti-rape movement. In F. Delacoste & F. Newman (Eds.), *Fight back: Feminist resistance to male violence.* San Francisco: Cleis Press.

Schauben, L. J., & Frazier, P. A. (1995). Vicarious trauma: The effects on female counselors of working with sexual violence survivors. *Psychology of Women Quarterly, 19,* 49-64.

Schechter, S. (1982). *Women and male violence.* Boston: South End.

Schmitt, F., & Martin, P. Y. (1999). Unobtrusive mobilization by an institutionalized rape crisis center: "All we do comes from victims." *Gender & Society, 13,* 364-384.

Spalter-Roth, R., & Schreiber, R. (1995). Outsider issues and insider tactics: Strategic tensions in the women's policy network during the 1980s. In M. M. Ferree & P. Y. Martin (Eds.), *Feminist organizations: Harvest of the new women's movement* (pp. 105-127). Philadelphia: Temple University Press.

Staggenborg, S. (1995). Can feminist organizations be effective? In M. M. Ferree & P. Y. Martin (Eds.), *Feminist organizations: Harvest of the new women's movement* (pp. 339-355). Philadelphia: Temple University Press.

Tyra, P. A. (1979). *Volunteer rape counselors: Selected characteristics—empathy, attribution of responsibility, and rape counselor syndrome.* Unpublished dissertation, Boston University School of Education.

Ullman, S. (1996). Do social reactions to sexual assault victims vary by support provider? *Violence and Victims, 11,* 143-156.

Wasco, S. M., & Campbell, R. (2000). *Emotional reactions of rape victim advocates: Experiences of anger and fear in helping rape victims.* Manuscript submitted for publication.

Wasco, S. M., Campbell, R., Barnes, H., & Ahrens, C. E. (1999, June). *Rape crisis centers: Shaping survivors' experiences with community systems following sexual assault.* Paper presented at the Biennial Conference of the Society for Community Research and Action, New Haven, CT.

Williams, J. E. (1984). Secondary victimization: Confronting public attitudes about rape. *Victimology, 9,* 66-81.

SEXUAL ASSAULT NURSE EXAMINER (SANE) PROGRAM

Linda E. Ledray

The Sexual Assault Nurse Examiner (SANE) model was developed as a part of the women's movement of the 1970s to better meet the needs of rape victims with a new model for providing medical care. The first programs were developed independently in Memphis, Tennessee, in 1976 (Speck & Aiken, 1995); Minneapolis, Minnesota, in 1977 (Ledray, 1993); and Amarillo, Texas, in 1979 (Antognoli-Toland, 1985). These programs were developed by medical professionals who recognized the need for more timely, sensitive, and comprehensive medical care and forensic evidence collection for sexual assault victims. These and similar programs have since become a national model for medical and forensic care of the rape victim (Ledray, 1998).

Sexual Assault Nurse Examiners (SANEs) are specially trained nurses who are on call to specified emergency departments, medical clinics, community agencies, or independent SANE facilities. SANEs typically work as a part of a Sexual Assault Response/Resource Team (SART). The team can vary greatly in makeup and coordinates its activities in a variety of ways. It is usually composed of a rape advocate, law enforcement officer, prosecutor, and the SANE. The SANE is paged by the police or medical facility whenever a sexual assault or attempted sexual assault victim reports to the police or comes to the medical facility within a specified time after the assault, usually 72 hours. Medical evidence exams are typically not completed beyond 72 hours, as it is unlikely that evidence will be found beyond that time. It is also too late to prevent a pregnancy.

The SANE may be on call to a hospital, clinic, or free-standing facility. When the victim arrives reporting a rape or attempted rape, the SANE is paged by the hospital triage staff and comes in to complete a medical and legal examination of the rape victim. The usual response time is one hour.

This exam typically has five essential components: (a) documentation and care of injuries, (b) collection of medical-legal evidence, (c) evaluation of risk and prophylactic treatment of sexually transmitted diseases (STDs),

(d) evaluation of risk and emergency pregnancy interception, and (e) crisis intervention (Ledray, 1998).

When the SANE arrives, she begins by completing a brief medical interview to determine where to examine the victim for evidence and potential injuries. She then collects any clothing that might be used as potential evidence and completes the medical and legal examination. If there was a vaginal assault, the SANE completes a vaginal speculum exam, and when a colposcope is available, she uses it to take pictures of genital injuries. The colposcope magnifies injuries for better visualization and documentation. Because this is an expensive piece of equipment, not all SANE programs have one available at every examination site. Although the use of a colposcope is, of course, preferable, good exams can be completed without one.

Once the medical and legal evidence exam is completed, the SANE refers the victim back to the emergency room medical staff for care, if any injuries require treatment. The medical treatment is always delayed when the injuries are not life-threatening so that evidence that may otherwise be lost can be collected first. If there are no injuries requiring additional treatment, the client is discharged by the SANE. When a police report has been made, the police may be called to provide her safe transportation home, to collect the evidence, or to complete their interview with the victim, if necessary. When an advocate is present in the emergency room, she is likely to assist with arranging transportation home for the victim or finding safe housing, in addition to providing crisis intervention.

In 1992, 72 individuals from 31 programs across the United States and Canada came together in Minneapolis for the first time at a meeting hosted by the Sexual Assault Resource Service, a Minneapolis-based SANE program, and the University of Minnesota School of Nursing. At that meeting, the International Association of Forensic Nurses (IAFN) was formed (Ledray, 1996). The American Nurses' Association (ANA) first recognized forensic nursing as a new specialty in 1995 (Lynch, 1995). SANE is a subspecialty of forensic nursing. At the 1996 IAFN meeting in Kansas City, Geri Marullo, executive director of ANA, predicted that within 10 years, the Joint Commission on the Accreditation of Hospitals (JCAHO) will require every hospital to have a forensic nurse available (Marullo, 1996).

Initial SANE development was slow, with only three programs operating by the end of the 1970s; however, development is progressing rapidly today (Ledray, 1996). When the *Sexual Assault Nurse Examiner (SANE) Development and Operation Guide* was published by the Office for Victims of Crime (OVC), 116 SANE programs were identified (Ledray, 1998). This number is expected to grow much more rapidly in the years to come.

Great strides have certainly been made in the SANE medical response to meeting the needs of sexual assault victims. Yet it is important to recognize that any examination after a sexual assault can still feel invasive and be anxiety-provoking for the assault victim. No one agency can effectively meet all the needs of sexual assault survivors. Rape crisis center advocates, SANEs, law enforcement personnel, and prosecutors have recognized the benefits of collaborative efforts in their work with sexual assault survivors. That is one of the reasons why the creation of SARTs is so important.

The SART concept has been demonstrated to be an effective model for providing better services to sexual assault victims, including crisis intervention and long-term counseling, investigation, and evidence collection, as well as a more sensitive initial medical response to rape victims (Ledray, 1998). SART membership may vary depending on the community and the needs of a particular rape survivor. At the least, it should include an advocate from the local rape crisis center, a SANE (or medical personnel when a SANE program is not available), a law enforcement officer, and a prosecutor. It may also include crime laboratory personnel, domestic violence advocates, clergy, and other social service agency personnel. In some communities, a core group of these individuals, usually the advocate, SANE, and law enforcement personnel, may respond together to the emergency room, or they may simply work cooperatively to better meet the needs of sexual assault survivors and their families/ significant others.

Although each SART member or agency may have a specific focus of attention and effort, each representative's expertise can facilitate the roles of other team members. The collaborative relationship of the SART goes far beyond the initial encounter with the rape victim. For instance, by understanding why a rape victim may fear reporting the rape, then providing her with accurate data with which to make an educated decision about reporting, the SANE can facilitate follow-through with reporting and prosecution. By understanding how the medical-legal evidence is used in the courtroom to prosecute, the SANE can collect better evidence for law enforcement and likely affect the ability to charge and prosecute the rapist.

References

Antognoli-Toland, P. (1985). Comprehensive program for examination of sexual assault victims by nurses: A hospital-based project in Texas. *Journal of Emergency Nursing, 11*(3), 132-136.

Ledray, L. E. (1993). Sexual assault nurse clinician: An emerging area of nursing expertise. *AWHONN's Clinical Issues in Perinatal and Women's Health Nursing. 4*(2), 180-190.

Ledray, L. E. (1996). Sexual Assault Nurse Examiner (SANE) programs. *Journal of Emergency Nursing, October 22 (5),* 460-465.

Ledray, L. E. (1998). Sexual assault: Clinical issues, SANE, and expert testimony. *Journal of Emergency Nursing, 24*(3), 284-287.

Lynch, V. A. (1993). Clinical forensic nursing: A new perspective in the management of crime victims from trauma to trial. *Critical Care Nursing Clinics of North America, 3,* 489-507.

Marullo, G. (1996). *The future and the forensic nurse: New dimensions for the 21st century.* Paper presented at the Fourth Annual Scientific Assembly of Forensic Nurses, Kansas City, MO.

Speck, P., & Aiken, M. (1995). 20 years of community nursing service. *Tennessee Nurse, 58*(2), pp. 15-18.

CHAPTER 13

Shelters and Other Community-Based Services for Battered Women and Their Children

Cris M. Sullivan
Tameka Gillum

Although this is somewhat difficult to believe today, community-based services designed specifically to help women with abusive partners were virtually nonexistent before 1976. Prior to the 1960s, battered women found themselves in the same shelters as catastrophe victims, alcoholics, and all other homeless individuals, as their only options for shelter were the Salvation Army, church homes, and other homeless shelters. In addition, many times, these assistance centers were full and turned battered women and their children away. Most of these shelters were also insensitive to the needs of women with abusive partners, often blaming the women for their victimization (Schechter, 1982).

The first shelters for women with abusive partners developed out of the feminist movement of the 1970s, during which consciousness-raising groups led to women talking, often for the first time, about the abuse they were experiencing in their homes. Feminists, community activists, and formerly battered women began organizing to develop new ways to meet the needs of battered women and to define the problem of what came to be called *domestic violence*. Early shelters often were no more than the private homes of women who opened their doors to battered women and their children, and none initially relied on governmental funding. Later, shelters often shared facilities with local YWCAs or used institutional settings such as motels or abandoned orphanages. Often, large old houses were set up to shelter women and children. Shelter staff did their best to make these settings feel like home for these women and children. Women in the shelter worked together, sharing household duties such as cooking and cleaning. Most often, women and children shared rooms in these shelters due to limited space. The allowable stay ranged from a few days to a few months.

Within the past 25 years, however, the battered women's shelter movement has been successful in educating the public and demanding an increase in services for women with abusive partners. Today, there are over 2,000 domestic violence programs across the United States (National Research Council, 1998). Most of these programs provide emergency shelter, 24-hour crisis lines, and numerous support services. Unfortunately, the number of programs available is still much lower than the need. Shelters are less likely to be available to women in rural areas, and most struggle continually for enough money to stay open. The National Coalition Against Domestic Violence estimates that for every woman who receives shelter, three are turned away for lack of space (R. Smith, personal communication, 1999).

The Shelter Experience

Although domestic violence shelter programs are not all alike, most share certain commonalties. Most shelter stays begin with a telephone call from a woman who has either just been assaulted or who knows she is in imminent danger of being assaulted.[1] The staff person or volunteer who answers the call is trained to assess the immediacy of the situation, to provide emotional support and understanding, and to arrange for the woman to come directly to the shelter, to receive medical attention at a local hospital, or to go to the home of a friend or relative.

If the shelter volunteer determines with the woman that the best option is for the survivor to enter the shelter, arrangements are made for her to get there safely. Most shelters have a policy that they will not pick women up from their homes, as doing so could result in danger to the woman and/or shelter volunteer if the perpetrator is still present. Not picking women up at their homes also minimizes the risk of perpetrators following the car to the shelter, which is generally in a confidential location. Some shelters allow their volunteers to pick women up from hospitals, hotels, or other locations deemed safe to both the volunteer and the family. Some women can arrange their own transportation to the shelter, either driving their own cars or taking public transportation.

It is important to understand that most women choose to enter shelter programs only as a last resort. The woman has likely just experienced a traumatic event, she is in both physical and emotional pain, and, if she has children, she is trying to comfort them and think of their needs as well. Entering a brand new environment that involves living collectively with many other women and children, having little to no privacy, and abiding by numerous rules that come with such a living situation is not something most women look forward to doing. If they can stay with friends or relatives, if they can secure their homes to feel safe living there, or if they can afford to move either temporarily or permanently, these choices are generally deemed more desirable and less traumatic for women and their children. Unfortunately, many women lack the social and economic resources to choose any of these options, and for them, a shelter is the best alternative.

Policies Regarding Children

Shelter programs differ in their policies regarding allowing women's adolescent children to stay as residents as well. Although most shelters allow all children under either age 12 or 14 to stay with their mothers, some ask that women find other accommodations for their male adolescents. This regulation was created for a number of reasons. First, some boys have already grown quite tall and muscular by early to middle adolescence, and they look more like men than children. This can alarm other women and children staying in the shelter, who do not expect to see men walking the hallways. Another reason this rule exists in some shelters is that some male adolescents have become violent toward their own mothers or other residents and have been difficult to restrain. Rules regarding the older male children of residents have been difficult to create and to implement because shelters do not want to discriminate against women or their children, nor do they want to overgeneralize the problematic behaviors of some adolescents. However, they also need to ensure the safety and comfort of all residents in the shelter. Many shelters balance this dilemma by dealing with situations on a case-by-case basis. Many teenagers—both male and female—do not want to reside in the shelter anyway, and they are happy to stay with friends or relatives as an alternative. In other cases, shelters have admitted male teenagers when the woman simply will not come otherwise. Creating rules that respect the diverse needs of many adults and children living together communally is far from simple or straightforward.

Other Shelter Rules

The typical domestic violence shelter resident is under 35 years of age, with two children, little income, and few options. When she arrives at the shelter, she is likely to be assigned to a room with at least one other woman and her children. Bathrooms are shared, and residents are expected to complete household chores to keep the shelter running smoothly. These chores might include cooking the evening meal, vacuuming, dusting, or helping with child care. Women are responsible for the whereabouts of their children at all times, with some shelters providing more respite from constant child care than others. Children have bed times, and adults must be in the shelter by a certain time at night unless they call and notify the staff. This way, staff knows if beds are available as new women call needing help.

Assistance Received

The typical maximum stay at a domestic violence shelter is 30 days, although most programs offer extensions as needed. During their stay, women are provided with much more than beds, meals, and laundry facilities. Counselor advocates work individually with women to identify the family's unmet needs and help women and their children in any way possible. Women are always informed about their legal rights and are assisted in obtaining personal protection orders, if they desire. Safety plans are discussed with women, and opportunities to talk with other women both formally and informally are provided. Counselor advocates help women with other needs they may have, such as finding housing, seeking employment, or obtaining health care.

Domestic violence shelter programs have been found to be one of the most supportive, effective resources for women with abusive partners, according to the residents themselves (Bowker & Maurer, 1985; Sedlak, 1988; Straus, Gelles, & Steinmetz, 1980; Tutty, Weaver, & Rothery, 1999). Most programs provide all ser-

vices free of charge, and they were created to empower and respect women
(Ridington, 1977-1978; Schechter, 1982).
Berk, Newton, and Berk (1986) reported
that, for women who were actively attempting other strategies at the same time,
a shelter stay dramatically reduced the
likelihood of further violence. More and
more communities are recognizing the
importance of domestic violence shelter
programs and are either establishing or
expanding such services in their communities.

Although shelters receive high effectiveness ratings in general from their residents, not all women feel that shelters are
options for them, and some are distrustful
of the experiences they might have there.
Lesbian women, for example, are much
more likely to have negative shelter experiences and/or to believe that shelters are
for heterosexual women only (Irvine,
1990; Renzetti, 1992). This is due to a
number of factors. Some lesbians perceive they will be discriminated against in
shelters, whereas others fear shelters
would be unsafe because their abusers,
also being women, could gain entry more
easily than could male batterers. Some
lesbians are even battered by women who
work within the shelter movement or who
know women who work within the shelter. Many shelters are beginning to deal
with these issues of safety and discrimination, but the complexity of the problem
makes it difficult to guarantee safety for
lesbian women at this time.

Another group of people underserved
by shelters are those women under 20 or
over 60 years old (see, e.g., Berk et al.,
1986; Gondolf, 1988; Hilbert & Hilbert,
1984; Okun, 1986; Schutte, Malouff, &
Doyle, 1988; Sullivan, Tan, Basta, Rumptz,
& Davidson, 1992). A study of all Florida

shelters found that, although 27% of all
Florida residents are senior citizens, less
than 1% of shelter residents were over 60
(Vinton, 1992).

The multitude of reasons that adult
teens being abused in dating relationships
do not access shelter services include
their lack of identification as being battered or abused, their access to protection
from their families if they still live at
home, their assumption that shelters are
for married or cohabiting women only,
and the belief that their abuse will not be
taken as seriously as abuse against older
women. Abused teens under the age of 18
are prohibited from most shelters unless
they are legally emancipated. This rule,
unfortunately, means teens have even
fewer options than adults who experience
violence in their relationships.

Older women share some of the same
reasons for not accessing shelter services
(lack of identification as battered, an assumption they are in the wrong age group
and do not qualify for services), but they
also have reasons distinct to their age.
Some older women may be less aware of
services available because services were
nonexistent when they were younger.
Some may feel more embarrassment or
shame about discussing their abuse because of their membership in a generation
that did not talk about such things as
freely. Still others might have special
health or physical ability needs that they
believe may not be adequately addressed
by shelter staff.

Some women of color, regardless of
age and sexual orientation, also hesitate to
use shelters for various reasons. Many
shelters are staffed primarily by white
women, who may be insensitive to needs
and issues within cultures other than their
own. For instance, some African Ameri-

can women are more hesitant to call the police because they fear their assailants will receive racist treatment from the criminal justice system (Williams, 1981). Language barriers prevent some women from seeking shelter, as do shelter policies that are more comfortable among those from the majority culture (e.g., chores need to be done at specific times; corporal punishment of children is banned). Migrant women are often working far from their homes and face multiple language, cultural, and structural barriers preventing their use of shelter programs (Rodriguez, 1998). Immigrant women face language, cultural, and sometimes legal barriers to accessing services (Bauer, Rodriguez, Quiroga, & Flores-Ortiz, 2000; Dasgupta, 1998). Many women of color have reported that when resources were not respectful of their ethnic group, they either did not use the services or used them for only a brief period of time (Sorenson, 1996). Because of this, many domestic violence programs report underrepresentation, lack of participation, and/or low completion rates by minorities (Williams, 1992). It is important to understand the context of experiences of partner abuse by varying cultures, particularly in the area of service delivery (Williams, 1993). In addition, Anglo women need to educate themselves about the different needs of all shelter residents, and shelter staff need to reflect the population whom they are serving.

Domestic Violence Programs Within Communities of Color

In response to the need for culturally specific services for survivors of domestic violence, an increasing number of domestic violence shelter programs are being designed specifically by and for women from their own communities. One example is the Asian Women's Shelter in San Francisco, California. The first domestic violence center to specifically serve the Asian and Asian American community, the shelter offers, among other things, a multilingual access model, which addresses the issue of language barriers that many Asian women face in seeking services from other shelters. Shelter services also are respectful of the values and traditions held by many Asian and Asian American women. For some Asian women, leaving an abusive man means leaving her children, family, and entire social network, as the act of leaving may not be respected by her larger community. To best help and assist women faced with difficult life choices, it is important to understand the cultural barriers, as well as the cultural strengths and supports, that are important components of women's experiences.

Another example of a culturally specific family violence intervention program is Asha Family Services, Inc., in Milwaukee, Wisconsin. Many programs developed and staffed by Anglo women specifically exclude any programs directed toward male perpetrators. Some in the African American community, however, believe it important to employ a holistic family approach, meaning that services are available for the batterer, the survivor, and the children and services are designed to promote the healing of mind, body, and spirit. Founded in 1989 to meet this need of the African American community, Asha Family Services is a nonprofit, spiritually based family violence intervention and prevention agency. The program strives to provide effective and comprehensive family violence intervention and prevention services. The agency also holds a state license as an outpatient mental health and substance abuse treatment facility.

Programs have also been designed to meet the needs of the Latina community more adequately. One such program, the Latina Domestic Violence Program of Congreso de Latinos Unidos, Inc., located in Philadelphia, Pennsylvania, is a community-based program offering services to Latina survivors of domestic violence. The program's services include court accompaniment and translation and expertise in international and territorial legal issues. It is important to note that interventions designed to target the Latina community should also have services available for Latino perpetrators, in addition to services for women and children. This is important because the community, in general, is family oriented. Respect for and loyalty to the family, as well as family unity, are strong values in this community. Traditionally, if a woman is to comply with treatment, a male figure in the home must be involved (Torres, 1998). In the case of survivors, this is the male partner. Hence, programs serving this community must recognize and be respectful of these values and provide services that are inclusive of the male perpetrators for those Latinas who need or want their partners to be involved.

One program that provides support services specifically to Native American battered women and their children is the Lac du Flambeau Domestic Abuse Program of Lac du Flambeau, Wisconsin. This program offers emergency transportation to and shelter at the statewide Native American shelter, support groups, individual counseling, advocacy, a 24-hour crisis line, restraining order assistance, domes-

tic abuse education, follow-up planning, community education, a Children's Services project, and transitional living. All services are provided by Native Americans, honoring the traditions and strengths of the Native community.

Another group of women excluded from most mainstream domestic violence programs in the United States is migrant farm workers. Migrant women, by necessity, are transient, unable to stay in one location for an extended period of time without losing their livelihood. Their children often work alongside them and may be prevented from fleeing with the women by their abusive partners. In 1995, the Lideres Campesinas Domestic Violence Outreach and Education Project was developed to meet the specific needs of migrant women being abused by partners and ex-partners. Through the collaborative efforts of the Centers for Disease Control, Lideres Campesinas, and the Migrant Clinicians' Network, this project was designed to assist migrant farm worker women to share information and resources. A select number of migrant farm worker women receive extensive training in domestic violence issues, legal options, and available services, and they then pass that information along to others through a variety of creative means. For example, information is shared at bus stops, in beauty shops, in the fields, and in stores. In the first year of the project, 17,000 migrant workers in California received information and assistance. The program's efforts continue to grow, and partnerships with service providers ensure that migrant farm worker women receive the attention, knowledge, and services they need in a culturally competent way (Rodriguez, 1998).

These projects are just a sampling of the culturally specific domestic violence service programs available across the United States. As both funding and cultural awareness increase, such programs are expected to expand in number and in scope.

Expansion of Services Within Domestic Violence Shelter Programs

The general public is often still under the misconception that the majority of domestic violence programs offer only crisis lines and residential (shelter) services. Although this may have been true when programs were beginning, today most domestic violence programs offer an array of services for women with abusive partners. These services include but are not limited to support groups for women who are not residing at the shelter, advocacy services, individual and group counseling, programs geared specifically toward children, referrals to other community-based services, and financial assistance.

Rainbow House (Chicago, Illinois) is just one example of a shelter program offering an array of services to both residents and nonresidents. In addition to residential services, Rainbow House offers intervention services to abused pregnant teens and their children; a comprehensive program of age-appropriate activities for preschool children; services to meet the educational needs and goals of teenage residents; health advocacy services; legal advocacy services; housing advocacy services; bilingual English/Spanish services; individual, family, and group counseling; employment assistance; children's services; and substance abuse prevention and education.

Domestic violence service programs have continually expanded their services over the years to better meet the diverse and complex needs of women escaping abusive partners. One innovation that is gaining popularity in many communities is transitional housing options. Lack of decent, affordable housing continues to be a problem for many women using domestic violence residential services (Correia, 1999; Sullivan et al., 1992), due in part to insufficient housing in many communities but also due to the fact that most shelters expect residents to leave within 30 days. This need has led more and more programs to create transitional housing alternatives in their communities. Transitional housing programs are designed to help survivors and their children as they make the transition from a domestic violence shelter to a more permanent residence. Such housing often is provided in apartment units where women can live for a set period of time or until they can obtain permanent housing. Women who live in these facilities pay only a small percentage of their income for rent. Some programs only allow women to stay 2 months, but it is more typical that women and their children can stay 18 to 24 months. Many transitional housing programs include other support services such as counseling, housing assistance, and employment assistance.

One model transitional housing program is Middle Way House, Inc., in Bloomington, Indiana. In 1998, Middle Way House opened a 28-unit facility for low-income battered women and their children. Each family that enters the program is assigned a case manager to work with throughout their stay. Additional services offered through this program include support groups, 24-hour child care, legal advocacy, parenting workshops, employment assistance, and community activities. Families can stay up to 2 years, and rent is determined by family income.

Another innovative program that some domestic violence agencies are now providing is the visitation center. Many batterers are able to maintain contact with women—and continue their abuse after a relationship has ended—through access to the children they have in common. Abusive men are often legally entitled to visit with their children, and they can use those visits to harass and harm their ex-partners. In response to this, a number of domestic violence programs have opened visitation centers where contact between the parents is minimized and the children are protected. These centers are designed in such a way that women do not have to have contact with their abusive ex-partners. Often, the women enter through one entrance of the building whereas the fathers enter through another. A neutral mediator (usually a center worker) takes the children to the visitation area and later returns them to their mother. All exchange between the two parties takes place through the center workers (McMahon & Pence, 1995)

The Duluth, Minnesota, Visitation Center, a model program that opened in 1989, is located in a YWCA building and includes family rooms, play areas, and a gym. In cases where abusive men have been granted unsupervised visitation by the courts, the visitation center can serve as a dropoff/pick-up site for parents. Women can bring their children in one door, while men use a separate door in a different section of the building. Staff oversees the exchange of the children and can ensure that perpetrators and victims do not have contact. In cases where batterers have been granted supervised visitation by the courts, staff remain in the same room with fathers and their children and are available to intervene if necessary to keep children safe (McMahon & Pence, 1995).

Expanding Services to Children of Women With Abusive Partners

As mentioned earlier, the majority of women using domestic violence shelter program services have children accompanying them (Jaffe, Wolfe, & Wilson, 1990). Until recent years, however, many programs had no services available specifically targeted toward children's needs. Lack of funding and human resources forced many domestic violence programs to focus exclusively on the women using their services. Today, many domestic violence agencies have comprehensive children's programs, including support groups, counseling, play rooms, and educational resources. The Women's Center and Shelter of Greater Pittsburgh, Pennsylvania, is one example of a program that offers an extensive array of services to children. Their children's program provides services to children of both shelter residents and nonresidents. These services include child care offered 9 a.m. to 8:30 p.m. Monday through Friday, age-appropriate structured activities for children in groups; school enrollment assistance, information and referrals to other agencies, weekly concurrent support groups for mothers and children, medical and dental screenings through the Healthy Tomorrows program; afterschool and summer recreation programs; and individual and systems advocacy.

A common intervention program for children exposed to domestic violence is the domestic violence support and education group. Groups generally run 10 to 12 weeks, and the curriculum is age-appropriate. Sessions include serious topics as well as fun activities and snacks, and children learn about labeling feelings, dealing with anger, and honing their safety skills. One evaluation of such a program revealed that children learned strategies for protection in times of emergency and regarded their parents in a more positive light. Mothers also reported a positive change in their children's behavioral adjustment (Jaffe, Wilson, & Wolfe, 1989). Gruszinski, Brink, and Edleson (1988) conducted a similar study, based on 371 children who attended a program over a 4-year period. They found that children improved their self-concepts, understood that violence in the home was not their fault, became more aware of protection planning, and learned new ways of resolving conflict without resorting to violence. Although the majority of support and education groups for children are currently being operated within domestic violence programs, most are open to children regardless of whether they are staying at the shelter.

Non-Shelter-Based Community Services for Battered Women and Their Children

Many services for battered women and their children are being offered not just within domestic violence programs but within a variety of systems throughout communities. Programs are growing in health care settings, in police stations and prosecutors' offices, in family service organizations, and on college campuses, just to name a few.

Programs in Health Care Settings

About 1.5 million women seek medical treatment for injuries sustained from abusive partners each year (Straus, 1986).

Unfortunately, physicians and nurses have traditionally received inadequate training to identify and assist victims of domestic violence appropriately (Stark & Flitcraft, 1988; Warshaw, 1993). Some hospitals and clinics have begun to address intimate male violence against women as a health issue and have initiated special training, protocols, and programs to respond to survivors of domestic abuse effectively.

AWAKE (Advocacy for Women and Kids in Emergencies) was the first program within a pediatric setting to link assistance for battered women with clinical services for their children. The program has its own satellite office in the Family Development Clinic at Children's Hospital in Boston, Massachusetts. Through this program, battered women and their children are paired with an advocate who assists them with everything from legal issues to safety planning. In 1994, the program expanded its services to include bilingual/bicultural advocates, who provide services at a health center located in a Jamaica Plains public housing development. The program also provides training to medical staff at Children's Hospital and the Martha Eliot Health Center, as well as across the state and the nation.

Another early domestic violence program in a public hospital was the Hospital Crisis Intervention Project founded at Chicago's Cook County Hospital in 1992. Staff and volunteers offer immediate assistance to battered women in the hospital and also train hospital staff to properly identify and treat domestic violence victims. In response to the cultural diversity of the patient population in Chicago, a multicultural staff is available to provide services in seven languages.

The Medical Advocacy Project at Mercy Hospital in Pittsburgh is unique in that the hospital offers an apartment on hospital grounds for survivors when local shelters are at capacity. In addition, all women who come through the emergency room are screened for domestic violence, and a full-time advocate is on staff to assist survivors.

Programs Located Within the Criminal Justice System

As laws and policies pertaining to domestic violence have improved, more women have contacted the criminal justice system for help in protecting themselves and their children. In response to this, some communities have implemented programs within police stations, prosecutors' offices, or legal offices to reach women in need of legal assistance, legal advocacy, and/or direct assistance.

One such response is a first-response team, which can but does not necessarily need to be housed within the criminal justice system. One first-response team, the Capital Area Response Effort (CARE), has been operating in mid-Michigan since 1995. When arrests are made in cases of domestic violence, the police call CARE, and two volunteers go to the home of the victim to offer immediate support and assistance. Depending on the need, volunteers can refer women to local shelter programs, inform them about the legal process that has begun, offer referrals, or simply provide immediate emotional support. As needed, CARE volunteers also provide advocacy and accompaniment through the legal process. CARE is housed within a police department but staffed by domestic violence advocates. The staff is overseen by an advisory board comprising police, prosecutors, service providers, and others from the community.

Although a first-response team can provide immeasurable assistance to women after the police have been called, such help is limited if the police, prosecutors, judges, and probation officers are not cooperative in holding perpetrators accountable for their behavior. In response to this, an increasing number of communities have designed what the Minneapolis Domestic Abuse Project first termed community intervention projects (CIPs). Under many different names across the country, these projects involve coordinating criminal justice system and community efforts to respond more effectively to domestic violence. The police agree to contact the CIP after responding to a domestic violence call, and perpetrators are held in jail for a set period of time (usually at least overnight). The CIP then sends female volunteers to the survivor's home and sends male volunteers to visit the perpetrator in jail. Survivors are given information, referrals, and transportation to a shelter, if needed, and perpetrators are encouraged to accept responsibility for their actions and to attend a batterer intervention program. Prosecutors agree to pursue domestic violence charges aggressively, and judges agree to order presentence investigations and to mandate jail time and/or batterer intervention. Probation officers also play an important role in this coordination. They agree to incorporate the perpetrator's violent history and the survivor's wishes in the pre-sentence investigation, and they hold perpetrators accountable if they do not attend their mandatory batterer intervention meetings.

There is some evidence that CIPs result in increased safety for survivors of domestic violence. One study found that CIPs resulted in increased arrests, increased successful prosecutions, and a larger number of perpetrators being mandated to attend batterer intervention programs (Gamache, Edleson, & Schock, 1988). Another study found that when police action was coordinated with other systems—a critical component of coordinated community intervention—perpetrators were significantly less likely to reoffend (Steinman, 1990). Equally important, when police action was *not* coordinated with other components of the system, perpetrators actually seemed to increase their use of violence against women.

Not all CIPs are identical, and some are much more comprehensive than others. Not all communities have gained the cooperation of all necessary players (police, prosecutors, judges, probation officers, and advocates), but thousands of communities have adapted components of this model, with varying degrees of success.

Programs Developed Through Family or Social Service Agencies

As more community members learn that domestic violence is a social problem requiring a comprehensive community response, programs are developing through a wider network of social service agencies. In 1980, for example, Dove, Inc. (Decatur, Illinois), a nonprofit social services agency organized by area churches as a cooperative community ministry, began its own domestic violence program. This program has developed an array of projects and services for battered women and their children, including support groups at schools for teenage survivors,

art therapy, support groups for lesbian and gay survivors, and HIV/AIDS education and support.

Other programs have been developed with the goal of preventing children of battered women from being placed in foster care, thus keeping battered women and their children together. One such program is Families First, located in and funded by the state of Michigan. Among the families eligible for the services are those with children at risk of homelessness or harm because of domestic violence but not yet at imminent risk of removal from the home because of abuse or neglect. Services of this program include assistance with relocation to safe housing; legal and medical advocacy; employment assistance; help developing safety plans; provision of transportation, clothing, and other concrete services; up to $300 to each family to aid with tangible needs; and facilitation of other ongoing social services to the families after Families First services have ended.

Programs Developed Through Universities

In 1994, Michigan State University became the first university to establish and fund its own on-campus domestic violence shelter and education program. One of the largest campuses in the country, Michigan State recognized that universities are communities unto themselves and, as such, experience the same social problems that other communities face. Their program, which includes shelter services, advocacy, counseling, support groups, and community education, serves as a prototype for other academic settings.

Michigan State University also houses a community advocacy program for battered women and their children. With funding from the National Institute of Mental Health as well as local support, female undergraduate students are trained through the community psychology program to work as community advocates for battered women and their children. This project, started in 1986, involves a collaborative relationship between the university and community-based organizations. Students earn college credits for participating, and battered women and their children receive free advocacy and support services. Students work in the community and are trained to provide advocacy across a variety of areas, including but not limited to housing, employment, education, transportation, child care, health care, legal assistance, and social support. An experimental longitudinal evaluation of the project has verified that women who worked with advocates reported higher quality of life, greater social support, and decreased difficulty obtaining community resources over time. Perhaps most important, they also experienced less violence over time than the women who did not work with advocates (Sullivan, 2000; Sullivan & Bybee, 1999).

Summary

Community-based services for battered women and their children have expanded exponentially in the last 25 years. As our knowledge about this complex issue has grown, as funding has increased, and as more community members are accepting responsibility for ending intimate male violence against women and children, community-based services have developed that reflect this growth. Today, most communities have at least some programs available for battered women and their children. Nonprofit domestic violence service programs offer an array of services to women and children, whether or not the family needs residential services. Many communities also have services provided through health care systems, the criminal justice system, and/or social service systems. Efforts have improved to ensure that services are culturally appropriate and respectful of the complex obstacles facing women with abusive partners. However, no community can be said to be doing enough. Too many survivors still receive insufficient help, and too many communities provide uncoordinated or inadequate assistance.

We have clearly come a long way, but our journey is far from over. Domestic violence victim support services will continue to develop and expand to meet the changing needs of women and children. At the same time, advocates nationwide eagerly anticipate the day when such support services for battered women and their children are no longer necessary.

Note

1. If the telephone number for the local program is not known, the toll-free National Domestic Violence Hotline (1-800-799-SAFE) can patch callers through to a program near them.

References

Bauer, H. M., Rodriguez, M. A., Quiroga, S. S., & Flores-Ortiz, Y. G. (2000). Barriers to health care for abused Latina and Asian immigrant women. *Journal of Healthcare for the Poor and Underserved, 11,* 33-44.

Berk, R. A., Newton, P. J., & Berk, S. F. (1986). What a difference a day makes: An empirical study of the impact of shelters for battered women. *Journal of Marriage and the Family, 48,* 481-490.

Bowker, L. H., & Maurer, L. (1985). The importance of sheltering in the lives of battered women. *Response to the Victimization of Women and Children, 8,* 2-8.

Correia, A. (1999). *Building comprehensive solutions to domestic violence. Publication #3: Housing and battered women: A case study of domestic violence programs in Iowa.* Harrisburg, PA: National Resource Center on Domestic Violence.

Dasgupta, S. D. (1998). Women's realities: Defining violence against women by immigration, race and class. In R. K. Bergen (Ed.), *Issues in intimate violence* (pp. 209-219). Thousand Oaks, CA: Sage.

Gamache, D. J., Edleson, J. L., & Schock, M. D. (1988). Coordinated police, judicial, and social service response to woman battering: A multibaseline evaluation across three communities. In G. T. Hotaling, D. Finkelhor, J. T. Kirkpatrick, & M. Straus (Eds.), *Coping with family violence: Research and policy perspectives* (pp. 193-209). Newbury Park, CA: Sage.

Gondolf, E. (1988). *Battered women as survivors: An alternative to learned helplessness.* Lexington, MA: Lexington.

Gruszinski, R. J., Brink, J. C., & Edleson, J. L. (1988). Support and education groups for children of battered women. *Child Welfare, 67,* 431-444.

Hilbert, J., & Hilbert, H. (1984). Battered women leaving shelter: Which way do they go? *Journal of Applied Social Sciences, 8*(2), 292-297.

Irvine, J. (1990). Lesbian battering: The search for shelter. In P. Elliott (Ed.), *Confronting lesbian battering* (pp. 25-30). St. Paul: Minnesota Coalition for Battered Women.

Jaffe, P. G., Wilson, S. K., & Wolfe, D. A. (1989). Specific assessment and intervention strategies for children exposed to wife assault: Preliminary empirical investigation. *Canadian Journal of Mental Health, 7*(2), 157-163.

Jaffe, P. G., Wolfe, D. A., & Wilson, S. K. (1990). *Children of battered women.* Newbury Park, CA: Sage.

McMahon, M., & Pence, E. (1995). Doing more harm than good? Some cautions on visitation centers. In E. Peled, P. G. Jaffe, & J. L. Edleson (Eds.), *Ending the cycle of violence: Commu-*

nity responses to children of battered women (pp. 186-206). Thousand Oaks, CA: Sage.

National Research Council. (1998). *Violence in families: Assessing prevention and treatment programs.* Washington, DC: National Academy Press.

Okun, L. (1986). *Woman abuse: Facts replacing myths.* Newbury Park, CA: Sage.

Renzetti, C. M. (1992). *Violent betrayal: Partner abuse in lesbian relationships.* Newbury Park, CA: Sage.

Ridington, J. (1977-1978). The transition process: A feminist environment as reconstitutive milieu. *Victimology: An International Journal, 2*(3-4), 563-575.

Rodriguez, R. (1998). Clinical interventions with battered migrant farm worker women. In J. C. Campbell (Ed.), *Empowering survivors of abuse: Health care for battered women and their children* (pp. 271-279). Thousand Oaks, CA: Sage.

Schechter, S. (1982). *Women and male violence.* Boston: South End.

Schutte, N. S., Malouff, J. M., & Doyle, J. S. (1988). The relationship between characteristics of the victim, persuasive techniques of the batterer, and returning to a battering relationship. *Journal of Social Psychology, 128,* 605-610.

Sedlak, A. J. (1988). Prevention of wife abuse. In V. B. Van Hasselt, R. L. Morrison, A. S. Bellack, & M. Hersen (Eds.), *Handbook of family violence* (pp. 319-358). New York: Plenum.

Sorenson, S. (1996). Violence against women: Examining ethnic differences and commonalities. *Evaluation Review, 20*(2), 123-145.

Stark, E., & Flitcraft, A. (1988). Violence among intimates: An epidemiological review. In V. B. Van Hasselt, R. L. Morrison, A. S. Bellack, & M. Hersen (Eds.), *Handbook of family violence* (pp. 293-317). New York: Plenum.

Steinman, M. (1990). Lowering recidivism among men who batter women. *Journal of Police Science and Administration, 17,* 124-132.

Straus, M. A. (1986). Medical care costs of intrafamily assault and homicide. *Bulletin of the New York Academy of Medicine, 62,* 556-561.

Straus, M. A., Gelles, R. J., & Steinmetz, S. K. (1980). *Behind closed doors: Violence in the American family.* New York: Anchor.

Sullivan, C. M. (2000). A model for effectively advocating for women with abusive partners. In

J. P. Vincent & E. N. Jouriles (Eds.), *Domestic violence: Guidelines for research-informed practice.* London: Jessica Kingsley.

Sullivan, C. M., & Bybee, D. I. (1999). Reducing violence using community-based advocacy for women with abusive partners. *Journal of Consulting and Clinical Psychology, 67*(1), 43-53.

Sullivan, C. M., Tan, C., Basta, J., Rumptz, M., & Davidson, W. S., II. (1992). An advocacy intervention program for women with abusive partners: Initial evaluation. *American Journal of Community Psychology, 20*(3), 309-332.

Torres, S. (1998). Intervening with battered Hispanic pregnant women. In J. C. Campbell (Ed.), *Empowering survivors of abuse: Health care for battered women and their children* (pp. 259-270). Thousand Oaks, CA: Sage.

Tutty, L. M., Weaver, G., & Rothery, M. A. (1999). Residents' views of the efficacy of shelter services for assaulted women. *Violence Against Women, 5*(8), 898-925.

Vinton, L. (1992). Battered women's shelters and older women: The Florida experience. *Journal of Family Violence, 7*(1), 63-72.

Warshaw, C. (1993). Limitations of the medical model in the care of battered women. In P. B. Bart & E. G. Moran (Eds.), *Violence against women: The bloody footprints* (pp. 134-146). Newbury Park, CA: Sage.

Williams, L. (1981). Violence against women. *Black Scholar, 12*(1), 18-24.

Williams, O. J. (1992). Ethnically sensitive practice to enhance treatment participation of African American men who batter. *Families and Society: The Journal of Contemporary Human Services, 73,* 588-595.

Williams, O. J. (1993). Developing an African American perspective to reduce spouse abuse: Considerations for community action. *Black Caucus: Journal of the Association of Black Social Workers, 1*(2), 1-8.

CHAPTER 14

Intervention Programs
for Men Who Batter

Larry W. Bennett
Oliver J. Williams

Batterer intervention programs are a distinct method of domestic violence prevention. These programs are designed for men arrested for domestic violence or for men who would be arrested if their actions were public. Batterer programs primarily use education or treatment groups but may include other intervention elements such as personal counseling or case management. They are usually offered by nonprofit or private agencies and less frequently by the criminal justice system. Programs may differ in theoretical orientation, structure, or auspice, but they share a common purpose of preventing men's violent, controlling behavior against women.

The typical batterer program accepts both voluntary or court referrals, although because domestic violence is a crime, most programs prefer that men are referred as a condition of their prosecution or probation. After an initial evaluation, the batterer attends weekly education or treatment groups for 3 to 6 months. Groups are almost always the preferred modality because they allow for peer feedback and reduce the isolation and private behavior common to batterers. The court is notified when the man either completes the program or fails to attend. Most batterer programs are linked to a coordinated community violence prevention effort, which also includes the criminal justice system, battered women's agencies, substance abuse treatment programs, behavioral health services, and other social service agencies.

History of Batterer Programs

Batterer intervention programs developed in the 1970s. Prior to the women's movement of that era, the social problem of domestic violence was widely ignored, so it was not deemed necessary to have special programs for men who batter. When it was identified at all, intimate partner violence was viewed as an emotional, addiction, or marital problem, and men who battered were treated in the mental health, substance abuse, or marital counseling practices of the time.

Profeminist men's groups provided the first batterer programs as a way of supporting the work of the women's antiviolence movement (Adams & McCormick, 1982). Although they did not deny that men who batter often have mental health, substance abuse, or relational problems, programs such as EMERGE in Boston, RAVEN in St. Louis, and AMEND in Denver viewed domestic violence as one means of male social control of women. At about the same time, marriage and family therapists began providing groups for couples when domestic violence was identified during assessment or treatment (Margolin, 1979). Marital or systemic therapists were initially inclined to view domestic violence as an interactional process. Feminists criticized this perspective because it blames the victim for her victimization, limits the causes of violence against women to problems in the nuclear family, and presents an additional risk to the victim (Bograd, 1984). In recent years, most systemic therapists have adopted the position that the batterer is fully responsible for his abuse (Lipchik, Sirles, & Kubicki, 1997).

A third influence on batterer programs was the application of cognitive-behavioral therapy for anger and aggression. This approach assumes that individuals learn to use aggression through observation and experience. Models for the use of aggression may be found in the family of origin, in the peer group, and in the public arena, such as arts and media. Use of aggression is reinforced by its success at getting a partner to behave differently, by physiological effects such as temporary stress reduction, and by the lack of nega-

tive consequences. Violent, controlling behavior is reinforced socially through lack of sanction and, in some cases, through overt support. The cognitive model of behavior suggests that cognition affects behavior: If cognition is modified, behavior may also be modified. The cognitive-behavioral approach helps batterers identify situations that trigger anger, alter their dysfunctional thinking, change their understanding about those situations, and learn more adaptive behavior in place of their controlling behavior. The social perspectives of feminism and cognitive-behavioral skill-building are frequently combined in contemporary models applied to batterer intervention programs (Ganley, 1989). The typical batterer program now uses a gender-based cognitive-behavioral approach.

Batterer programs are only one node in a coordinated, community-based effort to prevent violence. The Duluth model (Pence & Paymar, 1993), one of the most popular approaches in the United States, is a psychoeducational program built on an understanding that abuse—both physical and nonphysical—is one of many ways men exercise power and control over women. The Duluth approach emphasizes that intervention with batterers must be part of a coordinated community approach to domestic violence rather than an isolated program. Also critical to a community approach are, minimally, the criminal justice system and shelter plus services for battered women. Additional components of coordinated community responses include medical systems, child protection services, senior services, other social service and mental health providers, and clergy (Witwer & Crawford, 1995). Regardless of whether a batterer program is based on the Duluth model or not, most programs have accepted the importance of being linked to the community violence-prevention system. Research supports improved effectiveness of batterer programs operating within a coordinated community response (Babcock & Steiner, 1999; Murphy, Musser, & Maton, 1998).

Structure and Function of Batterer Intervention Programs

Goals for batterer programs include rehabilitation, justice, and victim safety. Batterer programs differ by their relative emphasis on each of these goals. Programs emphasizing rehabilitation focus on prosocial, nonviolent skill building, such as identification and management of anger and stress. Because many court-referred batterers have substance abuse problems, substance abuse screening and treatment are also integral to the rehabilitation goal. The approaches of rehabilitative programs may run the gamut of psychologically minded approaches to domestic violence, including cognitive-behavioral therapy (Hamberger, 1999), attachment theory (Stosny, 1996), process-oriented psychodynamic treatment (Saunders, 1996), and self-help (Goffman, 1984).

A batterer program stressing justice views its role as an extension of the justice system, emphasizing the batterer's accountability for his behavior during the program. In their U.S. Department of Justice survey of influential U.S. batterer programs and communities, Healy and her co-authors found that criminal justice professionals often view batterer programs not as treatment but as an extension of probation (Healy, Smith, & O'Sullivan, 1998). At one extreme of justice-oriented

programs are those conducted by court employees. In Chicago, for example, the Cook County Court Department of Social Services has conducted an in-house batterer program since 1979, working with over 1,000 probationers a year. Also included in this spectrum are nonprofit batterer programs that identify their mission as one of accountability.

Batterer programs that emphasize victim safety are usually managed by, or linked closely to, battered women's agencies. Safety-focused batterer programs also emphasize justice, viewing safety and justice as inseparable. Safety-focused programs often emphasize victim safety checks, employing a victim advocate to provide telephone follow-up and referral.

Elements of rehabilitation, justice, and victim-safety goals are present in most batterer programs. The most effective batterer programs are probably those that have intervention elements derived from all three goals. Batterer programs have changed over time. Whereas earlier batterer programs may have focused on a single goal, such as rehabilitation, the trend is toward multidimensional models that include elements of the feminist perspective, cognitive-behavioral skill-building, assessment-based intervention, attention to group process, and attention to both victim safety and batterer accountability (Healy et al., 1998).

Referral to Batterer Programs

Participants usually come to batterer programs either as a stipulation of probation or parole or as a diversion from prosecution or punishment. Because domestic violence is a crime in all 50 U.S. states, judges frequently order batterers to a program as a condition of probation. Prosecutors also use pretrial diversion as a tool to gain compliance from the offender in cases where the evidence or the victim is questionable and a conviction is deemed unlikely. In these diversion programs, the arrested batterer who meets certain criteria (e.g., first offense, less severe abuse) may enter a plea of guilty in exchange for agreeing to complete a batterer program. If he complies with the program, the charges are dropped. If he fails to comply with the program, the charges move forward. If convicted, he may return to the batterer program, have his sentence extended, or receive a variety of additional sanctions. Domestic violence advocates usually oppose diversion programs because they permit a criminal to escape having a police record and make reoffense a first offense.

On rare occasions, men come to batterer programs of their own accord. The word *voluntary* may technically describe the condition, but it would not usually describe their motivation. These men may be coming to the program for a variety of reasons other than their own behavioral change. Most often, self-referrals are either trying to influence their partner's behavior or responding to their partner's demand. This is usually labeled *wife referral.* Domestic violence advocates believe batterers will not go to a program of their own volition but only if they are coerced. The relative success of these divergent paths to batterer programs has not been extensively studied, but one study of 840 batterers in four cities found that voluntary participants were more likely to have re-assaulted their partners at 15-month follow-up than court-referred participants (44% versus 29%) (Gondolf, 1997).

Batterer programs may employ individual therapy, medication, case management, residential treatment, and other modes of intervention, but these program elements are rare. However, variations on six key elements are present in most batterer programs: evaluation, contact with victims, an orientation process, group, program-completion criteria, and post-completion maintenance.

Evaluation

Evaluation begins at the points of contact between the batterer, the batterer program, and the referral source. Evaluation usually requires gathering basic information from the batterer (including information from the court), educating the batterer about his contract with the program, and screening for problems with substance abuse, mental illness, and literacy. The relative amount of attention paid to these evaluation elements varies widely between programs. In addition to initial evaluation, programs may have a prolonged assessment period, including a formal evaluation of psychosocial functioning. Some educational programs do little individualized assessment, believing that such assessment frames the problem as a mental health issue rather than a criminal issue and supports a man's belief that forces outside his own control lead to his violent and controlling behavior. Other programs may do extensive evaluation over several sessions, including psychological assessment, drug screening, and partner interviews.

Future behavior of batterers (or anyone else) cannot be predicted with accuracy. Most batterer programs, however, make some estimate of the man's lethality, usually based on the chronicity, severity, and generality of his violence, coupled with his acceptance of responsibility for his abusive behavior and his apparent motivation to comply with the program. A lethality assessment is usually noted in his record, if such a record is kept, and is communicated to appropriate parties, such as his probation officer, his current partner, or his victim's advocate.

Contracts for participation are widely used in batterer programs. Key elements of a contract between a batterer and a program are (a) specification of participation required for him to complete the program (e.g., he must attend a minimum of 22 out of 26 group meetings); (b) identification of unacceptable behavior (e.g., coming to group intoxicated) and program actions if the unacceptable behavior occurs (e.g., removed from group and probation officer notified); (c) agreement on a fee arrangement (e.g., $15 per group); and (d) securing his consent to contact the victim, probation officer, or other authorities on either an as-needed or a regular basis. Contracts are more than formally signed documents; they are an intervention that educates the batterer about the nature and expectations of the program. Contracts provide a platform to hold the batterer accountable for his behavior, should he not participate adequately in the program. As such, contracts are linked to victim safety. Refusal to sign a contract usually results in the batterer being refused entry into the program, which may result in a violation of his probation, conditional discharge, or plea agreement. Contracts are controversial for some health and mental health professionals, because they appear to violate an individual's right to privacy. However, the victim's right to safety outweighs the batterer's right to privacy in the areas that directly effect victim safety, such as threats or failure to comply with the program.

Substance abuse is a special consideration for assessment and intervention in batterer programs. In most episodes of domestic violence, alcohol or drug use is not a factor (Kantor & Straus, 1987). However, abuse of alcohol and drugs by men referred to batterer programs has been well documented, with most studies finding a prevalence of over 50% (Bennett, 1995). The link between substance use or abuse and violence is complex, and in most cases, neither acute intoxication nor chronic substance abuse can be said to cause domestic violence (Pernanen, 1991). However, although alcohol or drug use may not be a direct cause of domestic violence, substance-abusing batterers are more likely to harm their victims severely, drop out of batterer programs, and fail to comply with court orders. In a study of 618 batterers in four U.S. cities, the best predictor of re-offense was a report of drunkenness during the batterers program (Gondolf, 1999).

Victim Contact

Victim contact is also part of most batterer programs, although the nature of the contact varies widely. Whereas some batterer programs solicit assessment and ongoing information from victims, many programs do not solicit information directly from the victim due to concerns about her safety, preferring to have a "firewall" between the victim and staff working with the batterer. Usually, this requires that an advocate have contact with the victim. When advocate and victim agree that it is safe for information about the batterer to be given to the batterer program, the victim advocate provides the information. The primary concern of a firewall approach is that information from the victim may get back to the batterer (or to his attorney) and become a threat either to the victim's safety or, in cases of divorce, to her role as a mother. Rather than solicit information *from* a victim, many batterer programs prefer to give information *to* victims. For example, victims may benefit from information about the local shelter or victim services, the batterer program expectations and curriculum, and the behavior expected of the batterer while he is in the program.

Some programs offer an orientation group for partners of batterers in the program. In addition to providing educational information about the batterers program, women may be warned not to relax, let down their guard, or expect unrealistic changes in the batterer's behavior. Programs offering an orientation program for victims should not offer counseling for victims unless they are a battered women's agency or are under the supervision of a battered women's agency. Counseling conducted by batterer intervention programs that are not battered women's agencies is prohibited by most state batterer program standards. Such counseling may convey, covertly or overtly, that the victim is somehow responsible for her partner's violence or that she could do something to prevent him from being violent. Battered women are not able to control or change the batterer's behavior; that is something he must do for himself.

Orientation

Most batterer programs offer some initial orientation to participants before they go into the main program. This may be a group meeting of several hours or an orientation program lasting several weeks. The goals of orientation are to socialize the batterer to the expectations of the program, increase his motivation to attend and participate, and conduct more in-depth assessment. Orientation programs reduce the dropout rates from batterer programs (Tolman & Bhosley, 1990).

Groups

Regardless of theoretical perspective, groups are the preferred mode of service delivery for batterer programs. Groups act to decrease a batterer's sense of isolation and belief that he is exceptional, improve his interpersonal skills, offer mutual aid, identify and develop his expertise in critical areas, maximize confrontation of denial and inappropriate behavior, help him develop a norm for personal and social change, and maximize rewards for change (Stordeur & Stille, 1989). Groups differ in focus and format, ranging from psycho-educational classes to process-oriented therapy groups. Most batterer groups are a combination of education and process. Self-help is another format for batterer groups, similar to Alcoholics Anonymous and other 12-step programs. However, due to concerns about batterer accountability and negative male bonding (Hart, 1988), self-help groups for batterers are not widely accepted. Self-help groups for batterers present a serious threat to victim safety unless a man has completed a more structured batterer program or has some other means of accountability to the community.

Batterer groups may be open-ended or closed-ended, structured or unstructured. The typical group is partially structured and time-limited. Batterer groups usually follow some form of curriculum or pattern, deviating from the curriculum on an as-needed basis. Curricula for batterer programs are widely available (see Domestic Abuse Project, 1993; Ewing, Lindsey, & Pomerantz, 1984; Pence & Paymar, 1993;

Sonkin & Durphy, 1997; Stordeur & Stille, 1989). Most programs propose that, in addition to managing anger and improving social skills, nonviolence requires an examination of socially sanctioned male dominance and a change in attitude toward women. In a coordinated community approach to preventing violence, these changes should occur at the community level as well as at the personal level.

Program Completion

All batterer programs have some formal definition of when the man has completed the program. Many programs use a "time-served" criterion to designate program completion. If the program is 26 weeks, for example, the batterer has completed the program after he attends 26 groups. However, determining when a man has completed a batterer program is not as simple as it first appears. For example, would a man fulfill his requirement if he attended all 26 weeks but did not participate? What if he missed 10 of 26 groups? Would he have completed the program if he attended all 26 weeks, participated, but still denied any responsibility for his abusive behavior? What if he was a model group member but battered his partner several weeks before his program completion date? To address these concerns, batterer programs are moving toward competency-based criteria in addition to the time-based criterion. Competencies may include his stated acceptance of responsibility for abuse, completion of homework and in-group tasks, compliance with collateral referrals, use of sensitive language, and so forth. Competency-based criteria are not as popular with criminal justice pro-

fessionals because of the pressure in many jurisdictions to move men through the legal system in a timely manner. Defense attorneys may object to such criteria on the grounds that they appear politically driven, lack studies supporting their utility, and require subjective evaluation by staff who may be paraprofessionals.

In the end, program goals may determine whether competency-based criteria are used for program completion. If the main goal is justice and the batterer program is viewed as an extension of probation, 26 weeks or 52 weeks may be deemed enough time in the program. If the program's goal features rehabilitation or victim safety, however, behavioral change and competence are expected. In particular, a safety-driven batterer program would not believe a man has completed the program unless he were violence-free for a period of time, articulated gender-sensitive ideas, and accepted responsibility for his violent, controlling behavior.

Maintenance

Many men make positive changes in behavior and attitude during batterer programs. Like other behavioral changes, however, these gains can be difficult to maintain once the program is completed. Whether they are called aftercare, drop-in, maintenance, or a booster program, such elements of batterer programs acknowledge that prosocial attitudes and noncontrolling behavior need reinforcement. Maintenance of gains in therapy has been found to be an important aspect of the change process in closely related areas such as substance abuse (Prochaska, DiClemente, & Norcross, 1992), but few

batterer programs have addressed the issues of continuing care or relapse prevention. Other than saying the man is welcome to return, maintenance programs
for batterers are in the early stages of development (Daniels & Murphy, 1997;
Jennings, 1990).

Effectiveness of Batterer Programs

The documented effects of batter programs
are modest. Reviews of batterer program
outcomes report, on the average, a recidivism rate of about 40% in the year after
the program (see Eisikovits & Edleson,
1989; Gondolf, 1991; Rosenfeld, 1992;
Tolman & Bennett, 1990; Tolman &
Edleson, 1995). The reported success of
batterer programs depends on how long
after the program the follow-up is conducted and how success is measured. We
expect recidivism will increase with time,
so success rates decrease the longer the
period between program completion and
follow-up. However, batterer program outcomes are more complicated than follow-
up time alone. For example, Dutton,
Bodnarchuk, Kropp, Hart, and Ogloff's
(1997) 11-year follow-up study of 446
batterers, using arrest records, found an
18% recidivism rate, whereas Gondolf's
(in press) follow-up of 618 batterers in
four U.S. cities, based on reports of female
partners, found that 41% had re-assaulted
their partners during the 30-month follow-
up period. The difference in recidivism
(18% and 41%) illustrates some of the
problems we have in commenting on the
success of batterer treatment programs:
Different definitions of recidivism and
different lengths of follow-up make comparisons between outcome studies difficult. The odds that a batterer will be arrested for his reassault are only a fraction

of the odds that he will reassault, so evaluations using law enforcement and
criminal justice records produce much
lower recidivism figures than evaluations
using partner reports. To understand the
outcome of batterer programs, we need
multiple outcome measures for each case.
Tolman and Edleson (1995) suggest outcome indicators might include (a) prevention of further injury to the victim,
rearrest, physical abuse, psychological
maltreatment, sexual abuse, or separation
abuse, as well as violence-supporting attitudes; (b) increase in a man's egalitarian
partnership, positive behaviors, social
skills, prosocial and anti-violence attitudes, or psychosocial functioning; and
(c) improvement in survivor or child well-
being (e.g., reduction of fear or trauma
symptoms).

Regardless of how effectiveness is
measured, assignment of cause for any
measured change in batterer programs is
also difficult. Although they may compare men who complete the program to
those who do not, few studies have compared outcomes between men completing a batterer program and men in a no-
treatment control group, or even to men in
comparison groups. Consequently, it is
difficult to determine whether the observed effects are due to the program or to
other factors. Most uncontrolled studies
have found small but statistically significant effects for batterer programs. Results
from the few controlled studies are equivocal. Several found no significant difference in outcome between men in the
batterer program and controls (Dunford,
1997; Feder, 1999; Harrell, 1991). Other
studies have found small but significant
differences (Taylor, Davis, & Maxwell,
in press; Palmer, Brown, & Barrera,
1992). However, the controlled studies to
date have all been hampered by serious
methodological problems, so conclusions

about the effectiveness of batterer programs remain an open question.

More useful than outcome studies, which focus on whether batterer programs are effective, are those studies identifying for whom batterer programs are effective. It is no surprise that batterer programs appear to be more effective with men who have a "stake in conformity" (Toby, 1957). Men who are employed, married, have children with their partner, and feel embarrassed about their abusive behavior are more likely to respond to a batterer program. However, these same men are also more likely to respond to criminal sanctions, to peer confrontation, to threats by their partner, or to other interventions.

Controversies Facing Batterer Programs

As suggested above, a key issue facing batterer programs is their effectiveness. Batterer programs face other issues as well, the most important being (a) criminal justice and mental health perspectives on domestic violence; (b) standards for batterer programs; (c) the link between batterer programs and other community services, especially programs for battered women; and, (d) the cultural competence of batterer programs and their staff.

Criminal Justice and Mental Health

How we view batterers determines how services are delivered, as well as the prioritization, funding, and evaluation of those services. Many of the cutting-edge issues in batterer intervention hinge on this perspective, for example, the possibility of creating batterer typologies and matching services with types of men, the link between battering and substance abuse, and the link between battering and mental illness.

Are there different types of batterers, or is it enough to define batterers by their illegal behavior? At present, most batterer programs have a "one size fits all" approach. This single approach to batterers is a product not only of a single theoretical perspective but also of the logistics and complexity of matching batterers with different sets of interventions in a group-based program. Early recognition of differences among batterers focused on men who were generally violent and men who battered only family members (Cadsky & Crawford, 1988; Shields, McCall, & Hanneke, 1988). Subsequent studies have proposed a threefold typology (Gondolf, 1988; Holtzworth-Munroe & Stuart, 1994; Saunders, 1992). The threefold typology includes (a) normal batterers, or men who are violent primarily in their family and do not usually have pronounced substance abuse or mental health problems; (b) batterers with mood regulation problems, unstable identities, and impulsive behavior, and (c) generally violent or antisocial batterers, who are violent outside the family as well as within the family. It remains to be seen whether such typologies based on behavioral indicators are useful in batterer intervention programs. Diagnostic-sounding categories such as *antisocial-generally violent* or *borderline-dysphoric* may lead some to regard battering as a mental health issue. However, a recent study of 840 batterers in four U.S. cities found them to be less pathological than had been previously reported and not well described by existing typologies (Gondolf, 1999; White & Gondolf, in press). Contrary to the matching program to person idea that underlies most efforts to create typologies of batterers, researchers have found that most batterers in their sample have personality characteristics that are well-suited to the typical gender-based cognitive-behavioral approach of batterer programs (White & Gondolf, in press).

Batterer Program Standards

By 1997, half of U.S. states had instituted standards for batterer programs. The stated purpose of batterer program standards is, in one example, "to guide new and existing programs toward the development and delivery of services which are safe, effective, and accountable" (Illinois Department of Human Services, 1994). Typical elements discussed by standards are (a) program philosophy, (b) program protocol, (c) view on whether contact with the victim is advisable, (d) staff ethics and qualifications, (e) fees, (f) intake procedures, (g) issues pertaining to intervention, and (h) discharge criteria (Austin & Dankwort, 1999). In those states regulated by law, the regulatory body may be a local judicial board, a criminal justice body, or another state code agency such as public health, human services, or child protection.

Mental health professionals often view standards for batterer programs as premature, politically driven government regulation operating without a scientific basis for its dictates and infringing on their right to practice according to their professional training. In opposition to the mental health perspective are domestic violence advocates, who view regulation as a necessary step to ensure safety for the victims of violence. Again, the goals of batterer programs inform the issue of program standards. Those programs emphasizing rehabilitation are more likely to view batterers as having behavioral health problems and to dispute standards seen as antithetical to mental health treatment. Those viewing the goal of batterer programs as victim safety are often proponents of standards, most of which articulate the primary goal of batterer programs to be victim safety. At present, there is no research to support either perspective, and the argument remains ideological. Research could test, for example, hypotheses that batterer program standards enhance the safety of battered women and that batterers treated in programs with credentialed mental health professionals are less likely to reoffend than those treated by other programs. However, given the difficulty of research with both batterers and victims, it is unlikely this will occur in the near future, and the standards debate will continue for some time.

Interaction With Victim Programs

What is the optimal relationship of programs for batterers with other community programs, especially programs for battered women? A related question is whether we should use public funds for batterer programs. In particular, in a time of declining public support for human services, does funding batterer programs take resources away from battered women's programs?

Most state standards for batterer programs require a working relationship with a battered women's agency. Historically, batterer programs have had a close working relationship with services for victims, and many batterer programs were operated by victim-service agencies. However, a combination of available government funding and increased frequency of mandated treatment for batterers has made batterer programming attractive to mental health and substance abuse agencies and to practitioners with no history in domestic violence programs and no connection to battered women's agencies. Some coordinated community violence-prevention efforts unwittingly support the erosion of the link between batterer programs and victim services by expanding the scope of batterer programs into mental health and substance abuse agencies.

The issue of public funding for batterer programs is quite controversial. With limited dollars, funding batterer programs may reduce funding for victim programs. On the other hand, proponents of public funding point out that the cost of batterer programs often prevents poor and minority men from attending, and these men represent populations that are disproportionately referred to batterer programs. Much of the public funding for batterer programs comes from sources that also fund services for victims. In Illinois, for example, public dollars for both perpetrator and victim services are channeled through the Department of Human Services. Some proponents of batterer program funding argue that programs conforming to state standards should receive public financial support for indigents and underserved populations, for program accountability, and for active linking to the community and case management. However, the natural source of funding for batterer programs is the criminal justice system, not human services, public health, or other streams that drain dollars for victim services.

Cultural Competence

Men of color have presented a problem for batterer intervention programs. People who design and conduct batterer programs are often mirror images of the people who are most likely to complete these programs—white, middle class, and educated. Although minority men are overrepresented among men arrested and prosecuted for domestic violence, they complete batterer programs at much lower rates than their white counterparts. In a study that compared men who complete treatment in either racially mixed or African American groups, race was a significant influence on trust, comfort, willingness to discuss critical subjects, and participation in treatment (Williams, 1995). Men in the African American groups felt more positive about their experiences and more willing to discuss issues associated with race that they considered as influences on their behavior.

Batterer programs address cultural and racial differences in one of five ways. In a *color-blind* group, differences do not make a difference. In a color-blind batterer group, differences due to race and ethnicity are viewed as unrelated to battering. A *culturally specific* milieu refers to a program where a critical mass of one minority group is present, but there is no attempt to raise or address concerns linked to diversity. A group consisting entirely of white, non-Hispanic men, for example, may employ a traditional batterer program curriculum and never make reference to the dominant culture. In contrast to the first two approaches, a *culturally centered* program puts culture or race at the center of treatment. An example of a culturally centered program is a program for Native American batterers using traditional healing rituals. In a *culturally focused* group, issues associated with diversity and the intersection of race, culture, gender, and violence are specifically addressed with a specific race/cultural group. Finally, in a *healthy heterogeneous* group, differences due to race and culture are addressed, both as they arise and at different times in the program, based on the ethnocultural makeup of the group. A national study of batterer programs found that most programs are deliberately color-blind and choose not to address the realities or concerns of men of color (Williams & Becker, 1994). This finding suggests one possible reason for ineffective batterer programs. Healthy heterogeneous, culturally centered, and culturally focused batterer programs with culturally competent staff will substantially increase the effectiveness of programs for men who batter.

Future Directions for Batterer Programs

Batterer programs, as part of a coordinated community response to domestic violence, are modestly successful at preventing further violence for certain types of men. To be more successful with a broader spectrum of abusers, batterer programs will need to refine and strengthen their programs within proactive communities. We believe the future of programs for men who batter depends on their ability to develop and apply new understandings of battering and related forms of social control, to develop culturally competent interventions, to advocate for responsible fatherhood across cultures, to redefine their role as one of a number of interventions for batterers, and to apply their knowledge of power and control to a broader social context.

New Knowledge

Although domestic violence is an underresearched field, even less is known about men who batter and about batterer intervention programs. Research and evaluation are stepping stones to more ef-

fective intervention. One outcome of research on batterers will be supplanting single-cause theories and overly simplistic notions about domestic violence. Increasingly, researchers and practitioners recognize that batterers come to their violence and control through a variety of paths. Some batterers have mental disorders, abuse alcohol or drugs, or suffer from the effects of poverty; other batterers do not bear these burdens. Some batterers hold patriarchal beliefs and misogynist feelings about women, whereas other batterers believe in gender equity. Some men are generally violent; their violence against their partner is an extension of their violence against society. Other men would never dream of being aggressive outside their home zone of safety. Many of the simple perspectives that we embraced early in the development of batterer programs have lost their capacity to explain what we see. A multicausal, multimodal perspective is needed, supported by solid research.

Additional understanding about batterers may also come from asking a different question: Why do most men *not* batter? Most men who abuse alcohol or drugs, for example, are not batterers. Most men get angry, but most do not batter their partners. Most men who witness violence in their family of origin do not grow up to be batterers. Identifying the protective factors in the environments of men who do not batter is one area that, when finally addressed, may yield new innovations. Another tack is focusing on the strengths of men who batter. Most of our attention has naturally been directed at the deficits of men who batter. Programs for batterers are often built on remediating batterer deficits, a limited approach. Some will find it unsettling to think about identifying and building on the strengths of batterers rather than—or in addition to—

challenging their weaknesses. We do not recommend this approach without adequate evaluation, but we do recommend that batterer programs provide opportunities for participants to identify and increase those strengths that are consistent with program philosophy and goals.

One final knowledge-building component is the systematic evaluation of effectiveness by batterer programs and the dissemination of those results to other programs. Few batterer programs monitor their outcomes beyond the process outcomes of attendance, program completion, satisfaction, and so on. We must look for and promote program models that have demonstrated effectiveness. Of course, traditional research and evaluation programs such as the ones cited in this chapter must also continue, but we believe batterer programs must evaluate their own effectiveness to advance the knowledge base. Networks of batterer intervention programs, with some government support, can greatly extend our knowledge of the effectiveness of these programs.

Cultural Competence

Definitions of racism, community structure and environment, social context, power, control, sexism, and masculinity are often based on a Eurocentric perspective rather than a minority reality. A batterer program that is unable to engage men of color increases the risk to battered women by engendering a man's resistance to getting help. For example, when a culturally insensitive program ignores the African American or Latino experience, a batterer may subsequently feel more justified in rejecting future help.

How might batterer interventions become more culturally competent? A link must be made between a batterer's social realities and his behavior toward his partner. Practitioners working with batterers must learn to confront, for example, African American men's scapegoating of African American women (hooks, 1995). If, as African American men often believe, oppression and environment produce violent behavior, why is his target a woman who, in most cases, experiences the same oppressive environment?

Responsible Fatherhood

Batterer programs should also place more emphasis on fatherhood and children. The co-occurrence of physical partner violence and child maltreatment in the same families is on the order of 30% to 60% (Appel & Holden, 1998; Edleson, 1999). Children who observe adult partner violence are more likely to become substance abusers, batterers, or victims of abuse. We can hope that programs will also assume more responsibility for identifying and helping the children who witness domestic violence. Although most programs have a module on parenting, this is likely to be an afterthought that is easily pushed aside for the seemingly more vital issues in the curriculum. In fact, helping a man develop skills to be a better parent may not be as useful as helping him understand the effect his violence has on his children (Carter & Schechter, 1997). Responsible fatherhood involves more than using good parenting skills. A responsible father is a man who, in addition to caring for and guiding his children, is a coequal to his children's mother, even if he does not live with her; contributes to the support of his children regardless of where they live; and accepts responsibility for his behavior, in particular for his controlling behavior, and its effects on his children and his children's mother. We hope batterer programs—and programs for men in general—will focus more on responsible fatherhood across cultures, and in a way that will enhance safety and security in the lives of children.

Responsible fathers are safe fathers. Some batterers can be safe fathers, and some cannot. In collaboration with child protection workers and battered women's advocates, batterer programs should develop ways to identify and intervene with men who present a risk to child safety. At the same time, batterer programs must ally with those elements in the men's movement that want to address the issue of men's violence against women and children. Some elements of the men's movement emphasize responsible fatherhood, along with their emphasis on men's personal growth. Other elements of the men's movement are reactionary, antifeminist, and motivated by their perception of imbalance between men's and women's rights in matters of mediation, divorce, custody, and visitation. A focus on the difficulty and pain of being a man may be useful, but viewing women or the women's movement as the source of men's pain is irresponsible and dangerous. We believe these reactionary elements present a threat to the safety and well-being of women and children. Batterer programs must not remain silent on this critical social issue.

Redefining Roles

One of the unintended problems engendered by batterer programs arises from their availability. When a batterer program is available, judges and prosecutors may stop thinking critically about what to do with batterers. It is an error to believe that batterer programs alone are a community's answer to men's violence against women. Instead, batterer programs should be one of several alternatives for sentencing batterers, not the only alternative (Frank, 1999). Batterer programs should be an integral part of the community response to violence against women, but they must not be the only response. In particular, they may not be the best response for those men who have multiple problems, who are repeat offenders, and who do not attend or participate in the batterer program.

The batterer program may be the community agency most likely to identify men for whom their program is inappropriate. It is important for batterer programs to become more fully integrated with other health, human service, and criminal justice agencies to facilitate the alternative responses necessary to manage the diversity of men entering batterer programs. Improving their partnerships with substance abuse agencies, mental health agencies, and the criminal justice system is the first order of business. Batterer programs that are not part of battered women's agencies must gain and maintain the trust of these agencies. In particular, batterer programs must find ways to hold both themselves and their work with batterers accountable to battered women's agencies. In addition, they must actively support funding and resources for victim services agencies.

An accountable batterer program is a program that views the safety of battered women as an integral part of all program activities. Accountable staff members in these programs make themselves available to battered women and their advocates because they believe such availability decreases the likelihood that they or their program will endanger victims. A batterer depends on isolation and privacy to maintain his control on his family, and this isolation increases the risk for violence to his partner and children. In the same way, a nonaccountable batterer program is conducted in isolation, increasing risk to the victims of the men in the program. Isomorphically, the same process holds for the isolation and privacy of individual staff in a batterer program, who avoid an active, consulting, or supervisory relationship with battered women's advocates.

Public Education

The burden of public education about domestic violence has been carried by battered women's agencies, later joined by medical and criminal justice agencies. Batterer programs usually confine their attention to education or treatment of batterers. Thus, the public is far more aware of battered women than they are of men who batter. An unintended effect of this imbalance is an overemphasis on the question "Why does she stay?" and an underemphasis on the question "Why does he batter?" and equally as important, "Why do *we* let him continue to batter?" Batterer programs are in an excellent position to correct this imbalance by collaborating with battered women's advocates to develop public education programs about domestic violence, with an emphasis on the perpetrator, male entitlement, and the social conditions that incubate and support men's abusive behavior. Batterer programs can expand the definition of battering as a means of social con-

trol to other mechanisms of social control. For example, the last decade of the 20th century witnessed an alarming rise in school violence, such as the 1999 murder of 13 students and faculty at a Littleton, Colorado, high school by two teenage boys, as well as similar shootings in Oregon, Arkansas, and Georgia. Although much of the response to this violence focused on the characteristics of the shooters—peer isolation, cult-like behavior— as well as the debate about guns and gun laws, one virtually ignored characteristic was that all the shooters were boys. Staffs from batterer programs are in an excellent position to lead a public discussion about the role of violence in the lives of boys and men. Alternate forms of gender-based abuse such as bullying, peer sexual harassment, and dating violence present a much earlier opportunity to enter the lives of potential batterers. Case finding, early intervention, risk reduction, public education, and primary prevention have, so far, been outside the range of batterer programs. However, these approaches may well represent the evolution of programs for men who batter.

References

Adams, D., & McCormick, A. (1982). Men unlearning violence: A group approach. In M. Roy (Ed.), *The abusive partner: An analysis of domestic battering* (pp. 170-197). New York: Van Nostrand Reinhold.

Appel, A. E., & Holden, G. W. (1998). The co-occurrence of spouse and physical child abuse: A review and appraisal. *Journal of Family Psychology, 12,* 578-599.

Austin, J., & Dankwort, J. (1999). Standards for batterer programs: A review and analysis. *Journal of Interpersonal Violence, 14,* 152-168.

Babcock, J. C., & Steiner, R. (1999). The relationship between treatment, incarceration, and recidivism of battering: A program evaluation of Seattle's coordinated community response to domestic violence. *Journal of Family Psychology, 13,* 46-59.

Bennett, L. (1995). Substance abuse and the domestic assault of women. *Social Work, 40,* 760-771.

Bograd, M. (1984). Family systems approaches to wife battering. *American Journal of Orthopsychiatry, 54,* 558-568.

Cadsky, O., & Crawford, M. (1988). Establishing batterer typologies in a clinical sample of men who assault their female partners. *Canadian Journal of Community Mental Health, 7,* 49-63.

Carter, J., & Schechter, S. (1997). *Child abuse and domestic violence: Creating community partnerships for safe families* [On-line, Family Violence Prevention Fund]. Available: www.mincava.umn.edu/link/fvpf1.htm

Daniels, J. W., & Murphy, C. M. (1997). Stages and process of change in batterers' treatment. *Cognitive & Behavioral Practice, 4,* 123-145.

Domestic Abuse Project. (1993). *Men's treatment manual.* Minneapolis, MN: Author.

Dunford, F. W. (1997, July). *The research design and preliminary outcome findings of the San Diego Navy Experiment.* Paper presented at the 5th International Family Violence Research Conference, Durham, NH.

Dutton, D., Bodnarchuk, M., Kropp, R., Hart, S., & Ogloff, J. (1997). Wife assault treatment and criminal recidivism: An 11-year follow-up. *International Journal of Offender Therapy and Comparative Criminology, 41,* 9-23.

Edleson, J. L. (1999). The overlap between child maltreatment and woman battering. *Violence Against Women, 5,* 134-154.

Eisikovits, Z. C., & Edleson, J. L. (1989). Intervening with men who batter: A critical review of the literature. *Social Service Review, 63,* 384-414.

Ewing, W., Lindsey, M., & Pomerantz, J. (1984). *Battering: An AMEND manual for helpers.* Denver, CO: AMEND.

Feder, L. (1999, July). *A test of the efficacy of court-mandated counseling for convicted misdemeanor domestic violence offenders: Results from the Broward experiment.* Paper presented at the 6th International Family Violence Research Conference, Durham, NH.

Frank, P. B. (1999, July). *Measuring the system, not individuals.* Paper presented at the 6th International Family Violence Research Conference, Durham, NH.

Ganley, A. L. (1989). Integrating feminist and social learning analyses of aggression: Creating multiple models for intervention with men who batter. In P. L. Caesar & L. K. Hamberger (Eds.), *Treating men who batter: Theory, practice, and programs* (pp. 196-235). New York: Springer.

Goffman, J. (1984). *Batterers Anonymous: Self-help counseling for men who batter.* San Bernadino, CA: B. A. Press.

Gondolf, E. W. (1988). Who are those guys? Toward a behavioral typology of batterers. *Violence and Victims, 3,* 187-203.

Gondolf, E. W. (1991). A victim-based assessment of court-mandated counseling for batterers. *Criminal Justice Review, 16,* 214-226.

Gondolf, E. W. (1997). Patterns of re-assault in batterers programs. *Violence and Victims, 12,* 373-387.

Gondolf, E. W. (1999). MCMI-III results for batterer program participants in four cities: Less "pathological" than expected. *Journal of Family Violence, 14,* 1-17.

Gondolf, E. W. (in press). A 30-month follow-up of court-referred batterers in four cities. *International Journal of Offender Therapy and Comparative Criminology.*

Hamberger, K. (1999). Cognitive behavioral treatment of men who batter their partners. *Cognitive & Behavioral Practice, 4,* 147-169.

Harrell, A. (1991). *Evaluation of court-ordered treatment for domestic violence offenders: Summary and recommendations.* Washington, DC: The Urban Institute.

Hart, B. (1988). Beyond the "duty to warn": A therapist's duty to protect. In K. Yllö & M. Bograd (Eds.), *Feminist perspectives on wife abuse* (pp. 234-248). Newbury Park, CA: Sage.

Healy, K., Smith, C., & O'Sullivan, C. O. (1998). *Batterer intervention program approaches and criminal justice strategies* (NJC168638). Washington, DC: Department of Justice, National Institute of Justice.

Holtzworth-Munroe, A., & Stuart, G. L. (1994). Typologies of male betterers: Three subtypes and the differences between them. *Psychological Bulletin, 116,* 476-497.

hooks, b. (1995). *Killing rage: Ending racism.* New York: Owl Books.

Illinois Department of Human Services. (1994). *Illinois protocol for domestic abuse batterers programs.* Springfield: Author.

Jennings, J. L. (1990). Preventing relapse versus "stopping" domestic violence: Do we expect too much from battering men? *Journal of Family Violence, 5,* 43-60.

Kantor, G., & Straus, M. A. (1987). The drunken bum theory of wife beating. *Social Problems, 34,* 213-230.

Lipchik, E., Sirles, E. A., & Kubicki, A. D. (1997). Multifaceted approaches in spouse abuse treatment. *Journal of Aggression, Maltreatment, & Trauma, 1,* 131-148.

Margolin, G. (1979). Conjoint marital therapy to enhance anger management and reduce spouse abuse. *American Journal of Family Therapy, 7,* 13-24.

Murphy, C. M., Musser, P. H., & Maton, K. I. (1998). Coordinated community intervention for domestic abusers: Intervention system involvement and criminal recidivism. *Journal of Family Violence, 13,* 263-284.

Palmer, S. E., Brown, R. A., & Barrera, M. E. (1992). Group treatment program for abusive husbands: Long-term evaluation. *American Journal of Orthopsychiatry, 62,* 276-283.

Pence, E., & Paymar, M. (1993). *Education groups for men who batter: The Duluth model.* New York: Springer.

Pernanen, K. (1991). *Alcohol in human violence.* New York: Guilford.

Prochaska, J. O., DiClemente, C. C., & Norcross, J. C. (1992). In search of how people change: Applications to addictive behavior. *American Psychologist, 47,* 1102-1114.

Rosenfeld, B. (1992). Court-ordered treatment of spouse abuse. *Clinical Psychology Review, 12,* 205-226.

Saunders, D. G. (1992). A typology of men who batter: Three types derived from cluster analysis. *American Journal of Orthopsychiatry, 62,* 264-275.

Saunders, D. G. (1996). Feminist-cognitive-behavioral and process-psychodynamic group treatments for men who batter: Interaction of abuser traits and treatment. *Violence and Victims, 11,* 393-414.

Shields, N. M., McCall, G. J., & Hanneke, C. R. (1988). Patterns of family and nonfamily violence: Violent husbands and violent men. *Violence and Victims, 3,* 83-97.

Sonkin, D. J., & Durphy, M. (1997). *Learning to live without violence: A handbook for men* (2nd ed.). Volcano, CA: Volcano Press.

Stordeur, R. A., & Stille, R. (1989). *Ending men's violence against their partners.* Newbury Park, CA: Sage.

Stosny, S. (1996). Treating attachment abuse: The Compassion Workshop. In D. Dutton (Ed.), *Treating abusiveness.* New York: Guilford.

Taylor, B. G., Davis, R. C., & Maxwell, C. D. (in press). The effects of a group batterer treatment program. *Justice Quarterly.*

Toby, J. (1957). Social disorganization and stakes in conformity: Complementary factors in the predatory behavior of hoodlums. *Journal of Criminal Law Criminology, and Political Science, 48,* 12-17.

Tolman, R. M., & Bennett, L. W. (1990). A review of quantitative research on men who batter. *Journal of Interpersonal Violence, 5,* 87-118.

Tolman, R. M., & Bhosley, G. (1990). A comparison of two types of pregroup preparation for men who batter. *Journal of Social Service Research, 13,* 33-43.

Tolman, R. M., & Edleson, J. L. (1995). Intervention for men who batter: A review of research. In S. Stith & M. A. Straus (Eds.), *Understanding partner violence: Prevalence, causes, consequences, and solutions* (pp. 262-274). Minneapolis, MN: National Council on Family Relations.

White, R., & Gondolf, E. (in press). Implications of personality profiles for batterer treatment: Support for the gender-based, cognitive behavioral approach. *Journal of Interpersonal Violence.*

Williams, O. J. (1995). Treatment for African American men who batter. *CURA Reporter, 25,* 610.

Williams, O. J., & Becker, L. R. (1994). Partner abuse programs and cultural competence: The results of a national study. *Violence and Victims, 9,* 287-295.

Witwer, M. B., & Crawford, C. A. (1995). *A coordinated approach to reducing family violence: Conference highlights* (NCJ155184). Washington, DC: Department of Justice.

CHAPTER 15

The Violence Against Women Act of 1994

The Federal Commitment to Ending Domestic Violence, Sexual Assault, Stalking, and Gender-Based Crimes of Violence

Roberta L. Valente
Barbara J. Hart
Seema Zeya
Mary Malefyt

In the 1970s, the phrases *battered woman* and *domestic violence* first entered the legislative lexicon. Before that time, the law dealt with emotional and physical abuse in extremely limited ways. Physical abuse and extreme mental cruelty were only rarely invoked as grounds for divorce, and police and prosecutors more often than not refused to deal professionally with battering incidents, dismissing them as "private matters" or "family squabbles." Rape and sexual assault were infrequently addressed as legal issues, even where there were laws on the books making these acts criminal. Stalking was rarely deemed a criminal activity, no

matter how imminent the danger posed by a stalker and no matter how disruptive the stalker's actions were to the victim. The small but growing number of victim advocates in the shelter and rape crisis movements reported that judges, lawyers, prosecutors, and police routinely failed to react to these crimes. State and federal legislators felt no pressure to pass laws to improve the legal system's capacity to respond. Neither the justice system nor the legislative system had conceived of "violence against women" as a problem.

Until three decades ago, few challenged the legal system's limited concept of women's rights. The law treated certain violent crimes, such as rape or domestic violence, as natural expressions of male authority when they occurred within the context of marriage or an intimate relationship, although the same violent attack against a neighbor, coworker, or stranger would be deemed criminal conduct. In cases of rape and sexual assault, if a woman tried to bring charges against an assailant, the legal system tended to focus its lens sharply on the victim's behavior rather than on the perpetrator's, devoting much of the criminal inquiry to what she had said, worn, or done to "lead on" the assailant.

Ironically, some of the well-intentioned protections the law offered to the average litigant and some of the well-meaning family law reforms initiated in the 1960s and 1970s had adverse effects on battered women. For example, the adoption by the states in the 1970s of "no-fault" divorce statutes (meant to ease the social stigma of divorce and to make divorce more broadly available) hurt battered women. Family law courts were reluctant, as a result, to consider wrong-doing by one spouse against another. Similarly, child custody reforms created a courtroom climate that discouraged spouses from reporting child or spousal abuse.

Generally speaking, the law prevented spouses from being compelled to testify against each other, although a wife could testify against her husband if she were the victim of his criminal actions (*Hawkins v. U.S.,* 1958). The reality was that the law did not encourage women seeking to invoke this testimonial exception. When battered women did decide to speak up about what their husbands had done, judges disallowed the testimony. Because of the great reliance of the law on rules discouraging negative spousal testimony, most courts and lawyers implicitly as-

sumed that a wife would not want to testify against her husband.

But it was not only the legal culture that hampered victims' efforts to find safety and independence from abuse or sexual assault. What many victims soon learned was that even those fortunate enough to obtain court orders of protection through the family and criminal courts were not really safe. When the offenders in these cases continued to beat their wives or committed other crimes of sexual assault or stalking, the legal system revealed itself to be unprepared to punish the perpetrators for violating the court orders, primarily because the American legal tradition reflected discomfort, until the latter third of the 20th century, with interfering in a husband's "management" of his family (*State v. Jones,* 1886). This problem still has fatal consequences for victims of domestic violence ("Warrant Unserved," 2000).

Nonlegal factors also limited the availability of options to victims of violence against women. Victim advocates realized that many married women, including many battered immigrant women, did not seek divorces because of religious beliefs or for fear their family or social groups would shun them (Goelman, Lehrman, & Valente, 1996). Others did not pursue divorce because it was costly and often left them without the economic means of survival, because alimony or "maintenance" awards were difficult to obtain.

Underlying all of these legal and social norms was the idea that when crimes of violence occurred against women, the victims of these crimes bore some responsibility for failing to prevent or manage the violence. This concept grew out of a long legal tradition from the Middle Ages until the 19th century. Few European women, for example, could own property.

In addition, in most Western legal traditions, when women marrried, their legal identity merged with that of their husbands; their actions, therefore, had to reflect the goals and desires of their husbands (Blackstone, 1765/1979, pp. 442-445). The management and ownership of property (and thus economic power) rested almost entirely in the hands of male family members, and so most women had no choice but to accept the precept that their role was to support, trust, and obey their "protectors."

When their male relatives violated that trust with violence, it was incumbent on the victimized women to change their behavior sufficiently to "earn" a less abusive response on the part of their protectors. Courts considered a broad range of female behaviors to be sufficiently "provoking" to justify male violence. For example, in the late 19th century in New York, an appeals court found that a wife who continued to receive a visitor whom her husband found objectionable had provoked her husband's violence. The court believed that "had the wife performed her duties towards her husband, she would have suffered no ill treatment at his hands" (*Rose v. Rose,* 1889). Even women's relationships to their children were proscribed, because children were the exclusive legal property of their fathers (*Welch v. Welch,* 1873).

Although women made great strides in the 20th century in accessing greater educational, financial, and social equality with men, many cultural biases, ingrained in the long history of the law, still burdened victims of domestic violence, sexual assault, and stalking. Many lawyers and judges still followed old court decisions that said a husband, as the superior legal and moral creature in the family, had the responsibility to discipline, control,

and chastise his wife. Until 1951, for example, California law gave husbands complete legal control over all of their wives' earnings, and as recently as 1988, the family law system in most states presumed that married women were legal dependents of their husbands, unless evidence to the contrary was presented in court (Kay, 1988).

Even up to the time of the passage of the Violence Against Women Act (VAWA) in 1994, many judges or juries expected victims to prove that they had tried to "manage" their behavior to avoid "provoking" male offenders to commit violence. A rape victim, for example, might have to show that she had not worn revealing clothing that "lured" the offender, or she might have to produce a witness to corroborate her testimony that she had told the offender she did not want to have sexual relations with him. It was not uncommon that a rape victim had to show evidence of bruises or scratches indicating that she had tried to fight off the attacker. If she did not fight (perhaps because she was afraid the attacker would seriously harm her), some judges or juries would assume that she had not said no with sufficient clarity. Because the law emphasized the victim's responsibility for managing the violence in these cases, rather than focusing on what the offender had done, offenders were rarely held accountable for their actions.

Creating Change on the State Level

In the early 1970s, the chief complaint of women calling crisis hot lines and seeking divorces at poverty law firms was that their husbands were battering and terrorizing them with impunity. Lawyers and advocates (who were both male and female) saw that these women could not rely on an inequitable legal system for justice. Many adopted a feminist viewpoint, which rejected the traditional constructs of women as being subordinate to their husbands. They rejected the idea that violent offenders could point to victims' behavior as an excuse for their criminal actions.

These lawyers and victim advocates brought their challenges in the courts and in the state legislatures, rewriting statutes and insisting that the law must no longer condone the subjection of women to the chastisement and coercive controls exercised by their husbands. Most important, these advocates, by pushing for new state laws, began to change the cultural climate that blamed women for the violence inflicted on them.

The lawyers and victim advocates doing this work made the first significant change in state law by developing and promoting statutes that allowed victims of domestic violence to go into family court to obtain civil protection orders.

Protection orders (also called injunctions, restraining orders, protection-from-abuse orders, harassment orders, stalking orders, stay-away orders, no-contact orders, protection orders incorporated into divorce decrees, conditions of release orders, and probation orders) are usually issued by a judge in family court. Under VAWA, a protection order can be issued by a civil or criminal court. It is defined broadly to include "any injunction or other order issued for the purpose of preventing violent or threatening acts or harassment against, or contact or communication with, or physical proximity to, another person" (18 U.S.C. § 2266).

For the order to be issued, one party (the victim) files a petition asking the court to protect her from acts of domestic violence, such as physical abuse, threats of harm, or harassing actions committed by a spouse, ex-spouse, or other intimate partner (depending on what state law allows). In many jurisdictions, the court then schedules a hearing and notifies the other party, the alleged abuser, to appear at the hearing. When both parties have presented their testimony and evidence, the judge makes findings about whether or not domestic violence occurred. If the judge finds that domestic violence has occurred, the judge then orders the remedies needed to protect the victim. The possible remedies are numerous, but the most common are ordering the abuser to refrain from further violence or threats, ordering the abuser to stay away from the victim, ordering the abuser to move out of the family home, and giving custody of children to the nonabusive parent. The civil protection order does not create a criminal record for the abuser, but it outlines what the abuser can and cannot do. The abuser is then put on notice that violation of the order could result in punishment, including possible criminal penalties.

Although the creation of the protection-order system constituted a simple addition to the body of family law, it made an enormous difference in the lives of battered women. For the first time, the victim controlled the initiation of the court process. She no longer had to wait and see if the local prosecutor would proceed with a criminal case. Instead, she could go to family court at any time after the abuser harmed or threatened her and ask for protection. Because these protection orders were issued in civil, not criminal proceedings, the amount of proof required was less, making it easier for victims to convince judges that abuse had occurred and that they were at continuing risk of more abuse. The other advantage of a civil protection-order system (as opposed to a criminal prosecution system) was that the victim was in the right court system to handle the other matters so integral to her safety: divorce, child custody, child support, spousal support, and division of marital property.

The passage of civil protection-order statutes precipitated a great change in social attitudes. In many states, for the first time, there was a legal recognition that a certain pattern of actions engaged in by a spouse or other intimate partner, including physical violence, sexual assault, financial deprivation, threats, stalking, and harassment, constituted a prohibited activity called domestic violence.

The Need for Federal Interventions to Address Violence Against Women

The Limits of State Authority to Legislate Change

The legislative change that created the civil protection-order system began on the state level. From the earliest days of the legal system in this country, the creation and implementation of family law legislation has been the province of the states, not the federal government (*In re Burrus,* 1890). Because of that legal division of labors, it was unthinkable in the 1960s and early 1970s that Congress would legislate in the arena of domestic violence, exclusively the responsibility of state legislative action, because domestic violence was considered a family law matter. Similarly, legislative changes addressing rape and sexual assault occurred for the most part on the state level, because criminal law, like family law, was a matter reserved to the states.

But it became clear that problems arose in domestic violence and sexual assault cases that could not be resolved entirely through changes to the states' family and criminal laws.

Shortly after the states passed their protection-order statutes, it became regrettably apparent that some of the men constrained from violence by court orders had no intention of adhering to the directives of the judges who issued them. As a result, state legislatures, at the urging of victim advocates, enacted enforcement provisions that gave the police and the courts greater authority to respond to abusers who violated protection orders.

If, for example, a protection order prohibited an abuser from contacting the victim, but the abuser turned up at her workplace to threaten her with further abuse, some state laws allowed the police and courts to treat this action as a criminal act, deserving of punishments such as jail time, probation, or other court-imposed restraints on his actions.

At the same time, states gave enhanced authority to police to enforce orders and arrest abusers. But the police, who had been trained to view domestic violence as a failure of communications and conflict-resolving skills within families, were reluctant to deal with domestic violence as a criminal matter. In addition, police hesitated to enforce court orders for administrative reasons: No databases were available to verify the court orders they were expected to enforce. To meet and counter this resistance, victim advocates negotiated first for local and countywide protection-order registries and then for statewide registries.

The effectiveness of these registries, however, was severely limited by geography. In the late 1980s, victim advocates began to realize that protection orders were not portable across state, tribal, or territorial lines. Some women lived in one state and worked in another, and many needed to relocate to enlist the support of family and friends in other states or on Indian land. Once these women left the state that had issued their protection order, they were seriously endangered because other states, tribes, or territories refused to enforce their protection orders.

Police officers, prosecutors, or judges, when presented with a violation of an order that had been awarded by a judge in a different state, claimed they lacked the authority to respond. State legislatures lacked the authority to pass laws compelling other states to enforce their orders. As a result, enforcement was uneven and worked well only in the locality where the order was granted.

Another problem impeded the effectiveness of the state protection-order system. Protection-order statutes had evolved separately in each state, resulting in a framework of similar but not identical laws. Some states would only protect heterosexual domestic violence victims or victims who had cohabited with the abuser, whereas other states would also protect victims in same-sex or dating relationships. The punishments for violations of these protection orders differed, too. In some jurisdictions, a violation would result in a criminal record and significant probation or jail time for the offender. In other states, a violation of a protection order was handled in family court, not criminal court.

Congressional Authority to Address Gaps in State Laws

Because the state laws were so uneven, victims in states with weaker protection-order statutes did not have access to the same protection as victims in other states.

Also, in many jurisdictions, judges failed to invoke or enforce their state protection-order laws because they still made judgments based on the historically subordinate view of women that had prevailed for so many centuries in the law. In both these situations, victims' civil rights were adversely affected.

To remedy these inequities, victim advocates turned to Congress for help. The opportunity for Congress to act on these issues opened up, as the U.S. Supreme Court had recognized situations in which federal law could better address some family law concerns than state law (*Hisquierdo v. Hisquierdo,* 1978).

The civil rights movement of the 1950s to the 1970s had raised national awareness that the states did not consistently protect individual rights. The Supreme Court cases that flowed from the civil rights movement established that the Constitution gave Congress the legislative authority to address discriminatory treatment and violations of civil rights. The discriminatory impact of state responses to domestic violence, sexual assault, and stalking could best be remedied by invoking Congress's constitutional authority to pass legislation to protect individuals from any state action that would "deny to any person within its jurisdiction the equal protection of the laws" (U.S. Constitution, XIV Amendment, Section 5).

Another line of Supreme Court cases led to the legal concept that states should encourage rather than limit interstate travel (*Shapiro v. Thompson,* 1968). Many victims had to move from one state to another, either to escape abusers or to find employment to establish economic independence from abusers. When states refused to recognize the protection orders issued by other states, victims were unable to engage safely in their "right to interstate travel." This required the passage of a federal law that would require all states to recognize out-of-state (also known as "foreign") protection orders. Only Congress had the authority to pass a law requiring every state, territory, and tribe to honor the protection orders issued by sister jurisdictions.

Most important, a line of cases starting from the Depression era and reaching up through the civil rights era had established that the Constitution gave Congress the authority to pass legislation on issues that affected interstate commerce (*Heart of Atlanta Motel, Inc. v. U.S.*, 1964; U.S. Constitution, Article I, Section 8, Clause 3). From 1990 to 1994, the U.S. Congress held hearings to determine whether domestic violence, sexual assault, and stalking affected interstate commerce sufficiently to trigger Congress's legislative authority to address these crimes (the Violence Against Women Act of 1990; Violent Crime Control and Law Enforcement Act of 1994; *Domestic Violence: Not Just a Family Matter,* 1994). As a result of these hearings, Congress found that 2 million to 4 million women in this country were victims of domestic violence each year, that women were six times more likely to experience violence by an intimate partner than men, that 70% of intimate-partner homicide victims were women, and that domestic violence was the leading cause of injury to U.S. women. Congress also found strong evidence that violence against women had substantial effects on interstate commerce, including costs attributable to health care, investigative and protective services, the criminal justice system, police forces, and lost worker productivity, all totaling between $5 billion and $10 billion annually.

The problems that so concerned victim advocates—the enforcement of out-of-state protection orders, the inconsistent protections offered to victims of violence against women within and across state lines, and the discriminatory attitudes displayed by the justice system—all added up to issues that Congress had the authority to address. Victim advocates, therefore, asked Congress to pass legislation that would rectify the inconsistencies and interstate gaps in state laws addressing violence against women. In addition, victim advocates asked Congress to provide funding to ensure that police, prosecutors, and courts would be trained about domestic violence, sexual assault, and stalking to improve responses of professionals to these crimes. This was the beginning of the work that would culminate in the passage of the VAWA in 1994.

The Violence Against Women Act (VAWA)

VAWA is a group of individually conceived legislative pieces that were joined together to create a package of federal laws and grant programs specifically addressing domestic violence, sexual assault, and stalking. Of the many portions of VAWA, five sections have the potential for having the greatest impact on improving the handling of crimes of violence against women in this country. These include

1. the full faith and credit provision (18 U.S.C. §§ 2265, 2266)
2. the interstate crimes of domestic violence (18 U.S.C. §§ 2261, 2262)
3. the battered immigrant women provisions [8 U.S.C. § 1154(a)(1)(A)(i), (ii), and (iii)]
4. the gun control provision [18 U.S.C. § 922(g)(8)]
5. the Violence Against Women grant programs, including the Grants to

Encourage Arrest (42 U.S.C. § 3796hh); the Law Enforcement and Prosecution Grants to Reduce Violent Crimes Against Women (popularly known as the STOP Violence Against Women Formula Grant Program and the STOP Violence Against Indian Women Grant Program, 42 U.S.C. § 3796gg); and the Rural Domestic Violence and Child Abuse Enforcement Assistance Grants (42 U.S.C. § 13971)

Another provision of VAWA, which has been used less frequently but which has generated more controversy, is the Civil Rights Remedy, a law giving victims of crime motivated by gender bias the right to sue the offenders in federal court (42 U.S.C. § 13981). A case brought under this law in federal court in Virginia has resulted in a legal challenge that has made its way to the U.S. Supreme Court. On May 15, 2000, the Supreme Court found that the Civil Rights Remedy was unconstitutional and struck that one provision of VAWA from the law books. The rest of VAWA, however, remains good law (*Brzonkala v. Morrison,* 1999).[1]

Full Faith and Credit Given to Protection Orders

The concept embodied in this relatively new federal law is simple. If one court issues a protection order, all other states, territories, and tribes must enforce it as vigorously and completely as they would enforce their own orders.

How would this help a particular woman who has been abused by her husband? Imagine that a woman named Mary

has resided with her husband, John, in State X. After years of abuse, Mary decides to leave her husband. She goes to the State X family court and obtains a protection order that prohibits John from physically abusing her, threatening her, or otherwise harassing her. The State X order also requires John to move out of the family home, stay 200 feet away from Mary, and refrain from contacting Mary by phone or through third parties. As a result of this order, John now lives one town away from Mary in State X. Both Mary and John commute into State Y every day for work.

One day, while John and Mary are working in State Y, John decides to disregard the prohibitions of the State X protection order. He turns up at Mary's workplace and demands of the receptionist that Mary come out and talk to him. When Mary refuses, John goes back to his workplace and spends the rest of the day calling her on the phone.

Prior to the passage of the Full Faith and Credit provision, Mary would have had difficulty asking for police or court help in State Y, the nonissuing state. Because her order was issued in State X but the violations occurred in State Y, neither the State X court nor the State Y police or courts would have responded. Thanks to VAWA's interstate protections, that gap can now be filled. Under the Full Faith and Credit provision, Congress has conferred the authority on State Y, through its police and courts, to honor the State X protection order as if it were an order that originated in State Y.

The sad reality, however, is that despite the best intentions of congressional lawmakers, most situations like Mary's are still not adequately addressed. Most law enforcement officers, prosecutors, family lawyers, and judges remain unfamiliar with the mandate established by the Full Faith and Credit provision and need training in how to implement this federal law in concert with existing state laws. Fortunately, VAWA also creates federal grant programs (described below) that provide the resources to train criminal justice system professionals in enforcing out-of-state orders.

The Requirements for Enforcing Out-of-State Protection Orders

The Full Faith and Credit provision directs enforcing states, tribes, and territories (the jurisdictions responding to the violations of the protection order) to enforce foreign protection orders as if they were issued in the enforcing jurisdiction.

The language of the Full Faith and Credit provision does not tell states, tribes, or territories exactly how to enforce foreign orders. Because the Full Faith and Credit provision is silent about these specifics, the states, tribes, and territories are free to establish their own enforcement procedures, provided they are consistent with the spirit of the federal law. One of the success stories of Full Faith and Credit is that many of the different enforcing authorities see the sense in developing common rules to ensure that victims receive uniform and consistent protection through protection-order enforcement procedures. Generally speaking, most states, tribes, and territories follow three basic rules.

First, states, tribes, and territories enforce all foreign protection orders, even if the parties protected by the orders would be ineligible for a protection order in the state to which they travel. Let's say Mary and John are dating partners. State X's law allows its courts to issue protection orders to victims in dating relationships, but State Y's law only allows courts to issue protection orders to married or formerly married intimate partners. Without the Full Faith and Credit provision, State Y's police and judges might say they had no authority to enforce an order covering a relationship not eligible for protection in State Y. With the Full Faith and Credit provision, it only matters that State X had the authority to issue the order. The only issue before State Y is enforcing the order.

The second rule is that State Y's courts must enforce all of the terms of State X's order, even if State X's order gives Mary protections that State Y is not allowed to offer. So, for example, the State X order might last for Mary's lifetime, because State X's law allows that. The court in State Y may only be allowed to issue orders that last for a year. Even if Mary's State X protection order is more than a year old, it is still enforceable under State X's laws. Under the Full Faith and Credit provision, State Y must still enforce the order, even though an order issued more than a year earlier in State Y would no longer be valid.

The third rule is that State Y must enforce the foreign order in the same manner it enforces its own orders. To punish a violation of State X's order, State Y must apply whatever penalties its own laws impose for violations of its own protection orders. It may be that a violation of a protection order in State X might result in a misdemeanor conviction requiring John to spend time in jail, whereas if the same violation occurs in State Y, the penalty may be a suspended sentence, so long as John attends a batterers' intervention program. If the violation occurs in State Y,

State Y's penalties will be applied in enforcing the order.

Changes Still Under Way

The development of consistent interstate enforcement procedures is a work in progress. Despite the best intentions of many victim advocates, judges, prosecutors, and police, the differences in eligibility, remedies, punishments, and procedures from state to state make it difficult to guarantee that battered women who relocate, travel, visit, work, or worship in another state, tribe, or territory will always be able to have the protection of their court orders enforced.

States have adopted legislation to make sure the basic rules of the Full Faith and Credit provision are followed. Both the federal government and the states have developed databases to make it easier for police, prosecutors, and the courts to track the issuance and validity of out-of-state protection orders. For example, on the federal level, information about protection orders is supposed to be entered in the National Criminal Information Center (NCIC) database, which is maintained by the FBI. When the system is finally completed and is fully operational, any law enforcement officer or court should be able to enter and verify protection orders from all participating states, tribes, and territories.

Protecting Due Process Rights Under Full Faith and Credit

The Full Faith and Credit provision allows states to enforce orders of protection, so long as both parties' constitutional rights to due process (notice of court proceedings against them and an op-

portunity to be heard in court) are honored (18 U.S.C. § 2265).

Three kinds of protection orders are generally issued. *Temporary* or *ex parte* orders usually last for anywhere from a few days to a few weeks and are issued on the testimony of a victim who is able to show that she is in sufficient danger that she needs temporary protection until a full court hearing can be scheduled at which both the victim and the abuser can present their own sides of the case. The alleged abuser is not present at an ex parte hearing. For that reason, it is essential that the temporary order be served on the alleged abuser, to ensure that he has had his constitutionally required notice of court action against him. At the same time, the Constitution requires that the court give him an opportunity to be heard in the near future. These requirements are called *due process,* and if they are not followed, the temporary order cannot be considered valid under the Full Faith and Credit provision.

A *final order* generally meets constitutional requirements of due process because it results from a scheduled court hearing; both the victim and the abuser had notice of the legal case and an opportunity to be heard by the court. Final orders generally may be enforced under the Full Faith and Credit provision.

The third type of protection order, commonly called a *mutual protection order,* is generally unenforceable under the Full Faith and Credit provision. A mutual protection order prohibits both the victim and the abuser from certain actions. These orders are often issued in a way that violates the victim's due process rights.

In Mary and John's case, for example, Mary may have petitioned State X for a protection order against John. During the course of the hearing, Mary may have testified that John hit her several times during an argument. John may have then testified that, during the argument, Mary was waving her arms around wildly and he thought she was trying to hit him, so that he attacked her in self-defense. The State X judge may not have probed further to find out whether John's statement about acting in self-defense was reasonable. In domestic violence cases, courts and law enforcement should not make decisions about who is at fault until they have analyzed who is really the primary or continuing aggressor in the relationship. In Mary's case, the judge may have abdicated his responsibility to determine the primary aggressor and may have, instead, spontaneously decided that it would be easier to issue an order requiring both Mary *and* John to refrain from hitting each other.

The problem with this scenario is that Mary went to court in the posture of a victimized party. She had no notice that John would ask the court to treat him as a victim, too. Her testimony and evidence had to do with the injuries John had done to her. She was not prepared to defend herself against charges by John that *she* had been an offender.

To protect Mary's constitutional due process rights, the judge hearing her case should have kept the hearing focused on her petition, not John's unexpected complaint of violence. The judge should have required John to file his own petition for a protection order, scheduled another hearing, and served Mary with notice of John's complaint. This would protect Mary's due process rights, just as John's had been protected.

Unfortunately, judges who have little understanding of domestic violence issues (such as what actions identify a primary or continuing aggressor or what ac-

tions constitute appropriate self-defense in a domestic violence case) may end up issuing these spontaneous mutual protection orders. A mutual order issued in this manner is not enforceable against the victim under the Full Faith and Credit provision. It is enforceable against the perpetrator because his due process rights were protected by notice and the opportunity to be heard. To be enforceable against the victim in another state, tribe, or territory, the mutual order must have resulted because *both* parties filed papers asking the court for a protection order, both parties had notice of each other's request, and both had an individual opportunity to prepare for and to be heard by the court.

Determining Jurisdiction Under the Full Faith and Credit Provision

For an order to be enforced under the Full Faith and Credit provision, the enforcing court must have jurisdiction, which refers to the court's authority to handle the case in question.

Jurisdiction can depend on the kind of case being handled. If the issue is a family law matter, such as a civil protection order or a divorce, the family law court, not the criminal court, will have the jurisdiction or authority to hear the case.

Jurisdiction also refers to the location of the violence. A woman who is battered in one state by her husband must initially ask that state's courts to issue an order for her protection and relief. Once the order is issued, another state, tribe, or territory may enforce the order under Full Faith and Credit.

In the case of Mary and John, if Mary has a State X order and John violates that order by harming Mary in State X, State X is the state with jurisdiction to address the violation. If Mary has a State X order and John violates that order by harming Mary in State Y, then State Y has jurisdiction to address the violation.

Enforcing Child Custody and Visitation Provisions in a Protection Order

In most cases where the victim of domestic violence has children in common with the abuser, a court issuing a protection order will also direct the parties as to who should have custody of the children and when and where the noncustodial parent may visit with the children.

Some victim advocates, courts, and legislators believe that custody and visitation provisions are integral to guaranteeing the safety of the victimized party and, therefore, should be enforced under the Full Faith and Credit provision. Other courts and legislators believe that this portion of a protection order is only enforceable under a different set of laws from the Full Faith and Credit provision.

The language of VAWA is vague as to whether custody and visitation provisions issued within the protection order are enforceable under the Full Faith and Credit provision. There is no legislative history about what Congress intended. Only future decisions by state, tribal, or territorial courts or clarifying language by Congress will settle this question.

Enforcing Criminal Orders

The Full Faith and Credit provision also applies to protection orders issued during criminal proceedings. For example, John may be charged in criminal court with assaulting Mary in State X. The criminal court may issue a restraining order prohibiting John from hurting, approaching, threatening, or harassing Mary during his pretrial release. The court may also issue a restraining order once John has been convicted and released on probation, parole, or suspended sentence. If John follows Mary into State Y and violates the terms of State X's order, the police in State Y should properly arrest and charge John with violation of the criminal order.

The reality is that Mary may obtain little in the way of protection in State Y. The criminal justice system, like the civil family law system, varies greatly from state to state. For example, some state statutes permit police to arrest violators of criminal protection orders without first seeking a warrant, and others do not. Until states, tribes, and territories make changes to their criminal laws and procedures that will make this process more consistent, police are not likely to enforce a criminal protection order from another jurisdiction.

Military Orders

The Full Faith and Credit provision of VAWA does not expressly cover orders issued on military bases. In fact, most military protection orders will not satisfy the due process requirements imposed by the Constitution. Military protection orders are usually issued by a commanding officer without giving the abuser an opportunity to be heard on the allegations of domestic violence. Because of this due process defect, orders issued on military bases will not be entitled to Full Faith and Credit in states, tribes, and territories. On the other hand, commanders on military bases have the authority to respond to violations of constitutionally sound civilian protection orders issued by any state, tribe, or territory that are intended to restrain the actions of military service members.

Federal Domestic Violence and Stalking Crimes

Some offenders commit acts of violence against women in the course of crossing state, tribal, or territorial boundaries, as they pursue, stalk, or harass intimate partners. Prior to the creation of three new federal crimes in VAWA, most of these cross-jurisdictional acts went unpunished.

To understand why these laws are so important, assume Mary has left State X to go to work in State Y. John sends a threatening e-mail (originating in State X) to her workplace (received in State Y). John then turns up at Mary's office and forces her to get into his car. He drives her around State Y, hitting her and threatening her with worse abuse. Without releasing Mary from the car, John then drives back into State X, forcing her to come to his house, where he commits further acts of domestic violence.

Which state should respond to John's actions? If both states wish to respond, how will each know exactly when one act of domestic violence began and when it ended, for the purposes of deciding which state will punish which act? Which state should prosecute the e-mail threat? What if Mary did not have a protection order? What if she already had a protection order against John? In tribal courts, what would happen if Mary were a Native American and John were not? The answers to all of these questions are crucial. In some cases, certain answers would mean that it would be impossible for any state, tribe, or territory to take steps to punish John.

Victim advocates and members of Congress realized that our increasingly mobile society creates nightmarish questions such as those presented above. The easy accessibility of instant, yet far-flung electronic and telephone communications networks has lengthened the reach of abusers. How can states, tribes, and territories sort out these complicated scenarios? What if an act straddling state, tribal, or territorial boundaries constitutes a serious rampage really deserving of a felony charge—but is only treated as two minor offenses, once its component parts have been divided up between the two jurisdictions?

States and territories only have the authority to address crimes committed completely within their borders. Tribes only have authority to arrest Native perpetrators committing crimes on Indian land. Victim advocates, then, had to turn to Congress to develop an effective response to crimes committed in this interstate no man's land. Congress crafted three new federal crimes. The first makes it a crime to commit domestic violence across state, territorial, or tribal lines (18 U.S.C. § 2261). The second makes it a crime to violate the terms of a protection order in the course of crossing state, territorial, or tribal lines (18 U.S.C. § 2262). The third new federal crime (which was created by a law passed in 1996) prohibits stalking across state lines or within special federal jurisdictions of the United States (18 U.S.C. § 2261A).

These new laws have proved useful because the federal prosecution system has superior resources and authority to investigate and prosecute offenses occurring in multiple jurisdictions. In addition, the sentences Congress devised for these crimes are far more serious than the punishments available on state, tribal, or territorial levels. An abuser can no longer use the confusion of multiple jurisdictions to evade justice.

Interstate Travel to Commit Domestic Violence [18 U.S.C. § 2261(a)(1)-(2)]

The first federal crime law of domestic violence covers actions that take place when a protection order has not been issued. An abuser may commit a crime of interstate domestic violence when he decides intentionally to travel from one state, tribal land, or territory to another to threaten or harm a spouse or an intimate partner. An abuser may also commit this crime by forcing a spouse or intimate partner to cross a state, tribal, or territorial line to threaten or harm that spouse or intimate partner. In both cases, the abuser has to commit a crime of violence that results in bodily injury to the victim. VAWA makes these actions federal crimes. An abuser can no longer evade prosecution just because it is unclear in which state, tribe, or territory the harm to the victim began. Federal courts have formally recognized the creation of this crime law as a way to end abusers' use of interstate travel "as a loophole in the system of law enforcement" (*United States v. Helem,* 1999; *United States v. Page,* 1999).

Interstate Violation of a Protection Order [18 U.S.C. §§ 2262(a)(1)-(2)]

This law recognizes the crime of traveling across a state, territorial, or tribal border with the intent to violate a protection order; when the violation of the order occurs, the crime is complete. Only violations of certain provisions within a protection order can trigger the application of this law—specifically, behavior constitut-

ing credible threats of violence, repeated harassment, or bodily injury to the protected person(s).

This law also makes it a federal crime for a person to force an intimate partner to cross state or territorial lines or enter or leave Indian country for the purpose of intentionally injuring the victimized intimate partner in violation of a valid protection order.

One of the first cases prosecuted under § 2262(a)(1) was *United States v. Casciano* (1997). This case illustrates how this new federal crime can occur. A woman from Massachusetts briefly dated a man named Michael Casciano. After he engaged in a variety of threatening and harassing behaviors toward her, she broke off their relationship and obtained a protection order from Massachusetts prohibiting him from harming or approaching her. A student, she spent some of her time in her home state, Massachusetts, and some time in New York, where she went to school. Michael Casciano tracked her whereabouts and violated the Massachusetts order by harassing her in New York via e-mail, phone calls, and appearances in her classes and the library. Some of his actions, like the e-mail and phone calls, originated in Massachusetts, but others occurred in New York. Because this case had multijurisdictional elements, neither New York nor Massachusetts had the resources to punish all of his actions. It was most appropriate to use the new federal law prohibiting interstate violations of protection orders to prosecute and convict him.

Interstate Stalking (18 U.S.C. § 2261A)

This new law makes it a federal crime to cross a state line or to travel within areas of special federal jurisdiction with the intent to injure or harass any person if, during the course of or as a result of the travel, the offender places the person or a member of the person's immediate family in reasonable fear of death or serious bodily injury. There is no requirement under this statute that actual bodily harm occur for a conviction to result.

Stalking is a crime that is only recently being taken seriously by legislatures, courts, and law enforcement. Both law enforcement and the courts have, unfortunately and incorrectly, viewed stalking as a potential crime rather than as a completed crime. Stalkers engage in behavior that is threatening or harassing, such as following victims to and from work, standing outside of their homes on public walkways or streets, and making repeated phone calls to terrorize the victim. In the past, the justice system ignored stalking on the grounds that stalking actions did not constitute complete crimes, such as assault, battery, or rape. Victims of this crime, however, knew its dangers only too well. In addition to placing victims at real risk of physical injury, stalkers create a climate of fear and harassment that actually harms victims by causing them extreme emotional distress and limiting their social and workplace movements.

A recent case prosecuted under the interstate stalking statute is *United States v. Young* (1999). The facts of this case clearly define stalking behavior. Young's former girlfriend obtained protection orders in both the District of Columbia, where she worked, and Maryland, where she resided after she ended the relationship with Young. Despite the protection orders, Young repeatedly threatened, harassed, and stalked his former girlfriend. On one occasion, he called her several times at home and at work early in the

morning to tell her he wanted to meet her at her office building at noon. She reluctantly agreed to meet him in the lobby of her office building but brought a coworker along with her because she was afraid to meet him alone. During the meeting, she repeatedly asked Young to leave. He eventually left after she accepted a ring he insisted she take back. Although Young did not physically harm his former girlfriend, she was justifiably afraid that he might do so at any time. Based on his past history of abusive behavior and his obsessive intrusions into her life, his former girlfriend reasonably believed she was in imminent physical danger.

Prosecution under the federal stalking statute provided an appropriate way to respond to behavior that, prior to the passage of VAWA, would have been difficult to prosecute. The VAWA statute provided two important elements to help Young's former intimate partner. First, the statute recognized stalking itself as a crime. The U.S. Attorney (the federal prosecutor) did not have to wait for Young to strike the first blow to charge him with a crime; his harassing and terrorizing behavior was enough to constitute a criminal action. Second, the statute gave the U.S. Attorney authority to address Young's actions in their entirety, rather than dividing the case up based on the jurisdiction in which actions occurred. This allowed the prosecutor to make clear to the court the pattern of his stalking behavior. The federal stalking statute made it possible to close the legal loophole that once made actions like Young's impossible to punish.

Gun Control Act Amendments

Advocates have long recognized that firearms pose a grave threat to the lives of victims of domestic violence. A woman is far more likely to be killed by her spouse, an intimate acquaintance, or a family member than she is to be murdered by a stranger (Violence Policy Center, 1997). Studies have also found that when males kill female intimates, more than half use firearms (Violence Policy Center, 1997). Victim advocates and law enforcement also provide overwhelming anecdotal evidence that firearms are often used to intimidate, as well as to injure or kill victims of domestic abuse.

In 1994, Congress recognized the risk that firearms present to victims of domestic violence when it amended the Gun Control Act (18 U.S.C. § 921, et seq.) to include four firearm prohibitions related to domestic violence. These amendments make it a federal crime for people to possess a firearm or ammunition if they are subject to certain types of protection orders or have been convicted of certain types of misdemeanor domestic violence crimes [18 U.S.C. § 922(g)(1)-(9)]. In some cases, this gun prohibition is triggered when the court has found that the person restrained by the protection order represents a "credible threat" to the victim protected by the order. In other cases, if the protection order specifically bars the abuser from using, attempting, or threatening use of physical force against the intimate partner protected by the order, the gun prohibition may apply. Law enforcement and military personnel who are subject to qualifying protection orders are exempt from this section while on duty.

A related provision [18 U.S.C. § 922(d)(8)] makes it a federal crime for a person to transfer a firearm or ammunition to a second person if the first person knows or has reasonable cause to believe the second person is subject to one of the types of protection orders covered by this law.

Like other laws limiting or prohibiting the use, possession, or sale of firearms, these domestic violence prohibitions have generated a flurry of court cases that have challenged these laws on the grounds that they violate numerous parts of the U.S. Constitution; the federal circuit courts have rejected these various challenges (*Fraternal Order of Police v. United States,* 1999; *Gillespie v. Indianapolis,* 1999; *United States v. Baker,* 1999; *United States v. Beavers,* 2000; *United States v. Meade,* 1999; *United States v. Myers,* 1999).

The Battered Immigrant Women Provisions

Advocates also recognized the severe problems faced by battered immigrant women under the provisions of the Immigration and Naturalization Service (INS) law and sought to reduce the barriers to permanent residency and citizenship for battered immigrant women through VAWA.

Immigrant women come to this country for many reasons. Some accompany husbands who want to study, work, or live here on a permanent basis. Some women immigrate to fulfill their own educational or economic goals. Many are sponsored by family members already in this country. Many of these women are here legally; many are not. Whatever their hopes and dreams prior to coming to the United States, whatever their economic status on their arrival, immigrant women face overwhelming cultural, linguistic, and social changes in their lives, once they arrive. It is not easy to be an immigrant in America. It is even harder to be a battered immigrant woman.

Battered immigrant women suffer many of the same problems that battered women who are U.S. citizens endure. Getting help from law enforcement or obtaining legal assistance is often difficult. Finding appropriate shelter, counseling, social service, and economic assistance is not easy. Finding work that pays well enough to allow a woman to leave the abuser, especially if she has children, is tough. Keeping a job and remaining safe, when the abuser is determined to harm her, may seem impossible. Battered immigrant women endure the same ordeals as their U.S. citizen sisters do. But a battered immigrant woman must also overcome a host of difficulties related to her status as an immigrant in this country.

For a woman coming from a less developed country, whose social fabric was a village-based, extended family environment, the time-urgent, automobile-based, individualistic culture of the United States can make her search for help absolutely terrifying. She may be a highly educated professional, someone of wealth and status in her home country, but bereft of earning potential in a country where she does not speak the language fluently and where her professional credentials are not recognized. As an immigrant, she may know no one except her abusive spouse, and she will not even think to look for help outside the home, because she has been raised to look for support only from her extended family or to view herself only in inextricable connection with her husband and his family. The battered immigrant woman who does locate a needed service may find that she cannot get there, because her abusive spouse has strictly forbidden contact with anyone outside of the home or has discouraged her from learning how to drive.

Even if she can identify and make her way to the services she needs, a battered immigrant woman may hesitate in the doorway of the agency where she is seeking help. She may be afraid of experiencing hostility because of her race or country of origin. She may speak no English or may not have the English language skills to express her needs, however eloquent she may be in her native tongue. She may try to use her children as interpreters, putting herself in the position of having to describe humiliating incidents to them so that they can render them into English for the agency staff trying to assist her.

A battered immigrant woman may be terrified to call the police for help because the police in her home country brutalize people, or she has heard stories in her immigrant community that have convinced her that the police will deport her. She may fear that using government benefit programs will reflect negatively on her application to the INS. She may be afraid of being forced to reveal that she has been working illegally, either because her abusive spouse required it or because her family could not survive without her economic contribution. Her husband, as part of the pattern of his abuse, may have told her that U.S. courts will not allow women to testify on their own behalf or that U.S. judges always give custody of children to men. She may remain silent because her husband has told her he will kidnap the children or disgrace her before her family if she seeks help.

Most important, she may not ask for help because her husband is using the immigration process to harass her and control her behavior.

Before the passage of VAWA, a spouse seeking permanent legal residence in the United States had to rely on a spouse who was a U.S. citizen or legal permanent resident to file and follow through on her immigration petition. Although this requirement was meant to prevent fraudulent marriages, it also became a tool for abusers to use to threaten and control their victimized spouses. The abusive spouse could file a petition on his partner's behalf and then withdraw it at will. He could refuse to appear at hearings or withhold documents to prevent the victimized spouse from "regularizing" her immigration status. His threats to hold up her petition process could coerce her into silence about the abuse, and his obstruction of the petition process could deprive her of the immigration status she needed to achieve economic independence.

In 1994, Congress responded to this untenable situation by passing the battered immigrant women provisions of the VAWA. The first of these provisions allows a battered immigrant to apply for legal permanent residency without the assistance of her spouse if she (a) is an eligible immigrant, (b) has been subjected to extreme cruelty by her husband, (c) is a person of good moral character, and (d) would suffer extreme hardship if forced to return to her country of origin. This process is called *self-petitioning,* and it disables the abusive spouse's capacity to control his immigrant wife's quest for legal permanent-resident status. When using this administrative process to apply for residency in the United States, the battered immigrant woman must show she is a person of good moral character.

A second provision, called *cancellation of removal,* was needed to help those women who could not meet the requirements of the self-petitioning process. Many battered immigrant women in this country are here illegally, either because

their temporary visas have expired or because they entered the country without inspection. Some battered immigrant women are subject to deportation because they have been divorced by their U.S. citizen or legal permanent-resident spouses.

With the passage of VAWA, battered immigrant women subject to deportation may now ask the INS to grant them cancellation of removal. Cancellation of removal takes away the threat of deportation, which most battered immigrant women fear nearly as much as the abuse, and it clears the way to seek legal permanent residency in the United States. A battered immigrant woman seeking legal permanent residency under this provision must show the INS that (a) she is deportable under law; (b) she or her child has been battered or subjected to extreme cruelty by her U.S. citizen or legal permanent-resident spouse; (c) she has been physically present in the United States for 3 years prior to the date of the application; (d) she has been a person of good moral character during this 3-year period; and (e) her deportation would result in extreme hardship to herself, her child, or her parent.

Whether a battered immigrant woman tries to regularize her immigration status through self-petitioning or cancellation of removal, she must show the INS that she would suffer extreme hardship if she had to return to her country of origin. She can present evidence of the domestic violence she has endured to illustrate why sending her back to her home country would create extreme hardship for her. She can show that her home country has no laws to protect her from domestic violence, so that deportation from the United States (with its strong laws regarding domestic violence) would place her in great physical danger. If her husband has also been abusive to her U.S. citizen children, she can show that her deportation would create extreme hardship for her and her children if she had to return to her home country and leave the children in the custody of the abuser.

These new provisions of VAWA have made an enormous difference in the lives of battered immigrant women. For the first time for many of these women, their immigration decisions and process are under their own control, not subject to the harassing whims of an abusive spouse. As a result of this new law, the INS has created a dedicated office staffed by personnel with specialized training on domestic violence to handle battered immigrant women's applications. With access to these new application procedures, battered immigrant women can envision a life in the United States on their own terms, free from abuse and at liberty to create the financial independence so many immigrants hope for when they come to this country.[2]

The Federal Grant Programs

One of the least heralded but most significant aspects of the VAWA was the creation of three new grant programs: the Grants to Encourage Arrest (42 U.S.C. § 3796hh); the Law Enforcement and Prosecution Grants to Reduce Violent Crimes Against Women (popularly known as the STOP Violence Against Women Formula Grant Program and the STOP Violence Against Indian Women Grant Program, 42 U.S.C. § 3796gg); and the Rural Domestic Violence and Child Abuse Enforcement Assistance Grants (42 U.S.C. § 13971).

These grant programs, which are administered by the U.S. Department of Justice's Violence Against Women Office, have delivered hundreds of millions of dollars to state, tribal, territorial, and local programs to provide direct services to victims of domestic violence, sexual assault, and stalking. The Grants to Encourage Arrest are used to fund programs in the law enforcement and criminal justice fields, including training for police officers, prosecutors, judges, and other justice system personnel. The Rural Program has funded programs in rural parts of the country that never before had the resources to offer adult and child victims of crimes of violence against women; through this program, new positions and programs have been created, including victim advocacy projects that protect victims' rights and safety. The STOP Formula Grant Program sends money directly to the states, as well as tribal and territorial governments, to disburse according to principles developed through a state plan meant to improve and coordinate services for victims of violence against women.

Of all of the changes created by VAWA, the grant programs have arguably had the greatest impact on social and system responses to domestic violence, sexual assault, and stalking. The projects funded through these programs must meet strict operating requirements, which guarantee consistent and safe services for victims of crimes of violence against women. Thousands of professionals in the criminal justice and victim advocacy systems have been trained using these funds. Not only have these trainees learned the changes wrought by VAWA, but they have also been thoroughly schooled in the emotional, psychological, financial, and legal problems confronted by victims of domestic violence, sexual assault, and stalking.

As a result, law enforcement, prosecution, judicial, legal assistance, and victim advocacy standards have evolved steadily since the passage of VAWA in 1994. Professionals addressing domestic violence have become accustomed to working in multidisciplinary groups to achieve real system change. The standards of service established by local law enforcement, courts, prosecutors' offices, and the private bar have greatly improved and have become more consistent with sister jurisdictions, thanks to the influence these grant programs have had. Most important, the lion's share of the funding from these programs has gone to expand direct services to victims of violence against women. Prior to 1994, there were few specialized units in police departments or prosecutors' offices or courts to address domestic violence, sexual assault, and stalking. Now, thanks to these grant programs, local jurisdictions view these specialized programs as institutional priorities, meaning that many more victims of these crimes will have qualified and energetic assistance and support.

The Civil Rights Remedy of VAWA

The Civil Rights Remedy was created to address the discriminatory injustices that too often prevailed in the state court systems. As described above, the uneven framework of laws that exist across the country often resulted in unjust differences in the outcomes of cases addressing violence against women. In addition, the historical bias of the law and the professionals in the legal system—the supposition that women were legally inferior to

men and the attitude that victims of these crimes had a responsibility to manage the behavior of the offenders—contributed to results in cases that left women financially and emotionally depleted. Congress, in adopting this provision of VAWA, made clear its commitment to protecting the civil rights of victims by giving them access to the federal court system, which was presumed to have better resources to address the needs of women victims than the state court systems had historically offered. Unfortunately, the majority of the U.S. Supreme Court, in *U.S. v. Morrison* (2000), found that Congress exceeded its legislative authority in passing this single provision of VAWA. It is important to note that the rest of VAWA remains good law, despite this ruling.

The Supreme Court did not dispute the need victims have for laws such as the Civil Rights Remedy; rather, the majority expressed the clear belief that states should address these problems. A description of the Civil Rights Remedy and the reasons Congress had for trying to offer this protection helps explain the great work that remains to be done on the state level, now that this federal law has been struck down.

The Civil Rights Remedy was primarily designed to give the victim of a gender-motivated crime the right to sue in federal or state court for monetary damages. This financial compensation is necessary to cover the costs borne by victims of violence against women, including medical and mental health treatment, job retraining, loss of property and assets, and a host of other financial and physical injuries arising from the offender's commission of crimes of violence.

Technically, the Civil Rights Remedy was gender-neutral, which means that

Congress assumed that men might have claims under this provision as well. The reality was that the cases filed under this statute had female plaintiffs and male defendants, indicating that women were the primary victims of gender-motivated crimes.

The congressional authors of the statute generally assumed that the crimes of violence most likely to trigger the use of the Civil Rights Remedy were domestic violence, sexual assault, or stalking. However, just proving that any of these forms of violence occurred was not enough to win under this law. Congress also required plaintiffs to show that these violent acts were motivated by gender bias.

This provision of VAWA could have helped many victims of violence against women. However, the U.S. Supreme Court's ruling on May 15, 2000 (*U.S. v. Morrison*) has rendered this form of relief unavailable as a federal protection.

Five of the justices on the Court decided that the Civil Rights Remedy should not be a federal law. In the majority opinion, Chief Justice Rehnquist wrote that the Constitution reserved certain areas of the law to states, such as criminal and family law, which are implicated in the Civil Rights Remedy. The majority essentially did not want to see domestic violence and sexual assault cases in federal court, because these are traditionally state issues, unless there is a clear interstate component to the activity regulated by the statute. The majority ruled that no interstate component existed to trigger Congress's legislative authority to pass the Civil Rights Remedy.

The four dissenting justices, like VAWA's primary sponsors in Congress, firmly expressed their opinion that the Civil Rights Remedy does address federal issues because violence against women has an adverse effect on interstate commerce. They noted the voluminous testimony collected by Congress, for example, showing that violence against women causes women to lose valuable productivity in the national workforce and drains money from government systems within and across state lines, because governments must provide expensive legal and social services to deal with it. They also observed that Congress had the legislative authority under Section 5 of the Fourteenth Amendment of the Constitution to write laws addressing violent acts of discrimination by private individuals.

This ruling is an important one. It is not so much a statement about violence against women as it is a vehicle to rein in congressional legislative authority. In fact, the majority agreed that the problems that this provision tried to address are real and that Congress heard substantial testimony to illustrate the breadth of the problem. *U.S. v. Morrison* (2000) is reflective of a growing line of cases that will be the legacy of the Rehnquist Court, a line of cases that began when the Court narrowed the constitutional interpretation of Congress's legislative authority in *U.S. v. Lopez* (1995). Many constitutional law experts believe that the Supreme Court will continue to issue decisions that further limit the expansive legislative authority Congress has exercised since the 1930s.

The rest of VAWA is still good law and not as vulnerable to constitutional challenge as the Civil Rights Remedy was. The other sections—which deal with interstate crimes of domestic violence; enforcement of protection orders across state, tribal and territorial lines; changes to INS law regarding battered immigrant women; and the federal grants programs—are all clearly within the limits of congressional legislative authority. They do not address issues generally reserved to the states; in fact, they provide for issues that the states do not have the capacity to address themselves.

Now that the Civil Rights Remedy has been invalidated by the Supreme Court, Congress may try to pass a new version that more closely meets constitutional tests, based on the limits the Supreme Court set in its decision. Alternatively, Congress may not resurrect this as a federal issue, and it may become necessary for states to adopt, on an individual basis, similar laws giving victims of gender-bias crimes a state cause of action against the perpetrators of those crimes. Not every state will decide to pass such laws, so the result may be an uneven patchwork of protections across the country, precisely what the Civil Rights Remedy was meant to prevent.

Conclusion

The VAWA of 1994 is a great experiment in the law. Victim advocates had gone to Congress hoping for change, and Congress focused intently on the heretofore unexamined crimes of domestic violence, sexual assault, and stalking. The hearings held on Capitol Hill to investigate the wide-ranging problems created by these crimes forever changed the national perception of violence against women. Domestic violence, sexual assault, and stalking were no longer unsubstantiated feminist "complaints." Statistical and empirical evidence was gathered and preserved in the public record to show that the suffering of victims of crimes of violence against women was real—and was substantial enough to qualify as a concern of national interest. The discoveries of Congress piqued the interest of the media,

the legal system, the justice system, and the public health system. The passage of VAWA created a radical change on the state, tribal, and territorial levels, as grant monies and technical assistance shaped the attitudes of professionals who came into contact with victims of crimes of violence against women every day. The prosecution of the new federal crimes and enforcement responsibilities created by VAWA also caused an enormous shift in how seriously these crimes were treated on the state level. VAWA defined new national standards and expectations regarding community responses to domestic violence, sexual assault, and stalking. With its legal authority and financial supports, VAWA has created a new climate, one that promotes victim safety, offender accountability, a responsive system of justice, and a community in which victims of crimes of violence against women can begin their personal searches for healing, safety, and justice.

Notes

1. Congress reauthorized the VAWA in October 2000, ensuring that the grant programs will continue. As part of this legislative package, Congress created a new statutory grant program that funds civil legal assistance for victims of domestic violence and sexual assault. In addition, VAWA 2000 made further improvements to Immigration and Naturalization Service law to help battered immigrant women.

2. For a comprehensive discussion of all of the immigration laws offering relief to battered immigrant women, see *Domestic Violence and Immigration: Applying the Immigration Provisions of the Violence Against Women Act* (Orloff et al., 1999), which was produced with a grant from the Office for Victims of Crime, U.S. Department of Justice, Grant No. 97-VF-GX-K019.

References

Blackstone, W. (1979). *Commentaries on the laws of England* (Book 1). Chicago: University of Chicago Press. (Original work published 1765)

Brzonkala v. Morrison, U.S. Supreme Court, Nos. 99-29 & 99-5 (1999).

Domestic violence: Not just a family matter (Hearing before the Subcommittee on Crime and Criminal Justice of the House Committee on the Judiciary), 103rd Congress, 2nd Session (1994).

Fraternal Order of Police v. United States, 173 F.3d 898 (D.C. Cir.), *cert. denied,* 120 S. Ct. 324 (1999).

Gillespie v. Indianapolis, 185 F.3d 693 (7th Cir. 1999).

Goelman, D. M., Lehrman, F. L., & Valente, R. L. (Eds.). (1996). *The impact of domestic violence on your legal practice.* Washington, DC: American Bar Association.

Hawkins v. U.S., 358 U.S. 74 (1958).

Heart of Atlanta Motel, Inc. v. U.S., 379 U.S. 241 (1964).

Hisquierdo v. Hisquierdo, 439 U.S. 572 (1978).

In re Burrus, 136 U.S. 586 (1890).

Kay, H. H. (1988). *Sex-based discrimination.* St. Paul: West.

Orloff, L., Kaguyutan, J., Pendleton, G., Goelman, D., Maher, H., Valente, R., & Garlow, B. (1999). *Domestic violence and immigration: Applying the immigration provisions of the Violence Against Women Act.* Washington, DC: American Bar Association.

Rose v. Rose, 4 NYS 856 (1889).

Shapiro v. Thompson, 394 U.S. 618 (1968).

State v. Jones, 95 N.C. 588 (1886).

United States v. Baker, 197 F.3d 211 (6th Cir. 1999).

United States v. Beavers, No. 99-1829, 2000, U.S. App. LEXIS 2080 (6th Cir. Feb. 16, 2000).

United States v. Casciano, 124 F.3d 106 (2d. Cir.), *cert. denied,* 522 U.S. 1034 (1997).

United States v. Helem, 186 F.3d 449 (4th Cir.), *cert. denied,* 120 S. Ct. (1999).

United States v. Lopez, 115 S. Ct. 1624 (1995).

United States v. Meade, 175 F.3d 215 (1st Cir. 1999).

United States v. Morrison, 120 S.Ct. 1740 (2000).

United States v. Myers, 187 F.3d 644 (8th Cir. 1999) (per curiam).

United States v. Page, 167 F.3d 325 (6th Cir.), *cert. denied,* 120 S. Ct. 496 (1999).

United States v. Young, No. 98-4742, 1999 U.S. App. LEXIS 32721 (Dec. 16, 1999).

Violence Against Women Act of 1990, 101 S. Rpt. 545 (U.S. Senate Committee on the Judiciary: October 19, 1990).

Violence Policy Center. (1997). *When men murder women: An analysis of 1996 homicide data.* Washington, DC: Author.

Violent Crime Control and Law Enforcement Act of 1994, 103 H. Rpt. 711 (U.S. House of Representatives Committee on the Judiary: August 21, 1994).

Warrant unserved, Maryland; Maryland killing mourned, questioned; judicial system failed slain wife, officials say. (2000, January 5). *Washington Post,* p. A1.

Welch v. Welch, 33 Wis. 534 (1873).

CHAPTER 16

Criminal Justice System Responses to Domestic Violence

Law Enforcement and the Courts

LeeAnn Iovanni
Susan L. Miller

In this chapter, we focus on recent developments in the criminal justice system's handling of domestic violence cases. Changes in criminal justice policy regarding domestic violence came about as a result of several occurrences in the 1970s and the early 1980s. The victim's rights movement and the women's movement took a stand against the entire criminal justice system's trivializing of violence committed against women. The battered women's shelter movement exposed how common and widespread domestic violence was and demonstrated that battered women were not pathologically ill. In the legal arena, class action civil suits against police departments argued successfully that police responded more slowly and with less seriousness to violent crimes committed between non-strangers than they did to stranger crimes. Finally, social science researchers published scientific evidence claiming that arrest was more effective in deterring domestic violence than were other police responses, a development that fell neatly in line with the already growing demands for more rigorous criminal justice system intervention in violence against women.

This chapter describes and analyzes the legal response to domestic violence by the criminal justice actors at each point in the process: police officers, prosecutors, judges, and probation officers. Among the recent developments reviewed are mandatory and presumptive arrest policies, no-drop prosecution policies, the increased granting of civil restraining orders, and integrated or unified courts. The positive and negative aspects of current policies are examined in terms of how well they are actually implemented, what effect they have on the recidivism of domestic violence perpetrators, and how well they address the needs and preferences of victims. Findings from relevant empirical research are discussed. Although serious intervention in domestic violence is now a widely accepted goal in the system, we also note how the practices and attitudes of criminal justice actors have not always kept pace with legislative and policy changes.

Police Practices

Historically, the criminal justice system treated domestic violence as a private issue, following a policy of nonintervention. Rather than respond to domestic violence as they would to other types of violence, police were encouraged to handle the situation as a civil matter, separating the parties or mediating the altercation. Until the mid-1980s, almost half of the states did not permit police to make arrests in domestic violence cases if there was no visible injury and if they had not witnessed the abuse (Sherman, 1992). In the last 15 years, however, great strides have been made to transform the beliefs and practices of the criminal justice system regarding domestic violence, with initial efforts being focused on the police. Most states now provide police with the option to arrest in misdemeanor domestic violence cases that they have not witnessed, but police officers may still rely on advising, mediating, possibly separating the couple, or issuing a citation to the offender requiring him to appear in court to answer specific charges. But in re-

sponse to demands for more aggressive criminal justice action in domestic violence cases, mandatory and presumptive arrest statutes, which either limit or strongly guide police discretion, have become increasingly popular in current law enforcement efforts. These policies state that police officers *have to* (mandatory) or *should* (presumptive) arrest domestic violence perpetrators when probable cause for misdemeanor violence exists, even if the violence does not occur in the officer's presence and even if the victim does not desire prosecution. In some jurisdictions, police may be required to use strict crime scene investigation and evidence-gathering techniques so that prosecutors can move forward without the victim's testimony. In addition to putting an emphasis on arrest in cases of domestic assault, many states also require officers to take more responsibility in handling these cases by providing victims with information on legal options and services and transporting victims to hospitals or shelters.

The Implementation of Mandatory and Presumptive Arrest Policies

Although a mandatory or presumptive arrest policy in the case of misdemeanor domestic assault may seem straightforward, these policies have not been without problems in actual practice, given the discretionary nature of police work. In maintaining public order, patrol officers must use their individual judgment in a variety of situations, one of the most difficult being interpersonal disputes. Requiring or strongly encouraging arrest represents a significant constraint on police discretion, one that officers may not readily accept. Several factors come into play when it comes to police discretion and the arrest decision. A major issue is the determination of probable cause. In an early evaluation of Phoenix's presumptive arrest statute adopted in 1984, for example, Ferraro (1989a, 1989b) found that officers' interpretations of what constituted probable cause differed greatly. Officers could consider the presence of visible injuries or property damage or witnesses. But many officers would accept only the presence of visible injuries to the complainant as evidence that an offense had occurred, and not property damage alone. Another factor affecting the arrest decision is officer attitudes, which may reflect stereotypes about domestic violence and battered women. Battered women are often viewed as inconsistent complainants who call the police to arrest and later drop the charges (Belknap, 1995; Ferraro, 1989a). Some officers also believe that women stay in violent relationships by choice or bring on the violence with their nagging or marital infidelity (Ferraro, 1989a; Saunders, 1995). In addition, domestic violence is sometimes viewed as normal among certain types of people, such as those from lower income groups, racial and ethnic minorities, the unemployed, and people with substance abuse problems (Ferraro, 1989a).

It has taken some time for police practice to catch up with policy changes. In Ferraro's study (1989b), it was found that arrests were made in only 18% of domestic battery cases, and police employed conciliation techniques in 51% of the cases. A similarly low arrest rate was observed in an early evaluation of the District of Columbia's 1987 mandatory arrest policy, where police made arrests in only 5% of domestic violence cases, regardless of the seriousness of the injury (Baker, Cahn, & Sands, 1989). A later survey of

victims revealed the arrest rate had increased to 41% (Keilitz, Hannaford, & Efkeman, 1997). Similarly, in research from London, Ontario, that assessed the effectiveness of a policy enacted in 1981 requiring police officers to file charges in probable cause cases of misdemeanor domestic assault, the filing of charges by police increased from a pre-policy 2.7% in 1979 to 67.3% in 1983 and then to 89.3% in 1990 (Jaffe, Hastings, Reitzel, & Austin, 1993). Zorza and Woods (1994, p. 12) also observed, in a survey of statistics from several jurisdictions that have adopted mandatory or presumptive arrest policies, that the overall number of arrests has increased, dramatically so in some jurisdictions such as the state of Connecticut; Duluth, Minnesota; and Kansas City, Missouri.

The implementation of mandatory arrest statutes has also been accompanied by some unanticipated consequences. These statutes were intended to protect women in domestically violent relationships, where men are almost always either the sole perpetrator or the primary physical aggressor (Hamberger & Lohr, 1994). But there is evidence that women are increasingly arrested, either as part of a dual arrest or as the sole arrestee, and that these arrests can occur even in jurisdictions where police have been instructed to arrest only the primary physical aggressor when they have probable cause to believe both parties have used violence (Zorza & Woods, 1994, p. 16). Statutes that require police to distinguish between the primary physical aggressor and the party who used violence in self-defense may not be enough to solve the problem of dual arrests. Hooper (1996) explains that the self-defense and primary aggression paradigms were developed to accommodate male (to male) violence and may not be the most helpful for women's violence, which is essentially different from men's violence. Women's violent acts are often not immediately precipitated by the violent acts of their partners (Hooper, 1996). Rather, domestically violent women can be viewed as caught up in a pattern of violence that they did not initiate and do not control (Hamberger & Potente, 1994). Indeed, women may "initiate" an assault motivated by a perceived need for self-protection or in retaliation for a non-immediate prior assault (Marshall & Rose, 1990, as cited in Hamberger & Potente, 1994), or in response to cues that seem to them to signal imminent violence.

Better training and education of police officers in both the dynamics of domestic violence and in communication with victims may help with the dual arrest problem (Saunders, 1995). In a study of police officers' attitudes in a state that, at the time, had a warrantless arrest statute for misdemeanor assault, Saunders (1995) found that officers who preferred to arrest the woman were less likely to feel comfortable talking with victims and more likely to harbor traditional stereotypes, believing that domestic violence was justified in the case of infidelity and that victims of domestic battery remained with their violent partners for psychological rather than practical reasons (Saunders, 1995). In contrast, in Massachusetts, where written justification for the arrest of both the offender and victim is required by law, Mignon and Holmes (1995) observed an increase in the overall number of arrests with the 1991 adoption of mandatory arrest in 24 police departments, but a lower rate of arrests of women than in other states with mandatory arrest statutes. These researchers noted that the relatively low number of dual arrests in Massachusetts made the phenomenon difficult to examine from their data, but they surmised that the low rates could be attributed to the combination of effective statutory, policy, and training efforts.

The Debate Surrounding Mandatory and Presumptive Arrest Policies

In addition to the dilemmas that mandatory and presumptive arrest policies can create for actual police practice, the increased use of arrest in cases of domestic violence has generated a great deal of controversy about what the goal of arrest should be and what is actually in the best interest of victims. For example, the current emphasis on arrest was influenced in part by social science research claims that arrest would have a specific deterrent effect on domestic violence, that is, the police intervention alone, in the form of an arrest, would prevent the individual offender from committing future assaults. But this idea is not well supported by the evaluation research. The claim initially came from results of the pioneering Minneapolis Domestic Violence Experiment (Sherman & Berk, 1984a, 1984b). In this controlled experiment, 314 cases of misdemeanor domestic assault were randomly assigned to three police interventions or treatments: arresting the offender, which included an overnight stay in jail; advising the couple with informal mediation in some cases; or separating the couple by ordering the suspect away for 8 hours. Based on an examination of both official police reports and victim interviews of a repeat police contact during a 6-month follow-up period, Sherman and Berk observed that the prevalence rate for subsequent offending (the percentage of suspects reoffending) was reduced by about half with arrest.

The widely publicized Minneapolis experiment was intensely criticized for its many methodological problems, such as the unrepresentative sample, the low officer participation rate, and the low percentage of follow-up interviews (see, e.g., Binder & Meeker, 1988, 1992; Fagan, 1989). The study was soon followed by replication experiments in six cities: Milwaukee, Wisconsin (Sherman et al., 1991, 1992); Omaha, Nebraska (Dunford, 1992; Dunford, Huizinga, & Elliott, 1990a); Charlotte, North Carolina (Hirschel & Hutchison, 1992; Hirschel, Hutchison, & Dean, 1992); Colorado Springs, Colorado (Berk, Campbell, Klap, & Western, 1992a, 1992b); Metro-Dade (Miami), Florida (Pate & Hamilton, 1992); and Atlanta, Georgia, all of which were sponsored by the National Institute of Justice's Spouse Abuse Replication Program (SARP).[1]

The SARP studies were still plagued by methodological problems (Zorza, 1994), particularly the low response rates for follow-up victim interviews, and they produced diverse and complex findings. Only two provided any direct support for the specific deterrent effect of arrest that was observed in the original Minneapolis experiment. Researchers in Metro-Dade found a statistically significant deterrent effect of arrest when they grouped cases simply into arrest or no-arrest categories and examined data from 6-month victim interviews; cases in the arrest group showed lower prevalence rates than those in the no-arrest group (Pate & Hamilton, 1992, p. 692). Researchers in Colorado Springs also observed evidence of a deterrent effect based on victim interviews. When arrest was compared to no-arrest, the use of arrest decreased the odds of the occurrence of new violence (Berk et al.,

1992a, p. 197). In contrast, in Omaha (Dunford, 1992; Dunford et al., 1990a) and in Charlotte (Hirschel & Hutchison, 1992; Hirschel, Hutchison, & Dean, 1992), researchers found no statistically significant differences in subsequent offending across the various treatment groups and concluded that arrest was no more effective as a deterrent than any of the other interventions. Other evidence of a deterrent effect came from an innovation in the Omaha study, in which researchers studied offenders who left the scene before the police arrived and were randomly assigned to receive or not to receive a warrant for their arrest. Interestingly, offenders assigned to the warrant treatment had lower prevalence and frequency rates than those in the non-warrant group (Dunford, Huizinga, & Elliott, 1990b, p. 642, as cited in Garner, Fagan, & Maxwell, 1995).

Surprisingly, the replications also produced evidence that arrest may actually increase the occurrence of future offending. For example, the Milwaukee researchers found that the use of a short arrest treatment resulted in an escalation in domestic violence at a 3-month follow-up (Sherman et al., 1991, p. 836). The escalation effect also held true after a 1-year follow-up. Similarly, in the Omaha data, those in the arrest group had a higher re-arrest frequency rate compared to those who received informal treatment (mediation and separation) after 1 year (Dunford, 1992, p. 123). Researchers, attempting to account for these different findings, hypothesized that arrest might better deter those suspects with high "stakes in conformity" (Toby, 1957), as indicated by their being married and/or employed. Indeed, in four sites, employed suspects were more likely to be deterred by arrest than unemployed suspects. Furthermore, arrest reduced the annual rate of future violence for married and employed suspects in Milwaukee, but for those with low stakes in conformity (unmarried and unemployed), arrest increased the annual rate of future violence (Sherman & Smith, 1992, p. 686). The Omaha data showed a similar effect for married and employed suspects (Sherman & Smith, 1992, p. 687). In Colorado Springs, arrest was also more likely to increase violence slightly among the unemployed and to decrease violence among employed suspects (Berk et al., 1992b, p. 702; Sherman & Smith, 1992, p. 687). The same was true in Metro-Dade (Pate & Hamilton, 1992, p. 695).

In addition to the problem of contradictory research results, the focus on police practice and specific deterrence led some scholars to attack the naive assumption that arrest alone will deter the complex behavior of domestic violence (Bowman, 1992; Lerman, 1992; Zorza, 1994). This notion directly conflicts with what is known about the phenomenon of domestic battery, a chronic behavior that stems from a complex set of individual as well as structural factors (see, e.g., Schecter, 1982) and is known to escalate in frequency and seriousness over time. Moreover, it has been noted that the solution to such a complex and enduring problem most likely lies in a coordinated response from the entire the criminal justice system and from a system of support services (see Chapter 23 in this volume).

In a different vein, Buzawa and Buzawa (1993) criticized the specific deterrence rationale generally; in their view, domestically violent outbursts are frequently impulsive acts from offenders who have a propensity toward violence, lack nonviolent communication skills, and may be in some type of pathological relationship with the victim. They believe the criminal justice system should focus on rehabilitation rather than deterrence when dealing with offenders with violent tendencies, if there is to be any success in controlling violence in the long term. They further note that hard-core abusers or chronic offenders will not be deterred by the threat of arrest, a threat that may in reality be remote, when officers are forced to carry out a policy that, as mentioned above, not only limits their traditional discretionary powers but also may conflict with their beliefs regarding domestic violence (Ferraro, 1989a; Stanko, 1989).

Finally, the constitutionality of the specific deterrence rationale has also been called into question (Binder & Meeker, 1992; Buzawa & Buzawa, 1993). An arrest for misdemeanor battery, accompanied by some period of initial incarceration that is meant to reduce recidivism, amounts to punishment without due process of law.

Still, battered women's advocates and other proponents of mandatory arrest argue that regardless of whether or not individual offenders are deterred from committing more violence, the general deterrent value of mandatory arrest laws should not be overlooked (Stark, 1996; Zorza, 1994). Mandating arrest communicates the seriousness of domestic assault, conveying that this behavior will not be socially or legally tolerated. Moreover, repeal of these laws could carry with it the danger that domestic violence will no longer be seen as a crime (Lerman, 1992).

Mandatory and presumptive arrest statutes also take into account the fact that it may be difficult for a woman to demand the arrest and prosecution of her husband or intimate partner. Arrest advocates have argued that the message of social condemnation implied in the criminalization of domestic violence would ultimately empower victims. Arrest policies serve not only to validate a woman's civil right not to be abused but also to protect the victim, who may be unable to make her own decision in a time of acute crisis. Stark (1996) noted that women in a condition of psychological and physical entrapment may be incapable of expressing a preference for arrest, or some women may simply not understand the nature of their risk. Stark (1996) also observed that mandatory arrest provides the practical benefits of immediate protection for the victim from the current violence and time to consider her options, such as leaving or obtaining a restraining order. But opponents of arrest policies such as Buzawa and Buzawa (1993) noted that relieving victims of their decision-making power by mandating arrest is ultimately patronizing to battered women. Often, victims simply want the violence to stop in the given instance or fear the consequences that may accompany arrest, such as retaliation by their spouse or loss of his income. Buzawa and Buzawa (1993) believe that true victim empowerment is achieved by giving victims control over the outcome of the police intervention and that a policy of victim preference is by far preferable to mandatory arrest.

Other scholars have called attention to the unique problems of lower class and minority women in dealing with domestic violence (Rasche, 1995), as well as the fact that mandatory arrest policies can have unanticipated and negative consequences for these women (Miller, 1989, 2000). Women from lower socioeconomic and minority groups may be more likely to call the police to solve problems in the private sphere, and this situation could result in disproportionately higher arrest rates of men in these groups (Hutchison, Hirschel, & Pesackis, 1994). On the other hand, lower class and minority women might be reluctant to call the police. According to Rasche (1995), African American women may be reluctant to seek relief from a criminal justice system that they perceive as dealing more severely with nonwhite men, whereas Asian women and Latinas may view expressing a preference for arrest as a betrayal of cultural norms that dictate privacy and deference to family authority. Lower class women may also be deterred from calling the police if it means the loss of an employed spouse's income.

Prosecutorial Practices

Changes in the police response to domestic violence in the past two decades have served as a catalyst for changes in prosecutorial policies. Prosecutors today strive to play a more active role in prosecuting domestic violence cases, a change that was facilitated by criticism that they remained a huge obstacle in case processing. Domestic violence cases now flood the system as a response to presumptive arrest or mandatory arrest policies, and this has led to tremendous increases in prosecutorial caseloads (Cahn, 1992). In some jurisdictions, prosecutors have responded with the use of "no-drop" policies, which allow prosecutors to proceed without victim cooperation, although some policies allow victims to drop charges after they have completed counseling and provided an official explanation to the court (Cahn, 1992; *The Legal*

Needs, 1988). Ultimately, however, there is no definitive evidence that no-drop policies and increased use of the criminal justice system are any more effective than prosecution policies that prioritize the victim's desires and let her wishes guide the prosecution efforts (Ford, 1991). Despite over a decade of changes in police arrest policies, prosecutorial reforms are best characterized by how little is known about their effectiveness.

Prosecutors, in general, exercise enormous discretion in making decisions about charges. Despite the criminalization of domestic violence and the accompanying policy changes, prosecutors often remain reluctant to file charges in domestic violence cases. First and foremost, prosecutors have traditionally assigned a lower threshold of seriousness to violent crimes committed between people who know each other, compared to violent crimes involving strangers (Buzawa & Buzawa, 1992). For example, the National Crime Survey demonstrated this disparity in case processing when it found that "more than one third of misdemeanor domestic violence cases would have been the felony offenses of rape, robbery, or aggravated assault if committed by strangers" (Buzawa & Buzawa, 1990, as cited in Hilton, 1993, p. 137). Furthermore, domestic violence cases are difficult to prosecute and are among the least likely to result in conviction. The low priority of domestic violence cases, coupled with time and resource constraints due to the enormous swell in the volume of cases, continues to minimize prosecutorial activity with battering cases. One domestic violence scholar has suggested that the overall rate of prosecution is typically less than 10% (Sherman, 1992). Some prosecutor's offices even go so far as to erect obstacles to case processing.

For example, in Omaha, Nebraska, victims must pay a fee to make their complaint directly to the prosecutor.

Domestic violence cases represent a particular challenge for prosecutors on several fronts, a key issue being the credibility and commitment of the victim. In addition to the prior arrest record of the batterer, severe injury to the victim makes prosecution more likely (Schmidt & Steury, 1989). On the other hand, if the victim has drug or alcohol problems, which could lead observers to question her status as a victim, the chances of prosecution are decreased (Rauma, 1984). Moreover, whenever cases are contingent on "he said/she said" reports with little independent evidence—a frequent occurrence in domestic violence cases—the appearance and credibility of the victim become even more crucial to the prosecution decision.

The relationship between the prosecutor and the victim can become complicated by conflicting agendas and assumptions. Prosecutors have a responsibility to assess victims' motivations because victims often rely on the prosecutor for reasons other than to obtain criminal conviction, such as to secure protection or to force repayment for damages (Ford, 1983; Ford & Regoli, 1993, p. 137). Victims are often grilled on their commitment to follow through with prosecution, their motivation in using the court process, and their relationship status with the defendant (Buzawa & Buzawa, 1990). Although some prosecutors anticipate the emotional impact and potential for increased hassles that court action may create for victims, most prosecutors have not made an effort "to understand the victim's situation as a whole, nor do they provide the time and resources necessary to enhance the cooperation and commitment of victims" (Ford & Regoli, 1993, pp. 137-138). Even for those victims willing and eager to pursue court action, prosecutors' organizational goals may conflict with victims' desires and their assumption that the prosecutor will represent their interests. This creates distrust and "victim disparagement [which] inevitably leads to high rates of voluntary dismissals" (Buzawa & Buzawa, 1996, p. 82). Furthermore, prosecutors' attitudes influence victims, so if prosecutors themselves are ambivalent about interfering in private matters, that ambivalence is communicated to victims and can be interpreted as a brush-off. Also, prosecutors have implicitly and explicitly blamed the victims with their questioning (i.e., "Why didn't you leave?"), thereby discouraging victims from continuing with a case.

It must be noted that prosecutors' frustrations with victims are not without merit. Victims frequently drop charges for reasons unrelated to prosecutorial behavior or refuse to show up to testify. Many factors are related to victim cooperation. A victim may simply forgive the abuse and decide she no longer wants to press charges, or she may hold on to the hope that her violent partner will change. Many victims suffer from low self-esteem and may blame themselves for the abuse. Others experience tremendous guilt over making the abuse public in court. In some cases, a victim may have left the relationship and negotiated a financial or custody settlement; in such cases, she may fear that prosecution will further anger her partner and jeopardize the agreement. One of the most significant factors in victim cooperation is a victim's fear of retaliation. Buzawa and Buzawa (1996) found, for example, that almost half of victims reported that their abusers threatened them with physical violence if they turned

to the criminal justice system for intervention. These researchers also noted that many abusers threatened to kidnap the victim's children or to lie or exaggerate her personal problems to protective services (Buzawa & Buzawa, 1996, p. 88), a situation that is further exacerbated if the victim has had a substance abuse problem or if she abused or neglected the children as a consequence of her own abuse (see Stark, 1992). Finally, for women who are unemployed or economically dependent on the batterer, the financial loss may be devastating. This financial loss extends to the costs of child care, the time taken off from the victim's own job if she has one, and so on (Ford, 1991).

Rebovich (1996) explains that many prosecutors' offices are committed to combating domestic violence, and they proceed with prosecution despite lack of victim cooperation—an action that has been criticized due to its failure to permit victims control over their own lives (Ford, 1991). The most extreme form of prosecutorial zeal is the no-drop policy, which completely removes responsibility and decision-making power from victims. Davis and Smith (1995, p. 547) have noted three compelling reasons for no-drop prosecution policies: The state has an obligation to send the message to batterers that domestic violence is wrong and will not be tolerated; the state has an interest in public safety, just as it does with other violent crimes; and batterers might be less likely to blame their victims for the prosecution, and so would be less likely to use intimidation tactics to get them to drop charges. These scholars also point out, however, that in the case of domestic violence, a prosecutor will be trying cases with a high proportion of reluctant witnesses, an enormous and difficult undertaking. Rebovich (1996) also notes that prosecutors have devised other methods to overcome victims' reluctance to testify, the most common method being the use of the subpoena, followed closely by the use of photographs of victims' injuries. Furthermore, if there is evidence such as family or neighbor testimony, 911 tapes, victim advocacy statements, or evidence of "excited utterances" at the crime scene, prosecutors introduce these, as well. Finally, prosecutors' offices rely on victim advocacy programs, which offer emotional and tangible support for victims to encourage their participation.

Although pursuing prosecution may be difficult, the advantages for victims can be substantial. Not only does prosecution convey the larger message that domestic violence is morally wrong, but tougher policies may, in fact, prove helpful in protecting victims and reducing violent behavior; vigorous prosecution will potentially encourage police not only to make more arrests and but also to provide victims with greater assistance (Lerman, 1981). Furthermore, Ford (1991) contends that the criminal justice system may operate more as a symbolic tool or "power resource" for the victim to use to gain control in a relationship; control can be achieved through the threats of prosecution, rather than actual prosecution.

Unfortunately, following through on a victim's preference for prosecution may not result in protecting her from further abuse; as with arrest, prosecution efforts are not always threatening to an offender, who may not fear engagement with the criminal justice system (Ford, 1991, p. 319). For example, in the Milwaukee mandatory arrest study, Sherman et al. (1992) found that offenders who were unemployed and who already possessed a criminal record did not consider an arrest for domestic violence to be a hardship.

This notion may also extend to other sanctions within the criminal justice system.

Several studies have examined prosecutorial effectiveness in domestic violence cases, and they found that prosecution programs had little effect on recidivism (Davis, Smith, & Nickles, 1998; Fagan, Friedman, Wexler, & Lewis, 1984; Ford & Regoli, 1992; Tolman & Weiscz, 1995). Still, despite the lack of a deterrent effect on offenders' violence—regardless of whether the offender received pretrial diversion with rehabilitative counseling; adjudicated guilt with counseling as a condition of probation; or other sentencing options such as fines, probation and jail time—the studies reveal a number of interesting outcomes. Victims reported that they felt more secure and in control of their situation 6 months after court disposition than they had prior to prosecutorial action (Ford & Regoli, 1992). Further abuse was more likely to occur when police used warrantless on-scene arrests: Rebattering within 6 months occurred with almost 40% of offenders (Ford & Regoli, 1992, pp. 62-63). With cases initiated by victims in prosecutor's offices, the re-offense rate was 29%. This particular research has been criticized, however, for the fact that random assignment of cases, an important component of an experimental design, occurred too soon in case processing (at case screening instead of at disposition), which resulted in the misassignment of many cases to the various prosecution options (Davis et al., 1998, p. 436).

Davis et al. (1998, p. 441) have suggested that evaluative prosecution studies are still in their infancy, and they are plagued by methodological problems that make it difficult to disentangle treatment effects from other factors that might influence recidivism. In addition, the research may be missing some victims because court populations tend to overrepresent poorer populations, suggesting that when domestic violence occurs in middle- and upper-class homes, victims may choose options other than going to court (Klein, 1996). Mills (1998, p. 313) also cautions against assuming that victim empowerment and recidivism are correlated without taking into account the effects of other variables, such as the victim's readiness to leave the relationship, characteristics of the battered woman in different prosecutorial treatment groups, and offenders' jail time. What appears consistent across the few studies conducted thus far is that there is no evidence that prosecution outcomes make a difference in recidivism in cases of domestic violence. Although researchers contend that innovative prosecutorial techniques can increase the number of cases prosecuted and could decrease recidivism, it is unclear which programs to embrace (see Cahn, 1992).

Civil Restraining Orders, Court Processing, and Judicial Behavior

Despite the heightened awareness and legislative reform of the last two decades, judges have also been reluctant to treat domestic assault as seriously as they treat violence between strangers. One type of court option for domestic violence victims is the civil restraining order. Civil restraining orders, or orders of protection, were developed in response to the reluctance of the criminal justice system to handle effectively the criminal nature of domestic violence (Klein, 1996). Because arrest, prosecution, and sentencing were rare events (Schechter, 1982), civil court remedies permitted victims to circumvent the criminal process, yet still obtain some relief or have an additional remedy at their disposal. Initially, these orders were difficult to obtain. Prior to the 1970s, women had to begin divorce proceedings to be eligible (Chaudhuri & Daly, 1992). Today, restraining orders are more accessible and can actually provide various types of relief. They not only establish limits to abusers' access to victims but may also include financial arrangements, restrictions on custody; they may limit access to residence, place of employment, children, and children's schools. Restraining orders also serve as an alternative form of victim protection if the level of evidence does not meet the standard of a criminal proceeding or if the victim would be a weak prosecution witness due to drug or alcohol abuse, for example (Finn & Colson, 1990). Because violation of a protective order is a criminal offense that can result in arrest, civil restraining orders expand police power and increase officers' ability to monitor repeat offenders (Finn & Colson, 1990). The effectiveness of civil orders ultimately rests on law enforcement's response, and it can be enhanced with serious prosecutorial and judicial actions and meaningful punishment for violators (Gelb, 1994).

Despite the potential effectiveness of civil orders, research that reviewed state statutory and case law, interviewed judges and victim advocates, and examined program documentation from several jurisdictions (Finn & Colson, 1990, 1998) identified many common weaknesses in the civil protection process. There are narrow eligibility categories for obtaining orders, victims may also have to pay filing fees and cannot obtain orders when courts are not in session (Finn & Colson, 1998, p. 44). The defendant must also be served before the order becomes effective, leaving the victim vulnerable in the interim. Moreover, despite simplified petitioning procedures and the assistance of lay advocates, victims not represented by counsel are less likely to obtain protection orders. Even if a victim is successful, the absence of counsel is more likely to result in an order that lacks the appropriate provisions regarding exclusion of the offender from the residence, as well as child custody, child support, and limitations on visitation rights.

Moreover, Klein (1996) points out that civil orders may represent a less meaningful legal response than a criminal response to offenders, particularly if they have histories of domestic and nondomestic arrests. With a sample of 663 cases that included both current and former partners, this researcher tracked every case brought to court for restraining orders in 1990 in Quincy, Massachusetts, to determine whether the defendants violated the original order and whether there were new incidents of threats or assaults. Klein found that almost half of the defendants re-abused within 2 years of the original restraining order, 34% were arrested for violations, and 95% became subject to new orders reflecting new incidents. New abuse was most strongly related to age and prior criminal history. Younger men and men with prior histories re-abused and re-offended at higher rates. Although it is unclear if the orders affected the severity of new abuse, restraining orders did not seem to protect women in almost 50% of the cases (the number of which is probably underreported because victims were not interviewed in this study). This finding is consistent with other research. In a study of couples involved in 500 restraining orders issued in a Colorado jurisdiction, the majority of defendants re-abused,

according to victim reports, despite the low arrest rate for new abuses or violations of the order (Harrell, Smith, & Newmark, 1993). Furthermore, in Klein's (1996) research, almost half of the women dropped the restraining order prior to the full year, with no change in the re-abuse. Klein concludes that civil options do not appear to provide a strong deterrent because of the long history of criminal involvement by abusers. In addition, almost 40% of abusers had significant substance abuse histories, which may have caused them to minimize the consequences of restraining orders. Klein's research also demonstrates judges' reluctance to deal harshly with violators. When orders were violated, only 25% of defendants were placed on probation, and 18% were jailed; the remaining cases were dismissed or diverted (Klein, 1996). These low percentages should not be surprising, however, because other research has found that most courts do even less with violations of restraining orders (Curtis, 1991). However, despite the reluctance of the courts to impose severe punishment, victims found some satisfaction in pursuing civil options because they continued to go to court for restraining orders, and almost one third of the sample took out new orders when the old ones expired.

Civil protection orders are valuable for the role they play in empowering victims. An order of protection requires contact with attorneys and judges, whose support to victims or admonishments to offenders might reinforce the message that battering is unacceptable (Ferraro & Johnson, 1983). Moreover, offenders are forced to admit publicly in court what is typically defined privately (Ferraro, 1995, p. 269). In interviews with victims who obtained temporary restraining orders and with their abusers, Harrell and Smith (1996) reported that the majority (86%) found restraining orders to be a valuable tool in documenting the occurrence of abuse. Most of the victims also believed the judge was "doing the right thing" for her and her children (Harrell & Smith, 1996, p. 218). It appears, then, that women believed restraining orders to be worthwhile, despite the fact that less than half the victims thought the offenders would actually believe they had to comply with the order. Interestingly, these researchers also reported that men greatly resisted court hearings, with over 75% denying abuse or attempting to persuade judges to deny permanent orders.

In a similar vein, a study conducted by the National Center for State Courts (Keilitz et al., 1997) showed that participants' well-being was positively affected by the protection orders, and these positive effects increased over time. At interviews with victims 1 month and 6 months after they received protection orders, 95% of the respondents said they would obtain a protection order again. Incidents of re-abuse were fairly low. However, of those participants who did experience severe abuse, more than one third had been threatened or injured with a weapon, more than half had been beaten or choked, and 84% had experienced milder physical abuse. The longer the victim was in a relationship, the stronger the possibility of severe violence. About 65% of the abusers had a prior criminal arrest history, and the women in these relationships were more likely to suffer severe violence. As in the earlier cited research, the protection orders obtained against such respondents were less effective in deterring future violence, but temporary protection orders served a useful purpose, even if victims did not pursue obtaining a permanent order. The court's attention seemed to influence offenders' behavior and also permitted safety planning and victim education (Keilitz et al., 1997, p. 11).

Restraining orders do not always mean a couple will completely cease contact. In Harrell and Smith's (1996) study, despite the issuance of a permanent order, about three quarters of the men and women reported having contact with each other, and 80% of women with temporary orders but without permanent restraining orders also reported contact. Reunion and reconciliation were reasons for contact, although more than half of the women reported unwanted contact within the first 3 months. Even with the high levels of contact, there was no difference in repeated violence among women who had a permanent restraining order, compared to those who did not. Continued abuse was primarily related to the severity of initial abuse incidents, the history of abuse, the criminal justice response, and the presence or absence of children. More specifically, the more abuse there had been 1 year prior to obtaining the restraining order, the greater the likelihood of re-abuse; if the offender was arrested, he would be less likely to commit serious abuse, although some abuse might continue; and women with children were 70% more likely to experience violence than women without children. The finding that an arrest could result in less severe re-abuse highlights the significance of a serious police response. However, when men violated orders, many women did not call the police. About 60% of the women felt they could get the men to stop their violence on their own, 25% were too afraid to call, and others felt that police would not do anything. Women with permanent orders felt empowered to call the police, and they expected police assistance. However, their satisfaction with police decreased between the first interview at 3 months and the second interview at 1 year (Harrell & Smith, 1996).

These studies demonstrate the equivocal nature of civil options. Pursuing restraining orders may empower the victim, particularly if she is not economically or emotionally dependent on her abuser, but the orders' ultimate effectiveness rests on a concerted effort by police to arrest and by courts to enforce these orders and impose meaningful sanctions when the orders are violated. In terms of the courts' treatment of domestic violence cases, the system's current best efforts are exemplified in two different courts that have attempted to provide more rigorous intervention in domestic violence cases and to be more sensitive to the needs of battered women.

In Massachusetts, the Quincy District Court Domestic Violence Program (QDC) provides what is actually an integrated criminal justice response to punish domestic violence offenders. According to Saltzman (1994), this highly acclaimed and nationally recognized program integrates the services of police officers, prosecutors, court clerks, judges, probation officers, and treatment counselors. An important feature of this integrated system is the monthly roundtable discussions, which keep the lines of communication open among all parties involved with the court. Integration is facilitated by information systems that track offenders and consolidate current case information. Links are also maintained to service providers, such as battered women's shelters and rehabilitation services for batterers.

As Buzawa, Hotaling, and Klein (1998) and Saltzman (1994) explain, al-

though it may not always be successfully carried out, the overall policy of the QDC is one of pro-intervention at all points in the system. A presumptive arrest policy guides Quincy police when they are called to the scene. The police are also instructed to conduct rigorous crime scene investigations, which help ensure successful prosecution even if victims are reluctant to testify. The district attorneys are meant to prosecute a majority of cases that reach their office. Judges should be willing to aggressively sentence and to aggressively revoke probation. Cases of repeat violence, including violations of restraining orders, are meant to receive heightened attention. Furthermore, judges are expected to handle requests for restraining orders promptly. Batterers who violate orders and have prior criminal convictions can face incarceration; otherwise, they may receive long probation, but a suspended sentence and short probation is more likely. Judges should hold regular probation revocation sessions for probation violators.

Saltzman (1994) further notes that sensitivity to the needs of victims is a priority, and the use of court advocates at key points is a significant feature of the Quincy court. Full-time specialized domestic abuse clerks, who are usually volunteer interns from law schools and social work programs at local universities, help victims negotiate the restraining order process. They disseminate information and assist in the complicated paperwork process. They also accompany victims to hearings to provide moral support. In Quincy, three times as many women return for the actual hearing as in other area courts, thanks to the individual assistance provided by these clerks (Saltzman, 1994, p. 341). When it comes to filing criminal charges, victim/witness advocates in the district attorney's office help victims file charges and accompany them to the hearing with the clerk-magistrate. The prosecutor's office also holds special daily briefing sessions to provide legal information as well as emotional support to victims. (For a more complete discussion of the importance of advocates, see Chapter 23 in this volume.)

The integrated procedures in the QDC appear to make a difference. Police arrest 75% of abusers when they are called to the scene of a domestic assault, and prosecutors successfully prosecute 70% of those arrested for domestic violence (Buzawa et al., 1998, p. 188); most of them are eventually convicted and sentenced to strict probation (p. 203). Based on 1995-1996 data, 40% of all assault charges were for domestic violence assaults, a figure that represented a huge increase compared to 20 years ago, when such charges were rare (Buzawa et al., 1998, p. 193).

However, despite increased arrests by police and rigorous prosecution, domestic violence cases in the QDC are usually brought before the court by the victim herself through the civil restraining order process, rather than by the police via a criminal charge. In 1995, the QDC issued 1,534 civil restraining orders, and 356 criminal cases were brought to the court, perhaps because victims prefer the control that the civil process gives them in the intervention rather than the arrest and aggressive prosecution of their abuser (Buzawa et al., 1998, p. 194). Furthermore, offenders who had restraining orders taken out against them had the most violent and abusive criminal histories and were among the greatest substance abusers, posing the highest risk to their victims for repeat violence, suggesting that restraining orders are not enough and that

more criminal charges are necessary (Buzawa et al., 1998, p. 203).

In a similar effort to improve the court process, Epstein (1999) explains that the District of Columbia Domestic Violence Court operates as a unified court, integrating the civil restraining order and the criminal charging processes—procedurally and physically—into a single, coordinated system. An important feature of this unified court is case coordination and information sharing from the point of intake to trial. In this way, if victims choose to pursue both means of intervention, they are assured access to the full range of civil and criminal remedies, while avoiding possible conflict between the two filing and hearing processes. In addition to the coordinated approach, advocates also play a major role in facilitating the entire process. In the D.C. court, civil intake counselors explain the protection order process and assist in filing the appropriate paperwork. They help the victim find legal representation if she so desires. At this point, the victim can also receive assistance regarding legal action for child support. She can then meet with a victim advocate to receive information and assistance for pursuing criminal prosecution. Lay advocates are also available to assist victims with obtaining access to a range of nonlegal support such as shelters, support groups, and counseling services. Following intake, specially trained domestic violence clerks schedule hearing dates and coordinate all cases—resolved and pending—that involve the same family, so that the judge can have a complete case history on hand. Judges servicing the court are assigned on a full-time basis for 1 year to ensure long-term judicial responsibility. Judges meet biweekly with representatives from all relevant agencies involved with the court.

Until recently, judges had been known to admonish battered women seeking legal remedies for taking up the court's valuable time. Although judges today are much more willing to grant restraining orders, they are not as willing to severely punish those offenders who violate orders, and they continue to demonstrate insensitivity to the needs of victims of domestic violence. The QDC and the D.C. Domestic Violence Court are innovative courts that represent some of the criminal justice system's best efforts in domestic violence intervention. But even these two model programs are not without problems, particularly when it comes to judicial attitudes. In her examination of the QDC, Saltzman (1994) said, "judicial misbehavior presents the most significant obstacle to the Quincy program's successful operation" (pp. 353-354). Saltzman reported that judges were hesitant to impose harsh sanctions against domestic violence offenders who violated restraining orders, and she speculated that they were either unaware of the range of sanctions available or were unclear about the judicial role in domestic violence. Judges were also reluctant to issue criminal complaints, perhaps because they had been more used to handling requests for civil restraining orders or they believed that issuing a criminal complaint was more the administrative duty of the court clerk. Judges who became frustrated with victims who had been no-show complainants in previous restraining order hearings sometimes displayed insensitivity toward victims by delaying the current hearing request, despite QDC policy to hold hearings promptly (Saltzman, 1994, p. 356).

In her more recent examination of the D.C. Domestic Violence Court, Epstein (1999) also observed that judges and court clerks continued to operate with an anti-victim bias and exhibited open hostility toward battered women. Some judges still accept the myth that a battered woman remains in the relationship by choice. Moreover, some judges continue to underestimate the seriousness of abuse and the potential danger for the victim, finding it difficult to think of domestic violence as a real crime worthy of their attention. Judges also became frustrated with victims who came before the court pro se (without legal representation), which they often do to request restraining orders, and may have not followed administrative procedures properly.

It appears, then, that in both the Quincy and District of Columbia courts, judges continue to harbor traditional stereotypes about domestic violence and demonstrate insensitivity with regard to battered women. These attitudes, which can adversely affect case handling, are likely to persist in other courts, as well. More judicial education and training on the psychological dynamics of battering and the special needs of battered women in court, given the obstacles they face, is of key importance if judges are to do their jobs effectively.

In terms of the criminal process, some evidence indicates that when judges treat domestic violence seriously, it can make a difference. For example, Thistlethwaite, Wooldredge, and Gibbs (1998) examined the effect of court dispositions on new arrests for a sample of 683 adults arrested on misdemeanor domestic violence charges in an Ohio county. The arrestees were tracked for 1 year after their sentences, if any, had been served. More severe sentences (jail combined with probation vs. either jail or probation alone) corresponded with a lower likelihood of recidivism. In addition, the effect of sanctions was different for different types of offenders. More severe sentences were more effective for people with greater stakes in conformity, that is, those offenders who were employed in one job longer and lived in one place longer and who lived in higher socioeconomic status neighborhoods.

In other research, Murphy, Musser, and Maton (1998) examined 253 offenders charged with domestic violence from prosecution files covering three police districts in Baltimore. They found that court orders for domestic violence counseling were associated with significantly lower criminal recidivism for battery or violation of a civil protection order. These researchers noted that their finding is consistent with other research, which evaluated a Minneapolis community intervention program and found that a court order for domestic violence counseling was associated with lower recidivism during a 12-month follow-up period than arrest alone (Syers & Edleson, 1992, as cited in Murphy et al., 1998). Moreover, in the Baltimore study, lower recidivism was also associated with the cumulative effects of successful prosecution, probation monitoring, a court order for counseling, attendance at counseling intake, and completion of counseling. Although the researchers cautioned that their methods were not rigorous, the results suggest a deterrent effect from a coordinated criminal justice response.

Probation

As an alternative to incarceration, probation begins after either a plea negotiation or a conviction. Probation is most commonly used to force offender participation in treatment programs. Typically, a sentence of incarceration will be imposed but then suspended if the offender suc-

cessfully completes other conditions, for example, he commits no further abuse, pays fines and victim restitution, or completes a treatment program (Ford, Reichard, Goldsmith, & Regoli, 1996). If the abuser is a repeat offender and has violated earlier probation requirements, he may face a split sentence of short incarceration followed by probation. This jail time can be fulfilled immediately or intermittently. Some jurisdictions are experimenting with short jail sentences to be served at halfway houses that also offer counseling (Ford et al., 1996, p. 260). Another probation program is called Intensive Supervision Probation, which extends the control of the criminal justice system through the use of curfews, house arrests, and frequent contacts with probation officers. It is often enhanced by the use of electronic monitors. Because of its heightened surveillance, Intensive Supervised Probation provides more protection for victims while permitting offenders to retain their employment.

As part of the criminal justice system, probation officers can play a major role in reinforcing the message that battering is a serious criminal offense—a message that abusers receive in treatment programs. Probation officers can also be trained about the dynamics of domestic violence, links to other resources, and ways to enhance victims' safety. Despite these potential benefits, probation has been criticized as another weak link in the criminal justice system's response to battering. Probation officers have been reluctant to accept as one of their central functions the mentioning or recording of abuse (Mullender, 1996). Domestic violence is often hidden, and some research reveals that probation officers seldom probe to find out more about a perpetrator's potential violence, displaying an overall lack of concern, often characterized by flippant and trivializing remarks (Swain, 1986).

Given the dynamics of battering—that it usually escalates in severity and frequency over time—it is even more important for probation officers to track abuse and keep accurate records. This situation may raise some role conflict for probation officers, because new criminal acts could result in jail or prison time, whereas probation is premised as an alternative to imprisonment. Moreover, there is the victim's safety to consider. On the one hand, a victim may benefit from the perpetrator's incarceration—she will be safer for a time and better able to consider her options. On the other hand, a perpetrator may become more enraged about the increased involvement of the criminal justice system and seek retaliation upon release.

Research on the attitudes of probation officers toward domestic violence reveals that they often discount the abuse and believe victim-blaming excuses, such as she provoked it, she asked for it, she stayed even though it was happening, and even, she enjoyed it—all of which reflect little or no understanding of the dynamics of battering (Mullender, 1996, p. 204; Swain, 1986). When probation officers harbor these kinds of misinformed and stereotypical attitudes, it will inevitably affect their work, as demonstrated by their failure to provide assistance to victims or to intervene in ongoing battering incidents. Typically, perpetrators minimize or deny their abusive behavior, and if probation officers sympathize, agree, or fail to hold perpetrators accountable for their violent acts, the overall impact on the victim and any children can be devastating.

With the national attention that domestic violence has received in recent years, it is likely that most probation officers do not condone domestic violence, but with their heavy caseloads, many still fail to look for it or act on it. However, there is still a crucial need to reinforce the message that abuse is a serious criminal offense and to train probation officers not to collude with perpetrators' denial of responsibility or victim-blaming rationalizations. Presentence investigation reports, for example, should not minimize domestic violence, and male officers may have to be particularly vigilant because they may be less able to identify with a woman's fear (Mullender, 1996, p. 210). These concerns point to the need for probation training about battering and gender dynamics (McWilliams & McKiernan, 1993). Victims have been particularly disappointed with probation, and they feel probation officers focus their efforts on male perpetrators to the disregard of victim safety. Probation officers need to be aware of victims' needs and issues regarding their safety. There may be times that victims should be consulted, warned, or protected, either during the probation period or once the time under supervision has been completed.

It is also important to note that just as there has been an increase in the number of women arrested for domestic violence, there has been a corresponding increase in the number of women placed on probation. First, probation officers need to understand that a woman may be acting in self-defense to stop abuse from escalating. In addition, they also need to recognize that although a woman may be convicted and under supervision, her safety is still in jeopardy. Probation officers should be well informed about court proceedings and civil protection orders, as well as battered women's shelters for women at risk.

Implications

Although mandatory and presumptive arrest statutes remain controversial, there is certainly no turning back from the criminalization of domestic violence and its more rigorous treatment in police encounters. But despite a policy emphasis on arrest, the practical realities are that the nature of police work is discretionary and that the victims themselves may not always desire an arrest. Furthermore, the diverse findings from the research on specific deterrence provide only weak support for the notion that arrest can actually prevent future domestic violence. Although some evidence suggests deterrence in the short term, other evidence indicates that arrest might increase assaultive behavior, putting some victims in increased danger, particularly when it comes to unemployed suspects.

It follows that mandatory and presumptive arrest policies that either completely remove or seriously reduce police discretion may not be in the best interest of all victims. It is likely that the future of police practice lies in mandated guidelines that emphasize the protection of victims (Ford et al., 1996) or in some type of structured discretion, where arrest is one of several mandated options that also consider victim preference (Schmidt & Sherman, 1996). Other commentators have recommended that if arrest is more likely to deter the suspect with high stakes in conformity, then perhaps the police should increase their arrests of those suspects whom they have been least likely to arrest in the past, that is, the middle-class, employed suspects (Bowman, 1992; Zorza, 1994). It also follows that for police to implement discretionary guide-lines effectively, training must be improved so that officers better understand the dynamics of domestic violence and the unique needs of battered women. Better training and education would also help officers to overcome stereotypical attitudes. In addition, police-initiated arrest warrants hold some promise as one of the options for preventing future violence. The Omaha offender-absent experiment demonstrated that some offenders who flee the scene might be deterred from committing future assault if police issue a warrant for their arrest.

Regarding police behavior, the process by which a police intervention is delivered may be more important for deterrence than the intervention itself. In an extended analysis of the Milwaukee data, Paternoster, Brame, Bachman, and Sherman (1997) found more deterrent effect for an individual who was warned than for one who was arrested but who perceived unfair treatment. Among arrestees, those who perceived unfair treatment were less likely to be deterred, regardless of time in custody and their stake in conformity. Although these researchers caution that "perceptions of procedural justice may not be particularly amenable to manipulation by the police" (Paternoster et al., 1997, p. 194), the focus on the manner in which treatment is delivered, a direct result of police attitudes and behavior, is a promising avenue for further study.[2] Procedural justice can also extend to other points in the system, such as the judiciary. Batterers may be more likely to comply with restraining orders, for example, if they feel they have been treated fairly (Epstein, 1999).

Police intervention will only be successful to the extent that it is supported by prosecutorial and judicial action. Indeed, many prosecutors' offices responded to the criticisms that they were the weak link in the system by reexamining their standard policies and developing strategies to enhance case-processing efforts. However, prosecutors' offices have instituted support and assistance programs for victims much more often than they have instituted innovative programs that have a significant effect on the recidivism of assailants. In fact, there is insufficient empirical support for policies that call for punishment or for policies that embrace the rehabilitation of batterers. At the same time, however, the research reveals that pursuing prosecution can be meaningful for victim empowerment. Victims feel supported by the system and gain a sense of control over their situation. These positive outcomes for victims often can be attributed to well-developed procedures designed to encourage victim participation, such as coordination with social service agencies, counseling, and court accompaniment. These prosecutor-backed efforts should be continued and evaluated. Researchers should also take into account a larger array of variables, such as the content of the relationship (seriousness of the abuse, victim's readiness to leave the relationship, and so forth), that may affect victim empowerment and recidivism (Mills, 1998).

Prosecutors have also developed ways to pursue cases without victim cooperation, despite a lack of empirical evidence suggesting that this strategy is any more effective than when victim cooperation is secured. Even so, two thirds of prosecutors' offices follow no-drop policies, which may be inappropriate. Victims are the experts of their own situations, and prosecutors should respect their decisions, even if victims' decisions conflict with case processing (Ford & Regoli,

1998). Prosecutors should strive to ensure victim safety by increased vigilance in tracking when warrants are served, monitoring warrants, tracking protection orders, aggressively enforcing them, and seeking penalties when they are abused. Future research should examine multiple outcomes of prosecution strategies and help to develop innovative alternatives to typical sentences of probation with short-term counseling, because the research demonstrates that probation with short-term counseling is no more effective in reducing recidivism than traditional sentences (Ford & Regoli, 1998). Prosecution programs that are well integrated into a coordinated community response may have greater success.

Civil orders of protection offer a potentially meaningful alternative for victims, especially when the evidence is not strong enough to sustain a criminal charge. The success of using civil options, however, depends on the ability of law enforcement to serve warrants quickly, of prosecutors to enforce violations, and of judges to mete out proportionate punishment for violators (Finn & Colson, 1998). As with the findings for mandatory arrest, civil options appear to be most effective with abusers who are employed, have no prior criminal history, use low levels of violence, and have no alcohol or substance abuse problems (Chaudhuri & Daly, 1992; Grau, Fagan, & Wexler, 1984). Victim support is essential. Prosecutors and the courts need to simplify forms, offer filing assistance, encourage and train lawyers to represent victims, and facilitate the process for victim advocates to continue supporting petitioners through the process of obtaining temporary and permanent orders. More work needs to be done to educate victims to use the contempt process to enforce orders and to expand community services and law enforcement support, such as victim counseling, shelters, pro bono legal services, and employment and education assistance (Keilitz et al., 1997). In addition, some jurisdictions do not yet include dating relationships, same-sex couples, and emotional and sexual abuse in their state statutes, clearly revealing that the protections offered by protection orders do not adequately cover all victims' circumstances. Prosecutors and judges need to be particularly cognizant of the additional danger associated with the batterer who has a long history of violent crime and/or alcohol and substance use; civil protection orders do little to deter an offender's behavior under these circumstances. Future research could focus on programs that deal with these high-risk offenders to determine what civil options (if any), such as no-contact orders, child custody, or financial arrangements, may work best to deter future occurrences of abuse.

Future research should also explore how prosecutors and judges can work more closely with probation officers to ensure successful probation outcomes. A few jurisdictions have prosecutors working with probation officers to track offender compliance with conditions of probation, although this tracking is rare. For example, according to a national prosecutor's survey conducted by the American Prosecutors Research Institution, only 28% of prosecutors monitor probation compliance (Rebovich, 1996, p. 187). Judges also need to hold offenders accountable by enforcing the conditions of probation and imposing meaningful sanctions for violations (Ford et al., 1996, p. 258). Because definitive evidence does not exist that batterer treatment programs actually rehabilitate abusers, these programs should be evaluated, and special-

ized treatments should be created that respond to the diversity of individual batterers.

Conclusion

For the last two decades, the criminal justice system's treatment of domestic violence has been subjected to close scrutiny and intense criticism. Whereas the initial emphasis was on police practice, observers quickly noted that policy and research must address intervention after the suspect is taken into custody, such as prosecutorial and judicial action. It was further noted that the exclusive focus on the suspect must give way to more focus on the needs of the victim, such as her preference for arrest and prosecution, and her security at all points in the system. More recently, it has been pointed out that a coordinated criminal justice and community-based response is required to combat the complex problem of domestic violence.

Despite heightened awareness and policy changes, the criminal justice system, with its inherent focus on the individual offender, can achieve only so much in the struggle to end domestic violence. This is not to say that arrest, prosecution, and civil remedies should be discarded, but their effectiveness is limited.

> Women are being told that police will arrest, that temporary protection orders will keep abusers away, and that judges will send them to prison if the women will only be consistent and cooperative with prosecutors. In the majority of cases, women do not experience these outcomes and continue to be abused, harassed, and threatened. (Ferraro, 1995, p. 269)

This is a realistic consequence of the limitations of the state's power to combat a problem whose roots lay in the structured gendered inequality of our society. Despite women's economic progress in recent decades, the legacy of male domination and the conditions that foster it persist. Battering is just one means by which male domination is maintained. As long as cultural and economic inequalities endure, violence committed by men against women will not be eliminated through statutory changes and police and court reforms.

Notes

1. At this writing, we were unable to find any published results from the Atlanta replication.

2. Perceived procedural justice was based on the suspect's perception that his side of the story was adequately heard, absolutely and relative to the victim's, and that his arrest was consistent with his expectations, as well as his report on the use of handcuffs and physical force, a more objective fact.

References

Baker, K., Cahn, N., & Sands, S. J. (1989). *Report on District of Columbia police response to domestic violence.* Washington, DC: D.C. Coalition Against Domestic Violence and the Women's Law and Public Policy Center, Georgetown University Law Center.

Belknap, J. (1995). Law enforcement officers' attitudes about the appropriate responses to woman battering. *International Review of Victimology, 4,* 47-62.

Berk, R. A., Campbell, A., Klap, R., & Western, B. (1992a). A Bayesian analysis of the Colorado Springs spouse abuse experiment. *Journal of Criminal Law and Criminology, 83*(1), 170-200.

Berk, R. A., Campbell, A., Klap, R., & Western, B. (1992b, October). The deterrent effect of arrest in incidents of domestic violence: A

Bayesian analysis of four field experiments. *American Sociological Review, 57,* 698-708.

Binder, A., & Meeker, J. (1988). Experiments as reforms. *Journal of Criminal Justice, 16,* 347-358.

Binder, A., & Meeker, J. (1992). Arrest as a method to control spouse abuse. In E. S. Buzawa & C. G. Buzawa (Eds.), *Domestic violence: The changing criminal justice response* (pp. 129-140). Westport, CT: Auburn House.

Bowman, C. G. (1992). The arrest experiments: A feminist critique. *Journal of Criminal Law and Criminology, 83*(1), 201-208.

Buzawa, E. S., & Buzawa, C. G. (1990). *Domestic violence: The criminal justice response.* Newbury Park, CA: Sage.

Buzawa, E. S., & Buzawa, C. G. (1992). *Domestic violence: The changing criminal justice response.* Westport, CT: Auburn House.

Buzawa, E. S., & Buzawa, C. G. (1993). The scientific evidence in not conclusive: Arrest is no panacea. In R. J. Gelles & D. R. Loseke (Eds.), *Current controversies on family violence* (pp. 337-356). Newbury Park, CA: Sage.

Buzawa, E. S., & Buzawa, C. G. (1996). *Do arrests and restraining orders work?* Thousand Oaks, CA: Sage.

Buzawa, E., Hotaling, G., & Klein, A. (1998). The response to domestic violence in a model court: Some initial findings and implications. *Behavioral Sciences and the Law, 16,* 185-206.

Cahn, N. (1992). Innovative approaches to the prosecution of domestic violence crimes. In E. S. Buzawa & C. G. Buzawa (Eds.), *Domestic violence: The changing criminal justice response* (pp. 161-180). Westport, CT: Auburn House.

Chaudhuri, M., & Daly, K. (1992). Do restraining orders help? Battered women's experience with male violence and the legal process. In E. S. Buzawa & C. G. Buzawa (Eds.), *Domestic violence: The changing criminal justice response* (pp. 227-252). Westwood, CT: Auburn House.

Curtis, S. (1991). *Criminal enforcement of restraining orders: A study of four district courts.* Cambridge, MA: Harvard Law School.

Davis, R. C., & Smith, B. E. (1995). Domestic violence reforms: Empty promises or fulfilled expectations? *Crime & Delinquency, 41*(4), 541-552.

Davis, R. C., Smith, B. E., & Nickles, L. B. (1998). The deterrent effect of prosecuting domestic violence misdemeanors. *Crime & Delinquency, 44*(3), 434-442.

Dunford, F. W. (1992). The measurement of recidivism in cases of spouse assault. *Journal of Criminal Law and Criminology, 83*(1), 120-136.

Dunford, F. W., Huizinga, D., & Elliott, D. S. (1990a). The role of arrest in domestic assault: The Omaha police experiment. *Criminology, 28*(2), 183-206.

Dunford, F. W., Huizinga, D., & Elliott, D. S. (1990b). Victim-initiated warrants for suspects of misdemeanor assault: A pilot study. *Justice Quarterly, 7,* 631-653.

Epstein, D. (1999). Effective intervention in domestic violence cases: Rethinking the roles of prosecutors, judges, and the court system. *Yale Journal of Law and Feminism, 11,* 3-50.

Fagan, J. (1989). Cessation of family violence: Deterrence and dissuasion. In L. Ohlin & M. Tonry (Eds.), *Family violence* (pp. 427-480). Chicago: University of Chicago Press.

Fagan, J., Friedman, E., Wexler, S., & Lewis, V. (1984). *National family violence evaluation final report* (Vol. 1). San Francisco: Ursa Institute.

Ferraro, K. (1989a). The legal response to woman battering in the United States. In J. Hanmer, J. Radford, & E. A. Stanko (Eds.), *Women, policing, and male violence: International perspectives* (pp. 155-183). London: Routledge & Kegan Paul.

Ferraro, K. (1989b). Policing women battering. *Social Problems, 36,* 61-74.

Ferraro, K. (1995). Cops, courts, and woman battering. In B. R. Price & N. J. Sokoloff (Eds.), *The criminal justice system and women: Offenders, victims, and workers* (pp. 262-271). New York: McGraw-Hill.

Ferraro, K., & Johnson, J. M. (1983). How women experience battering. *Social Problems, 30*(3), 325-229.

Finn, P., & Colson, S. (1990). *Civil protection orders: Legislation, current court practice, and enforcement* (Issues and practice report). Washington, DC: National Institute of Justice.

Finn, P., & Colson, S. (1998). Civil protection orders. In *Legal interventions in family violence: Research findings and policy implications* (pp. 43-47). Washington, DC: National Institute of Justice.

Ford, D. A. (1983). Wife battery and criminal justice: A study of victim decision-making. *Family Relations, 32,* 463-475.

Ford, D. A. (1991). Prosecution as a victim power resource: A note on empowering women in violent conjugal relationships. *Law & Society, 1*(2), 313-334.

Ford, D. A., & Regoli, M. J. (1992). The preventive impact of policies for prosecuting wife batterers. In E. S. Buzawa & C. G. Buzawa (Eds.), *Domestic violence: The changing criminal justice response* (pp. 181-207). Westport, CT: Greenwood.

Ford, D. A., & Regoli, M. J. (1993). The criminal prosecution of wife assaulters: Process, problems, and effects. In N. Z. Hilton (Ed.), *Legal responses to wife assault: Current trends and evaluation* (pp. 127-164). Newbury Park, CA: Sage.

Ford, D. A., & Regoli, M. J. (1998). The Indianapolis domestic violence prosecution experiment. In National Institute of Justice and American Bar Association (Eds.), *Legal interventions in family violence: Research findings and policy implications* (pp. 62-64). Washington, DC: Department of Justice.

Ford, D. A., Reichard, R., Goldsmith, S., & Regoli, M. J. (1996). Future directions for criminal justice policy on domestic violence. In E. S. Buzawa & C. G. Buzawa (Eds.), *Do arrests and restraining orders work?* (pp. 243-265). Thousand Oaks, CA: Sage.

Garner, J., Fagan, J., & Maxwell, C. (1995). Published findings from the spouse assault replication program: A critical review. *Journal of Quantitative Criminology, 11*(1), 3-28.

Gelb, A. (1994). *Quincy court model domestic abuse program manual.* Swampscott, MA: Productions Specialties.

Grau, J., Fagain, J., & Wexler, S. (1984). Restraining orders for battered women: Issues of access and advocacy. *Women and Politics, 4* 13-28.

Hamberger, L. K., & Lohr, J. M. (1994). The intended function of domestic violence is different for arrested male and female perpetrators. *Family Violence and Sexual Assault Bulletin, 10*(34), 40-44.

Hamberger, L. K., & Potente, T. (1994). Counseling heterosexual women arrested for domestic violence: Implications for theory and practice. *Violence and Victims, 9*(2), 125-137.

Harrell, A., & Smith, B. E. (1996). Effects of restraining orders on domestic violence victims. In E. S. Buzawa & C. G. Buzawa (Eds.), *Do arrests and restraining orders work?* (pp. 214-242). Thousand Oaks, CA: Sage.

Harrell, A., Smith, B. E., & Newmark, L. (1993). *Court processing and the effects of restraining orders for domestic violence victims* (Final report to the state justice institute). Washington, DC: The Urban Institute.

Hilton, N. Z. (1993). *Legal responses to wife assault: Current trends and evaluation.* Newbury Park, CA: Sage.

Hirschel, J. D., & Hutchison, I. W. (1992). Female spouse abuse and the police response: The Charlotte, North Carolina, experiment. *Journal of Criminal Law and Criminology, 83*(1), 73-119.

Hirschel, J. D., Hutchison, I. W., & Dean, C. W. (1992). The failure of arrest to deter spouse abuse. *Journal of Research in Crime and Delinquency, 29*(1), 7-33.

Hirschel, J. D., Hutchison, I. W., & Pesackis, C. E. (1992). Family violence and police utilization. *Violence and Victims, 9,* 299-313.

Hooper, M. (1996, February). When domestic violence diversion is no longer an option: What to do with the female offender. *Berkeley Women's Law Journal,* pp. 168-181.

Hutchison, I. W., Hirschel, L. W., & Pesackis, C. E. (1994). Family violence and police utilization. *Violence and Victims, 9,* 299-313.

Jaffe, P. G., Hastings, E., Reitzel, D., & Austin, G. W. (1993). The impact of police laying charges. In N. Z. Hilton (Ed.), *Legal responses to wife assault: Current trends and evaluation* (pp. 62-95). Newbury Park, CA: Sage.

Keilitz, S. L., Hannaford, P. L., & Efkeman, H. S. (1997). *Civil protection orders: The benefits and limitations for victims of domestic violence: Executive summary.* Washington, DC: Department of Justice.

Klein, A. R. (1996). Re-abuse in a population of court-restrained male batterers: Why restraining orders don't work. In E. S. Buzawa & C. G. Buzawa (Eds.), *Do arrests and restraining orders work?* (pp. 192-213). Thousand Oaks, CA: Sage.

The legal needs of battered women: Hearing before the New York City Council, Committee on Women. (1988, March 15). (testimony of E. Holtzman, King County District Attorney).

Lerman, L. G. (1981). Criminal prosecution of wife beaters. *Response to Violence in the Family, 4,* 1-19.

Lerman, L. G. (1992). The decontextualization of domestic violence. *Journal of Criminal Law and Criminology, 83*(1), 217-240.

Marshall, L. L., & Rose, P. (1990). Premarital violence: The impact of family of origin violence, stress, and reciprocity. *Journal of Family Violence, 5,* 51-64.

McWilliams, M., & McKiernan, J. (1993). *Bringing it out in the open: Domestic violence in Northern Ireland.* Belfast: Her Majesty's Stationery Office.

Mignon, S. I., & Holmes, W. M. (1995). Police response to mandatory arrest laws. *Crime and Delinquency, 41*(4), 430-442.

Miller, S. L. (1989). Unintended side effects of pro-arrest policies and their race and class implications for battered women: A cautionary note. *Criminal Justice Policy Review, 3*(3), 299-316.

Miller, S. L. (2000). Mandatory arrest and domestic violence: Continuing questions. In R. Muraskin & T. Alleman (Eds.), *It's a crime: Women and justice* (pp. 287-310). New York: McGraw-Hill.

Mills, L. G. (1998). Mandatory arrest and prosecution policies for domestic violence: A critical literature review and the case for more research to test victim empowerment approaches. *Criminal Justice and Behavior, 25*(3), 306-318.

Mullender, A. (1996). *Rethinking domestic violence: The social work and probation response.* London: Routledge.

Murphy, C. M., Musser, P. H., & Maton, K. I. (1998). Coordinated community intervention for domestic abusers: Intervention system involvement and criminal recidivism. *Journal of Family Violence, 13*(3), 263-284.

Pate, A. M., & Hamilton, E. E. (1992, October). Formal and informal deterrents to domestic violence: The Dade County spouse assault experiment. *American Sociological Review, 57,* 691-697.

Paternoster, R., Brame, R., Bachman, R., & Sherman, L. W. (1997). Do fair procedures matter? The effect of procedural justice on spouse assault. *Law and Society Review, 31*(1), 163-204.

Rasche, C. E. (1995). Minority women and domestic violence: The unique dilemmas of battered women of color. In B. R. Price & N. J. Sokoloff (Eds.), *The criminal justice system and women: Offenders, victims, and workers* (2nd ed., pp. 246-261). New York: McGraw Hill.

Rauma, D. (1984). Going for the gold: Prosecutorial decision-making in cases of wife assault. *Social Science Research, 13,* 321-351.

Rebovich, D. J. (1996). Prosecution response to domestic violence: Results of a survey of large jurisdictions. In E. S. Buzawa & C. G. Buzawa (Eds.), *Do arrests and restraining orders work?* (pp. 176-191). Thousand Oaks, CA: Sage.

Saltzman, E. (1994). The Quincy District Court Domestic Violence Prevention Program: A model legal framework for domestic violence intervention. *Boston University Law Review, 74,* 329-364.

Saunders, D. G. (1995). The tendency to arrest victims of domestic violence: A preliminary analysis of officer characteristics. *Journal of Interpersonal Violence, 10*(2), 147-158.

Schecter, S. (1982). *Women and male violence: The vision and struggles of the battered women's movement.* Boston: South End.

Schmidt, J. D., & Sherman, L. W. (1996). Does arrest deter domestic violence? In E. S. Buzawa & C. G. Buzawa (Eds.), *Do arrests and restraining orders work?* (pp. 43-53). Thousand Oaks, CA: Sage.

Schmidt, J. D., & Steury, E. (1989). Prosecutorial discretion in filing charges in domestic violence cases. *Criminology, 27*(3), 589-610.

Sherman, L. W. (1992). *Policing domestic violence: Experiments and dilemmas.* New York: Free Press.

Sherman, L. W., & Berk, R. A. (1984a). The Minneapolis domestic violence experiment. *Police Foundation Reports, 1,* 1-8.

Sherman, L. W., & Berk, R. A. (1984b, April). The specific deterrent effects of arrest for domestic violence. *American Sociological Review, 49,* 261-272.

Sherman, L. W., Schmidt, J. D., Rogan, D. P., Gartin, P. R., Cohn, E. G., Collins, D. J., & Bacich, A. R. (1991). From initial deterrence to long-term escalation: Short custody arrest for poverty ghetto domestic violence. *Criminology, 29*(4), 821-850.

Sherman, L. W., Schmidt, J. D., Rogan, D. P., Smith, D. A., Gartin, P. R., Cohn, E. G., Collins, D. J., & Bacich, A. R. (1992). The variable effects of arrest in criminal careers: The Milwaukee domestic violence experiment. *Journal of Criminal Law and Criminology, 83*(1), 137-169.

Sherman, L. W., & Smith, D. A. (1992, October). Crime, punishment, and stake in conformity: Legal and informal control of domestic violence. *American Sociological Review, 57,* 680-690.

Stanko, E. A. (1989). Missing the mark? Policing battering. In J. Hanmer, J. Radford, & E. A. Stanko (Eds.), *Women, policing, and male violence: International perspectives* (pp. 46-69). London: Routledge & Kegan Paul.

Stark, E. (1992). Framing and reframing battered women. In E. S. Buzawa & C. G. Buzawa (Eds.), *Domestic violence: The changing criminal justice perspective* (pp. 271-292). Westport, CT: Auburn House.

Stark, E. (1996). Mandatory arrest: A reply to its critics. In E. S. Buzawa & C. G. Buzawa (Eds.), *Do arrests and restraining orders work?* (pp. 115-149). Thousand Oaks, CA: Sage.

Swain, K. (1986). Probation attitudes to battered women: Apathy, error, and avoidance? *Probation Journal, 33*(4), 132-134.

Syers, M. A., & Edleson, J. L. (1992). The combined effects of coordinated criminal justice intervention in woman abuse. *Journal of Interpersonal Violence, 7,* 490-502.

Thistlethwaite, A., Wooldredge, J., & Gibbs, D. (1998). Severity of dispositions and domestic violence recidivism. *Crime and Delinquency, 44*(3), 388-398.

Toby, J. (1957). Social disorganization and stakes in conformity. *Journal of Criminal Law, Criminology, and Police Science, 48,* 12-17.

Tolman, R. M., & Weiscz, A. (1995). Coordinated community intervention for domestic violence: The effects of arrest and prosecution on recidivism of woman abuse perpetrators. *Crime & Delinquency, 41*(4), 481-495.

Zorza, J. (1994). *Must we stop arresting batterers? Analysis and implications of new police domestic violence studies.* New York: National Center on Women and Family Law.

Zorza, J., & Woods, L. (1994). *Mandatory arrest: Problems and possibilities.* New York: National Center on Women and Family Law.

CHAPTER 17

Advocacy on Behalf of Battered Women

Ellen Pence

Over the past 25 years, reform efforts for battered women have produced two distinct yet interwoven forms of advocacy. The first, *individual case advocacy,* is characterized by an advocate who tries to help one woman get what she wants and needs—either from a local agency or an entire institution, representing a complex system of community agencies that help the state regulate the lives and conflicts of ordinary citizens. This advocate takes up the woman's situation as one case to be managed and resolved by the state. In the second form of advocacy, often called *systems* or *institutional advocacy,* an advocate takes up many cases as one representative unit and tries to alter the practices that produce unfair outcomes for battered women as a group. My mother, who has been engaged in both forms of advocacy since the mid-1970s, defines the difference this way:

> When I advocate for an individual woman, I am trying to help her over-come the many obstacles on her path to effectively using the courts and police to protect her. When I do systems advocacy, I am trying to build a new path. I come to understand what I need to do in systems advocacy by my work with individual women.

In this chapter, I will offer some observations about the current state of institutional advocacy in the U.S. battered women's movement. Specifically, I want to discuss advocacy efforts to create civil and criminal court responses that effectively protect women who are being battered and to examine our efforts to correct the criminal court system's historic hands-off approach to men who beat their wives and partners.

Almost three decades after the first battered women's shelters opened in the United States, we face a critical juncture in our work as advocates. As our programs and agendas for social change become mainstreamed into the legal system, we risk losing our most powerful tool—our position of solidarity with women who are beaten. Today, advocates witness alarming numbers of battered women being arrested for assaults that, given a slightly different set of circumstances, would be hailed as acts of heroism. The legal system has reluctantly granted us interventions that gain control over offenders. However, in many communities, advocates are not positioned to argue that applying those strategies to women who are battered and fight back neither protects public safety nor meets any reasonable standard of justice. Women are being charged with child neglect for failing to stop their batterers from using force against them. New laws require shelter advocates to report women for child neglect when they fail to stop their batterers' use of violence and are unable to leave them. At the same time, judges grant unsupervised visitation to men who have brutally assaulted their children's mothers, but judges themselves are not charged with failure to protect children. More and more women are being aggressively prosecuted for crimes committed on behalf of drug dealers who regularly beat them. Immigration policies are changing—for example, the 1985 Marriage Fraud Act and H1 work permit rules make foreign-born women more vulnerable to their partners' violence (Dasgupta, 1998). Finally, shelters once open to all battered women are increasingly screening out "inappropriate" women from their life-saving resources. These are not problems that cannot be overcome or transformed, but doing so requires a critical examination of our present course, a more sophisticated understanding of how institutions—such as the legal system—continuously reproduce relationships of domination between men and women, and a commitment to finding new ways to stand in solidarity with women.

I was asked to write this chapter because I have been around since the earliest days of our collective work. I have been a part of the Duluth Domestic Abuse Intervention Project, the most often cited example of an effective, locally organized, criminal justice reform effort. I have also had the opportunity to visit similar projects in the United States and abroad to learn about their successes and frustrations in using the legal system to protect women from continued abuse. These experiences give me an insight into our history that can be important for those who are working to move our collective efforts forward. Still, I am limited in my experience, both personally and politically. A chapter such as this should be written by a group of advocates from different states, representing different communities. As I describe the history of advocacy, I will use terms such as *we, us,* and *our* as if there were a universal "we," but there never was. I use these terms to represent the social movement of the 1970s and 1980s, in which women worked toward common goals, even while holding different views on how to reach those goals.

The Early Years of Institutional Advocacy—The 1970s

The women who organized the first shelters for battered women described themselves as advocates. The term *advocate* means mouthpiece; it connotes one who speaks for or takes up the cause of another. The *others* in this context were women who were being beaten by their husbands, lovers, or partners. The notion of speaking out was a core theme of the women's movement, the same movement in which local women's groups opened shelters and articulated a message to a community that was alternately half-hostile and half-listening. However, we did not use the term *advocate* to distinguish between those who were beaten and those who fought for new institutional responses to battered women, particularly because many advocates themselves had experienced violence in their lives. As advocates, we intended to stand in solidarity with shelter residents. Working at a shelter did not so much require a college degree as a willingness to speak out in often hostile institutional environments. We hoped that battered women differentiated the role of advocates from the role of social workers or other professionals who managed their situations as cases. By the 1970s, social workers had long left their radical roots and were fully entrenched in the institutional processes of regulating and managing the lives of poor people and, in particular, the lives of poor women. As advocates, we claimed the role of articulating the needs of women to the system, not the reverse.

Social movements are characterized by the changes they demand in their formative years. The women's movement in the United States was preceded by over a decade of progressive organizing by black civil rights activists to strike down the Jim Crow laws, organizing by migrant farm workers to get decent wages and health protection, organizing by welfare recipients to get rid of patronizing vendor payments and secure a guaranteed annual income, organizing by Native American activists to assert tribal rights as sovereign nations, and organizing by antiwar protesters to end the draft and the Vietnam War. Many early women's advocates had worked in or were heavily influenced by these struggles.

As women filled shelters to the rafters, they told their stories. Women were devastated by the personal betrayal of their abusers but perhaps equally harmed by the seemingly endless ways that police officers, clergy, welfare workers, judges, family members, landlords, attorneys, and therapists found to blame them for their partners' violence. Advocates heard the same stories in every state. Of course, every story had its parochial twist, but the overarching theme of community collusion with batterers was starkly visible. Like activists in all of the progressive social movements of the 1960s, we sought a paradigm shift. We wanted practitioners in agencies that battered women needed for protection to refrain from finding fault with the victims and instead to understand and eliminate the social facilitators of this violence. We wanted to train the eye of scrutiny away from a woman's so-called "healthy" response to being beaten, on to both the abuser and the institutional practices that failed to help women.

Our demands as a social movement emerged from what women needed: They needed to be safe. Women needed exceptions to the legal aid rule that determined eligibility through the family's income level. Women needed new welfare intake rules that recognized their need to hide from the father of their children. Women needed police to keep records of repeated calls to their homes. To control the use of violence against them and their children, women needed a revision of most of the social service system's rules. In a sense, we were breaking new ground. We were using legal strategies inspired by the civil rights movement and strategists such as

Thurgood Marshall, but at the same time, we were trying to alter the case management practices of the court and human service systems. This dual role of outside agitator and inside reformer characterized our early years of advocacy.

When we listened to a woman's experience of being beaten and then turned with her to the legal system for help that was not forthcoming, her anger became ours. Although this empathy with women was seen as "unprofessional," in those days being called unprofessional was not an insult; we had no desire to be professionals. In fact, many of us were glad someone noticed the difference. We were also labeled "man-haters," a name that struck a more divisive cord among us. For some, it was not much of an insult, although it seemed unfair that our indignation over men beating women was interpreted as *our* problem with men rather than men's problem with women. Nevertheless, some women felt that the accusation questioned their loyalty to their sons, fathers, and husbands. Our critics often coupled these accusations with claims that we were all lesbians, unable to get a man, biased because we had been in bad marriages, or alarmists because we had not yet healed from our personal traumas. The list of what made us biased—and, by default, made the practitioners objective—seemed endless, and it was a powerful tool of resistance to our efforts. The accusations eventually fueled divisions in advocacy organizations and added to the complex set of circumstances in which many activists stepped back and stopped critiquing institutional collusion with batterers. Still, although the seeds of division were already being sewn, so, too, were the fundamental principles of good advocacy. The notion of basing our critique on the experiences of real women was fully en-

trenched by the late 1970s. Our strength at the state legislatures, with the media, and in efforts to counter bogus research lay in our connection to what was happening to women and our willingness to speak out.

Some workers in the movement identified themselves as feminists, but feminists hardly constituted the majority of volunteer and paid staff. It was a personal commitment rather than a political ideology that inspired large numbers of women to start and maintain local shelters. Many workers in the movement had themselves escaped violent partners or were still living in or attempting to leave violent relationships. Others were daughters, sisters, or mothers of women who had been or were being beaten. Middle-class, working-class, and poor women all joined the working committees and carried out the work of the newly organized shelters. The presence of so many women who had used these systems enriched our movement. Whereas many white middle- and working-class feminists offered a political analysis important to our work, those same women tended to be somewhat naive about how the state regulated the private lives of women. The term *feminist* was used mostly by white women who offered an important gender analysis to our work. Progressive African, Native, Asian, and Latin American women in the movement were less likely to use the term *feminist*. Nevertheless, women of color brought a deeply historical and far less naive understanding of relationships of domination and exploitation—and, correspondingly, of the pitfalls we would face in using institutions of social control to benefit women.

Progressives in the movement offered a crucial analysis of the violence we all abhorred, but because they did not make up the majority of workers, they did not control the movement's politics. This broad spectrum of movement workers was not unanimous on how to talk about families, marriage, and women's roles within those institutions. We did, however, agree that—contrary to what was portrayed in Hollywood and women's magazines, in romance novels and from the pulpit— women were not safe within the family setting. We agreed that community agencies responsible for controlling criminal and antisocial behavior made the widespread abuse of women possible, and even worse when they engaged in practices that either ignored violence or treated it as a symptom of defective relationships. Practices that assumed that violence was the result of a relationship gone sour were particularly problematic because of the resulting intervention activities that focused on changing women. These practices were not simply misguided or ineffective; they were often dangerous. We perceived safety as every woman's right, as the goal of our work, and most important, as the responsibility of the community to ensure. Safety was to this social movement what liberation was to the larger women's movement.

In response to the specific needs of women entering shelters, we developed legal avenues of protection in both civil and criminal courts. A number of activists argued that pursuing civil remedies to this violence undermined our long-term goal of getting the police and court systems to view domestic violence as a serious crime against women. However, some civil solutions, such as court restraining orders, held great promise for women who needed immediate state intervention with "teeth" that achieved the same level of relief afforded by a divorce without the long, drawn-out process. On the criminal side, we pushed for greater enforcement of criminal statutes, which had, for almost a century, been ignored when the offender was the husband or lover of the victim.

Seeking a Civil Remedy

In 1976, the Pennsylvania Coalition against Domestic Violence became the first advocacy organization to approach its state legislature for a civil relief tailored specifically to the needs of battered women. Within 5 years of the coalition's success, more than 30 other states had passed legislation allowing courts to grant immediate restraining orders; among other protections, these orders could exclude an abusive party from the petitioner's home. Few people working in courthouses and advocacy programs today are aware of the historical significance of this accomplishment. For more than 10 centuries, women in Western society futilely sought and went without state protection from the violence of brutal husbands. By the late 1970s, we had garnered the political strength and the social consciousness to undermine the husband's "king of the castle" privilege. Women could now tell their story in a courtroom and if a judge were convinced, by a preponderance of the evidence, that she was being physically or sexually abused, the judge could order the man to leave his home and have no contact with her until the court lifted the order. This achievement is on par with the victories of the first wave of feminists, who struggled for almost a century for the right to divorce, sue for custody of their children, use birth control, and vote.

The protection order replaced the old peace bond and divorce restraining order. It was more powerful—most states made the violation of a protection order a misdemeanor—and gave police the authority to arrest violators without requiring women to return to court. In average-size cities such as Minneapolis, Minnesota, literally thousands of women filed for this protection every year, and hundreds of men were arrested for not obeying the orders.

Criminal Intervention Strategies

Activists in the battered women's movement were deeply conflicted over an agenda for criminal system reforms. Yet we did find common ground in the problems women faced as a cumbersome and adversarial criminal court system slowly processed their abusers' cases. We knew it was not in the best interests of women to have laws that effectively required them to arrest their abusers, so we advocated for—and achieved—police authority to arrest in misdemeanor cases without witnessing the assault. We knew that taking part in hostile court actions against their abusers was dangerous for women, so we successfully argued for several evidentiary rule changes, as well as police documentation practices that gave prosecutors the ability to bring the victim's story into the courtroom without relying exclusively on her testimony.

Women wanted and needed many things from the justice system, including police protection, orders for their abusers to leave them alone or even leave the house, limits placed on their abusers' contact with them, financial help from him or the state, freedom to stay in their own homes safely, and a way to make abusers' contact with children safe for both the women and the children. Moreover, some women wanted the most hotly contested

and controversial of wishes: someone to help him change.

Few women said they wanted their abusers punished, jailed, or put in prison. Most battered women saw imprisonment as a last resort, whereas advocates were more likely to pursue jail as an intervention goal. However, even many advocates recognized jails or prisons as hostile to women and felt that little was to be gained by sending men already fully engaged in antiwoman behaviors into an environment that would only reinforce their hatred of women. Many activists were reluctant to adopt a strategy that used imprisonment against men who were already overly criminalized in our society. Not surprisingly, Native American and African American women offered particularly strong arguments for alternative strategies.

As advocates, we had all seen or heard police officers, prosecutors, probation officers, social workers, or judges shake their heads sympathetically and say, "she's just not ready to testify," "she's reluctant," "she's still stuck in the honeymoon phase," or "she's too dependent on him." While we relentlessly educated professionals in training sessions and courthouse hallways about the personal struggles of battered women, we also tried to maintain the premise that the problem lies not in a woman's response to being beaten but in the community's response to the beating. Adhering to the notion that women's experiences should form the foundation of our agenda, we asked a fundamental question. Why would a woman who is being punched by her husband take an adversarial action against him that (a) will take up to a year to resolve; (b) will likely result in her being cross-examined by a lawyer who will try to make 12 perfect strangers think that she is an evil, wicked, lying, wretched woman; (c) will focus exclusively on the violence in this one incident and rule as irrelevant the countless blows, insults, threats, and disloyalties she has endured over the years; (d) may result in him being sent to jail—but probably will not; (e) may result in him being sent to a batterers' group that he will hate and probably not finish; (f) may result in him being fined by the court—a fine he could coerce her into paying; and (g) will very likely not penalize him if he fails to follow through on any of the court orders that presumably protect her?

We pursued an agenda of criminalization, not because women in shelters were saying, "I want my partner prosecuted," but because many activists believed that men would not stop battering women until the community thought of and treated doing so as a crime. We knew that no group of people who systematically dominated others quit doing so because of a spiritual or ethical revelation. Historically, excessive power—the freedom of dominators to act without consequence— has only been curbed by the oppressed who organize to take it away. Our strategy was inspired by the assumption that to make wife beating a crime would profoundly alter the premise of male dominance in marriage. Prosecuting an individual batterer does not necessarily protect the woman he is beating. In fact, sometimes, she becomes subjected to even more intimidation and abuse. Pursuing a criminal agenda meant using individual cases to make a social point. We tried to create some safeguards so that this agenda would not be used against women, but even from the beginning, we faced an uphill battle. When we criticized the almost universal problem of low conviction rates, some prosecutors—instead of

improving investigations and police evidence gathering—responded by criminally charging women who refused to testify or who changed their testimony when subpoenaed to testify against their wishes. Today, many advocates have lost sight of this history, and they join other practitioners in viewing the primary barrier to holding offenders accountable as the failure of women to cooperate with prosecution efforts. Criminal consequences for individual men who batter—prosecution and convictions—have become goals of advocates, and many of us see battered women who do not share our enthusiasm for this presumed deterrence strategy as problematic. We label them as reluctant, in denial, recalcitrant, recanters. Note that using the legal system to right a historic wrong is rarely free of risk to those whom the reformed laws are intended to protect.

Eventually, efforts to enhance the state's control over offenders translated into laws that expanded police powers of arrest, strengthened a prosecutor's ability to present evidence, and allowed jailers to hold suspects longer. This type of reform is typically supported by the political right, not people of color, progressives, and/or feminists. We pursued every reform effort only cautiously; as I mentioned earlier, each gain has itself been used against some battered women in ways we tried, but were unable, to avoid.

Training and Conversion Efforts

In the late 1970s and early 1980s, on the heels of new legislation, we had the notion that if we trained practitioners to understand the new laws, things would change. We put together training packages—for police officers, social workers, therapists, doctors, judges, and anybody who would let us into their training rooms. I still remember every detail of the first training I did at a police station. In 1977, we had successfully lobbied the Minnesota legislature to pass a law saying that if, during their investigation, police officers reasonably established that one adult household member had assaulted another, the officers could arrest and charge the suspect without the victim initiating the legal action. However, 6 months after its passage, advocates from every shelter in the state were reporting that the new law was rarely used. Police were still asking women at the scene of the assault if they wanted to arrest and prosecute their abusers. Women, of course, continued to say, "No, just get him out of the house."

It was common in those days for us to train in a group. Usually, one woman went as the expert and gave a speech full of statistics and the feminist analysis of battering. Then, three or four other women—the "victim's panel"—talked about their personal experiences of being abused. The expert speaker got dressed up and carried a briefcase. If she had been battered, she would not necessarily talk about it. The other women dressed innocently—no low-cut blouses or tight pants. We all tried to look very heterosexual, because police and others in the system had branded us as man-hating lesbian radical feminists who had been turned off men by some bad experience with a guy. We even stooped to coaxing pregnant shelter workers into accompanying us on these training sessions to improve our image.

On this occasion, in August 1978, I got dressed up as the expert. Three former residents of the Duluth shelter, all of whom had called the police within the past year, dressed innocently. We went off to the police department for a 2-hour training, having spent the early part of the day drinking coffee in the shelter lounge and talking with four or five of the current residents, discussing exactly what the police needed to hear. We planned for me to talk for about 20 minutes on the new arrest law and the "dynamics" of battering. Specifically, I was to say that women who lived with men who battered were not sick, crazy, masochistic, or products of bad families but were being controlled by violence and constrained by the inadequate backing of police and the courts. Then, each woman was to talk for about 15 minutes about the kinds of violence her husband used against her and the impact that the police response had on her and on her husband. Then, we would open it up for questions.

The speech would open their minds, the panel their hearts. On leaving, we would know that, through our efforts, the police had seen the light and the state—instead of women—would start to take responsibility for arresting men who battered. We were all nervous but determined to do our task well. When we arrived at the police station, the desk sergeant directed us to a basement training room and said "Good luck" as we turned to the staircase. I remember thinking, "How nice." Downstairs, the training officer introduced us as "the girls from the shelter" to 25 or so uniformed officers, and we began.

I started by answering the question police always ask: Why do women stay? About 5 minutes into this little speech, an officer named Tommy Cich—a name etched into my memory—raised his hand and said, "I'll tell you why *these* women get hit—they let their alligator mouths outrun their hummingbird brains." I was a bit shocked, but I said, "Thank you, Officer Cich, for that analysis. Mine was slightly different," and I went back to my planned remarks. Then, another officer raised his hand; I ignored him, but he spoke anyway. "You know, there is something about a battered woman that just makes you want to hit her." For the second time in as many minutes, the room filled with laughter, and I found myself at a complete loss for words. I finally blurted out in a high-pitched tone, "Well, let's take a short break here, and you boys can all go get yourselves a cup of coffee!" I motioned to the victim panel, which looked as stunned as I felt, and we slipped off to the women's toilet. The Duluth Police Department in 1977 did not boast a large women's restroom with several stalls. Instead, the women's restroom was a converted closet with a stool in the middle and a tiny sink off to the side. Nevertheless, we hovered around the toilet and said, "Now what?" I remember one woman asking, "Why do they hate us so much?" None of us attempted an answer. None of us knew what to do, nor did we want to try anything. So, we walked out the back door, drove back to the shelter, called the desk sergeant, who no longer seemed so nice, and told him we had left.

Advocates from shelters across the state spent the next few years subjecting themselves to these types of training experiences. We quickly learned how to make witty comebacks to officers who acted like they had been recruited from caves. We occasionally converted an officer or two to be sympathetic to the plight of beaten women. Almost every shelter found a couple of allies in its local police department: someone they could go to with complaints. In some cities, police

chiefs agreed to ongoing training programs for officers. Several departments ordered their dispatchers to make calls from the shelter a top priority for sending a squad car. In city after city, police became active participants in the increasing number of task forces and commissions addressing the problem. Nevertheless, none of these accomplishments seemed to substantially alter the way that police responded to calls. In fact, many of us felt that our newly formed cooperative relationships were drawing us into the police way of thinking more than we were persuading them to ours.

Eventually, we recognized the futility of these educational efforts. We began to understand that patriarchy is not simply a mind-set or just a function of attitudes—patriarchy is a practice. We needed to change it at the level of practice. This realization led to the development of criminal justice reform projects in cities across the United States and Canada. These projects were marked by the attention their organizers paid to drafting and lobbying for the enactment of procedures and policies that defined what practitioners could and could not do when responding to cases involving women abuse.

Intervention and Coordinated Community Response Projects— The 1980s

Every community has its own advocacy story. No single strategy was employed by everyone, but innovators created common visions for those of us who attended the growing number of regional and national gatherings. Seattle and San Francisco developed early prosecution programs. The state of Oregon took the lead in requiring police to make an arrest when violence reached a certain level. Pennsylvania shaped the dual track agenda of civil and criminal interventions. Courageous lawsuits against police inaction in New York, California, and, later, Connecticut, gave countless advocacy programs access to police training rooms for the first time.

Advocates in Duluth, who organized the first community-wide intervention project, capitalized on the work of dozens of other programs when defining their multiagency approach to intervention, and they introduced some of their own innovations. They organized a local effort to implement legal strategies conceived at state, regional, and national gatherings. Most state domestic violence coalitions had already obtained new arrest laws, civil protection legislation, and welfare regulations. Duluth's contribution was organizing a project with advocates at the center of a planning and implementation strategy for law enforcement, courts, and human service agencies, responding to the mounting criticism of inadequate protection for battered women. We met with policy makers from key intervening agencies and somehow convinced them to let us help write a comprehensive policy for their agencies on responding to domestic violence cases. Toward that end, we called a series of small interagency meetings to work out the overlap in policy language, and ultimately, we became the central group encouraging interagency relationships for cases involving domestic violence. We immersed ourselves in the intricacies of case processing and, by so doing, learned to stop pointing at practitioners with poor attitudes and a lack of understanding about battered women and focus instead on the institutional work routines, policies, and procedures that produced an inattention to women's safety.

From the 911 dispatcher to the probation officer, scores of system workers—representing agencies from federal, state, county, or city government—will act on one woman's case before it is closed. Each action taken, beginning with that call to the police, is an opportunity to centralize or marginalize women's safety. When Duluth advocates started raising questions gleaned from the reality of our own and other women's lives, we were brought deep into the daily workings of the justice system. We began to take note of literally hundreds of institutional steps used to process a case while listening to women's stories, observing courtroom procedures, riding along with police, and attending meetings between women and prosecutors. We found opportunities to enhance women's safety in dispatch and patrol response procedures, booking procedures, and bail hearings; when decision were being made to prosecute, defer, or drop a case; during pretrial maneuvers, trial tactics, sentencing hearings, and revocations of probation. We proposed changes at every stage of a case's journey through the system. We proposed new legislation, new notions of practitioners' job duties, new department policies, new interagency protocols, and new administrative forms. Although never instrumental in achieving landmark legal decisions, we were pioneers in fighting for their enforcement, and we succeeded in rearranging how the system processes each aspect of a case. In doing so, we carved out a role for ourselves that few grassroots groups before us had done.

This intervention model eventually became known as a Coordinated Community Response (Shepard & Pence, 1999).

In 1987, the Hilton Foundation awarded close to a million dollars to a national judicial organization to coordinate an intensive summit of interdisciplinary teams from all 50 states. After the 5-day conference, teams returned home with the message that effective coordination should be spearheaded by community councils and that the judiciary should play a key role in organizing those councils. Advocates should be present at the table, but not in the central, agenda-setting role that Duluth and other grassroots groups had envisioned. Coordinating councils proliferated, and advocates became increasingly marginalized in identifying problematic practices in a community. Even more significantly, the agenda of change focused more on increased efficiency, arrests, and convictions than on critiquing the impact of institutional responses on the safety, autonomy, and integrity of battered women.

While "systems-driven" reform efforts were taking shape, shelter and nonresidential advocacy programs were maturing in several unfortunate ways. Urban programs started placing their workers into limited and specialized roles. Some advocates were restricted to accompanying women to civil protection court—day after day, month after month—or to working the criminal court, or to finding housing. Such a development has many implications for our effectiveness. First, advocates began to talk about women in noticeably different ways. Opportunities for advocates to problem-solve larger issues disappeared as administrators in the increasingly stratified workforce took on the roles of agency spokespersons. Without full responsibility, advocates lost the ability to respond fully. Second, a growing attraction to being professional left fewer opportunities for shelter residents to have meaningful ways of joining the struggle. Finally, funding relationships started to shape advocacy programs in several problematic ways. Foundations and local government funding sources began to link dollars to units of services provided. Women coming into shelters became clients, advocates became counselors, and the distinction between the shelter programs and the institutions that regulate women's lives became far less pronounced. The federal government finally supported institutional advocacy on a large scale in 1994 with the passage of the Crime Bill's Violence Against Women Act. However, grant guidelines funneled a substantial amount of Violence Against Women Act funds through police and prosecutors, whom they required to collaborate with local advocacy programs. In some communities, local advocacy programs received subcontracts from the police or prosecutors' offices, but in other communities, the police department or prosecutor's office built its own advocate staff positions into the budget. In cities and towns across the country, advocates started being managed by or working directly for the very agencies we had originally organized to change.

The crux of advocacy is identifying the site of problems and the standpoint from which to articulate and pose solutions to those problems. An advocate, therefore, places herself at the position of interaction between the battered woman and the system and makes her agenda the problematic ways in which the woman experiences that interaction. This standpoint of advocacy is unattainable when the advocate has only partial loyalty to the woman. Advocates must offer absolute confidentiality, a clear commitment to the safety needs of a woman, and the ability to speak out on behalf of women without risking reprisal—conditions that do not exist when we merge with the institutions that we are committed to changing.

Advocacy in the New Millennium: Reclaiming Our Roots

I want to propose five concrete actions that can return advocacy programs to our more radical roots while still capitalizing on our growth of the past three decades. I offer each of these proposals as a point of departure—an action plan that should quickly transform our waning attachment to the viewpoint of women and, in doing so, map out a new course of advocacy for the next decade.[1]

Build critical reflection into the structure of advocates' work. At the core of my proposal is increasing an advocate's ability to develop critical perspectives about her work. This program will be successful if advocates can nest their efforts in the larger political understanding of violence against women and move away from atomized tasks. Advocates from all around the country complain about how little time they get to think. Their activities on behalf of battered women seem to take them from crisis to crisis. As a result, advocates rarely get the chance to pursue theoretical questions that arise from their work, scrutinize the fundamental philosophies of their programs, debate policy issues, or link domestic violence work with other oppressions in society. Nor do they get the space or time to acquire information that is vital to connecting theory with practice. This lack of opportunity to think critically makes advocates fall into traditional and fragmented work patterns, lose their connection to women's realities, and

prioritize their tasks according to bureaucratic expediency. We can take several simple steps to recapture our perspective. First, schedule regular discussions—at least every 2 months—for advocates and battered women to think through issues they are facing. Second, assemble a video and article library to expose workers to new ideas for ending oppression from a broad range of progressive efforts. Finally, set aside at least a half hour of every staff meeting for one advocate to summarize an article or documentary and lead a short discussion on its local implications.

Build community-organizing activities into advocates' job duties. Ultimately, we must guarantee a battered woman's safety *within* her community, not away from it. The community is a battered woman's life source; removing her from it may be a temporary solution to her problems but never a permanent one. The success of the battered women's movement, therefore, hinges on changing minds and society. Organizing communities must become central to our advocacy work. However, in the melee of our frenetic activities to ensure the safety of individual battered women, we have increasingly ignored this basic understanding. Even when we recognize community organizing as an important part of our program, most of us do not quite comprehend what it entails, nor the skills it requires. We must acknowledge community organizing as the complex activity that it is and prepare ourselves. The work of transforming our communities is the work of all women, including battered women. It is our community and, therefore, our historic task to change the conditions that make women unsafe in their homes. Again, simple steps will make this a reality. Every advocate should attend at least one community-organizing training a year. We should restructure women's groups to introduce ways for battered women to organize around their common problems, which means that group facilitators should plan to spend more than 2 hours a week in each group. Every group should lead into subsequent sessions to act on an issue, and women attending the groups should be provided with the basic resources of community organizing, such as paper, stamps, and transportation funds.[2]

Give battered women and advocates decision-making control over the work methods used by advocacy programs. The battered women's movement was founded on the reclamation of decision-making power by the women whose lives were affected by program policies. Over time, most programs abandoned their efforts to include battered women's opinions and voices in the decisions being made on their behalf. The same thing eventually happened to advocates, as programs moved from cooperative management structures to increasingly hierarchical ones. It is time to reverse this condition. I propose that each program develop a decision-making committee in which battered women occupy prominent positions, holding veto power over every proposed policy. The decision-making tree might even allow advocates who work closely with battered women to have a central role in developing program policies. Ultimately, the reference point of all policies would be the interests of battered women.[3]

Strengthen the collective advocacy efforts of progressives in the community by linking the antiviolence work of marginalized groups. A significant problem of the contemporary battered women's movement is that it has drifted away from other types of violence against women, as well as the oppressions under which other marginalized groups struggle. Unless we understand the relationships between various social oppressions, our movement runs the risk of working in isolation and perhaps even in opposition to other social change campaigns. We can overcome this by developing an accountability committee made up of community members and activists from other progressive groups working against oppression. This committee would not only help the domestic violence program make decisions but also act as the watchdog of official institutions such as the courts and police. Thus, if a judge makes a decision that endangers a woman or her children, the committee—rather than a "special interest program"—would assume the responsibility for public confrontation. Today, advocacy programs have been reduced to the status of special interest groups, separated from the concerns of the larger community. An accountability committee could create connections among progressive organizations to enhance our collective work toward a society free of relationships of domination and deepen our commitment to the whole experience of women.

Rebuild our programs to minimize our dependence on institutions that subjugate women. It is impossible for us to be truly free of the influence of institutions that produce and maintain patriarchal privilege. We can, however, be far more conscious of how our relationships to our funding sources and other institutions that manage women's cases might subvert our ability to stand in solidarity with battered women. The first step to reclaiming our grass roots is to ensure that every community's advocacy program for battered women is independent from local law enforcement and criminal and civil court systems. That does not mean we cannot work cooperatively with court-employed victim assistants, nor that we compete with staff in other institutions for the role of victim advocate. It simply means that we must be clear about the differences between people who help manage victims' participation in legal proceedings, such as prosecutors, and people who are mouthpieces for the goals and needs of battered women. The second step is to set standards for fund raising that give our relationship with battered women priority over our financial stability. The politics of money plays out differently in each state and philanthropic setting. However, we collectively face similar challenges in our approaches to federal funding. We must not have unspoken agreements, if we get money from funding sources, to not speak out about their failures to protect battered women. State and federal sources—the largest being the U.S. Department of Justice—now provide some of the most influential advocacy programs in the country with significant financial support. Yet we are almost silent on the Justice Department's role in increasing the vulnerability of immigrant and undocumented women to abusive partners through their immigration policies, practices, and laws. We have mounted no unified voice against the failure of the Justice Department to offer guidelines to prosecutors on working with women living under the control of drug dealers—women who are easy game for major convictions in federal court. We have no national plan to confront the dismal charging and conviction rates of prosecutors charged with upholding the law on reservations and federal lands. I only mention these as examples of how subtle collusion can be and how easily the system co-opts our voices. The decision to apply for and accept funding must always be accompanied by an analysis of how a funding source contributes to women's vulnerability to male violence. Although we are not obliged to be penniless by taking a position of only accepting clean money, we must not be silent about funders' institutional practices that are harmful to battered women.

Conclusion

Today, we are miles away from where we started. Although we are weaker in some ways, we are stronger in others. We have established a foundation of important legislation, we enjoy more resources and a more diverse leadership, we have more experience, we have a more sophisticated understanding of how institutions affect our lives, and we have greater access to inner chambers of power. Nevertheless, we must actively pursue an agenda of reclamation if we are to continue to be a force of liberation for women who are battered. The suggestions I have made for immediate actions toward reclamation are only starting points. As we discuss the possibilities in our state coalitions and local programs, a more contextually appropriate course of action will emerge.

Thirty years ago, we faced incredibly hostile reactions to our insistence on the most basic protections for women: sending a squad when she calls or arresting men who brutally beat their partners. Because of our work and the important and courageous work of allies in the system, these institutional responses are now normal. However, these institutions are still the guardians of men's power over women. Our role is never to help the legal system manage cases or women's lives—it is to continue to make women's real experiences visible and to make women's safety a goal of legal intervention and the responsibility of the community. We must resist the forces that swallow up social movements and their transforming agendas.

Notes

1. A special thanks to Shamita Das Dasgupta who helped me think through these five points and eliminate others that would have cost so much money as to further compromise our autonomy.

2. A wonderful resource for thinking like organizers in a women's group is *Training for Transformation: A Handbook for Community Workers* by Anne Hope and Sally Timmel. This manual can be ordered from the Grailville Art & Bookstore, 932 O'Bannonville Rd., Loveland, OH 45140, 1-888-683-2302.

3. In 1990, when the Domestic Abuse Intervention Project faced the problems discussed here, we adopted such a decision-making tree. To obtain a copy, write to DAIP, 202 East Superior Street, Duluth, MN 55802.

References

Dasgupta, S. D. (1998). Women's realities: Defining violence against women by immigration, race, and class. In R. Bergen (Ed.), *Issues in intimate violence* (pp. 209-219). Thousand Oaks, CA: Sage.

Shepard, M. F., & Pence, E. L. (1999). *Coordinated community responses to domestic violence: Lessons from Duluth and beyond.* Thousand Oaks, CA: Sage.

CHAPTER 18

Health Interventions With Battered Women

From Crisis Intervention to Complex Social Prevention

Evan Stark

This chapter focuses on health interventions with battered women.[1] The first section reviews the empirical rationale for intervening and the barriers to doing so effectively. The next section outlines interventions by individual clinicians, health care institutions, and communities, roughly paralleling the traditional public health divisions of tertiary, secondary, and primary prevention. Promising initiatives, policies, and program models are described. But the dearth of outcome evaluations in the field means these must be taken as illustrative rather than as proven models of "best practice." As with other health problems that derive from complex social and behavioral processes that lie outside traditional models of disease, successful health intervention depends on linking all three levels of response through collaborative efforts with social service, criminal justice, and community-based providers, what is called a coordinated community response. The conclusion addresses future challenges to clinical violence intervention.

An underlying theme in this chapter is that health programs are most likely to succeed when they normalize and mainstream clinical violence intervention. *Normalization* implies that work with battered women builds on the skills and patient education techniques clinicians successfully employ in other medical or behavioral health areas: smoking, child abuse, or sexually transmitted disease (STD), for instance. *Mainstreaming* refers to making clinical violence intervention part of routine patient care.[2] Given high rates of staff turnover at hospitals and community health centers, the institutionalization of domestic violence training is a critical component of mainstreaming. Mainstreaming also entails integrating sensitivity to partner abuse into the clinical response to a spectrum of medical and behavioral problems that can be caused or aggravated by battering.

The Need For Clinical Violence Intervention

Normally, the need for health services is determined by identifying the number of new cases of a problem in the population (i.e., its *incidence*), the duration of a typical case, and how many people are suffering its effects at a given time (its *prevalence*). Problems can have a low incidence—HIV disease is an example—and still pose major challenges to intervention because of their duration and serious effects. By contrast, although the flu has a high seasonal incidence, it makes only minimal demands on health services because it resolves quickly. Primary prevention aims to reduce the incidence of new cases. But most interventions are designed to reduce prevalence through acute care or early intervention.

Confusion about whether to define a case of domestic violence by each abusive episode or a woman's continuing exposure to battering makes it difficult to agree on the incidence, prevalence, or duration of the problem in the general population. Without this basic information, it is impossible to accurately gauge the level of services needed to treat battered women, to say with certainty what portion of the population of battered women is being served, or to determine whether interven-

tions are reducing the incidence or prevalence of the problem. The rationale for health care's involvement has come largely from surveys and health research on the use of services by battered women and the medical response.

The database for an expanded health response was provided by research conducted in the late 1970s and 1980s, largely with funding from the National Institutes of Mental Health (NIMH). Studies in urban, rural, emergency, primary care, and family practice settings demonstrated that battered women used health resources in large numbers for injuries and for a range of other emergent and nonemergent problems linked to domestic violence (Appleton, 1980; Hamberger, Saunders, & Hovey, 1992; Stark & Flitcraft, 1996). Research also laid the groundwork for professional education and improved training by disclosing how rarely medical personnel identified the problem, linked it to its medical or behavioral consequences, or selected abuse as the focus of intervention (Hilberman & Munson, 1977-1978; Stark, Flitcraft, & Frazier, 1979). Illustrating neglect of the problem in the medical community were the few sentences devoted to deliberate injury in a 1985 survey of *Injury in America* (Committee on Trauma Research, 1985) conducted under the joint auspices of the National Research Council and the National Academy of Medicine.

Despite early claims that battered women rarely sought help for their problems (Walker, 1984), population surveys revealed that a substantial proportion use health services. For example, 17% of the abused women participating in a Kentucky Harris poll reported using emergency medical services (Schulman, 1979). In Texas, 358,595 women reported that they required medical treatment at some point in their lives because of abuse (Teske & Parker, 1983). Based on these and similar findings, the American Medical Association (AMA, 1992) conservatively estimates that more than 1.5 million women nationwide seek medical treatment for injuries related to abuse each year. Looking only at the most severe cases, a National Crime Victimization Survey for 1991 concluded that partner assaults cost medicine more than $44 million annually and resulted in 21,000 hospitalizations with 99,800 patient days, 28,700 emergency department visits, and 39,900 visits to physicians each year (U.S. Department of Justice, 1992). Importantly, battered women seek help even more promptly than people injured in automobile accidents (Stark & Flitcraft, 1996).

Although the above estimates refer primarily to emergent injuries, studies based on actual use of health services show that battered women commonly seek help at all major medical sites, suffer a wide range of nonemergent as well as emergent problems, and are typically frank about their source. Reviews of medical records suggest that between 18.7% and 30% of female trauma patients have a history of battering (McLeer & Anwar, 1989; Stark, 1984; Stark et al., 1979). But when women are directly questioned in emergency medical settings, as many as 54.2% disclose such abuse (Abbott, Johnson, Kozial-McLain, & Lowenstein, 1995), contradicting physician claims that abused women are evasive. In addition to their prevalence among injury patients, battered women are disproportionately represented among rape victims, homeless women, women who attempt suicide, alcoholics and drug users, mothers of abused children, psychiatric patients, and women with HIV disease (Browne & Bassuk, 1997; Cohen, Deamant, Barkan, Richardson, & Young, 2000; Muelleman, Lenaghan, & Pakieser, 1998; Roper, Flitcraft, & Frazier, 1979; Stark & Flitcraft, 1991, 1988b, 1996; Stark et al., 1979). The proportion of battered women using obstetrical and general medical services for nonemergent health problems equals or exceeds their proportion among emergency patients. Prevalence estimates for current intimate partner violence among women in primary care settings range between 7% and 29% (Bullock, 1989; Freund, Bak, & Blackhall, 1996; Gin, Rucker, Frayne, Cygan, & Hubbell, 1991; Rath, Jarratt, & Leonardson, 1989). Indeed, 55.1% of 1,443 women seeking medical care in two university-associated family practice clinics in Columbia, South Carolina, had experienced some type of intimate partner violence in a current, most recent, or past intimate relationship with a partner. Although the majority of these women (77.3%) experienced physical or sexual violence, 22.7% were suffering the consequences of nonphysical abuse (Coker, Smith, & McKeown, & King, 2000). Conversely, 38.8% of the women in a midwestern community-practice setting reported they had been abused at least once (Hamberger et al., 1992). These approximations establish targets for screening protocols in hospitals and other health care institutions.

A Philadelphia study revealed another important facet of help-seeking by abuse victims: that injuries from domestic violence occur at every point in the life cycle. The typical victim of battering is a single, separated, or divorced young woman (under 30) with a child. However, 34% of injuries to girls 16 to 18 are caused by battering; so are 18% of the injuries to women over 60 (McLeer & Anwar, 1989).

The hallmarks of abusive injuries are their sexual nature and their frequency. Battered women are 13 times more likely than nonbattered women to be injured in the breast, chest, and abdomen and three times as likely to be injured while pregnant (Stark & Flitcraft, 1996). Of the 37.6% of female primary-care patients who have been victims of intimate partner violence, almost half (18.1% of the total) were also sexually assaulted (Coker et al., 2000). A third of all rapes are committed in abusive relationships (Roper et al., 1979). Still, abusive injuries are no more likely to result in hospitalization than nonabusive injuries, underlining the fact that in itself severity is not a good indicator of abuse. A woman who comes to a health facility three times with injuries has an 80% chance of being a battered woman, whether those injuries require sutures or not. Frequency and the central pattern of injury combine to constitute an Adult Trauma History (ATH) typical of woman battering.

In addition to injury, medical problems indirectly related to partner assault account for 14% to 20% of women's visits to ambulatory care or internal medicine clinics. The bulk of these presentations involve headaches from head trauma, joint pains from twisting injuries, abdominal or breast pain following blows to the torso, dyspareunia or recurrent genitourinary infections from sexual assault, dysphagia following choking, or chronic pain syndromes that are often elicited by nonviolent coercive tactics used in battering. Up to 53% of the female patients visiting pain clinics have reported physical and/or sexual abuse, primarily by their partners (cited by Schornstein, 1997), although the

battered women were also twice as likely as nonabused women to report pain unrelated to injury, or "spontaneous" pain (Haber & Ross, 1985). As the result of forced sex, battered women are also at elevated risk for HIV infection and other STDs. Repeated presentations of somatic complaints are also a common presentation of battering at primary care clinics, particularly among obstetrical patients (American College of Obstetricians and Gynecologists, 1995).

The psychosocial sequelae of abuse are as important as its or medical consequences. Compared to a baseline population of nonbattered patients, for example, battered women were 5 times more likely to attempt suicide, 15 times more likely to abuse alcohol, 9 times more likely to abuse drugs, 6 times more likely to report child abuse, and 3 times more likely to be diagnosed as depressed or psychotic (Stark & Flitcraft, 1988a, 1996). Absolute numbers are as important as the relative frequencies of these problems. For example, 19% of battered women attempted suicide at least once, 38% were diagnosed as depressed or having another situational disorder, and 10% became psychotic (Stark & Flitcraft, 1996). Because these problems only became disproportionate after the presentation of an abusive injury, battering is clearly their cause. The result is that battering is a major factor in each of these caseloads: Battered women compose an estimated 45% of female alcoholics, 45% of the mothers of abused or neglected children, 29.5% of women who attempt suicide, and 48.8% of the black women who attempted suicide (Stark & Flitcraft, 1996).

A second important set of findings suggests the potential utility of clinical violence intervention in this caseload. In marked contrast to its institutional prevalence (between 18% and 54%), only 3.2% of all cases represent a woman's first presentation of abuse (Flitcraft, 1993; Stark & Flitcraft, 1996) between 1 in 6 and 1 in 18 cases. The discrepancy between the high prevalence of battering and its low incidence is accounted for by the duration of battering for most victims seen in the health setting. Where nonbattered women had an average of 1.9 trauma visits to the hospital, for example, at-risk women averaged 5.7 injury visits ($p < .0001$) and had an average abusive trauma history of 7.1 years (Stark & Flitcraft, 1996). Almost one battered woman in five has presented to the emergency room at least 11 times with trauma. The fact that woman battering is ongoing in the vast majority of cases dramatizes the ineffectiveness of current interventions. But it also indicates that early intervention could reduce subsequent use of medical services for domestic violence and its sequelae by somewhere between 80% and 95%. This translates into huge cost savings.

The importance of professional training and education was underscored by a third discovery, that only a tiny proportion of health professionals recognize the signs or consequences of domestic violence, perhaps as few as 1 in 20, even when physicians believed it was their responsibility to do so (Hilberman & Munson, 1977-1978; Kurz & Stark, 1988; Stark & Flitcraft, 1996; Stark et al., 1979). A 1991 survey of emergency departments in Massachusetts revealed that 80% had no written protocol in place to identify domestic violence, and 58% reported that they identify five or fewer battered women each month, far below research estimates (Isaac & Sanchez, 1994).

Instead of identifying domestic violence, clinicians respond inappropriately to battered women. Failure to recognize abuse has traditionally been accompanied by symptomatic treatment, which does little to address the underlying issue. In response to pain, headaches, multiple injuries, and somatic complaints, battered woman disproportionately receive pain or sleep medications, anxiolytics, and frankly punitive referrals to psychiatry or Child Protective Services. Instead of being viewed as a persistent help-seeker, the woman who returns multiple times to the medical clinic is typically misidentified as someone who is overusing health resources or using them inappropriately. In this situation, clinicians often resort to labels such as "frequent visitor," "hypochondriac," or "hysteric" to validate their frustration and lack of intervention. These medical practices isolate the woman from further health resources, reinforce her isolation, and validate the batterer's claim that *she* has the problem, not him. When battered women develop drug, alcohol, or other problems in response to the stress that accompanies ongoing abuse, these are mistaken for their primary problem, and they are referred to treatment settings that are unresponsive to domestic violence and, therefore, ineffective in stopping the secondary problem. Over time, these interventions further entrap abused patients and contribute to the escalation of battering, rather than to its resolution (Kurz & Stark, 1988; Schecter, 1978; Stark & Flitcraft, 1996). Given this pattern of response, it is not surprising that battered women rate medical professionals the least effective among service providers (Bowker & Maurer, 1987).

In sum, in woman battering, health professionals encounter a widespread and seemingly chronic health problem with a low spontaneous cure rate, more closely resembling AIDS than the flu. In lieu of effective intervention, battering is likely to be a significant issue throughout the life course, evoking a range of nonemergent, general medical, and psychosocial problems, requiring repeated injury visits, and eliciting significant costs wherever and whenever women seek health care. Whereas early intervention might dramatically reduce the duration and prevalence of these problems, current practice is largely ineffective and may even aggravate a victim's predicament.

Barriers to Change

Confronted by the data on woman battering and evidence that the failure of physicians to intervene appropriately leads to increased suffering, the AMA Council on Ethical and Judicial Affairs (1992) suggested that domestic violence intervention be rooted in the medical principles of beneficence (doing good) and nonmalfeasance (to do no harm). In the same year (1992), the Joint Commission on the Accreditation of Health Care Organizations (JCAHO) required all emergency and ambulatory care services to develop domestic violence protocols, and in 1996, the standards were upgraded to include objective criteria to identify, assess, and refer victims of abuse (Schornstein, 1997). Furthermore, most victims of domestic violence report they would welcome inquiries about abuse from clinicians (Caralis & Musialowski, 1997; Mayden, Barton, & Hayden, 1997).

The health response to battered women has improved dramatically since these initiatives. But it was naive to assume that clinical violence intervention would be-

come routine simply because health practitioners were shown its utility or because hospitals adapted domestic violence protocols. Despite widespread public awareness campaigns by major professional health organizations, providers are still more likely to screen for health problems that are less prevalent or serious than for battering. Training improves the clinical response (Bullock, 1989), but it is unclear whether changes are sustained (McLeer & Anwar, 1989). A study at four Philadelphia emergency rooms identified a propensity for physicians to "discredit" victims who disclosed domestic violence and to avoid dealing with abuse, even when they had been trained to identify battering and believed it was their responsibility to do so (Kurz, 1987; Kurz & Stark, 1988). These findings have been confirmed in other settings (Caralis & Musialowski, 1997).

The limited efficacy of training is not hard to understand. Apart from the lack of clinical guidelines and other practical barriers to routine screening, health intervention in battering touches on a range of political concerns with which medical care and public health are uncomfortable. These include the implications of sexual inequality, the competing rights of husbands and victims as well as of battered women and their children, involvement with criminal justice, and the sentiment that medical intervention in private life is justified in only the most extreme instances. Beyond this, the status structure of medicine, its traditional male bias, the strict hierarchical organization of health training, and a commitment to a narrow disease paradigm that excludes so-called social problems present further barriers to participation by physicians in efforts to prevent domestic violence. Nursing, social work, public health, and the allied health professions embrace more holistic concepts of health but are no less wedded to stereotypes that attribute blame to victimized individuals and preclude public advocacy where the roots of problems lie in politically charged issues such as sexual inequality.

Even when clinicians are highly motivated to intervene, they may not be able to do so, as the Commonwealth Fund's Community Health Center Domestic Violence Initiative (discussed below) illustrates. Individual clinicians control only a small part of what takes place in the physician-patient encounter. The rest is molded by the "social and cultural context, the policies and resources of health care institutions, and the beliefs, values, and professional norms of the medical community" (Flitcraft, 1993, p. 156). In turn, this context is inseparable from local competition among health care institutions and the larger structure of health care delivery and finance. The substitution of managed care for traditional payment arrangements can limit the access of battered women because their problems often fall outside the purview of what are considered legitimate medical concerns. In addition, some insurance companies exclude women known to be battered from coverage, a practice known as "pink lining." Studies by the Insurance Commissioners in Pennsylvania and Kansas revealed that 24% of the responding companies reported using domestic violence as an underwriting criterion when issuing and renewing insurance (cited in Fromson & Durborow, 1997). Even where victims have financial access to health services, capitation arrangements and pressure for primary care providers to serve as gatekeepers aggravate widespread concern about time constraints, making it even more difficult for these frontline professionals to address the ongoing health needs of battered women and their children. Add the absence of strong federal leadership in primary care or public health and the huge number of families without adequate health coverage to start and it is easy to explain why a health problem that affects 20% or more of the adult female population has elicited a medical response that is uneven at best, even from those practitioners specializing in injury.

To move health care into the mainstream of political and community life where domestic violence is unacceptable, prevention efforts must address both the substance of professional norms and their organizational context. At present, such efforts are rare (Warshaw, 1989).

Clinical Violence Interventions

In identifying violence as a public health problem, former U.S. Surgeon General C. Everett Koop (1991) challenged health providers to "recognize violence as their issue" (pp. v-vi). Defining what this means has not always been easy.

The Clinician-Patient Encounter

The earliest medical responses to woman battering relied on the initiatives of individual health professionals, most of them nonphysicians. In 1977, building on the success of hospital-community collaborations in establishing rape crisis teams, the Ambulatory Nursing Department of the Brigham and Women's Hospital in Boston formed a multidisciplinary committee to develop a therapeutic intervention for victims of domestic violence. The intervention at Brigham—like a parallel program developed at Harborview

Hospital in Seattle—relied on a Social Service Trauma Team composed initially of volunteer social workers who met weekly with nursing staff. Although efforts to expand hospital-based rape crisis teams to include domestic violence were sporadic and their volunteer base was difficult to sustain, clinician-advocates introduced free-standing domestic violence services at hospitals in Chicago, Hartford, San Francisco, and Philadelphia, in Minnesota and Wisconsin, and elsewhere, most of them centered in emergency departments. In the wake of these changes, the San Francisco-based Family Violence Prevention Fund (FUND) and the Pennsylvania Coalition Against Domestic Violence collaborated in testing a model health response in hospitals and clinics in California, Pennsylvania, and Michigan. As important, they disseminated model domestic violence protocols from around the country.

Initiatives among hospital staff generated attempts to mobilize private practitioners. Following a unique Surgeon General's Workshop on Violence and Public Health in 1985, as well as the revelation that battering was a problem for a significant number of pregnant women, the American College of Obstetricians and Gynecologists mounted a national campaign to educate its members. In 1991, the AMA followed suit, developing and disseminating diagnostic and treatment guidelines on child abuse and neglect, child sexual abuse, domestic violence, and elder abuse and neglect. In the wake of the AMA initiative, many state medical societies distributed diagnostic, reporting, and intervention guidelines to their membership. The AMA also played a key role in the formation of the National Coalition of Physicians Against Family Violence,

with institutional membership from more than 75 major medical organizations. In 1985, the Nursing Network on Violence Against Women was formed and successfully lobbied the American Nurses Association to make domestic violence a priority. The American Medical Women's Association, the American Academy of Family Practice, and the American College of Emergency Physicians have also participated in the creation of a comprehensive medical response to family violence. Domestic violence was also introduced into standard medical education. Of the 126 U.S. medical schools responding to a 1993 survey, 101 reported incorporating material on domestic violence as part of required course material.

Responding to these initiatives, health providers offered various rationales to explain why they distanced themselves from domestic violence. One early theory suggested that identification in medical settings was difficult because battered women were reluctant to discuss the real cause of their injuries. Yet researchers have used simple interview techniques and questionnaires to uncover substantial rates of domestic violence in various medical settings, suggesting that identification is not so difficult, after all. Next was concern that some patients would be offended by questions about violence at home; in deference, health providers were reluctant to discuss the issue. Again, high rates of patient participation in domestic violence research have belied this concern. In fact, clinicians routinely probe issues involving sexuality and other seemingly delicate issues. More recent explanations explore the health providers' projected helplessness and their belief that domestic violence is a Pandora's box of problems without solution (Friedman, Samet, Roberts, Hudlin, & Hans, 1992; Kurz & Stark, 1988; Sugg & Inui, 1992; Warshaw, 1989). This rationale is inconsistent with clinicians' usual determination when faced with near-certain failure in other areas. Nevertheless, clinicians are more likely to intervene when they believe they can make a difference (Kurz & Stark, 1988).

At first glance, it seems intuitively obvious that physician intervention in domestic violence must be modeled after physician involvement in other abuse situations or in other criminal investigations, such as homicide or rape. Indeed, as reflected in the JCAHO guidelines, the current strategy is to expand the identification of domestic violence seen primarily in emergency departments, assess for trauma-related problems, and implement referrals that place a high priority on immediate safety (such as to shelters). Protocols based on this approach use the medical encounter largely for case finding and evidence gathering for subsequent criminal proceedings and typically frame assessment by a calculus of physical harms that highlights severe injury (Schornstein, 1997).

As we have seen, the vast majority of health visits by battered women involve unimpressive injuries, repeated presentations of nonemergent medical problems, or psychosocial and/or behavioral problems elicited by the ongoing experience of coercive control. Because of this profile, approaches focused solely on violence and its consequences or its implications for criminal justice are unlikely to identify or respond appropriately to more than a small proportion of victims. By contrast, primary care models of intervention are particularly suited to the ongoing nature of most domestic violence and can draw on experience with issues that overlap with law enforcement and criminal justice concerns, including alcohol and drug use, HIV disease, tuberculosis and syphilis treatment, birth control, prenatal testing, and pregnancy termination, as well as the assessment and confinement of people who are a danger to themselves or others. Meanwhile, because of its emphasis on patient empowerment, domestic violence intervention converges with many contemporary challenges in medical practice also addressed in primary care settings—including smoking cessation, cancer screening, HIV prevention, occupational and environmental health, and the care of terminally ill patients— where new models of physician-patient relationships are emphasized. In these areas, health care providers integrate periodic crisis intervention with ongoing monitoring, patient education, patient-centered planning, and liaison with community-based service organizations, including battered women's shelters. Adapting a primary care model also facilitates the incorporation of clinical violence intervention into routine practice throughout the health system.

Clinical Intervention

At present, the elements of clinical interventions with battered women typically include identification and treatment of medical needs; assessment of service and mental health needs, clear documentation, and safety assessment; and case management, including referral to law enforcement and/or community-based domestic violence services.

Identification

Health management with battered women begins with identifying a history of domestic violence and meeting immediate medical needs. Providing medical care in the context of the violence reinforces an understanding that the abuse is the major issue at hand, minimizes the feeling of being overwhelmed by a list of seemingly unrelated issues, and focuses care, particularly for residents and medical students.

In health settings, the most effective operational approach to identification relies on an inclusive notion of coercion and control, regardless of the marital status or sexual orientation of the patient, the severity of injury inflicted, or whether the current presentation involves injury, medical or psychosocial problems, or simply fear. Because the clinician's concern is with future health risks, the important distinction is between an anonymous assault, mugging, or other street crime, where future assault or control by the criminal is unlikely, and assault, intimidation, forced isolation, or control by any social partner.

The integration of a brief screen for battering into the basic patient interview with all female patients avoids the problem of identifying abuse only after the extent and nature of injuries make the diagnosis tragically obvious. In one primary care setting, a single question, "At any time has a partner ever hit you, kicked you, or otherwise hurt you?" was added to a self-administered health history form: Domestic violence identification rose from 0% (with discretionary inquiry alone) to 11.6% (Freund et al., 1996). Another study reported that the use of two simple questions—"Do you ever feel unsafe at home?" and "Has anyone at home hit you or tried to injure you in any

way?"—has a sensitivity of 71% in detecting domestic violence and a specificity of almost 85% (Feldhaus et al., 1997).

To get at battering situations where violence may be less prominent than other coercive behaviors, a clinician can ask, "Is there anyone in your life who is controlling what you do?" When questioned frankly in a confidential setting, battered women are forthright, cooperative, and willing to engage in joint safety planning for themselves and their children (Olson et al., 1996) Thus, after staff training and the introduction of an identification protocol in the emergency department at the Medical College of Pennsylvania, the percentage of women found to be battered increased almost sixfold, from 5.6% to 30% (McLeer & Anwar, 1989).

In reviewing a woman's medical history, in addition to the adult trauma history, suspicion that battering has occurred is raised by headache or nonspecific pain, the abuse of licit or illicit substances, sleep disorders, anxiety, dysphagia, hyperventilation, and other signs of living in a stressful environment. A careful history of substance abuse, for instance, often reveals that use became addictive only through efforts to self-medicate the fear attendant on battering. Self-induced or attempted abortions, multiple therapeutic abortions, miscarriages, and divorce or separation during pregnancy are important presentations of abuse, especially in obstetrical or gynecological admissions. Persistent gynecological complaints, particularly abdominal pain and dyspareunia in the context of normal physical examinations, are frequently overlooked manifestations of domestic violence. However, the strongest clues of abuse are the clustering and repetition of presentations and complaints rather than isolated events.

Just as routine questions regarding a patient's smoking habits identify smoking-related problems and reinforce a patient's decision not to smoke, routine questions about violence identify the problems of abused women, underline that violence is a concern for health, assess current safety of women who were battered in the past, and heighten the awareness of women who have not been in an abusive relationship.

Assessment

Following identification, a confidential assessment of service needs can progress from validation of a woman's concern to a careful history of adult trauma, an overview of the dynamics in the relationship (patterns of control, strategies for resistance), a review of health and mental health problems that may be associated with abuse, and consideration of risk to any children involved.

Domestic violence can be seen from a clinical perspective as a staged experience that involves injury, illness, isolation, and complex psychosocial problems. The complexity of interventions varies depending on the stage at which a woman presents. The needs and resources of the woman who comes into primary care or the emergency room with her first episode of violence contrast markedly to the needs and resources of a 45-year-old mother who is abusing alcohol and is seriously depressed. Relatively straightforward patient education may help the first use appropriate family and community supports, whereas the second woman will need complex case-management strategies to find safety and to address her substantial mental health problems.

Shorter, repeated interviews are the best way to take an accurate adult trauma history. In lieu of this, it is useful to identify the first, most serious, most recent episode and typical pattern of violence. The possibility of life-threatening violence must always be considered. Significant risk is indicated if injury has caused a previous hospitalization; if a woman's believes her life is in danger or it is unsafe for her to leave the facility; if the batterer has used a gun or knife, stalked her, or threatened to kill her or himself; or if the couple is in the throes of divorce, separation, or conflict over children. An equally important prompt for enhanced advocacy is a sudden change in the abusive pattern, an escalation in violence, newly introduced restrictions on a woman's freedom, or an increased level of fear, prompted by the introduction of a gun for instance, even if there is no immediate injury (Alpert & Albright, 2000).

In assessing risk and service needs, a woman's capacity for self-protection, separation, or escape is as important as the level of violence. A useful way to frame the client's concerns is to help her identify her degree of entrapment by specifying elements of isolation, intimidation, and control that might prevent her from defending herself, escaping, or using helping resources when she is threatened or hurt again. Whether focusing on those areas of a woman's life from which she derives social connection (isolation), her level of fear and self-worth (intimidation), or her material or emotional deprivation (control), providers must make every effort to "walk in the victim's shoes" by putting her responses in the context of what she is experiencing. Open-ended questions about coercive control (e.g., Does your partner ever make you do things about which you are ashamed?) often reveal the subtle forms of domination that make a woman feel like a hostage.

Rapid weight loss, malnutrition, and chronic fatigue may reflect attempts to cope with stress or the emergence of a posttraumatic disorder. But they may also be the direct result of an escalation of control, intimidation, or isolation strategies in a relationship. Similarly, missed appointments, failure to comply with medical regimens, reports of behavior that seems contrary to a person's character, or presentations symptomatic of obsessions, compulsions, or other psychiatric disorders may also reflect coercive control by a partner.

A patient's risk may be summarized by the overall levels of injury, fear, and entrapment she is experiencing. Even where injury is relatively minor, enhanced advocacy and/or emergency intervention may be required for patients who present with high levels of fear (or intimidation) or are extremely isolated or controlled by their partner (entrapment).

Suicidality is also a risk that must be weighed, particularly if there are previous suicide attempts or the woman is severely depressed, anxious about the fate of her children, isolated from friends or family, or feels trapped or hopeless. The use of tranquilizers, antidepressants, antianxiety agents, and pain medication in some circumstances may genuinely facilitate a woman's ability to function effectively, but these are too often prescribed indiscriminately, leading to misuse, addiction, or reinforcement of the batterer's claim that the victim is "crazy."

Children's Safety

Cross-assessment for woman battering and child abuse is an essential component of any domestic violence procedure, as well as of interviews with mothers in pediatric or obstetrical settings. The risks children face in abusive relationships as victims, co-victims, or witnesses elicit symptoms that run the gamut from low self-esteem in girls and aggression and behavior problems in boys and girls to sleep or anxiety disorders and a range of somatic disorders in preschool children. Any or all of these problems may interrupt age-appropriate developmental tasks. The overall risk to children in a battering situation is a function of the absolute level of violence and coercion in the relationship, regardless of whether the child has been physically hurt by the abuser or whether his tactics are aimed primarily at the mother, the child, or both. In one case, a man who had previously snapped his belt before assaulting his partner began snapping it when he was displeased with the children, indicating their need for emergency protection. In addition, the coercive control elements of battering may so disable the mother that neglect of basic child needs is a distinct risk. In these cases, the mother's trust can be gained, and accurate information secured, only if she is assured that revealing her own victimization will not jeopardize her parental rights and that she will be involved in whatever decisions are made to protect the child.

Documentation

Careful documentation, using direct quotes from the client or photographs of injuries where appropriate, can sensitize subsequent health care providers to the importance of domestic violence in a patient's life and provide an ongoing record for the client of resources and survival strategies she has explored and used. Because the medical chart may also support the woman in criminal or civil proceedings, descriptions of domestic violence should clearly include evidence of injury, illness, and distress; identify the perpetrator (e.g., injured in assault by boyfriend); and summarize other information pertinent to the client's vulnerability or safety. Euphemisms such as "stormy relationship" or "marital discord" should be avoided. Even if the patient rejects the clinician's offers of support, the suspicion or disclosure of abuse should be documented in the medical record, and the patient should be provided with the information she will need if she decides to accept help on another occasion.

A secondary role of documentation is to provide data needed to demonstrate hospital resources necessary for comprehensive care of this client population and to monitor improvements in clinical practice. Medical records may also help to determine the extent and consequences of abuse as well as comorbidity, to document the patient's previous attempts to find aid, or to build a clinical history when patient recall is unreliable. However, the best source of aggregate data is anonymous questionnaires or simple screens administered at intake or during routine health exams.

Case Management and Advocacy

The objectives of case management with battered women are to review the woman's priorities in relation to available options and resources, facilitate the implementation of a safety plan for the woman and her children, and plan for ongoing support. The empowerment strategies appropriate with battered women differ markedly from the protective service orientation that characterizes intervention with vulnerable populations of children or the elderly. Because her risk may be great whether she decides to remain with the abusive partner or leave, for instance, emphasis should be placed on expanding her

options rather than convincing her to adopt a specific course of action. Nor should interventions around woman battering be confused with strategies used to resolve family conflicts such as couples' counseling or parenting education, although these may be appropriate choices after safety and empowerment strategies have been fully used.

Safety Planning

A safety plan is a shared understanding, sometimes written and sometimes not, of how the woman can be best protected when confronted by a dangerous partner. The presumption underlying safety planning is that a woman's current vulnerability to battering can be reduced by reinforcing strategies she is already using to prevent, minimize, or avoid being hurt or controlled and by increasing her autonomy whether she decides to stay or to leave the relationship. Questioning proceeds from how she has managed so far, to what has worked, to what she sees as the next step. Confidentiality in all aspects of working with a battered woman is a precondition to implementing a safety plan. Independent safety planning for children in abusive homes is also suggested, where possible. In addition to shelter and other emergency housing, legal services, and treatment for substance abuse, planning for safety with battered women often includes women's groups, ongoing physical therapy, job changes, continuing education, welfare or emergency assistance, links to 12-step addiction treatment groups, counseling for children, work with child and/or adult protective services, and programs for the disabled. Future risks if the patient is discharged home should be jointly determined. Safety planning is an evolving process that should be reviewed and modified as experience dictates.

Protocols should clearly outline the responsibilities of clinical staff who have identified abuse to refer cases to police, domestic violence services, child protective services, social services, and mental health treatment programs. Domestic violence is a crime, although only a few states mandate hospital authorities to report cases to legal authorities; they should do so only at the patient's request. Health providers are not expected to have in-depth legal knowledge regarding domestic violence. However, they should communicate the criminal nature of battering to the patient, as well as the options state law affords in criminal and civil court to initiate formal separation and have the offender arrested, removed from the home, or ordered into counseling for his violence. A working relationship with local police and court agencies will facilitate appropriate handling of domestic cases within the legal system as well as link the patient to agencies that can provide legal advocacy.

If the clinician suspects a life-threatening risk, the patient should be informed and enhanced advocacy initiated, beginning with her options. Even in today's fiscal climate, a hospital admission or extension of a hospital stay may be justified by the absence of another safe option. Although going to a battered woman's shelter, leaving the area, or going into hiding may be the most protective options available, there may be many reasons why a woman cannot choose them.

The Three As

Clinical violence intervention is summarized by the three As: *ask, assess,* and *advocate.*[3] The success of this strategy de-

pends on accountability achieved through monitoring and feedback, including follow-up to determine what has actually changed in relation to what a woman hopes to gain through each step in her plan. Even if things turn out differently than she hoped, the sense of control a woman gains from having identified her problem and developed a plan to manage it is a significant step toward her recovery.

Institutional Intervention

Clinical violence intervention requires health care organizations to commit resources to crisis intervention, emergency hospitalization, counseling, support groups, and advocacy; they must also bolster staff resources to complement identification and assessment. Such a comprehensive approach will require changes in medical practice that rival those seen in law enforcement (Flitcraft, 1993). In marked contrast to the public and hierarchical nature of the criminal justice system, however, the U.S. health system is a decentralized mix of private office-based practices, managed care corporations, community-based facilities, and private, nonprofit, and public hospitals. This structure largely explains why health care organizations have changed more slowly and with less consistency than criminal justice services and in response to a more diffuse array of state, professional, and local initiatives.

Hoping to document the need for services and to use reporting requirements to induce hospitals to invest in training, Wisconsin and Connecticut initially required medical services to compile monthly statistics on their census of battered women. Reporting rates were extremely low, however, because hospitals lacked a framework for identification and there were no sanctions for noncompliance. Although aggregate reporting was quickly abandoned, state support for health training stimulated the creation of the University of Connecticut Health Center's Domestic Violence Training Project (DVTP), Womankind in Minnesota, and similar organizations in Alabama, Colorado, New Jersey, New York, and Wisconsin. Often rooted in partnerships with state battered women's coalitions, universities, and state departments of health or public health, these organizations have trained thousands of health providers, developed domestic violence manuals and other widely disseminated information, and provided the technical assistance hospitals needed to initiate and sustain programs. In 1990, through its Office of Domestic Violence Prevention, New York became the first state to require that licensed hospitals establish protocols and training programs to identify and treat domestic violence. The New York Office also placed domestic violence advocates in New York City hospitals. Meanwhile, guided by the recommendation of a Governor's Task Force on Domestic and Sexual Violence in 1993-1994, Florida passed legislation requiring 1 hour of instruction on domestic violence as a condition of licensing and relicensing for health providers. Shortly thereafter, California required hospitals and clinics to screen all patients for domestic violence; subsequently, it went further, becoming the first state to require health personnel to report individual cases to authorities, a controversial policy that has been widely debated.

Private practitioners, community health centers, and managed care organizations have proved the most difficult to reach. But progress has also been made in these arenas. A model effort to help private practitioners reach an office-based clientele was Project SAFE (Safety Assessment for Everyone), a Connecticut-based collaboration between the state's medical society, Connecticut's Coalition Against Domestic Violence (CCADV), and the Domestic Violence Training Project. The emphasis in Project SAFE was on graphically attractive patient information (posters and brochures, for example), physician handbooks, and other office resources that were disseminated by the medical society to its membership and followed by grand rounds across the medical and surgical subspecialties. Even more ambitious was a Physicians' Campaign Against Family Violence launched with a special issue devoted to domestic violence by the *Maryland Medical Journal.* With seed funding from the state medical society, the Maryland program produced training materials, a physicians' manual, and patient information brochures, and it stimulated legislation to develop on-site victim advocacy programs at four diverse hospitals.

Despite myriad domestic violence program initiatives in health settings and the increasing emphasis on outcomes by federal, state, and private funders, there are few reports that evaluate these programs. McFarlane, Christoffel, Bateman, Miller, and Bullock (1991) found that implementation of a program for health professionals in a Texas obstetrical service resulted in a statistically significant gain in knowledge of domestic violence. Of those who completed training, 86% stated they intended to assess for signs of abuse among pregnant patients. More important, at 6 months follow-up, it was reported that about 75% of participating health service centers were assessing pregnant patients for signs of battering. The combination of community outreach, public education, and health professional training was linked to a noted increase in calls to information centers by battered women who had been referred by a health care provider. The value of training was also demonstrated. Identification of domestic violence increased by 20% when nurse interviews replaced reliance on patient self-reports of abuse.

The sustained effects of training demonstrated by the Texas study stand in marked contrast to the Philadelphia studies reported earlier (Kurz, 1987; Kurz & Stark, 1988; McLeer & Anwar, 1989). Unfortunately, there is insufficient information to determine whether the differences were serendipituous or explained by the setting (obstetrical vs. emergency department), training methods, staff turnover, or some other factor. How much the responsiveness of health providers to domestic violence has improved over time is unclear.

Connecticut's Community Health Center Domestic Violence Initiative

One of the few evaluated efforts to institutionalize domestic violence intervention was Connecticut's Community Health Center Domestic Violence Initiative, a collaboration between the Domestic Violence Training Project (DVTP) and the Connecticut Primary Care Association (CPCA) supported by the Commonwealth Fund. The project's goal was to incorporate domestic violence assessment for underserved populations at the state's nine community health centers (CHCs). It hoped to accomplish this by eliciting CHC buy-in through a working group of CHC representatives, using a patient path-model and patient questionnaires to identify potential barriers to domestic vi-

olence screening, developing a model staff-administered education program in the health centers, and incorporating domestic violence into a continuous quality-improvement program to reinforce organizational commitment to the use of the screen and protocol. Nationwide, CHCs have adapted a life-cycles approach, which divides patients into perinatal, pediatric, adolescent, adult, and geriatric subgroups. Records are periodically sampled from each stage to fulfill JCAHCO requirements for quality review. Working with the Clinical Issues Committee of the CPCA, DVTP designed the curriculum to respond to the needs of each subgroup (as well as to provide basic information to all staff) and added a domestic violence clinical outcomes measure to each of the five cycles. In addition, the 3-year project funded half-time positions and provided multidisciplinary expertise at two model CHCs to see if a more intensive effort would substantially improve outcomes. DVTP provided education for selected trainers from each CHC and ongoing technical assistance.

The independent evaluation (Brody & Weiser, 1998) identified strengths and weaknesses of the CHC initiative that have broad applicability to efforts elsewhere. Improvement was most dramatic in the perinatal and adolescent stages, but over time, total assessment rates improved for all centers in four of the five life cycles. Patients experienced fewer barriers to care than staff suspected. But whereas patients saw domestic violence as a legitimate health concern, medical staff, whether through bias or time constraints, frequently sidestepped domestic violence for issues they felt were more important. Staff turnover during the project period was considerable and included several of the staff educators trained to deliver the curriculum. Because the CHCs do not have a culture that supports research, existing methods for collecting and analyzing data, although useful for minimal documentation, were not adequate for research purposes. More important, the project was implemented at the same time as the largely Medicaid patient populations were required to become members of managed care organizations (Schauffler & Wolin, 1996). This transformation pressured the CHCs to engage in revenue-generating activities (giving training a low priority) and to employ their resources strategically to maintain their patient base. Although the onset of managed care elicited more careful data collection and analysis, without a clear demonstration that clinical violence intervention is cost-effective, there was little time and few resources to invest in training, building collaborative relationships, documenting, collecting data, and developing materials.

Lessons for Institutional Change

Despite its limits, the CHC project made it clear that mainstreaming and normalization hold the key to the successful institutionalization of clinical violence intervention. *Mainstreaming* involves making clinical violence intervention part of routine patient care. *Normalization* implies that work with battered women builds on the skills and patient education techniques clinicians successfully employ in other medical or behavioral health areas. Lessons drawn from these interrelated strategies included the following.

- *Accommodate the institutional culture.* Understanding the distinctive features of the CHCs made it possible to integrate domestic violence

education and quality assurance tools into routine patient care. At the same time, one size does not fit all. This means affording flexibility in how protocols are adapted by each health care organization.

- *Involve leadership.* Representatives from the CHCs participated in every phase of project implementation and provided DVTP with legitimacy, critical access to health staff, and information about practice realities that were vital to success. In turn, the provision of technical assistance helps strengthen the leadership of identified domestic violence liaisons.

- *Respect existing skills.* Successful introduction of the domestic violence screen into each life-cycle chart was possible only because practitioners saw the link between domestic violence and other important problems they were already treating (such as AIDS and substance use) and because the questions (not only what was asked but when) were adapted to their specific clinical setting and existing practice.

- *Build local capacity.* The "training the trainers" approach transferred educational skills to indigenous experts. The most successful training programs facilitate patient disclosure by sensitizing all staff to the issue, including security, maintenance, secretarial, and triage personnel, and by communicating the seriousness with which the facility takes the problem through prominently displayed educational materials, posters, and the like.

- *Establish accountability for outcomes.* Incorporating a domestic violence outcome measure into existing quality-assurance procedures ensured that clinical violence intervention would become a routine part of CHC culture for which staff was accountable.

- *Provide outside support.* Outside technical assistance proved critical to ongoing staff education, particularly because of staff turnover, to data collection and analysis, and to liaison with community resources.

Linking Domestic Violence to Related Health Problems

A critical facet of institutionalizing clinical violence intervention is outreach to all health programs that target women, particularly where problems are known to be aggravated by battering. Project AWAKE (Advocacy for Women and Kids in Emergencies), a pioneering effort in this respect, started at Children's Hospital in Boston in 1986 to broaden child abuse programming to include intervention on behalf of battered women and to unite services that are often offered separately, and in conflict, to women and children. Providing the battered mothers of abused children with a domestic violence advocate has dramatically improved the likelihood that mother and child will stay together and remain safe.

Another example of linkage grew out of the clinical trial of the medicine ACTG 076, which showed that perinatal transmission of HIV could be significantly reduced by the administration of zidovudine. This underscored the importance of educating, counseling, and testing women of childbearing age. Partner violence may significantly constrain a woman's choice of sexual partners and compromise her capacity to negotiate for safe sex or safe drug use, to comply with other risk-reducing behaviors and to use health services. This is why the Health Resources and Services Administration (HRSA) has built education about abuse and its consequences into the training curriculum for professional and community providers in its HIV programs. Similarly, in dozens of communities, prevention of abuse has been recognized as a critical piece of Healthy Start, Healthy Mothers, Healthy Babies, and other programs whose primary objective is child health and improved parenting. Similarly, the Center for the Advancement of Mothers and Children at MetroHealth Medical Center in Cleveland, Ohio, is using an interdisciplinary team approach to link high-risk drug-abusing women and their children to available domestic-violence intervention services in the community (Hambleton, Clerk, Sumaya, Weissman, & Horner, 1997).

Community Interventions: Toward Complex Social Prevention

There is virtually no research on the primary prevention of domestic violence (Chalk & King, 1998). In part, this reflects the consensus among policy makers, echoing the emphasis among advocates, that domestic violence is a criminal justice problem and that reform should focus on the response by police and the courts. Despite the health research supported by NIMH and the publication of several health monographs by a short-lived Office of Domestic Violence under

President Carter, until recently, the key federal agencies responsible for health policy, grouped under the Department of Health and Human Services, did relatively little to address domestic violence in medical education, primary care, public health, or other related health areas. A marked exception was the effort by the Centers for Disease Control (CDC) to define domestic violence as a public health problem through a newly created National Center for Injury Prevention.[4]

A turning point occurred in 1985, when Surgeon General C. Everett Koop convened an unprecedented workshop on violence and public health with a special emphasis on domestic violence. Follow-up regional conferences disseminated violence prevention strategies to the larger public health community. In the wake of these initiatives, the nascent CDC center received support to fund community-based prevention projects on the problem, Health and Human Services funded a national Health Resource Center on Domestic Violence at the San Francisco-based Family Violence Prevention Fund, and domestic violence reduction was included among the national health objectives for the year 2000.[5] Despite a limited staff commitment at Health and Human Services, in 1995, HRSA developed an Action Plan to Prevent Family and Intimate Partner Violence, and implementation of the plan has been encouraged in agencies responsible for maternal and child health, primary care, medical education, minority health, and AIDS. Still, no additional funding to support Health and Human Services intervention was provided by the path-breaking Violence Against Women Act (VAWA) in 1994, and the CDC was designated as the fulcrum for federal action in the area rather than the HRSA, the

umbrella for government departments with the greatest experience in health education and service delivery.

By contrast with the relative dearth of federal or state initiatives in prevention, community-wide efforts to address domestic violence have grown dramatically over the past 20 years. At present, health care providers in several hundred U.S. communities have joined with a broad spectrum of service providers and community-based groups in a coordinated community response (CCR) to coordinate local services and promote domestic violence prevention.

The Coordinated Community Response: An Example of Complex Social Prevention

The CCR is based on the recognition that changing one facet of the service response without changing the system as a whole can actually make the situation worse. For example, a battered woman may be identified by health providers but not protected, and so she is at greater risk than before abuse was disclosed. The CCR may be developed by an informal, community-based network, or it may emerge from a formal Family Violence Council facilitated by the public health or police department or by the mayor, a judge, or other public figure. In all of these cases, the body implementing the process provides a public forum within which agencies with different levels of institutional power (large teaching hospitals, courts, and battered women's programs, for example) can address each other as relative equals. In this process, advocates and survivors of family violence provide crucial feedback on how the system operates in ways that may not be visible—or may be visible only very slowly—from official data, from institutional records, or to decision makers. The CCR allows the community to take ownership of the problem of woman battering, and it is a vehicle to move the service response from crisis management of violent episodes to prevention.

In most communities, the objectives of the CCR are to address three broad areas of work: ensuring safety and support for victims and accountability for perpetrators, coordinating and evaluating existing services and developing new services where needed, and initiating community-wide prevention by promoting zero tolerance for coercion and control. The effort includes public education, professional training, and policy change. Missouri's Educational Center on Family Violence recommends that local councils stage their work according to priorities roughly corresponding to these objectives, that is, proceeding from the establishment of emergency programs for victims (such as shelters and hot lines) (Priority 1) to support groups and protocol development (Priority 2) to prevention efforts (Priority 3) such as gun safety, parent education, and school-based programs.

Although professional staff assist in the development of community-wide prevention strategies in some states, and federal or state funding is playing an increasing role, the infrastructure of the CCR is provided by volunteers and frontline service providers.

In some areas, state-level councils have taken the lead in prevention. For example, the Illinois Council for the Prevention of Violence successfully shepherded the Illinois Violence Prevention Act of 1995 through the General Assembly, creating a new state entity, the Illinois Violence Pre-

vention Authority, which will plan, coordinate, fund, and evaluate public health and public safety approaches to violence prevention in the state. Community Intervention Projects are another form of coordinated community response. Started in Duluth, Minnesota, these projects are private-sector grassroots efforts designed to enhance the service system response to domestic violence by working with all sectors of the justice, mental health, and health systems. Elements of the work include the development, implementation, and monitoring of protocols and practice guides with each component; training of justice and treatment staff; outreach to batterers in the justice system; batterer education; outreach to enhance victim safety; and community education.

Many councils coordinate the health response through subcommittees that include major providers. Projects of these subcommittees have included area-wide health training; development of standardized screening instruments and response protocols; Mortality and Morbidity Review teams to respond proactively to poor outcomes by closing gaps in the service response; and Community Without Violence initiatives, where area health organizations collaborate to distribute packets on family violence to patients, professionals, and other staff.

Challenges to Clinical Violence Intervention

Whatever kept individual clinicians from responding appropriately to battered women in the past, experience suggests that health providers are willing to take violence as their issue when required behavioral changes are incremental and consistent with existing values, practices, and skills. The proper aim of clinical violence intervention is to prevent the progression of problems, largely by restoring a woman's sense of control over her material resources, social relationships, and physical environment, a process called *empowerment*. This is best approached by considering battering as an ongoing concern for primary care, rather than as an acute event requiring crisis intervention. Developing early intervention strategies will involve the skills of many medical disciplines, including nursing and social work, and will call on the expertise of a broad range of clinicians.

From Emergency Medicine to Primary Health Care

The JCAHO guidelines were part of a broad-based strategy to expand the identification of victims of domestic violence seen predominantly in emergency departments. Meanwhile, a national health objective for the year 2000 is for at least 90% of hospital emergency departments to have domestic violence protocols (objective 7.l2). Similarly, the protocols most frequently employed at hospitals and other health facilities rely heavily on a calculus of physical harms to identify, assess, and refer victims, and many orient information gathering in the medical encounter to the demands of criminal proceedings. As we have seen, this strategy is based on an extremely limited picture of domestic violence; fails to assess for the more subtle forms of domination in battering relationships; lacks cognizance of the multiple presentations of woman battering or its numerous medical, psychosocial, or behavioral sequaelae; and offers a conception of medicine's response that is at odds with the multifaceted capacities

evident in the clinical response to AIDS, addiction, and a range of health problems similarly rooted in complex social processes. The relative lack of clinical experience with victims of domestic violence is a limitation. Current domestic violence protocols will need to be disseminated to all primary health sites and updated based on ongoing evaluation in clinical settings and growing knowledge about the importance of coercive tactics other than physical abuse (AMA Council on Ethical and Judicial Affairs, 1992; Burge, 1989; Mehta & Dandrea, 1988; McFarlane, Parker, Soecken, & Bullock, 1992).

Garnering New Resources

Blue Cross/Blue Shield of Pennsylvania estimates that at least $32 million a year is spent in Pennsylvania alone to treat domestic violence injuries. As we have seen, to the costs of injury must be added the disproportionate demand that domestic violence places on prenatal care, alcohol and drug treatment, mental health, and pediatric, adolescent, and general medical services. These costs rival the costs of other widely recognized problems to which vast health resources have been devoted, HIV disease, for example, or substance use. However, current institutional programs and protocols rarely allot additional health care resources to victims of domestic violence, nor do they contribute to shifting resources (in alcohol treatment, intensive care unit trauma admissions, or adverse birth outcomes, for example) to include specific domestic violence interventions. Moreover, in the current fiscal climate of managed care, it is unlikely that health care organizations will shift needed resources to clinical violence intervention without compelling evidence that these expenditures are cost-effective. To generate this evidence, public or private research dollars must be invested to show that innovative programs can, in fact, significantly reduce health care-system use by battered women. Because the disproportionate use by battered women is due almost entirely to the duration of the problem, the potential contribution of early intervention is enormous.

The Dilemmas of Collaboration

In community collaboration to implement primary prevention, health care is challenged to broaden its traditional perspective, recognize the strengths of parallel systems with alternative and even conflicting perspectives, and yet maintain its core values and its commitment to patient care. Nowhere is this more apparent than in current moves to subordinate the medical response to the needs of criminal justice by requiring health providers in California and several other states to report identified cases of domestic violence to police.

From the start, the battered woman's movement has struggled to reconcile the radical critique of state services as punitive and oppressive with the need to end the marginalization of domestic violence by service professionals. Mandates to arrest and pressure to prosecute offenders have attempted to address this dilemma at two decision points where marginalization was most apparent. But where a legalistic approach that includes mandates is appropriate in certain situations, including those involving dependent classes such as children and the frail elderly in the medical system, it is inconsistent with the patient-centered model of empowerment that has been used to enhance bat-

tered women's options by community-based services, social work, and medicine.

It would be a mistake, however, to conclude from this example that clinicians can significantly contribute to the welfare of battered women by remaining locked in their particular subspecialties or health settings.

As with other health problems—HIV infection and alcoholism are examples—victims and their advocates played a key role in bringing the scope and consequences of woman battering to the attention of medicine and public health. More than other branches of medicine, public health has a long tradition of working closely with community-based groups in prevention efforts. Moreover, without such alliances, the forceful political action and creative programming needed to challenge the entrenched beliefs and practices that give rise to woman battering will not materialize. Medicine brings to the table a long tradition that values professional confidentiality, extensive experience in multidisciplinary cooperation, dogged and continued engagement against seemingly insuperable odds, and a commitment to beneficience and nonmalfeasance. Rather than respond defensively to the challenges posed by the long road ahead, the appropriate response of health providers is to mobilize behind the growing realization that freeing our citizens from coercion and control is a vital part of the public health mission.

Notes

1. The chapter is geared toward the general reader rather than the health specialist. For a more technical summary, see Eisenstat (1999) and Stark and Flitcraft (1997).

2. To the extent that clinical violence intervention has been normalized and mainstreamed, work with battered women has not been surrounded by the controversy that attends parallel efforts to intervene in pregnancy termination or the promotion of safe sex, for instance.

3. *The 3As Response to Domestic Violence, Connecticut's Domestic Violence Education for Health and Human Service Providers.* (1998). Domestic Violence Training Project. New Haven, CT.

4. Leadership of the CDC center was recently decimated in response to pressure from congressional opponents of gun control.

5. A screening packet is available from the Health Resource Center on Domestic Violence (toll-free 1-888 Rx-Abuse)

References

Abbott, J., Johnson R., Kozial-McLain, J., & Lowenstein, S. R. (1995). Domestic violence against women: Incidence and prevalence in an emergency population. *Journal of the American Medical Association, 273*(22), 1763-1767.

Alpert, E., & Albright, C. (2000). Domestic violence, Part II: Risk assessment and safety planning. *Hippocrates, 14*(4), 33-37.

American College of Obstetricians and Gynecologists. (1995). *The abused woman* (ACOG Patient Education Pamphlet No. APO83). Washington, DC: Author.

American Medical Association, Council on Ethical and Judicial Affairs. (1992). Physicians and domestic violence: Ethical considerations. *Journal of the American Medical Association, 267,* 3190-3193.

Appleton, W. (1980). The battered woman syndrome. *Annals of Emergency Medicine, 9*(2), 84-91.

Bowker, L. H., & Maurer, L. (1987). The medical treatment of battered wives. *Women's Health, 12,* 25-45.

Brody & Weiser, Inc. (1998). *Evaluation of the Connecticut Community Center domestic violence initiative.* Branford, CT: Author. (Contact at 250 Main Street, Branford, CT. 06405)

Browne, A., & Bassuk, S. S. (1997). Intimate partner violence in the lives of homeless and poor housed women: Prevalence and patterns in an ethnically diverse sample. *American Journal of Orthopsychiatry, 67*(2), 261-278.

Bullock, L. (1989). Characteristics of battered women in a primary care setting. *Nurse Practitioner, 14,* 47-55.

Burge, S. K. (1989). Violence against women as a health care issue. *Family Medicine, 21,* 368-373.

Caralis, P. V., & Musialowski, R. (1997). Women's experiences with domestic violence and their attitudes and expectations regarding medical care of abuse victims. *Southern Medical Journal, 90*(11), 1075-1080.

Chalk, R., & King, P. (Eds.). (1998). *Violence in families: Assessing prevention and treatment programs.* Washington, DC: National Academy Press.

Cohen, M., Deamant, C., Barkan, S., Richardson, J., Young, M. (2000). Domestic violence and childhood sexual abuse in HIV-infected women and women at risk for HIV. *American Journal of Public Health, 90*(4), 560-565.

Coker, A. L., Smith, P. H., McKeown, R. E., & King, M. J. (2000). Frequency and correlates of intimate partner violence by type: Physical, sexual, and psychological battering. *American Journal of Public Health, 90*(4), 553-560.

Committee on Trauma Research. (1985). *Injury in America: A continuing health problem.* Washington, DC: National Academy of Medicine.

Eisenstat, L. B. (1999). Primary care: Domestic violence. *New England Journal of Medicine, 341*(12), 887-892.

Feldhaus, K. M., Kozial-McLain, J., Armsbury, H. L. Norron, J. M., Lowenstein, S. R., & Abbott, J. T. (1997). Accuracy of three brief screening questions for detecting partner violence in the emergency department. *Journal of the American Medical Association, 227,* 1357-1361.

Flitcraft, A. (1993). Physicians and domestic violence: Challenges for prevention. *Health Affairs, 12*(4), 154-161.

Freund, K. M., Bak, S. M., & Blackhall, L. (1996). Identifying domestic violence in primary care practice. *Journal of General Internal Medicine, 11*(1), 44-46.

Friedman, L. S., Samet, J. D., Roberts, M. S., Hudlin, M., & Hans, P. (1992). Inquiry about victimization. *Archives of Internal Medicine, 152,* 1186-1190.

Fromson, T., & Durborow, N. (1997). *Insurance discrimination against victims of domestic violence.* Philadelphia: Women's Law Project &

Pennsylvania Coalition Against Domestic Violence.

Gin, N. E., Rucker, L., Frayne, S., Cygan, R., & Hubbell, A. (1991). Prevalence of domestic violence among patients in three ambulatory care internal medicine clinics. *Journal of General Internal Medicine, 6,* 317-322.

Haber, J., & Ross, C. (1985). Effects of spouse abuse and/or sexual abuse in the development and management of chronic pain in women. *Advances in Pain Research and Therapy, 9,* 889-895.

Hamberger, L. K., Saunders, D., & Hovey, M. (1992). Prevalence of domestic violence in community practice and rate of physician inquiry. *Family Medicine, 24,* 283-287.

Hambleton, B. B., Clerk, G., Sumaya, C. V., Weissman, G., & Horner, J. (1997). HRSA's strategies to combat family violence. *Academic Medicine, 72*(1), S110-S114.

Hilberman, E., & Munson, K. (1977-1978). Sixty battered women. *Victimology: An International Journal, 2*(3-4), 460-470.

Isaac, N. E., & Sanchez, R. L. (1994). Emergency Department response to battered women in Massachusetts. *Annals of Emergency Medicine, 23*(4), 855-858.

Koop, C. E. (1991). Foreword. In M. L. Rosenberg & M. A. Fenley (Eds.), *Violence in America: A public health approach.* New York: Oxford University Press.

Kurz, D. (1987). Responses to battered women: Resistance to medicalization. *Social Problems, 34*(1), 501-513.

Kurz, D., & Stark, E. (1988). Not so benign neglect. In K. Yllö & M. Bograd (Eds.), *Feminist perspectives on wife abuse* (pp. 249-265). Newbury Park, CA: Sage.

Mayden, S. R., Barton, E. D., & Hayden, M. (1997). Domestic violence in the emergency department: How do women prefer to disclose and discuss issues? *Journal of Emergency Medicine, 15,* 447-451.

McFarlane, J., Christoffel, K., Bateman, L., Miller, V., & Bullock, L. (1991). Assessing for abuse: Self-report versus nurse interview. *Public Health Nursing, 8*(4), 245-250.

McFarlane, J., Parker, B., Soecken, K., & Bullock I. (1992). Assessing for abuse during pregnancy: Severity and frequency of injuries and associated entry into prenatal care. *Journal of*
the American Medical Association, 267, 3176-3178.

McLeer, S. V., & Anwar, R. (1989). A study of women presenting in an emergency department. *American Journal of Public Health, 79,* 65-67.

Mehta, P., & Dandrea, A. (1988). The battered woman. *American Family Physician, 37,* 193-199.

Muelleman, R. L., Lenaghan, P. A., & Pakieser, R. A. (1998). Nonbattering presentations to the ED of women in physically abusive relationships. *American Journal of Emergency Medicine, 16*(2), 128-131.

Olson, L., Anctil, C., Fullerton, L., Brillman, J., Arbuckle, J., & Sklar, D. (1996). Increasing emergency physician recognition of domestic violence. *Annals of Emergemcy Medicine, 27*(6), 741-746.

Rath, G. D., Jarratt, L. D., & Leonardson, G. (1989). Rates of domestic violence against adult women by male partners. *Journal of the American Board of Family Practice, 2,* 227-233.

Roper, M., Flitcraft, A., & Frazier, W. (1979). *Rape and battering: An assessment of 100 cases.* Unpublished manuscript, Department of Surgery, Yale Medical School, New Haven, CT.

Schauffler, H. H., & Wolin, J. (1996). Community health clinics under managed competition: Navigating uncharted waters. *Journal of Health Politics, Policy, & Law, 21*(3), 461-488.

Schecter, S. (1978, October). *Psychic battering: The institutional response to battered women.* Paper presented at Midwest Conference on Abuse of Women, St. Louis, MO.

Schornstein, S. L. (1997). *Domestic violence and health care.* Thousand Oaks, CA: Sage.

Schulman, M. A. (1979). *Survey of spousal violence against women in Kentucky* (Harris Study No. 7092701, conducted for Kentucky Commission on Women). Washington, DC: Government Printing Office.

Stark, E. (1984). *The battering syndrome: Social knowledge, social therapy, and the abuse of women.* Doctoral dissertation, Department of Sociology, SUNY–Binghamton.

Stark, E., & Flitcraft, A. (1988a). Personal power and institutional victimization: Treating the dual trauma of woman battering. In F. Ochberg (Ed.), *Post-traumatic therapy and victims of violence* (pp. 115-152). New York: Brunner/Mazel.

Stark, E., & Flitcraft, A. (1988b). Women and children at risk: A feminist perspective on child abuse. *International Journal of Health Services, 18*(1), 97-118.

Stark, E., & Flitcraft, A. (1991). Spouse abuse. In M. Rosenberg & J. Mercy (Eds.), *Violence in America: A public health approach.* New York: Oxford University Press.

Stark, E., & Flitcraft, A. (1996). *Women at risk: Domestic violence and women's health.* Thousand Oaks, CA: Sage.

Stark, E., & Flitcraft, A. (1997). Woman battering. In J. Last (Ed.), *Maxcy-Rosenau public health and preventive medicine* (14th ed.). Norwalk, CT: Appleton-Century-Crofts.

Stark, E., Flitcraft, A., & Frazier, W. (1979). Medicine and patriarchal violence, the social construction of a private event. *International Journal of Health Services, 9*(3), 461-493.

Sugg, N. K., & Inui, T. (1992). Primary care physicians' response to domestic violence: Opening Pandora's box. *Journal of the American Medical Association, 267,* 3157-3160.

Teske, R. H. C., & Parker, M. L. (1983). *Spouse abuse in Texas: A study of women's attitudes and experiences.* Huntsville, TX: Sam Houston State University, Criminal Justice Center.

U.S. Department of Justice. (1992). *Crime in the U.S., 1991* (Uniform Crime Reports). Washington DC: Author.

Walker, L. (1984). *The battered woman syndrome.* New York: Springer.

Warshaw, C. (1989). Limitations of the medical model in the care of battered women. *Gender and Society, 3,* 506-517.

CHAPTER 19

Religious Issues and Violence Against Women

Marie M. Fortune

The rape crisis advocate received a middle-of-the-night crisis call from a woman who had just been raped. The advocate went immediately to the woman's home and found her seated on the sofa reading from her Bible. The advocate proceeded to inquire as to her well-being and to offer support and information about reporting to the police and seeking medical care. The victim decided to go to the emergency room. The advocate accompanied her as she read her Bible in the car on the way.

When they arrived, the victim was shown to an exam room to wait. When the doctor came in and saw the woman reading from her Bible, she said, "Is there something you want to discuss before I do the exam?"

"Yes," the woman replied. "I'm a Jehovah's Witness, and I just want to read a few passages of scripture before you examine me." She read the passages, closed the Bible, and put it aside. The

doctor proceeded. Afterward, she informed the woman that she was at high-risk for pregnancy due to the rape. Would she like to receive the morning-after treatment to prevent pregnancy?

The woman said she thought that would be best, but she would have to have permission from her church to do so. So the advocate telephoned each of the church's 12 elders in the early morning hours to ask their permission. They agreed, and the woman received the treatment.

The victim had given clear signals that she was a religious woman and had concerns. The advocate, although she observed these signals, was not comfortable responding to them initially. The doctor realized the importance of the woman's religious concerns and, by acknowledging and affirming her, provided the space that the woman needed to deal with the immediacy of her medical care.

Overview

Religion is a personal and institutional reality in the lives of the majority of the population. Whether one's experience came only in childhood or extends into adulthood, religious training and affiliation provide a significant context for many women as they address experiences of personal violence and victimization. This context is often dramatically shaped by the institutional presence of church, synagogue, temple, or mosque. Expressed in doctrine, teachings, scripture, or polemics, values and belief systems are communicated by religious communities and institutions to their members. In addition, members often have direct support relationships with religious leaders who may provide counseling or instruction.

So it is no surprise that many people, whether currently active in a particular religious group or not, will turn to their faith and/or religious leader in a time of crisis for support and for help in discerning the meaning of the experience and in determining what action they should take. The Jehovah's Witness woman who was raped was looking in scripture for the reassurance of God's presence to her and for some sense of meaning: Why does someone do these kinds of things to another person? And why did he do it to me? She consulted with the leadership of her church to gain their support for her choice to deal with the risk of pregnancy.

In this chapter, I will offer in broad strokes the basic issues and questions that face religiously affiliated women who are victims of violence. I will attempt to be reasonably inclusive, given my limitations of expertise and experience as a Protestant clergywoman. (Within the pluralistic societies of North America, we need to be aware of Roman Catholic, Protestant, Jewish, Orthodox, Muslim, Buddhist, Hindu, and Native American or First Nations beliefs and practices, as well as many others.) The reality is that, regardless of the particular religious affiliation, a majority of women will be dealing with some aspect of a religious context alongside the trauma of the violence. Most of these women will find their religious group or leadership to be either helpful (a resource) or unhelpful (a roadblock) in their healing.

Too often, the religious community has been a roadblock for victims and survivors. Many women have been abandoned by their faith communities, left to experience shame and guilt, whereas their perpetrators have had license to continue their abusive behavior. The final consequence of all of this has been the destruction of families and of individuals and an erosion of people's trust in their religious institutions. If our religious institutions are to enter this conversation, we must begin with a confession. Historically and today, our religious institutions have failed. Some parts of the church, for example, have even been able to name and confess complicity in the abuse of women: The Catholic Bishops of Canada stated that the church must take some responsibility for the abuse of women when it has directed abused women to remain in relationships with batterers and when it has taught women's subordination in marriage (Poronovich, 1989). Priests were urged to refer battered women and abusers to community agencies with the resources to help them. This was a major step forward in changing the institutional and cultural understanding of violence against women. It created the necessary context for finding ways to be a resource to victims, survivors, and perpetrators.

No woman should ever be forced to choose between safety and her religious community. She should be able to access the resources of both community-based advocacy and shelter *and* faith-based support and counsel. These two resources should be working collaboratively to provide consistent advocacy and support for safety and healing for victims and survivors, as well as accountability for perpetrators. If a woman is put in the position of having to choose, she will often choose her religious affiliation and community because it is familiar and a high priority in her life. If she finds there leadership that does not understand her experience, does not empathize with her experience, and proceeds to blame and shame her, she will be further cut off from the resources she needs for healing.

This chapter will examine the historical context of patriarchal religious traditions in which the everyday experiences of congregants occur. We will also look at the contemporary context, which often reflects the historical. Finally, we will consider the possibilities of collaboration between religious and secular resources, which truly focus on the needs and concerns of women who are victimized. This will, then, move us to suggest necessary institutional changes and to outline the possibilities for changing community norms to confront violence against women as a social problem.

Historical Context of Patriarchal Religions: The Tasks of Deconstruction and Reconstruction

Dominant Cultural Norms

The dominant cultural norms of Western societies accept men's violence against women as normative, that is, just the way things are. The old adage, "boys

will be boys," although adamantly denied on the one hand, functions to explain and justify male behavior on the other. A theological norm is operative in this cultural framework as well. Theologically, our understanding of violence against women reflects our understanding of God and of the nature of people. If the world as we know it is the created order intended by God, then one might conclude that God created two categories of people, victims and victimizers, and these categories are generally gender-specific. But there are societies in which sexual violence does not exist; the people, male and female, do not comprehend the concept as described by anthropologists. Some examples are the Ashanti of West Africa (Benderly, 1982) and indigenous tribes living near Mount Banahaw in the Philippines (Arche Ligo, personal communication, 1994). What is most interesting about these societies is the way in which their gender relationships are organized: women are respected, share power equally with men, and participate fully in religious leadership. Religion includes a female deity and/or a male/female deity, and the community seeks harmony with the environment. Thus, in these societies, sexual violence is unnatural, not part of the created order or the nature of humans, and not ordained by God as inevitable. But in Western postindustrial societies, sexual violence is a cultural norm and is generally accepted as "just the way things are."

To Be a Victim

In Western culture, the meaning of the word *victim* in English is revealing. Webster's Dictionary in 1987 defines victim as "1. a living being sacrificed to a deity or in the performance of a religious rite 2. one that is acted on and usually adversely affected by a force or agent, e.g., one that is subjected to oppression, hardship, or mistreatment." Our understanding of the word *victim* is tied to religion, a sacrifice to a deity as part of a religious practice. This practice is the common denominator among Western religious traditions, which are fundamentally patriarchal. Women and children are sacrificed in the worship of patriarchy.

The second definition is more concrete: "one that is acted on, usually adversely affected by a force or agent"—that is, the recipient of the actions of someone else with adverse consequences, for example, being raped, battered, molested, or harassed. To be a victim is to be made powerless, at least momentarily, because someone is doing something to us that we did not choose and cannot stop them from doing. When we are victimized, we feel powerless and afraid.

So it is reasonable that we do not like to think of ourselves as victims; we do not like to use that word because when we do, we are acknowledging our temporary powerlessness, which is scary. Even in a scary, life-threatening situation, we want to believe that we are not totally powerless, that we do have some resources to defend ourselves. And we do.

But this dynamic can also trap us in denial: This isn't really happening to me, this isn't really abuse. This denial is our psychological defense against acknowledging our powerlessness. It is perfectly reasonable, but it may not serve us well. It can also tempt us to distance ourselves from each other. When we hear a friend describe her experience of abuse or read a story in the newspaper that details an attack on a woman, we often try to identify everything about her that is different from us. If I am white, she is African American; if I am older, she is young and foolish; if I live in the north end of town, she lives in the south; she was doing something stupid like hitchhiking, and I would never do something like that. This is a psychological defense we employ to protect ourselves from the knowledge that it was she, but it could have been me.

This is why women are not good on rape juries. Many women spend all their time noting their differences from the victim and so are unsympathetic and often unwilling to convict the rapist. It is also why some women in congregations are not sympathetic to the women who come forward to disclose that the pastor is sexually abusing them. While this denial and refusal to identify are understandable, they are not helpful to us. Separating ourselves from each other is not helpful and will not protect us.

Of course, the extension of this method is blaming the victim. Let's figure out what she did wrong that can explain why she got raped or beaten. Women are well-trained in trying to figure out what they did wrong that caused this problem. If we can explain why she got raped or beaten based on *her* behavior, we reason that we can learn never to engage in those behaviors and so think that we can immunize ourselves against violence. The victim believes it, too. If we can just figure this out, we can make sure it does not happen again. It does not work; it is only a highly developed practice of superstition.

Deconstructing the Traditions

Specifically, in Hebrew and Christian scriptures, we find story after story of violence against women: Dinah (Genesis

34), Tamar (2 Samuel 13), the Levite's concubine (Judges 19), Jephthah's daughter (Judges 11), Vashti (Esther 1), Suzannah (Daniel 13), and, probably, the persistent widow in Luke's Gospel (Luke 18). These stories tell us that our forebears in the faith knew what it is like to be physically and sexually abused.

Traditionally, sexual violence committed against women and children was regarded as a property crime against the husband or father of the victim. Hence, laws focused only on the possibility of male assault of an adult female or child; the assault on an adult male by a male was often confused with homosexuality.

Historically, theological discussion about sexual violence has been minimal. Hebrew scripture discusses rape as a property crime in the Deuteronomic passages and describes acts of sexual violence in the stories of the rape and murder of the unnamed concubine in Judges 19, the rape of Dinah in Genesis 34, and the incestuous abuse of Tamar in II Samuel 13. The issue of false accusation of rape is described in the story of Joseph and Potiphar's wife in Genesis 39. The threat of rape against men is described in Judges 19 and Genesis 19 (and subsequently is misinterpreted as homosexuality). In both of these stories, the men seek protection by offering virgin daughters to the assailants.

The understanding of sexual violence in the Christian tradition perpetuated a tendency to blame the victim and not to find the offender culpable for his actions. From the Malleus Maleficarum (Robbins, 1959) in the 16th century to the canonization of St. Maria Goretti (Young, 1995) in the 20th century, misogyny and the lack of accountability of men prevented religions from addressing the ethical or theo-

logical implications of rape. Augustine discussed rape in the context of whether or not suicide is an appropriate action for a victim of rape (Pellauer, 1995).

The dualistic view of the mind-body split assigned the sexual or carnal self to women and provided justification for women's subordination. Tertullian's view of women as "the devil's gateway" was only one example (Bussert, 1986). Protestant reformers used the framework of marriage as the context to assert women's subordination. Luther and Calvin justified wife-beating, unless it was life-threatening (Bussert, 1986). The right to chastise enforced women's subordination in marriage. In the "Rules of Marriage" compiled by Friar Cherubino in the 15th century (Bussert, 1986), we find the careful instruction to a husband to first reprimand his wife, "and if this still doesn't work . . . take up a stick and beat her soundly . . . for it is better to punish the body and correct the soul than to damage the soul and spare the body" (p. 13).

Unfortunately, these doctrines have been viewed as consistent with scriptures, interpreted to confirm male dominance over women:

> Wives be subject to your husbands as you are to the Lord. For the husband is the head of the wife just as Christ is the head of the church, the body of which he is the Savior. Just as the church is subject to Christ, so also wives ought to be, in everything, to their husbands. (Ephesians 5.22-24 NRSV)

Either by its silence or its instruction, the church has too often communicated to battered women that they should stay in abusive relationships, try to be better wives, and forgive and forget. To batterers, the church has communicated that their efforts to control their wives or girlfriends are justified because women are to be subject to men in all things. Men have been permitted to "discipline" their wives and their children, all for the "good of the family." Christian history is filled with examples of church leaders justifying abuse of women by men. Church fathers such as Martin Luther described their own physical violence toward their wives, without apology (Smith, 1911).

Likewise within Judaism, we find texts and teachings that have been cited to justify the abuse of women. Within Judaism, we find texts and teachings that are specific to the abuse of women. Rabbi Julie Spitzer (1985), the first Jewish leader in the United States to discuss wife abuse publicly, draws this conclusion:

> On the whole, the rabbinic literature . . . deals fairly with domestic violence. A surprising exception is Maimonides' ruling in the Mishneh Torah permitting a woman to be beaten by her husband because she refuses to do her household chores. Unlike Terumat ha-Deshen in which a woman may be beaten to keep her from cursing her parents or her in-laws (a significant transgression), the Mishneh Torah passage permits use of force for a relatively minor infraction. Even the Ramban's contemporaries did not all agree with his opinion.
>
> On the lenient side, Rabbi Meir of Rothenberg's [responses] are the most supportive of the woman's position in wife abuse cases. He even would go as far as to recommend excommunication if the case were to come before him. The Shulchan Aruch also rules sensitively in this matter, noting that wife beating was not to be tolerated, but pro-

viding a fair manner in which to adjudicate the charges (see also Graetz, 1998; Twersky, 1996).

Selective use of texts and teachings has allowed some to justify abuse of women. But as Spitzer also points out, there were some who clearly spoke against wife abuse.

The expectation among Jews of maintaining *shalom bayit* (peace in the home) has also been misused by some. Shalom Bayit refers to the ideal that the Jewish home should be harmonious and functional. Often, primary responsibility for this expectation has fallen to women, so that if there is disharmony (or violence) in the home, it is seen as her responsibility. In addition, shalom bayit has also, on occasion, served to hide the fact of violence behind the facade of a "peaceful home." This public/private split has always been to the detriment of women who are victims of domestic violence.

Within Islam, we also find texts and interpretations of texts that have been used by abusive men to justify their behavior, according to Muslim scholar and activist Sharifa Alkhateeb (1998).

> The most abused verse is ayah 34 of Surah four: "Men are the protectors and maintainers of women because Allah gave more to the one than the other, and because they support them from their means. So devout women are extremely careful and attentive in guarding what cannot be seen in that which Allah is extremely careful and attentive in guarding. Concerning women whose rebellious disloyalty (nusbooz) you fear, admonish them, then refuse to share their beds, then hit them; but if

they become obedient, do not seek means of annoyance against them. For Allah is Most High, Great. (p. 18)

Alkhateeb argues that this passage instructs Muslim men to financially and physically protect women (given their greater physical strength) and instructs Muslim women to guard their fidelity in obedience to Allah. She points out that to translate the word "to hit" contradicts the explicit teachings of the Prophet:

The prophet vehemently disapproved of men hitting their wives, and . . . he never in his entire life hit any woman or child. In the prophet's last sermon, he exhorted men to "be kind to women— you have rights over your wives, and they have rights over you." He also said, "Treat your women well, and be kind to them, for they are your partners and committed helpers." (p. 18)

Then Alkhateeb concludes,

The wording of this verse emphasizes the woman's obedience to Allah's desires, and not to those of another human being, but those who misinterpret this verse would assign men the duty of being eternal surveillance police over their wives. . . . In short, this verse has been used as a tool of control and abuse completely opposed to the Islamic foundation of marriage and family. (p. 18)

The stated purpose in each of these traditions has been preservation of marriage and the family—at any cost. The real purpose has been the preservation of male control of women and children within patriarchy.

Reconstruction Within the Traditions

The contemporary theological discussion of sexual and domestic violence emerged from feminist theologians, beginning in the early 1980s (see Adams, 1994; Adams & Fortune, 1995; Bussert, 1986; Cooper-White, 1995; Eugene & Poling, 1998; Fortune, 1983; Graetz, 1998; Nason-Clark, 1997; Poling, 1991; Spitzer, 1985). Here, we begin to see the deconstruction of the patriarchal traditions and then the question, is there any resource within our traditions to be redeemed that can support women who are victims of sexual or domestic violence?

To explore possible resources within Western religious traditions, we must include ethics along with theology, scripture, and doctrine. Ethics is the framework of right action derived from a particular theological understanding of humans in relation to God and each other. In this context, many of the stories that appear in Hebrew and Christian scripture describe the reality of violence against women and describe a patriarchal response to the victim and perpetrator. This is not, however, a prescribed response for those of us seeking a non-patriarchal approach to sexual and domestic violence. In other words, scripture may accurately describe the historic and contemporary experiences of many women and girls. It need not be regarded as establishing justification for the way they are treated. The value of these stories lies in their validation of common experiences of women and girls, which we find clearly articulated in sacred texts. But we must consider further what response is required, taking into account theology, ethics, doctrine, and scripture.

Likewise, in dealing with domestic violence, the scriptural justifications for women remaining in abusive relationships (subordination in marriage, e.g., Ephesians 5.20; prohibition of divorce, e.g., Malachi 2:13-16) must be considered in the fuller context of ethics, theology, and doctrine. Prooftexting (the selective use of a text, usually out of context, to support one's position) is a common ploy by those who seek to justify their actions. It is not difficult to prooftext a man's prerogative to dominate and control a woman within patriarchal Western religious traditions. But this, nonetheless, does not represent the whole story.

Early in the development of religious responses to sexual and domestic violence, Bussert (1986) clearly stated the agenda: "We need . . . to begin articulating a faith that will provide women with resources for strength rather than resources for endurance. We must articulate a theology of empowerment rather than a theology of passive endurance" (p. 65). This approach requires a critique (or deconstruction) of the roadblocks that can be created by patriarchal interpretations of religious teachings, as well as a development (or reconstruction) of useful resources that empower victims and survivors to address their experiences.

Thus, sexual and domestic violence must be understood theologically and ethically as sin, that is, as the physical, psychological, and spiritual violation of a person by another person; as such, it violates the bodily integrity of the victim and shatters any possibility of right relationship between the victim and abuser. Any

form of personal violence can destroy trust in the other person (with an acquaintance or family member) or trust in the basic security of one's world (with a stranger). So, the secondary effect is to isolate or cut the victim off from her community.

Within Western cultures today, to assert that sexual violence is unnatural and unacceptable runs counter to the dominant norms. Yet this assertion is consistent with the portrayal of God, for example, in Hebrew and Christian scriptures, as one who stands with the vulnerable and powerless and speaks judgment against those who choose to use their power in ways that harm others. Likewise, Alkhateeb notes that in the Qur'an, the marital relationship specifically is mandated to be one of "mutual kindness and mercy" (30:21; 9:71).

It is also important to distinguish ethically between sexual violence and sexual activity, condemning the first and affirming the second. To make this distinction, one must assert an ethical norm for sexual relationships that affirms shared power, equality, authentic consent, and shared responsibility. This context precludes coercion, aggression, physical force, and domination and seeks to protect those who are vulnerable due to particular life circumstances (e.g., age). Condemning sexual violence requires assertion of justice in its aftermath: support for victims/survivors and accountability for offenders within both religious and secular communities.

Likewise, we must assert family values as the foundation of our work on domestic violence: respect, equality, freedom from fear, support, love, freedom from violence, responsibility for self and others. These values apply to our families, no matter how our family is described: a couple, a single person relating to extended family, one or two parents with children, three or four generations together, by blood or by choice. These are the values that support and sustain healthy, just relationships devoid of violence and abuse. These are the values we learn from the Jewish teaching of shalom bayit (peace in the home) as well as from Jesus' ministry, in his profound regard for the well-being of the other person, and from the Qu'ran in the framework for an Islamic marriage.

To understand how traditional religious teachings dramatically shape the experiences of women and men in relationships where there is violence and abuse, we need only look to the daily newspaper. A convicted wife abuser tried to use the First Amendment protection of his religious beliefs to support his right to abuse his wife (Abrahamson, 1996). Ramiro Espinosa believed that the teachings of the Roman Catholic Church gave him the right to have sex with his wife whenever he chose, because the marriage vows they exchanged signaled her consent to have sex with him, and, once given, this consent was somehow permanent. Espinosa, 54, seemed to equate breaking into his wife's locked room, slapping her, and ripping her clothes with legitimate foreplay. Thankfully, this time the court was not swayed by this defense. He was convicted of attempted marital rape. This is yet another tragic example of an appeal to church doctrine to justify wife abuse. When interviewed, church leaders rejected Espinosa's argument, saying that Roman Catholic doctrine teaches that sex should be part of a loving relationship. But they did not go further to point out the harm done to the woman (which is a sin) and the need to call the husband to account for his abusive behavior (offering the possibility of his repentance).

Contemporary Context: Moving From Mistrust to Collaboration

I received a call from an advocate at the battered women's shelter asking for help. She reported that Linda had come into the shelter after receiving medical care at the emergency room. Having just talked with her pastor, Linda indicated that he had instructed her to return home to her husband immediately. The advocate knew that it would be very dangerous for Linda to return home at this time. She requested that I call up the pastor and "straighten him out." I said that I would consider her request and get back to her immediately.

As I sat and discussed the call with another staff member, the phone rang. It was the pastor calling to say that there was a member of his congregation at the shelter and that the shelter advocate had told her that she had to get a divorce. He said that we knew how his church viewed divorce and would I call up the advocate and "straighten her out." I said that I would consider his request and get back to him immediately.

The result of these inquiries was that we all sat together and talked: the battered woman, the advocate, the pastor, and me. This made it possible for there to be an exchange of awareness. The pastor did not comprehend that if the woman went home that night, she would be in great physical danger. The advocate did not understand the gravity of the issue of separation and divorce for this particular woman, because her church did not believe in divorce. (Also, the shelter advocate did not tell the woman that she had to get a divorce. That is inappropriate under any circumstances. The woman's anxiety about go-

ing to the shelter and separating from her abusive husband, coupled with the pastor's concern about possible divorce, led him to overstate what, in fact, had been told to the woman.)

By the time we were finished meeting, the pastor understood and supported the woman's staying in the shelter. The advocate understood that the issue of possible divorce would require much more reflection for the woman and that she needed her pastor's support through this experience. Everyone was finally on the same team, which was good news for the battered woman. This meant that she did not have to choose between her faith and safe shelter as she struggled to protect herself and her children.

This experience between the shelter advocate and pastor is far too common. Uninformed and insensitive religious leaders have created roadblocks for victims and survivors when they have not supported their need for safety and support in protection from violence and abuse. On the other hand, on occasion, religious leaders' mistrust of secular services has been well-founded: The insensitivity and lack of awareness on the part of advocates and counselors regarding women's religious beliefs and practices has also been a roadblock to the women. It has meant that religious women have not felt safe in the places where they have sought safety from their abusers or with agencies designed to respond to the violence they have suffered.

The mistrust may have developed from simplistic assumptions or erroneous beliefs on both sides of this equation. Religious leaders may see a secular program as "breaking up families" or "undermin-

ing a woman's faith." Secular advocates may see religious leaders or congregations as "sexist" or "unhelpful" to the woman.

Breaking through this mistrust requires some risk-taking from both sides and a commitment to the well-being of the victim or survivor. If we stay focused on her, we realize that no single organization or person can provide all that she needs. We need the resources of others in our community to provide for her and to empower her to be safe and to find the healing she needs.

For battered women, healing begins with making justice, and making justice begins with creating a place where she can disclose the fact of her abuse and find support. When she comes to her religious leader, she should find an informed, compassionate person who can hear her and immediately refer her to community resources to provide safe shelter, advocacy, legal options, and so on. The religious leader then should be able to help her reflect spiritually on her experience so that she can gain understanding and sustenance from her faith. We must reassure her that God stands by her side, that God understands her suffering and confusion and will not abandon her, and that God can give her courage to find protection for herself and her children. As she sorts through her options, we must support her priority for safety.

Most important, we must stop asking her to forgive her abuser. Forgiveness is the single most common expectation that is placed on Christian battered women: "Forgive and forget; go back to him; he needs you;" or "Don't you think it's time you forgave him?" Never mind that it is impossible to forget the things he did; never mind that "forgive and forget" appears in Shakespeare's *King Lear*, not the Bible. Never mind that it is the worst advice we can give her. She takes it seriously and tries very hard to forgive, absent any acknowledgment on the batterer's part of the harm he has done, not to mention any effort on his part to change. Forgiveness is the last step in a long process. It is possible if an abuser truly repents (which unfortunately does not often happen) or if we stand by her and support her healing process, clearly acknowledging what was done to her and trying to prevent it from happening again.

Changing Social and Cultural Norms

Our religious institutions have a profound impact on the social norms of our communities. As religious leaders, for better or worse, we help shape our society's understandings of experiences. The majority of our people relate in some significant way to a religious tradition: In childhood and/or adulthood, religious teachings matter, and the support of our religious communities in times of crisis matters. But most important, religious doctrines and teaching significantly shape the values of our society, which determine our social and cultural norms. This is certainly the case regarding values about intimate relationships, family, the position of women, and sexuality. Even though at times the popular discussion seems to be disconnected from the discussion within religious institutions, religious values, nonetheless, shape the discussion, if only just under the surface.

How can our values support and move us forward in addressing violence against women or, at the very least, not be used by the dominant culture to continue to minimize and justify this violence?

I was presenting in Alaska a number of years ago and in dialogue there with native Alaskan members of the Tlingit tribe. I heard them reflect on their history. They have a memory of a time 100 years ago when, in their tribe, wife abuse was forbidden. The reason for this was that every member of the tribe was vital to the tribe's survival. The women were not expendable. The community norm was clear: You didn't beat your wife. If you violated the norm, there was a predictable response: Your family had to make material restitution to your wife's family in a public gathering called a "potlatch." Consequently, there was rarely ever an incident of wife abuse. It was shameful and expensive. Now, 106 years later, after the arrival of white settlers and alcohol, those community norms have been badly damaged. Hence, the incidence of wife abuse and alcoholism equals that in the rest of the United States. But the advantage that the Tlingit people have is that they have a memory of a time when the norm of their community supported safety for women. They are now seeking to recover this norm and these values for their community. And thankfully, they have a tradition to recover.

For most Western women, the history of the Western traditions of church and law are part of the problem: The church, as a dominant cultural institution, has significantly shaped law and public policy. For example, regarding women as chattel is still a dominant theme operating just below the surface of public discourse on issues of violence against women. We have to look harder to find the values in our traditions that support seeking an end to violence against women.

Our religious organizations can no longer deny the reality of sexual and physical abuse. Perhaps we are beginning to understand that our religious institutions are part of the problem. Either explicitly or implicitly, religious doctrine and practice have contributed mightily to the context that has long tolerated the abuse of women. It can certainly be argued that justifications from religious sources are a result of wrongheaded interpretations of texts or doctrines. But they still dramatically affect social values because they coincide with the dominant norms of patriarchal culture. It is religion in service to patriarchy.

Because their acts of sexual violence have been minimized as normal male behavior ("boys will be boys") and often overlooked by the legal system, religious communities, and the community in general, males traditionally have presumed that they have sexual access to women and children. Victims of sexual violence have often been blamed for their own victimization: What was she wearing/doing/thinking? Seldom have men been held accountable for their acts of sexual violence against others.

The rhetoric of the 1970s brought with it new awareness: Rape is violence, not sex; that is, acts of sexual violence are not the result of uncontrollable male sexual urges toward attractive women. The traditional understanding had meant that sexual violence was sexual and therefore natural and acceptable. The shift in understanding asserted that sexual violence is an act of violence and aggression, in which sex in used as a weapon. Although this was an important insight at the time, it failed to comprehend that violence has

been made erotic in the dominant patriarchal culture; sexual violence began to be understood as sexual and violent but not acceptable. The 1990s brought even further awareness: In a culture in which violence is made erotic and sexuality is largely defined by what men choose to do sexually, there is an inevitable blurring of the line between sexual activity and sexual violence. This understanding presents a particular challenge to those who want to draw a qualitative distinction between sex and sexual violence (see also Adams, 1994; Fortune, 1995).

In biblical sources, we find little to challenge the norms of male sexual privilege and use of power to control women's behavior. Instead, we find stories of women's experience of violence, but the moral teaching revolves around the violation of male property rights that her violation represents. One exception is the story of Susannah, in which Susannah is sexually harassed by two elders in the community. When she resists, they falsely accuse her of adultery to save themselves. Daniel appears on the scene to defend her and indict the elders. The only problem is that this story did not appear in the original Canon but only in the Apocrypha. So it is not a story that is familiar to most churchgoers.

On the other hand, the story of Vashti is familiar to most Jews. She was the Queen who preceded Esther, and her story appears in the Book of Esther. It seems the king threw a party for his cronies and ordered Queen Vashti to appear before them, so that he could show off her beauty. She refused to be objectified in this way and said no. This enraged the king, who was worried that if the people found out that the queen had disobeyed him, other wives might disobey their husbands, and chaos would ensue. So he fired the queen, sending her away because she refused him. Esther then became queen, working inside the system to save her people, the Jews. Both Vashti and Esther are celebrated each year during the Festival of Purim. Stories like Vashti's remind us that women have always engaged in acts of resistance to male violence and domination.

Making Changes Where We Are

In spite of the powerful messages from the dominant culture that reinforce men's violence against women, our religious institutions have the potential to reframe the conversation and help to shift the community norms to respect women's bodily integrity and right to live free from fear in the home, school, and workplace and on the street. We also have a captive audience, in effect, who are looking for guidance in addressing intimate relationships and family.

Seminaries are in a key position to prepare those in training for ministry to understand the issues of violence against women so that they can respond appropriately to victims, survivors, or perpetrators and take leadership in the community in raising the issues. Coursework in various areas (including scripture, history, theology, and pastoral care) can address violence against women (see Adams & Fortune, 1996, for materials useful in a theological education curriculum).

Within congregations, a commitment to ensuring a safer environment for women (and children) means policies and procedures addressing professional misconduct by clergy and lay leaders, as well as education and discussion about violence against women. The congregation can partner with local programs to provide meeting space, volunteers, and material support.

The clergy have a regular opportunity to give clear signals that they are informed and available to talk with congregants. Remembering victims and survivors in public prayer, preaching sermons that name the issues of violence against women (McClure & Ramsey, 1998), and encouraging religious education for all ages that addresses the issues—these are clear indicators from clergy of their concern and availability. Clergy also have access to public forums to raise public policy issues regarding direct services to women or changing social norms. For example, they can provide a letter to the editor or media interview in support of a battered woman who finally defends herself from her abuser and ends up in jail.

Congregations and clergy can build genuine, supportive relationships with local programs that address violence against women. Then, clergy can make direct referrals when needed to an individual person in a particular program, and congregations can learn from those who staff and benefit from the program.

Advocates in a secular setting can reciprocate these relationships and also gain some reliable referrals for women they serve who are seeking a pastoral resource. In addition to making available specific resources needed by victims or survivors (safe shelter, legal information and advocacy, job training, transitional housing, counseling, and support), advocates can take steps to ensure that women who have religious concerns are comfortable in their programs. They can also be sensitive to the particular needs of religious women by affirming their expression of those needs and helping them find the religious resources they need. Shelters and rape crisis agencies can have helpful literature available for those who use their services (Fortune, 1987). They can maintain a list of local religious leaders who are trained and sensitive to abuse issues and who are available to meet with victims or survivors. They can ensure that women who are in residence for a period of time are able to celebrate their religious holidays.

Training is useful for identifying allies and building collaborative relationships with religious leaders in the community. Training for religious leaders should include religious allies in the planning and should focus on the basics of the issues, as well as how to make appropriate referrals and work together with secular advocates and counselors (Fortune, 1991).

If we are to succeed in the goal that Bussert asserts, "articulating a faith that will provide women with resources for strength rather than resources for endurance," we must work where we are to maximize women's resources and minimize the roadblocks that either our religious or secular efforts may offer.

Our social norms are established and reinforced by values and belief systems that are often part of our religious traditions. For many years, many of us in religious communities have been deconstructing the religious belief systems that have promoted the subordination of women and violence against women, and we have been reconstructing and retrieving the stories, teachings and doctrines in terms of the values of our traditions that affirm women living our lives free from violence. As an organizing tool, one of the few remaining institutions in our communities is our religious groups. Youth groups, children's programs, women's groups, men's groups—these are ready audiences every week in all of our communities. Although there is an historic ambivalence toward our religious tradi-

tions within our movements, we cannot afford any longer to overlook these institutions and to leave out the religious issues and the role of religious communities in responding to sexual and domestic violence.

Finally, religious leaders have a significant opportunity to collaborate with the wider community in doing what we do best: seeking to bring healing and wholeness where there has been brokenness and violence. We have much to learn from and much to bring to this common effort to end violence against women. If we believe that the way things are is not the way they have to be, then we must join with our allies to ensure that violence against women becomes a peculiar, odd, and unusual occurrence in the 21st century.

References

Abrahamson, A. (1996, January 29). Defendant says he has right to sex with wife. *Los Angeles Times.*

Adams, C. (1994). *Woman battering.* Minneapolis, MN: Fortress Press.

Adams, C., & Fortune, M. (Eds.). (1996). *Violence against women and children: A Christian theological sourcebook.* New York: Continuum.

Alkhateeb, S. (1998, January). Ending domestic violence in Muslim families. *Sisters!, 1*(4), p. 18.

Benderly, B. L. (1982, October). Rape free or rape prone. *Science,* pp. 40-43.

Bussert, J. (1986). *Battered women: From a theology of suffering to an ethic of empowerment.* Minneapolis, MN: DMNA of the Lutheran Church in America.

Cooper-White, P. (1995). *The cry of Tamar: Violence against women and the church's response.* Minneapolis, MN: Fortress.

Eugene, T. M., & Poling, J. N. (1998). *Balm for Gilead: Pastoral care for African American families experiencing abuse.* Nashville, TN: Abingdon.

Fortune, M. (1983). *Sexual violence: The unmentionable sin.* Cleveland, OH: Pilgrim.

Fortune, M. (1987). *Keeping the faith: Guidance for Christian women facing abuse.* San Francisco: Harper.

Fortune, M. (1991). *Violence in the family: A workshop manual for clergy and other helpers.* Cleveland, OH: Pilgrim Press.

Fortune, M. (1995). *Love does no harm.* New York: Continuum.

Graetz, N. (1998). *Silence is deadly: Judaism confronts wifebeating.* Northvale, NJ: Jason Aronson.

McClure, J., & Ramsey, N. (1998). *Telling the truth: Preaching about sexual and domestic violence.* Cleveland, OH: United Church Press.

Nason-Clark, N. (1997). *The battered wife: How Christians confront family violence.* Louisville, KY: Westminster John Knox.

Pellauer, M. (1995). Augustine on rape: One chapter in the theological tradition. In C. Adams & M. Fortune (Eds.), *Violence against women and children: A Christian theological sourcebook.* New York: Continuum.

Poling, J. N. (1991). *The abuse of power: A theological problem.* Nashville, TN: Abingdon.

Poronovich, W. (1989, December 22). Canadian bishops: Church teaching abets wife abuse. *National Catholic Reporter.*

Robbins, R. H. (1959). Malleus maleficarum. *Encyclopedia of Witchcraft and Demonology, S.V.* New York: Crown.

Smith, P. (1911). *The life and letters of Martin Luther.* Boston: Houghton Mifflin.

Spitzer, J. (1985). *Spousal abuse in rabbinic and contemporary Judaism.* New York: National Federation of Temple Sisterhoods.

Twersky, A. (1996). *The shame born of silence: Spouse abuse in the Jewish community.* Pittsburgh, PA: Mirkov.

Young, K. Z. (1995). The imperishable virginity of Saint Maria Goretti. In C. Adams & M. Fortune (Eds.), *Violence against women and children: A Christian theological sourcebook.* New York: Continuum.

CHAPTER 20

School-Based Education and Prevention Programs

Mary K. O'Brien

This chapter reviews school-based programs designed to prevent violence against women. Because of the increasing number and diversity of programs now available, only primary prevention programs are reviewed in this chapter. Primary prevention programs are defined as those that combat risk factors for problems before the problem ever has a chance to develop. Most primary prevention programs involve an educational component designed to increase knowledge and improve attitudes, with the hope that these changes will affect behavior.

A common search strategy was used to find programs to review for this chapter. A number of databases (including Medline, HealthStar, Eric, Psychinfo, and the Internet) were searched, using a variety of terms combining basic elements such as *violence prevention programs, violence against women,* and *school-based programs.* Once the reports and programs were identified from the database searches, only those that were school-based, primary prevention programs with evaluation plans were included in this chapter. Many exciting adolescent violence-prevention programs are not school-based or primary prevention (e.g., The Youth Relationships Project by Wolfe et al., 1996) and, therefore, will not be included in this review. Other violence prevention programs that are not school-based include mentoring programs, peer counseling programs (usually implemented as intervention in treatment facilities rather than preventive settings such as schools), and victim support groups. These programs also are beyond the scope of this chapter and, therefore, are not included in this review.

The Evolution of School-Based Violence Prevention Programs

Single-Audience and Single-Component Programs to Multi-Audience and Multi-Component Programs

Violence-against-women prevention programs have evolved from single-component programs consisting of one didactic presentation, with the sole goal of increasing knowledge, to multicomponent programs with multigoal curricula that have several interactive and didactic sessions, school-wide activities, parent and teacher participation, or community interaction. The National Center for Injury Prevention and Control of the Centers for Disease Control and Prevention (CDC) (1993) recently reviewed several youth violence prevention programs with multi-factor and multisession curricula designed to provide students with information and to teach new skills. Multifactorial curricula are designed with the underlying premise that new knowledge and new skills will have a greater chance of changing attitudes and behaviors, which will then reduce the perpetration of violent behaviors or the likelihood that an individual becomes a victim of violence. However, the combination of new knowledge and skills is still not sufficient to effect change (National Center for Injury Prevention and Control, 1993). Behavior changes do not occur immediately after the acquisition of knowledge. In addition, behavior changes require time and repeated effort. In addition, the National Center for Injury Prevention and Control asserts that behavior change is more likely to occur if students' physical and social environments support and encourage the behaviors that reduce violence.

Recognizing that multifactorial approaches are needed, more recent programs have been developed that include a combination of many of the following strategies: conflict resolution, peer education/mediation, training in social and life skills, education to prevent injuries from firearms, adult mentoring, parenting centers, afterschool recreation activities, job training, and public information and education campaigns. Powell and colleagues (1996) have more formally categorized these many different strategies into four different levels of primary prevention. The first and most common strategy is educational programming directed toward the students themselves. This is usually manifested in didactic teaching sessions that take place in school classes and involve teacher implementation. The next level of prevention involves family members and peers. These programs, composed of various activities that involve parents and classmates, are designed to reinforce the messages that the students receive in the classroom. Such programs also involve counseling services directed toward those students who may be involved in harmful relationships. The next prevention level works with students' social groups and organizations, such as schools and neighborhoods. These efforts include activities designed to promote cultural changes in the schools and at home that optimize nonviolence behaviors. The last level of programming focuses on societal macro systems such as economic opportunities, firearm availability, and media exposure. This typically involves physical activities such as cleaning up neighborhoods as well as creating job skills programs and developing businesses to enhance neighborhood job opportunities. Many of the programs reviewed in this chapter have taken extraordinary steps to include components from the first three levels. The fourth level is beyond the capacity of most programming efforts because it entails policy and legislative modifications at the local, state, and federal government levels to promote broader social change that will address violence in general.

Recognition of Developmental Stages of Target Audiences

In addition to evolving from single- to multicomponent programs, violence prevention programs have changed their curricula to address the developmental stages of the target audience. For instance, in elementary schools, violence-prevention programs emphasize generalized antiviolence knowledge, attitudes, and behaviors toward peers. As children get older, the programs become more and more oriented to dating and intimate partnerships, as students progress through middle and high school. Characteristics of school-based violence-prevention programs, therefore, are age-appropriate. That is, they reflect the reality of interpersonal relationships that children and adolescents experience during that stage of development. It is important to touch on the possibilities of future relationships, however, even if children are not at the dating stage.

The Evaluation of School-Based Violence Prevention Programs

One of the most fundamental problems with violence-prevention programs is the lack of theoretically driven program development and the paucity of carefully planned evaluation studies that measure programmatic impact on violence outcomes. It was with this in mind that Powell and his colleagues (1996) examined a number of programs taking place across the United States. They assert that few quantitative evaluations of violence-prevention programs have been conducted, which means this type of work is still needed. They describe the current efforts of 15 different research teams around the United States, who have designed primary prevention programs that are theoretically driven by social learning theory, attribution theory, or resilience theory. Those who developed their programs from social learning theory believe that violence is a learned behavior, and thus, they provide skills, present alternative behavior models, and review options and choices. The programs developed from attribution theory offer training to help students understand that adversity does not come from the intentional behaviors of others but that conflict may arise from their own responses to others. This theory purports that a common misconception may trigger aggressive behaviors. For example, when students believe that others' behaviors are deliberately hostile, they may respond aggressively, thus triggering and escalating conflict, an outcome that was not inevitable. Resilience theory suggests that students can lead healthy and productive lives despite the challenges and violence they face. To provide the opportunity for students to be resilient, a program needs to offer caring, supportive, adult contact; meaningful activities; and expectations of productive, healthy behaviors. Each of these programs in Powell et al.'s (1996) review has plans to conduct rigorous evaluations to assess its impact on interpersonal youth violence. Baseline data from all of the programs indicate the presence of violent events and violent behaviors, justifying and confirming the need for these programs.

This chapter is divided into three sections according to school level: elementary school, middle school, and high school. Under each of these sections, programs that met the search criteria are described, along with the methods used for evaluation and analysis. Table 20.1 presents an overview of the programs included in this analysis.

Elementary School Programs

The overall approach of violence-prevention programs in elementary schools is to target general interpersonal violence prevention rather than dating or domestic violence prevention. The students are still young enough not to have formulated solidified opinions and beliefs about dating relationships, and yet they still experience violence in their lives and, therefore, need strategies to deal with violence.

The most common strategy for elementary school children—and the one with the least supportive evidence—has been skills-building programs. Skills that are addressed in these programs include assertiveness training, self-control, problem solving, and conflict resolution. Conflict mediation and peer counseling are also included. The programs were designed in light of the association found between weak conflict-management skills and youth aggression in general, as well as partner violence specifically (Foshee et al., 1996). Several violence-prevention programs based in elementary and middle schools have been developed and implemented based on this premise and thus focus on skills building. The skill most often targeted has been conflict resolution, often using peer mediation as the strategy to resolve conflicts. Peer-mediation programs are usually implemented in conjunction with conflict-resolution curricula, and they target mostly elementary and middle school students. Peer-mediation programs, designed to reach consensus, maintain confidentiality, and avoid blame, involve student peers who mediate disputes.

These peer mediators are usually trained to help the parties in the dispute to examine the components of the conflict and reach a nonviolent solution.

However, remarkably little evidence to date suggests that school-based curricula designed to target conflict-resolution skills or other social skills reduce aggressive and violent behavior among children in schools or neighborhoods in either the short term or the long term (Grossman et al., 1997; Kellermann, Fuqua-Whitley, Rivara, & Mercy, 1998). Nine projects using this approach to reduce violence are described and evaluated by Powell, Muir-McClain, and Halasyamani (1995). They report finding a wide variation in implementation of the skills-building programs across these nine projects. There also is very little outcome data to support the advocacy of these programs (Powell et al., 1995).

Because of the confusion in the violence-prevention literature about the distinction between social skills training (e.g., problem solving, conflict resolution, communication skills) and violence prevention (Larson, 1994), and because of the lack of evidence to support the effectiveness of this approach in preventing violence, these programs are not reviewed here. Although many violence-prevention programs include skills building in their repertoire of activities as a way to affect violence outcomes directly, it cannot be concluded that general social skills-building programs will naturally lead to reductions in intimate partner violence unless such programs are specifically designed to do so.

Not the most common strategy—but arguably the most effective strategy—for violence prevention in the elementary school setting is a schoolwide effort, rather than class-based curricular programs. This schoolwide approach includes activities that promote safe, nonviolent environments

(text continued on page 394)

TABLE 20.1 Summary of School-Based Violence-Prevention Programs

Program Name	Author	Goals of the Program	Number of Sessions	Program Description	Program Evaluation
ELEMENTARY SCHOOLS					
Peace Programs					
PeaceBuilders	Embry et al. (1996)	To promote positive behavior change using common language and activities throughout the school	0	Multiple activities incorporated into everyday life at schools, rather than a curriculum	Pre- and post-program documentation of visits to the school nurse, as well as home and delinquent behaviors
Comer School Development Program	Haynes (1996)	To create a safe environment at school that promotes and supports personal development and optimal learning	Not clear	Activities for students, teachers, parents, family, and school staff	Observations and anecdotal reporting procedures
My Family and Me	Minnesota Coalition for Battered Women (1991)	To increase students' understanding about effects of family problems and improve skills to handle family problems	6	Curricular activities led by teachers that address affective knowledge, skills building, and violence education	Pre- and post-program survey to assess knowledge and attitudes
Affective Education Programs					
Second Step: A Violence Prevention Curriculum	Grossman et al. (1997)	Empathy training, impulse control, and anger management	30	Classroom-based sessions led by teachers involving scenarios that challenge students' new emotion skills	Teacher ratings, parent ratings, and behavioral observations
MIDDLE SCHOOLS					
A Dating Violence Prevention Program for Middle School Students	Macgowan (1997)	To help students recognize dating violence, understand its causes, and make decisions about relationships in the future	5	Classroom-based didactic and discussion sessions led by teachers	In progress

(Continued)

TABLE 20.1 Summary of School-Based Violence-Prevention Programs *(Continued)*

Program Name	Author	Goals of the Program	Number of Sessions	Program Description	Program Evaluation
Healthy Relationships: A Violence Prevention Curriculum	Safer (1994)	To educate adolescents about the dynamics of healthy and unhealthy relationships and provide prosocial skills for long-lasting healthy relationships; to increase awareness, knowledge, and skills; and to explore the role and impact of gender and society in violence	53	Classroom-based didactic and discussion sessions led by teachers	Three-year longitudinal study under way
STOP: School Targeting Operation for the Prevention of Interpersonal Violence	Rodgers (1997)	To provide information about the causes of violence and offer skills instructions to prevent violence	9	Classroom-based didactic and discussion sessions led by teachers	Pre- and post-program knowledge and attitude survey; teachers' form to evaluate implementation
Safe Dates	Foshee et al. (1996)	To prevent dating violence by changing norms about violence and gender stereotyping, building skills, and increasing help-seeking behaviors	10	School activities: ten classroom-based didactic and discussion sessions led by teachers, one play, one contest Community activities: multiple activities including provision of counseling services at a community agency for adolescents in harmful relationships and materials for parents	Pre-, post-, and 1-year follow-up survey to assess knowledge, attitudes, and dating behaviors
HIGH SCHOOLS					
The London Family Court Clinical Violence Prevention Program	Jaffe et al. (1992)	To increase knowledge about intimate partner violence and assist students in developing an action plan	One, plus discussion sessions	A full or half-day program consisting of one 90-minute didactic presentation followed by a series of discussion sessions led by community professionals	Pre-, post- and 6-week follow-up survey to assess knowledge, attitudes, and behavioral intentions

Program	Author	Objectives	Sessions	Description	Evaluation
The Minnesota School Curriculum Project	Jones (1991)	To increase knowledge about domestic violence, examine reasons for abuse, and teach skills to prevent violence	Not available	The curriculum was designed for teachers to use in the context of their standard courses such as English, math, and science	Pre- and post-program knowledge survey
A Dating Violence Prevention Program	Avery-Leaf et al. (1997)	To provide information about dating violence, to change attitudes that accept the use of aggression in relationships, and to enhance skills	5	Classroom-based didactic and discussion sessions in health classes by the teachers	Pre- and post-program survey
A Prevention Program for Violence in Teen Dating Relationships	Lavoie et al. (1995)	To increase students' awareness of the different forms of dating violence	2-4	Classroom-based didactic and discussion sessions led by community members	Pre- and post-program knowledge and attitude survey
The Youth Relationships Project: A Violence Prevention Curriculum for Adolescents	Prothrow-Stith (1987)	To increase students' understanding of the nature of anger, homicide, fighting, and conflict	10	Classroom-based didactic and discussion sessions in health classes led by teachers	Pre- and post-program knowledge and attitude survey and self-reported fighting behaviors
The Dating Safely Group: A Psycho-Educational Program for Teenage Girls	Becky & Farren (1997)	To help students understand the definitions and nature of abusive dating relationships, how to avoid them, and the long-term impact of abusive dating relationships on self-esteem and the ability to make decisions	8	Group-based sessions for girls only, outside the classroom setting, led by two psychologists	Plans are under way to administer pre- and post-program surveys of knowledge and behaviors
Step by Step: Developing Respectful and Effective Ways of Working With Young Men to Reduce Violence	Denborough (1996)	To increase boys' understanding of gender issues in relationships	14	Group-based sessions for boys only, outside the classroom setting, led by members of the community agency	Process evaluation took place; outcomes evaluation in planning stages
Helping Teens Stop Violence: A Practical Guide for Counselors, Educators, and Parents	Creighton & Kivel (1990)	To increase students' awareness of interpersonal violence with related issues of racism, adultism, sexism, and other forms of power and control	2	Classroom-based didactic and discussion sessions; not clear who runs the sessions or in which class it takes place	Pre- and post-curriculum test

at schools, with rules of behavior for everyone (students, teachers, staff, and parents). This schoolwide approach includes teaching children to be peacemakers and focuses on positive behaviors rather than negative behaviors. A major goal of this strategy is to create a school culture that supports peaceful behaviors and rewards students for engaging in healthy interpersonal behaviors. Another category of approaches, identified by Gamache and Snapp (1995), is commonly referred to as affective education programs. These programs strive to enhance self-esteem and teach children to recognize and label feelings as a way to handle emotional distress and avoid confrontation. These two forms of elementary school programs are described in more detail below with specific examples.

Peace Programs

Peace programs are generally used to change the social culture at the schools and involve more than classroom-based education programs. For instance, activities used to promote peaceful behaviors among the students include schoolwide contests to see which students are the most peaceful and peace slogans hung up throughout the school. Three programs used this approach: PeaceBuilders, the Comer School Development program, and My Family and Me.

PeaceBuilders (Embry, Flannery, Vazsonyi, Powell, & Atha, 1996)

A perfect example of a peace-building program for nonviolence in elementary schools is the program called Peace-Builders. Embry et al. (1996) developed a school-based violence-prevention program for students in kindergarten through fifth grade. PeaceBuilders activities are built into the overall school environment. PeaceBuilders uses broad behavior-change techniques including the development of a common language for peace building, a language used by students, their teachers, and office staff. Stories and live models of positive behavior reinforce the messages of peace and peaceful behaviors. Environmental cues to signal peaceful behaviors are placed throughout the class and school. To increase students' range of responses and positive peaceful behaviors, students frequently engage in role-plays and rehearse positive solutions after negative events occur. Group and individual rewards are used to strengthen positive behavior, and punishments are used for negative behaviors. Students are encouraged to monitor themselves and each other for positive behavior. Efforts also are made to promote the generalization of peace behaviors in other aspects of the children's lives, at home and in the neighborhood. The goal of this effort is to increase the maintenance of positive behavior change across time, place, and people. These strategies are meant to change school climate, including everyday interactions of students with staff and family. PeaceBuilders was designed as a way of life for students in school, home, and neighborhood environments. The prevention plan also includes activities performed by teachers, students, parents, family members, and the principal and assistant principal. Members of the support staff, such as bus drivers, hall monitors, and lunch monitors, are encouraged to coach peace-building activities throughout the day. Students are identified as Peace-Builders because they praise people, avoid put-downs, seek wise people, notice hurts they have caused, and right wrongs.

The PeaceBuilders program was evaluated using a multicomponent evaluation strategy. The outcome evaluation assessed aggressive and delinquent behavior, social competence at home and at school, parent-child relationships, school discipline, and peace-building behaviors. One report published recently investigated the impact of the PeaceBuilders program on visits to the school nurse (Krug, Brener, Dahlberg, Ryan, & Powell, 1997). The overall weekly number of nurse visits, visits for all injuries, and visits for injuries caused by fights were compared between four PeaceBuilders schools and three control schools. The rate of nurse visits decreased 12.6% in the schools implementing a PeaceBuilders program and remained unchanged in the control schools. The same trend was detected for injury-related visits. Whereas the rate of fighting-related injuries changed little in the schools implementing the Peace-Builders program, the rate of visits for fighting-related injuries increased 56% in the control schools. These data show that PeaceBuilders may decrease violence in the school setting. They also suggest that school nurse visits may be a useful evaluation tool for elementary school-based violence-prevention programs. No other PeaceBuilders evaluation data have been reported.

Comer School Development Program (Haynes, 1996)

Haynes (1996) described yet another peace-building program for elementary schools, which is similar in design to the PeaceBuilders program. The Comer School Development Program is designed to "embrace children within a web of personal relationships and activities" (Haynes, 1996, p. 308). The school-based program is designed to create a safe haven that supports students' healthy development, fosters optimal learning, and discourages interpersonal violence. This program also engages teachers, parents, family, and elementary school staff. Haynes (1996) believes that when the school climate is "reconfigured with attention paid to each of these areas, schools are better able to address the problem of violence more effectively" (p. 310). The 12 precepts critical to the program's success include the following: (a) order and discipline, (b) respect trust and kindness among students, (c) caring and sensitivity among the school personnel, (d) fair and equal treatment for students, (e) equal access to resources for all students, (f) high expectations for student achievement, (g) parental involvement, (h) maintenance of the school building's physical appearance, (i) academic focus, (j) collaborative decision making, (k) productive school-community relations, and (l) an absence of finger pointing.

Haynes (1996) reported anecdotal evidence suggesting an improvement in the school environment for parents and children as a result of the program. One parent described the positive change in dismissal procedures, and a student reported feeling safer at the school. The multifactor approach is consistent with the trend in the literature that suggests more than an education program is warranted in the fight against violence. More outcome evaluations of these multifactor strategies are required.

My Family and Me: Violence Free (Minnesota Coalition for Battered Women, 1991)

This program uses several peace strategies in combination with affective and violence education. The curriculum, entitled *My Family and Me: Violence Free,* has six learning goals and activities for students in kindergarten through third grade and fourth through sixth grades. The first goal of the curriculum was to raise awareness of students' concept of family and the effects that problems have on all family members. The second goal was to encourage students to label and define the different forms of violence in families and to understand the effects of this violence on the different family members. The third goal was to establish a safety plan. Teachers assisted students in the development of their own personal safety plan to use in violent and abusive emergency situations in the family. The fourth goal was to teach students how to express their feelings, opinions, and behaviors based on the values of respect and sharing of power. The fifth goal focused on assertive skills. Students were taught to practice assertiveness skills that are aimed to solve problems without violence. And, finally, the sixth goal aimed to help students gain a sense of their own uniqueness and worth. Students are encouraged to understand and believe that they can always make choices for themselves in the future regardless of problems that happen in the family.

This curriculum was evaluated using pre- and posttests administered by teachers. Of 40 teachers trained to deliver the curriculum, 22 teachers administered the pre- and the posttest in their classrooms. Results indicate that students showed an increase in knowledge about violence. Attitude changes were not statistically significant, although they were in the desired direction of change.

Affective Education Programs

Second Step: A Violence Prevention Curriculum (Grossman et al., 1997)

The previous program, My Family and Me: Violence Free, made the connection between peace programs and affective ed-

ucation. The Second Step program is designed to be more exclusively oriented toward teaching children about their feelings and how their feelings play a role in relationships. Three separate curricular packages are prepared for preschool to kindergarten children, children in Grades 1 to 3, and children in Grades 4 and 5. This review focuses on the results of a study by Larson (1994), which implemented the curriculum for second and third grade students. The main goals of the program for the second and third grade students are "to reduce impulsive and aggressive behavior in young children and increase their level of social competence" (Larson, 1994, p. 152). Although these goals imply that the program may not be a primary prevention program, the syllabus and actual implementation suggest otherwise. Therefore, this program will be reviewed here as a primary prevention program.

There are 30 lessons in the program, arranged in three units: empathy, impulse control, and anger management. The first unit, empathy training, involves students identifying their own feelings and those of others, learning to take others' perspectives, and showing care and concern for each other. The second unit explores issues of impulse control. Students are presented with a problem, a way to solve the problem, and behavioral skills for effective solution implementation. The third unit, anger management, challenges students to learn and use new skills. Students are presented with a tense scenario and then with coping strategies and behavioral skills to handle the potentially anger-provoking situation. Each session lasts the length of a class period, about 35 to 40 minutes. The sessions are taught once or twice a week by teachers in the classroom. Each lesson is constructed around a black-and-white photograph of a situation, which is used to generate discussion and provide an opportunity for students to practice new appropriate skills in response to and in the context of the scenario. Each lesson has activities that help students generalize their skills for that one scenario to other environments, such as home and neighborhood. Role-playing and other conceptual activities are an important part of the curriculum.

Teacher ratings, parent ratings, and direct behavior observations of student behavior (specifically ability to identify problems, ability to solve problems, and the use of assertive versus aggressive responses) were outcome assessment measures used to evaluate the impact of the Second Step program. Grossman et al. (1997) reported that scores did not differ significantly between the intervention and control schools for any of the parent-reported or teacher-reported behavior scales. However, the direct behavior observation scales did reveal an overall decrease in physical aggression and an increase in neutral prosocial behavior in the intervention group, compared with the control group. These significant differences were noted 2 weeks after the curriculum was completed, and most of these effects persisted 6 months later. The duration of this effect after 6 months, and its implications for violent behavior in later life, are unknown (Kellermann et al., 1998).

It is clear from the literature that elementary school programs have had some success in changing knowledge and attitudes about violence. However, it is still not clear to what extent these programs have an impact on the children's behaviors and behavioral intentions in regard to violence in general and violence against women in particular. The next section reviews a number of educational programs designed for middle school students. In general, these programs focus more directly on the prevention of violence against women in the form of dating violence.

Middle School Programs

Unlike elementary school-based programs, middle school programs more directly target dating behaviors. Hence, there has been a dramatic increase in the number of violence-prevention programs that focus specifically on dating and dating violence in the middle school setting. Two reasons come to mind for this increase. One, to reduce the prevalence of high school dating violence, students need to be reached at a younger age, before serious dating begins. Two, even though many teachers and parents may not like to accept this, the fact is that many middle school students are starting to explore the dating game. Therefore, the need for and relevance of dating and dating violence-prevention curricula in the middle schools emerges from the age-appropriateness of the topic of dating. This is the natural and logical direction of school-based primary prevention programs. The programs described below are all, in some way, addressing the concerns of dating and dating violence in the middle school population.

A Dating Violence Prevention Program for Middle School Students (Macgowan, 1997)

A five-session relationship violence-prevention program was developed by the Domestic Violence Intervention Services of Tulsa, Oklahoma. The curriculum is designed to help students recognize dating violence, understand its causes, and make decisions about relationships in future. Such decisions include avoiding abusive relationships or ending a current relationship. This program primarily focuses on knowledge and skills development. It is not clear if the sessions are 1 hour in length and taught each day for 5 consecutive days or whether the sessions are designed for delivery once a week for 5 weeks. The first session focuses on violence in society in general and in different kinds of relationships. The role of self-esteem in interpersonal violence is also discussed. The second session focused on the different forms of abuse, including sexual, physical, and emotional. The role of power and control in abusive relationships is explored and discussed in the third session. The fourth session gets students talking about the characteristics of healthy and unhealthy relationships and how healthy relationships can be developed based on the principles of mutuality, dignity, and self-worth. Communication skills and problem-solving skills are the main objectives of the fifth session, along with helping students to understand where they can go to for help if they find themselves in an abusive relationship.

Parents, who are oriented to the curriculum 1 week before the students begin the sessions, are encouraged to discuss issues with their children and help them with homework assignments throughout the program.

This curriculum was presented to 802 middle school students at one school in Dade County, Florida. A 22-item survey based on the curriculum was designed to tap four main domains: (a) knowledge about relationship violence, (b) attitudes about nonphysical violence, (c) attitudes

about physical/sexual violence, and (d) attitudes related to dealing with dating violence. Students also rated the program on a scale of 1 = *poor* to 5 = *superior*: the program's score, 3.8. In addition, teachers presenting the curriculum were given a checklist of objectives and activities for each session as reminders. This ensured reasonable standardization of program implementation so that the results could be attributed to the program. Significant improvements in knowledge about relationship violence and attitudes about nonphysical violence were noted in the posttest scores for students in the treatment group as compared to the control group. Within the treatment group, posttest scores were also significantly higher than pretest scores. In addition, male students with a higher level of academic ability made the most improvements. However, no changes were noted in attitudes about physical violence or in methods of dealing with an abusive relationship.

Healthy Relationships: A Violence Prevention Curriculum (Safer, 1994)

This curriculum is designed to educate adolescents about the dynamics of healthy and unhealthy relationships and provide the prosocial skills necessary for creating lasting and healthy relationships (Safer, 1994). The program, a three-volume curriculum developed by Men for Change in cooperation with The Halifax County-Bedford District School Board in Nova Scotia, Canada, distinguishes itself from other school-based programs because of its emphasis on gender analysis. Men for Change believe the Healthy Relationships curriculum uses a more holistic approach by using

gender analysis as a powerful tool for exposing the roots of violent and aggressive behaviors. By empowering students to analyze the culture of violence that condones abusive behavior, we are taking the necessary step towards helping them to create the violence-free society of tomorrow. (p. FAQ 3)

There are 53 activities; each is designed to be administered within a 45-minute to 1-hour session. The activities are intended to build thematically; however, teachers can choose to construct "mini-modules" to suit their time constraints and the needs of their students. The program can be integrated into existing curricula, or it can be taught as a stand-alone program. The three volumes are typically taught in three sequential grades, but they can also be taught in 1 year, if time allows. The first two volumes of the program are best integrated into health classes (or personal development and relationship classes, if they exist). Activities can also be used in English and social (family) studies programs. If necessary, these two volumes can be used in individual counseling sessions or small groups within school- or community-based settings. The third volume is designed for extended group work to provide a place and context for communication skills practice and team building.

"Volume 1: Dealing With Aggression" is intended to increase adolescents' ability to identify the emotions they experience (emotional literacy), help adolescents recognize and effectively handle their anger and someone else's anger, explore their choices in conflict situations, and learn communication skills. The activities in Volume 1 "help students to recognize the range of emotions that can lead to outbursts, and they teach the basic communication skills needed to choose

healthy alternatives to solve their problems" (Safer, 1994, p. FAQ 2).

"Volume 2: Gender Equality and Media Awareness" examines the impact of gender stereotypes and influences of North American culture on attitudes and behaviors. Students are encouraged to critically analyze the messages in popular media, especially TV and music, for issues of power and control that can lead to violence in relationships. There are several goals of Volume 2: to increase students' awareness of how, and the extent to which, media influences attitudes, behaviors, and mores; to increase students' awareness of the impact of television on their lives; to explore the link between sexism and violence with students; to help students recognize the pervasiveness of gender stereotypes; to highlight the damaging effects of violent role models; and to help students recognize their talents and gifts.

"Volume 3: Building Healthy Relationships" works with students to demonstrate the connection between sexist attitudes and violent behaviors and the pivotal role that this connection plays in teen dating violence and domestic violence. Students explore another link, one that is more positive: the link that exists between respect, safety, equality, trust, empathy, and a sense of personal value and responsibility and healthy relationships. Groups of four students (two boys and two girls if possible), called Gender Justice Action Groups, should be formed for this set of activities. The intention of the Gender Justice Action Groups is to work toward gender equality in all areas of life, ending all forms of gender-related violence and oppression (i.e., justice). The groups achieve this by exploring how male-female relationships may be compromised by unrealistic expectations and sexist attitudes and by practicing respectful and open communication skills with each other. The authors believe that the skills and issues addressed in Volume 3 should result in students being better prepared to handle the multiplicity of relationships throughout their lives.

This is one of the few programs that extend over a long period of time. Others are typically one to five or six sessions. Health Relationships has 56 sessions and can extend over 3 academic years or 75 teaching hours, if all components and handouts are used. Although no formal evaluation of this program has been published to date, the Manitoba Research Centre on Family Violence and Violence Against Women has selected the Men For Change Healthy Relationship curriculum as the focus of a 3-year longitudinal study because of its integrated, long-term approach and attractive curriculum. This longitudinal study was to have begun in 1996; we eagerly await the results.

STOP: School Targeting Operation for the Prevention of Interpersonal Violence (Rodgers, 1997).

Sponsored by the Partnership Against Domestic Violence in Atlanta, Georgia, this curriculum provides information about the causes of violence and offers skills instruction in an effort to prevent violence. The program, described by Rodgers (1997), is divided into nine units and is presented once a week, in 1-hour sessions, over a 10 to 12-week period. The units are designed to proceed in a logical sequential format. The units can, however, be extracted and presented independently of the whole curriculum. Units 1 and 2 are introductory units that explore the seriousness of the problem of family violence and examine the myths, atti-

tudes, and beliefs about interpersonal violence, respectively. Unit 3 continues with the presentation of preliminary information about interpersonal violence, such as the definition of various terms and forms of abuse. Unit 4 begins to explore the roots and causes of violence, seven in particular: sex role stereotyping, the media, unrealistic expectations, lack of communication skills, poor self-esteem, lack of parenting skills, and stress. It typically takes several sessions to cover all the material in this unit. Unit 5 is designed to have students think about why victims of interpersonal violence may stay in abusive situations. Resources and agencies that can be called on to help with abusive situations are the focus of Unit 6. Students are also asked to suggest ways that people can prevent violent behaviors and to begin to explore the patterns of abuse that may exist in dating relationships. Unit 7 confronts the topic of sexual assault. Students are taught that rape is an act of violence with the primary goals of power and dominance. Finally, students explore the notion of victim blaming in the context of rape in all its forms (stranger rape, marital rape, and date/acquaintance rape). Unit 8 continues to address issues surrounding dating relationships and dating violence, and Unit 9 explores elder abuse.

No data have yet been reported, so it is difficult to gauge the impact of this program on knowledge and attitudes. However, it is important to note that an evaluation process is in place. Teachers are asked to administer the Attitude Survey and Violence Concept Test before they began the curriculum and again on its completion and to send the completed forms to the STOP Program coordinator at the Partnership Against Domestic Violence in Atlanta, Georgia. The Attitude Survey consists of 10 questions in which students are asked to indicate whether they agree or disagree or if they are not sure. Questions include stereotypical sex-role behaviors ("When two people are married, the man should have control over the woman in their relationship"), incidence of abuse ("Violence in the family, such as when a husband hits his wife, does not happen very often in the United States"), and acceptability of abuse ("It is never OK for a husband to hit, kick, push, or shove his wife, no matter what happens"). The Violence Concepts Test consists of 10 multiple-choice questions and 10 true/false questions. These questions are designed to measure the impact of the program on students' knowledge about violence in the home, especially between husband and wife. Teachers are also asked to complete a facilitators' evaluation form, which provides an opportunity for teachers to give feedback on the sessions. The form includes questions such as "What portions of the curriculum did you find particularly effective or had a particular impact on your students?" "How did you present the curriculum to your students? How long did it take to complete the program? Did you choose to present all of the text?"

Safe Dates (Foshee et al., 1996)

This program bridges middle and high school and is, therefore, presented as the last program in the middle school section. It also addresses the multifactor approach in the curriculum (i.e., attitudes and knowledge and behaviors).

The Safe Dates program is designed to prevent dating violence by changing (a) violence norms, (b) gender stereotyping, (c) conflict-management skills, (d) help-seeking, and (e) cognitive factors associated with help-seeking. This is accomplished through school-based and community-based activities. The major theoretical underpinning of the approach appears to be directly derived from the Health Belief Model constructs of perceived susceptibility and severity as cues to action. That is, adolescents' beliefs in the need to get help with dating and dating violence issues are influenced by their perceived susceptibility to dating problems and the perceived severity of those problems. Foshee (1998) speculates that adolescents may not feel susceptible to dating violence problems if they do not label the violence as abusive. She also suggests that it is the perception of being abused that will result in adolescents seeking help for dating violence issues rather than the actual occurrence and seriousness of the dating violence.

This program is unique in that it is designed to address both victims and perpetrators of relationship violence and does not assume that girls are the victims and boys are the perpetrators. The Safe Dates program includes activities for school and community.

School-based activities. There are three major components to the school activities: (a) a theater production performed by peers, (b) a 10-session curriculum (the Safe Dates curriculum), and (c) a poster contest.

The theater production is a 45-minute play performed by eight students enrolled in a theater course at one of the schools involved in the study. The play, performed at each of the seven schools, is about a girl who is a victim of dating violence, and it shows how she tries to get help for her situation. The play was designed to address the mediating variables related to help-seeking behaviors, including her belief in the need to seek help, her perception of the seriousness of the violence in her relationship, and her perception of susceptibility to further violence in the dating relationship. The play also looks at the fact that this female student has difficulty labeling the relationship as abusive because the characteristics of her relationship do not match her stereotypes of abuse. Finally, the play explores her attributions for violence.

The play kicks off the 10-session Safe Dates curriculum. Each session is designed to be taught in one classroom period (about 45 minutes). Some teachers taught the curriculum on 10 consecutive days, and others taught it on alternate days until the sessions were covered. Still other teachers taught the curriculum in five 1½-hour sessions (thus covering two sessions per day), and one teacher taught it once a week for 10 weeks.

Session 1 promotes discussions of the characteristics of healthy relationships, including caring behaviors, ways people would like to be treated in a relationship, and the choices students have in how they are treated and how they treat someone in a relationship. Session 2 defines dating abuse, describes harmful dating behaviors, and differentiates between harmful and abusive behaviors, as well as different forms of abusive behaviors. Session 3 includes the reasons people use abusive behaviors, the role of power and control in abusive relationships, the difference between jealousy and love, and warning signs of dating violence. Session 4 is designed to help students understand why people do not leave abusive relationships and explores ways in which friends can help friends in abusive situations, including the use of community resources. The premise for encouraging the use of community resources in Session 4 is that adolescents will be more likely to seek help if they are aware of resources available and believe that these resources are effective. Session 5 provides an opportunity for students to practice the skills required for effective discussions with friends who may be victims or perpetrators of dating violence. Session 6 explores how gender stereotyping forms students' images of relationships and how these stereotypes can lead to abusive relationships. Students practice conflict-resolution skills and communication skills in Session 8. They are also given an opportunity to generate nonviolent strategies to use when their dating partners do not use communication effectively. Session 9 examines sexual assault and ways to reduce the risk of rape in dating relationships. Session 10 is used to obtain feedback from students and to initiate the poster-contest activities.

Another piece of the school-based activity set is the schoolwide poster contest. The poster contest is designed as another forum to expose students to messages about dating violence. Interested students develop posters that address themes in the Safe Dates curriculum, and these are displayed in the classrooms. Students judge the posters and choose three winners, who receive cash prizes.

Community-based activities. Community activities are included in the program to improve resources for adolescents, and specifically for those adolescents involved in abusive dating relationships. These activities include special services for adolescents in violent relationships at a community agency called Harbor, Inc. These services include a domestic violence and rape crisis phone line and support groups. The crisis hot line had been in existence before the Safe Dates project but was updated to provide services specifically for adolescents. Community service providers received training from Safe Dates staff on how to provide adolescent counseling on the phone and in small groups. In addition, materials for parents were prepared and made available for distribution.

About 1,200 eighth and ninth graders in seven schools in a rural North Carolina setting participated in a study to evaluate the impact of the curriculum. Students completed a 116-item questionnaire before the program and 1 month after the completion of the program (7 months later). They also completed questionnaires 1 year later, although this data is not yet available. The questionnaires were designed to assess demographics, presence of dating and dating violence, knowledge of dating-violence issues and services provided to assist with adolescent dating-violence situations, dating-violence behaviors including victimization and perpetration, and theoretically driven mediating variables such as dating violence beliefs. Conflict-resolution and communication skills, among others, were also assessed. Foshee (1998) hypothesized that, compared with students exposed to community activities only, those students exposed to both school and community activities would be less likely to initiate dating violence, more likely to leave a dating-violence relationship, and more likely to stop perpetrating dating violence. Results indicate that students in the treatment group reported significantly less psychological abuse perpetration, less sexual violence perpetration, and less violence perpetration against a current dating partner. Students in the treatment group were also more significantly aware of services available for adolescents in abusive dating relationships.

High School Programs

High schools are "uniquely positioned to reach a large proportion of our communities' youth, to challenge and shape their attitudes, and to teach them skills for nonviolent relationships" (Sudermann, Jaffe, & Hastings, 1995, p. 252). Preventing violence in relationships is an important issue for high schools to address because high school students are dating. Sudermann and colleagues believe that in the high school years, adolescents experiment with different behaviors in relationships and, based on these experiences and their social milieu, develop beliefs and values about relationships.

Given the age of high school students and the proximity to adult working lives, several program developers took a different approach to violence prevention. Instead of addressing violence prevention directly, tangential topics were addressed in the hopes of focusing adolescents' attention on practical skills of everyday living and working. With this in mind, many types of school-based violence-prevention programs for high school students have been developed, including problem-solving skills programs, peer mediation and conflict resolution programs, and vocational training and employment programs. Problem-solving skills programs include the Interpersonal Cognitive Problem-Solving Curriculum and a program called Providing Alternative Thinking

Strategies (PATHS). These are designed to counter early antisocial behaviors by encouraging cognitive and social skills development. It is not clear what impact these programs have on general or specific violence prevention in the long term. Another type of education-based program designed for high school students is vocational training and employment programs. These are designed to provide adolescents with a sense of accomplishment, a stable and legal income, and justification for further education, all of which were hoped to have a connection in preventing violent behaviors. Many of these types of programs did not achieve their goals. Nine vocational training programs were designed specifically to address crime and delinquency prevention. Six of them were found to have no effect; one reported an increase in the rate of adolescents' criminal offenses (Kellermann et al., 1998). Other programs have shown similarly disappointing results. Mentoring programs attempt to build stable, competent, and caring relationships between children and adults to reduce or prevent violence in general and particularly in relationships. Although these programs may be prevention oriented, quantitative research studies that measure the impact of this prevention strategy do not seem to exist; instead, there are feedback studies about the quality of the relationships. It is not clear if mentors follow any educational prescription, and this makes evaluation challenging. Also, the impact of mentoring programs may be highly dependent on the nature of the relationships, which makes evaluation even more difficult (Kellermann et al., 1998).

Given the unimpressive results of these education-based programs for high schools students, a more direct strategy is required for violence prevention, as was found in the elementary school setting. In their review, Sudermann et al. (1995) identified key components of successful high school violence-prevention programs. Student programs should include student violence-awareness events such as school planning committees, large-group violence-awareness events, small-group discussions, and integrated curricula. Partnerships among students, teachers, support staff, parents, administrators, board members, survivors, and community agencies are also key. This approach is consistent with the multifactor approach used in elementary and middle schools. Several programs are described below that represent this successful approach.

The London Family Court Clinic Violence Prevention Program (Jaffe, Sudermann, Reitzel, & Killip, 1992)

Jaffe et al. (1992), from the London Family Court Clinic in London, Ontario, Canada, describe their efforts to implement and evaluate a high school program developed to address intimate partner violence. All students in four senior high schools receive a full day or half-day intervention designed to address wife assault and dating violence. The program is composed of a large-group presentation on wife assault and dating violence, followed by classroom discussions facilitated by community professionals. Unlike many of the other school-based programs, this one does not use school teachers to implement a set curriculum. Instead, teachers facilitate classroom discussions with representatives from community organizations such as antiviolence agencies, the Police Department, and the Board of

Education. The auditorium session, which lasts 90 minutes, entails didactic presentations on the myths and facts about domestic and dating violence. This is followed by 1-hour discussions in classrooms for the half-day program. The full day program includes the auditorium session and group discussions; however, the group discussions last the whole school day and allow students to develop actions plans.

Knowledge, attitudes, and behavioral intentions were assessed 1 week before the program was implemented, immediately afterward (i.e., 1 week after program implementation), and again at 5 or 6 weeks post-intervention. The 48-item London Family Court Clinic Questionnaire on Violence in Intimate Relationships was used to assess attitudes about sex roles, wife assault, and dating violence; knowledge about domestic violence; and behavioral intentions.

Significant positive gains were found on knowledge, attitude, and behavioral intention scores (i.e., students report what they do in hypothetical situations) at posttest for both groups. Most gains were maintained at 6 weeks following the intervention. Girls significantly improved on more items, especially attitudes, than did boys. Most of the positive changes for boys and girls were maintained at follow-up. It should be noted that, for some of the male students, there was an increase in the acceptance of violence. The authors hypothesized that these male students may have already been involved in abusive behaviors and thus may require more than primary prevention. Unfortunately, these changes for boys were also largely maintained at follow-up. Because the authors do not report separate results for the two types of programs, one assumes that the results from the two forms of the program were collapsed into one database for analysis. Therefore, it is not clear whether the program differences resulted in different levels of impact.

The Minnesota School Curriculum Project (Jones, 1991)

The Southern California Coalition on Battered Women published *Skills for Violence-Free Relationships,* a curriculum designed for 13- to 18-year-olds. This curriculum served as the basis for the curriculum in the Minnesota School Curriculum Project (Jones, 1991). The Minnesota Coalition for Battered Women developed this school-based curriculum and designed it so that teachers could incorporate the curricular content and activities into their regular courses and classes. So, instead of teaching "The Course," teachers use the curriculum in the context of their standard courses, such as English, math, and science. The overall goals of the project are to (a) increase young people's knowledge about the problem of domestic violence, (b) examine reasons for abuse, and (c) teach skills that reduce the likelihood that students will find themselves in an abusive relationship.

A total of 560 junior high school students and 382 senior high school students completed curriculum pre- and posttests to evaluate their knowledge about domestic violence and available resources. Jones (1991) found that students in the treatment group significantly increased their knowledge scores compared to those in the control group.

Five items were also administered to measure attitudes about violence. These attitude items were designed to reflect societal attitudes about sex roles (e.g., "In serious relationships between men and women, men should be the leaders and decision-makers") and acceptance of violence in male and female relationships ("It's no one else's business if a husband hits a wife"). Jones (1991) found little to no change in attitudes for the control and treatment groups and concluded that this curriculum "had done little to affect attitudes toward domestic violence" (p. 264). However, there were large and statistically significant differences between males and females on four of the five attitude questions. Female students consistently showed more desirable attitudes than their male peers. In general, a high degree of uncertainty across all five attitude questions was noted among the male responses as compared with the girls' responses. Jones suggests that this may be due to a fair amount of ambivalence in the boys' opinions about dating and dating violence at this point in their lives. At this juncture of ambivalence in boys' thinking processes, an antiviolence educational program may have the greatest impact. It may be easier to educate someone who is still open to new ideas and possibilities.

> To the extent that undesirable responses on these attitude items undergird or support a tolerance for violence in male-female relationships and indicate a stance supporting traditional sex-role behavior for men and women, these responses among boys may be cause for concern. (Jones, 1991, p. 266)

The results from this study suggest that the Minnesota School Curriculum Project achieved the goal of increasing knowledge about domestic violence. Attitudes concerning issues of domestic violence, however, do not seem to have been affected by the curriculum. Given the fact that this curriculum was heavily geared toward building knowledge about domes-

tic violence and that it was presented in a relatively short period of time, the lack of changes in attitudes is not surprising. This continues to support the multifactor and long-term approach that seems to be required for changes in attitude about violence and subsequent behavior change.

A Dating Violence Prevention Program (Avery-Leaf, Cascardi, O'Leary, & Cano, 1997)

This five-session curriculum is designed to provide information about dating violence, change attitudes that accept the use of aggression in relationships, and enhance skills. Teachers are trained in one 8-hour session 1 week before they begin teaching 11th- and 12th-grade students. The sessions are taught in required health classes and last the full period (about 40 minutes). The goals of the program are achieved through several objectives and activities. A unique objective of this program is the promotion of "equity in dating relationships by demonstrating how gender inequality may foster violence" (Avery-Leaf et al., 1997, p. 12). Other objectives include challenging the use of violence as a strategy to resolve conflict, focusing on communication and help-seeking skills, and identifying available resources to assist those in at-risk or difficult dating relationships. The curriculum development is driven by a number of different perspectives, including social learning theory and sociological and feminist theories. Avery-Leaf and her colleagues (1997) posit that "individuals who experience violence in their families or origin, those with aggressive personalities, or those who maintain attitudes which justify the use of dating violence may be at risk for using aggression in dating relationships" (p. 12). They also suggest that, whereas gender-based power inequities in the American culture are linked with male abuses of power and control within dating relationships, there has been a failure to examine aggression perpetrated by females against male partners. Their curriculum, therefore, is designed to implement preventive efforts for both males and females.

The main goal of one reported evaluation effort was to assess students' acceptance of violence as a means of resolving conflict. This was accomplished using the Justification of Interpersonal Violence questionnaire (Avery-Leaf et al., 1997), in which students were asked to rate the aggressive acts of pushing, slapping, and punching. Separate scales were computed for female perpetration of dating aggression and male perpetration of dating aggression. Another scale, called the Justification of Dating Jealousy and Violence scale, was used to assess students' attitudes about aggressive behaviors in dating relationships. Students were asked to asked to rate assertions about vignettes as *not at all justifiable* to *completely justifiable*. Results showed that the curriculum was successful in reducing overall attitudes justifying aggression in dating relationships. Furthermore, on completion of the program, both male and female students who received the curriculum were significantly less accepting of aggression during an argument between girl friends and boyfriends. There was no change in attitude for students who did not receive the curriculum. The authors of this research believe that their program has promise for effective change but caution against celebration just yet. This is because of the profound floor effect they found on both attitude measures at the pre-program assessment point. Many students already believed that pushing, slapping, and punching were never acceptable

activities in a dating relationship and therefore, the program could not move their scores any lower.

A Prevention Program for Violence in Teen Dating Relationships (Lavoie, Vezina, Piche, & Boivin, 1995)

Two curricula were implemented to increase high school students' awareness of the different forms of dating violence, including issues of control and physical, emotional, and sexual abuse. One curriculum, considered the short form, consists of two classroom sessions for a total of 120 to 150 minutes; a team of two representatives from a community organization present these sessions. Session 1 is designed to identify the problem of dating violence in general and, in particular, to explore the different forms of control. Other objectives include highlighting the inappropriate use of control in dating relationships and distinguishing between the concepts of control over one's self, control over one's environment, and control over another person. The second session encourages students to identify their rights and responsibilities in a relationship as well as those of their dating partner and to link the concept of rights and responsibilities to violence prevention. Students also explore the concept of victim blaming and ways to avoid such thought processes. The long form of the curriculum consists of these two sessions plus two more activities, for a total of 240 to 300 minutes. Students are asked to view a film on dating violence and to write letters to fictional characters in a violent dating relationship (the perpetrator and the victim).

Two Canadian high schools participated in this project. They were randomly assigned to either the short or long form of the curriculum. Knowledge and attitudes were assessed before and after program implementation, using a 25-question survey. Seventeen items composed the attitude scale, and nine questions assessed knowledge; the knowledge questions were analyzed individually. Results indicated that boys and girls in both conditions significantly improved their attitude and knowledge scores on the posttest as compared with their pretest scores. In addition, girls consistently scored higher than boys on the posttest evaluations. Finally, Lavoie and her colleagues found that students who received the short form of the curriculum (i.e., the two-session curriculum) improved more on the knowledge items than those students who received the long form. These authors questioned the quality of the two additional activities and suggested that, because the students in the long form had lower pretest scores than students in the short form, more work might have been required to increase knowledge and change attitudes. The results, along with those reported by Avery-Leaf et al. 1997, emphasize the importance of noting students' starting point (pre-program attitude and knowledge scores) and how these pre-program scores can affect the degree of change achieved by a program. Floor and ceiling effects of pre-program scores must be considered when analyzing program effects.

The Youth Relationships Project: A Violence Prevention Curriculum for Adolescents (Prothrow-Stith, 1987).

The Violence Prevention Curriculum for Adolescents (Prothrow-Stith, 1987) is designed for implementation in high school health classes. The curriculum has five main sections and is presented across 10 sessions. The first part provides basic information, in the form of statistics mostly, on adolescent violence and homicide. Students are encouraged to examine homicide statistics locally and nationally. The next section focuses on anger and encourages students to recognize anger as a normal emotion with both constructive and destructive outcomes. In particular, the connection between anger and fighting is explored. The next two sections of the curriculum focus on fighting. The focus of the third section of the curriculum is the analysis of risks and benefits of fighting and explores alternatives to fighting. The fourth section encourages students to understand and identify the factors that may lead to fighting and provides an opportunity to practice skills to avoid fighting. Over the course of several sessions, students develop their own scripts showing how fights occur, and they enact and videotape the scenarios. The whole class then analyzes the videotape to identify alternatives to fighting in that situation. Through this and other exercises, students are taught that a typical fight has intrapersonal and peer-influenced components. The last section challenges students to develop and implement principles of nonviolence for the classroom.

Knowledge; attitudes about anger, violence, and homicide; and the number of fights students engaged in were measured before and after the implementation of the curriculum. Results showed significant differences in 106 tenth-grade students. It appears that there was no control group for this evaluation. In another study of 347 high schools students, the number of fights significantly decreased for the students in the treatment schools. Significantly fewer self-reports of fights were noted by the students who received the curriculum compared with those who did not receive the curriculum (DeJong, Spiro, Wilson-Brewer, Vince-Whitman, & Prothrow-Stith, 1988). Long-term effects are not known.

The Dating Safely Group: A Psychoeducational Program for Teenage Girls (Becky & Farren, 1997)

This program was designed by two school psychologists in a Boston-area high school for small groups of six to eight girls. The overall goals of the program are to help students understand (a) the definitions and nature of abusive dating relationships and how to avoid them and (b) the long-term impact of abusive dating relationships on self-esteem and ability to make decisions. The program is co-facilitated by two female school psychologists, although a male-female co-facilitation team is also appropriate and creates opportunities for modeling other types of behaviors. Students from Grades 9 through 12 are included if they can tolerate group settings, are willing to try to articulate and share their thoughts and feelings, are emotionally stable, and have permission from their parents. Sessions are held in the middle of the week to avoid holidays on Mondays and Fridays and at various times during the day to reduce time missed in one particular class. Becky and Farren recommend a diverse age range for the group participants because it facilitates discussion. They found that older students tend to be less inhibited in discussing dating issues, and this may encourage more participation from younger students.

Eight sessions are held, one per week during one class period (about 50 minutes). Session 1 reviews the purpose and format of the group sessions, reinforcing the notion that the girls are there to learn skills. Definitions of abuse and the five categories of abuse (verbal, physical, emotional, financial, and sexual) are explored through discussions. Session 2 explores male and female stereotypes, the role the media play in perpetuating these stereotypes, and the impact these stereotypes have on violent behaviors in relationships. The third session focuses on warning signs and risk factors for dating violence, including jealousy, possessiveness, and controlling behaviors. Sessions 4 and 5 explore the issue of date rape. A videotape is shown in Session 4 and intermittently stopped to allow time for discussion about a variety of issues generated by the film, including victim blaming, rape in long-term relationships, and the differences of popular versus legal definitions. The fifth session focuses on prevention of date rape. Sessions 6 and 7 are geared toward teaching conflict-management and communication skills, respectively. The final session is used to wrap up. The girls provide feedback about the group process and program content and are encouraged to continue working together and seek support from community agencies when necessary.

Although no evaluation data are available yet, the authors describe plans to conduct a pre- and post-treatment assessment of knowledge and behaviors. At the beginning of the 8-week course, girls will complete a brief questionnaire that assesses knowledge of dating violence, knowledge of strategies for protection, and dating habits and involvement in abusive dating relationships. Girls' knowledge will be assessed immediately following the completion of the program and again at 6 and 12 months after the completion of the program.

Step by Step: Developing Respectful and Effective Ways of Working With Young Men to Reduce Violence (Denborough, 1996)

Denborough (1996) describes a program that was developed by a community organization in Sydney, Australia, called Sydney Men Against Sexual Assault (MASA). Their program is derived from several theoretical frameworks, including gender stereotypes for masculine behaviors and masculinity, as well as subsequent culture-bound male-generated power and control issues in relationships. MASA is usually invited into high schools to work with a "problem" class, usually ninth-grade boys. Because of the existing problem, the Step by Step program is not truly primary prevention. However, as Denborough points out, "Year 9 boys are not the problem—the problem is the ways in which gender, race, class, and sexuality dynamics are organized in our society" (p. 100). The program is presented across 14 sessions, but it is not clear how long each session is or how long the total program is. Session 1 is used to make introductions and set rules for the group. Session 2 provides the time for boys to reflect on the extent of violence in their own lives, and Session 3 is used to elicit agreements from boys to work on these issues for the rest of the program. Sessions 4 and 5 focus on "gendered violence" and the cultural pressure for boys to be tough because they are male (i.e., gender stereotypes). Session 6 expounds on this theme by linking male-stereotyped aggression with its impact on an individual's health as well as that of others. The seventh session invites the boys to ac-

knowledge that changes must be, and can be, made. The eighth session presents a new challenge: Boys are asked to explore the meaning of their existence and the meaning of hope.

The next five sessions explore how boys can counter the negative cultural expectations of male aggression through discussing the strengths of being male, building skills, developing support networks, and engaging participation from people within their world (family, school, neighborhood, etc.) to promote positive behaviors. The last session provides an opportunity for boys to summarize and evaluate the program messages.

Although process evaluations have been conducted to make improvements to the program, no outcomes evaluation efforts have thus far been reported. Given the length and intensity of this program, it would be helpful to know its impact on boys' knowledge of, attitudes toward, and behaviors of dating violence.

Helping Teens Stop Violence: A Practical Guide for Counselors, Educators, and Parents (Creighton & Kivel, 1990).

The high school curriculum presented here is one component of a larger effort to prevent and intervene with interpersonal violence. Other components include community-based workshops and teen support groups; these will not be reviewed here. This program is the result of collaborative efforts between two community organizations located in Contra Costa County, California: the Battered Women's Alternatives and the Oakland Men's Project. The goals of the 2-day curriculum are to increase students' awareness of interpersonal violence with related issues of racism, adultism, sexism, and other forms of power and control. Co-facilitators from community agencies present the curriculum to high school students in their classroom. The sessions last the duration of the class period. The first session is designed to examine gender stereotypes for men and women, boys and girls and how these stereotypes can negatively affect relationships. Activities such as discussions, role-plays, and writing exercises achieve these objectives. Session 2 explores power and control issues in depth. Discussions and role-plays are used to achieve the goal of increasing students' understanding of the connection between power, control, and abuse.

No outcome evaluation data have been reported to date. However, the authors have designed a curriculum pre- and posttest for students to complete that should indicate changes in knowledge and attitudes.

Overall Observations

Although this is but a brief overview of some of the important work being done in school-based violence-prevention programs, some general observations can be made to enhance the perspective for future work.

Curricular Diversity

There is a wide range of, and much diversity within, school-based violence-prevention programs. Some curricula are designed to be taught as they are presented, in consecutive, sequential style, most likely in health classes. Other pro-

grams are taught by staff members from community agencies, and some are taught by school teachers who have been specially trained by staff from community agencies. Other programs are designed with more built-in flexibility. For instance, teachers are taught the curriculum, and then, they choose how and where and when to implement the curriculum throughout their regular teaching courses. Some of the curricula involve more than just classes; there are small-group sessions with the school social worker or school psychologist, plays, and other schoolwide activities such as poster contests.

Community and Academic Collaborations

The collaborations between community and educational organizations are evident, promising, and appropriate. These collaborations highlight the recognition and acknowledgment of at least two areas of expertise (violence prevention and intervention programming with teaching) coming together to work on a problem. That in itself is a wonderful role model and sets a high standard for students.

Several of the programs in this chapter were developed by teams consisting of agency members and academic staff. Also, many programs involved staff of community organizations making presentations to students. These efforts indicate an emphasis on and commitment to integrating violence-prevention activities into school programs rather than making a perfunctory presentation that has little if any impact in the short term or the long term. More efforts could be undertaken to integrate these programs into school systems more fully and on a permanent rather than "special guest appearance" basis.

Program Evaluation

Progress has been made in terms of identifying programs that successfully improve students' knowledge about interpersonal violence. Sustained changes in attitudes are difficult to achieve, but these attitude changes may be the route to ensure long-term impact on behaviors. It is important and necessary to continue to promote changes in attitude and behaviors at the same time, because one does not necessarily follow the other.

It is clear that many efforts are being made to evaluate these programs. We await the outcome data from many projects. It is important to ascertain the impact of these programs and share both the successes and failures to avoid unnecessary duplication of effort. The next step in this process will be to replicate the impact of some of these programs in different settings with the same and different target groups. Perhaps, we can develop a core number of school-based violence-prevention programs that can be integrated into elementary, middle, and high schools throughout the country.

The Future of School-Based Programs

The growth in peer-mediation and conflict-resolution programs as strategies for violence prevention is confusing because it is not clear that these programs reduce interpersonal violent and aggressive behaviors. They may be important components of a multifactor antiviolence program, but they are probably not enough to affect change on their own. In addition, to be made relevant to prevention of violence against women, an explicit link of peer mediation and conflict resolution with dating violence is recommended. One way in which this can be accomplished is through the discussions that take place in class about expectations in a dating relationships and the rights and responsibilities of each member of that relationship. If this link is not made explicit, will students get it? Given the stages of cognitive development, it may be that younger students are still concrete enough in their thinking that they may not understand that (a) this could apply to them later, even if they're not dating right now; and (b) peer-mediation skills can be used in multiple settings (family, friends, boyfriends, and girl friends).

Given the age of global communication, the next step in school-based violence-prevention programming could include the use of the Internet to continue to spread the culture of peace. However, efforts to include participation from the local community in an effort to reduce violence have yet to be fully achieved. Perhaps, this step needs successful completion before we begin to consider opening programs to wider audiences.

Single-factor approaches are not promoted or recommended, mostly because they do not work. Multifactor violence-prevention strategies should include classroom sessions that explore knowledge, attitudes, skills, and behavioral intentions. Program components that involve teacher, staff, and parent training, students groups, and schoolwide environmental changes should also be considered. Of course, this multicomponent approach can pose challenges for evaluation. However, component analyses are the next step in evaluation research to ascertain the benefits of various component combinations. That is, which components are essential for the most positive impact on knowledge, attitudes, skills, and behaviors? How much effort is required to minimize undesirable behavior and maintain behavior changes that promote peace?

Violence against women per se does not seem to be the focus of elementary school-based violence-prevention programs. This is age-appropriate and sets the stage for further and more specific work in violence prevention as children get older. This general antiviolence approach also reflects the primary prevention nature of these programs. Even community organizations dedicated to violence-against-women prevention and intervention programs have designed and implemented programs that address interpersonal violence for elementary students, without specifying dating or domestic violence or violence against women. In addition, given the increasing number of reports in the literature that indicates an upward trend in girls' perpetration of aggressive behaviors toward their peers and their boyfriends, a general approach to interpersonal violence may be more reflective of societal conditions. A generalized antiviolence approach is, therefore, recommended at an early age, with explicit reference to dating partners and interpersonal adult relationships as the children get older and these topics become more salient. The continuing problem is that, although these programs have been found to have a positive impact in the right direction, we still do not know if they work in the long term.

A more global antiviolence approach may also decrease the likelihood of male defensiveness about the topic of preventing violence against women. Few programs have directly addressed this challenge. Foshee (1998) makes an attempt to avoid male defensiveness; she points out that her curriculum is designed to address both victims and perpetrators of relationship violence and does not assume that girls are the victims and boys are the perpetrators. Avery-Leaf et al. (1997) also address male and female perpetration of dating violence. Sudermann et al. (1995) caution that some students nonetheless will perceive violence-prevention programs as "male bashing." This can be avoided using a number of different approaches:

- Emphasize the role that nonviolent men can play in finding solutions to the problem
- State that most men do not batter their spouses
- Focus on responsibility, not blame
- Suggest that men will benefit from a less violent school and society

Finally, once these curricular programs have been thoughtfully developed and carefully evaluated, they should be packaged and made readily accessible to school districts for implementation. Although ongoing evaluation should take place to note progress, more formal and expensive academic research designs should not always be necessary if we have accumulated enough evidence to support a program. However, replication studies are needed so that we can determine if existing programs are valuable in different parts of the United States and perhaps different parts of the world. Part of this effort will include the standardization and documentation of guidelines for curriculum delivery. The research question becomes, are the same results achieved if a curriculum is delivered in a manner different from its designed intention? Therefore, currricula need to be structured *and* flexible so that teacher style and class personality add to the impact of the program rather than detract from it.

Conclusions

We definitely need to keep working with school-based programs because we have seen their impact on short-term outcomes. With such powerful outcomes in a short time, there is hope that these school-based programs will have a long-term impact, as well. Although many school-based violence-prevention programs are available, none to date have reported long-term results. Continued evaluation efforts and longitudinal studies will help us understand the long-term impact these curricula have on the incidence of interpersonal, dating, and domestic violence.

References

Avery-Leaf, S., Cascardi, M., O'Leary, K. D., & Cano, A. (1997). Efficacy of a dating violence prevention program in attitudes justifying aggression. *Journal of Adolescent Health, 21,* 11-17.

Becky, D., & Farren, P. M. (1997). Teaching students how to understand and avoid abusive relationships. *The School Counselor, 44,* 303-308.

Creighton, A., & Kivel, P. (1990). *Helping teens stop violence: A practical guide for counselors, educators, and parents.* Alameda, CA: Hunter House.

DeJong, W., Spiro, A., Wilson-Brewer, R., Vince-Whitman, C., & Prothrow-Stith, D. (1988). *Evaluation summary: Violence prevention curriculum for adolescents.* Newton, MA: Education Development Center.

Denborough, D. (1996). Step by step: Developing respectful and effective ways of working with young men to reduce violence. In C. McLean, M. Carey, & C. White (Eds.), *Mens' way of being.* New York: Westview.

Embry, D. D., Flannery, D. J., Vazsonyi, A. T., Powell, K. E., & Atha, H. (1996). Peace-Builders: A theoretically driven, school-based model for early violence prevention. *American Journal of Preventive Medicine, 12*(Suppl 2), 91-100.

Foshee, V. A. (1998). Involving schools and communities in preventing adolescent dating abuse. In X. B. Arriaga & S. Oskamp (Eds.), *Addressing community problems: Psychological research and interventions* (pp. 105-129). Thousand Oaks, CA: Sage.

Foshee, V. A., Linder, G. F., Bauman, K. E., Langwick, S. A., Arriaga, X. B., Health, J. L., McMahon, P. M., & Bangdiwala, S. (1996). The Safe Dates project: Theoretical basis, evaluation design, and selected baseline findings. *American Journal of Preventive Medicine, 12*(Suppl 2, No. 5), 39-47.

Gamache, D., & Snapp, S. (1995). Teach your children well: Elementary schools and violence prevention. In E. Peled, P. G. Jaffe, & J. E. Edleson (Eds.), *Ending the cycle of violence: Community responses to children of battered women* (pp. 209-231). Thousand Oaks, CA: Sage.

Grossman, D. C., Neckerman, H. J., Koepsell, T. D., Yu Liu, P., Asher, K. N., Beland, K., Frey, K., & Rivara, F. (1997). Effectiveness of a violence prevention curriculum among children in elementary school. *Journal of the American Medical Association, 277*(20), 1605-1611.

Haynes, N. M. (1996). Creating safe and caring school communities: Comer School development program schools. *Journal of Negro Education, 65*(3), 308-314.

Jaffe, P. G., Sudermann, M., Reitzel, D., & Killip, S. M. (1992). An evaluation of a secondary school primary prevention program on violence in intimate relationships. *Violence and Victims, 7*(2), 129-146.

Jones, L. E. (1991). The Minnesota School Curriculum Project: A statewide domestic violence prevention project in secondary schools. In B. Levy (Ed.), *Dating violence: Young women in danger* (pp. 258-266). Seattle, WA: Seal.

Kellermann, A. L., Fuqua-Whitley, D. S., Rivara, F. P., & Mercy, J. (1998). Preventing youth violence: What works? *Annual Review of Public Health, 19,* 271-292.

Krug, E. G., Brener, N. D., Dahlberg, L. L., Ryan, G. W., & Powell, K. E. (1997). The impact of an elementary school-based violence prevention program on visits to the school nurse. *American Journal of Preventive Medicine, 13*(6), 459-463.

Larson, J. (1994). Violence prevention in the schools: A review of selected programs and procedures. *School Psychology Review, 23*(2), 151-164.

Lavoie, F., Vezina, L., Piche, C., & Boivin, M. (1995). Evaluation of a prevention program for violence in teen dating relationships. *Journal of Interpersonal Violence, 10*(4), 516-524.

Macgowan, M. J. (1997). An evaluation of a dating violence prevention program for middle school students. *Violence and Victims, 12*(3), 223-235.

Minnesota Coalition for Battered Women. (1991). *Teacher's guide to the prevention curriculum: Skills for violence-free relationships.* St. Paul: Author.

National Center for Injury Prevention and Control. (1993). *The prevention of youth violence: A framework for community action.* Atlanta, GA: Centers for Disease Control and Prevention.

Powell, K. E., Dahlberg, L. L., Friday, J., Mercy, J. A., Thornton, T., & Crawford, S. (1996). Prevention of youth violence: Rationale and char-acteristics of 15 evaluation projects. *American Journal of Preventive Medicine, 12*(Suppl 2, No. 5), 3-12.

Powell, K. E., Muir-McClain, L., & Halasyamani, L. (1995). A review of selected school-based conflict resolution and peer mediation projects. *Journal of School Health, 65*(10), 426-431.

Prothrow-Stith, D. (1987). *Violence prevention curriculum for adolescents.* Newton, MA: Education Development Center.

Rodgers, A. B. (1997). *STOP: School targeting operation for the prevention of interpersonal violence.* Atlanta, GA: The Partnership Against Domestic Violence.

Safer, A. (1994). *Healthy relationships: A violence-prevention curriculum.* Nova Scotia, Canada: Men for Change.

Sudermann, M., Jaffe, P. G., & Hastings, E. (1995). Violence prevention programs in secondary (high) schools. In E. Peled, P. G. Jaffe, & J. E. Edleson (Eds.), *Ending the cycle of violence: Community responses to children of battered women* (pp. 232-254). Thousand Oaks, CA: Sage.

Wolfe, D. A., Wekerle, C., Gough, R., Reitzel-Jaffe, D., Grasley, C., Pittman, A. L., LeFebre, L., & Stumpf, J. (1996). *The youth relationships manual: A group approach with adolescents for the prevention of women abuse and the promotion of healthy relationships.* Thousand Oaks, CA: Sage.

CHAPTER 21

Getting the Message Out

Using Media to Change Social Norms on Abuse

Marissa Ghez

The 20th century has witnessed monumental shifts in the way Americans perceive and respond to the problem of violence against women. Although the movement at large has made significant gains, the domestic violence-prevention movement in particular has made historic and monumental strides, which are the subject of this chapter. Today, more than ever before, the public recognizes domestic violence as a costly and pervasive problem that affects women all over the country—often with devastating consequences. Never before has there been such a unified national consensus that domestic violence is wrong, it is inexcusable, and it must be stopped.

This has not always been the case. As recently as 20 years ago, institutional response to the problem was largely ineffective, jeopardizing women's lives at every turn. Typically, police did not take the problem seriously, rarely arresting perpetrators. When battered women persevered and tried to press charges, district attorneys often refused to support their cases. Those cases that *did* make it to court were likely to be dismissed. Attitudes throughout the criminal justice system questioned "what she did to provoke him" and why she didn't just leave "if it was really so bad."

These kinds of institutional failings reflected widespread public indifference to the problem of spousal battery. At a time when major attitudinal, legal, and institutional changes were being called for and enacted to establish racial equality, public dialogue about the problem of domestic violence was virtually nonexistent. When domestic violence was discussed at all, it was done so with the pervasive assumption that such occurrences were really "family matters" best dealt with at home.

Friends of perpetrators and policy makers alike felt the problem was a private affair, "not their business." These kinds of pervasive norms among the general public helped to explain the lack of institutional response to victims of abuse: Not only was there no public pressure to reform, but institutional leaders held attitudes that simply reflected norms within the larger community.

Within the last three decades, however, the organized domestic violence movement has achieved a powerful public presence in the broader women's movement. As a result of the tireless work of thousands of individuals nationwide, a well-organized network of shelters and local domestic violence programs has sprung up in every community to provide women with safety options and places to go when they are in danger. Advocates have successfully worked with government officials to have domestic violence recognized as criminal behavior and to hold perpetrators accountable for it. By and large, criminal justice sanctions have taken root in the judicial system, and more batterers are being prosecuted.

Furthermore, journalists have begun to turn their attention to the issue in unprecedented numbers, culminating in the national "teach in" on domestic violence that resulted from massive coverage of O. J. Simpson's trial for the murder of his ex-wife and the revelation of his history of abusing her. During this time period, coverage of domestic violence graced the front pages, and lead stories appeared in every major media outlet in the country, from *People* magazine to *The New York Times,* from *The Oprah Winfrey Show* to CNN. Indeed, the 1990s proved a watershed decade for the issue of domestic violence, due in large measure to the quantity and character of media coverage the issue generated during this time.

During this time, historic gains were made in raising awareness about the prevalence and seriousness of domestic violence and in increasing people's understanding of their role in stopping it. At the same time, advocates today face a significant challenge: how to continue generating public dialogue on spousal abuse during a time when many journalists feel they have already "done" the issue of domestic violence and when gaining access to the public's attention is intensely competitive. Every issue seeking to gain widespread public recognition and support faces the same challenge: how to reach the general public to influence mass perceptions, attitudes, and behaviors related to that issue. Clearly, because of their massive reach, media outlets can play a key role in delivering high-impact messages about domestic violence, as well as other social and health issues affecting women. The question for advocates remains, how do we continue to ensure the kind of exposure to domestic violence prevention messages that is likely to influence social norms about the problem and, ultimately, actual rates of violence against women?

This chapter will discuss how effective messages can be developed for broad dissemination through public education campaigns to change attitudes and behaviors about domestic violence. It will also highlight some of the innovative ways that advocates around the country are using media to disseminate social norm-change messages related to abuse, including several national efforts run by the Family Violence Prevention Fund, as well as the valuable lessons that have emerged from such efforts over time. The chapter will also address some of the problems advocates face in seeking exposure for domestic violence prevention messages in an increasingly crowded media marketplace and make recommendations for potential strategies that could help generate the kind of media coverage necessary to change social norms permitting domestic violence to persist.

Developing Messages That Resonate

Consider the following fictional scenario:

> *Martin's friend Linda has become more and more withdrawn. Martin runs into Linda at the market, and she has a black eye. "It's nothing. I ran into a door," she tells him. Martin accepts her explanation. However, that afternoon, he sees a poster on a city bus about domestic violence. Alarmed, he writes down the number of a shelter and goes to see Linda, who tells him that yes, her husband beats her up. She admits that she'd been too ashamed to tell Martin earlier. Linda decides to seek help at a local domestic violence program, where a professional counselor is available to help her.*

This is a communications outcome advocates and educators are hoping for. Martin, like most Americans, probably knew something about domestic violence. However, the poster connected the issue to Linda's problem and prompted him to offer help. Ideally, public education campaigns promulgate messages people can use. Television and radio public service announcements (PSAs), posters, and flyers can be valuable tools for helping victims, getting people involved, and building a society that does not tolerate abuse. Given limited resources, advocates putting together such efforts must ask themselves how to choose which messages are right for their communities.

Historically, the public health community has placed tremendous importance on developing, testing, and promulgating discrete messages that resonate with the general public on various health issues. When reaching out to the public about different health risks, health educators have long struggled with what has been called "the disconnect between knowledge and behavior." Awareness of a health risk will not automatically lead to at-risk audiences taking protective action. Most people, for example, know smoking causes cancer and other adverse health consequences, yet many people still smoke. The majority of Americans understand that HIV is a sexually transmitted and fatal disease, but not all of those people who are at risk will protect themselves. Similarly, surveys reveal that most people consider domestic violence an important social issue, yet comparatively few have done something to help stop it. To promote awareness and action, health communicators must understand the complex social environment of the individuals whose behaviors they want to change. Communicators must define whom they are trying to reach, what the target audience already knows, and what they can do to help.

In thinking about how to put together a media campaign on domestic violence, advocates generate many message ideas. Each slogan and each image is based on an assumption about what needs to be communicated to turn awareness into action. Three models of behavior change provide advocates an opportunity to think critically about how they expect their messages to work and how knowledge can be turned into behavior that matters (Hornik, 1991). These conceptual frameworks, developed over the years by leading behavioral scientists, are outlined below.

Social Expectation: The Power of Public Opinion

In the first conceptual model, individual behavior is recognized as deeply influenced by the expectations of others. The theory of reasoned action posits that the decision to take a particular action step is determined by an individual's intention to perform that action, which is in turn influenced by the individual's belief about what social norms are related to that behavior (Ajzen & Fishbein, 1980; Fishbein & Ajzen, 1975). In other words, the decision to take action is deeply influenced by perceptions of normative behaviors. From this viewpoint, domestic violence continues because society has not clearly articulated strong social norms against it, and these norms must be made more powerful to compel people to get involved. By changing the norms around domestic violence, social expectation campaigns create the circumstances people need to act (although the campaigns do not necessarily tell people what to do).

A recent grassroots campaign in Dover, New Hampshire, used an innovative strategy to spread a social expectation message. The slogan, "Dover Does Not Tolerate Domestic Violence," was boldly printed on garbage bags sold by the community. Because municipal trash collectors were required to use these bags, every resident of Dover was exposed to a strong message against domestic violence.

Not far away, on Long Island, New York, a print campaign launched by Retreat, Inc., targeted boys and men for a social expectation message. The campaign, titled "Heroes Don't Hit," included a newspaper advertisement featuring the names of 100 local men who publicly condemned domestic violence. The banner read, "These residents all believe that if you're a man who abuses women you're a despicable coward. And you will be held accountable." This advertisement emphasized that men of the community agree that domestic violence is inexcusable. The advertisement supported social norms against engaging in abuse; it also provided social support for speaking out against it.

The audience for social expectation messages is broad, and the message itself is general. By itself, it should not be expected to change behavior directly. However, as part of a larger campaign, a simple supportive slogan lays the groundwork for action. If people know what to do but are holding back because they don't think intervening is socially acceptable, a social expectation message can encourage action. In an atmosphere saturated with social expectation messages, individuals will be more likely to turn knowledge into action by helping a victim, exposing a perpetrator, or speaking out to friends and neighbors.

Changing Behavior by Changing Beliefs

In the second conceptual framework, communicators consider what factors influence a person's decision about whether or not to take a particular action. These factors include beliefs about the risk, the consequences of taking (or not taking) a particular action to address that risk, and the perceived costs of taking such an action (Becker, 1974; Rosenstock, 1974). Many different opinions and beliefs affect different kinds of behavior; depending on the particular behavior being addressed, some are more influential than others and can be used to affect the decision to take action. Using this framework, communicators try to determine which beliefs most powerfully correlate with behavior, so that they can strengthen those that positively correlate to desired behavioral goals and weaken those beliefs that negatively correlate. By successfully changing the way people think, these messages might also change how they behave.

Imagine that the goal is to persuade people to reach out and speak to victims of spousal abuse. First, advocates might use knowledge and intuition, or interviews and focus groups, to explain why a person may or may not approach a friend she suspects is being abused. What considerations might inform her decision?

Does she understand the severity of the situation? Many health educators believe that preventative behavior will take place only if a health risk is considered severe. Even if a person can identify a domestic violence situation, she may not understand the potentially serious consequences of abuse. She may not think things are "bad enough" to step in.

Does she have reasons for taking action? If a person knows the serious consequences of domestic violence, she will probably have reasons to intervene. She may fear for her friend's safety, and for the physical and emotional health of her friend's children. She may worry that the abusive man could end up in deep trouble—possibly in jail—for his abusive behavior. She may feel a moral obligation to speak up.

Does she have reasons not *to take action?* On the other hand, even if she understands the seriousness of domestic violence and wants to intervene, a person might also have strong reasons for not speaking up. She might be afraid of em-

barrassing or angering her friend if her suspicions turn out to be false. She might think she doesn't know her friend well enough to butt in. She might think that her friend would be in greater danger if she tries to leave. She might fear for her own safety if the abusive man finds out about the conversation.

Does she know what to do? An important barrier to action is ignorance. If a person simply does not know what to do, then she probably will not take any action. Access to information about how to talk with a victim and how to help make a safety plan encourages safe intervention. People also need to know about local shelters and how to contact them so they can pass this information along to women in need. Health educators must grapple with ways to widely disseminate "how to" information and deal with the increased demand for services that may result.

How do communicators decide which of these sets of beliefs will most deeply influence the final decision about whether or not to take action? Public opinion polling and focus groups are good ways to examine which ways of thinking are associated with positive behavioral outcomes.

Many grassroots education campaigns focus on people's beliefs about domestic violence. For example, the Marin Abused Women's Services in Marin County, California, has produced a 23-minute video as a conversation-starter for community, school, and church meetings. Dramatic vignettes explore the pros and cons of intervention in different situations taking place in the community. When characters have misgivings about intervening, other characters emphasize important and persuasive reasons for taking action. In each vignette, the characters ultimately do the right thing by intervening to help battered women, thereby sending the message to viewers that no consideration is more powerful than the responsibility to help victims of abuse. By allowing viewers to examine the thought process people go through as they make the decision to intervene, the video provides topics for group discussion.

Building Confidence by Demonstrating the Tools of Change

Even if educators build a strong campaign to change beliefs, people might still be unwilling or unable to take action against domestic violence. Self-efficacy may be missing, a third conceptual framework, referring to the belief that one has the skills and ability to perform a particular action in a variety of circumstances (Bandura, 1986, 1992). Even if people understand that domestic violence is a terrible problem with devastating consequences, and even if they know what can be done to stop it, they may not feel that they themselves are capable of action. Overwhelmed by the enormity of the problem, or simply convinced they wouldn't know how to talk with an abused woman even though they know they should, people may just turn away. To avert this response, educators must offer messages that give people the concrete doable skills that allow them to act.

Health educators have found that one of the best ways to increase confidence to take action is through demonstration. Effective campaigns and messages against domestic violence can include modeling of recommended behaviors. Demonstration serves two purposes: First, it provides information on how to do something. Second, it increases the sense that "If the average person can do it, so can I." Interactive role-playing and dramatic video and theater interventions all draw on the notion of demonstration to build people's skills and confidence.

This kind of approach is being used successfully by some domestic violence programs in local public education initiatives. For example, in Sacramento, California, WEAVE (Women Escaping a Violent Environment) has developed a statewide campaign against domestic violence designed to facilitate intervention by increasing the self-efficacy of Californians to take action against it. Advertisements and action kits produced through the campaign promote such actions as talking with a victim about abuse. As the campaign's kick-off advertisement points out, "In ads like this over the next year, we'll *show* you what you can do, safely and effectively, to put a stop to domestic violence." By teaching people how to discuss the issue and telling them what to expect, the campaign aims to increase viewers' self-efficacy to intervene.

In thinking about how to develop the best messages for domestic violence-prevention campaigns, advocates know that these three conceptual approaches are not mutually exclusive. A message might use one dominant approach while including elements from others. The three approaches provide a framework for understanding how we expect our messages to work, and not a formula for execution. Analyzing and understanding the expectations behind campaign ideas will improve the focus of domestic violence-prevention campaigns and keep messages consistent and behavior-focused.

Clarifying the conceptual basis for campaign messages also facilitates the process of pretesting messages, an important phase in the development of public education campaigns. Using survey and focus groups to test ideas will help create messages that are effective with the community. This process of testing is called formative research. Eye-catching, thought-provoking advertisements can be daring, creative, and intuitive, but formative research ensures that the concepts and messages of the campaign remain realistic, culturally sensitive, and effective. Such research ultimately helps us determine whether the messages we have decided to use in our public education initiatives persuasively compel people to do something about domestic violence—such as seeking help at a shelter, speaking with a friend who is being battered, or putting up a poster at the office.

Public education can help bring a taboo subject into the light and make what was once considered a private, family problem an issue of community concern and public responsibility. Social attitudes do change, and the impact can be life-saving. Friends once let their friends drive drunk, never thinking to intervene, and now designated drivers are commonplace and socially reinforced. In the same fashion, public education campaigns against domestic violence, using effective messages, can create a society in which victims of domestic violence find support everywhere they turn—at work, at church, from their neighbors and friends.

However, messages, no matter how effective, can only make such a broad impact when they are broadly promulgated. Ingrained public attitudes and behavior about abuse will change only when people receive repeated exposure to messages supporting that behavior change. We turn our attention to this subject in more detail later in this chapter.

Constructing a National Effort: *There's No Excuse for Domestic Violence*

One of the greatest challenges facing the domestic violence movement in the United States today is the widespread perception that domestic violence is a private matter. In a country that values individualism, where privacy is valued as sacred and is protected by the Constitution, domestic violence is often perceived as private business between two individuals that requires therapy rather than political action and intervention.

In the early 1990s, the Family Violence Prevention Fund (FVPF), a national organization based in San Francisco, California, began to explore ways to shift the paradigm toward recognition of domestic violence as a public problem, combining media and community-based activism into an overall approach. During this time, the FVPF began convening and talking with a diverse group of long-time leaders in the domestic violence and allied social justice movements about how to galvanize broad-based support for change. Overwhelmingly, these activists had the same vision of the movement's next important step: to have a public conversation about domestic violence through the media, which engaged ordinary individuals in efforts to end abuse.

"After years of hard work to reform the criminal justice response to abuse and ensure services for victims, we had a new imperative: to engage the general public on the issue of domestic violence through a large-scale media campaign," said FVPF Executive Director Esta Soler (Marin, Zia, & Soler, 1998, p. 61). "To this day, this strategy holds enormous, untapped potential for the movement," she continued. "Media campaigns and grassroots organizing can have a profound impact over time on target issues and communities—particularly when they are effective in generating outrage about a problem and concrete ways to address it."

In 1994, the FVPF launched the first national domestic violence-prevention campaign, called *There's No Excuse for Domestic Violence*. Several years in development, the effort seeks to galvanize popular support for anti-domestic-violence activities and build a broad constituency for change. Prior to *There's No Excuse*, domestic violence programs had waged dozens of local public education initiatives designed to let victims know where they could find help in the community, as well as to alert the larger community to the severity of the problem. However, no national effort had been mounted to challenge the pervasive social norms that allow the problem to persist. *There's No Excuse* was designed to address that gap.

Unlike previous efforts, *There's No Excuse* targets not the victim or perpetrator of abuse but rather the friends, family, and coworkers who sanction the violence with their silence. The campaign focuses national attention on community responsibility for stopping domestic violence and is designed to make every American feel that they have not only the responsibility to help stop domestic violence but also social permission to intervene. The campaign includes PSAs and educational materials that trumpet the campaign's key messages that "Domestic violence is ev-erybody's business" and "There's no excuse for it." The campaign made a significant leap in addressing domestic violence not from a victim-assistance perspective but from a true preventive approach, working to change the social norms that foster an environment in which abuse can exist in the first place. In this sense, the campaign drew heavily on social expectation themes, seeking to convey that Americans not only have the right to get involved, but that society *expects* them to do so.

These themes led to the creation of hard-hitting advertising meant to compel intervention on behalf of victims of abuse. In one powerful 60-second television PSA called "Neighbors," viewers see a couple in their bed listening to the sounds of a man brutally beating a woman in the apartment above them. The couple exchange anxious looks, but when the husband reaches over to the night table, instead of picking up the phone to call the police, he turns off the light. The screen fades to black and viewers read: "It is your business." A companion *There's No Excuse* print advertisement addresses social expectations for action, as well: Over an image of a man beating a woman, the tagline reads, "If the noise coming from next door were loud music, you'd do something about it."

The campaign draws much of its strength from the power of public opinion. Recognizing the power of the media in reaching large audiences, the FVPF initiated research in collaboration with The Advertising Council, the Ford Foundation, and others in the early 1990s. Focus groups and polling conducted nationwide in the formative research phase of the *There's No Excuse* campaign revealed that despite public recognition of domestic violence as a serious problem, few Americans had actually taken action against it, especially compared to other issues (Klein, Campbell, Soler, & Ghez, 1997). Research conducted for the FVPF in 1994 showed that whereas 18% of respondents reported having taken some action against domestic violence in the previous year, 56% had helped save the environment, and 43% had helped children living in poverty during the same time period (Klein et al., 1997). The same study revealed the shocking fact that although 29% of respondents said they knew a woman who was being battered, only 9% had actually talked with an abused woman. These surveys found a frightening divide between knowledge and action: Two out of three of Americans who said they knew a victim of domestic violence nevertheless had failed to even talk with her about the abuse.

To close the gap between knowledge and action and encourage friends and family members of abuse victims to reach out and help, the FVPF created print advertisements designed to emphasize the reasons it is important to talk with victims of abuse. At the same time, the advertisements argue persuasively against the beliefs that might present barriers to taking such an action. Over an image of a bruised woman, the headline reads, "While you're trying to find the right words, your friend may be trying to stay alive." The text of the advertisement stresses the severity of the danger (she could be killed), while also giving important reasons why action is necessary (you have a responsibility to your friend; we all have a responsibility to take action against domestic violence), dismissing the barrier (the feeling of "not knowing what to say" can be overcome), and providing concrete suggestions for what to do (speak to your friend, no matter what).

Polling data collected by the FVPF also indicated that a fairly complex web of factors stops people from getting involved in this issue. Not only did the campaign need to create social permission for action and a set of beliefs compelling enough to encourage intervention, but the campaign also had to create self-efficacy for these interventions, the sense that the average person had the skills to make a difference. Early on, the campaign team learned that they had to address two major reasons people give for not taking action against domestic violence: First, more than half (55%) of the people surveyed said they didn't know what to do to reduce domestic violence in their communities. Second, the majority (84%) said they would fear for their personal safety if they tried to intervene in a specific domestic violence situation (Klein et al., 1997). From a communications point of view, the challenge was clear: The campaign needed to create and promulgate simple, safe, and doable interventions that would encourage people to take action.

As a result, the FVPF created a toll-free number that interested individuals could call for information on how they can help stop domestic violence in their communities. This number (1-800-END-ABUSE) is publicized on each PSA that is part of *There's No Excuse* and on all companion educational materials. Callers to this number receive a Take Action! kit, which outlines safe, simple, and effective ways of reaching out to victims—for example, by putting victim-safety cards in restrooms, where they can be taken anonymously. The materials walk readers step-by-step through how to have a conversation with a friend suspected of being abused, including tips on what to do if she denies the problem. More recently, the FVPF has developed organizing tools for individuals who want to get more involved, including the Neighbor to Neighbor, Worker to Worker, and Person to Person Domestic Violence Action Kits. These materials give people the tools and resources they need to make it easy to reach out and take group action. The kits combine educational materials to raise awareness with easy-to-use tools that enable people to speak out and carry the message that domestic violence is wrong, it is not a private matter, and it is never acceptable.

Since its launch, *There's No Excuse* has generated more than $100 million of donated time and space in media markets across the country for domestic violence prevention PSAs. Due in large measure to the interest in the issue generated in the 1990s, *There's No Excuse* print, radio, and television PSAs have appeared in national news magazines, on prime time television, in national and local newspapers, and on radio stations nationwide. In local communities across the country, domestic violence advocates use the PSAs to publicize local resources by adding local hot-line numbers and lobbying for local airplay. As a result of this environment, during the first 4 months of the campaign, the campaign's television spots were aired 14,000 times, compared to the monthly average of 1,100 for The Advertising Council's other campaigns (Klein et al., 1997).

Evidence collected as part of the campaign evaluation indicates that during the period of heavy exposure, these messages had a positive effect on consumer attitudes and behavior on the issue of domestic violence. Research conducted for the FVPF found that in the media markets with heaviest exposure to campaign messages, people were more likely than those in other markets to recall the PSAs and report increased action against domestic violence. In addition, they were more likely than others to perceive domestic violence as an important social issue and to believe that perpetrators should be arrested and incarcerated. In these exposed markets, the percentage of people who said they had recently taken action against domestic violence increased by 12 percentage points to 26% between July 1994 and November 1995 (Klein et al., 1997).

Culturally Specific Approaches: *It's Your Business*

The second phase of *There's No Excuse for Domestic Violence* was an investigation into culturally specific approaches to prevention. After the initial launch of *There's No Excuse,* focus groups were held in several cities, which indicated that a culturally specific initiative might be more effective than a general campaign in reaching the African American community. Building on the campaign's earlier successes, the new initiative sought to determine how to package information in ways that resonate even more within the African American community. With assistance from The Advertising Council, a talented team of freelance writers with experience in writing dramatic material for African American audiences was recruited for script writing. UniWorld Group, Inc., the nation's largest African American-owned and -oriented advertising agency, would produce the spots. Thus *It's Your Business* was born.

Early on—in an effort to create original material that might excite radio stations—the FVPF decided to abandon traditional PSA formats in favor of a social drama that used an entertainment-education approach to reaching audiences. This approach has been extensively used, with much success, outside the United States, in such formats as soap operas to deliver important health messages (Advocates for Youth, 1998; Maibach & Holtgrave, 1995; Montgomery, 1990; Nariman, 1993). The *It's Your Business* campaign sought to use such a format, in the form of a dramatic radio serial, to deliver domestic violence-prevention messages to the African American community, believing that such a format would capture audience interest and generate involvement with the characters' problems. The campaign team believed that this kind of audience involvement would be key to the impact of the campaign (Bandura, 1986; Hoffner, 1996; Rubin & Perse, 1988).

Launched by the FVPF in 1999, after 3 years of research and development, *It's Your Business* is a 12-part radio microdrama in 90-second episodes that uses a soap opera-like format. Its culturally specific messages are centered around a fictional domestic violence trial, as reported and discussed on a popular African American radio call-in show hosted by Ma B. With pointed commentary and dare-to-air tactics, Ma B makes no topic taboo and speaks out on the sensitive issue of domestic violence against African American women. Each *It's Your Business* episode is self-contained, but as a whole, the series develops the story of the characters Charlise and James, fictional listeners of Ma B's show. As the episodes progress, Charlise acknowledges and escapes from James's violence, and the cou-

ple's friends and family help ensure her safety and let James know in no uncertain terms that "20 eyes are watching" him and "20 feet will come" to protect Charlise and her children.

"This is Ma B Lady Queen Sistah Friend," one episode begins. Ma B continues,

> News flash! Local business wonder, Damon DeCur, was arraigned on near-fatal assault of live-in girlfriend, Denise Champion. After a party, a neighbor saw girlfriend fly though the glass patio door. DeCur says Denise ran through; the neighbor thinks she was thrown. People, I lived it, almost died it, got out, and survived it! Better to air the dirty laundry in public than lose your sister-friend-mother-child. Gotta talk about it! Stop domestic violence! It *is* your business!

Formative research commissioned by the FVPF and conducted by the Annenberg School for Communication at the University of Pennsylvania showed that many African Americans were quite supportive of speaking with other people about domestic violence (Nabi & Mehan, 1998). However, about half the sample reported that they did not like talking with others about their personal lives and that it would be easier to talk with a woman than a man about domestic violence. Furthermore, the research showed that whereas many people who know victims of abuse talk with them about the violence, some do so in ways that could be construed as judgmental. For example, one out of every three said they would tell victims of abuse to "stop doing whatever is making him so angry." Therefore, the program sought to portray characters modeling two kinds of behaviors—speaking out about the problem and speaking compassionately with victims—in the hopes that listeners might perceive their own ability to take similar action.

More than a media outreach campaign, *It's Your Business* was designed to spur grassroots activity to end domestic violence in the African American community. The FVPF worked with advocates to help them use the campaign as an organizing tool locally. Each radio episode concluded with a toll-free number listeners could call for a free *It's Your Business* Community Action Kit. This kit provided callers with background information on the issue, tips on how to talk with someone who is abused and how to raise awareness in the community, and special advice for men who want to reach out and help.

In April 1999, the FVPF distributed the *It's Your Business* campaign to dozens of African American-oriented stations nationwide, with assistance from American Urban Radio Networks, and mounted an intensive lobbying campaign to encourage station managers to play the series. Stations were asked to air the 12-part series over the course of 12 weeks, rotating each new episode several times before unveiling a new episode every week, to allow listeners to follow the story and understand the messages as they evolved over time.

The innovative campaign, the first of its kind, was well received by listeners who heard the series. However, the campaign team experienced tremendous obstacles in trying to convince radio stations to air the program in the serial way it was intended. In the end, despite the fact that the spots were entertaining, lively, and professionally produced, the *It's Your Business* campaign was not able to convince gatekeepers at radio stations to play the program as conceived, even in those markets where commitments had been made by stations in advance. As a result, an independent evaluation conducted by the Annenberg School for Communication at the University of Pennsylvania revealed that few people were even exposed to the series (Hornik et al., 1999).

The simplest and most likely explanation is a financial one—the "ask" was too big and stations could not afford to give so much time to PSAs when they must give priority to paying customers. The time commitment required—12 episodes of a 90-second PSA, which is longer than a standard PSA, to be aired 12 times repeatedly and in sequence—was more than most stations were able to give. Yet, *It's Your Business* was conceived in a serial manner in an attempt to generate the kind and quantity of media exposure that might actually change social norms on abuse among listeners, in a way that an isolated 30-second PSA cannot hope to do. In the end, the media advocacy campaign had an Achilles heel: reliance on donated time. For this reason, the project shed important light on some of the challenges of exposure that a media campaign must confront, challenges that many public interest campaigns currently face. This will be discussed in more detail later in this chapter.

Getting the Message Out: Grassroots Organizing

Getting the message out doesn't just mean airing PSAs. Exposure to a behavior change can and should occur on the grassroots level, as well. In the best examples of grassroots organizing, activities are created on the ground that attract and generate the kind of media coverage that can reach large numbers of people and create attitudinal and institutional change. Innovative efforts that combine grassroots organizing and media are popping up nationwide:

■ In San Francisco, spontaneous grassroots organizing in the Bay Area Filipino community followed the vicious and near-fatal attack on Irma Chingcuangco and her parents by her ex-husband, in full view of their 8-year-old son. The controversy began when some members of the community reacted with sympathy for the batterer, soliciting donations for his bail. In response, activists organized community leaders, students, and others to speak out at meetings and other forums to educate the community about the seriousness of domestic violence. The group formed a speaker's bureau, generated media coverage about the case, and ultimately put a stop to the money collection that might otherwise have freed Irma's attacker.

■ In Texas, an innovative judge is sentencing batterers to "shame sentences," ordering one abusive husband to publicly apologize to his wife on the steps of City Hall and another to go to a shopping mall carrying a sign that read, "I went to jail for assaulting my wife. This could be you." Both activities generated media coverage far beyond Texas borders.

■ In Alabama, advocates created the first Governor's Challenge on Domestic Violence, an event at the state capitol where the governor signed a proclamation urging that every state vehicle should have a "There's No Excuse for Domestic Violence" bumper sticker put on it—and challenging other states to do the same. The event was widely covered throughout the state, and the publicity reached Florida, which was the first state to meet the challenge.

Grassroots public education campaigns are a critical supplement to PSAs and messages in the media. The end result could be a situation like this: A woman sees an anti-domestic violence PSA, which reminds her of an article about the problem she just read in her local newspaper. It spurs her to ask her friend, who she thinks may be in a violent relationship, if she is being abused. The friend, who indeed is being beaten, has just seen a bumper sticker against domestic violence on her way to work and a stack of victim safety cards in her workplace restroom. That victim is more likely to reach out and ask for help in escaping a violent situation, instead of feeling isolated, overwhelmed and alone. It is the combination of these tactics, creating multiple exposures to domestic violence messages, that creates an environment of support for victims and zero tolerance for abuse.

The Million Dollar Question: How to Get Past the Gatekeeper

If a PSA airs on television and nobody sees it, did it really air at all? This is a new twist on an old saying, but a relevant question to ask in today's increasingly competitive media markets. The domestic violence movement has placed a tremendous amount of collective attention on developing messages that will "move" people to care about the problem and take action against it. However, less collective energy has been placed on an area of equal or even greater challenge—that is, how we can ensure mass exposure to our messages. This is by no means a simple question for any public interest movement (Hornik, 1997; Hornik & Woolf, 1998), and it is a particular challenge for the domestic violence community, during a time when many journalists feel they have already covered the issue extensively.

At the same time the *There's No Excuse* campaign was launched, events in the news were occurring that increased exposure of the issue—and the campaign—dramatically. American football legend O. J. Simpson was on trial for the murder of his ex-wife, Nicole Brown Simpson, and her friend Ron Goldman, after a documented history of abusing her. Although he was eventually acquitted, the case generated massive media attention on the issue of abuse.

Because the launch of the campaign coincided with a period of heightened national interest in the issue, *There's No Excuse* PSAs were aired during this period 300% more frequently than typical Advertising Council campaigns (Klein et al., 1997). During fall 1999, immediately after the arrest of Simpson and the coincidental launch of the *There's No Excuse* campaign, events in the news led to increased interest on the part of public service directors in airing domestic violence PSAs. That fall, the campaign generated $38 million in donated time, compared to a mere $9 million generated by the campaign in all of 1995. Donated time spiked again in 1996, to more than $31 million, at the same time that the civil trial of Simpson was capturing the nation's atten-

tion. Airtime dropped again in 1997 to $12 million, and again in 1998, to just over $9 million.

Despite the impressive cumulative dollar amounts donated to *There's No Excuse* in the years when the trials were in the news, even then (at the zenith of popularity for domestic violence PSAs), *There's No Excuse* PSAs were largely aired during "graveyard shifts" with low viewer rating points. According to an Advertising Council analysis of donated time on television network and cable stations between 1994 and 1999, the significant majority of *There's No Excuse* PSAs ran during the lowest rated part of the day (called a *daypart*)—late night (1:00-6:59 a.m.)—every single year since the campaign's inception (The Advertising Council, 2000). During this time period, between 65% and 70% of all *There's No Excuse* television spots ran during this daypart. Conversely, the lowest percentage of *There's No Excuse* spots (between 0% and 10% across all years) ran in the highest rated daypart, prime time (8:00-10:59 p.m.).

It is instructive to examine even more closely the time period when O. J. Simpson's arrest hit the news, generating massive coverage of the issue of domestic violence, beginning in June 1994 and lasting through that fall. The Advertising Council's analysis of this time period reveals that even between August and October 1994, the vast majority of *There's No Excuse* spots were placed during the late night daypart on both network and cable television (69% on the networks and 67% on cable). On the other hand—and perhaps most telling of all—the spots were least likely to air during prime time (3% on the networks and 0% on cable), even during this time period.

Historically, PSAs have tended to be aired during these time slots, which broadcasters have difficulty selling because of the limited audience share they deliver. The experience of the *There's No Excuse* campaign is no exception to the rule; it is simply a striking example of the odds advocates face trying to gain exposure for their issues, even when there is a major event related to that issue shaping the news cycle. Yet, from the media gatekeepers' perspective, the decision to relegate such spots to "remnant space" simply makes good business sense. Media outlets today face fierce competition as the number of ways to reach similar audience shares multiplies exponentially, particularly in print and cable media. In this environment, when gatekeepers must decide between supporting important causes and supporting their own bottom line, they will invariably choose the side of the paying customer. A full-page advertisement in *The New York Times* can cost upward of $50,000; an advertisement on NBC's highly rated *ER* can cost as much as $1 million. Competing with such lucrative paying customers, even the most well-crafted PSAs will inevitably air in the dark of night, in time slots with very low audience shares.

For this reason, domestic violence advocates are reliant on the goodwill of media gatekeepers to get their message out, and they often end up reaching limited numbers of people because of the times available for donated advertising. The similar experiences of leaders in related public interest areas who also work with media reveal that the challenge of generating exposure for our issues is a daunting one. Lessons from interactions with media gatekeepers tell us that organizations without the financial means to purchase

advertising space cannot possibly compete against corporations with seemingly limitless advertising budgets, such as Coca Cola or Nike. In such an environment, how can a public education campaign on domestic violence or any other public interest issue successfully strive to get adequate media exposure to be able to hope for an impact?

Similarly daunting challenges operate on the news side of the media business. During the period when Simpson's trials were taking place, Americans were exposed to anti-domestic-violence messages through news media as well as through PSAs. In June and July 1994, 54 network news stories and 454 print stories referred to domestic violence, as compared to just two network news stories and 206 print article references in the 2 months before the killings. Non-news media outlets saturated readers with messages, as well. *People* magazine ran a cover story in February 1995 called "Why Nobody Helped Nicole: Friends, family, and police saw her bruises but failed to stop O.J.'s abuse. What went wrong?" The November issue of *Self* magazine ran an article called "60 Ways to Stop Domestic Violence," and *Men's Fitness,* in October 1994, included a special report called "Is Someone You Know a Batterer? Domestic abuse is every man's problem. Here's how to spot it and stop it" (Klein et al., 1997). Coverage of the issue reached historic highs.

This context greatly shapes the environment in which domestic violence advocates do their work today. Although journalists remain interested in and committed to covering the issue of spousal abuse, they have turned their collective attention to other pressing social issues that have emerged due to events in the news. In recent times, these issues have included such worthy topics as violence in schools, the environmental impact of world trade, and evolving efforts to reform the health care system. The reality of a limited (and even, some say, shrinking) "news hole" is that, however worthy they are, public interest issues such as domestic violence prevention cannot expect to be in the limelight without a companion large-scale news event to make them relevant to media gatekeepers and the public alike.

How, then, can advocates hope to keep the issue of domestic violence prevention front and center in the public consciousness so that social norms on this issue will continue to evolve? *That's* the million dollar question.

Recommendations for the Future

What does all this teach us? We know that gatekeepers will air PSAs most often when they coincide with natural news events, over which campaign planners have little or no control—and that even then, these messages are often relegated to remnant, undesirable space. Therefore, relying on PSAs and media gatekeepers is not enough to guarantee public exposure to a message. Public attitudes toward abuse and social norms that tolerate and excuse domestic violence *can* change. But only if we can find ways to break through media gatekeepers and expose mass audiences to our messages.

Following are some recommendations for innovative ways to work with or bypass media gatekeepers, deliver exposure of large numbers of people to domestic violence prevention messages regardless of events in the news that support or dis-

tract attention from this issue, and compete with paying customers vying for the public's attention.

Work With Them, Not Against Them: Involve Corporate America and Benefit From Their Advertising Budgets

Many of our corporate citizens have enormous advertising budgets. Both small and large corporations literally spend millions of dollars putting together and executing media plans that are intended to attract potential consumers to their products. Often, these projects are executed by advertising agencies that create commercials for the companies or by media buyers who are employed in-house or contracted with externally to do so. The individual media buyers who execute multimillion-dollar media plans for corporations develop close relationships with the sales representatives for different media outlets, who are vying for advertising revenue for their media outlets.

For example, we can safely assume that The Coca Cola Company annually allocates a specific dollar amount that will be spent on Coca Cola advertising. The company's marketing department would, then, instruct its advertising agency to create compelling commercials for the product, which are then placed in various media by media buyers. These buyers develop close relationships with sales representatives for different media outlets, who are vying for prime-time advertising revenue that might otherwise go to their competitors.

The media buyers start by developing a media plan for which media outlets should be targeted with these advertisements and at what amount. The company's media buyers then begin the dance of negotiating with different media outlets about how much money will be paid for airing the advertisements. If an agreement can be reached, the media outlet is put on the company's media plan, which means that the advertisements will be run on that media outlet at the agreed-upon rate. In today's competitive market, all but the most elite media outlets are in the position of having to bargain with the company's media buyers as they compete for the business, usually lowering their asking price for advertisements in the process. Creative deals are cut routinely by media outlets in their quest to "get on the plan;" for example, many media outlets will give companies frequency discounts that allow companies to get more exposure for less money.

This competitive environment represents a tremendous opportunity for public interest advocates in general, and for domestic violence advocates in particular. In the past, both local and national domestic violence organizations have forged relationships with corporate America to achieve mutual benefits. For example, advocates have received financial contributions that help keep their operations afloat, and corporate leaders have received tax deductions for responding to the problem, as well as counsel on how to help victims of abuse at the workplace. Few groups, however, are working directly with corporate advertising departments to take advantage of bargaining that could take place when corporate media buys are executed.

Instead of approaching companies and asking simply for a donation to fund a domestic violence program or project, advocates could encourage their corporate partners to instruct whoever is buying their advertising time to leverage time for domestic violence PSAs when they do their media buys. Media buyers acting on behalf of their corporate clients could negotiate not just for better rates, but for a different deal structure that gives visibility to domestic-violence-prevention messages. For example, media buyers could go to the sales representatives at a particular media outlet (i.e., *People* magazine) and demand that if significant purchases are made, then the outlet must also donate airtime to domestic violence PSAs as part of the deal and place those PSAs prominently. To maintain ties with paying corporations, media outlets are likely to agree.

Preliminary conversations with sales representatives of some media outlets indicate that this is potentially an extremely effective way of garnering wide exposure for domestic-violence-prevention messages, and that sales representatives are likely to cut such deals to win the account and the revenue it brings. If advocates are working with a company that has, for example, a $100 million media plan, and negotiators could arrange a 4:1 ratio of purchased-to-donated time, then the efforts of one company alone could yield $25 million in free airtime for domestic-violence-prevention messages.

Such efforts don't have to take place only on the national level with multimillion-dollar companies; local agencies could lobby local businesses to negotiate time on area stations when they do their media buys, on a smaller scale. This strategy creates a win-win situation: Domestic violence groups gain exposure for their messages and corporations don't lose a penny. In fact, they can publicize their efforts as a social marketing program of their company, which may in fact attract new customers (particularly for corporations whose target audience is largely female). Companies might even be able to convince gatekeepers to allow them to include a corporate logo on the domestic violence PSA, so that in fact their exposure would be increased through the program and tied publicly to a good cause.

The FVPF has evidence that such a strategy might be extremely effective in garnering exposure for domestic-violence-prevention messages. In 1999, the FVPF received substantial funding to buy airtime throughout California for anti-domestic violence television and radio spots. The California Department of Health Services provided $210,000 to purchase time for the *It's Your Business* radio serial, in addition to $500,000 to place locally produced broadcast-quality television PSAs. To do the job, the FVPF contracted with two advertising agencies that annually execute millions of dollars of media buys in California, one for the radio campaign and one for the television campaign.

Because of their relationships with sales representatives at California's major media outlets, media buyers at the advertising agencies were able to leverage the funds to yield even greater airtime. In both cases, the sales representatives were happy to cut such deals to keep good relations with companies that bring them big corporate business. In the radio buy, media buyers were able to negotiate a 3:1 ratio of purchased-to-donated advertising time in three California markets with heavy African American concentrations. In the television buy, media buyers were able to negotiate a 2:1 ratio.

Clearly, there is tremendous potential to expand this type of approach by reconceptualizing the way that domestic vio-

lence programs can partner with their corporate neighbors.

Making Friends: Advertising Agencies Can Be Powerful Allies

Corporations are not the only ones with the power to instruct media buyers to cut deals that might benefit domestic violence groups. Advertising agencies also have tremendous power and should be cultivated as important allies in efforts to stop domestic violence. Most media buyers are employed by advertising agencies, not by corporations. That means that their "marching orders" can come either from the corporation whose advertising they are placing or from the head of the advertising agency. Too often, advertising agencies create public interest PSAs pro bono and then consider their contribution complete, when, in fact, they could play a significant and important role getting the spots on the air.

Advertising agencies generally have a portfolio of clients that they work with at any one time, some of whom may be associated with causes and some of whom may not. Advertising agencies develop close relationships over time with their clients (particularly on the marketing side). The agencies could play a tremendous role by taking the domestic violence PSAs they have created to their corporate clients and asking whether or not the client would agree to allow their media buyers to negotiate deals benefitting these PSAs when corporate media buys are made. Even companies that are not officially linked to the issue of domestic violence may be persuaded to allow the media buyers acting on their behalf to negotiate placements for the domestic violence PSAs because the advertising agency feels so strongly about the issue. It would be well worth the effort for domestic violence advocates to encourage the advertising agencies they work with to begin thinking about how their media buyers can help—and how the clients they work with can use their advertising budgets to leverage time for these spots.

Recently, a large advertising agency purchased a significant amount of prime-time television space for one of their corporate clients; however, when the time came, the new advertisements the company expected to be able to use during this time were not ready. The ad agency was able to convince the company to donate the purchased airtime to public interest issues (among them, domestic violence prevention), and as a result *There's No Excuse* PSAs were aired during prime time on such channels as CNN, reaching millions. Advocates can encourage the advertising agencies they work with to do the same, should such situations occur in local markets, as they often do.

You Get What You Pay For: Generating Revenue for Purchased Time

If the public service community cannot continue to generate exposure for its messages in a media advocacy (that is, donated) context, then one obvious alternative is to seek a source of revenue for actually purchasing time. This strategy would free the domestic violence community from a heavy reliance on the goodwill of public service directors.

In California, the State Department of Health Services is running a multifaceted tobacco-control campaign that is widely trumpeted as one of the public health community's best success stories, in large part because the advertisements that are at its heart have been purchased on prime-time media outlets throughout the state. Television advertisements and billboards discouraging smoking are seemingly everywhere, and evaluations have shown that these advertisements have demonstrably reduced rates of smoking in California: Since the campaign began, rates of smoking declined from 26% in 1987 to 21% in 1990 (Kizer & Honig, 1990). The initiative was financed through a tax placed on cigarettes, and the millions of dollars this tax generated helped finance prime-time placement of antitobacco messages.

Such a model could be applied to the domestic violence movement by creating a funding stream that would allow states to develop provocative advertising campaigns that ensure the visibility of the issue, regardless of events in the news. The question that remains, of course, is what to tax to generate sufficient revenue for such a project. Fees are already levied on marriage licenses in every state, and these provide critical funding to local shelters. Other creative alternatives should be explored.

Fiction Tells a Powerful Story: Working With Hollywood

Recently, an online magazine called *Salon* broke a story that was subsequently reported in *The Washington Post,* the *Los Angeles Times,* and other publications about a program developed by the White House's Office of National Drug Control Policy in an effort to generate exposure for antidrug messages. Recognizing the limitations of a pro bono environment, in 1997, Congress allocated an unprecedented $1 billion to advertising and outreach programming aimed at discouraging youth from taking drugs and encouraging drug-using teens to quit. As part of the arrangement, the government added a clever stipulation that requires a "media match" from media outlets on which airtime is purchased for PSAs related to drugs and other issues affecting children today. Television stations wanting to avoid the match requirement were allowed by the White House to get credits if they included antidrug themes in primetime programming instead.

Although the deal raised some eyebrows, sparking concern over the issue of government censorship of television content, the idea of financial incentives for positive programming is a good one. The White House correctly realized that the exposure value of an entire plot or subplot on a highly rated television show far exceeds that of a PSA aired during a commercial break. Furthermore, this arrangement has the additional advantage of allowing viewers to see appropriate behaviors being modeled by popular characters with whom they might identify. The approach is an interesting one and reflects that the government is at least recognizing the importance of issues of exposure and experimenting with innovative solutions.

Whether or not the domestic violence community has the political power to convince the White House to create a similar program on issues related to domestic violence (or on the broader issue of violence prevention), there is clearly room for advocates to work directly with producers and scriptwriters in Hollywood. Should such outreach result in domestic-violence-prevention messages being interwoven more frequently in highly rated programs, the reach of such messages would be enormous. At a minimum, such programs would lead to peer dialogue about the shows and how they dealt with the problem; perhaps, they would even prompt viewers to model positive interventions in their own lives.

Conclusion

Domestic violence exists for a myriad of complex reasons. One factor, however, significantly contributes to the perpetuation of domestic violence, enabling men to continue beating and killing their partners and stigmatizing women who are desperately seeking to escape and rebuild their lives. That factor is society's tacit acceptance of abuse. Public education campaigns, particularly those using media, can play a critical role in creating a cultural shift on abuse. Whereas much time has been spent thinking about what messages can effectively change behavior related to domestic violence, less time has gone into crafting effective strategies for bringing those messages to mass audiences and ensuring that exposure happens repeatedly over time. But based on lessons learned by advocates across the country, we know that there are emerging strategies that can leverage opportunities the media present to reach vast numbers of people with carefully crafted messages.

During the past 20 years, it has largely been domestic violence advocates who have worried about how to galvanize the general public with such messages. Today, as the domestic-violence-prevention movement matures and broadens, it is time for others to get involved and to partner with advocates in collective efforts to reach broad segments of society with social norm-change messages. As demonstrated in this chapter, advertising agencies, corporate giants, journalists, and government innovators alike each have powerful roles to play, and can make a lasting difference by using their institutional relationships and vehicles to disseminate strong anti-domestic-violence messages. Indeed, there is a role for each of us.

The time is right for such efforts. Each time someone laughs at a joke about abuse, each time a newspaper explains a domestic homicide as a "lover's quarrel," each time a friend accepts the explanation that bruises were caused by walking into a door, each time we as a society do not intervene and proclaim that abuse is never acceptable, never excusable—domestic violence will continue to thrive unabated. If attitudes about abuse shift to that of zero tolerance for abusers and community-wide support for victims, then the social norms that today condone abuse can work tomorrow, instead, to eliminate it.

References

The Advertising Council. (2000). *Media support for domestic violence campaign 1994-1999*. New York: Author.

Advocates for Youth. (1998). *The use of mainstream media to encourage social responsibility: The international experience*. Menlo Park, CA: Kaiser Family Foundation.

Ajzen, I., & Fishbein, M. (1980). *Understanding attitudes and predicting social behavior*. Englewood Cliffs, NJ: Prentice Hall.

Bandura, A. J. (1986). *Social foundations of thought and action: A social cognitive theory*. Englewood Cliffs, NJ: Prentice Hall.

Bandura, A. J. (1992). Exercise of personal agency through the self-efficacy mechanism. In R. Schwarzer (Ed.), *Self-efficacy: Thought control of action* (pp. 3-38). Washington, DC: Hemisphere.

Becker, M. H. (1974). The health belief model and personal health behavior. *Health Education Monographs, 2,* 324-508.

Fishbein, M., & Ajzen, I. (1975). *Belief, attitude, intention, and behavior: An introduction to theory and research*. Reading, MA: Addison-Wesley.

Hoffner, C. (1996). Children's wishful identification and parasocial interaction with favorite television characters. *Journal of Broadcasting and Electronic Media, 40,* 389-402.

Hornik, R. (1991). Alternative models of behavior change. In J. N. Wasserheit, S. O. Aral, & K. K. Holmes (Eds.), *Research issues in human behavior and sexually transmitted diseases in the AIDS area* (pp. 201-218). Washington, DC: American Society for Microbiology.

Hornik, R. (1997, June 5-6). *Health communication: Making sense of contradictory evidence*. Paper presented at the Annenberg Public Policy Center Public Health Communication Meeting, Philadelphia.

Hornik, R., Gandy, O., Wray, R., Stryker, J., Ghez, M., & Mitchell-Clark, K. (1999). *Preventing domestic violence in the African American community: The impact of a dramatic radio serial*. Paper submitted by the Annenberg School for Communication at the University of Pennsylvania to the Health Communications Division of the 50th International Communication Association Annual Conference, Philadelphia (May 2000).

Hornik, R., & Woolf, K. (1998, April 23). *Complementing message theory with exposure theory: Is it worth it?* Paper presented at the Kentucky Health Communication Conference, Lexington, KY.

Kizer, K., & Honig, B. (1990). *Toward a tobacco-free California: A status report to the California Legislature on the first 15 months of California's tobacco control program*. Sacramento, CA: Department of Health Services.

Klein, E., Campbell, J., Soler, E., & Ghez, M. (1997). *Ending domestic violence: Changing public perceptions/halting the epidemic*. Thousand Oaks, CA: Sage.

Maibach, E., & Holtgrave, D. R. (1995). Advances in public health communication. *Annual Review of Public Health, 16,* 219-238.

Marin, L., Zia, H., & Soler, E. (1998). *Ending domestic violence: Report from the global frontlines*. San Francisco: Family Violence Prevention Fund.

Montgomery, K. (1990). Promoting health through entertainment television. In C. Atkin

& L. Wallack (Eds.), *Mass communication and public health.* Newbury Park, CA: Sage.

Nabi, R., & Mehan, T. (1998). *It is your business: Report on formative research survey findings.* Unpublished paper produced by the Annenberg Public Policy Center of the University of Pennsylvania, Philadelphia.

Nariman, H. N. (1993). *Soap operas for social change, toward a methodology for entertainment-education television.* Westport, CT: Praeger.

Rosenstock, I. M. (1974). The health belief model and preventive health behavior. *Health Education Monographs, 2,* 354-385.

Rubin, A. M., & Perse, E. M. (1988). Audience activity and soap opera involvement. *Human Communication Research, 14*(2), 246-268.

PART IV

Continuing and Emerging Issues

The chapters in this park elaborate on some of the issues raised in previous sections and also address topics that are just beginning to capture the attention of researchers on violence against women.

Jody Raphael examines how recent welfare "reform" measures may be detrimental to women in violent intimate relationships. Specifically, women who receive Temporary Assistance to Needy Families (TANF) benefits are now required to meet welfare-to-work stipulations. Besides facing child care concerns and relatively unattractive job prospects, these women may also find their work options blocked by abusive partners.

Significantly, Raphael's chapter highlights the importance of examining the intersection of social class and racial inequalities with gender inequality in researching violence against women. For the most part, research on violence against women, although it emphasizes the role of gender inequality in the etiology of violence and responses to violence, has been both class- and color-

blind. Research like Raphael's shows that poor women, and especially poor women of color, are at greater risk of victimization by intimates than more affluent and white women, and they also have greater difficulties obtaining the multilevel services they need. Clearly, more work is needed that examines how these intersecting inequalities—along with age, sexual orientation, and disability—affect victimization risk and experiences, so that more responsive and culturally competent prevention and intervention programs can be developed. Certainly, the studies cited by Raphael, along with the some of the collaborative projects discussed by Edleson and Bible in Chapter 5 (this volume), are an important start, as is the work of the Institute on Domestic Violence in the African American Community, housed at the University of Minnesota's School of Social Work (see Williams, Griffin, & Saunders, 2000; see also Renzetti, 1999b; Richie, 1996). We hope such studies will inspire others to more closely examine these multiple, diverse pathways to victimization and recovery.

An emerging issue in violence against women research is the link between victimization and offending. Traditionally, researchers and others have conceptualized offenders and victims as two distinct or dichtomous groups. However, recent feminist research shows that there is often an overlap between female victimization and offending. For example, criminologist Meda Chesney-Lind (1997) reports that many young women charged as runaways by the juvenile justice system are actually attempting to escape from physically and sexually abusive homes. Studies of young people entering the juvenile justice system show that girls are more likely than boys to have been abused. Similarly, Davis (1993) has found that homeless women and girls, who sometimes engage in petty theft and street hustling to survive, are often victimized by men and boys on the streets as well as by the police who may harass them (see also Miller & Jayasundara, Chapter 23, this volume).

In the Special Topic, Drew Humphries briefly discusses how women drug users may be doubly victimized: by intimates and by the criminal justice system. Research indicates that women, like men, are usually introduced to drugs by men: their fathers or stepfathers, uncles, brothers, and, for women, boyfriends (Chesney-Lind, 1997; Inciardi, Lockwood, & Pottieger, 1993). Once initiated into drug use, however, men are more likely to continue to use drugs for thrills or pleasure, whereas women are more likely to continue to use drugs as a kind of self-medication. And women who use drugs regularly are more likely than regular male drug users to have a history of physical and sexual abuse (Chesney-Lind, 1997; Fullilove, Lown, & Fullilove, 1992; Inciardi et al., 1993). Nevertheless, as Humphries

shows, women drug users, especially those who are pregnant, have been demonized by the media and the criminal justice system, which ignore the relationship between their illicit drug use and their victimization experiences.

Another connection between women's victimization and offending, which is not addressed in this *Sourcebook* but which warrants greater attention from researchers, is women's use of violence in intimate relationships. As Jasinski (Chapter 1, this volume) and others (e.g., DeKeseredy & Schwartz, Chapter 2, this volume) note, some studies, but particularly those that use the Conflict Tactics Scales, indicate that women use violence against their intimate partners at a rate similar to men. Of course, these findings have been challenged, largely on methodological grounds. Brush (1990) and Saunders (1989), for example, point out that the claim that women are as violent as men is overstated if one factors in injurious outcomes; domestic assaults by men are six times more likely to cause injury than domestic assaults by women. One must also determine the context in which the violence occurred, the motivations underlying the use of violence in a specific situation, and the meanings actors give to specific actions (i.e., the individual actor's subjective interpretations of an action and how these interpretations vary from individual to individual). In focusing on incidence rates, there is the faulty assumption that all violence is the same when, in fact, there are important differences between initiating violence, using violence in self-defense, and retaliating against a partner. Moreover, this is not simply an issue of who hits first, because individuals may be motivated to strike first because they believe violence against them is imminent (see Saunders, 1989).

Gender differences in context, motivation, and meaning have not been the subject of many studies by violence researchers (Crowell & Burgess, 1996). The few studies that have examined these variables indicate that men are more likely to use violence against an intimate partner when they perceive themselves losing control of the relationship or when they interpret their partners' words or behavior as challenges to their authority, whereas women are more likely to use violence against an intimate partner in self-defense or in retaliation when attacked (Barnett, Lee, & Thelan, 1997; Cascardi & Vivian, 1995; DeKeseredy, Saunders, Schwartz, & Alvi, 1997; Dobash, Dobash, Cavanagh & Lewis, 1998). More research is needed that examines gender differences in context, motivation, meaning, and other situational variables (e.g., the use of drugs or alcohol) among those who have used violence against an intimate partner and those who have not (see Renzetti, 1999a).

Another area in which women's victimization and offending are linked is sex work. In Chapter 23, Jody Miller and Dheeshana Jayasundera discuss prostitution in the United States and internationally, particularly in economically underdeveloped countries, where the sex tourism industry is flourishing. They are careful to point out that not all sex workers are at equal risk of victimization, and they also emphasize that sex workers are victimized not only by "clients" and pimps but also by police and state officials. Although their focus is on adult women, the authors also briefly discuss the child sex trade. They note that they hold different views about how to resolve these problems, and readers no doubt will find themselves weighing the pros and cons of the various intervention strategies presented. Nevertheless, this chapter also

makes clear the important intersections between gender, race, class, and age inequalities, not only in the United States but on a global scale.

Finally, Johanna Bond and Robin Phillips expand the international focus introduced by Miller and Jayasundera by examining violence against women as a human rights issue. Their chapter discusses the growing recognition internationally of violence against women as a human rights abuse, while also bringing attention to forms of violence not often discussed in the United States, including female infanticide, bride burning, mass rape as a warfare strategy, and honor killings. Much of this chapter looks at violence against women in the context of human rights law, and the authors discuss various organizations that have been established to monitor and respond to violence against women internationally and in specific countries or regions of the world. Attention to violence against women in its multitude of forms has been a catalyst in linking domestically based women's movements in various countries, thereby spawning an international women's rights/human rights movement. According to Bond and Phillips, this global network "has successfully moved violence against women to the top of the international community's policy agenda" (p. 498). Still, we wait anxiously for evidence documenting the effective translation of policy into practice.

References

Barnett, O. W., Lee, C. Y., & Thelan, R. (1997). Gender differences in attributions of self-defense and control in interpartner aggression. *Violence Against Women, 3,* 462-481.

Brush, L. (1990). Violent acts and injurious outcomes in married couples: Methodological issues in the National Survey of Families and Households. *Gender & Society, 4,* 56-67.

Cascardi, M., & Vivian, D. (1995). Context for specific episodes of marital violence: Gender and severity of violence differences. *Journal of Family Violence, 10,* 265-293.

Chesney-Lind, M. (1997). *The female offender.* Thousand Oaks, CA: Sage.

Crowell, N. A., & Burgess, A. W. (1996). *Understanding violence against women.* Washington, DC: National Academy Press.

Davis, N. J. (1993, Summer). Female youth homelessness—systematic gender control. *Socio-Legal Bulletin,* pp. 22-31.

DeKeseredy, W. S., Saunders, D. G., Schwartz, M. D., & Alvi, S. (1997). The meanings and motives for women's use of violence in Canadian dating relationships: Results from a national survey. *Sociological Spectrum, 17,* 199-222.

Dobash, R. P., Dobash, R. E., Cavanagh, K., & Lewis, R. (1998). Separate and intersecting realities: A comparison of men's and women's accounts of violence against women. *Violence Against Women, 4,* 382-414.

Fullilove, M., Lown, A., & Fullilove, R. (1992). Crack hos and skeezers: Traumatic experiences of women crack users. *Journal of Sex Research, 29,* 275-287.

Inciardi, J. A., Lockwood, D., & Pottieger, A. E. (1993). *Women and crack-cocaine.* New York: Macmillan.

Renzetti, C. M. (1999a). The challenges to feminism posed by women's use of violence in intimate relationships. In S. Lamb (Ed.), *New versions of victims: Feminist struggle with the concept* (pp. 42-56). New York: New York University Press.

Renzetti, C. M. (1999b, April). *Violence against women living in public housing.* Paper presented at the Second Trapped by Poverty, Trapped by Abuse Conference, sponsored by the Taylor Institute and the Poverty Research and Training Center, Ann Arbor, MI.

Richie, B. E. (1996). *Compelled to crime: The gender entrapment of battered Black women.* New York: Routledge.

Saunders, D. G. (1989, November). *Who hits first and who hurts most? Evidence for greater victimization of women in intimate relationships.* Paper presented at the Annual Meeting of the American Society of Criminology, Reno, NV.

Williams, O. J., Griffin, L. W., & Saunders, A. (Eds.). (2000). Domestic violence in the African American community [Special issue]. *Violence Against Women, 6,* 467-549.

CHAPTER 22

Domestic Violence as a Welfare-to-Work Barrier

Research and Theoretical Issues

Jody Raphael

Although national surveys estimate that domestic violence is a factor in about 6% of all U.S. households (Plichta, 1996; Straus & Gelles, 1990; Tjaden & Thoennes, 1996), during the last 5 years, researchers have consistently found that 20% to 30% of women receiving welfare benefits are current victims of domestic violence. Research has also demonstrated that abusers deliberately employ violence to sabotage women's efforts to become self-sufficient; threatened by their partners' participation in education, training, or work, many men make use of a variety of violent strategies calculated to prevent the women from successfully completing training courses or getting to work.

The research generated a legitimate concern about welfare reform. With its mandatory work requirements, welfare reform might exacerbate the domestic violence already present in many women's lives. Some of these women might not be able to conform to the work-related requirements of welfare reform due to domestic violence, and they would lose welfare benefits, becoming financially more dependent on their abusing partner. For these reasons, the Family Violence Option (FVO), proposed by Senators Paul Wellstone (Democrat, Minnesota) and Patty Murray (Democrat, Washington), was added to the federal welfare reform legislation as a state option. Under the

AUTHOR'S NOTE: The author is greatly indebted to Richard M. Tolman of the University of Michigan School of Social Work, with whom she has worked over the past 3 years. Many of the conclusions and ideas in this chapter are the result of this fruitful collaboration.

FVO, (Section 402[a][7] of Title I, Temporary Assistance to Needy Families, 1996), states may temporarily waive federal work requirements and any other provisions to keep battered women safe through the welfare-to-work journey. Identification of or assessment of domestic violence and referral to needed services prior to workforce activities, when necessary for safety, became a reality in the majority of states that adopted the FVO.

The information about the relationship of current domestic violence and welfare receipt has been explosive. Corroborated by national crime statistics indicating that the rate of intimate violence against women generally decreases as household income levels increase (Greenfeld & Rand, 1998), this research is helping to destroy the myth that domestic violence is equally present in all households, a mantra that anti-domestic-violence advocates have long maintained. Squarely confronting the overrepresentation of domestic violence in low-income homes provides an opportunity to learn more about the causes of domestic violence. What is there about the low-income abuser, or the dynamics in welfare households, that causes so much domestic violence? Some thoughtful researchers have the sense that answers to these questions, as they elucidate the relationship between domestic violence, welfare receipt, and household income, will advance our knowledge of the basic causation of domestic violence itself (Riger & Krieglstein, 2000).

This chapter will detail the results of recent research efforts about domestic violence on issues of prevalence, effects on employment, and consequences for physical and mental health as they affect employment as well as quality of life. Then, the implications of this research for welfare reform policy will be briefly addressed. Finally, I will discuss the implications of the research to date for theories of the causation of domestic violence.

Prevalence of Domestic Violence

Researchers whose work appeared between 1996 and 1999 have largely answered the question about the prevalence of current domestic violence in welfare caseloads, finding remarkably consistent levels of current domestic violence, between 20% and 30%, with two thirds of the caseloads consisting of past victims. These results are likely to be serious underestimates because of many women's inability to admit to the domestic violence in their lives. As studies employ diverse definitions of domestic violence, measurement differences account for some of the dissimilar prevalence rates. Not surprisingly, the more inclusive the definition of violence, and the greater the number of behavior-specific items used to measure violence, the higher the prevalence rate that is reported (Riger & Krieglstein, 2000; Tolman, 1999).

The first research on one state's entire welfare caseload (Allard, Albelda, Colten, & Cosenza, 1997) occurred in a random sample of 734 women in Massachusetts, surveyed between January and June 1996, in state welfare department offices. Although the interview was conducted orally, when it came time for abuse questions, respondents listened through headphones to an audiotape and used an answer sheet to enhance their willingness to answer questions about domestic violence without the embarrassment of disclosure to interviewers. When a six-item index of physical abuse was used, 19.5%

of the women revealed that such an episode had occurred within the past year. One indication of the seriousness of these occurrences was the fact that 18% of the women admitting to abuse ever in their lives stated that they had called the police to their home within the past year; 18% of those ever abused also had a restraining order in effect during the past year.

The Worcester Family Research Project (Bassuk et al., 1996), a 5-year study of 436 women, most of whom were welfare recipients, both homeless and housed, was conducted by the Better Homes Fund and the University of Massachusetts Medical Center between 1992 and 1997. Nearly one third of the sample (32%) had experienced severe violence from their current or most recent partner within the prior 2 years.

In a random survey of 824 women in one low-income neighborhood in Chicago conducted between September 1994 and May 1995, Northwestern University researcher Susan Lloyd (Lloyd & Taluc, 1999) asked women face-to-face in their own homes about domestic violence in their lives. Although rates of current domestic violence were high for the entire neighborhood sample (11.8%), welfare recipients experienced three times the amount of physical violence within the past year (31.1%) as did their nonwelfare counterparts, and two and a half times the amount of severe physical aggression within the past year (19.5% compared with 8.1%). Three other studies have corroborated this higher prevalence of domestic violence within households of women on welfare. In 1993, the Commonwealth Fund's Survey on Women's Health (Plichta, 1996) undertook a telephone survey of over 2,000 women ages 18 and over nationally. Researchers asked whether certain behaviors had occurred

within the past 5 years with the partner with whom they were currently living. Although 24% of the welfare recipients admitted to domestic violence in the past 5 years with their current partner, only 6.8% of other respondents reported domestic violence. In a random survey of 1,000 Utah residents undertaken by the Governor's Commission for Women and Families (Dan Jones, 1998), researchers found that 17.6% of the welfare-eligible women answered positively about domestic violence, as compared to 7.4% of noneligible women.

The University of North Texas's Health Outcomes of Women Study (Marshall & Honeycutt, 1999) is a multiwave longitudinal study of low-income women begun in 1995; some of the women were not receiving welfare benefits but had income within 175% of poverty guidelines. The 836 women in the sample all had been in a serious relationship with a man that lasted at least 1 year. The study employed numerous questions to measure psychological as well as physical abuse.

Nearly equal proportions of the sample had nonviolent partners (31.6%) as had boyfriends who committed at least one potentially life-threatening act of violence (31%). The remainder (37.3%) reported mild or moderate acts of violence. The study found, however, that the severity of violence women had sustained from their current partner was associated with welfare receipt. For example, nearly three fourths of women in both the moderate and severe violence groups reported having received two or more types of governmental financial assistance.

The University of Michigan's Women's Employment Study (Tolman & Rosen, 1998) surveyed a random sample of 753 single mothers with children who were on the welfare rolls in a small urban Michigan county in February 1997, interviewing them again in late 1998 and for a third time in early 2000. Respondents were asked about their current employment status, work history, demographic characteristics, schooling, experience with domestic violence, substance dependence, and physical and mental health status. The first wave of interviews found that about 15% of the women reported being severely physically abused by a husband or partner in the previous 12 months, with 20.6% reporting moderate physical violence within the past year.

In interviewing 122 women on welfare enrolled in a mandatory 4-week county welfare-to-work program for women whom the county considered to be work-ready in Allegheny County, Pennsylvania, in 1998, Lisa Brush (2000) found that 38% of those enrolled reported that their current or most recent partner hit, kicked, or threw something at them; 27% were cut, bruised, choked, or seriously physically abused by an intimate; and 18% were forced or coerced into sex. In a random sample of 325 women on welfare in Utah, 12.3% had experienced domestic violence in the previous 12 months (Barusch, Taylor, & Derr, 1999).

It is important to caution that the large bulk of this research occurred before welfare reform had its greatest effects. Caseloads have and are precipitously declining, and as they face more barriers, including that of domestic violence, women may be more likely to remain on welfare, resulting in a higher percentage of women on welfare now experiencing work sabotage by their partners. Research now also needs to be carefully linked to individual state welfare policies in effect at the time of the study. As these now differ from state to state, the general applicability of conclusions based on caseload

research may be severely compromised (Tolman, 1999).

Employment

As states began to transition welfare recipients into employment, reports from welfare-to-work programs about domestic violence as an employment barrier began to surface. From the anecdotal evidence, it became clear that the domestic violence seemed, in most cases, calculated to sabotage the women's efforts to become self-sufficient through education, job training, or employment. Interviews with women documented the many ways that their partners deliberately interfered with welfare-to-work activities (Raphael, 1995, 1996). These included destroying books and homework assignments; keeping women up all night with arguments before key tests or job interviews; turning off alarm clocks; destroying clothing or winter coats in the winter; inflicting visible facial injuries before job interviews; deliberately disabling the family car, removing the battery, or hiding the car keys; threatening to kidnap the children from child care centers, which prevented the mothers from using outside child care, making work impossible; failing to show up as promised for child care or transportation for job interviews; and a whole host of additional abusive behaviors, including in-person harassment on the job that led to their partners being fired (Raphael, 1995, 1996, 2000). One welfare recipient, for example, realized only after her right arm was broken for the second time before the practice test that her partner was deliberately preventing her from getting her high school equivalency certificate. Another reported that her boyfriend promised to drive her to a job interview in the suburbs but began to beat her around the face in the car and then dumped her off on the side of the road (Raphael, 2000).

Psychological or emotional coercion also plays a part. Welfare-to-work participants reported concerted attempts to undermine self-confidence, attempts that interfered with their learning, as well as continuous efforts to make them feel guilty about leaving children with outside child care providers.

Although some women dropped out of the welfare-to-work programs rather than risk serious injury from their partners or confront all the complicated issues that violence from a long-term intimate partner entails, domestic violence did not work as an absolute barrier to employment. Many battered women struggled to work, and some succeeded, whereas others could not sustain the employment over time. Some programs identified abuser behaviors that present a more nuanced understanding of how domestic violence serves as a welfare-to-work barrier. For example, some reported that women's abusers allowed their partners to complete job training programs but drew the line at their seeking employment. This was because the training programs consisted mostly of women but jobs in the wider world would put women into contact with employed men with whom the women might become intimately involved. Likewise, jobs in settings where no men were present were easier for some partners to accept (B. Haynes, personal conversation, August 14, 1997).

Many providers noticed that domestic violence increased or was exacerbated when women sought education, training, or work. For example, one domestic violence provider remarked that domestic violence was not a factor in many relation-ships until the women were required by their welfare workers to learn English as part of welfare reform (B. Hinojosa, personal conversation, February 12, 1997). Some program staff noticed that many of the abusers were unemployed or underemployed and reasoned that if the men were assisted with jobs or job training, the unequal economic balance might be remedied, perhaps leading to less sabotage and violence (Raphael, 1996, 2000).

A number of quantitative studies corroborate that direct interference with employment occurs with some frequency in the lives of battered women on welfare. First, some studies measure abusers' attitudes toward education, training, and employment. The University of Massachusetts Boston survey (Allard et al., 1997) found that abused women were 10 times more likely than their never-abused counterparts to have a current or former partner who would not like them going to school or work. In their study of women on welfare in one urban county in Michigan, Tolman and Rosen (1998) found that 22.9% of their entire sample reported that they needed to miss work or school because of interference from their partners, with 5.6% reporting that this occurred in the past year.

In an assessment of 1,082 new applicants for public assistance in four Colorado welfare offices between April and December 1997, the Center for Policy Research (Pearson, Thoennes, & Griswold, 1999a) found that 44% of the victims of domestic violence reported that their abusive ex-partners had prevented them from working.

Most researchers have found that women who are abused have worked no more or less than those who are not victims; in other words, the existence of domestic violence does not predict which women in a sample will be working (Lloyd & Taluc, 1999; Tolman & Rosen, 1998). However, there are grounds to believe that the nature and severity of the domestic violence could predict this. In a recent analysis, Riger, Ahrens, and Blickenstaff (in press) correlate abusers' interference with education and employment with the severity of the abuse the women suffered. They found that the more physical and psychological abuse a woman suffered, the more the abuser interfered with her work or school participation. As would be expected, women who missed work or who were forced to quit as a result of abuse reported significantly higher scores on the restraint scale (used to measure domestic violence) than those women who did not stop working. The researchers' sample was small and drawn from a population of women in domestic violence shelters. However, it may well be proven over time that there is a link between the severity of abuse and the likelihood of the woman's being able to undertake work activities.

Researchers who determine respondents' employment history over time provide the opportunity, through multivariate analyses, to obtain a better understanding of how domestic violence may interfere with long-term workforce involvement. Susan Lloyd's (Lloyd & Taluc, 1999) neighborhood survey found that women who experienced domestic violence in their adult relationships were more likely to have experienced spells of unemployment and to have had more job turnover, even though women who were abused were employed in roughly the same numbers as those who were not victimized at the time of the survey. Lloyd also discovered that respondents who reported having experienced domestic violence within the past 12 months and who stated that

their partners had directly prevented them from going to school or work or had threatened to harm their children were less likely to be employed than women who did not experience these particular forms of abuse. Likewise, women whose partners had threatened to kill them at some point in time were less likely to be currently employed.

After interviewing 122 women in a mandatory welfare-to-work program in Pittsburgh in 1998, Lisa Brush (2000) made some basic correlations between domestic violence and employment outcomes. Only a small minority of the women (16%) were able to find a job within the 20 program days, and 14 women (11%) dropped out. The vast majority (73%) completed the program, thus complying with the work requirements imposed by their welfare department.

Brush (in press) isolated those aspects of domestic violence that she demonstrated had a controlling effect on ability to complete the program or obtain employment. She found, for example, that women who had sought an order of protection as a result of the domestic violence dropped out at six times the rate of women who did not, strong evidence that battered women facing a safety crisis in the short term will be unable to comply with welfare reform requirements. However, women who reported being hit, kicked, or coerced into sex, if they worked at all, had significantly higher job-placement rates than their peers whose partners did not batter or harass them in these ways. This finding confirms the results of other studies (e.g., Lloyd & Taluc, 1999) that concluded that some battered women try to use work as a way to escape domestic violence. Brush (2000) also discovered that those women whose intimate partners objected to their going to work because of conformity with traditional expectations about motherhood and housewifery experienced statistically significant higher dropout rates than those whose partners did not. Women who stated that their intimate partners told them that working mothers are bad mothers dropped out five times as frequently as women not subjected to these messages.

The first longitudinal analysis of domestic violence and employment is found in the Worcester Project. In one of its first analyses (Salomon, Bassuk, & Brooks, 1996), researchers discovered an interesting relationship between domestic violence, welfare usage, and employment. A fluid pattern of welfare use became apparent, with about one third of the sample reporting more than one stay on welfare. These welfare cyclers were three times more likely to have worked in the past year than were continuous welfare users. Cyclers, however, used welfare for longer total durations than those who stayed on welfare continuously did. Cyclers were more likely to have experienced violence than were continuous users. To examine the relationship between domestic violence and welfare use, the study sorted participants into two groups, short/moderate-term users and long-term users of welfare. Rates of violent victimization, both in childhood and in adulthood, high across the sample, were uniformly higher in the long-term welfare group for all types of victimization.

Of the 436 women in the Worcester baseline study, 356 were reinterviewed between May 1994 and November 1996, and 327 were again interviewed between September 1995 and August 1997. Researchers asked detailed questions pertaining to income, jobs, welfare usage, and domestic violence during the follow-up time periods, enabling them to correlate domestic violence with maintaining employment at least 30 hours per week for 6 months or more in this first study demonstrating in a multivariate analysis the independent power of recent partner violence in predicting women's capacity to maintain work.

In a recent research report from the Worcester Project (Browne & Bassuk, 1999), the work experiences of 285 women were reported. When women were simply asked whether they had worked at all in the past 12 months, there were no significant differences between women who were victims of domestic violence and those who were not in the past year. It was only when the level of work was defined with more specificity that the effects of partner violence emerged. Controlling for a variety of demographic, psychosocial, and health variables that were significantly associated with recent physical aggression or violence, women who experienced physical aggression during the first 12-month follow-up period had about one third the odds of working at least 30 hours per week for 6 months or more during the following year as did women who had not experienced such aggression. Recent (past 12 months) experiences with physical violence by male partners—rather than earlier partner violence—predicted reduced capacity to maintain work the subsequent year.

The Worcester researchers caution, however, that the dates of onset and termination of each violence episode and of each work experience were not available within the 12-month periods. They believe that new research must follow women for longer periods of time, with designs that date the onset and termination of all episodes of violence and employment so that temporal relationships between violence and employment can be more precisely assessed.

It is clear that subsequent research needs to focus on employment over time. Longitudinal data and measures of employment that include job stability, as well as those that can correlate severity of violence experienced with employment, will yield more revealing analyses of how domestic violence truly affects the employability of women. The University of Michigan's Women's Employment Study, with its three waves of interviews over a multiyear period, holds the promise of being able to make these vital analyses in future years.

Researching domestic violence as an employment barrier now has also become more complex due to mandatory work requirements contained in state welfare plans. Federal law requires all women to be involved in some work activity within 24 months or face loss of welfare benefits. Because most women will attempt to comply with these work requirements, it is also important for researchers to gather more nuanced information about the nature of these employment activities. For example, are battered women able to participate in certain kinds of education, job training, or employment, as compared with other women? Will their abusers allow them to take jobs in low-paying sectors in which women are the main employees (such as child care) but prohibit them from entering better paying professions where they will encounter more men, such as nontraditional jobs for women in the trades or manufacturing? Do abusers go along with women's participation in education and training but draw the line at employment? Is maintaining employment over time, as opposed to obtaining work, more difficult for battered women? In short, during this time of welfare reform, domestic violence may limit

the terms and conditions of employment, its duration, or sustainability, rather than employment itself. Longitudinal studies of women on welfare over time, taking these factors into account, will yield important information for both policy and program design for battered women on welfare.

The quantitative data thus reflect the complex pattern presented by qualitative evidence, showing that low-income battered women have many different responses to the abuse: Some struggle to work, others work but cannot sustain employment over time, and still others do not or cannot obtain a job at all. Longitudinal data and measures of employment that include job stability will yield more revealing analyses of how domestic violence affects the employability of women.

Health and Mental Health Issues

Several research studies demonstrate that battered women on welfare are more likely to report adverse physical health and higher prevalence of mental health problems. In the Worcester sample (Bassuk et al., 1996), 43% of the housed women and 44.9% of the homeless women suffered from a major depressive disorder, as compared to 21.3% of the general female population; 15.5% of the housed and 17.5% of the homeless women were currently suffering from posttraumatic stress disorder (PTSD). Of those experiencing physical violence, 32.6% reported drug and alcohol problems, compared to 16.5% of those who did not experience violence. About 10% of women who had experienced physical aggression had mental health hospitalization in the past year, as compared to 1.4%

of those who were not abused by a partner.

In their Michigan sample, Tolman and Rosen (1998) found that women who experienced domestic violence in the past 12 months had nearly three times as many mental health problems as their non-abused counterparts; almost two thirds of the recent victims (61.6%) qualified for one of the five psychiatric diagnoses measured by the research. About 38% of women battered within the past 12 months were currently suffering from PTSD, as compared to 17.6% of the sample that had been battered in the past and 5.1% of the sample that had never been abused. One third (34%) of Brush's (in press) sample had at least one symptom from three PTSD symptom categories (intrusion, constriction, and hyperarousal).

Not only do these studies provide strong support for the relationship between domestic violence and physical and mental symptoms, but they also demonstrate how these mental health problems can affect women's employment. For example, multivariate analysis in the Worcester sample (Browne & Bassuk, 1999) revealed that women struggling with mental health problems had only half the odds of maintaining work as women without mental health problems, and women who had spoken to a clinician about mental health problems in the past 6 months had about one third the odds of maintaining work. In the Michigan sample (Tolman & Rosen, 1998), both health problems and major depression were associated with lower rates of employment. Brush (in press) found that women who said they had trouble concentrating had similar dropout rates but significantly higher job-placement rates than women who did not report that symptom. However, women who reported angry outbursts dropped out more than women who

did not report this symptom. Brush's work is the first to establish a link between domestic violence and a particular traumatic symptom affecting work, and it militates against making overgeneralized assumptions about mental health symptoms.

Clearly, mental health problems, the results of trauma from violence, have been proven to interfere with women's ability to obtain or maintain employment. Many battered women with these health and mental health problems are, however, struggling to work. Findings about health and mental health among samples of battered women on welfare are thus cause for grave concern, especially as we have seen that domestic violence is often exacerbated during women's efforts to seek employment. The data also force us to broaden our inquiry beyond the issue of employment. We need to be measuring whether, as a result of going to work, poor women are becoming victims of domestic violence in greater numbers. Thus, we should be concerned about domestic violence as well as employment, and we need to be worried that although working, many battered women are suffering from mental health problems that gravely interfere with the quality of their lives and their ability to provide good parenting to their children. Although many research projects are structured to measure work outcomes during welfare reform and to make correlations with domestic violence as a welfare-to-work barrier, few have been designed to capture increases in domestic violence or to gauge the effects of that violence on the physical and mental health of women and their children. Unfortunately, as many welfare researchers are unfamiliar with the issue of domestic violence, they may be unequipped to measure its effects on physical and mental well-being. It is, thus, vital for domestic violence experts to team with welfare re-searchers to study domestic violence, one of the unintended effects of welfare re-form (Riger & Krieglstein, 2000). The in-tegration of the two previously separate fields—welfare and domestic violence—is more imperative than ever (Meier, 1997).

Implications for Welfare Reform

The research data build the case for indi-vidualized attention for battered women through the welfare-to-work process. Some abused women can and will want to work, especially as a way to escape the vi-olence permanently. Others will attempt work but may not be able to sustain it, and still others may not be able to comply with work requirements due to sabotage or severe mental health effects from that violence. The FVO, which directs welfare workers to screen for domestic violence and refer battered women to domestic vi-olence services, allows states to tempo-rarily waive federal work requirements to provide battered women time to resolve issues of domestic violence that are serv-ing as work barriers. As of the spring of 1999, only a handful of states had failed to adopt the FVO or to craft policies sen-sitive to the needs of battered women (Ra-phael & Haennicke, 1999).

Early research (Raphael & Haennicke, 1999) indicates that low percentages of women are disclosing domestic violence to welfare caseworkers. In states consid-ered more successful, 5% to 10% of the caseload has disclosed, much lower num-bers than the higher rates of acknowledg-ment of domestic violence obtained by researchers. Information gleaned from evaluations of FVO demonstration projects and interviews with TANF caseworkers point up several salient differences be-tween research and actual practice. In two demonstration sites, women on welfare told researchers that they did not disclose for fear of being pitied by their welfare caseworker. Another frequently cited fac-tor was fear that the abuser would find out (Raphael & Haennicke, 1999). Presum-ably, this sense of shame or fear of the abuser is overcome when confidential and anonymous research is taking place. Do-mestic violence advocates housed or co-located at welfare department offices ob-tain four and five times the number of dis-closures obtained by welfare caseworkers (Raphael & Haennicke, 1999). Concerns about trust, expertise, and confidentiality work against disclosure to welfare case-workers, issues that seem to be eased through use of trained domestic violence advocates.

Because women fail to disclose the vi-olence, caseworkers are unable to help them get to work in a manner that is safe for them. Because welfare workers can-not help keep women safe unless they know about the violence, the discrepancy between the two disclosure rates—in research and in practice—remains a cause for concern. Welfare departments will have to put considerably more time, ef-fort, and funds into the task of increasing the domestic violence disclosure rates if women and children are to be safe during welfare reform (Raphael & Haennicke, 1999).

Federal welfare reform also requires women to establish paternity and cooper-ate with child-support collection. There has been a concern about the danger that child-support collection could pose to do-mestic violence victims or survivors, whose partners or ex-partners might retaliate or gain custody or visitation rights as a result of established paternity. The FVO does allow states to exempt participants from child-support enforcement due to domestic violence.

Until recently, there was little research information about domestic violence and child-support enforcement, but data emerging from three demonstration projects funded by the federal Office of Child Support Enforcement in three states—Colorado, Massachusetts, and Minnesota—provide a first indication of the extent of the problem. In Colorado, when a sample of 1,082 new applicants for public assistance were screened for domestic violence, 40% disclosed current or past abuse. Only 3% believed they needed to apply for a good-cause waiver of child-support enforcement. In Massachusetts, 36% of the sample of 2,584 disclosed domestic violence, and 8% wanted a waiver. About 52% of the 83 women sampled in Minnesota disclosed domestic violence, with 2.4% of these expressing interest in the good-cause waiver (Pearson, Thoennes, & Griswold, 1999b). The conclusion is that most women on welfare who are victims of domestic violence do, in fact, want to collect child support and believe that it is safe to do so. However, the fact that a small percentage believes it is unsafe to collect child support makes it imperative that child support enforcement offices learn how to effectively screen women or give them the opportunity to disclose the domestic violence so that they may make an informed choice about the safety of participating. It is the general sense that child support enforcement agencies are lagging behind other governmental entities in knowledge about domestic violence and ability to effec-tively deal with the issue (Raphael & Haennicke, 1999).

Implications for the Causes of Domestic Violence

Why is there so much domestic violence in welfare households? And what does the answer tell us about the causes of domestic violence? Historically, the battered women's movement has not focused on issues of class or race (Kanuha, 1996) but has emphasized that battering is embedded in all levels of society, where norms condoning male dominance need to be radically changed (Meier, 1997; Riger & Krieglstein, 2000). Thus, theories of domestic violence causation have not, to date, adequately dealt with poverty issues. In addition, the thinking has been that as women's resources—and their power in the relationship— increase, the incidence of domestic violence will necessarily decrease. However, the evidence from research on welfare and domestic violence demonstrates the opposite effect: As women gain greater economic resources through welfare reform, increasing the economic disparity between their income and that of their partner, they may be at far greater risk for domestic violence (Riger & Krieglstein, 2000).

Battered women on welfare say their partners sabotage their work efforts for two basic reasons. If the women obtain employment, they will have the economic resources to leave the relationship. Thus, maintaining welfare receipt is a key means of power and control for abusers. In addition, the women say their partners fear that in the workplace, they will meet someone more attractive, undoubtedly because these men in the workplace are employed and probably will have more economic resources than the women's current partners (Raphael, 2000). These comments of battered women may well contain the clues we need to understand the dynamics of domestic violence in welfare homes.

Disparity of income appears to be the salient factor. Lisa Brush (2000) found some factors that confirm the hypothesis that positive effects of education and training can precipitate or aggravate controlling behavior of intimates: In her sample, women who had less than a high school diploma or its equivalent reported significantly lower rates of work-related jealousy than those with these minimal educational credentials. Brush's conclusion is corroborated by other domestic violence research studies that have analyzed women's economic resources vis-à-vis those of their partners. Hotaling and Sugarman (1986) found that domestic violence increased when the wife had more education or higher income than her husband. In a sample of 365 women in Tucson, Arizona, researchers found that total family income, per se, had no influence on domestic violence, but income disparity did. Violence against women increased as the interspousal income gap closed. The less disparity in income, or the more resources the woman had relative to her husband, the more frequent and escalated the violence. Violence appears to be an equalizing tactic used by some men in an attempt to establish control over their partners' lives (McCloskey, 1996). Analysis of a sample of 102 women in San Francisco, California, also found that receipt of no income from the male partner was significantly correlated with increased relationship abuse within the past 3 months Women's relative economic power increased the men's likelihood of being abusive (Raj, Silverman, Wingood, & DiClemente, 1999). The working hypothesis is that when the economic differential leans in favor of the woman in the relationship, domestic violence is exacerbated.

Absent from this analysis is any conclusive explanation for the frequent usage of violence by low-income men aimed at their intimate partners. One might expect emotional coercion or sabotage of work-related efforts, but higher prevalence of violence in low-income households has yet to be adequately explained. As one author has postulated (McCloskey, 1996), low occupational standing may index a number of other descriptors, including low educational attainment, low self-esteem, lower social skills, and alcohol and drug problems; these characteristics may also contribute toward more domestic violence perpetrated by men of lower economic means. Others believe that the shame of not being able to support one's family causes hate that turns to violence (Gilligan, 1996). One analyst (L. Brush, personal conversation, August 9, 1999) points to the explosive double bind that confronts the partner of a woman on welfare. If the abuser is low-income or unemployed, he knows that his partner's working will assist the family economically. When he does not permit her to work, the family will become even poorer through loss of welfare benefits. Yet the abuser legitimately fears that if he allows her into the workplace, she will ultimately leave him. The conflicting emotions may well be a tinderbox that ignites the violence. Although other factors certainly contribute to domestic violence, primarily strong cultural norms supporting and condoning battering, the data about domestic violence and welfare make it clear that economic variables need to be better incorporated into the current theoretical mix than they have been heretofore (Meier, 1997; Riger & Krieglstein, in press; Walby, 1990). Research on domestic violence and welfare will continue to push the domestic violence movement toward a more complex and integrated theory of the causation of domestic violence.

References

Allard, M. A., Albelda, R., Colten, M. E., & Cosenza, C. (1997). *In harm's way? Domestic violence, AFDC receipt, and welfare reform in Massachusetts.* Boston: University of Massachusetts, McCormack Institute.

Barusch, A., Taylor, M. J., & Derr, M. (1999). *Understanding families with multiple barriers to self-sufficiency.* Salt Lake City: University of Utah Graduate School of Social Work.

Bassuk, E. L., Weinreb, L. F., Buckner, J. C., Browne, A., Salomon, A., & Bassuk, S. S. (1996). The characteristics and needs of sheltered homeless and low-income housed mothers. *Journal of the American Medical Association, 276,* 640-646.

Browne, A., & Bassuk, S. (1999). The impact of recent partner violence on poor women's capacity to maintain work. *Violence Against Women, 5,* 393-426.

Brush, L. (2000). Battering, traumatic stress, and welfare-to-work transition. *Violence Against Women, 6*(10), 1039-1065.

Dan Jones and Associates. (1998). *Domestic violence incidence and prevalence study.* Salt Lake City, UT: Governor's Commission on Women and Families.

Gilligan, J. (1996). *Violence: Our deadly epidemic and its causes.* New York: G. P. Putnam.

Greenfeld, L., & Rand, M. (1998). *Violence by intimates: Analysis of data on crimes by current or former spouses, boyfriends, and girlfriends.* Washington, DC: Department of Justice, Bureau of Justice Statistics.

Hotaling, G. T., & Sugarman, D. B. (1986). An analysis of risk markers in husband to wife violence: The current state of knowledge. *Violence and Victims, 1,* 101-124.

Kanuha, V. (1996). Domestic violence, racism, and the battered women's movement in the United States. In J. Edleson & Z. Eisikovits (Eds), *Future interventions with battered women and their families* (pp. 34-49). Thousand Oaks, CA: Sage.

Lloyd, S., & Taluc, N. (1999). The effects of male violence on female employment. *Violence Against Women, 5*(4), 370-392.

Marshall, L., & Honeycutt, T. (1999). *Women, domestic abuse, and public assistance.* Denton: University of North Texas.

McCloskey, L. (1996). Socioeconomic and coercive power within the family. *Gender & Society, 10,* 449-463.

Meier, J. (1997). Domestic violence, character, and social change in the welfare reform debate. *Law & Policy, 19,* 205-263.

Pearson, J., Thoennes, N., & Griswold, E. A. (1999a). Child support and domestic violence: The victims speak out. *Violence Against Women, 5,* 427-448.

Pearson, J., Thoennes, N., & Griswold, E. A. (1999b). *New approaches to self-sufficiency and safety in public assistance and child support agencies: Preliminary findings from three demonstration projects.* Denver, CO: Center for Policy Research.

Personal Responsibility and Work Opportunity Reconciliation Act of 1996 (PRWORA), P.L. 104-193, 110 Stat. 2105 (1996).

Plichta, S. B. (1996). Violence and abuse: Implications for women's health. In M. M. Falik (Ed.), *Women's health: The Commonwealth Fund survey* (pp. 237-270). Baltimore, MD: Johns Hopkins University Press.

Raj, A., Silverman, J., Wingood, G., & DiClemente, R. (1999). Prevalence and correlates of relationship abuse among a community-based sample of low-income African American women. *Violence Against Women, 5,* 272-291.

Raphael, J. (1995). *Domestic violence: Telling the untold welfare-to-work story.* Chicago: Taylor Institute.

Raphael, J. (1996). *Prisoners of abuse: Domestic violence and welfare receipt.* Chicago: Taylor Institute.

Raphael, J. (2000). *Saving Bernice: Battered women, welfare, and poverty.* Boston: Northeastern University Press.

Raphael, J., & Haennicke, S. (1999). *Keeping battered women safe through the welfare-to-work journey: How are we doing: A report on the implementation of policies for battered women in state temporary assistance for needy families (TANF) programs.* Chicago: Taylor Institute.

Riger, S., Ahrens, C., & Blickenstaff, A. (in press). Measuring interference with employment and education reported by women with abusive partners: Preliminary data. *Violence and Victims.*

Riger, S., & Krieglstein, M. (2000). The impact of welfare reform on men's violence against women. *American Journal of Community Psychology, 28,* 631-647.

Salomon, A., Bassuk, S., & Brooks, M. (1996). Pattern of welfare use among poor and homeless women. *American Journal of Orthopsychiatry, 66,* 510-525.

Straus, M. A., & Gelles, R. J. (Eds.). (1990). *Physical violence in American families: Risk factors and adaptations to violence in 8,145 families.* New Brunswick, NJ: Transaction.

Tjaden, P., & Thoennes, N. (1996). *Stalking in America: Findings from the national violence against women survey.* Denver, CO: Center for Policy Research.

Tolman, R. (1999). Guest editor's introduction. *Violence Against Women, 5,* 355-369.

Tolman, R., & Rosen, D. (1998, October). *Domestic violence in the lives of welfare recipients: Implications for the Family Violence Option.* Paper presented at the annual meeting of the Association for Public Policy Analysis and Management, New York.

Walby, S. (1990). *Theorizing patriarchy.* Oxford, UK: Basil Blackwell.

CRIMINALIZATION OF PREGNANCY

Drew Humphries

Intimate violence and sexual assault typify the kinds of force used against women. But what happens when women who have been so victimized also find themselves reviled as monsters, charged as felons, and threatened with punishment? As the "criminalization of pregnancy" shows, such women are doubly victimized. The war on drugs has eliminated any notion of personal victimization—for example, intimate violence, poverty, sexual assault, or the desperation of drug use—from public debate. The war on drugs has also turned that debate into a one-sided punitive attack on drug users, directed in part against women who use drugs during pregnancy.

In the 1980s and early 1990s, women were almost as likely as men to use crack, a smokable form of powder cocaine. Although this observation might otherwise have gone unnoticed, the war on drugs had created a climate in which politicians, drug experts, medical researchers, law enforcement officials, and the media sensationalized every new indication of drug pathology. If women of childbearing age used drugs, it seemed obvious that drug use would have a harmful impact on reproduction. Once exploited, fears about a drug-reproduction connection were used to justify criminal prosecutions of women who continued to use crack/cocaine during pregnancy.

On national network news, poor women of color, who numbered among crack users, exemplified the mindless addiction associated with this drug. Claims of an epidemic of pregnant drug users raised concerns about their capacity to mother. Women were widely believed to smoke crack with the full knowledge that the drug would adversely affect their unborn babies. Images of suffering babies made it difficult to ignore their mothers' responsibility, especially after the network news linked prenatal cocaine exposure with neonate addiction, premature birth, low birth weight, sudden infant death syndrome, cerebral palsy, death, birth defects, developmental delay, and retardation.

For a handful of county prosecutors, it was time to hold the mothers accountable for their damaged babies. The first cases attributed infant death to prenatal cocaine exposure. For example, Melanie Green's baby had tested positive for drugs at birth. When the baby died, an Illinois county attorney, Paul Logli, filed manslaughter charges against Green. The 1989 grand jury that was convened to hear the charges, however, refused to indict.

Drug-trafficking charges figured in other cases. After giving birth to a second cocaine-exposed baby in 1989, Jennifer Johnson, for example, was convicted on two counts of felony distribution of cocaine to a minor. Cocaine ingested by the mother crossed the placenta barrier and flowed through the umbilical cord to the fetus. The prosecutor, Jeffrey Deen, argued that cocaine continued to flow to the baby after it had passed through the birth canal but before the umbilical cord was cut; hence, Johnson distributed a controlled substance to a living baby, a minor.

As the war on drugs wound down, cooler heads prevailed. Research physicians pointed out that the adverse effects of prenatal cocaine exposure were based on studies of questionable design, with deficient samples and inappropriate control groups. Public health leaders challenged the deterrent value of the prosecutions. Far from forcing women into drug-rehabilitation programs, the threat of prosecution drove women away from prenatal care and drug-treatment programs. Feminists and civil rights attorneys raised issues of discrimination. In singling out pregnant women, the prosecutions violated principles of equal protection, especially because laws barring the sale and possession of illicit drugs apply to everyone. The prosecutions provided opportunities for antiabortion activists to chip away at *Roe v. Wade*. Several attempts had been made to equate prenatal cocaine exposure to child abuse, but these failed. And although lower courts were more likely to uphold convictions, higher courts reversed them, finding that prosecutors had stretched the meaning of statutes beyond legislative intent.

Stepping back for a moment, we can consider the significance of events labeled as "the criminalization of pregnancy." The convergence of images of gender, race, and social class with depictions of addiction, its locale, and disorder painted a powerful and enduring picture of social menace. Threatening enough to trigger criminal prosecutions, the menace blurred the distinction between offending and being victimized. Charged by prosecutors as felons, crack mothers were also victims in the war on drugs. The incarceration rate for women increased so much during the war on drugs that it has been called the war on women. In addition, the social menace evoked by "crack mothers" has persisted, making it difficult to address the needs of women who use drugs. When providers view them as unfit mothers, the quality of service declines. As state governments decide whether to use federal funds to finance the drug-treatment centers created for women with children, correcting misconceptions is even more important.

CHAPTER 23

Prostitution, the Sex Industry, and Sex Tourism

Jody Miller
Dheeshana Jayasundara

The adage "prostitution is the world's oldest profession" may read as a tired cliché, but it highlights key issues salient for understanding women's experiences in the commercial sex industry. Explicit in the adage is recognition that prostitution is an enactment of sexual *labor,* and one that is deeply rooted across societies. The particular nature of the industry takes a variety of forms historically as well as within and across nations. However, a common thread in the organization and control of the sex industry is that it is characterized by gender, race, and class inequalities, as well as power imbalances resulting from colonial and imperialist relations across nations (see Maher, 1997; Truong, 1990). As sociologist Eleanor Miller (1991) notes, prostitution "is work that would have no value were it not for the conditions of economic and sexual inequality under which it is performed" (p. 8; see also Overall, 1992).[1]

In recent years, there have been a number of significant shifts in the organization of the commercial sex industry, each relevant to women's experience of violence within prostitution. In the United States, the arrival of crack cocaine in urban markets in the mid 1980s considerably altered the conditions under which sex work is performed, with many scholars suggesting that these changes have been to women's detriment (see Maher, 1997; Miller, 1995a; Ratner, 1993). Internationally, the last decades of the 20th century witnessed a tremendous growth in what is known as "sex tourism": the development and expansion of industries providing sexual services, catering primarily to Western and Japanese men who travel to Third World countries for business or leisure activities (see Truong, 1990). In conjunction with the development and expansion of sex tourism has been a rise in trafficking of individuals for prostitution and the widespread involvement of children in the sex-tourism industry.

This chapter provides an overview of the commercial sex industry within the United States and internationally, highlighting the impact of legal responses and organizational features in shaping women's experiences within prostitution, particularly their experiences of violence. Linda Fairstein (1993), a Manhattan sex crimes prosecutor, argues that "it is unlikely that any occupation or lifestyle exposes a woman to the threat of assault and gratuitous violence as constantly and completely as prostitution" (p. 171). Our goal is to illuminate how and why this is the case.

Definitional Concerns

Definitions of prostitution, along with appropriate interventions, are hotly contested. Social definitions largely concentrate on the exchange of sexual relations for monetary payment or barter, characterized by promiscuity or lack of emotional attachment (Flowers, 1998, p. 6). However, contemporary debate centers on the issue of prostitution as forced or chosen: violence against women versus a form of work. In recent years, women engaged in the sex industry have been at the forefront in arguing that prostitution should be defined as *sex work* (see Bell, 1987; Jenness, 1993; Kempadoo & Doezema, 1998). For example, the U.S.-based prostitutes' rights movement, COYOTE (Call Off Your Old Tired Ethics), asserts that laws against prostitution are at the heart of sex workers' victimization and that prostitution is voluntary. COYOTE argues that prostitution should be decriminalized, destigmatized, and

recognized as a legitimate form of service work (Jenness, 1993). In sharp contrast, some feminist groups, most notably WHISPER (Women Hurt in Systems of Prostitution) and CATW (Coalition Against Trafficking in Women), characterize prostitution by definition as a form of violence against women. Drawing on the language of the antirape movement, they refer to women as "survivors of prostitution" and reject the claim of prostitution as work (see Barry, 1979, 1995; Giobbe, 1991).

Although many feminists do not take the hard-line stand of groups such as WHISPER, they nonetheless have difficulty accepting wholeheartedly the position of groups such as COYOTE and some international sex workers' rights organizations (see Kempadoo & Doezema, 1998, for a number of examples). Most feminists highlight the larger patriarchal contexts in which prostitution occurs, suggesting that prostitution both results from and contributes to the sexual objectification of women and the sexual double standard. Moreover, given economic and employment inequalities based on gender, race, class, and nation, they argue that it is difficult to know how many women would choose sex work, if a wider range of employment options were available. Thus, while maintaining "a crucial moral distinction between prostitutes as sex workers and prostitution as a practice and institution" (Overall, 1992, p. 708), many feminists "defend prostitutes' entitlement to do their work but [do not] defend prostitution itself as a practice under patriarchy" (Overall, 1992, p. 723; see also Chancer, 1993; Cooper, 1989).

These debates are played out within the international arena, as well. Early international conventions distinguished between prostitution as a personal choice and slavery-like prostitution due to coercion or trafficking in people. These conventions prohibited international trafficking and regarded prostitution as a human rights violation only if it involved overt coercion or exploitation (Lim, 1998). Successive international instruments also followed this approach. However, the Convention for the Suppression of Traffic in Persons and the Exploitation of the Prostitution of Others, adopted by the United Nations in 1949, took an abolitionist approach. This convention viewed the prostitute as a victim and did not distinguish between forced and voluntary prostitution (Lim, 1998).

After the 1949 Convention, "both feminist and international concern for prostitution and the traffic in women abated for a time" (Doezema, 1998, p. 36). It was not until the 1980s, in conjunction with the rise in sex tourism, that trafficking and prostitution again received international attention. Some more recent international instruments also take the abolitionist approach outlined in the 1949 Convention (Lim, 1998). However, supporters of sex workers' rights argue that many adults make relatively free decisions to enter the trade; thus, voluntary prostitution should be distinguished from prostitution resulting from trafficking, which involves overt pressure or coercion from third parties in the form of deception, violence, or debt bondage (Foundation Against Trafficking in Women, International Human Rights Law Group, and Global Alliance against Traffic in Women, 1999).

In fact, some argue that the tendency to view Third World sex workers primarily as victims, while accepting that Western women can choose sex work, is a continuation of colonial legacies that define Third World women as inferior, "needing guidance, assistance, and help" (Kempadoo, 1998, p. 11). Instead, these authors argue that "despite the marginality and vulnerability of sex workers internationally" (Kempadoo, 1998, p. 8), the conceptualization of Third World sex workers exclusively as victims should be rejected. Consequently, even the forced/voluntary dichotomy recently has been challenged. A number of activists argue that this remains a limited framework for dealing with sex work, as it often results in policies aimed only at rescuing trafficked women; women who are voluntarily involved in the sex industry continue to face exploitation and human rights violations that remain unaddressed by current intervention strategies (Doezema, 1998).

Our own position parallels that of Kempadoo and Doezema. Although we use the terms *prostitution* and *sex work* interchangeably throughout the chapter, we nonetheless recognize prostitution as a form of sexual labor and sex workers as human agents despite their subjection to stigma, victimization, and exploitation. Without taking an ethical position on the legitimacy of prostitution or its functions in support of patriarchal capitalism,[2] our concern in this chapter is with the legal, social, and economic conditions under which prostitution occurs within racist, patriarchal, capitalist systems. Again, our particular focus is how these conditions promote and contribute to violence against sex workers.

Legal Responses to the Sex Industry

Four legal paradigms have been identified to address prostitution: prohibition, abolition, legalization/regulation, and decriminalization (Coomaraswamy, 1997). In fact, these paradigms speak to the definitional concerns highlighted in the previous section. In the prohibitionist model, prostitution is a crime. Technically, all parties involved are criminalized, including the sex worker, client, and others who profit (e.g., pimps, brokers, traffickers, managers). However, with few exceptions, it is primarily sex workers themselves who are arrested and prosecuted under these laws. The United States currently adopts the prohibitionist model, as do China, Iceland, Japan, Malta, Nepal, the Philippines, Romania, Slovenia, Sri Lanka, Tanzania, Uganda, and Vietnam (Wijers & Lap-Chew, 1997).

The prohibition model is widely believed to be the most oppressive for sex workers (see Scibelli, 1987). This approach leaves women with no legal apparatus to defend themselves. Rarely do states enforce laws against traffickers, pimps, or clients, although women are routinely subject to arrest and incarceration. Moreover, because of the illegal nature of their work, many women are hesitant to go to law enforcement when they are crime victims and conduct their work so as to conceal their activities, which increases their risk of victimization (Miller, 1997).

The abolitionist approach calls for the elimination of laws against prostitution itself. It criminalizes third parties, rather than the actual transaction. As noted earlier, this is the approach adopted by the U.N. Convention of 1949. Abolitionism decriminalizes women's involvement in prostitution and does not distinguish between voluntary and forced prostitution. Instead, prostitutes are defined as victims. As such, the abolitionist approach does not recognize women's right to choose prostitution as a legitimate occupation. Most countries in Western Europe adopt a predominantly abolitionist approach, in-

cluding Belgium, Denmark, Finland, France, Ireland, Italy, Norway, Portugal, Spain, Sweden, and the United Kingdom. In addition, Bangladesh, Bulgaria, Cameroon, Canada, Czechoslovakia, Colombia, the Dominican Republic, Hong Kong, India, Lithuania, Nigeria, Poland, Thailand, and the Ukraine follow a primarily abolitionist model (Hoigard & Finstad, 1992; T. Peterrsson, personal communication, September 12, 1999; Wijers & Lap-Chew, 1997). In fact, in January 1999, Sweden, which previously only criminalized third parties, passed a new law that criminalizes sex workers' clients. Although other Scandinavian countries are considering the legislation, there was just one successful conviction in the year following passage of the legislation (Peterrsson, personal communication, September 12, 1999).

It is important to clarify that no country has adopted a purely abolitionist approach; typically, whereas the act of prostitution itself is not criminalized, such acts as street solicitation, loitering, and "kerb-crawling" remain criminal offenses (e.g., see Hatty, 1989, regarding Australia; Lowman, 1990, regarding Canada; Scibelli, 1987, regarding France and Thailand). Thailand is a notable case in this regard. Some authors classify Thailand as adopting a prohibitionist approach (Scibelli, 1987), in part because of the contradictory nature of laws governing the industry there. In her detailed analysis of sex tourism in Thailand, social researcher Thanh-Dam Truong (1990) documents these contradictions:

> Sexual services are produced on the edge of legal ambiguity. Prostitution is criminalized under the Penal Code. At the same time, it is formalized under the law governing industries. Under the

Penal Code it is defined as "a crime of promiscuity." It is defined as "personal services" under business law, and as "special services" by the Police Department. The law recognizes "personal services" as a business and ensures privileges to investors, and at the same time criminalizes workers in the business. Given the contradiction between the legality of "personal service" enterprises and the illegality of prostitution, the relations of power and production in prostitution are . . . complex and diverse. (p. 180)

Legalization/regulation is the third legal paradigm dealing with prostitution. This is the predominant approach in a number of Western countries, including Australia, Austria, Germany, Greece, the Netherlands, and Switzerland, as well as Curacao, Ecuador, Peru, and Turkey (Wijers & Lap-Chew, 1997). This is also the approach found in some counties in Nevada (Scibelli, 1987). Under this model, there is state tolerance of prostitution through government regulatory schemes. Regulation includes direct government interventions such the registration of brothel houses, as well as neo-regulatory systems such as mandatory health exams and taxation. Under this model, sex workers rather than other parties are subject to regulation. Registration is often compulsory, and unregistered women are considered to be committing an illegal act. And whereas sex workers are typically required to undergo medical exams for sexually transmitted diseases (STDs), their customers are not. Failure to attend mandatory medical exams makes women liable to prosecution (Wijers & Lap-Chew, 1997). Moreover, women's mobility is severely restricted, with regulations governing when and with whom they can be in public space (see Scibelli, 1987).

Decriminalization is the paradigm advocated by many sex workers' rights organizations, including COYOTE (Jenness, 1993). In contrast to the abolitionist model, the argument for decriminalization emphasizes the view that prostitution is work and rejects the notion that sex workers are by definition victims. Instead, this model aims to criminalize exploitation, coercion, and violence against sex workers by third parties, while defining sex work as a legitimate occupation. To highlight the distinction between decriminalization and the abolitionist approach, consider again Sweden's new law against clients. Under the decriminalization paradigm, such laws are discriminatory, even though sex workers themselves are not targeted. The laws challenge the legitimacy of the work, may deter clients from seeking the services of sex workers, and thus have an adverse effect on their business. Moreover, the abolitionist model has been critiqued for failing to distinguish between pimps and brokers, on the one hand, and women's partners and boyfriends, on the other. Anyone who profits from sex workers' labor legally qualifies as a "pimp," even if the relationship is not based on coercion (see Hoigard & Finstad, 1992).

Decriminalization is a fundamentally liberal approach; key issues include challenging the sexual double standard of morality as a means to destigmatize prostitution, as well as combating discriminatory labor practices and exploitative working conditions (see Truong, 1990, pp. 48-50). Some advocates do not critique the sex industry as a feature of patriarchal capitalism (see Jenness, 1993), whereas others view decriminalization as a short-term solution to improve sex workers' lives, with the goal of eliminating prostitution in an ideal nonpatriarchal society (see Chancer, 1993; James, 1978; Overall, 1992; Scibelli, 1987).

Before moving on, two additional legal issues are noteworthy. First is the harmful impact of immigration laws on transnational sex workers; second, we will briefly discuss current legal interventions on the international child sex trade. A number of sex workers' rights organizations have argued that besides laws against prostitution, immigration laws also contribute to the coercive, exploitative features of the transnational sex industry (see Kempadoo & Doezema, 1998). Many Third World and Eastern European women who are trafficked or go abroad to work in the sex industry do so as illegal immigrants. Thus, the threat of deportation remains a serious concern that keeps many sex workers in dependent relationships with third parties. Even though deportation at first glance appears to be a solution, in many cases, women find that traffickers are waiting for them when they arrive home, or they face rejection from their families and communities when the nature of their work is discovered. As Kempadoo and Doezema (1998) summarize,

> It is important to recognize that trafficked women are first and foremost migrants—persons seeking economic, social, and political opportunities away from home—yet, due to restrictive laws and policies and limited opportunities for women, [they] are relegated to informal sector work. State policies and laws furthermore serve to position migrant women as "undesirable aliens" and criminals, yet yield benefits for traffickers. (p. 32)

Moreover, these laws allow third parties to dispense with women who are no longer viewed as economically viable (for instance, if they contract STDs such as HIV) by turning them in to authorities for arrest and/or deportation (see Kempadoo & Doezema, 1998; Truong, 1990).

With regard to children's involvement in the sex industry, there is near uniform agreement that an abolitionist model is best, at least in theory. Children are defined as victims of the sex industry, and third parties as well as clients should be criminalized and prosecuted. Child sex tourism has become a grave international concern, resulting in both national and international efforts to ameliorate it. The United Nations Convention on the Rights of the Child has as one goal the protection of children from sexual exploitation. A number of Western nations have passed new laws to prosecute citizens for sex crimes against children committed abroad; however, evidentiary and cross-jurisdiction problems have thus far made these efforts difficult (Berkman, 1996; Bureau of International Labor Affairs, 1996; Healy, 1995).

In addition, most of the countries where child sex tourism occurs have adopted stringent laws prohibiting the trade. In Sri Lanka, for example, new laws were passed in 1995 to curb child sex tourism by raising the minimum age of consent to 18 for boys and 16 for girls, making sexual activities with youths under those ages a crime, and providing a minimum 5-year jail term for pimps and clients (Gunasekera, 1996; Samarasinghe, 1996, 1997). Several European tourists have been prosecuted under the new laws, although there is no evidence in the short term of a significant deterrent effect of the laws. For the most part, enforcement has been quite lax in most countries.

In addition, it is important to note that some argue that the issue of children's involvement in the sex industry should be defined more broadly to explicitly emphasize poverty and economic inequalities exacerbated by Western imperialism. Developmental processes have contributed to a rise in the earning activities of children globally; attempts to ameliorate children's participation in the sex industry without addressing the global exploitation of children's labor more broadly provide a truncated approach, with likely harmful effects for the children involved (see Kempadoo, 1998; Montgomery, 1998).

In the remaining sections of this chapter, we will provide overviews of the sex industry in the United States, as well as sex tourism, child sex tourism, trafficking, and transnational sex work. As we do so, we turn our attention to the exploitation of and violence against sex workers in these contexts. We will pay particular attention to the impact of legal and social responses to sex work as entrenched features of the industry's organization, further highlighting the role these play in contributing to sex workers' exploitation and abuse. Particularly in the West, the extent of violence and of women's ability to protect themselves varies across sectors of the industry, with women working in indoor settings generally afforded greater protection, at least from violence at the hands of clients.[3] Within the sex-tourism industry and among transnational sex workers, this distinction is less meaningful. As we will discuss further below, sex workers in these contexts often face a wide range of abuses in the context of brothel and other indoor work, including illegal confinement, forced or coerced labor, and sexual and physical abuse (Kempadoo & Doezema, 1998).

Prostitution and Violence Against Street Sex Workers in the United States[4]

As noted above, with the exception of several counties in Nevada, prostitution remains criminalized in the United States. Because of the illicit nature of prostitution, it is not possible to obtain accurate estimates of its prevalence. In 1996, there were 48,591 arrests of women for prostitution or commercialized vice in the United States (Maguire & Pastore, 1997, p. 336). This increase from 33,306 arrests 20 years earlier (see James, 1978) is not necessarily a result of a rise in prostitution; it may rather be an outcome of the dominant law-and-order philosophies characteristic of criminal justice policies in the 1980s and 1990s. In 1996, the bulk of these arrests (61%) were of women between the ages of 25 and 39 (Maguire & Pastore, 1997, p. 335); African Americans accounted for 38% of those arrested for prostitution and commercialized vice in 1996 (Maguire & Pastore, 1997, p. 338).[5]

These figures are of limited utility, however, as they only document arrests (and may include multiple arrests of the same women) and are widely recognized as overrepresenting women working on the streets, who are most vulnerable to law enforcement efforts. Priscilla Alexander (1988), a sex workers' rights advocate and researcher, estimates that only 10% to 20% of sex workers work in this sector of the industry. In addition, sex work occurs in massage clinics, bars, hotels, brothels, and outcall sectors (e.g., escort services, "call girls") (see Alexander, 1988). Scholars estimate that from 250,000 to 500,000 women are involved in prostitution in the United States (Scarpitti & Andersen, 1989; Scibelli, 1987).

However, most research on prostitution in the United States has focused on women's experiences in the lower echelons of the sex industry—the streets, and more recently crack houses and other drug environments (see Carmen & Moody, 1985; Inciardi, Lockwood, & Pottieger, 1993; Maher, 1997; Miller, 1986; Ratner, 1993; Zausner, 1986). This is partly a result of greater ease of access to these populations, as other forms of sex work remain hidden. In addition, it is because street prostitution has often been defined as the most problematic form of sex work in the United States and elsewhere because it occurs in public settings and often in areas characterized by high rates of crime. Street prostitution is also widely recognized as the most dangerous setting for sex workers themselves, a topic we will return to shortly. Notably, social definitions of prostitution in the United States so pervasively emphasize the actions of only sex workers that virtually no research has been conducted on clientele (see Chancer, 1993; but see Prasad, 1999).

The sex industry is not only characterized by different sectors but by status and economic hierarchies across them. Generally speaking, women working on the streets are among the lowest paid and socially stigmatized, with the recent exception of women engaged in sex-for-crack exchanges and/or who work in crack houses. Women working through escort services or as call girls are at the high end. Not surprisingly, poor women and women of color are disproportionately represented on the streets and in the lower levels of prostitution, in part because of the "low value assigned to their sexuality" within racist constructs of desire (Austin,

1992, p. 272; see also Kempadoo, 1998). In fact, in her ethnography of a Brooklyn drug market, sociologist Lisa Maher (1997) reports hierarchy among street-level sex workers, with white women able to attract more and higher-paying clientele than their African American and Latina counterparts.

Most scholars, activists, and sex workers agree that, in the United States and elsewhere, women's primary motivation for involvement in the industry is economic. In markets characterized by intense gender, race, and class hierarchies, prostitution provides a sometimes viable economic alternative among the limited options available. Both in the United States and abroad, despite the risks associated with sex work, no other occupation available to unskilled women provides an income comparable to that provided by prostitution. It is also important to note that "in one person's lifetime, sex work is commonly just one of the multiple activities employed for generating income, and very few stay in prostitution for their entire adulthood" (Kempadoo, 1998, p. 4; see also Austin, 1992, p. 272; Maher, 1997; Miller, 1986). Nonetheless, *prostitute* often becomes a master status for women involved in sex work, contributing to problems such as law enforcement discrimination, stigmatization, and violence.

In the United States, street prostitution is widely believed to be the most dangerous setting for sex work. Women engaged in street prostitution face widespread physical and sexual violence. For example, in the early 1980s, researchers Mimi Silbert and Ayala Pines (1982) conducted one of the largest studies of violence against street prostitutes in the United States, interviewing 200 women and girls in the San Francisco Bay area. They reported that 70% of their sample had been raped by clients, 65% were beaten by clients, 66% were physically abused by pimps, and 73% "had experienced rapes totally unrelated to their work as prostitutes" (p. 128). When women were identified as prostitutes by their rapists, the rapes tended to be more brutal, and the victims sustained more serious injuries.

Likewise, sociologist Jody Miller's (1997) study of street prostitution in Columbus, Ohio, in the early 1990s reported that 94% of the women had been sexually assaulted, including 75% who were raped by clients and 63% who were raped in other contexts on the streets. In addition, 88% reported having been physically assaulted: 61% had been beaten up, nearly a third had been stabbed or slashed, a quarter had been hit with an object such as a baseball bat or brick, and 38% reported having been kidnapped and held captive. In this sample of just 16 women, "two reported having been choked, three had suffered serious injuries such as broken bones, one had her head rammed through a glass door, and one had been tortured with electric shock" (Miller & Schwartz, 1995, p. 8).

These studies report the prevalence of violence, but this is only the tip of the iceberg, as women working on the streets describe much of this kind of violence as routine (E. Miller, 1986; J. Miller, 1997; Miller & Schwartz, 1995; Silbert & Pines, 1981; Zausner, 1986). Moreover, street-level sex workers experience violence, not just at the hands of clients, but also from pimps, drug dealers and users, the police, and others within the street environment (see Bracey, 1983; Maher, 1997; Miller, 1995a). Outside the United States, similar findings have also been reported, for instance, in the United Kingdom (Cunnington, 1984), Scotland (McKeganey & Barnard, 1996), Canada (Lowman & Fraser, 1995), and Norway (Hoigard & Finstad, 1992).

As noted previously, a wealth of evidence suggests that shifts resulting from the introduction of crack cocaine into the U.S. urban street scene have had detrimental effects on women engaged in sex work in these settings. For example, in her monograph, *Sexed Work,* Lisa Maher (1997) documents a rigid gender division of labor in the crack economy, shaped along racial lines, in which women find sex work one of the only available options for supporting their drug use. Changes in the economy brought about by crack have disadvantaged street sex workers further, resulting in lower payments, increased competition between women, and an intensification of their degradation and mistreatment. In addition, sexual exchanges in crack houses, particularly sex-for-crack exchanges, are believed to be among the most exploitative for drug-addicted women (see Bourgois & Dunlap, 1993; Goldstein, Ouellet, & Fendrich, 1992; Inciardi et al., 1993).

The intensity of violence against women working on the streets is a result of at least two sets of factors. First is the way in which the organization and criminalization of street prostitution make women particularly vulnerable to violent attack. Often, women who work on the streets have as one primary goal the avoidance of police detection. So, for example, they get into cars with clients hurriedly to minimize the possibility of being seen, they conduct transactions in isolated spots such as dark alleys or side streets, and they have clients drop them off in these areas to decrease visibility. However, these strategies often put women in greater physical danger. Because they are unable to conduct their work openly, their vulnerability to violence is increased. Although women also have strategies to avoid victimization, the nature of the work makes vulnerability to violence a structural feature (see Miller, 1997). Consequently, street-level sex workers are primary targets for serial killers as well (D. Linger, personal communication, October 27, 1999). In the 8 months following Miller's research in Columbus, Ohio, five street sex workers were murdered by a serial killer who was never caught (see also The Black Coalition Fighting Back Serial Murders, n.d; Cunnington, 1984; Lowman & Fraser, 1995).

Additional contributions to violence are ideologies that stigmatize sex workers, and street sex workers in particular (see Austin, 1992), "marking violence against them as insignificant, deserved, and/or justified" (Miller, 1995a, p. 437). Miller and Schwartz (1995) suggest that a particular set of ideological beliefs or "rape myths" concerning prostitution allow clients to justify or excuse their sexual violence against sex workers and also limit sex workers' access to legal assistance. First is the belief that prostitutes cannot be raped: "The fact that prostitutes are available for sexual negotiation [is interpreted to] mean that they are available for sexual harassment or rape" (Hatty, 1989, p. 236; see also Rubin, 1984). Second is the belief that no harm was done: Through a confusion of sex with violence, rape is defined simply as a bad business transaction. Third is a belief that prostitutes deserve violence against them because of their violation of normative expectations of appropriate femininity.

Finally, the notion of "collective liability" (see Black, 1983; Scully, 1990) is brought to bear on sex workers. For instance, women in Miller and Schwartz's (1995) study reported being held respon-

sible for the actions of their counterparts: A client angry at one sex worker would pick up another woman and take his aggression out on her. Although they recognized the pervasiveness of these beliefs, the women in Miller and Schwartz's study rejected each of them. As one put it, "being prostitutes, we still know the difference between rape and not getting raped." Another said, "Just because I'm working the streets, it's not casual to me, it's still a traumatic thing."

Besides overt violence, women working on the streets encounter a number of additional problems. Most notable is discriminatory law enforcement, both with regard to the sometimes indiscriminate arrest of street sex workers and the handling of (and participation in) their victimization by criminal justice officials. We will begin with a focus on the latter. As other chapters in this volume illustrate, the extent of women's legal protection from sexual violence is shaped by the extent to which they adhere to the standards of normative femininity. In the United States, this means being white, middle class, and chaste; as Bumiller (1990) suggests, protection is governed by women's ability to present themselves as "fallen angels" (see also Estrich, 1987; Frohmann, 1997). Because sex workers fall at the far end of this continuum, some scholars have suggested that rape of prostitutes goes unpunished (see Frohmann, 1997; Miller & Schwartz, 1995). Fairstein (1993) reports that in many U.S. communities, complaints brought by sex workers are automatically dismissed. Moreover, many sex workers do not go to the police when they are victimized for fear of criminal sanctions, because they have outstanding warrants for prostitution-related charges, or simply because they don't believe the criminal justice system will take their victimization seriously (Miller, 1997).

As noted, attitudes about sex workers play an important role in this process. When Miller was completing her research in Columbus, one vice officer told her that the attitude among police when a prostitute is found dead is, "Who really cares? You're dealing with a girl who's a zero." The Black Coalition Fighting Back Serial Killers (n.d.) was formed in the mid-1980s to raise awareness about police inattention and mishandling of the case of the Southside Slayer, a serial killer in South Central Los Angeles who targeted primarily African American women working as street sex workers. The police didn't bring the murders to public attention until 10 women had been killed and, specifically, until white women had been targeted. Moreover, early in the investigation, several officers referred to them as "cheap homicides," and one officer was overheard saying, "The slayer is doing a better job cleaning up the streets than we are" (Prescod, 1990).

In addition, as noted earlier, discriminatory law enforcement also occurs when it comes to the arrest and prosecution of street-level sex workers. There are often reports of police officers demanding free sex in exchange for avoiding arrest. In fact, in Miller's (1997) study, nearly half of the women she spoke with reported having been forced or coerced into having sex with men who identified themselves as police officers (see also Carmen & Moody, 1985). Other problems are noteworthy as well. As stated previously, sex workers bear the brunt of laws against prostitution, even where there is formal equality under the law criminalizing all parties involved (see Lowman, 1990). Even when clients are arrested, the penal-

ties they face are not as harsh, and charges often are dropped if they agree to testify against the sex workers (Scibelli, 1987). In some places, entrapment is legal, so that an undercover officer can approach a woman, quote a sexual act and a price, and if she consents, she is subject to arrest for solicitation.

Even when entrapment is not legal, it is nearly impossible for a "known" prostitute to credibly challenge the word of a police officer. Consequently, women often plead guilty rather than undergo prosecution. Once a woman has a record for prostitution, she is subject to indiscriminate arrest under loitering laws, which criminalize the movement of known prostitutes in public spaces (Scibelli, 1987). There is evidence of a great deal of abuse in the application of loitering laws, with police using arbitrary arrest tactics to harass women who are known prostitutes. Women have reported being arrested for walking to the store, for dressing a certain way, and for carrying condoms with them (Carmen & Moody, 1985; Miller, 1997). The process becomes cyclical: The more often women are arrested, the longer their record of prostitution becomes, making it more and more difficult to escape criminal labeling (Scibelli, 1987).

This section has documented some of the myriad problems faced by women working at the lower levels of the sex industry, particularly in the United States. In the remainder of the chapter, we turn our attention to the international sex industry, focusing on sex tourism, as well as trafficking and transnational sex work. Although many of the problems documented in the previous section apply to women working in the international sex industry, sex workers in the transnational sexual economy face a number of unique dangers tied to organizational features of the global industry.

Violence, Coercion, and Exploitation Within the International Sex Industry

Sex Tourism and Child Sex Tourism

According to the United Nations World Tourism Organization, tourism is fast becoming "the single most important global economic activity" (Enloe, 1989, p. 20). Tourism has been promoted extensively as a developmental strategy, resulting particularly from Western developmental policies, the influence of multinational corporations, and the economic impact of the U.S. military presence abroad (Campagna & Poffenberger, 1988; Enloe, 1989; Mies, 1986; Truong, 1990; Wood, 1981). Local governments, too, have actively promoted tourism, as it has become increasingly important in sustaining their economies. Worldwide, tourism is a $3.4 trillion industry (Kattoulas, 1995).

This is the context in which sex tourism has flourished. As we have defined it, sex tourism generally refers to the development and expansion of industries providing sexual services, catering primarily to Western and Japanese men who travel for business or leisure activities. Although prostitution and sex tourism are global phenomena, the growth in sex tourism in recent decades has been particularly pronounced in Asia. Prostitution has a long history in the region, but sex tourism is in part an outgrowth of U.S. military bases and "rest and recreation" centers established there during the Vietnam War (Enloe, 1989; Mies, 1986; Phongpaichit, 1982). The growth in international tourism, linked to the production of leisure services, occurred simultaneously with the placement of American troops in the region. The infrastructures put in place were well suited to the expansion of the tourist industry when the soldiers withdrew (see Truong, 1990).

Western imperialism, colonial legacies, and racialized notions of sexuality continue to shape the structure and operation of the sex-tourism industry (Kempadoo & Doezema, 1998). For instance, the promotion of tourism and sex tourism, including packaged sex tours, advertises the sexual availability of young women and girls to tourists, highlighting the notion that Asian women are submissive, exotic, and thus sexually desirable. Moreover, sex tourism is often framed as beneficial to both Third World economies and individual sex workers and their families, thus assuaging possible guilt on the part of sex tourists (see Kempadoo & Doezema, 1998; Miller, 1995b; Truong, 1990). Sex tourism is well documented in a number of countries, including Thailand, the Phillipines, China, Vietnam, Laos, Cambodia, Brazil, and the Dominican Republic (Flowers, 1998).

In Thailand, for instance, an estimated 500,000 to 700,000 women work in the commercial sex industry, the vast majority in Bangkok (Lim, 1998; Scibelli, 1987). A third are believed to be minors (Lim, 1998). If these estimates are accurate, upward of 10% of young women in Thailand between the ages of 15 and 25 are involved in the industry (see Scibelli, 1987). Young women from impoverished rural areas migrate or are trafficked to Bangkok to work in the sex industry as a means of supporting their families. There are direct routes from villages in the North to brothels in red-light zones in the Suthisarn and Saphan Kwai and from all regions to Patpong and Pattaya. Often, these young women are the main or even sole breadwinners in their families. It is important to note that estimates of the size of the commercial sex industry in various places do not distinguish between women working in tourist versus local markets. Although the thrust of public and research attention has been on sex tourism, many sex workers in Third World countries also provide services to local clientele (see Kempadoo & Doezema, 1998; Miller, 1999).

There is evidence that many young women are sold, outright or into debt bondage, in exchange for money provided to their families (Lim, 1998). Growing consumerism in the Third World is also cited as a factor; families in rural areas, able to purchase consumer goods from the profits of their daughters' labor, often obtain status within their communities (see Kempadoo & Doezema, 1998; Truong, 1990). As in other Southeast Asian countries, young women's sense of obligation to their families, and in some cases the economic benefits they receive, often result in their acceptance of the circumstances of their work. Moreover, as will be discussed shortly, they often have little recourse to resist because of the stigma attached to the work, its criminalization, and the coercive features of the industry.

Linked with tourism, prostitution is often recognized as a way to increase foreign revenue to a country, despite the fact that the majority of profits generated from tourism are channeled to Western multinationals (Truong, 1990). For example, a recent study conducted in Thailand suggests that prostitution is the largest underground industry in that country, generating between 10% and 14% of the country's gross national product (see Lim, 1998). The result is a tacit acceptance of the industry, despite the criminalization of sex workers (see Truong, 1990). Consequently,

whereas women and other providers of sexual services are stigmatized and face law enforcement sanctions, the infrastructures of the industry and those who profit from it remain untouched. This is not just the case in Thailand; it is a global phenomenon (see Kempadoo & Doezema, 1998).

One outgrowth of sex-tourism industries has been a rise in the involvement of children in these markets. Experts suggest that child sex tourism in particular has grown in recent years, as Western tourists who fear AIDS among adult prostitutes increasingly demand younger children (Boyes, 1996; Kattoulas, 1995). In addition, there is some evidence of organized pedophile networks in the West, exacerbated by the Internet, which provide information and organize tours abroad for the purpose of sexually abusing children (Boyes, 1996; EPCAT, 1997; McGirk, 1996). Moreover, developmental processes within the global economy have contributed to a rise in the earning activity of Third World children in a variety of settings. Thus, the rise in children's involvement in sex tourism and prostitution must be addressed "in the context of the global exploitation of child labor" (Kempadoo, 1998, p. 7).

Again, most available data focus on the Asian context, whereas child prostitution remains a global problem. According to a recent estimate by the U.N. International Labor Organization, upward of 1 million children in Asia are involved in the sex trade (Kaban, 1996; see also Healy, 1995). Thailand, Sri Lanka, the Philippines, Cambodia, and India are believed to be among the main centers of child sex tourism (Boyes, 1996; McGirk, 1996). Evidence suggests that in contrast to the West, where most child prostitution involves runaways (Davis, 1993), in Asia, many youths work in the sex industry to support their families (Montgomery, 1998; Truong, 1990). Sex tourists from Western Europe as well as Australia, Japan, and the United States travel to Asia to partake in the child sex trade. There is evidence that the production of pornographic publications featuring children has increased as well.

As is the case with the sex-tourism industry more generally, the root causes of the problem appear to be a host of economic, social, and cultural factors that developing countries face, as well as the demand generated by thousands of men who travel to the region annually to purchase sexual services from children; multinational infrastructures support the trade. Poverty is often cited as a primary cause for the increase in the number of children involved. This is the case both for parents who are induced to sell their children and for youths who see the sex industry as a viable means of earning money when compared to the limited alternatives available (see Montgomery, 1998). Gender discrimination and the lesser value of female children also contribute to a climate in which the sexual exploitation of girls flourishes, although there is evidence of the involvement of boys in the sex industry, as well (Montgomery, 1998). As previously discussed, a number of legal remedies have recently been introduced to curtail child sex tourism in particular; however, there is limited evidence of their success.

Trafficking and Transnational Sex Work

In conjunction with globalization and sex tourism, there has been a documented rise in trafficking and the movement of sex workers across international borders. The most recent definition given by the Global Alliance Against Traffic in Women, in cooperation with other agencies, defines *trafficking* as all acts and attempted acts involved in the recruitment, transportation within or across borders, purchase, sale, transfer, receipt, or harboring of a person (a) involving the use of deception, coercion, or debt bondage, (b) for the purpose of placing or holding such person, whether for pay or not, in involuntary servitude, in forced or bonded labor, or in slavery-like conditions, in a community other than the one in which such person lived at the time of the original deception, coercion, or debt bondage (Foundation Against Trafficking in Women, International Human Rights Law Group, and Global Alliance against Traffic in Women, 1999).

However, as noted previously, a number of activists argue against the voluntary versus forced dichotomy, noting that it remains a limited framework for dealing with transnational sex work. For example, as a result of both immigration laws and laws against prostitution, women who voluntarily migrate for prostitution often find themselves in situations of coercion, dependence, and debt bondage. Because their decision to engage in sex work was voluntary, they receive less public sympathy and inadequate assistance or support (Kempadoo & Doezema, 1998). Thus, it is important to note that many of the problems associated with trafficking are also faced by women who migrate voluntarily for prostitution.

Evidence suggests that every year, hundreds of thousands of women are trafficked and exploited within the transnational prostitution industry. Although accurate data are difficult to come by, the

International Organization for Migration estimates that traffickers move as many as 4 million illegal migrants each year. Trafficking may take place within national boundaries as well as across international borders. International trafficking involves both legal and illegal migration. Although much attention is currently paid to international trafficking, particularly across Asian countries, rural-urban migration patterns are long established within national boundaries, as noted above with regard to Thailand. Calcutta is a well-known receiving zone in India, with land routes through West Bengal, Bombay, and Punjab.

Although the trafficking of women for prostitution is a global activity, trafficking is believed to be highest within and from Asia. Nonetheless, trafficking can be found in Latin America and the Caribbean, in Africa, and to and from North America, the Middle East, Europe, and Australia. The collapse of the Soviet Union, with the resultant opening of borders and economic decline, has resulted in highly organized Russian crime groups that also send women abroad to work in the commercial sex industry. Russian sex workers are found throughout the world, most notably in Japan, China, the Middle East, and Western Europe (Brussa, 1998; Flowers, 1998). Although there are common patterns in sex workers' experiences in various locations, cultural patterns and differences in laws pertaining to migration and prostitution also create unique problems that are site-specific for sex workers (see Kempadoo & Doezema, 1998). We will touch on some of these issues below.

Where trafficking across borders is concerned, it is notable that the same country can serve as a sending, destination, or transit country. For example, in Thailand, there is evidence that women are trafficked from China to Hong Kong, from Burma to Thailand, and from Thailand to Japan (Wijers & Lap-Chew, 1997). Thus, there does not appear to be one set pattern to trafficking. Instead, trafficking routes change in response to economic and political changes. Typically, women and girls are trafficked to a destination via overland routes; where more sophisticated crime groups are involved, they are also transferred by air to overseas markets.

In most instances, developed or developing countries with well-established sex industries are receiving countries. These include Japan, Germany, the United States, and the Netherlands, along with Thailand, Taiwan, Korea, and India. For instance, evidence suggests that the majority of sex workers in Western Europe today are migrants from Third World and Eastern European countries (Brussa, 1998). Poorer countries, with the lowest levels of development, are more likely to send women and children abroad; the historical pattern continues to be outmigration from poorer to wealthier countries. Wealth disparities between First and Third World countries, as well as the marginalization of women in the latter, are factors. As mentioned with regard to sex tourism more broadly, developmental strategies have contributed immensely to the growth in international trafficking. In addition, Western notions of the exotic sexuality of Asian, African, and Latin American women contribute to demand (Kempadoo & Doezema, 1998; Miller, 1995b).

The extent and nature of trafficking is best documented in Asia. It encompasses a large spectrum of countries, with diverse cultures and economies. Within the region, Japan is a major receiving country. It is estimated that 150,000 non-Japanese women, mainly from Thailand and the Philippines, are working as prostitutes in Japan. Japanese men constitute the largest number of sex tourists in Asia (Lim, 1998). Thailand is also a major receiving country in Asia, in part because of its well-developed tourism industry. It receives women mainly from the Philippines, China, Hong Kong, and Burma. In South Asia, Bangladeshi women are usually trafficked via India to Pakistan, and massive trafficking of women and girls takes place across Nepal into India. It is estimated that over 100,000 Nepalese women and girls work in brothels in India. About a quarter of sex workers in India are believed to be underage (Lim, 1998).

Asia includes a large number of poor countries as well as economically well-developed countries. This, along with the growth in tourism, helps explain the high rate of trafficking within the region. High rates of illiteracy; lack of employment opportunities; and cultural religious ideologies and patriarchal family structures that place unmarried, separated, divorced, or widowed women outside the protective confines of the social system make them most liable for trafficking. Trafficking usually takes place from rural to urban settings and from cities to other countries. Unfamiliarity with their surroundings makes it difficult for women to return home.

It is important to note that women who are trafficked and/or who migrate for sex work are not only found in tourist markets. Instead, their sexual services are made available to indigenous men, too (Kempadoo & Doezema, 1998). In Sri Lanka, for instance, where a great deal of

internal trafficking occurs (e.g., women migrate and are tricked or coerced from rural to urban areas within the country), the vast majority of women describe their clientele as almost exclusively local men, despite Sri Lanka's reputation for sex tourism. Moreover, women who migrate into the country from Russia, Thailand, and elsewhere routinely provide sexual services to Sri Lankan businessmen (Miller, 1999).

It is estimated that traffickers generate gross earnings of $5 billion to $7 billion per year (Office for Drug Control and Crime Prevention, United Nations Interregional Crime and Justice Research Institute, and Centre for International Crime Prevention, 1998). Trafficking today is well structured and is often controlled by organized crime groups. Recruiting agents may be job agencies, acquaintances, family friends, or relatives. Recruitment methods usually involve deceit or debt bondage, but they can also involve violence. Most often, women are deceived about the conditions of work rather than its nature, although it is not uncommon for women to be deceived about the nature of the work, as well. Some are brought over with promises of jobs as waitresses, domestic helpers, or similar service workers; sometimes, false marriages are promised or arranged.

Even when women know they are migrating for sex work, they are often unprepared for the working conditions they discover. For example, trafficking often generates a system of debt bondage. This occurs when women borrow money for the cost of travel, visas, false documents, and employment location; they are, then, charged exorbitant interest and required to work off the debt before accumulating their own earnings. It is not uncommon for women's debt to be sold by one employer to another, or for women's visas and passports to be confiscated as security on the loan. In some instances, particularly cases involving the traffic in young women or children, an advance payment is given to the family, which the individual is required to pay off with interest. Even when migration is voluntary, women's status as illegal immigrants makes them vulnerable to exploitation and coercion in these markets (Kempadoo & Doezema, 1998).

Violence and Exploitation Within Sex Tourism and Transnational Sex Work

Evidence regarding sex tourism and transnational sex work tends to be more anecdotal than the research discussed above from the United States. Nonetheless, it consistently points to similar patterns of violence and discriminatory law enforcement, in addition to coercion, exploitation, and violence in the context of "inside" work (e.g., brothels, lodges, outcall services) as a result of the structural features of the international sex industry. Trafficking, as we have previously discussed, is "a process through which migrant women are brought into prostitution through the use of violence, coercion, deceit, [or] abuse, and are denied human rights and freedoms" (Kempadoo & Doezema, 1998, p. 21). As noted, trafficking can occur within or across national borders. In addition, women who voluntarily migrate for sex work also sometimes find themselves working in slavery-like conditions in which their mobility is restricted and they are not given the right to control the conditions of their work, including the choice of which or how many customers they see. Moreover, many women

work under conditions of debt bondage, as previously described.

Documenting "how slavery finds its way into the sex industry," sex workers' advocate Jo Bindman (1998) notes,

Most people who work in [sex] establishments lack formal contracts with the owners or managers but are subject to their control. Those who work in the sex industry are commonly excluded from mainstream society. They are thereby denied whatever international, national, or customary protection from abuse is available to others as citizens, women, or workers. The lack of international and local protection renders sex workers vulnerable to exploitation in the workplace and to violence at the hands of management, customers, law enforcement officials, and the public. (p. 67)

As a consequence of conditions of illegal confinement and forced labor, women are subject to a range of abuses, including physical and sexual assault, as well as exposure to HIV and other STDs. Health care is minimal, and women who contract diseases are often simply discarded. For instance, Truong (1990) reports that in Thailand, brothel owners often arrange police raids and the arrest of unwanted women. Sex workers are often blamed for the spread of AIDS and other STDs. Just as historian Judith Walkowitz (1980) documented regarding the spread and control of syphilis in the 19th century, sex workers today "are placed under scrutiny, subject to intense campaigning and . . . define[d] as the vectors and transmitters of disease" (Kempadoo, 1998, p. 18). In some countries, such as Sri Lanka, women found to have STDs are remanded to detention facilities (Miller, 1999). Most often, migrant women are deported on discovery that they are HIV-positive, and they face intense stigma on return to their homelands. In fact, "there is a fairly well-substantiated rumor that HIV-positive Burmese women returned to Burma [e.g., deported] have been executed by the ruling SLORC authorities" (Murray, 1998, p. 56).

Again, many argue that strict migration laws in conjunction with legal statutes governing the sex industry allow this system to flourish and increase sex workers' dependence on outside agents (Kempadoo & Doezema, 1998). Brokers, managers, traffickers, recruiters, and middle men, as well as legitimate businesses such as hotels and travel agencies, continue to profit from the industry, whereas sex workers face distinct disadvantages that undermine their ability to control their labor and make them dependent on individuals and organizations who exploit them (see Kempadoo & Doezema, 1998; Truong, 1990). In addition, police corruption, bribery schemes, and government collusion are well documented (Miller, 1999; Truong, 1990). Several particularly gruesome cases highlight the seriousness of violence against women in the international sex industry. One is a well-publicized brothel fire in Thailand, where the charred remains of women were found chained to beds. Legal analyst Margaret Healy (1995) opens her analysis of laws against child sex tourism with the horrifying case of a 12-year-old Filipino girl who was brutalized by an Australian doctor, who "forcibly inserted an electric vibrator into [her] vagina" (p. 1985), where it broke and became lodged. The girl did not receive medical treatment and died 7 months later. Although the doctor originally received a life sentence for the crime, the

Supreme Court in the Philippines eventually reversed the decision and acquitted the doctor, who remains a free man. It is difficult to know how typical cases such as these are, but clearly, around the world, sex workers are "imprisoned and detained, subjected to cruel and degrading mistreatment, [and] suffer violence at the hands of the state or by private individuals with the state's support" (Doezema, 1998, p. 46). Because many of the women subject to this exploitation made the initial decision to engage in sex work, they do not receive public support. "As yet, no international conventions or anti-trafficking organizations exist that explicitly support sex workers' human rights" (Kempadoo & Doezema, 1998, p. 30), particularly if they are voluntarily involved in the industry.

Conclusion

This chapter has provided an overview of the commercial sex industry in the United States and internationally, focusing on how the organization and control of the industry facilitates the abuse and mistreatment of sex workers. The sex industry is built on gender, race, and class inequalities, as well as power imbalances between Western and Third World nations. Profits generated from the sex industry, as well as a sexual double standard that defines sex workers as deviant and therefore outside the realm of legitimate society and its protections, allows the industry to thrive on the backs of sex workers themselves. As we have detailed, "the law plays a critical role in determining the physical vulnerability of prostitute women" (Hatty, 1989, p. 235). Legal responses, whether they emphasize prohibition, abolition, or regulation, jeopardize the rights and safety of women involved in the industry in various but systematic ways.

As noted, most activists and researchers agree that the key to improving the situation of women in the sex trade is to recognize the legitimacy of their work and to sanction those who exploit them. Sometimes, this approach is viewed merely as a short-term solution by people who remain critical of the industry itself (see Overall, 1992), and in other cases, it is a long-term goal that seeks recognition of prostitution as a legitimate service industry (see Jenness, 1993). Given the economic benefits derived from sex workers' exploitation by individuals, multinational corporations, and governments, as well as the gendered hierarchies on which the industry is built, the likelihood of this occurring in the short term is minimal. Nonetheless, the recent development of sex workers' rights organizations throughout the world is reason to maintain hope.

Notes

1. Here, we should clarify precisely what our chapter will and will not cover. Although we recognize that a minority of sex workers are men, our focus is on women in the sex industry. In addition, although we will provide a brief overview of children's involvement in sex-tourism markets, it is beyond the scope of this chapter to deal systematically with the array of distinct and additional problems associated with this facet of the industry. Thus, our primary emphasis is on adults. Finally, although a number of activities fall under the umbrella term *sex work,* including pornography, erotic dance, stripping, and phone sex work, we limit our analysis to prostitution.

2. This is necessary, as the coauthors do not share an identical position regarding these questions. One is more sympathetic to feminist critiques of prostitution as an institution that contributes to women's oppression; the other's position falls closer to that of prostitutes rights' groups,

which posit that prostitution is legitimate service work. Moreover, to focus on this debate at length distracts from the primary goal of this chapter, which is to highlight the contemporary nature of violence against sex workers. The authors agree, however, that the terms of the previous debate are inadequate to address the child sex trade.

3. An ironic exception is the recent case of Queensland, Australia, where laws were changed in a seeming move to afford greater control to sex workers. As a result, women were legally permitted to work as call girls, but third-party involvement was strictly prohibited. A number of call girls were subsequently murdered by clients in their apartments, acting on the knowledge that the women were working alone (A. Arnot-Bradshaw, personal communication, April 14, 1999).

4. We do not have data to address estimated prevalence rates of prostitution in other Western industrialized countries. Where data are available, various facets of the commercial sex industry in these countries will be discussed.

5. The *Sourcebook of Criminal Justice Statistics—1997* did not provide a breakdown of arrests by race and gender; thus, this figure includes both male and female arrestees.

References

Alexander, P. (1988). Prostitution: A difficult issue for feminists. In F. Delacoste & P. Alexander (Eds.), *Sex work: Writings by women in the sex industry* (pp. 184-214). London: Virago.

Austin, R. (1992). "The Black community," its lawbreakers, and a politics of identification. *Southern California Law Review, 65,* 1769-1817.

Barry, K. (1979). *Female sexual slavery.* New York: New York University Press.

Barry, K. (1995). *The prostitution of sexuality.* New York: New York University Press.

Bell, L. (Ed.). (1987). *Good girls/bad girls: Feminists and sex trade workers face to face.* Seattle, WA: Seal.

Berkman, T. (1996). Responses to the international child sex trade. *Boston College International and Comparative Law Review, 19,* 397-416.

Bindman, J. (1998). An international perspective on slavery in the sex industry. In K. Kempadoo

& J. Doezema (Eds.), *Global sex workers: Rights, resistance, and redefinition* (pp. 65-68). New York: Routledge.

Black, D. (1983). Crime as social control. *American Sociological Review, 48,* 34-45.

The Black Coalition Fighting Back Serial Murders. (n.d.). *Counting women's lives: Organizing for police accountability in black communities.* Los Angeles: Author.

Bourgois, P., & Dunlap, E. (1993). Exorcising sex-for-crack: An ethnographic perspective from Harlem. In M. S. Ratner (Ed), *Crack pipe as pimp: An ethnographic investigation of sex-for-crack exchanges* (pp. 97-132). New York: Lexington.

Boyes, R. (1996, August 22). How the sex tourists evade justice. *The Times.*

Bracey, D. H. (1983). The juvenile prostitute: Victim and offender. *Victimology, 8,* 149-162.

Brussa, L. (1998). The TAMPEP project in Western Europe. In K. Kempadoo & J. Doezema (Eds.), *Global sex workers: Rights, resistance, and redefinition* (pp. 246-259). New York: Routledge.

Bumiller, K. (1990). Fallen angels: The representation of violence against women in legal culture. *International Journal of the Sociology of Law, 18,* 125-142.

Bureau of International Labor Affairs. (1996). *Forced labor: The prostitution of children.* Washington, DC: U.S. Department of Labor.

Campagna, D. S., & Poffenberger, D. L. (1988). *The sexual trafficking in children: An investigation of the child sex trade.* Westport, CT: Auburn House.

Carmen, A., & Moody, H. (1985). *Working women: The subterranean world of street prostitution.* New York: Harper & Row.

Chancer, L. S. (1993). Prostitution, feminist theory, and ambivalence: Notes from the sociological underground. *Social Text, 37,* 143-171.

Coomaraswamy, R. (1997, February 12). *Report of the Special Rapporteur on Violence Against Women: Its causes and consequences.* Paper presented at the 53rd Session of the United Nations Economic and Social Council, New York.

Cooper, B. (1989). Prostitution: A feminist analysis. *Women's Rights Law Reporter, 11,* 99-119.

Cunnington, S. (1984). Aspects of violence in prostitution. In J. Hopkins (Ed.), *Perspectives on rape and sexual assault* (pp. 25-36). London: Harper & Row.

Davis, N. J. (Ed.). (1993). *Prostitution: An international handbook on trends, problems, and policies.* Westport, CT: Greenwood.

Doezema, J. (1998). Forced to choose: Beyond the voluntary v. forced prostitution dichotomy. In K. Kempadoo & J. Doezema (Eds), *Global sex workers: Rights, resistance, and redefinition* (pp. 34-50). New York: Routledge.

Enloe, C. (1989). *Bananas, beaches, and bases: Making feminist sense of international politics.* Berkeley: University of California Press.

EPCAT (End Child Prostitution in Asian Tourism). (1997, April 20). The paedophile's club. *The Sunday Leader.*

Estrich, S. (1987). *Real rape.* Cambridge, MA: Harvard University Press.

Fairstein, L. A. (1993). *Sexual violence: Our war against rape.* New York: William Morrow.

Flowers, B. R. (1998). *The prostitution of women and girls.* Jefferson, NC: Macfarland.

Foundation Against Trafficking in Women, International Human Rights Law Group, and Global Alliance against Traffic in Women. (1999). *Human rights standards for the treatment of trafficked persons.* Bangkok, Thailand: Global Alliance against Traffic in Women.

Frohmann, L. (1997). Discrediting victims' allegations of sexual assault: Prosecutorial accounts of case rejections. In P. A. Adler & P. Adler (Eds), *Constructions of deviance* (2nd ed., pp. 211-228). Belmont, CA: Wadsworth.

Giobbe, E. (1991). Prostitution and sexual violence. *Center for Advanced Feminist Studies* (University of Minnesota), *8,* 6-7.

Goldstein, P. J., Ouellet, L. J., & Fendrich, M. (1992). From bag brides to skeezers: A historical perspective on sex-for-drug behavior. *Journal of Psychoactive Drugs, 24,* 349-361.

Gunasekera, R. (1996, October 27). Sri Lanka says orphanages used in child-sex trade. *Reuters World Service.*

Hatty, S. (1989). Violence against prostitute women: Social and legal dilemmas. *Australian Journal of Social Issues, 24,* 235-248.

Healy, M. A. (1995). Prosecuting child sex tourism at home: Do laws in Sweden, Australia, and the United States safeguard the rights of children as mandated by international laws? *Fordham International Law Journal, 18,* 1852-1871.

Hoigard, C., & Finstad, L. (1992). *Backstreets: Prostitution, money and love.* University Park: Pennsylvania State University Press.

Inciardi, J., Lockwood, A. D., & Pottieger, A. E. (1993). *Women and crack cocaine.* New York: Macmillan.

James, J. (1978). The prostitute as victim. In J. R. Chapman & M. Gates (Eds.), *The victimization of women* (pp. 175-201). Beverly Hills, CA: Sage.

Jenness, V. (1993). *Making it work: The prostitutes' rights movement in perspective.* New York: Aldine de Gruyter.

Kaban, E. (1996, November 12). ILO says 250 million children are workers. *Reuters World Service.*

Kattoulas, V. (1995, November 30). World tourism industry dodges child sex-tour issue. *Reuters North American Wire.*

Kempadoo, K. (1998). Introduction: Globalizing sex workers' rights. In K. Kempadoo & J. Doezema (Eds.), *Global sex workers: Rights, resistance, and redefinition* (pp. 1-28). New York: Routledge.

Kempadoo, K., & Doezema, J. (Eds.). (1998). *Global sex workers: Rights, resistance, and redefinition.* New York: Routledge.

Lim, L. L. (Ed.). (1998). *The sex sector: The economic and social bases of prostitution in southeast Asia.* Geneva: International Labor Organization.

Lowman, J. (1990). Notions of formal equality before the law: The experiences of street prostitutes and their customers. *Journal of Human Justice, 1,* 55-76.

Lowman, J., & Fraser, L. (1995). *Violence against persons who prostitute: The experience in British Columbia* (Technical report). Canada: Department of Justice.

Maguire, K., & Pastore, A. L. (Eds.). (1997). *Sourcebook of criminal justice statistics—1997.* Washington, DC: Bureau of Justice Statistics.

Maher, L. (1997). *Sexed work: Gender, race, and resistance in a Brooklyn drug market.* New York: Oxford University Press.

McGirk, T. (1996, May 12). Their latest holiday destination. *The* [Colombo, Sri Lanka] *Independent.*

McKeganey, N., & Barnard, M. (1996). *Sex work on the streets: Prostitutes and their clients.* Buckingham, UK: Open University Press.

Mies, M. (1986). *Patriarchy and accumulation on a world scale: Women in the international division of labor.* London: Zed Books.

Miller, E. M. (1986). *Street woman.* Philadelphia: Temple University Press.

Miller, E. M. (1991, August). *Thinking about prostitution discourse as a way of thinking about gender as a principle of social organization.* Paper presented at the Annual Meeting of the American Sociological Association, Cincinnati, OH.

Miller, J. (1995a). Gender and power on the streets: Street prostitution in the era of crack cocaine. *Journal of Contemporary Ethnography, 23,* 427-452.

Miller, J. (1995b). Sex tourism in Southeast Asia. In A. Thio & T. Calhoun (Eds.), *Readings in deviant behavior* (pp. 278-283). New York: HarperCollins.

Miller, J. (1997). Victimization and resistance among street prostitutes. In P. A. Adler & P. Adler (Eds), *Constructions of deviance* (2nd ed., pp. 500-515). Belmont, CA: Wadsworth.

Miller, J. (1999). *The commercial sex industry in Sri Lanka: Some preliminary observations.* International Centre for Ethnic Studies Lecture Series, Colombo, Sri Lanka.

Miller, J., & Schwartz, M. D. (1995). Rape myths and violence against street prostitutes. *Deviant Behavior, 16,* 1-23.

Montgomery, H. (1998). Children, prostitution, and identity: A case study from a tourist resort in Thailand. In K. Kempadoo & J. Doezema (Eds.), *Global sex workers: Rights, resistance, and redefinition* (pp. 139-150). New York: Routledge.

Murray, A. (1998). Debt-bondage and trafficking: Don't believe the hype. In K. Kempadoo & J. Doezema (Eds.), *Global sex workers: Rights, resistance, and redefinition* (pp. 51-64). New York: Routledge.

Office For Drug Control And Crime Prevention, United Nations Interregional Crime and Justice Research Institute, and Center for International Crime Prevention. (1998). *Global programme against trafficking in human beings: An outline for action.* Geneva: United Nations.

Overall, C. (1992). What's wrong with prostitution? Evaluating sex work. *Signs, 17,* 705-724.

Phongpaichit, P. (1982). *From peasant girls to Bangkok masseuses.* Geneva: International Labor Office.

Prasad, M. (1999). The morality of market exchange: Love, money, and contractual justice. *Sociological Perspectives, 42,* 181-198.

Prescod, M. (1990, June). Paper presented at the annual meeting of National Women's Studies Association, Akron, OH.

Ratner, M. S. (Ed.) (1993). *Crack pipe as pimp: An ethnographic investigation of sex-for-crack exchanges.* New York: Lexington.

Rubin, G. (1984). Thinking sex: Notes for a radical theory of the politics of sexuality. In C. Vance (Ed.), *Pleasure and danger: Exploring female sexuality.* London: Pandora.

Samarasinghe, M. (1996, October 30). Sri Lanka cracking down on child sex abuse. *Reuters World Service.*

Samarasinghe, M. (1997, February 11). Sri Lanka deports Swiss facing child abuse charges. *Reuters World Service.*

Scarpitti, F. R., & Andersen, M. L. (1989). *Social problems.* New York: Harper & Row.

Scibelli, P. (1987). Empowering prostitutes: A proposal for international legal reform. *Harvard Women's Law Journal, 10,* 117-157.

Scully, D. (1990). *Understanding sexual violence: A study of convicted rapists.* Boston: Unwin Hyman.

Silbert, M. H., & Pines, A. M. (1981). Occupational hazards of street prostitutes. *Criminal Justice and Behavior, 8,* 395-399.

Silbert, M. H., & Pines, A. M. (1982). Victimization of street prostitutes. *Victimology, 7,* 122-133.

Truong, T. (1990). *Sex, money, and morality: Prostitution and tourism in southeast Asia.* London: Zed Books.

Walkowitz, J. (1980). *Prostitution and Victorian society.* Cambridge, UK: Cambridge University Press.

Wijers, M., & Lap-Chew, L. (1997). *Trafficking in women, forced labour and slavery-like practices in marriage, domestic labour and prostitution.* The Netherlands: Foundation Against Trafficking in Women.

Wood, R. E. (1981). The economics of tourism. *Southeast Asia Chronicle, 78,* 2-12.

Zausner, M. (1986). *The streets: A factual portrait of six prostitutes as told in their own words.* New York: St. Martin's.

CHAPTER 24

Violence Against Women as a Human Rights Violation

International Institutional Responses

Johanna Bond
Robin Phillips

In Armenia, a man locked his young wife and their infant daughter in the bedroom after the woman threatened to leave him. The man repeatedly beat and raped his wife until she escaped one day when he forgot to lock the door before he went to work.

A 15-year-old girl in Jordan was killed by her father when he discovered that she was pregnant. Later, it was discovered that the father was the person who impregnated her.

A young female secretary in Bulgaria was repeatedly raped by her boss. The man threatened to kill the woman if she reported the rape.

A young woman in Bangladesh was blinded and severely disfigured when a jilted lover threw corrosive battery acid in her face.

In the United States, a 9-year-old girl was forcibly taken from the playground in her suburban community and forced to engage in prostitution in South America. Although she begged her "clients" to help her, she did not escape until her captors sent her back to the United States as part of an international prostitution ring when she was in her mid-20s.

Violence against women is almost certainly the most pervasive human rights violation in the world. Women around the world experience violence in their families, in their workplaces, and in their communities. They experience violence both at the hands of the state and at the hands of private individuals. This violence includes domestic violence, rape, sexual assault, forced prostitution, female genital mutilation, female infanticide, and sexual harassment. Other lesser known forms of violence against women include honor killing, which is the murder of a woman by family members because they believe her behavior has brought shame to the family; dowry violence, the murder or maiming of a woman by her husband or his family because her family has not provided the expected or desired dowry for her; and sex trafficking in women, which in its most narrow sense means the movement of women to other countries by fraud for the purpose of forced or coerced prostitution.

The statistics are overwhelming. In the United States, a woman is abused by her partner every 9 seconds. Around the world, more than 130 million women and girls have undergone female genital mutilation (FGM), with an additional 2 million girls undergoing FGM each year. More than 5,000 women are killed each year in dowry murders in India. In the 1994 genocide in Rwanda, more than 15,000 women were raped in 1 year. In South Africa, 50,000 rapes are reported each year. Rape-crisis researchers there estimate only 1 in 35 rapes is reported to the authorities. An estimated 250,000 women from Central and Eastern Europe and the former Soviet Union are trafficked to Western Europe in the sex trade each year.

In spite of the pervasive nature of the problem, the United Nations was slow to respond. In 1993, almost 50 years after its creation, the United Nations finally formally recognized women's rights as human rights and violence against women as a human rights abuse. It promised to integrate gender issues throughout the systems of the United Nations to ensure that women enjoy human rights on an equal basis with men. Through individual women's stories of abuse and organized lobbying efforts, activists from around the world persuaded the United Nations to recognize the forms of violence women most commonly experience as violations of international human rights. Increased attention to violence against women around the world was also the catalyst for the United Nations' broader recognition of the impact of gender on human rights issues. This chapter outlines the development of women's human rights within the United Nations and the international institutional recognition of violence against women as a human rights abuse.

Overview of Human Rights Law: The International Bill of Human Rights

Human rights are the rights that all people have simply because they are human beings. Contemporary human rights standards were developed in the aftermath of World War II. Countries around the world organized an international body to develop universal human rights standards and monitor implementation of these standards to protect the human rights of all people. This organization, the United Nations, was created in an effort to ensure that the atrocities of the Nazi regime would never be repeated. It was founded on the principle that each member nation of the United Nations must protect all of its citizens against violations of their fundamental human rights.

The United Nations Charter was signed in 1945. Under the Charter, members of the United Nations have an obligation to promote human rights and fundamental freedoms "without distinction as to race, sex, language, or religion." The General Assembly of the United Nations adopted the Universal Declaration of Human Rights in 1948 and proclaimed it the "common standard of achievement for all peoples and all nations." The Universal Declaration states that the "recognition of the inherent dignity and of the equal and inalienable rights of all members of the human family is the foundation of freedom, justice, and peace in the world." The Universal Declaration established core human rights principles, including among others, the rights to life, liberty, security, and equal protection of the law. These rights fall into two broad general categories: civil and political rights and economic, social, and cultural rights.

Eighteen years after it adopted the Universal Declaration, the General Assembly adopted two international human rights treaties, the International Covenant on Civil and Political Rights and the International Covenant on Economic, Social, and Cultural Rights. Together with the Universal Declaration, these documents form what has become known as the International Bill of Human Rights.

Civil and political rights include rights such as the right to life; the right to nondiscrimination; the right to liberty and security of the person; the right to live free of torture or cruel, inhuman, or degrading treatment or punishment; freedom of thought, conscience, and religion; and freedom of association. Traditionally, commentators have characterized civil and political rights as negative rights (Steiner & Alston, 1996). To be in compliance with these obligations, governments merely had to refrain from doing something. A government, for example, had to cease torturing political prisoners or cease blocking labor unions from organizing. Traditionally understood, the In-

ternational Covenant on Civil and Political Rights did not require governments to take any affirmative action. States parties, countries that ratified the treaty and agreed to be bound by its terms, could, therefore, theoretically implement their obligations under the treaty immediately and without delay.

Economic, social, and cultural rights, on the other hand, were traditionally understood as positive rights, requiring the state to take some action. Economic, social, and cultural rights include rights to work, to health, and to education. The International Covenant on Economic, Social, and Cultural Rights requires that a state party "take steps . . . to the maximum of its available resources, with a view to achieving progressively the full realization of the rights recognized in the present Covenant." Because the treaty requires progressive implementation, states parties commit to incremental rather than immediate implementation of most of the economic, social, and cultural rights contained therein.

The distinction between civil and political rights and social, economic, and cultural rights has resulted in a hierarchy of rights (Meyer, 1999). Historically, the United Nations and international human rights organizations have placed a higher priority on civil and political rights. The example of the tortured political prisoner became the quintessential picture of human rights violations.

In recent years, the traditional distinctions between civil and political and economic, social, and cultural rights have begun to break down. Many commentators recognize that the protection of civil and political rights often requires that the state take affirmative measures to ensure the enjoyment of those human rights. Similarly, there is a consensus within the international community that civil and political and economic, social, and cultural rights are interdependent and indivisible. Full enjoyment of civil and political rights is not possible without economic, social, and cultural rights—and vice versa. Subsequent human rights conventions adopted by the United Nations, such as the Convention on the Elimination of All Forms of Discrimination Against Women adopted in 1979, the International Convention on the Elimination of All Forms of Racial Discrimination adopted in 1969, and the Convention on the Rights of the Child adopted in 1990, represent a blend of civil, political, economic, social, and cultural rights.

Human Rights Violated by Systemic Violence Against Women

In addition to gender-based human rights violations, women may suffer other human rights violations that have nothing to do with gender. Women may, for example, die as a result of armed conflict or be imprisoned because of their political opinions. Violence against women, however, specifically refers to violence women suffer *because* they are women or to forms of violence that women suffer disproportionately.

The rights embodied in the major human rights treaties are directly relevant to violence against women. Many of these rights are violated by systemic violence against women but have not traditionally been invoked in this context. Women generally have not, for example, asserted complaints involving violence against women under the Optional Protocol to the International Covenant on Civil and Political Rights, a process that would allow them to bring complaints before the United Nations Human Rights Committee.

International treaties provide a catalog of universal human rights. The most basic of all human rights is the right to life. Extreme forms of violence often result in women losing their lives. In some cultures, a strong preference for sons may lead families to commit female infanticide. For example, after the government in China instituted a policy restricting families to only one child, the birth rate for female children dropped precipitously. According to a 1987 survey by the State Statistical Bureau of China, there were half a million fewer female infants than one would predict given the expected biological ratio of male to female births (Heise, Pitanguy, & Germain, 1994).

In countries such as Brazil, Egypt, Jordan, Pakistan, and Turkey, communities tolerate and condone "honor" crimes, in which women and girls are murdered or maimed by their families in an effort to regain family honor after the victim has allegedly shamed the family. In Pakistan, for example, in 1999, a man set his sister, Ghazala, on fire because he suspected she was having sexual relations with a neighbor (Amnesty International, 1999, p. 5). According to witnesses, her burned and naked body lay in the street for 2 hours because no one wanted to have anything to do with it. Amnesty International outlines the responsibility of the government of Pakistan, stating,

> As state institutions—the law enforcement apparatus and the judiciary—have dealt with such crimes against women with extraordinary leniency, and as the law provides many loopholes for murderers in the name of honour to get away, the tradition remains unbroken. (Amnesty International, 1999, p. 5)

When the state fails to act diligently to prevent these and other types of violence, women suffer grave human rights violations, including violations of the right to life.

Similarly, violence against women, including FGM, domestic violence, forced prostitution, and many other forms of violence, violates the right to live free of torture or cruel, inhuman, or degrading treatment. Definitions of *torture* under international law generally include four elements: "(1) severe physical and/or mental pain and suffering; (2) intentionally inflicted; (3) for specified purposes; and (4) with some form of official involvement, whether active or passive" (Copelon, 1994, p. 122). In cases of violence against women, the last element, official involvement, is satisfied through governmental inaction or passive involvement in the violence.

The purpose and methods of domestic violence, for example, and traditional forms of torture are similar in many ways. Perpetrators of domestic violence often use violence and control to dominate the victim in much the same way as the traditional perpetrator of torture, who represents the state. These perpetrators may use torture to elicit information, punish the victims, or diminish their capacity (Copelon, 1994).

The World Organization Against Torture, an international coalition of nongovernmental organizations (NGOs) fighting against torture and other inhumane treatment, has also detailed the similarities between public forms of torture and private forms of torture.

> Just as torture by a state official typically takes place when the victim is in *incommunicado* detention, at the unsupervised mercy of his interrogators or captors and without access to the outside world, battered women, because of their domestic situation, live isolated

from family and friends and others. (Benninger-Budel & Lacroix, 1999, p. 43)

The World Organization Against Torture also equates torture with other forms of violence against women, including among others, rape and sexual assault, dowry violence, and honor crimes.

Violence against women also violates the right to liberty and security of person. Gender-based violence, such as rape or domestic violence, involves some form of physical assault or intrusion. As a result, these forms of violence inherently violate the rights of bodily integrity and security of the person. Women's accounts of rape and sexual violence within war-torn areas provide extreme examples of violations of the right to liberty and security of person. For example, Beverly Allen (1996), author of the book *Rape Warfare,* describes the war in the former Yugoslavia and the systematic use of rape and "ethnic cleansing." Allen describes three different methods of genocidal rape used by the Serbian military in the conflict: (a) armed forces entered a village, took several women from their homes, raped them in public areas, and left the village; (b) armed forces held women in concentration camps, where they chose women at random and raped them as a form of torture—often followed by murder; and (c) armed forces arrested women and held them in rape/death camps, where they systematically raped the women for prolonged periods of time (p. 62).

Throughout Africa, rape has been a common feature of ethnic conflict (Human Rights Watch, 1996). The United Nations High Commissioner for Refugees, among others, confirms the practice of systematic, politically motivated rape in Somalia, Sierra Leone, and Rwanda (Green, 1999). In each instance of rape, the armed forces violated women's right to liberty and security of person by abducting women and committing acts of sexual violence against them.

Similarly, in some cases of domestic violence, the perpetrator may restrict the victim's liberty through violence and control. For example, female victims of domestic violence often report being locked inside their homes, an obvious restriction on their liberty and freedom of movement. Sopheap, a Cambodian woman, told representatives of a local women's organization about her harrowing experience of being locked inside her house every day by her husband (Zimmerman, 1994). Victims of trafficking for the purpose of forced labor, including prostitution, often experience similar restrictions on their liberty. Many victims of trafficking are held captive by traffickers, who either physically lock the victims up or withhold personal identification, such as passports, to prevent any travel or escape.

In some cases, the state itself may infringe on the right to liberty in a misguided effort to "protect" women victims of violence. For example, in Jordan, police have imprisoned a number of women, allegedly to protect them from their own families. In those cases, the government suspects that family members will engage in honor crimes.

Violence against women, by definition, interferes with the enjoyment of the right to physical and mental health. The International Covenant on Economic, Social, and Cultural Rights guarantees the right to the "highest standard attainable of physical and mental health." Violence against women can have devastating physical effects on women, as well as lasting and debilitating psychological effects.

FGM, for example, may cause devastating and potentially deadly health consequences for women and girls. The physical and psychological effects of FGM can include hemorrhage, infection, psychological dysfunction, urine retention, tetanus, and blood poisoning, the worst of which may be fatal. No issue of violence against women has caused more controversy in the implementation of strategies to eliminate it. Some NGOs, such as the Foundation for Women's Health, Research, and Development (FORWARD International), recognize FGM as an issue of violence against women, but they have had more success eradicating the practice at the local level by treating it as a health and development problem (Green, 1999, p. 209).

Other NGOs have focused their efforts on law reform. NGOs in Senegal, Egypt, Guinea, Burkina Faso, Ghana, and Tanzania have fought to criminalize the practice. Most NGOs, however, recognize that legal reform alone will be meaningless. These NGOs simultaneously work on education, training about human rights, alternative income generation for midwives who perform FGM, and other economic empowerment projects.

Rights Guaranteeing Women Effective Remedies

The International Covenant on Civil and Political Rights guarantees individuals the right to an effective remedy when their human rights are violated. Female victims of violence, by virtue of being victims of human rights violations, must have adequate access to justice. Victims of violence may be seeking prosecution of the perpetrators, protection from future violence in the form of a restraining order, or compensation for the injuries that they have suffered. In every case, women victims must have fair and effective access to the legal system in the state in which they reside.

Some states violate the right to an effective remedy by creating obstacles that block a woman's access to the court system. In many countries around the world, women victims of domestic violence may not be able to document their injuries adequately due to onerous rules of evidence in court (Thomas, 1999). For example, in Macedonia, women seeking to prosecute their batterers must obtain medical documentation of their injuries, which can cost as much as a month's salary (Minnesota Advocates for Human Rights, 1998). These rules deny women an effective remedy by preventing the prosecution of crimes of violence against women.

In some countries, rules of evidence discount the testimony of women. In Pakistan, for example, Article 17 of the *Qanun-e-Shahadat* Order of 1984 (Law of Evidence Order) diminishes the weight of women's testimony in some circumstances to that of half of a man's testimony (Human Rights Watch, 1999). The Qanun-e-Shahadat Order also allows for the admission of evidence to show that the victim was "immoral." Prior to the passage of rape shield laws in the United States, which prohibited harmful testimony about a victim's prior sexual conduct, victims of sexual assault were often criticized, blamed, and discredited by the legal system. Such state-sanctioned discriminatory rules of evidence violate women's rights to seek redress for their injuries.

In many countries, police refuse to respond to calls relating to domestic violence or to investigate assault claims when they discover the victim and the perpetrator of the assault are related. Even if the police investigate and file a report, prosecutors often do not pursue the cases. In some instances, when a woman successfully maneuvers through the criminal justice system to have her case heard before a judge, the judge dismisses the case or imposes only a nominal fine. For example, in Albania, a woman who attempts to prosecute a domestic assault meets with extreme resistance at each step of the criminal justice system. The police, prosecutors, and judges view their role as facilitating reconciliation, and they pressure women to "pardon" their husbands. Not surprisingly, in a review of the Tirana, Albania, district court records over a 6-month period, not a single case of domestic assault was fully prosecuted. In this same 6-month period, prosecutors estimated that about 300 women presented claims to the prosecutor's office. The prosecutor's office did not pursue any of the cases. Ten women filed claims in the court without the prosecutor's assistance. These claims were dismissed at the first hearing (Minnesota Advocates for Human Rights, 1996). Because they are often denied access to justice and legal remedies, women victims of violence may suffer further human rights abuses at the hands of a legal system that purports to offer assistance.

Development of Women's Rights Within the United Nations

Although the United Nations Charter recognized the equal rights of men and women when it was adopted in 1945, women around the world experienced discrimination in many facets of life. In most societies, women did not have rights equal to those of men. Notably, only 30 of the 51 countries that signed the Charter allowed women to vote or hold public office. From its inception, the United Nations recognized that special measures would be necessary if women were ever to enjoy human rights on an equal basis with men.

One of the most striking features of the human rights movement from 1945 to the present has been the relative inattention to women's human rights within mainstream institutions of the United Nations. The International Bill of Human Rights provides the outline of the fundamental human rights necessary for the full protection of women's human rights, including the freedom from violence. If these rights were applied as they were originally intended—without discrimination—there would be no need for further action. Unfortunately, however, the human rights of women and girls have not been equally recognized and protected in the implementation of international human rights law.

Activists from around the world have worked diligently for over three decades to make the United Nations more responsive to the human rights abuses women face. These activists have lobbied for the development of new international laws and for changes in procedures for monitoring compliance with human rights treaties to reflect the role that gender plays in the realization of human rights. Although slow, these efforts have been successful on several fronts, including (a) the adoption of United Nations treaties and declarations that more clearly define women's human rights, (b) the development of procedures to monitor implementation and

enforcement of the treaties, and (c) the increased recognition of women's human rights issues within mainstream gender-neutral human rights treaties and forums. In addition to improvements within the United Nations, changes in international human rights law and policy have provided new tools for growing regional and national networks of activists to employ in working to protect women's human rights and reduce violence against women.

Development of International Law Within the United Nations

The Commission on the Status of Women

In 1946, the United Nations created the Commission on the Status of Women to begin implementing the goals of gender equality articulated in the United Nations Charter. Despite the creation of the Commission on the Status of Women, progress toward improving the status of women has been slow. In its early years, the United Nations focused on women's legal rights and addressed conditions of legal inequality. The Commission on the Status of Women conducted a series of studies on the status of women's legal rights in its member states. It found that women around the world experienced discrimination both in law and in fact. This discrimination included inequality in laws and customs relating to marriage and family. Women and girls were denied the same educational opportunities as men and boys. Many experienced obstacles to advancement in the workplace and did not receive equal pay for equal work. In many countries, women were not allowed to own or inherit property. The United Nations responded with a series of treaties aimed at resolving some of these inequalities. These treaties included the Convention on the Political Rights of Women, adopted by the General Assembly in 1952, and the Convention on the Nationality of Married Women, adopted in 1957.

After its initial focus on women's legal rights, the United Nations shifted its focus in the early 1960s to economic development. There was a growing recognition in the United Nations that legal rights without development were meaningless. The international community recognized that development was essential to real—substantive rather than formal—equality for women. The United Nations increasingly structured its development assistance programs to meet this challenge. The United Nations broadened its focus to include policy formulation, attitude change, political commitment, and institution building. Later, the United Nations expanded its programs to integrate women into the development process. It recognized not only that development was essential *for* women but that meaningful development could not occur *without* the full participation of women.

The Convention on the Elimination of All Forms of Discrimination Against Women

One of the most significant developments for protection of women's human rights was the adoption of the United Nations Convention on the Elimination of All Forms of Discrimination Against Women in 1979. The Women's Convention prohibits discrimination against women in areas such as employment, education, health, public life, family life, and other facets of life. Although it is comprehensive, the Women's Convention does not include some forms of discrimination against women that have gained international attention since it was adopted in 1979. The Convention, for example, does not explicitly provide protection for lesbian women or explicitly protect against violence as a human rights abuse.

General Recommendation No. 19

Although the Women's Convention does not specifically prohibit violence against women, its monitoring body, the Committee on Elimination of Discrimination Against Women (CEDAW), issued a general recommendation in 1992 to explain the Convention's prohibition on violence. CEDAW's General Recommendation No. 19 describes gender-based violence as a form of discrimination that "seriously inhibits women's ability to enjoy rights and freedoms on a basis of equality with men." It categorically states that violence against women is a human rights abuse and a form of discrimination prohibited by the Women's Convention. It outlines the types of violence that violate international human rights standards, including domestic violence, sexual harassment, rape, dowry violence, sex trafficking in women, forced sterilization, and FGM.

Declaration on the Elimination of Violence Against Women

In December 1993, the General Assembly adopted the Declaration on the Elimination of Violence Against Women. This declaration is a comprehensive document outlining the responsibilities of governments, international organizations, and NGOs in eliminating violence against women. Unlike a United Nations convention, a declaration is not a legally binding document. Rather, it is hortatory and expresses the consensus of the General Assembly.

The Declaration on the Elimination of Violence Against Women defines *violence against women* broadly to include more than just physical aggression:

> Violence against women shall be understood to encompass, but not be limited to, the following:
>
> a) Physical, sexual, and psychological violence occurring in the family, including battering, sexual abuse of female children in the household, dowry-related violence, marital rape, female genital mutilation, and other traditional practices harmful to women, nonspousal violence, and violence related to exploitation;
>
> b) Physical, sexual, and psychological violence occurring within the general community, including rape, sexual abuse, sexual harassment, and intimidation at work, in educational institutions, and elsewhere, trafficking in women and forced prostitution;
>
> c) Physical, sexual, and psychological violence perpetrated or condoned by the State, wherever it occurs.

The Declaration on the Elimination of Violence Against Women also sets forth the obligations of governments and NGOs in protecting the human rights of women and girls. These obligations include (a) refraining from engaging in violence against women; (b) preventing, investigating, and appropriately punishing acts of violence against women; (c) developing laws and procedures to create just and effective remedies for women victims of violence and informing women of their rights to these remedies; (d) training law enforcement officials to be sensitive to issues of violence against women; and (e) providing adequate resources for activities related to the elimination of violence against women. The Declaration also calls on governments to promote research, collect data, and compile statistics relating to violence against women.[1]

State Responsibility

The CEDAW Committee's General Recommendation No. 19 and the Declaration on the Elimination of Violence Against Women are significant in the evolution of women's human rights law, because they explicitly recognize the role of governments in preventing, investigating, and punishing violence against women. The United Nations has always accepted the notion that a government is responsible for its actions that directly result in violations of human rights. This responsibility includes official government policies, as well as actions by individual representatives of the government. The United Nations now recognizes that governments are also responsible for inaction in the face of human rights violations. In cases in which the state does not directly commit a human rights violation, it is still possible to hold the state responsible *if* the state has not made diligent efforts to prevent or protect against the human rights violation in question. For example, even though a perpetrator of domestic assault may be a private citizen with no affiliation to the state, the state may be responsible for violating international human rights standards when it has not taken actions to systematically prevent domestic violence and it has not investigated and punished the perpetrator for the assault.

CEDAW's General Recommendation No. 19 and the Declaration on the Elimination of Violence Against Women, among other documents, outline the state's responsibility for human rights violations committed by private, nonstate actors. The Declaration on the Elimination of Violence Against Women requires governments to "exercise due diligence to prevent, investigate, and punish acts of violence against women, *whether those acts are perpetrated by the State or by private actors.*" This expansion of responsibility recognizes that women are often victims of human rights violations that do not occur directly at the hands of the state. Women are often beaten, raped, and tortured in their homes by private individuals. The state is responsible when it has failed to protect women from these human rights violations.

Optional Protocol to the Women's Convention

The expansion of the concept of state responsibility has opened the door for greater recognition of violence against women as a human rights abuse. Another major advancement in the women's human rights movement was the adoption of the Optional Protocol to the Women's Convention. Although the Women's Convention contains strong language protecting the rights of women, it does not contain a mechanism to enforce its provisions. In 1999, after many years of debate, the United Nations adopted an Optional Protocol to the Women's Convention.

An optional protocol is a separate treaty that provides an enforcement mechanism for an existing treaty. The en-

forcement mechanism may only be used against states that have separately ratified the optional protocol treaty. As of April 3, 2000, 34 countries had signed the Optional Protocol to the Women's Convention. The Optional Protocol allows complaints to be filed with the United Nations against states that do not protect the human rights of women. The Protocol contains two separate procedures: a communications procedure that allows individual women or groups to submit claims of violations to the Committee on the Elimination of Discrimination Against Women and an inquiry procedure that allows the Committee to initiate inquiries into grave or systematic violations of women's human rights. Claims and inquiries may only be brought against states that are parties to the Protocol. By allowing women to bring gender-based human rights complaints, including claims involving violence against women, in an international forum, the Optional Protocol provides a significant new vehicle through which women may seek redress, compensation, or vindication of their rights.

United Nations World Conferences

International Women's Year and the World Conferences

The United Nations declared 1975 International Women's Year and sponsored the first world conference on women in Mexico City, Mexico, to address issues related to women in an international forum. The conference included both an official meeting of the General Assembly of the United Nations and a parallel conference for NGOs. At the parallel conference, NGOs conducted workshops on a wide range of human rights issues and met to develop strategies to affect the plan of action being adopted by the General Assembly.

At the end of the conference, the governmental delegates had adopted a plan of action and declaration on women's equality. These documents focused on equality for women and their involvement in development and peace efforts. Although the document was revolutionary in its approach to women's equality, it did not address violence against women. Even more important than the documents were the connections women were making with other activists and the networks that developed as a result of these meetings.

After the Mexico City conference, the General Assembly declared 1976 through 1985 the United Nations Decade for Women. The activities associated with the Decade for Women helped to promote the international women's movement and bring worldwide attention to women's issues. The United Nations held two world conferences on women during the Decade for Women. In 1980, halfway through the decade, the United Nations held a second conference on women in Copenhagen, Denmark. The next world conference, called the United Nations Third World Conference on Women, was held in Nairobi, Kenya, in 1985. These conferences also included formal sessions of the General Assembly and parallel conferences for NGOs. The conferences provided an opportunity for women to exchange experiences and forge ties to support future international work. Violence did not appear in the official document from the Copenhagen conference and was only nominally addressed in the Nairobi conference document, the Nairobi Forward Looking Strategies on the Advancement of Women.

Although violence against women was not included in the official documents resulting from the Mexico City or Copenhagen conferences, NGOs at both parallel forums were beginning to discuss the issue and form connections with one another. By 1976, the International Women's Information and Communication Service (Isis), headquartered in Chile and Italy, had begun to work on violence against women and was acting as a documentation center (Joachim, 1999). Other NGOs were organizing regional and international meetings on violence against women. For example, women active in various NGOs organized a meeting on FGM in 1982 and another on trafficking in women in 1983. By the time many women's groups reached Nairobi in 1985, they had identified violence against women as a major problem. The Nairobi NGO forum played a crucial role in bringing those groups together to network and to raise awareness about violence against women for the first time in a global human rights conference.

1993 Vienna Conference on Human Rights

The first world conference to categorize violence against women as a human rights abuse was the World Conference on Human Rights in Vienna in 1993. The Vienna Declaration and Program of Action declared in Article 18:

> The human rights of women and of the girl-child are an inalienable, integral, and indivisible part of universal human rights. . . . Gender-based violence and all forms of sexual harassment and exploitation, including those resulting from cultural prejudice and international trafficking, are incompatible with the dignity

and worth of the human person and must be eliminated.

At the Vienna conference, as with other world conferences, the United Nations sponsored a separate forum for NGO meetings. At this parallel conference, women's NGOs organized a public meeting where women from around the world spoke about the violence they had experienced in their lives. At this meeting, more than 1,000 people heard compelling testimony of human rights abuses against women around the world. The women's stories illustrated the failure of existing human rights mechanisms to adequately address violations of women's human rights.

The Vienna conference is widely recognized as one of the most important milestones in the international women's human rights movement. The women's movement is credited with successfully persuading the governmental delegates to add a women's human rights agenda to the work of the United Nations. Governmental delegates agreed to include women's human rights and violence against women as major themes of the conference and to begin a process of integrating gender issues into all of the human rights mechanisms of the United Nations.

In 1994, the United Nations Committee on Human Rights responded to the new attention and concern given to violence against women by appointing a special rapporteur on violence against women (Coomaraswamy & Kois, 1999). The Special Rapporteur, Radhika Coomeraswamy of Sri Lanka, reports each year to the United Nations Commission on Human Rights on issues of violence against women around the world. The Special Rapporteur collects research conducted on violence against women around the world and conducts original research on specifically identified issues each year. For example, in 1996, the Special Rapporteur's report focused on domestic violence. In 1998, she reported on violence against women in times of armed conflict.

Beijing Conference

The importance of the issue of violence against women in the international community was reiterated at the United Nations Fourth World Conference on Women in Beijing, China, in 1995. At the Beijing conference, the United Nations reaffirmed that women's rights are human rights and that violence against women is a human rights violation. In the Beijing Declaration and Platform for Action, the United Nations identified violence against women as among 12 critical areas of concern for women around the world. This document includes comprehensive recommendations to states, international organizations, and NGOs for the elimination of violence against women.

Violence Against Women: NGO Activity at the International, Regional, and National Levels

Global Campaign for Women's Human Rights

The formal recognition of violence against women as a human rights abuse and the subsequent speed with which it gained international attention can be attributed to the tireless efforts of a large network of international activists. These activists organized around the U.N. meetings, gaining momentum during the U.N. Decade for Women. The actions of the

United Nations in recognizing women's rights as human rights and violence against women as a human rights abuse was the culmination of years of lobbying efforts by these women's organizations around the world.

Between the conferences at Nairobi in 1985 and at Vienna in 1993, NGOs began to explore issues of violence against women in greater depth and in greater numbers. The Vienna conference would not have had the impact it did were it not for NGOs organizing around the issue of violence against women as a human rights abuse. Building on the groundwork laid in Nairobi, many organizations and networks around the world organized the Global Campaign for Women's Human Rights in preparation for the World Conference on Human Rights in Vienna in 1993. The conference became a vehicle to highlight women's issues and the failures of the existing United Nations human rights bodies to address violence against women.

The Global Campaign included an initiative called the Sixteen Days of Activism Against Gender-Based Violence. The Sixteen Days campaign referred to the days between November 25, 1993, the International Day Against Violence Against Women, and December 10, 1993, International Human Rights Day. Organizers designed the Sixteen Days campaign to link gender violence with human rights. Around the world, NGOs organized activities during these days to raise awareness about and combat violence against women. In Costa Rica, for example, representatives from 50 women's organizations convened a meeting to develop a policy paper on violence against women to be used by policy-making agencies throughout the country (Joachim, 1999).

In preparation for the Vienna conference, the Center for Women's Global Leadership at Rutgers University in New Jersey and the International Women's Tribune Center, a New-York based NGO, circulated a petition calling on the conference to comprehensively address women's human rights issues and recognize gender violence as a human rights abuse. The campaign successfully gathered almost half a million signatures from 124 countries. The petition and campaign became a tool for organizing women on the grassroots level around the world. It sparked a new dialogue and activism around the failure of the United Nations to adequately address women's human rights issues.

After the Vienna conference, the Global Campaign for Women's Human Rights focused on lobbying for full implementation of the Vienna Declaration's commitments to women. The campaign built on its success in the petition drive and gathered more than 1 million signatures from women's human rights supporters around the world. The new petition called on the United Nations to assess the progress toward implementation of the Vienna Declaration's commitments to women's human rights and to ensure that the principles were included in the Beijing Declaration and Platform for Action.

The success of the networking efforts of the Global Campaign were apparent at the United Nations Fourth World Conference on Women in Beijing. National, regional, and international networks of women organized around a broad range of women's human rights issues in preparation for the Beijing conference. At the parallel NGO forum, violence against women was a unifying theme that cut across race, culture, ethnicity, class, age, and all other identifying criteria. Participants in the NGO forum held hundreds of workshops, ranging from public education for domestic violence issues to direct services to women victims of violence in war. In Beijing, NGOs held another tribunal for women victims of violence to testify about their experiences.

The result of the conference, the Beijing Declaration and Platform for Action, is a blueprint for the advancement of women. It reasserts that women's rights are an integral part of human rights and outlines the obligation of governments, international agencies, and NGOs to ensure that women's human rights are promoted and protected in all spheres.

International and Regional Networks

Although the international conferences did not create women's networks, they legitimized the issues and brought together unprecedented numbers of women from around the world. These large meetings of women provided the opportunities for information sharing and coalition building around common issues, creating the basis for organized networks. The world conferences provided the forum for women to share experiences with violence and strategies for eliminating it.

The success of global consciousness-raising and mobilization around women's human rights and violence against women can be attributed to the convergence of several events in the early 1990s: (a) preparations and organization for the World Conference on Human Rights in Vienna in 1993, (b) international news coverage about the use of rape in wartime as an instrument of ethnic cleansing in the former Yugoslavia, (c) proactive funding of antiviolence efforts by foundations, (d) the

crucial catalyst role played by NGOs (Keck & Sikkink, 1998, p. 181). The continued success of the international women's human rights movement later in the decade was fueled, in part, by improved technology and the growth of the Internet. Women around the world had greater access to information and to methods of communication with others in the developing women's movement.

Ending Violence Against Women: The Importance of Regional Networks

Active regional networks of NGOs contribute to the success of efforts to combat violence against women at the international, national, and local levels. By collaborating with other NGOs from the region, antiviolence organizations benefit from one another's programmatic strengths and pooled resources. Regional networks also provide an opportunity to coordinate activities and build on the experiences, both positive and negative, of other organizations. Networks or coalitions also allow NGOs to demonstrate more powerfully that many constituencies are concerned about the problem.

Since the early to mid-1990s, many regional networks have made gender-based violence a priority for human rights activity. For example, in Latin America, NGOs formed the Southern Cone Network Against Domestic Violence in 1989 and the Latin American and Caribbean Network Against Sexual and Domestic Violence in 1990. The Latin American and Caribbean Network Against Sexual and Domestic Violence held its first meeting in 1992, which brought together antiviolence activists from 21 Latin American and Caribbean countries. The inaugural meeting provided an opportunity to establish the network's priorities, which included: coordinating the activities of NGOs in the five subregional focal points, facilitating the exchange of information within and among subregions, developing or strengthening national networks, raising awareness about violence against women, and ensuring that violence against women is a priority on the agendas of public and private institutions (Ortiz, 1997).

The Latin American and Caribbean Network Against Sexual and Domestic Violence has been successful in implementing many of its initial priorities. The network has been successful in raising awareness about violence against women through widespread media coverage, judicial training, and police training. Through the sharing of legislative models and "best practices," the network has also had a direct impact on antiviolence legislation or policies in many countries in the region.

Similar networks exist in other regions around the globe. In Africa, for example, a network called Women in Law and Development in Africa (WiLDAF) developed in the wake of the 1985 Women's Conference in Nairobi. Representatives from 14 African countries originally formed WiLDAF in 1990 when they realized they shared common goals and obstacles in their women's rights work (Kuenyehia, 1995). The network has continuously facilitated an exchange of information among NGOs in the region. As a result, WiLDAF has been able to raise awareness about broad patterns of violence (Bunch, Frost, & Reilly, 1999). WiLDAF has prioritized the issue of violence against women since the early 1990s and has given special consideration to issues of violence against women in areas of armed conflict.

Ending Violence Against Women: Efforts at the National Level

In addition to their work organizing around the international conferences and their participation in regional networks, NGOs were simultaneously pursuing antiviolence campaigns in their own countries and regions. These national activities both supported and were supported by activities at the global level. At the international conferences, NGOs were able to emphasize the centrality of violence against women as a human rights abuse by pointing out the number of national and international groups around the world that had begun to focus on the issue.

At the same time, NGOs were able to use the documents that came out of the conferences, the Nairobi Forward-Looking Strategies, the Vienna Declaration and Programme of Action, and the Beijing Platform for Action, as tools to demonstrate to national governments and private funding agencies that violence against women was an important problem warranting public attention, government action, and financial resources. The antiviolence work at the national level and international level was, and continues to be, mutually reinforcing.

The national campaigns around the world share common themes but vary widely in their emphasis. For example, women in Bulgaria have created a national network to provide services to women victims of violence and to advocate for legal reform to combat violence against women. In Ghana, women are organizing to end the practice of *trokosi,* a traditional practice in which a family offers a young virgin to a "fetish priest" to be the priest's sexual slave in an effort to atone for the family's alleged sins. Recognizing the link between women's economic empowerment and violence, women in Nepal are organizing to increase women's property rights so that, among other things, an abused woman will have the financial ability to leave her abusive spouse. In 1997 in Peru, women successfully lobbied for changes in the law that previously allowed a man to be exonerated for rape if the rapist offered to marry the victim.

Although the specific approaches vary from country to country and from NGO to NGO, antiviolence activities in most countries combine efforts to reform the legal system with efforts to educate the public about violence against women. These efforts often involve grassroots organizing and legal literacy campaigns. In addition, NGOs in most countries are attempting to use international human rights standards to improve the situation for women in the domestic context. They are using international women's human rights standards to persuade government officials and legislators to change national laws on issues related to women.

Conclusion

Since the days of the drafting of the Universal Declaration of Human Rights, the notion that human rights apply universally has been a central principle of human rights law. Universal application of human rights norms precludes states from applying human rights principles selectively. At least in theory, states must conform to fundamental human rights norms, regardless of who is seeking protection or under what circumstances.

One of the major barriers to the widespread recognition of violence against women as a violation of international hu-

man rights standards is the reluctance of some people to accept that human rights standards are universal when applied to women. Many opponents of women's human rights still argue that culture and religion justify harmful practices that violate women's human rights. These arguments of cultural relativism directly contradict the principle of universality. Like any other human rights, women's human rights are universal; culture and tradition, therefore, cannot be used to defend practices that violate women's human rights.

Women who have organized and asserted their human rights have often encountered a backlash at the local, national, and even international level. Because women who assert their rights are inherently challenging the existing power structure, there are many forces that stand in opposition. Those forces rely on the rhetoric of cultural relativism to forestall progressive changes. By arguing that external influences, particularly a Western notion of human rights, are driving the push for women's rights, conservatives and fundamentalists are able to galvanize public support. Women's human rights activists have found the human rights framework, and particularly the universal nature of human rights, to be effective in countering this rhetoric.

Recognizing the universality of women's rights does not—and should not—preclude thinking about the differences among women. A number of factors, including race, class, ethnicity, sexual orientation, and geopolitics, affect the ways that women experience and respond to violations of their human rights. The universality of women's human rights does not undermine the rich diversity among women.

A mere 20 years ago, violence against women was not widely recognized as a significant global problem. Due to the efforts of countless activists around the world, that situation has begun to change. Activists organized networks and targeted lobbying efforts to affect international human rights law and the policy agenda of the United Nations. The tribunals in which women from across the globe gathered to share their painful stories of human rights violations awakened the international human rights community. Victim/survivors and activists began to see similarities in the violence women suffered under patriarchal systems that transcend geographic borders.

As women's human rights activists began the fight to eradicate violence against women, a new social movement was created. The international women's human rights movement has successfully moved violence against women to the top of the international community's policy agenda. Activists have used advanced technology, such as the Internet, to build coalitions that would not have been possible a decade ago. Through these networks and other means, women have begun the struggle to eliminate violence against women as a human rights abuse. The road will undoubtedly be long, but the successes to date are encouraging.

Note

1. In addition to General Recommendation No. 19 and the Declaration, the Americas region has benefitted greatly from the work of the Inter-American Commission on Women. The Inter-American Commission on Women is the body that enforces implementation of the Inter-American Convention on the Prevention, Punishment, and Eradication of Violence Against Women, which came into effect in March 1995. The treaty, which has been ratified by 28 countries in the region, defines violence against women broadly and recog-

nizes it as a human rights abuse. The Commission and the Inter-American Convention on Violence Against Women have provided critical tools for women's rights organizations in Latin America to help eliminate violence against women.

References

Allen, B. (1996). *Rape warfare: The hidden genocide in Bosnia-Herzegovina and Croatia.* Minneapolis: University of Minnesota Press.

Amnesty International. (1999). *Pakistan: Violence against women in the name of honor.* New York: Amnesty.

Benninger-Budel, C., & Lacroix, A. (1999). *Violence against women: A report.* Geneva: World Organisation Against Torture.

Bunch, C., Frost, S., & Reilly, N. (1999). Making the global local: International networking for women's human rights. In K. Askin & D. Koenig (Eds.), *Women and international human rights law* (Vol. 1., pp. 91-113). Ardsley, NY: Transnational Publishers.

Bunch, C., & Reilly, N. (1994). *Demanding accountability: The global campaign and Vienna tribunal for women's human rights.* New Brunswick, NJ: Center for Women's Global Leadership.

Coomaraswamy, R., & Kois, L. (1999). Violence against women. In K. Askin & D. Koenig (Eds.), *Women and international human rights law* (Vol. 1, pp.177-217). Ardsley, NY: Transnational Publishers.

Copelon, R. (1994). Intimate terror: Understanding domestic violence as torture. In M. Schuler (Ed.), *From basic needs to basic rights* (pp. 116-152). Washington, DC: Women, Law, & Development International.

Green, D. (1999). *Gender violence in Africa: African women's responses.* New York: St. Martin's.

Heise, L., Pitanguy, J., & Germain, A. (1994). *Violence against women: The hidden health burden.* Washington, DC: The World Bank.

Human Rights Watch. (1996). *Shattered lives: Sexual violence during the Rwandan genocide and its aftermath.* New York: Human Rights Watch.

Human Rights Watch. (1999). *Crime or custom? Violence against women in Pakistan.* New York: Human Rights Watch.

Joachim, J. (1999). Shaping the human rights agenda: The case of violence against women. In M. Meyer & E. Prügl (Eds.), *Gender politics in global governance* (pp. 142- 160). Lanham, MD: Rowman & Littlefield.

Keck, M., & Sikkink, K. (1998). *Activists beyond borders*. Ithaca, NY: Cornell University Press.

Kuenyehia, A. (1995). Organizing at the regional level: The case of WiLDAF. In M. Schuler (Ed.), *From basic needs to basic rights* (pp. 515-527). Washington, DC: Women, Law, & Development International.

Meyer, M. (1999). Negotiating international norms: The Inter-American Commission of Women and the Convention on Violence Against Women. In M. Meyer & E. Prügl (Eds.), *Gender politics in global governance* (pp. 58-71). Lanham, MD: Rowman & Littlefield.

Minnesota Advocates for Human Rights. (1996). *Domestic violence in Albania*. Minneapolis: Author.

Minnesota Advocates for Human Rights. (1998). *Domestic Violence in Macedonia*. Minneapolis: Author.

Ortiz, M. (1997). Violence against women: A regional crisis. In A. Brasileiro (Ed.), *Women against violence breaking the silence* (pp. 16-27). New York: UNIFEM.

Peters, J., & Wolper, A. (Eds.). *Women's rights, human rights: International feminist perspectives*. New York: Routledge.

Phillips, R. (1999). Violence in the workplace: Sexual harassment. In K. Askin & D. Koenig (Eds.), *Women and international human rights law* (Vol. 1, pp. 257-285). Ardsley, NY: Transnational Publishers.

Schuler, M. (Ed.). (1992). *Freedom from violence: Women's strategies from around the world*. New York: UNIFEM.

Steiner, H., & Alston, P. (1996). *International human rights in context: Law, politics, morals*. Oxford, UK: Clarendon.

Thomas, C. (1999). Domestic violence. In K. Askin & D. Koenig (Eds.), *Women and international human rights law* (Vol. 1., pp. 219-256). Ardsley, NY: Transnational Publishers.

The United Nations and the advancement of women 1945-1995 (United Nations Blue Book Series, Vol. VI). (1995). New York: United Nations Department of Public Information.

Women, Law, & Development International. (1998). *Gender violence: The hidden war crime*. Washington, DC: Author.

Zimmerman, C. (1994). *Plates in a basket will rattle: Domestic violence in Cambodia*. Phnom Penh, Cambodia: Asia Foundation.

Author Index

Abbey, A., 11, 17, 122-122, 124, 137
Abbott, J., 347, 367
Abbott, J. T., 354, 367
Abel, R., 210, 221
Abraham, M., 150, 166, 172
Abrahamson, A., 379, 384
Achenbaum, W. A., 190
Acierno, R., 122, 124, 139
Acker, M., 125, 126, 136, 140
Adams, C., 377, 382, 383, 384
Adams, C., D., 262, 275
Adams, C., M. M., 162, 173, 171n5
Adelman, S. A., 10, 20, 21
Adlerstein, L. K., 16, 16-17
Ahrens, C., 456
Ahrens, C. E., 231-235, 237-241
Aiken, M., 243, 246
Aitken, L., 180, 181,190
Ajzen, I., 420, 437
Albelda, R., 444, 447, 455
Albright, C., 355,367
Alcott, Louisa Mae, 209, 219, 220
Aldarondo, E., 12, 19, 154, 165, 172, 174
Alder, C., 24, 33
Alexander, P., 465-466, 477
Alford, P., 151, 172
Alkhateeb, S., 376, 378, 384
Allard, M. A., 444, 447, 455
Allen, B., 485, 498
Alpert, E., 355, 367
Alston, P., 483, 499
Altholz, J. A., 182, 186, 192
Alvi,, S. 441, 442
Amir, M., 24, 33
Ammerman, R. T., 39, 51
Anctil, C., 354, 368

Andersen, M. L., 466, 480
Anderson, J., 109, 112
Anderson, K. L., 14, 15, 17
Anderson, L., 127, 128, 133, 137
Antognoli-Toland, P., 243, 245
Anwar, R., 347, 348, 350, 354, 360, 368
Anwar, R. A. H., 168, 170, 175
Aponte, G., 232, 238, 239
Appel, A. E., 273, 275
Applebaum, P. S., 64, 71
Appleton, W., 346, 367
Arbuckle, J., 354, 368
Arias, I., 7, 17, 39, 51, 151, 158, 168, 170, 172, 176
Armsbury, H. L., 354, 367
Armstrong, J. G., 66, 70
Arriaga, X. B., 390, 392, 401-403, 414
Arthur, C., 77, 83, 85-86, 91, 92
Asch, A., 193, 206
Asgard, U., 40, 51
Asher, K. N., 390, 391, 396-397, 415
Atha, H., 391, 394-395
Attala, J. M., 46, 51
Austin, G. W., 305, 326
Austin, J., 270, 276
Austin, R., 466, 468, 477
Avery-Leaf, S., 393, 406-407, 413-414
Avis, J. M., 77, 78, 84, 91, 92

Babcock, J., 10, 19
Babcock, J. C., 263, 276
Bachar, Karen, 98, 117-142
Bachman, G. A., 105, 113
Bachman, R., 143, 164, 165, 168-169, 172, 321, 326
Bacich, A. R., 307, 312, 327
Bak, S. M., 347, 367

501

Baker, C. K., 230, 235, 239
Baker, D., 218, 223
Baker, K., 305, 324
Ballard, T. J., 160, 162, 172, 173, 171n5
Bambawale, U., 109, 113
Bandura, A., 6-7, 17
Bandura, A. J., 422, 427, 437
Bangdiwala, S., 390, 392, 401-403, 414
Barbour, L. S., 160, 177
Barkan, S., 347, 367
Barkan, S. E., 162, 176
Barling, J., 158, 176
Barnard, M., 467, 479
Barnes, C., 193, 205
Barnes, G., 125, 126, 136, 140
Barnes, H., 235, 241
Barnes, H. E., 231, 234, 240
Barnett, O. W., 6, 17, 168, 172, 182, 190, 441
Baron, L., 14, 17
Baron, S., 183
Barrera, M. E., 268, 277
Barry, K., 460, 477
Bart, P., 180, 190
Bartholemew, K., 8, 19
Barton, E. D., 350, 368
Barush, A., 446, 455
Basile, K. C., 150, 172
Basinait-Smith, C., 151, 169, 175
Bassuk, E. L., 445, 450, 455
Bassuk, S., 449, 451, 455
Bassuk, S. S., 347, 367, 445, 450, 455, 456
Basta, J., 163, 177, 250, 253, 260
Bastian, L. D., 120, 121, 141
Bateman, L., 359, 368
Bauer, H. M., 251, 258
Bauman, K. E., 390, 392, 401-403, 414
Bayer, R., 68, 70
Beach, S. R., 39, 51
Beasley, R., 9, 17
Becker, H., 203, 205
Becker, L. R., 272, 277
Becker, M. H., 420, 437
Becker-Lausen, E., 105, 112
Becky, D., 393, 409-410, 414
Beebe, D. K., 119, 137
Beeman, Sandra, 73
Begum, N., 196, 203, 205, 205n15
Beland, K., 390, 391, 396-397, 415
Belknap, J., 305, 324
Belknap, R. A., 143, 169, 172
Bell, L., 460, 477
Belluci, P. A., 157, 174
Bench, S., 118, 138, 233, 240
Benderly, B. L., 373, 384
Bending, R. L., 74, 76, 77, 80, 83, 95
Bennett, L., 265, 276
Bennett, L. W., 9, 21, 75, 83, 85-87, 89, 95, 268, 277
Bennett, Larry W., 224, 261-277

Benninger-Budel, C., 485, 498
Benson, D., 211, 216, 218, 220
Berg, B. J., 151, 152, 173
Berg, D. R., 127, 128, 131, 133, 134, 135, 137, 140
Bergen, R. K., 27, 33, 66, 70, 150, 151, 154, 163, 172
Berger, R. J., 236, 239
Bergman, L., 162, 172
Berk, R., 65, 70
Berk, R. A., 250, 259, 306, 307, 308, 324, 327
Berk,S., 65, 70
Berk, S. F., 250, 259
Berkman, T., 464, 477
Berkowitz, A., 122, 125, 133, 135, 137
Berkowitz, A. D., 161, 172
Berliner, L., 105-106, 112
Berns, S., 158, 174
Bernstein, D., 119, 142
Bersani, C. A., 11, 17
Beskow, J., 40, 51
Best, C. L., 122, 124, 139
Best, J., 27, 33
Best, M. C., 196, 207
Bhosley, G., 266, 277
Bible, Andrea L., 3, 73-95, 439
Binder, A., 307, 308, 324
Bindman, J., 475, 477
Bjorn, L., 211, 215, 221
Black, D., 468, 478
Blackhall, L., 347, 367
Blackstone, W., 281, 300
Blazer, D. G., 151, 173
Blickenstaff, M., 456
Block, C. R., 58, 66, 70, 81, 82, 83-84, 86, 87, 89-90, 92
Block, M. R., 182, 190
Blood, R. O., 12, 17
Bloom, D. E., 32, 33
Blowers, B. R., 478
Boddy, J., 116
Bodnarchuk, M., 268, 276
Bograd, M., 12, 17, 31, 33, 262, 276
Boivin, M., 393, 407-408, 415
Bond, Johanna, 441, 481-499
Boney-McCoy, S., 30, 34, 44, 52
Bonge, D., 157, 174
Bordt, R., 230, 239
Boswell, A. A., 122, 137
Bourg, S. E., 161, 172
Bourgois, P., 467, 478
Bowker, L. H., 8, 9, 14, 17, 154, 159, 172, 249, 259, 349, 367
Bowman, C. G., 308, 321, 324
Boyes, R., 471, 478
Bracey, D. H., 467, 478
Brame, R., 321, 326
Brand, P. A., 167, 172
Brandl, B., 182, 185, 190
Breen, R., 164, 176
Breitenbecher, K. H., 122, 128-129, 134-135, 137-138

Brener, N. D., 118, 119, 121, 127, 136, 138, 396, 415
Brienza, J., 215, 220
Briere, J., 102, 112
Briere, J. N., 104, 112
Brillman, J., 354, 368
Brink, J. C., 79, 93, 255, 259
Broadhurst, D. D., 101-102, 107, 113
Brody Field, M., 153, 178
Brookover-Bourque, L., 121, 138
Brooks, M., 449, 456
Brooks, N. A., 193, 206
Brown, C. L., 180, 190
Brown, R. A., 268, 277
Browne, A., 118, 124-125, 139, 155, 172, 220, 221, 347,
    367, 445, 449-451, 455
Browning, J., 9, 17
Brownmiller, S., 117, 138
Bruce, F. C., 162, 173, 171n5
Bruno, R. L., 197, 202, 205
Brush, L., 440, 442, 446, 448, 451, 454, 455
Brussa, L., 473, 478
Brydon-Miller, M., 74, 94
Brygger, M. P., 79, 92, 93
Buckner, J. C., 445, 450, 455
Bularzik, M., 209, 220
Bull, C., 215, 220
Bullock, I., 365, 368
Bullock, L., 162, 175, 347, 350, 359, 367, 368
Bumiller, K., 468, 478
Bunch, C., 115-116, 496, 498
Burge, S. K., 365, 367
Burgess, A., 143
Burgess, A. W., 19, 117-118, 121, 125, 127, 136, 138,
    170, 173, 441, 442
Burgess, R. L., 6, 10, 17
Burke, L. K., 166, 172
Burke, P. J., 145, 172
Burkhart, B. R., 161, 172
Burkhart, S. A., 196, 206
Burnam, M. A., 231, 240
Burt, M. R., 122, 138, 228, 229, 230, 240
Bush, J., 167, 175
Buss, D. M., 122, 138
Bussert, J., 377-378, 384
Butler, R., 180, 190
Butler, R. N., 180, 191
Buzawa, C. G., 308-311, 324
Buzawa, E., 316-317, 324
Buzawa, E. S., 308-311, 324
Bybee, D., 231, 232, 234, 235, 239
Bybee, D. I., 78, 95, 258, 260
Byington, D., 229, 241
Byington, D. B., 228, 229, 235, 236, 239

Cadsky, O., 269, 276
Cahn, N., 305, 309-310, 313, 324
Cahn, T. S., 9, 19

Calvin, John, 375
Campagna, D. S., 470, 478
Campbell, A., 308, 324
Campbell, D. T., 49, 52
Campbell, D. W., 61, 71
Campbell, J., 60, 70, 74-76, 77, 82-84, 84, 86, 89, 93,
    95, 160, 162, 163, 168,
172-173, 176, 425-426, 430-431, 437
Campbell, J. A., 43, 52
Campbell, J. C., 58, 61, 65, 70, 71, 76, 78, 82, 84-85, 87,
    90, 93, 143, 151,
153, 155, 169, 172
Campbell, Jacquelyn C., 2-3, 57-72
Campbell, R., 90, 95, 230, 232, 233, 234, 235, 237, 238,
    239, 240, 241, 307
Campbell, Rebecca, 223, 227-241
Cancian, F., 74, 76, 93
Candell, S., 127, 129, 133, 135, 138
Cano, A., 393, 406-407, 413
Caralis, P. V., 350, 367
Carey, R. G., 81, 94
Carlson, B. E., 168, 173
Carmen, A., 466, 469, 478
Carrillo, T. P., 79, 94
Carter, J., 273, 276
Cascardi, M., 393, 406-407, 413-414, 441, 442
Cash, T., 182, 192
Cauble, A. E., 15, 19
Causby, V., 167, 175
Cavanagh, K., 441, 442
Cazenave, N. A., 164, 173, 181, 190
Cervantes, N., 148, 174
Chalk, R., 171, 173, 362, 367
Chalmers, L. J., 122, 140
Chancer, L. S., 460, 464, 466, 478
Charney, D., 220, P. 217
Chaudhuri, M., 313, 322, 324
Chen, H. T., 11, 17
Chesney-Lind, M., 440, 442
Christie, J. L., 188, 190
Christoffel, K., 359, 368
Clerk, G., 362, 368
Cleveland, H. H., 122, 138, 139
Clinton, William J., 117
Coble, C. N., 122, 138
Cockerham, W. C., 180, 190
Cohan, D. J., 77, 82, 86, 90, 91-92, 93
Cohan, Deborah, 91
Cohen, M., 347, 367
Cohen, M. A., 118, 138
Cohen, R. L., 120, 121, 141
Cohn, E. G., 307, 312, 327
Coker, A. L., 347, 348, 367
Cole, S., 205n15, 206
Cole, S. S., 195, 206
Coles, F., 216, 220
Collins, B. G., 228, 229, 240
Collins, B. S., 9, 20

Collins, D. J., 307, 312, 327
Collins, M. E., 122, 138
Collins, P., 213, 214, 220
Colson, S., 313, 322, 325
Colten, M. E., 78, 84-91, 94, 444, 447, 455
Comeau, J. K., 15, 19
Conte, A., 218, 220
Conte, J. R., 106, 112
Cook, A. S., 65, 70
Cook, K., 211, 220
Cook, S., 97, 99
Coomaraswamy, R., 461, 478, 493, 498
Cooper, B., 460, 478
Cooper-White, P., 377, 384
Copelon, R., 485, 498
Cornell, C. P., 28, 33
Correia, A., 253, 259
Cosenza, C., 444, 447, 455
Cowan, B., 110, 112
Coxell, A. W., 119, 138
Coyle, B. S., 119, 138
Coyne, K., 58, 70
Craven, D., 143, 153, 164, 174
Crawford, C. A., 262, 277
Crawford, M., 269, 276
Crawford, S., 388-389, 415
Creighton, A., 393, 411, 414
Crenshaw, K. W., 164, 173
Crockett, W. H., 180, 190
Croer, M. W., 164, 177
Crossmaker, M., 195, 196, 206
Crowell, N. A., 5, 18, 117-118, 121, 125, 127, 136, 138,
    143, 170, 173, 441, 442
Crull, P., 221, 217
Crystal, S., 181, 190
Cullen, F. T., 120, 121, 138
Cunnington, S., 467, 478
Currie, D. H., 28, 33, 145, 146, 173
Curtis, S., 314, 324
Cygan, R., 347, 367

Dahlberg, L. L., 388-389, 396, 415
Daly, J., 76, 94
Daly, K., 313, 322, 324
Daly, M., 63, 72, 163, 178
Dandekar, N., 221, P. 217
Dandrea, A., 365, 368
Daniels, J. W., 268, 276
Dankwort, J., 270, 276
Dasgupta, S. D., 166, 173, 251, 259, 330, 343
D'Augelli, A. R., 119, 141
Davidson, W. S., II, 90, 95, 163, 177, 232, 238, 239,
    250, 253, 260
Davies, J., 81, 93
Davis, D., 94, 202, 204n4
Davis, N. J., 440, 442, 471-472, 478
Davis, R., 118, 138, 233, 240

Davis, R. C., 268, 276, 311, 312, 324, 325
de Lamo, C., 110-111, 112
De Nitto, D
Deamant, C., 347, 367
Dean, C. W., 307, 326
Dean, K. E., 122, 138
DeBord, K. A., 127, 130, 139
DeCoster, S., 214, 215, 221
Deegan, M. J., 193, 206
Defour, D., 212, 213, 216, 221
DeJong, W., 409, 414
DeKeseredy, W. S., 11, 14, 16, 20, 25-29, 31, 33, 38, 52,
    152, 161, 173, 440, 441, 442
DeKeseredy, Walter S., 1-2, 23-34
DeMaris, A., 164, 173
Denborough, D., 393, 410-411, 414
DeNitto, D., 229, 241
DeNitto, D. M., 228, 239
Dermen, K. H., 123, 124, 141
Derr, M., 446, 455
Desai, Sujata, 2, 25, 35-52
DeVillis, R., 47, 52
Dhanoa, J., 110, 112
DiClemente, C. C., 267, 277
DiClemente, R., 454, 455
DiClemente, R. J., 151, 178
Dienemann, J., 65, 70, 76, 78, 82, 84-85, 87, 90, 93
Dienemann, Jacqueline D., 2-3, 57-72
Dillman, D. A., 42, 52
DiMaggio, P. J., 230, 240
Dimeff, L. A., 122, 123, 124, 141
Dinero, T. E., 122-124, 127, 139
Dines, G., 206, 204n5
DiNitto, D., 232, 241
DiNitto, D. M., 229, 235, 236, 239
Dobash, R. E., 8, 12, 13-14, 19, 28, 29, 31, 33, 74, 83,
    93, 206, 205n14, 441, 442
Dobash, R. P., 8, 12, 13-14, 19, 28, 29, 31, 33, 74, 83,
    93, 206, 205n14, 441, 442
Doe, T., 196, 203, 207
Doezema, J., 460, 461, 464, 465, 470, 471, 472, 473,
    473, 474, 475, 476, 478, 479
Doucette, J., 196, 206
Douglas, K. A., 118, 119, 121, 127, 136, 138
Douglass, R. L., 182, 190
Dowdall, G. W., 121, 142
Dowse, L., 193, 206
Doyle, J. S., 250, 259
Draper, P., 10, 17
Dubois, C., 213, 221
Duffy, A., 27-28, 33
Duggan, P., 127, 128, 133, 137
Dunford, F. W., 268, 276, 307, 325
Dunlap, E., 467, 478
Durand, E., 67, 72
Durborow, N., 351, 367
Durphy, M., 267, 277
Dutton, D., 9, 17, 268, 276

Dutton, D. G., 8, 9, 13, 19, 31, 33, 39, 52, 157, 173
Dutton, M. A., 119, 138, 233, 240
Dworkin, A., 201, 206

Earls, F., 61, 71
Earp, J. A., 145, 176
Earp, J. L., 47, 52
Eberth, L. D., 233, 240
Eby, K. K., 90, 95
Edleson, J. L., 79, 85-86, 92, 93, 94, 95, 255, 257, 259,
    268, 273, 276, 277, 319, 327, 439
Edleson, Jeffrey L., 3, 73-95
Efkeman, H. S., 305, 315, 323, 326
Eisenstat, L. B., 367, 366n1
Eisikovits, Z., 74, 83, 93
Eisikovits, Z. C., 268, 276
Ekcstrum, J., 203, 206
El Saadawi, N., 115-116
Elden, M., 77, 82, 93
Elliot, D., 31, 34, 105-106, 112
Elliot, D. M., 104, 112
Elliot, M. N., 127, 131, 133, 135, 140
Elliott, D. S., 307, 325
Elliott, F. A., 10, 19
Ellis, C., 213, 223
Ellis, D., 26, 27, 33
Ellis, L., 7, 13, 19
Ellsberg, M., 62, 71
Elman, Amy, 99
Elman, R. A., 194, 196, 201, 206
Elman, R. Amy, 193-207
Elwell, M. E., 106, 112
Embry, D. D., 391, 394-395, 414
Engel, B., 58, 66, 70, 81, 82, 83-84, 86, 87, 89-90, 92
Enloe, C., 470, 478
Ephross, P. H., 106, 112
Epstein, D., 317-318, 321, 325
Epstein, S. R., 182, 190
Ertl, M., 152, 175
Estes, S. B., 214, 215, 221
Estok, P. J., 67, 71
Estrich, S., 212, 221, 468, 478
Eugene, T. M., 377, 385
Ewing, W., 266, 276

Faden, R., 59, 66, 70
Faden, R. R., 162, 173
Fagan, J., 11, 19, 157, 173, 307, 312, 322, 325
Fairstein, L. A., 460, 468, 478
Faison, F., 237, 241
Fanslow, J. L., 26, 30, 34, 37-38, 51, 52
Fantuzzo, J. W., 45, 52
Farley, C., 210, 221
Farley, R., 213, 221
Farren, P. M., 393, 409-410, 414
Farrington, K., 15, 19

Feder, L., 268, 276
Federman, D., 59, 66, 70
Fekete, J., 26, 28, 33
Feld, S. L., 158, 173
Feldbau-Kohn, S., 9, 19
Feldhaus, K. M., 354, 367
Felstiner, W., 210, 221
Fendrich, M., 467, 478
Fenton, G. W., 11, 19
Ferracuti, F., 14, 21
Ferraro, K., 305, 308, 314, 324, 325
Ferree, M. M., 227, 235, 240
Fields, M. D., 182, 190
Figley, C. R., 233, 240
Finder, A., 215, 221
Fine, M., 193, 206
Fineran, S., 77, 82, 86, 90-93
Finkelhor, D., 102-103, 105-106, 112, 143, 150-151,
    154, 163, 170, 173, 178, 184, 185, 190, 191
Finn, P., 313, 322, 325
Finstad, L., 462, 463, 467, 478
Fischer, D. H., 179-180, 190
Fischer, K., 236, 238, 240
Fishbein, M., 420, 437
Fisher, A., 220, 221
Fisher, B. S., 120, 121, 138
Fisher, E., 76, 83, 85-88, 90-93
Fisher, E. R., 8, 19
Fisher, Ellen, 80, 82, 92
Fiske, D., 49, 52
Fitzgerald, L., 212, 216, 220, 221
Fitzgerald, L. F., 118, 122, 124-125, 127, 128, 133-135,
    137, 139, 140
Fitzpatrick, D., 29, 33
Flannery, D. J., 391, 394-395, 414
Fletcher, K. E., 10, 20, 21
Fletcher, S., 168, 173
Flitcraft, A., 64, 71, 143, 146, 150, 153, 159-160, 168-
    169, 177, 255, 259, 347- 359, 366n1, 368-369
Flores-Ortiz, Y. G., 251, 258
Flowers, B. R., 460, 470, 473
Foa, E. B., 118, 138
Follingstad, D. R., 151, 152, 166, 172, 173
Ford, C. V., 180, 191
Ford, D. A., 76, 93, 310, 310-312, 319, 321-323, 325
Ford, J. S., 68, 70
Fortune, M., 377, 382-384, 385
Fortune, Marie M., 224, 371-385
Foshee, V. A., 390, 392, 401-403, 413, 414
Foster, Bob, 92
Foubert, J. D., 129, 133, 135, 138
Fowler, F. J., 42, 52
Fox, B. J., 26, 33
Fox, J. A, 143, 153, 164, 173, 174
Frank, P. B., 274, 276
Fraser, L., 467, 479
Frayne, S., 347, 367
Frazier, P., 127, 129, 133, 135, 138

Frazier, P. A., 232, 233, 240, 241
Frazier, W., 346, 347, 348, 368, 369
French, M., 115-116
Freund, K. M., 347, 367
Frey, K., 390, 391, 396-397, 415
Frick, C., 79, 93
Friday, J., 388-389, 415
Friedman, D. H., 9, 20
Friedman, E., 312, 325
Friedman, L. S., 352, 367
Frintner, M. P., 123, 138
Fritz, S., 180, 192
Frohmann, L., 231, 240, 468, 478
Fromson, T., 351, 367
Frost, S., 496, 498
Fullerton, L., 354, 368
Fullilove, M., 440, 442
Fullilove, R., 440, 442
Fuqua-Whitley, D. S., 390, 397, 404, 415
Furey, E. M., 196, 206
Furman, F. K., 181, 190

Galinsky, M. J., 75, 77, 85, 86, 93
Gamache, D., 394, 414
Gamache, D. J., 79, 93, 257, 259
Gamble, N., 218, 221, 231, 234, 240
Gamson, W. A., 236, 240
Gandy, O., 428, 437
Ganley, A. L., 262, 276
Gardner, G., 119, 142
Gardner, W., 59, 62, 70
Garfield, G., 86, 93
Garfield, Gail, 79-80, 88, 92
Garlow, B., 300, 301
Garner, J., 307, 325
Garnets, L., 119, 138
Gartin, P. R., 307, 312, 327
Gary, L. T., 162, 176
Gavazzi, S. M., 125, 140
Gazmararian, J. A., 160, 162, 171n5, 172, 173
Gelb, A., 313, 325
Gelfand, A. N., 119, 141
Gelfand, M. D., 119, 141
Gelles, R. J., 5-7, 13, 15, 19, 20-21, 28-29, 33, 51, 52,
        143, 144, 146, 149, 160, 162, 164, 165, 173, 174,
        177, 184, 192, 249, 259, 443, 456
Gentlewarrier, S., 167, 175
George, L. K., 151, 173
Gergen, M. M., 74, 93
Gerike, A. E., 181, 190
Germain, A., 484, 498
Gershuny, B. S., 130, 133, 133-135, 139
Ghez, M., 425-426, 428, 430-431, 437
Ghez, Marissa, 225, 417-438
Gibbs, D., 318, 327
Gidycz, C. A., 24, 34, 47, 52, 118, 119, 121-123, 127,
        128, 131, 133-139, 141

Gielen, A. C., 65, 70, 162, 173
Gilbert, N., 26, 33
Giles-Sims, J., 168, 173
Gilfus, M. E., 77, 82, 86, 90, 91-92, 93
Gillespie-Sells, K., 202, 204n4
Gilligan, J., 454, 455
Gillum, Tameka, 223, 247-260
Gin, N. E., 347, 367
Giobbe, E., 460, 478
Giusti, L. M., 24-25, 32, 34
Glassner, B., 32, 33
Gledhill-Hoyt, J., 121, 142
Godkin, M. A., 182, 192
Goelman, D., 300, 301
Goelman, D. M., 280, 301
Goffman, J., 263, 276
Gold, S. R., 120, 122, 140
Goldberg, V., 199, 206
Golding, J. M., 231, 240
Goldsmith, S., 319, 321, 323, 325
Goldstein, P. J., 157, 174, 467, 478
Gondolf, E., 250, 259, 265, 277
Gondolf, E. W., 8, 9, 19, 58, 70, 74, 75-76, 76, 77,
        80, 82-86, 89-92, 93, 159, 174, 264, 268, 269-
        270, 276
Gondolf, Edward, 80, 92
Goode, W. J., 12, 19
Goodman, L., 118, 119, 138, 220, 221
Goodman, L. A., 118, 119, 124-125, 138-139, 143, 174
Goodstein, L., 125, 141
Gordon, L., 185, 190
Gordon, M., 36, 40, 51, 52
Gordon, M. T., 118, 139
Gorey, K. M., 102, 112
Gornick, J., 228, 229, 230, 240
Gortner, E., 158, 174
Gottman, J., 156, 174
Gottman, J. M., 10, 19, 158, 174
Gough, R., 387, 415
Graetz, N., 376, 377, 385
Grasley, C., 387, 415
Grau, J., 322, 325
Gray, J. N., 69, 70
Green, D., 485, 498
Green, S. K., 180, 190
Greenblat, C. S., 184, 190
Greenfeld, L., 444, 455
Greenfeld, L. A., 143, 153, 164, 174
Greenwood, D. J., 74, 81, 93
Griffin, G., 180, 181, 190
Griffin, L. W., 181, 191, 439, 442
Griffin, S., 97, 99
Griswold, E. A., 447, 455
Groff, A., 218, 221
Grossman, D. C., 390, 391, 396-397, 415
Gruber, J., 211, 213, 215, 216, 218, 221, 223
Grubstein, L., 232, 238, 239
Gruenbaum, E., 116

Gruszinski, R. J., 79, 93, 94, 255, 259
Gulledge, K. M., 119, 137
Gunasekera, R., 464, 478
Gunter, L. M., 180, 191
Guralnik, J. M., 65, 70
Gutek, B., 218, 221
Guthrie, D., 122, 142

Haber, J., 348, 368
Haennicke, S., 452-453, 455
Halasyamani, L., 390, 415
Hale, Nancy, xii
Hall, B., 74, 94
Hall, B. L., 82, 94
Hall, R., 33
Halliday, C., 29, 33
Hallinan, T., 153, 174
Hamberger, K., 263, 276
Hamberger, L. K., 9, 19, 157, 174, 305, 306, 325, 346, 347, 368
Hambleton, B. B., 362, 368
Hamby, S. L., 30, 34, 44, 52
Hamilton, E. E., 307, 308, 326
Hampton, R. L., 164, 174
Haney, B., 232, 240
Hannaford, P. L., 305, 315, 323, 326
Hanneke, C. R., 154, 174, 269, 277
Hans, P., 353, 367
Hansen, M., 148, 174
Hanson, K., 122, 123, 136, 138
Hanson, K. A., 134, 139
Hanson, R. F., 119, 121, 141
Harkavy, I., 81, 93
Harney, P. A., 11, 19
Harnish, R. J., 122, 123, 124, 137
Harrell, A., 268, 276, 314-316, 326
Harris, L., and Associates, 180, 191
Harris, M., 119, 138
Harris, S. B., 182, 186, 191
Harrison, D., 232, 239, 241
Hart, B., 74, 76, 77, 91, 94, 167, 174, 266, 276
Hart, Barbara J., 224, 279-301
Hart, S., 268, 276
Hartwick, L., 77, 82, 86, 90, 91-92, 93
Harvey, M., 230, 237, 240
Harvey, M. R., 118, 140, 228, 229, 240
Harway, M., 148, 174
Haskall, L., 151, 176
Hastings, E., 305, 326, 403, 404, 413, 415
Hastings, J. E., 9, 19, 157, 174
Hatty, S., 462, 468, 476, 478
Hause, E. S., 151, 152, 173
Hayden, M., 350, 368
Hayes, R. O., 116
Haynes, B., 447
Haynes, N. M., 391, 395, 415
Health, J. L., 390, 392, 401-403, 414

Healy, K., 263, 276
Healy, M. A., 464, 471, 476, 478
Heavey, C. L., 125, 126, 136, 140
Heesacker, M., 127, 132, 133, 141
Hegeman, K. E., 127, 131, 133, 135, 140
Heise, L., 62, 71, 484, 498
Hemphill, K. J., 39, 52
Hendricks, Charles (Terry), xi-xii
Hennessy, M., 77, 84, 95
Heppner, M. J., 127, 130, 133, 133-135, 139
Herek, G. M., 119, 138
Herman, D., 97, 99
Heron, W. G., 16, 16-17, 19
Hersen, M., 39, 51
Hervig, L. K., 120, 140
Heslet, L., 118, 140
Heyman, R. E., 9, 19
Hickey, T., 182, 190
Hickman, S. E., 127, 139
Hicks, D., 122, 141
Hieger, B., 127, 128, 133, 137
Hilberman, E., 346, 349, 368
Hilbert, H., 250, 259
Hilbert, J., 250, 259
Hillenbrand-Gunn, T. L., 127, 130, 139
Hilton, N. Z., 310, 326
Himelein, M. J., 122, 123, 124, 127, 130, 134, 136, 139
Hinojosa, B., 447
Hirschel, L. W., 307, 309, 326
Ho, C. K., 165, 174
Hoffner, C., 427, 437
Hoge, S. K., 10, 20, 21
Hoigard, C., 462, 463, 464, 467, 478
Holamon, 164, 175
Holcombe, B., 211, 221
Holden, G. W., 273, 275
Holmes, W. M., 306, 326
Holt, M. G., 183, 191
Holtgrave, D. R., 427, 437
Holtzworth-Munroe, A., 8, 9-10, 19, 156-158, 174, 269, 277
Homans, G. C., 11, 19
Hondagneu-Sotelo, P., 76, 77, 94
Honeycutt, T., 445, 455
Honig, B., 435, 437
hooks, b., 273, 277
Hooper, M., 305-306, 326
Hoover, S. A., 152, 175
Hooyman, N. R., 181, 191
Hope, Anne, 343n2
Horner, J., 362, 368
Hornik, R., 419, 428, 430, 437
Horton, C. B., 195, 207
Hotaling, G., 316-317, 324
Hotaling, G. T., 6-7, 19, 156, 157, 159, 160-161, 174, 177, 454, 455
Hovey, M., 346, 347, 368
Howell, M., 164, 176

Howell, N., 118, 141
Hubbell, A., 347, 367
Hudlin, M., 353, 367
Hudson, W. W., 45-46, 51, 52, 144, 174
Hugentobler, M. K., 75, 76, 77, 86, 94
Huizinga, D., 307, 325
Hummert, M. L., 180, 190
Humphrey, C. F., 127, 130, 139
Humphries, Drew, 440, 457-458
Hutchings, G., 109, 112
Hutchinson, G., 9, 19, 157, 174
Hutchison, I. W., 174, 307, 309, 326
Hwalek, M., 181, 182, 192

Illman, S. M., 153, 178
Immelt, S., 58, 70
Inciardi, J., 466, 467, 479
Inciardi, J. A., 440, 442
Inui, T., 353, 369
Iovanni, LeeAnn, 224, 303-327
Irvine, J., 250, 259
Isaac, A., 167, 175
Isaac, N. E., 349, 368
Israel, B. A., 76, 77, 86, 94
Itzin, C., 181, 191

Jackson. T., 74, 94
Jackson. T. L., 118, 139
Jacobs, C. D., 131, 133, 135, 141
Jacobson, A., 119, 139
Jacobson, N., 156, 174
Jacobson, N. S., 10, 19, 158, 174
Jaffe, P. G., 79, 94, 254, 255, 259, 305, 326, 392, 403,
    404-405, 413, 415
James, J., 464, 465, 479
Janssen-Jurreit, M., 109-110, 112
Jarratt, L. D., 347, 368
Jasinski, J. L., 12, 19, 156, 165, 174, 440
Jasinski, Jana L., 1, 5-21
Javier, R. A., 16-17, 19
Jayasundera, Dheeshana, 440, 441, 459-480
Jenness, V., 460, 463, 477, 479
Jennings, J. L., 268, 277
Jensen, G. F., 237, 240
Jensen, S. A., 77, 82, 86, 90, 91-92, 93
Joachim, J., 492, 494, 499
Johnson, C. H., 162, 173, 171n5
Johnson, H., 26, 30, 33, 34, 63, 72
Johnson, H. C., 10, 19
Johnson, J. M., 99, 314, 325
Johnson, M. P., 6, 19, 146, 154, 174
Johnson, R., 347, 367
Johnson, S. M., 180, 191
Joinson, C., 233, 240
Jones, A., 148, 174
Jones, A. S., 65, 70

Jones, Dan, 445, 455
Jones, L. E., 393, 405-406, 415
Jorgensen, L. B., 180, 191
Jouriles, E. N., 9, 19
Joy, C. B., 15, 19
Juliá M., 74, 82, 94
Julian, T. W., 9, 19, 125, 140
Jurik, N., 211, 214, 221

Kaban, E., 471, 479
Kaguyutan, J., 300, 301
Kallish, C. B., 118, 139
Kalmuss, D., 7, 19
Kane, R. L., 10, 20
Kanin, E., 24, 33
Kantor, G., 265, 277
Kantor, G. K., 156, 174
Kanuha, V., 74, 76, 77, 80, 83, 95, 164, 166, 174, 176,
    454, 455
Kapadia, A., 127, 131, 133, 135, 140
Karabatsos, G., 123, 124, 141
Karpos, M., 237, 240
Kass, N. E., 162, 173
Katon, W. J., 119, 141, 142
Kattoulas, V., 470, 479
Katzenstein, M. F., 235, 240
Kaufman, J., 7, 19
Kaufman Kantor, G., 11-12, 15, 19, 21, 165, 174
Kay, H. H., 281, 301
Keck, M., 495, 499
Keegan, D., 119, 142
Keenan, L., 74, 76, 77, 80, 83, 95
Keilitz, S. L., 305, 315, 323, 326
Keita, G., 220, 221
Keita, G. P., 118, 124-125, 139
Kellermann, A. L., 390, 397, 404, 415
Kelly, K., 152, 173
Kelly, K. D., 26, 33
Kelly, L., 23-24, 28, 33
Kelly, R., 214, 221
Kempadoo, K., 460, 461, 464, 465, 466, 470, 471, 472,
    473, 474, 475, 476, 479
Kempe, C. Henry, 97
Kendall-Tackett, K. A., 102-104, 106, 112
Kendall-Tackett, Kathleen A., 98, 101-113
Kenig, S., 216, 223
Kennedy, L., 31, 33
Kepler-Youngblood, P., 164, 177
Kerr, J., 201, 206
Kerr, M. E., 67, 71
Kidd, A. H., 167, 172
Killip, S. M., 392, 404-405, 415
Kilpatrick, D. G., 119, 121, 122, 124, 139, 141
King, C., 61, 71
King, M. B., 119, 138
King, M. J., 347, 348, 367
King, P., 362, 367

King, P. A., 171, 173
Kirkwood, C., 28, 34
Kivel, P., 393, 410-411, 414
Kivlighan, D. M., 130, 133, 133-135, 139
Kizer, K., 435, 437
Klap, R., 307, 308, 324
Klaus, P. A., 120, 121, 141, 143, 153, 164, 174
Klaw, E. L., 127, 131, 133, 135, 140
Klein, A., 316-317, 324
Klein, A. R., 313, 313-314, 326
Klein, E., 425-426, 430-431, 437
Klein, F., 221, P. 217
Kling, K. H., 127, 128, 133, 137
Klinger, D., 468
Knapp, D., 213, 221
Knight, R. A., 137, 141
Knuepel, G. M., 182
Koepsell, T. D., 390, 391, 396-397, 415
Kogan, N., 180, 191
Kois, L., 493, 498
Kondrat, M. E., 74, 82, 94
Konial-McLain, J., 354
Koop, C. E., 351, 363, 368
Kopper, B. A., 122, 139
Kosberg, J. I., 182, 191
Koss, M., 97, 99, 220, 221, P. 217
Koss, M. P., 24, 31, 34, 46, 47, 52, 59, 62, 70, 118-127,
    136, 138-143, 152, 174, 178, 228, 229, 237, 240
Koss, Mary P., 98, 117-142
Koss, P. G., 118, 119, 121, 140
Kothari, C., 127, 131, 133, 135, 140
Kowalski, R. M., 125, 142
Kozial-McLain, J., 347, 367
Krieglstein, M., 444, 452-453, 455, 456
Kropp, R., 268, 276
Krosnick, J. A., 39, 41, 52
Krug, E. G., 396, 415
Kub, J., 60, 65, 70, 76, 78, 82, 84-85, 87, 90, 93, 143,
    160, 163, 169, 172-173
Kubicki, A. D., 262, 277
Kuenyehia, A., 496
Kupek, E., 31, 34
Kurcharski, L. T., 180, 191
Kurtz, M. E., 180, 191
Kurz, D., 14, 19, 148, 153, 163, 175, 349-350, 353,
    360, 368
Kustis, G., 213, 221

La Taillade, J. J., 10, 19
Lacroix, A., 485, 498
Lalumiere, M. L., 122, 140
Lang, A. R., 123, 141
Langwick, S. A., 390, 392, 401-403, 414
Lanier, C. A., 127, 131, 133, 135, 140
Lap-Chew, L., 462, 463, 473, 480
Larson, J., 390, 396, 415
Larzelere, R. E., 14, 21

Latham, L., 122, 127, 138
Lather, P., 69, 70
Lau, E. A., 182, 191
Lavoie, F., 393, 407-408, 415
Layman, M. J., 122, 123, 127, 136, 138
Lazorick, S., 160, 162, 172, 173, 171n5
Ledray, L. E., 238, 239, 240, 245-246
Ledray, Linda E., 223, 243-246
Lee, C. M., 119, 137
Lee, C. Y., 441
Lee, H., 121, 142
Lees, S., 195, 206
LeFebre, L., 387, 415
Lefley, H. P., 122, 141
Leggett, M. S., 25, 34
Lehrman, F. L., 280, 301
Lenaghan, P. A., 347, 368
Lenihan, G. O., 131, 135, 140
Lennett, J., 78, 84-91, 94
Leonard, K. E., 158, 176
Leonardson, G., 347, 368
Lerman, L. G., 308, 312, 326
Leslie, D. R., 102, 112
Leveille, S. G., 65, 70
Leventhal, B., 166, 175
Levin, M., 74, 93
Levin, R., 75, 76, 83, 84, 94
Levinson, D., 12, 19
Levy, B., 119, 138
Lewin, K., 74, 94
Lewis, M. I., 180, 191
Lewis, R., 441, 442
Lewis, V., 312, 325
Lidz, C., 59, 62, 70
Lidz, C. W., 64, 71
Lie, G. Y., 167, 175
Lieberman, E. S., 162, 176
Lightfoot-Klein, H., 115-116
Ligo, Arche, 373
Lilly, G., 105, 113
Lim, L. L., 461, 470, 471, 474, 479
Linder, G. F., 390, 392, 401-403, 414
Lindsey, M., 266, 276
Linton, M. A., 123, 140
Linz, D., 125, 126, 136, 140
Lipchik, E., 262, 277
Lira, L. R., 121, 140
Liss, M., 61, 68-69, 70
Lloyd, S., 445, 448, 455
Lobell Bosch, T., 182, 186, 192
Lockhart, L. L., 164, 167, 175
Lockwood, A. D., 466, 467, 479
Lockwood, D., 440, 442
Loe, M., 213, 221
Lohr, J. M., 157, 174, 305, 325
Long, P. J., 122, 140
Lonsdale, S., 196, 206, 204n7

Lonsway, K. A., 122, 127, 128, 131, 133-135, 137, 140, 238, 240
Loseke, D. R., 25, 34, 65, 70
Lowenstein, S. R., 347, 354, 367
Lowman, J., 462, 467, 469, 479
Lown, A., 440, 442
Loy, E., 76, 78, 82, 84-85, 87, 90, 93
Lu, C., 120, 121, 138
Lundgren, E., 206, 205n14
Lundy, S. E., 166, 175
Lunn, D., 168, 173
Lurie, N., 203, 206
Luther, Martin, 375
Lynch, V. A., 244, 246
Lynott, P. P., 181, 191
Lynott, R. J., 181, 191
Lyon, E., 81, 93
Lyons, J., 122, 138

McAuslan, P., 122-123
McCall, G., 154, 174
McCall, G. J., 134, 140, 269, 277
McCann, I. L., 118, 140, 233, 241
McCarthy, M., 195, 206
McCloskey, L., 454, 455
McClure, J., 383, 385
McCormick, A., 262, 275
McCormick, M. C., 162, 176
McCubbin, H. I., 15, 19
McDaniel, S., 217, 218, 222
McDonald-Gomez, M., 16-17, 19
McDuffie, D., 122-123, 137
McEwen, M. K., 129, 133, 135, 138
McFarlane, J., 162, 164, 175, 359, 365, 368
MacFlynn, G., 11, 19
McGee, S., 85, 94
McGirk, T., 471, 479
McGovern, P., 203, 206
MacGowan, M. J., 391, 397-398, 415
McIntosh, S. R., 45, 52, 144, 174
McKeel, A. J., 148, 175
McKenry, P. C., 9, 19, 125, 140
McKeown, R. E., 347, 348, 367
McKibben, M., 182, 186, 191
McKiernan, J., 320, 326
McKinney, K. A., 180, 191
MacKinnon, C., 193, 196, 206, 212, 221
McLeer, S. V., 168, 170, 175, 347, 348, 350, 354, 360, 368
MacLeod, L., 28-29, 33
McMahon, M., 254, 259
McMahon, P. M., 26, 30, 34, 37-38, 51, 52, 118, 119, 121, 127, 136, 138, 390, 392, 401-403, 414
McMillen, C., 107, 113
McNamara, J. R., 152, 175
McPhedran, M., 203, 206

McSweeney, M., 46, 51
McWilliams, M., 320, 326
Madigan, L., 231, 234, 240
Madigan, M., 218, 221
Maenner, G., 121, 142
Magruder, B., 161, 177
Maguire, K., 465, 479
Maguire, P., 82, 94
Maher, H., 300, 301
Maher, L., 459, 466, 467, 479
Mahoney, P., 154, 158, 175
Mahoney, Patricia, 98, 143-178
Maibach, E., 427, 437
Maiuro, R. D., 9, 19
Malamuth, N. M., 122, 125, 126-127, 136, 138, 140
Malefyt, Mary, 224, 279-301
Mallon-Kraft, S., 105, 112
Malone, J., 9, 21, 157, 158, 176
Malouff, J. M., 250, 259
Margolin, G., 262, 277
Margolis, K., 203, 206
Marin, B. V., 60-61, 70
Marin, G., 60-61, 70
Marin, L., 424, 437
Marks, J. S., 162, 172, 173, 171n5
Marks, L. S., 160, 162, 173, 171n5
Markson, E. W., 181, 191
Marques, J. K., 118, 140
Marshall, L., 445, 455
Marshall, L. L., 46, 52, 149, 151-152, 175, 306, 326
Marshall, R., 104, 112
Marshall, Thurgood, 331
Martin, D., 19
Martin, D. W., 127, 131, 133, 135, 140
Martin, P. Y., 227, 228, 229, 231, 232, 235-241
Martin, S., 211, 214, 221
Marullo, G., 244, 246
Marx, B. P., 118, 140
Maston, C., 143, 153, 164, 174
Mastrioianni, A. C., 59, 66, 70
Matoesian, G. M., 231, 241
Maton, K. I., 263, 277, 319, 326
Matthews, N. A., 228, 229, 241
Maurer, L., 154, 172, 249, 259, 349, 367
Maxwell, C., 307, 325
Maxwell, M. S., 228, 229, 230, 235, 236, 239, 241
Maxwell, S. M., 232, 239, 241
Mayall, A., 122, 140
Mayden, S. R., 350, 368
Mazurek, C. J., 127, 131, 133, 135, 140
Mazurek, T., 230, 235, 239
Meeker, J., 307, 308, 324
Meekosha, H., 193, 206
Meglin, D. E., 75, 77, 85, 86, 93
Mehan, T., 427, 438
Mehta, P., 365, 368
Meier, J., 454, 455
Meier, R. F., 121, 141

MeKeganey, M., 479
Meloy, R. J., 153, 177
Melton, G. B., 69, 70, 71
Mennen, F. E., 106, 113
Menzel, L., 67, 71
Mercer, G., 193, 205
Mercy, J., 390, 397, 404, 415
Mercy, J. A., 388-389, 415
Merrill, L. L., 120, 140
Merrill, S. E., 180, 191
Messerschmidt, J., 211, 215, 221
Messman, T. L., 122, 140
Meyer, M., 483, 499
Meyer, S. L., 9, 19
Meyerson, L. A., 118, 140
Miedema, B., 76, 83, 94
Mies, M., 74, 82, 94, 470, 479
Mignon, S. I., 306, 326
Mihalic, S. W., 31, 34
Milburn, A. K., 105, 113
Millea, S., 195, 207
Miller, B. A., 122, 123, 124
Miller, B. D., 107, 110-111, 113
Miller, E. M., 466, 467, 479
Miller, J., 459, 462, 467-471, 473-476, 479
Miller, Jody, 440, 441, 459-480
Miller, S. L., 9, 19, 309, 326
Miller, Susan L., 224, 303-327
Miller, T., 157, 174
Miller, T. R., 118, 138
Miller, V., 359, 368
Miller-Perrin, C. L., 6, 17, 168, 172, 182, 190
Mills, L. G., 313, 322, 326
Milner, J. S., 120, 140
Miranda, R., 118, 140
Mirande, A., 164, 175
Mitchell, V., 182, 191
Mitchell-Clark, K., 428, 437
Moeller, J. R., 105, 113
Moeller, T. P., 105, 113
Molina, L. S., 151, 169, 175
Momirov, J., 27-29, 33
Monahan, J., 64, 71
Money, J., 197, 201, 206, 205n10
Montagne, M., 167, 175
Montgomery, E. A., 11, 19
Montgomery, H., 464, 472, 479
Montgomery, K., 427, 438
Monti-Catania, D., 81, 93
Moody, H., 466, 469, 478
Moore, D. W., 15, 21
Moore, K. A., 119, 140
Moore, M., 109, 112
Morelli, P., 74, 76, 77, 80, 83, 95
Morgan, P., 214, 216-219, 221
Morgan, Phoebe, 99, 209-222
Morris, J., 196, 206
Moss, J., 214, 216, 221

Muehlenhard, C. L., 11, 19, 24-25, 32, 34, 123, 127, 139, 140
Muelleman, R. L., 347, 368
Mueller, C. M., 236, 237, 241
Mueller, C. W., 214, 215, 221
Muir-McClain, L., 390, 415
Mullan, P., 205n15, 206
Mullender, A., 319-320, 326
Mulvey, E., 59, 62, 70
Mulvey, E. P., 64, 71
Munhill, P. L., 69, 71
Munson, K., 346, 349, 368
Murphy, C. M., 9, 19, 59, 71, 152, 175, 263, 268, 276, 277, 319, 326
Murphy, J. E., 161, 175
Murray, A., 476, 479
Murray, Patty, 443
Musialowski, R., 350, 367
Musser, P. H., 263, 277, 319, 326
Myers, B., 167, 175
Myers, T., 76, 94

Nabi, R., 427, 438
Nariman, H. N., 427, 438
Nason-Clark, N., 377, 385
Naureckas, S. M., 58, 66, 70, 81-84, 86-87, 89-90, 92
Neckerman, H. J., 390, 391, 396-397, 415
Nedd, D., 60, 70, 160, 163, 173
Needle, R. H., 15, 19
Neff, J. A., 164, 175
Neidig, P. H., 9, 20
Neimeyer, G. J., 127, 132, 133, 141
Nenadic, Natalie, 193
Neufeld, J., 152, 175
Neuman, W. L., 236, 239
Neville, H. A., 130, 133, 133-135, 139
Newberger, E. H., 162, 176
Newcomb, M. D., 123, 142
Newell, C. E., 120, 140
Newmark, L., 314, 326
Newton, P. J., 250, 259
Nickles, L. B., 312, 325
Noel, C., 182, 190
Norcross, J. C., 267, 277
Nord, C. W., 119, 140
Norris, J., 122, 123, 124, 141
Norron, J. M., 354, 367
Nosek, M. A., 206, 204n3
Notgrass, C., 122, 142
Nuessel, F. H., 180, 191
Nurius, P. S., 122, 123, 124, 141

O'Brien, Mary K., 224, 387-415
O'Campo, P., 162, 173
O'Campo, P. J., 65, 70
O'Donohue, W., 125, 127, 132, 133, 135-136, 141

Ogloff, J., 268, 276
O'Hara, M. W., 105, 113
O'Keefe, M., 164, 176
Okun, L., 26, 29, 34, 250, 259
OLeary, D., 7, 9, 20
O'Leary, K. D., 7, 9, 17, 19, 59, 71, 152, 157, 158, 175,
    176, 393, 406-407, 413-414
Olson, L., 354, 368
O'Malley, H. C., 182, 191
Orcutt, J. D., 237, 241
Orlandi, M. A., 60, 71
Orloff, L., 301
Ormerod, A., 212, 221
Oros, C. J., 46, 52
Ortega, D., 74, 76, 77, 80, 83, 95
Ortiz, M., 496, 499
O'Shea, Sarah, 92n1
O'Sullivan, C. O., 263, 276
O'Sullivan, E. A., 228, 229, 241
Ouellet, L. J., 467, 478
Ouimette, P. C., 122, 141
Overall, C., 459, 460, 464, 477, 479

Pagelow, M., 154, 176
Pagelow, M. D., 8, 9, 12, 20
Pakieser, R. A., 347, 368
Palmer, S. E., 268, 277
Palmore, E. B., 180, 191
Pape, K. T., 151, 172
Park, P., 74, 94
Parker, B., 63, 71, 162, 164, 175, 365, 368
Parker, M. L., 347, 369
Parks, K. A., 122, 123, 124, 141
Pastore, A. L., 465, 479
Pate, A. M., 307, 308, 326
Paternoster, R., 172, 321, 326
Patterson, J. M., 15, 19
Paymar, M., 75, 94, 262, 266, 277
Payne, J. P., 127, 128, 133, 137
Pearlman, L. A., 118, 140, 233, 241
Pearson, J., 447, 455
Peled, E., 74, 79, 83, 93, 94
Pellauer, M., 375, 385
Pence, E., 75, 94, 170, 176, 254, 259, 262, 266, 277
Pence, E. L., 338, 343
Pence, Ellen, 224, 329-343
Pendleton, G., 300, 301
Pendo, E., 197, 206
Pennebaker, J. W., 66, 71
Perez, P., 164, 175
Perez, R., 182, 191
Perkins, C. A., 120, 121, 141
Pernanen, K., 265, 277
Perrin, R. D., 6, 17, 168, 172, 182, 190
Perse, E. M., 427, 438
Pesackis, C. E., 309, 326
Peters, J., 499

Peterson, J. L., 119, 140
Peterrsson, T., 462
Pettiway, L., 213, 222
Pharr, S., 167, 176
Phelps, J. L., 24-25, 32, 34
Phillips, L. R., 182, 191
Phillips, R., 499
Phillips, Robin, 441, 481-499
Phongpaichit, P., 470, 479
Piche, C., 393, 407-408, 415
Pierce, L. H., 106, 113
Pierce, R. L., 106, 113
Pilkington, N. W., 119, 141
Pillemer, K., 182-185, 189-192
Pillemer, K. A., 182, 192
Pines, A. M., 466, 467, 480
Pino, N. W., 121, 141
Pinzone-Glover, H. A., 127, 131, 133, 135, 141
Pirog-Good, M. A., 145, 172
Pitanguy, J., 484, 498
Pittman, A. L., 387, 415
Pittman, K. J., 228-230, 240
Pittman, N. E., 124, 141
Pitts, V. L., 24, 34
Plichta, S., 149-150, 154, 159, 168-170, 176
Plichta, S. B., 443, 445, 455
Poffenberger, D. L., 470, 478
Polek, D. S., 151, 152, 173
Poling, J. N., 377, 385
Pomerantz, J., 266, 276
Poronovich, W., 372, 385
Porter, C., 60, 71
Posavac, E. J., 81, 94
Potente, T., 306, 325
Potter, S. H., 108, 113
Pottieger, A. E., 440, 442, 466, 467, 479
Powch, I. G., 24-25, 32, 34
Powell, K. E., 388-389, 390, 391, 394-395, 396, 415
Powell, M. R., 227, 231, 241
Powell, W. W., 230, 240
Prasad, M., 466, 479
Prescod, M., 469, 480
Pride, A., 228, 229, 241
Prochaska, J. O., 267, 277
Prothrow-Stith, D., 393, 408-409, 414, 415
Punch, M., 64, 71

Quam, Powell,L., 203, 206
Quigley, B. M., 158, 176
Quinn, M. J., 182, 183, 191
Quinsey, V. L., 122, 140
Quiroga, S. S., 251, 258

Radford, J., 23, 28, 33
Raj, A., 454, 455
Ramanamma, A., 109, 113

Ramsey, N., 383, 385
Ramsey-Klawsnick, H., 183
Ramsey-Klawsnik, H., 191
Rand, M., 444, 455
Rand, M. R., 143, 153, 164, 170, 174, 176
Randall, M., 151, 176
Raphael, J., 439, 446-447, 452-455
Raphael, Jody, 443-456
Rappaport, S. R., 196, 206
Rasche, C. E., 309, 326
Rath, G. D., 347, 368
Rathbone-McCuan, E., 182, 191
Ratner, M. S., 459, 466, 480
Raudenbush, S. W., 61, 71
Rauma, D., 65, 70, 310, 327
Rawlins, M. E., 131, 133, 135, 140
Ray, D. C., 180, 191
Ray, R. E., 181, 191
Raymond, J., 182, 185, 190
Reason, P., 74, 82, 94
Rebovich, D. J., 311-312, 323, 327
Reed, J. G., 181, 191
Reed, S., 164, 175
Regoli, M. J., 310-311, 312, 319, 321, 322, 323, 325
Reichard, R., 319, 321, 323, 325
Reilly, N., 496, 498
Reinharz, S., 74, 94, 181, 191
Reiter, R. C., 105, 113
Reith, L., 168, 173
Reitzel, D., 305, 326, 392, 404-405, 415
Reitzel-Jaffe, D., 387, 415
Renzetti, C., 76, 82, 84, 89, 94
Renzetti, C. M., 166, 167-168, 176, 250, 259, 439,
 441, 442
Renzetti, Claire, 73
Replogle, W., 119, 137
Resick, P. A., 118, 141
Resnick, H. S., 119, 121, 122, 124, 139, 141
Reutter, L. I., 68, 70
Reyes, L., 167, 175
Rice, S., 180, 191
Richardson, B., 119, 139
Richardson, J., 347, 367
Richey, C. A., 74, 76, 77, 80, 83, 95
Richie, B., 86, 89, 91, 92
Richie, B. E., 166, 176, 439, 442
Richie, Beth, 79-80
Rideout, G., 107, 113
Ridington, J., 250, 259
Riederle, M. H., 123, 142
Riger, S., 74, 75, 76-77, 78, 81, 83, 86-87, 90, 94-95,
 118, 139, 444, 452-453, 455, 456
Ringel, C., 143, 153, 164, 174
Riordan, K. A., 58, 66, 70, 81-84, 86-87, 89-90
Rivara, F., 390, 391, 396-397, 415
Rivara, F. P., 390, 397, 404, 415
Robbins, P. C., 64, 71
Robbins, R. H., 375, 385

Roberts, M. S., 353, 367
Rodenburg, F. A., 45, 52
Rodgers, A. B., 392, 400-401, 415
Rodriguez, M. A., 251, 258
Rodriguez, R., 251, 252, 259
Rogan, D. P., 307, 312, 327
Ronai, C., 213, 223
Roper, M., 347, 348, 368
Rose, L., 60, 70, 160, 163, 173
Rose, P., 306, 326
Rosemond, J. K., 14, 21
Rosen, D., 445, 447, 448, 451, 456
Rosenbaum, A., 10, 11, 20, 21, 39, 52, 158, 176
Rosenfeld, B., 268, 277
Rosenstock, I. M., 420, 438
Rosenthal, E. H., 127, 132, 133, 141
Rosenthal, E. R., 180, 192
Ross, C., 348, 368
Ross, L. T., 122-123, 137
Rosswork, S. G., 120, 140
Rotatori, A. F., 196, 206
Rothenberg, K. H., 65, 71
Rothery, M. A., 249, 260
Rounsaville, B., 9, 20
Rouse, L. P., 164, 176
Rubin, A. M., 427, 438
Rubin, G., 468, 480
Rubinson, L., 123, 138
Rubinstein, F. L., 233, 240
Rucker, L., 347, 367
Rudy, E. B., 67, 71
Rumptz, M., 250, 253, 260
Rumptz, M. H., 90, 95
Runeson, B., 40, 51
Runtz, M., 102, 112
Rushe, R. H., 10, 19
Russell, D. E., 118, 141
Russell, D. E. H., 106, 113, 143, 150, 151, 154, 163, 176
Russell, G., 182, 190
Russell, R., 220, 217
Russo, F. N., 143, 174
Russo, N., 220, 221
Russo, N. F., 118, 121, 124-125, 139, 140
Rutherford, W. H., 11
Rutledge, L. L., 151, 152, 173
Rutter, P., 216, 217, 223
Ryan, G. W., 396, 415
Ryan, J., 61, 71, 216, 223
Ryan, K., 9, 20

Sacco, V. F., 26, 30, 34
Sackett, L. A., 152, 176
Safer, A., 392, 398-399, 415
Saloman, A., 445, 449, 450, 455, 456
Saltzman, E., 316-318, 327
Saltzman, L. E., 26, 30, 34, 37-38, 51, 52, 143, 160, 162,
 168-169, 172, 173, 171n5

Saltzman, Linda E., 2, 25, 35-52
Samarasinghe, M., 464, 480
Samet, J. D., 352, 367
Sampson, R. J., 61, 71
Sanchez, R. L., 349, 368
Sanday, P. R., 24, 34
Sandfort, T., 102, 113
Sands, S. J., 305, 324
Sarat, A., 210, 221
Saunders, A., 439, 442
Saunders, B. E., 119, 121, 122, 124, 139, 141, 158, 175
Saunders, D., 25, 34, 346, 347, 368
Saunders, D. G., 39, 52, 152, 176, 263, 269, 277, 305, 306, 327, 440, 441, 442
Saunders, K., 8, 19
Scarce, M., 129, 134-135, 137, 138
Scarpitti, F. R., 466, 480
Schauben, L. J., 233, 241
Schauffler, H. H., 361, 368
Schechter, S., 162, 176, 182, 192, 228, 229, 241, 247, 250, 259, 273, 276, 313
Schecter, S., 308, 327, 349, 368
Scheper-Hughes, N., 107, 113
Schewe, P., 127, 133, 141
Schewe, P. A., 125, 132, 135-136
Schilit, R., 167, 175
Schlecter, S., 12, 20
Schluter, T. D., 164, 175
Schmidt, J. D., 307, 310, 312, 321, 327
Schmitt, D. P., 122, 138
Schmitt, F., 235-238, 241
Schneider, B., 212, 216, 223
Schneiderman, K., 207
Schock, M. D., 79, 93, 257, 259
Schollenberger, J., 65, 70
Schonfield, D., 180, 192
Schornstein, S. L., 348, 350, 353, 368
Schratz, M., 180, 191
Schreiber, R., 231, 241
Schuler, M., 499
Schulman, M. A., 346, 368
Schultz, V., 220, 223
Schulz, R., 180, 192
Schurman, S. J., 75, 76, 77, 86, 94
Schutte, N. S., 250, 259
Schwartz, A., 77, 78, 85
Schwartz, Abby, 78, 81, 87, 92
Schwartz, D. G., 440, 442
Schwartz, L., 195, 197, 207
Schwartz, M. D., 11, 14, 16, 20, 24, 25, 27, 31, 33, 34, 65, 71, 441, 467, 468, 479
Schwartz, Martin D., 1-2, 23-34
Scibelli, P., 462, 463, 465, 469, 470, 480
Scott, C. S., 122, 141
Scully, D., 468, 480
Searles, P., 236, 239
Seaver, C., 182, 185, 188, 192
Sedlak, A., 101-102, 107, 113

Sedlak, A. J., 249, 259
Sefl, T., 231, 234, 240
Segars, H., 182, 191
Senchak, M., 158, 176
Sengstock, M. C., 181, 182, 192
Seto, M. C., 122, 140
Seygried, S., 74, 76, 77, 80, 83, 95
Shakespeare, T., 193, 202, 204n4, 205, 207
Sharps, P. W., 168, 176
Shelley, G. A., 26, 34, 37-38, 51, 52
Shen, H., 164, 165, 176
Shepard, M. E., 170, 176
Shepard, M. F., 43, 52, 338, 343
Sherman, L. W., 304, 306, 307, 308, 310, 312, 321, 326, 327
Shields, N. M., 154, 174, 269, 277
Short, L., 77, 84, 95
Shortt, J. W., 10, 19, 158, 174
Shotland, R. L., 125, 141
Siegel, J. M., 177, 231, 240
Sikkink, K., 495, 499
Silbert, M. H., 466, 467, 480
Silva, C., 164, 175
Silva, M., 59, 71
Silverman, J., 454, 455
Silvern, L., 182, 190
Simcoe, K. W., 197, 201, 206, 205n10
Simon, A. F., 102, 106, 112
Sinnott, J. D., 182, 190
Sirles, E. A., 262, 277
Skinner, B. F., 6, 20
Sklar, D., 354, 368
Slater, J., 203, 206
Slater, V., 164, 177
Sloan, J. J., 120, 121, 138
Small, S. A., 83, 88, 95
Smart, C., 220, 223
Smith, B., 314-316
Smith, B. E., 311, 312, 324, 325, 326
Smith, C., 164, 177, 263, 276
Smith, D., 308
Smith, D. A., 312, 327
Smith, J., 145, 176
Smith, K., 130, 133, 133-135, 139
Smith, M. D., 12, 20, 27, 31, 32
Smith, P., 376, 385
Smith, P. H., 47, 52, 145, 176, 347, 348, 367
Smith, R., 248
Snapp, S., 394, 414
Sobsey, D., 196, 203, 207
Sockloskie, R. J., 125, 126, 140
Soecken, K., 365, 368
Soeken, K., 162, 164, 175
Sohng, S. S. L., 74, 76, 77, 80, 83, 95
Soler, E., 424-426, 430-431, 437
Solomon, S. D., 61, 68-69, 70
Song, Y. I., 166, 176
Sonkin, D. J., 267, 277

Sontag, S., 180, 192, 194, 207
Sorenson, S., 251, 259
Sorenson, S. B., 164, 165, 176, 231, 240
Sorrell, J. M., 67, 71
Souza, C. A., 161, 176
Spade, J. Z., 122, 137
Spalter-Roth, R., 231, 241
Spath, R., 77, 82, 86, 90, 91-92, 93
Speck, P., 243, 246
Spencer, M., 74, 76-77, 80, 83, 95
Spiro, A., 409, 414
Spitz, A. M., 160, 162, 172, 173, 171n5
Spitzer, J., 376, 377, 385
Sporakowski, M. J., 148, 175
Spunt, B. J., 157, 174
Staggenborg, S., 235, 236, 241
Stallings, R., 61, 71
Stambaugh, P., 211, 217, 220
Stambaugh, P. M., 214, 216, 219, 223
Stanko, B., 214, 223
Stanko, E. A., 26, 34, 308, 327
Stanley, L., 215, 223
Stark, D., 143, 177
Stark, E., 64, 71, 146, 150, 153, 159-160, 168, 169, 177,
    255, 259, 308-309, 311, 327, 347-349, 349-350,
    353, 360, 368, 368-369, 366n1
Stark, Evan, 224, 345-369
Starzomski, A., 8, 18
Starzomski, A. J., 8, 18
Stashinko, E., 58, 70
Stein, J. A., 231, 240
Steiner, H., 483, 499
Steiner, R., 263, 276
Steinman, M., 257, 259
Steinmetz, S., 5, 7, 21, 164, 165, 177
Steinmetz, S. K., 182, 192, 249, 259
Stets, J. E., 14, 20, 145, 172
Stets, M. E., 161, 169, 177
Steury, E., 310, 327
Stille, R., 266, 267, 277
Stimpson, L., 196, 207
Stoelb, M. P., 127, 128, 133, 137
Stoltenberg, C. D., 9, 17
Stordeur, R. A., 266, 267, 277
Stormo, K. J., 123, 141
Stosny, S., 263, 277
Stout, K. D., 155, 177
Strachan, C. E., 9, 19
Straus, M., 9, 164, 173, 181, 183, 190, 192
Straus, M. A., 5-7, 7, 12, 13, 14, 14-15, 17, 19, 20-21,
    21, 26, 28, 29, 30, 31, 33, 34, 39, 44-45, 52, 143,
    144, 146, 149, 154, 156, 158, 160, 161, 164, 165,
    169, 172, 173, 174, 177, 184, 192, 249, 255, 259,
    265, 277, 443, 456
Stringer, E. T., 74, 95
Stritzke, W. G., 123, 141
Ström, Katinka, 193, 204n1
Strom, K., 170, 176

Strube, M. J., 160, 177
Stryker, J., 428, 437
Stuart, G. L., 8, 9-10, 19, 156-158, 174, 269, 277
Stuifbergen, A., 203, 205
Stumpf, J., 387, 415
Sudermann, M., 392, 403, 404-405, 413, 415
Sugarman, D. B., 6-7, 19, 30, 34, 44, 156, 157, 159, 160-
    161, 174, 177, 454, 455
Sugg, N. K., 353, 369
Suitor, J. J., 183, 192
Sullivan, C., 76, 92
Sullivan, C. M., 78, 79, 81, 84, 87, 90-91, 95, 163, 177,
    250, 253, 258, 260
Sullivan, Cris M., 223, 247-260
Sullivan, M., 119, 142
Sumaya, C. V., 362, 368
Swain, K., 320, 327
Sweet, S., 28, 34
Syers, M., 79, 93, 95
Syers, M. A., 319, 327
Symons, P. Y., 164, 177

Taluc, N., 445, 448, 455
Tan, C., 163, 177, 250, 253, 260
Tanaka, J. S., 125, 126, 140
Tatara, T., 184, 192
Taylor, B., 118, 138, 233, 240
Taylor, B. G., 268, 276
Taylor, M. J., 446, 455
Taylor, R. G., 124, 141
Templin, T. N., 169, 172
Terpestra, D., 218, 223
Teske, R. H. C., 347, 369
Tessaro, I., 47, 52
Testa, M., 123, 124, 141
Tharinger, D., 195, 207
Thelan, R., 441
Thistlethwaite, A., 318, 327
Thoennes, N., 5, 21, 29-30, 34, 41-42, 52, 63, 71, 97, 99,
    118, 119, 121, 141, 143, 149, 151, 153, 168, 177,
    443, 447, 455, 456
Thomas, C., 487, 499
Thompson, D., 195, 206
Thomson, G., 211, 216, 218, 220
Thornhill, N. W., 125, 140
Thornton, S. R., 120, 140
Thornton, T., 388-389, 415
Tilley, C., 204n4, 207
Timmel, Sally, 343n2
Tinkle, M., 203, 205
Tjaden, P., 5, 21, 29-30, 34, 41-42, 52, 63, 71, 97, 99,
    118, 119, 121, 141, 143, 149, 151, 153, 154, 168,
    177, 443, 456
Toby, J., 269, 277, 307, 327
Tolin, D. F., 157, 174
Tolman, R., 443-448, 451, 456
Tolman, R. M., 9, 21, 266, 268, 277, 312, 327

Tomita, S. K., 182, 183, 191
Torbert, W. R., 74, 82, 95
Torkelson, N., 119, 142
Torres, S., 61, 71, 177, 252, 260
Toubia, N., 115-116
Touchette, N., 65, 71
Truong, T., 459, 462, 463, 464, 470, 471, 472, 475, 476, 480
Tsui, A., 218, 221
Turk, A. T., 28, 34
Turnbull, J. E., 75, 77, 85, 86, 93
Tutty, L. M., 249, 260
Twersky, A., 376, 385
Tyra, P. A., 233, 241
Tyree, A., 157, 158, 176

Uehara, E. S., 74, 76, 77, 80, 83, 95
Ullman, S., 231, 234, 241
Ullman, S. E., 123, 124, 137, 141, 151, 177
Ulrich, Y., 63, 71
Upchurch, D. M., 164, 165, 176
Urban, B. Y., 75, 83, 85-87, 89, 95
Urquiza, A. J., 62, 71

Vadas, Melinda, 193
Valente, R., 300, 301
Valente, R. L., 280, 301
Valente, Roberta L., 224, 279-301
Valenti-Hein, D. C., 195, 197, 207
Valentine, D., 182, 192
Valtinson, G., 127, 129, 133, 135, 138
Van Horn, A. S., 119, 138
Van Roosmalen, E., 217, 218, 222
Vazsonyi, A. T., 391, 394-395, 414
Venkatramani, S. H., 110-111, 113
Vezina, L., 393, 407-408, 415
Villarruel, A., 60, 71
Vincent, S. D., 105, 113
Vince-Whitman, C., 409, 414
Vinton, L., 98-99, 179-192, 182, 185, 186, 189, 192, 250, 260
Vitaliano, P. P., 9, 19
Vivian, D., 9, 21, 441, 442
Vogel, R. E., 123, 127, 139

Wachowiak, D. G., 123, 127, 139
Wagner, B. C., 9, 19
Walby, S., 455, 456
Waldner-Haugrud, L. K., 161, 177
Waldo, C. R., 127, 131, 133, 135, 140
Walker, E. A., 119, 141-142
Walker, L., 346, 369
Walker, L. E., 7, 21, 28, 34, 153, 155, 169, 177
Walker, M. E., 119, 121, 141
Walkowitz, J., 475, 480

Walling, M. K., 105, 113
Waltz, J., 10, 19
Warchol, G., 143, 153, 164, 174
Ward, S., 172
Warnken, W. J., 10, 20, 21
Warren, C. A. B., 180, 192
Warren, C. W., 118, 119, 121, 127, 136, 138
Warshaw, C., 255, 260, 351, 369
Wasco, S. M., 231, 232, 234, 235, 238, 239, 240, 241
Wascok, S. M., 234
Watts, C., 62, 71
Waxman, B. F., 196, 197, 207
Weaver, G., 249, 260
Websdale, N., 53-55
Websdale, Neil, 2, 53-55
Wechsler, H., 121, 142
Weinraub, B., 207, 205n12
Weinreb, L. F., 445, 450, 455
Weis, J., 144, 177
Weiscz, A., 312, 327
Weissman, G., 362, 368
Wekerle, C., 387, 415
Welkos, R., 207, 205n13
Wellington, C., 211, 221
Wellstone, Paul, x, 443
Wellstone, Sheila, x
Welsh, S., 216, 223
Welty, A., 183
Wendell, S., 193, 207
West, C. M., 164, 167, 177
West, Carolyn M., 98, 143-178
Western, B., 307, 308, 324
Wexler, S., 312, 322, 325
Whalen, M. B., 228, 229, 240
White, B. W., 167, 175
White, Byron, 197
White, E., 166, 178
White, J. W., 125, 142, 152, 178
White, R., 269-270, 277
White, R. M., 180, 191
Whyte, W. F., 81, 93
Wiehe, V. R., 182, 192
Wijers, M., 462, 463, 473, 480
Williams, J. E., 231, 234, 241
Williams, L., 251, 260
Williams, L. M., 102-103, 106, 112, 154, 158, 175
Williams, Linda M., 98, 143-178
Williams, O. J., 181, 191, 251, 260, 271, 272, 277, 439, 442
Williams, Oliver J., 224, 261-277
Wilner, M. E., 75, 77, 85, 86, 93
Wilson, A. V., 148, 178
Wilson, D. G., 148, 178
Wilson, M., 63, 72, 163, 178
Wilson, S. K., 254, 255, 259
Wilson, Tamar Diana, 98, 101, 115-116
Wilson-Brewer, R., 409, 414
Wilt, S. A., 153, 178

Wineman, N. M., 67, 72
Winfeld, I., 151, 173
Wingood, G., 454, 455
Wingood, G. M., 151, 178
Winston, J., 212, 215, 223
Wise, S., 215, 223
Wisniewski, N., 118, 119, 121, 127, 136, 139
Wisniewski, W., 24, 34
Witwer, M. B., 262, 277
Wolak, J., 170, 178
Wolan, D. L., 119, 138
Wolf, R. S., 182, 192
Wolfe, D. A., 254, 255, 259, 387, 415
Wolfe, D. M., 12, 17
Wolfgang, M. E., 14, 21
Wolin, J., 361, 368
Wolper, A., 499
Womendez, C., 207
Wong, E., 203, 207
Wood, R. E., 470, 480
Woodruff, W. J., 118, 119, 121, 140
Woods, L., 305, 327
Wooldredge, J., 318, 327
Woolf, K., 437, 430
Wray, R., 428, 437
Wright, C., 163, 178
Wurmser, T., 76, 78, 82, 84-85, 87, 90, 93
Wyatt, G., 122, 142
Wyatt, G. A., 123, 142

Wyatt, G. E., 60, 72, 106, 113, 121, 142
Wynne, E. C., 65, 70

Xue, X., 162, 173

Yancey Martin, Patricia, 223, 227-241
Yllö, K., 12, 21, 58, 70, 74, 75-76, 77, 89, 82-84, 86, 93, 143, 145-146, 150-151, 154, 162, 163, 173, 176, 178
Young, K. Z., 375, 385
Young, M., 347, 367
Yount, K., 211, 213, 223
Yu Liu, P., 390, 391, 396-397, 415

Zahniser, S. C., 162, 173, 171n5
Zaragoza-Diesfeld, Y., 231, 234, 240
Zausner, M., 466, 467, 480
Zawitz, M. W., 153, 173
Zegree, J. B., 9, 19
Zetes-Zanatta, L. M., 124, 141
Zeya, Seema, 224, 279-301
Zia, H., 424, 437
Ziegler, E., 7, 19
Zimmerman, C., 486, 499
Zorza, J., 143, 170, 178, 305, 307, 308, 321, 327
Zuravin, S., 107, 113

Subject Index

Abolitionist approach to prostitution, 462
Abortion, sex-selective, 107-108
Abuse, defining, 2
Abused children. *See* Child abuse; Children
Abused women. *See* Battered women
Abusive Behavior Inventory (ABI), 43-44
Abusive men. *See* Batterers
Accountability:
    in batterer program, 275
    to battered women, 91
Acrotomophiles, 197
Acute flare-up, 145
Administration on Aging, 188
Adult Trauma History (ATH), 348, 354
Advertising Council, The, 424, 426, 430, 437
Advocacy:
    civil remedy and, 333-334
    clinical violence intervention and, 357-358
    criminal intervention strategies, 334-335
    crux of, 339
    forms of, 329
    in new millennium, 340-342
    institutional, early years, 330-333
    intervention, 337-339
    religious leaders and, 380
    research process metaphor, 81-82
    training and conversion efforts, 335-337
Advocates for Youth, 437
African Americans:
    battered women shelters and, 251
    child sexual abuse and, 106
    criminal intervention strategies and, 334
    elder abuse among, 181
    intimate violence, 164
    scapegoating of female, 273
    See also Women of color

African American Task Force on Violence Against
    Women, 79-80, 88, 90
Ageism, 180
Agenda of criminalization, 335
Aggression:
    confluence model of, 126
    stability of, 158-159
AIDS, 363, 471. *See also* HIV
Alcohol:
    Harvard study on, 120-121
    male peer-support model and, 16
    role in violence against women, 11
    vulnerability to rape and, 123-124
Alcohol, Drug Abuse, and Mental Health Administration
    (ADAMHA), 65
Alcoholics Anonymous, 266
Alcoholism:
    battered women and, 169, 348, 366
    batterers and, 156-157
AMEND, 262
America Online, "Bunion Love" bulletin board, 202
American Academy of Family Practice, 352
American Association for Retired Persons (AARP), 186,
    189
American College of Emergency Physicians, 352
American College of Obstetricians and Gynecologists,
    348, 352
American Medical Association (AMA), 59, 70, 347,
    350, 352, 367
American Medical Women's Association, 352
American Nurses Association (ANA), 244, 352
American Prosecutors Research Institution, 323
American Psychiatric Association, 217
American Psychological Association, 59, 70, 103
American Urban Radio Networks, 428
Amnesty International, 498

Amputee Times magazine, 197-199, 201-202, 205n8
Amsterdam Treaty, 204n7
Anger:
    borderline personality organization and, 8
    rape crisis centers and, 228
Antirape movement, 228-231
    evolution of, 229-231
    Violence Against Women Act and, 237
    See also Rape crisis centers
Anxiety, in battered women, 169
Armed forces:
    military protection orders, 290-291
    sexual harassment in, 214
    U.S. Naval Recruit Study, 120
Arrest statutes, 304-309
Asha Family Services, Inc., 251
Asian Women's Shelter, 251
Avoidance behavior, child sexual abuse and, 104-105
AWAKE (Advocacy for Women and Kids in Emergencies), 255, 362

Battered child syndrome, 97
Battered parents, 182
Battered women:
    accountability to, 91
    anxiety in, 169
    child neglect and, 348
    non-shelter-based services, 255-258
    See also Victim
Battered women, shelters for:
    assistance from, 249-251
    children and, 248-249, 254-255
    communities of color and, 251-253
    criminal justice system programs, 256-257
    expansion of services within, 253
    origins of, 247
    rules in, 249
    the shelter experience, 248-251
    social service agency programs, 257
    university programs, 257-258
Battered Women as Survivors: An Alternative to Treating Learned Helplessness (Gondolf & Fisher), 80
Battered Women's Syndrome (BWS), 169
Batterer:
    assaultive and nonassaultive behaviors, 145
    classifications, 10
    drug and alcohol use, 156-157
    dysphoric/borderline, 156
    early childhood experiences, 157-158
    head injury of, 10
    intervention programs for. *See* Batterer intervention programs
    intimate violence, 155-159
    personality disorders and, 157
    psychological pathology in, 8-10
    risk markers, 156-159
    stability of aggression, 158-159

    threefold typology of, 269-270
    typologies of, 155-156
    See also Abusive men
Batterer intervention programs:
    completion of, 267
    contracts for, 265
    controversies facing, 269-270
    cultural competence and, 271-273
    effectiveness of, 268-269
    evaluation for, 264-265
    future directions for, 272-275
    goals of, 263, 267
    group delivery in, 266-267
    history of, 261-263
    interaction with victim programs, 270-271
    maintenance of, 267-268
    orientation to, 266
    public education and, 275
    referral to, 263-264
    responsible fatherhood emphasis, 273-274
    role redefinition, 274-275
    standards, 270
    victim contact and, 265-266
Battering, defined, 145
Battering Syndrome, The, 169
Behavior:
    avoidance, 104-105
    battering, 145
    changing beliefs and, 420-423
    coercive control, 145
Belmont Report, 64, 71
Bias, retrospective or recall, 39
Biological explanations, 10-11
Birth planning in China, 108-109
Black Coalition Fighting Back Serial Murders (n.d.), 468-469
Blue Cross/Blue Shield of Pennsylvania, 365
Borderline personality organization, 8
Boxing Helena, 200
Bureau of International Labor Affairs, 464
Bureau of Justice Statistics, 26, 31
Bureau of National Affairs, 210-211, 218

Canadian National Survey, 26
Canadian Urban Victimization Survey, 26
Capital Area Response Effort (CARE), 256
Catalytic validity, 69
CATW (Coalition Against Trafficking in Women), 460
Center for International Crime Prevention, 479
Centers for Disease Control and Prevention (CDC), 30, 37, 52, 76, 363
    National Center for Injury Prevention and Control, 388
    migrant women shelters, 252
    Violence Against Women Survey, 119
Centre for International Crime Prevention, 474
Certificate of confidentiality (COC), 68-69

Change, tools of, 422-423
Chester the Molester, 195
Chicago Women's Health Risk Survey, 87
Child abuse:
    cross-assessment for woman battering and, 356
    See also Child sexual abuse
Child Abuse and Prevention and Treatment Act
    of 1974, 62
Child custody, enforcing in protection order, 290
Child neglect, battered women and, 348
Child Protective Services, 349
Child sexual abuse:
    among U.S. girls, 101-102
    difference in response to, 105-107
    effects of, 102-105
    other maltreatment vs., 106-107
    posttraumatic stress disorder and, 103-104
    severity of, 106
    sexualized behavior and, 103
    See also Child abuse
Children:
    Asian, abuse of, 106
    battered women shelters and, 248-249, 254-255
    elementary school, 390
    non-shelter based services, 255-258
    sex industry and, 464
    sex tourism and, 471-472
    who observe adult violence, 273
    See also Abused children
China:
    birth planning in, 108-109
    female infanticide in, 107-111, 484
Civil restraining orders, 313-317. *See also* Court orders;
    Protection orders
Classical conditioning, 6
Clinical violence intervention:
    assessment and, 355-356
    barriers to change, 350-351
    case management and, 357-358
    challenges to, 364-366
    children's safety and, 356
    clinician/patient encounter, 351-353
    documentation with, 356-357
    identification, 354-356
    institutional intervention, 358-362
    need for, 346-350
    normalization and, 345
    three As, 358
Clothesline Project, 237
Code of ethics, 59, 64
Code of Federal Regulations (CFR), 66
Coercive control, 145
Cognitive processes:
    of batterers, 157
    of sexually abused children, 104
Cognitive-behavioral therapy, for batterers, 263
Collaboration:
    community, dilemmas of, 366

    with religious leaders, 379-380
Collaborative research:
    accountability to battered women, 91
    as forced bonding, 73
    assumptions in, 81-83
    best practices, 80-88
    challenges to, 75-78
    complementary talents with, 90
    "coresearchers" in, 82
    defined, 74-75
    differences between disciplines, 77
    enhancement of research with, 88-92
    environment differences and, 87-88
    funding access and, 83-84
    incentives and, 85
    larger social movement and, 91-92
    legitimacy and, 90-91
    objectivity and, 83
    ongoing communication and, 85-86
    problem-solving flexibility and, 87
    research implementation, 89-90
    research questions and, 89
    retention strategies and, 90
    roles in, 86-87
    skill differences, 77-78
    successful, 83-88
    survivor involvement and, 84
    time commitment and, 76-77
    value-based science and, 82-83
College:
    National College Health Risk Behavior Survey,
      119-120
    See also Universities
Comer School Development Program, 395-396
Committee on Science, Engineering, and Public
    Policy, 70
Committee on Trauma Research, 367
Common couple violence, 6, 98
Community, as research participant, 60-61
Community Advocacy Project, 78-79, 81, 84-85, 90
Community collaboration, dilemmas of, 366
Community intervention, 362-364
Community intervention projects (CIPs), 256
Community Involvement Model (CIM), 80
Compassion fatigue, 233
Complex social prevention, 362-364
Computer-assisted telephone interviewing (CATI), 40
Conditioning, classical and operant, 6
Confidentiality:
    research, 67-69
    safety plan and, 357
Conflict Tactics Scale (CTS), 14, 25, 26, 30, 39, 44, 65,
    183-184
Conflict Tactics Scale 2 (CTS2), 44
Confluence model, 125-126
Congress:
    protection legislation, 284
    See also Legislation

Connecticut, Community Health Center Domestic Violence Initiative, 360-361
Continuum of abuse, corrupt, 28
Continuum of unsafety, 26
Continuum of violence, 26, 98, 211-212
Control theory, 15
Coordinate Community Response project, 337-339
Coordinated community response (CCR), 363-364
Corrupt continuum of abuse, 28
Court cases:
    Fraternal Order of Police v. United States, 294
    Gillespie v. Indianapolis, 294
    Hawkins v. U.S., 280, 301
    Heart of Atlanta Motel, Inc. v. U.S., 285, 301
    Hisquierdo v. Hisquierdo, 284
    Meritor Savings Bank v. Mechele Vinson, 211
    In re Burrus, 283
    Roe v. Wade, 458
    Rose v. Rose, 281, 301
    Shapiro v. Thompson, 284, 301
    State v. Jones, 280, 301
    U.S. v. Morrison, 298-299, 301
    United States v. Baker, 294, 301
    United States v. Beavers, 294, 301
    United States v. Casciano, 292, 301
    United States v. Helem, 292, 301
    United States v. Meade, 294, 301
    United States v. Myers, 294, 301
    United States v. Page, 292, 301
    United States v. Young, 293, 301
    Welch v. Welch, 281
Court orders:
    police enforcement of, 283-284
    See also Civil restraining orders; Protection orders
COYOTE (Call Off Your Old Tired Ethics), 460, 463
Crack cocaine, prostitute rape and, 467
Creating Collaborations, 85, 93
Crime in the Ivory Tower study, 120
Criminal justice system:
    battered women programs, 256-257
    civil restraining orders, 313-317
    data from, 48
    Full Faith and Credit Provision and, 290
    implications of research, 321-323
    intervention strategies by, 334-335
    judicial behavior, 318-319
    police practices and, 304-309
    probation, 319-321
    prosecutorial practices, 309-313
    sex industry and, 461-465
    statistics from, 36-37
    street sex workers and, 468-469
    as victim's "power resource," 312
    See also Legal system
Crisis hot lines, rape, 231
Cultural competence:
    batterer intervention programs and, 271-273
    conducting research and, 60-62

Cultural congruence with research, 61
Culture:
    acceptance of violence and, 14-15
    changing norms and, 381-385
    dominant Western norms, 373
    intimate violence and, 163-166
    media campaigns and, 426-428
    patriarchal, 12
    rape, 16
    sexual violence in Western, 378
Cycle of violence, 155

DAP Research & Training Update, 79
Dating:
    intimate violence and, 160-162
    See also Teen dating
Dating Safely Group, 409-140
Dating violence prevention program:
    high school, 406-408
    middle school, 398-403
Decriminalization of prostitution, 463
Depression:
    abusive men and, 9
    battered women and, 169, 450-451
    child sexual abuse and, 104
Diagnostic and Statistical Manual (DSM-IV), 217
Disability Now newspaper, 202
Disability pornography:
    examples of, 194-201
    genre of, 197-198
    mainstreaming, 198-201
    political implications, 201-204
Disability rights movement, 194
Disclosure (movie), 211
Dissociation, child sexual abuse and, 104
District of Columbia, 305, 317-318
Divorce:
    "no-fault," 280
    prohibition of, 378
Domestic Abuse Project, 79, 83, 88, 256, 266
Domestic violence:
    early shelters, 247
    employment and, 446-450
    interstate travel to commit, 292
    older women and, 185-186. *See also* Older women abuse
    prevalence of, 444-446
    relation health problems and, 362
    welfare reform and, 452-455
Domestic Violence Action Kits, 426
Domestic Violence Intervention Services of Tulsa, 398
Domestic violence movement, 182-183
Domestic Violence Training Project (DVTP), 360
Domestic Violence: Not Just a Family Matter, 285
Drug abuse:
    batterers and, 156-157
    double victimization and, 440

pregnancy and, 457-458
    See also Substance abuse
Due process rights, 288
Duluth Domestic Abuse Intervention Project, 330
Duluth model, 262
Duluth Visitation Center, 254
Dysphasia in battered woman, 354
Dysphoric/borderline batterers, 156

Education:
    batterer programs as, 275
    rape crisis centers and, 238
    sexual assault, 135
Elder abuse movement, 183-184. *See also* Older women
    abuse
EMERGE, 262
Employment:
    domestic violence and, 446-450
    intimate violence and, 170
Entrapment, psychological and physical, 309
Ethical issues:
    codes of ethics, 59
    gender, 59-60
    religion and ethics, 377
    research paradigms and, 58-59
Ethnicity:
    child sexual abuse and, 106
    cultural congruence and, 61
    intimate violence and, 165
    See also Women of color
Evolutionary perspective, 10
Exchange theory, 11, 15

Face-to-face interviews, 42
Families First program, 257
Family and Intimate Violence Prevention Team, 30
Family violence, definition of, 23
Family Violence Council, 363
Family Violence Option (FVO), 443-444
Family violence perspective, 13-14
Family Violence Prevention Fund (FVPF), 351-353, 363,
    418, 423-428
    toll-free number, 425
    Web site, 69
Fatherhood, emphasis on responsible, 273
Fear, rape crisis centers and, 228
Female genital mutilation (FGM), 98, 115-116, 482,
    485-486
Female infanticide, 107-111
    in China, 484
    in India, 109-111
Femicide, 153. *See also* Homicide
Feminist (term), 332
Feminist theory, 12-13, 43, 125, 145-146, 216, 247, 282
    Abusive Behavior Inventory and, 43-44
    and older women, 181

prostitution and, 460
rape crisis centers and, 228-231
Fetish Letters magazine, 198-200, 202, 205n11
Ford Foundation, 424
Foundation Against Trafficking in Women, 472, 478
Foundation for Women's Health, Research, and Devel-
    opment (FORWARD International), 486
Fraternal Order of Police v. United States, 294
Funding, collaborative research and, 83-84

Gallery magazine, 203
Gender:
    as ethical issue, 59-60
    inequality, institutionalization of, 212
    violence and, 15-16
    See also Feminist theory; Men
Gender-specific roles, 12
General Social Survey, 26, 30-31
Gillespie v. Indianapolis, 294
Girls, teenage, 409-410
Global Alliance Against Traffic in Women, 472, 478
Global Campaign for Women's Human Rights, 493-495
Granny bashing, 182
Grants to Encourage Arrest, 297
Growing Old in America (Fischer), 179
Gun Control Act, 293-294

Harvard School of Public Health College Alcohol
    Study, 120-121
Hawkins v. U.S., 280, 301
Head injury, batterers and, 10
Headache, in battered women, 354
Healing, 380
Health care settings, battered women services in,
    255-258
Health intervention. *See* Clinical violence interventions
Health Omnibus Programs Extension of 1988, 68
Health problems:
    child sexual abuse and, 105
    domestic violence and, 362
    sex slavery and, 475-476
Health Resource Center on Domestic Violence, 367n4
Healthy Relationships: A Violence Prevention Curricu-
    lum, 398-400
Healthy Tomorrows, 254-255
Heart of Atlanta Motel, Inc. v. U.S., 285, 301
Heterosexual relationships, violence by women and, 13
Heterosexuality, sexual harassment and, 215
Hippocratic oath, 205
HIV:
    clinical interventions and, 353, 365, 366
    exposure risk, 170
    low incidence problem, 346
    prostitution and, 463
    public awareness of, 419
    rape victims and, 232

risk for, 348
trafficking of women and, 475-476
See also AIDS
Home, as dangerous place, 97
Homicide, intimate violence and, 153-155
Homophobia, sexual harassment and, 215-216
"Honor" crimes, 484
Hope, rape crisis centers and, 228
Hospital records, 47-48
Hostile environments, 211
Human rights:
  systemic violence against women and, 484-486
  violence against women as violation of, 481
  See also Rights
Human Rights Watch, 485, 498-499
Hustler magazine, 195
Hyperventilation, of battered woman, 354

Illinois Department of Human Services, 270
Immigrant women:
  intimate violence and, 166
  provisions in VAWA, 294-297
  self-petitioning process, 296
  survey respondents, 32
Immigration and Naturalization Service (INS), 294
Immigration policies, 330
In re Burrus, 283
Incidence:
  need for clinical intervention and, 346
  variance in rates, 30
  See also Prevalence
Index of Spouse Abuse (ISA), 45
India, female infanticide in, 107-111, 109-111
Infibulation, 115-116. *See also* Female genital mutilation
Injuries:
  domestic assaults and, 440
  hallmarks of abusive, 348
Injury in America, 346
Institutional Review Board (IRB), 57
Inter-American Commission on Women, 498n1
Inter-American Convention on the Prevention, Punishment, and Eradication of Violence Against Women, 498n1
Intergenerational transmission of violence, 6
International Association of Forensic Nurses (IAFN), 244
International Bill of Human Rights, 482-487
International Human Rights Law Group, 472, 478
International Organization for Migration, 473
International sex industry, 470-476
  child sex tourism, 471-472
  sex tourism, 470-472
  trafficking, 472-475
International Women's Information and Communication Service (Isis), 492
International Women's Year, 491-492
Intervention:
  advocacy and, 337-339

battered women shelters and. *See* Battered women, shelters for
beginnings, 223
clinical violence, 345-369
community, 362-364
criminal justice system, 334-335
institutional, 358-362
media campaigns, 417-438
need for federal, 283-285
older women abuse, 187-188
police, 321-322
preventive rape, 127-136
with batterers. *See* Batterer intervention programs
Interviews, 42-43
Intimate partner violence:
  incidence of, 5
  uniform definitions, 37-38
  See also Intimate violence
Intimate Partner Violence Surveillance: Uniform Definitions & Recommended Data Elements, 37
Intimate violence:
  batterer characteristics, 155-159
  characteristics of, 146-148
  chronicity of, 153-155
  common couple violence, 154. *See also* Common couple violence
  costs and consequences of, 168-170
  culture and, 163-166
  defining, 144-146
  effects of, 143
  ethnicity and, 165-166
  immigrant women and, 166
  low-income men and, 454
  new research directions, 170-171
  ongoing, multidimensional and changing, 146-147
  ongoing relationship and, 147
  patterns of, 155
  pregnancy and, 162-163
  prevalence and incidence, 164-165
  racial difference and, 164
  relationship stage and, 160-162
  same-sex relationships and, 166
  separation and, 163
  shared lives and, 147-148
  types of, 148-153
  victim responsibility and, 148
  women survivors of, 159-160
  See also Intimate partner violence
Intimate violence, types of, 148-153
  homicide, 153-155
  overlap of, 153-155
  physical abuse, 149-150
  psychological abuse, 151-152
  sexual abuse, 150-151
  stalking, 152-153
Intra-individual theory, 6-8
It's Your Business, 426-428, 434

Jealousy, male sexual, 10
Joint Commission on the Accreditation of Health Care
    Organizations (JCAHO), 48, 350, 353, 365
Joint Commission on the Accreditation of Hospitals
    (JCAHO), 244
Journal of the American Medical Association, 97
Journal of Interpersonal Violence, 1
Journal of Religion and Abuse, 1
Judicial behavior, 318-319
Justice, 380

"Kitchen table factor," 88

Lac du Flambeau Domestic Abuse Program, 252
Latin American and Caribbean Network AG Sexual and
    Domestic Violence, 495-496
Latina Domestic violence Program, 252
Law Enforcement assistance Administration (LEAA),
    229
Law Enforcement and Prosecution Grants to Reduce
    Violence Crimes Against Women, 297
Learned helplessness, 7-8
Legal Needs, The (Cahn), 310
Legal system:
    protection orders, 282-283
    state laws, 281-285, 291
    treatment of mentally retarded, 197
    women's rights and, 279-280
    See also Criminal justice system
Legalization of prostitution, 463
Legislation:
    Child Abuse Prevention and Treatment Act, 62
    Gun Control Act, 293-294
    Marriage Fraud Act, 166, 330
    National Hate Crimes Statistics Act, 197
    Older Americans Act, 180
    Public Health Service Act, 68
    Social Security Amendments, 180
    Victims of Crime Act, 231
    Violence Against Women Act (VAWA), 279-301
    Violent Crime Control and Law Enforcement Act,
        117, 285
Lesbians, shelter experiences of, 250
Lesbian violence, 13, 98, 166-168
Likert scale format, 41
London Family Court Clinic Violence Prevention Pro-
    gram, 404-405
London Telegraph, The, 109
Los Angeles Times, 435

Mainstreaming:
    clinical violence intervention and, 361
    sexualization of disability, 198-201
    use of term, 345-346
Male health practitioners, abuse of disabled women, 203

Male peer-support model, 16
Malleus Maleficarum, 375
Mandatory arrest statutes, 304-309
Marriage:
    subordination in, 378
    traditional, 12
Marriage Fraud Act, 166, 330
Maryland Medical Journal, 359
Massachusetts:
    AFDC Working Group, 88
    arrest statute, 306
    Governor's Commission on Domestic Violence, 88
    Mothers Survey, 89-90
    Quincy District Court Domestic Violence Program
        (QDC), 316-318
Measure of Wife Abuse (MWA), 45
Measurement strategies, 38-49
    Abusive Behavior Inventory (ABI), 43-44
    Conflict Tactics Scales (CTS), 44-45
    future directions, 51
    hybrid, 49
    implications, 50-51
    Index of Spouse Abuse (ISA), 45
    Measure of Wife Abuse (MWA), 45
    Partner Abuse Scales (PAS), 46
    selecting, 50
    Severity of Violence Against Women Scales
        (SVAWS), 46
    Sexual Experiences Survey, 46-47
    Women's Experience with Battering Scale
        (WEB), 47
Measurement strategies, individuals:
    interviews, 42-43
    observation, 40
    peer reports, 40
    self-administered surveys, 41-42
    surveys, 40-41
Measurement strategies, record reviews:
    civil and criminal justice records, 48
    hospital records, 47-48
    service provision records, 48-49
Media, O. J. Simpson trial and, 418, 430
Media campaigns:
    advertising agencies and, 434-435
    corporate America's and, 432-433
    culturally specific, 426-428
    fiction and, 435-436
    gatekeepers and, 429-432
    generating revenue for, 435
    grassroots organizing, 428-429
    messages that resonate and, 419-423
    national, 423-426
    public service announcements (PSAs), 419
    recommendations for future, 432-434
Men:
    abusive. *See* Batterers
    profiles of violent, 9
    rape intervention with, 133-134

researching violence against women, 53-55
    working with young, 409-410
Men Against Sexual Assault (MASA), 409-410
Men's Fitness, 431
Meritor Savings Bank v. Mechele Vinson, 211
Mexican Americans, intimate violence and, 164
Michigan Community Advocacy Project, 78-79
Middle Way House, Inc., 253
Migrant women:
    battered women shelters, 252
    shelter experiences and, 251
Military orders, Full Faith and Credit provision and,
    290-291
Milwaukee Women's Center, Older Abused Women's
    Program, 188
Minneapolis Domestic Violence Experiment, 306-307
Minnesota:
    Advocates for Human Rights, 487, 499
    Coalition for Battered Women, 415
    Domestic Abuse Project, 79
    School Curriculum Project, 405-406
Modeling, concept of, 6
Morning-after pill, 232
Movies:
    disabled women and, 199-200
    violent, 14
Multidimensional theories, 15-17
Multiple personality disorder, child sexual abuse
    and, 104
My Family and Me: Violence Free, 395-396

Nairobi Forward Looking Strategies on the
    Advancement of Women, 492
Nairobi Forward-Looking Strategies, 496
National Academy of Medicine, 346
National Association of Student Personnel Administra-
    tors, 127
National Center for the Injury Prevention and Control,
    30, 388
National Center for State Courts, 315
National Coalition Against Domestic Violence, 248
National Coalition of Physicians Against Family Vio-
    lence, 352
National College Health Risk Behavior Survey,
    119-120
National Commission, 58-59
National Council for Research on Women, 99, 210-
    213, 221
National Crime Survey, on misdemeanor cases, 310
National Crime Victimization Survey, 164, 168-169, 247
National Criminal Information Center (NCIC)
    database, 288
National Family Violence Resurvey, 149, 185
National Family Violence Surveys, 183-184
National Institute of Justice (NIJ), 76, 94
    Spouse Abuse Replication Program (SARP), 307
    Violence Against Women Survey, 119, 26, 31

National Institutes of Health (NIH), 64-65, 71
National Institutes of Mental Health (NIMH), 258, 346
National Research Council, 35, 52, 259, 346
    battered women shelters, 248
    Panel on Research on Violence Against Women,
        117
National Victim Center, 119, 232, 241
National Violence Against Women Survey, 29
Native Americans:
    criminal intervention strategies and, 334
    shelters, 252
    stalking crimes and, 291
Nebraska Coalition Against Domestic Violence, 92
Neglect, sex-selective, 109-111
New England Journal of Medicine, 203
New York Times, The, 199, 214, 431
New Yorker, 199
"No-drop" policies, 309
No-fault divorce statutes, 280
Nongovernmental organizations (NGOs):
    activities of, 493-495
    FORWARD International, 485-486
    Global Campaign for Women's Human Rights,
        493-495
    international and regional networks, 495-497
    national level efforts, 496
    obligations of, 490
    parallel conferences, 491-493
    World Organization Against Torture, 485
Normalization, 345, 361
Nuremberg Code, 58-59, 64-67, 71
Nursing Network on Violence Against Women, 352

O. J. Simpson trial, 418, 430
Observation, as measurement strategy, 40
Older Americans Act, 180
Older women abuse:
    contemporary American society and, 179-182
    domestic violence and, 185-186
    domestic violence movement and, 182-183
    elder abuse movement and, 183-184
    future research directions, 188-189
    information about, 98
    programs and services, 186-188
    shelter experiences, 250
Omaha offender-absent experiment, 321
Operant conditioning, 6
Orders of protection. *See* Civil restraining orders;
    Court orders; Protection orders

Paradigm:
    defined, 1-2
    research, 58-60
Parents, battered, 182
Partner, use of term, 45
Partner Abuse Scales (PAS), 46

Partner Violence Surveillance, 51

Patriarchal culture, 12
   risk for violence and, 16
   sexual harassment and, 215

Patriarchal religions, 373-379

Patriarchal terrorism, 6, 98, 146

PeaceBuilders, 394-395

Peer reports, as measurement strategy, 40

Peer-mediation programs, 390

Pennsylvania Coalition Against Domestic Violence, 333-334, 352

Penthouse Forum magazine, 194-195

People magazine, 431

Personality characteristics, psychopathy and, 8-10

Personality disorders, of batterers, 157

Pharaonic circumcision, 115

Physical abuse, intimate violence and, 149-150

Physical health problems, child sexual abuse and, 105

Physical injury, intimate violence and, 168

Physiological explanations, 10-11

Piano, The, 199

Pimps, 463

Plan to Prevent Family and Intimate Partner Violence, 363

Playboy magazine, 194-195

Police:
   arrest policies, 304-309
   domestic violence practices, 304-309
   enforcing court orders, 283-284
   intervention, 321-322
   warrantless on-scene arrests, 312

Politics, disability pornography and, 201-204

Pornography:
   child sexual abuse and, 103
   dead women in, 201
   disability. *See* Disability pornography
   sadomasochistic, 201
   sexual abuse and, 194

Posttraumatic stress disorder (PTSD):
   battered women and, 450-451
   sexually abused children and, 103-104

Power:
   defined, 11-12
   excessive, 335

Pregnancy:
   criminalization of, 457-458
   intimate violence and, 162-163

Prevalence of violence:
   of domestic violence, 444-446
   intimate violence, 164-165
   need for clinical intervention and, 346
   rape, 118-121
   variance in rates, 30

Prevention of violence:
   complex social, 362-364
   focus on, 118
   school-based violence, 387-389
   use of term, 135

Probation, 319-321

Probation officers, 319-321, 323

Process-oriented psychodynamic treatment, for batterers, 263

Prohibition model for sex workers, 462

Prosecutorial practices, 309-313, 322

Prostitution, 459
   "call girls," 466
   child sexual abuse and, 103
   definitions of, 460-461
   legal paradigms to address, 461-464
   rape and, 467
   "rape myths" about, 468
   street, 466-467
   tourism and, 471. *See also* Sex tourism
   violence and, 465-470

Protection orders, 282-283
   civil, 313-317
   enforcing child custody in, 290
   enforcing visitation in, 290
   Violence Against Women Act on, 286-291
   welfare-to-work programs and, 448
   See also Civil restraining orders; Court orders

Psychological abuse, intimate violence and, 151-152

Psychological autopsies, 40

Psychological and physical entrapment, 309

Psychopathy, personality characteristics and, 8

Public funding, of batterer programs, 271

Public Health Service Act, 68

Public opinion, power of, 420

Public policy, violence research and, 65

Public service announcements (PSAs), 419

Quanun-e-Shahadat Order, 487

Quid pro quo, 210-211

Rainbow House, 253

Rape:
   abusive relationships and, 348
   as violence, 382
   evolutionary perspective, 10
   fear of, 97
   feminist perspective on, 12-13
   intervention with men, 133-134
   interviewing women about, 24
   male peer-support model and, 16
   medical needs of victims, 232
   prevalence of, 5, 118-121, 135
   preventive interventions, 127-136
   prostitutes and, 467
   vulnerability to, 121-127

Rape crisis centers (RCC):
   community connections, 238-239
   effects on society, 235-237
   effects on survivors, 234-235
   educational campaigns by, 238

emergence of, 228-220
mainstream organizations and, 238
mobilizing strategies and tactics, 237-239
"occupy and indoctrinate" strategy, 238
services provided by, 231-233
what are?, 227
working in, 233-234
See also Antirape movement
Rape culture, 16
Rape kit, 232, 239
Rape Trauma Syndrome (RTS), 236
Rape Warfare (Allen), 485
RAVEN, 262
Recidivism, batterer programs and, 268
Recommended Data Elements, 30
Record reviews, 47-49
Refugees. *See* Immigrant women
Relationships:
    between woman and harasser, 216
    of domination, 332
    ongoing, 147-148
    same-sex, 166-168
    stage of, 160-162
Religion:
    changing norms and, 381-385
    Christianity, 375-378
    ethics and, 377
    Islam, 376-377, 487
    Jehovah's Witnesses, 371-372
    Judaism, 376-378
    overview, 372-373
    patriarchal, 373-379
    religious counseling, 372
Research:
    case studies, 78-80
    collaborative. *See* Collaborative research
    confidentiality, 67-69
    cultural competence and, 60-62
    cultural congruence and, 61-62
    dissemination, 69-70
    ethical challenges, 57-72
    freedom to withdraw, 66-67
    immigrant and refugee respondents, 32
    incentives for participation, 67
    informed consent and, 64-67
    methodology difficulty, 24
    paradigms, 58-60
    participant safety and, 62-64
    public policy and, 65
    sensitive nature of inquiry, 65
    trauma from participation, 65-66
    useful, 88
    validity problems, 331
Research on Older Women: Where Is Feminism?
    (Hooyman), 181
Research questions, 38, 89
Resource theory, 11-12

Restraining orders. *See* Civil restraining order; Court orders; Protection orders
Retention strategies, 90
Retrospective or recall bias, 39
Rights:
    disability, 194
    due process, 288
    effective remedies, 486-487
    hierarchy of human, 483
    violation of human, 481-499
Roe v. Wade, 458
Rose v. Rose, 281, 301
Rural Domestic Violence and Child Abuse Enforcement
    Assistance Grants, 297

Safe Dates program, 401-402
Safety, research participant, 62-64
Safety plan, 357-358
Safety Planning With Battered Women: Complex Lives,
    Difficult Choices (Davies et al.), 81
Salon magazine, 435
Same-sex relationships:
    intimate violence and, 166
    See also Lesbian violence
School-based violence prevention:
    affective education programs, 396-397
    community and academic collaborations, 411-412
    curricular diversity and, 411
    elementary programs, 390-391, 394
    evaluation of programs, 389-390
    evolution of programs, 387-389
    future of programs, 412-413
    high school programs, 403-411
    middle school programs, 397-403
    peace programs, 394-396
    program evaluations, 412
    summary of programs, 391-393
Secondary victimization, 231
Self-esteem, damage to victims, 29
Self-help for batterers, 263
Self-help groups for batterers, 266
Self magazine, 431
Self-petitioning process, 296
Serial killers, sex workers and, 468-469
Service provision records, 48
Severity of Violence Against Women Scales (SVAWS),
    46
Sex industry, 459
    international, 470-476
    legal responses to, 461-465
    lower echelons of, 466
Sex tourism, 459, 470-472
    child, 471-472
Sex work, 460, 477n1
    crack cocaine and, 467
    victimization, offending and, 441
    violence and, 465-470

Sexed Work (Maher), 467
Sex-selective abortion, 107-108
Sex-selective neglect, 109-111
Sexual abuse:
    among disabled women and girls, 196-197
    frequency of, 106
    intimate violence and, 150-151
    pornography and, 194
    severity of, 106
    U.S. girls, 101-102. *See also* Child sexual abuse
Sexual assault education, 135
Sexual Assault Nurse Examiner (SANE), 238, 243-246
Sexual Assault Response/Resource Team (SART),
    243, 245
Sexual Experiences Survey, 46-47
Sexual harassment:
    challenging male dominance and, 215-216
    continuum of violence and, 211-212
    distressing experience, 217-218
    effects of, 216-219
    hostile environments, 211
    information about, 98
    male domination and, 213-214
    reporting, 218-219
    risk of victimization, 212-216
    sex discrimination, 212
    sexual blackmail, 210-211
    sexualization of work and, 213
    surviving, 219
    what is?, 210-212
Sexual partners, multiple, 122-123
Sexual Politics of Disability, The (Shakespeare et al.), 202
Sexually transmitted diseases (STDs):
    as consequence of assault, 170
    prostitution and, 463-464
    rape victims and, 232
    risk for, 348
    trafficking of women and, 475
    See also AIDS; HIV
Shapiro v. Thompson, 284, 301
Slam magazine, disability pornography in, 195-196,
    204n6
Sleep disorders, in battered women, 354
Social etiological model, 16-17
Social learning theory, 6-8
Social movements, 64, 91, 194, 303, 329-342, 384, 417
    formative years of, 331
    international, 441, 498
    outcomes of, 236
    prostitution and, 461
    women's movement, 97-98, 227-230, 243, 247, 366
Social psychological theory, 6
Social Security Amendments, 180
Socialization, gender-specific roles and, 12
Sociocultural theories, 6, 12-15
Socioeconomic status (SES):
    cultural competence and, 61
    risk of victimization and, 42

Southern Cone Network Against Domestic violence, 495
Sporting events, violent, 14
Stalking:
    behavior, 293
    importance of measures, 29-30
    interstate, 292-293
    intimate violence and, 152-153
    Violence Against Women Act and, 291-293
State laws, 281-285
State v. Jones, 280, 301
STOP Violence Against Indian Women Grant Program,
    297
STOP Violence Against Women Formula Grant Pro-
    gram, 297
STOP: School Targeting Operation for the Prevention of
    Interpersonal Violence, 400-401
Stress:
    as risk factor, 15
    signs of, 354
Subculture of violence, 14
Substance abuse:
    in battered women, 354
    batterer intervention programs and, 265
    See also Drug abuse
Suicidality:
    battered women and, 169, 348
    risk of, 356
Supreme Court cases, 284. *See also* Court cases; U.S.
    Supreme Court
Surgeon General's Workshop on Violence and Public
    Health, 352
Surveys, 40-42
Survivorship model, 8
Survivors of intimate violence, 159-160
Sweden:
    anti-prostitution law in, 195
    forced sterilization in, 196
Sydney Men Against Sexual Assault (MASA), 410-411
Systems-driven reform, 339

Take Back the Night March, 237
Teens:
    Dating Safely Group for, 409-410
    dating violence, 161
    shelters and abused, 250
Telephone interviews, 42
    computer-assisted, 40
    danger with, 63
Temporary Assistance to Needy Families (TANF),
    439, 444
Texas Council on Domestic Violence, 80
Texas Department of Human Services, 80, 90
Theory of Flight, The 200
There's No Excuse program, 424-426, 430-431
Third National Incidence Study of Child Abuse and
    Neglect (NIS-3), 101, 107
Time Out magazine, 201

Trafficking of women, 472-475
Training:
    for health professionals, 349-350
    religious ministry, 383-384
Training for Transformation: A Handbook for Community Workers (Hope and Timmel), 343
Transitional housing programs, 253
Trokois, 496-497
12-step programs, 266

U.S. Bureau of the Census, 192
U.S. Constitution:
    Article I, Section 8, 284
    due process requirements and, 288
    Fourteenth Amendment, Section 5, 299
    privacy and, 423
    Sixteenth Amendment, Section 5, 284
U.S. Department of Defense, 222, 211
U.S. Department of Health and Human Services, 59, 71, 363
U.S. Department of Justice, 347, 369
    Office of Justice Assistance, 69
    Office on Violence Against Women, 117
    Violence Against Women Office, 297
U.S. Department of State, 108-109, 113, 222
U.S. Equal Employment Opportunity Commission, 210, 213, 222
U.S. Merit Systems Protection Board, 212-214, 218, 222
U.S. National Hate Crimes Statistics Act of 1990, 197
U.S. Naval Recruit Health Study, 120
U.S. Office for Drug Control and Crime Prevention, 474, 479
U.S. Office for Victims of Crime (OVC), 244
U.S. Office of Child Support Enforcement, 453
U.S. Office of Civil Rights, 210, 222
U.S. Supreme Court:
    cases, 284, 298. *See also* Court cases
    sexual harassment, 211
Understanding Violence Against Women, 117
United Nations:
    Charter, 482-483, 487-488
    Commission on the Status of Women, 488-489
    Committee on Elimination of Discrimination Against Women (CEDAW), 489-491
    Committee on Human Rights, 492-493
    Convention on the Elimination of All Forms of Discrimination Against Women, 484, 489
    Convention on the Nationality of Married Women, 489
    Convention on the Political Rights of Women, 489
    Convention on the Rights of the Child, 464, 484
    Decade for Women, 492
    Declaration on the Elimination of Violence Against Women, 489-491
    development of women's rights within, 487-497
    Fourth World Conference on Women, 493-494

    High Commissioner for Refugees, 485-486
    Human Rights Committee, 484
    International Bill of Human Rights, 482-487, 488
    International Covenant on Civil and Political Rights, 483, 486
    International Covenant on Economic, Social, and Cultural Rights, 483, 486
    International Labor Organization, 471
    International Convention on the Elimination of All Forms of RD, 484
    Interregional Crime and Justice Research Institute, 474, 479
    Optional Protocol to the Women's Convention, 491
    prostitution and trafficking in women, 461-462
    Third World Conference on Women, 492
    Universal Declaration of Human Rights, 483
    World Conferences, 491-493
    World Tourism Organization, 470
United States v. Baker, 294, 301
United States v. Beavers, 294, 301
United States v. Casciano, 292, 301
United States v. Helem, 292, 301
United States v. Meade, 294, 301
United States v. Morrison, 298-299, 301
United States v. Myers, 294, 301
United States v. Page, 292, 301
United States v. Young, 293, 301
United Way, 229
Universities:
    battered women programs, 257
    See also Colleges
UniWorld Group, Inc., 426

Validity:
    catalytic, 69
    problem of, 31
Values, sexual, rape and, 123
Victim:
    blaming, 382
    disparagement, 311
    effects of intimate violence on, 168-170. *See also* Intimate violence
    empowerment, 322
    responsibility in intimate violence, 148
    Western culture and, 373-374
    See also Battered women
Victimization:
    drinking and, 124
    link between offending and, 440
    past, vulnerability and, 122
    repeated, 146
    risk of sexual harassment, 212-216
    secondary, 231
    self-esteem damage and, 29
Victims of Crime Act, 231
Victim's panel, 336
Vienna Conference on Human Rights, 492-493

Violence:
  acceptance of, 14-15
  borderline personality organization and, 8
  continuum of, 211-212
  control mechanism, 11
  cycle of, 155
  defining, 23-29
  gender and, 15-16
  subculture of, 14
Violence and Abuse Abstracts, 1, 23
Violence against women:
  definitions, 36-38
  measurement of, 35
  men researching, 53-55
  role of alcohol, 11
Violence Against Women Act (VAWA)
  antirape movement and, 237
  as institutional advocacy, 339
  as legislative frame, ix
  Civil Rights Remedy, 286, 298-300
  federal grant programs, 297-298
  Full Faith and Credit provision, 286-290
  Gun Control Act amendments, 293-294
  important sections, 285-286
  of 1990, 285
  passage of, 117
  protection orders and, 286-291
  services intervention and, 363
  stalking crimes, 291-293
  victims prior to, 281
Violence Against Women Survey (Canada), 26
Violence Against Women Survey (U.S.), 119
Violence Against Women journal, 1, 74
Violence Prevention Curriculum for Adolescents,
  408-409
Violence and Victims journal, 1
Violence by women, 13
Violent Crime Control and Law Enforcement Act,
  117, 285

Visitation, enforcing, in protection order, 290
Visitation center, 254
Vogue magazine, 199

Washington Post, The, 109, 435
Welch v. Welch, 281
Welfare cyclers, 449
Welfare reform, 452-455
Welfare-to-work programs, 446-447
WHISPER (Women Hurt in Systems of Prostitution),
  460
White House, Office of National Drug Control Policy,
  435-436
Wife referral, 264
Wisconsin Bureau on Aging, 188
Wisconsin Coalition Against Domestic Violence
  (WCADV), 183, 188
Women Against Pornography, 204n6
Women of color:
  battered women shelters and, 250-253
  intimate violence and, 164
  relationships of domination and, 332
Women and Disability (Lonsdale), 204n7
Women in Law and Development in Africa (WiLDAF),
  496
Women's Center and Shelter of Greater Pittsburgh, 254
Women's Experience with Battering Scale (WEB), 47
Worcester Family Research Project, 445, 449-451
Working women's Institute, 217
Workplaces, male-dominated, 214
World Health Organization, 101
  female infanticide, 111, 113
  sex-selective abortion, 107-108
World Organization Against Torture, 485
World Vision, 109, 111

Youth Relationships Project, 387, 408-409

About the Authors

Karen Bachar is a doctoral candidate in the Program Evaluation Research Methodology Program and is pursuing a master's degree in public health at the University of Arizona, where she is director of the Arizona Rape Prevention Education Data and Evaluation Project. She is a member of the Evaluation Group for the Analysis of Data (EGAD) and a founding member of Proyecto Interacional Sobre la Estructura Familiar (PIEF), a multinational domestic violence project at the University of Arizona Department of Psychology. She recently participated on the Governor's Taskforce on Sexual Assault for the State of Arizona.

Larry W. Bennett is Associate Professor, Jane Addams College of Social Work, University of Illinois at Chicago. Previously, he was a member of the faculty at Carthage College in Kenosha, Wisconsin, and he worked for 15 years in social service agencies. His research and publications focus on the relationship between substance abuse and domestic violence, the structure and effectiveness of community-based batterer-intervention programs, and the link between various forms of men's violence such as sexual harassment, dating violence, and adult partner abuse.

Raquel Kennedy Bergen is Assistant Professor of Sociology at St. Joseph's University in Philadelphia, Pennsylvania. She is the author of several scholarly articles and book chapters on wife rape and the book, *Wife Rape: Understanding the Response of Survivors and Service Providers*. She edited the book *Issues in Intimate Violence* and a special issue of *Violence Against Women* on the subject of marital rape. A crisis counselor for battered and sexually abused women, her current work is on sexual violence against women during pregnancy.

Andrea L. Bible works at the National Clearinghouse for the Defense of Battered Women in Philadelphia. She previously worked at the Minnesota Center Against Violence and Abuse as a cofacilitator of the Applied Research Forum of VAWnet—The National Electronic Network on Violence Against Women and at the Battered Women's Justice Project Criminal Justice

Center. She has worked as a legal advocate with a community-based intervention project, volunteered as a crisis advocate at a women's shelter, and volunteered in a hospital-based advocacy program.

Johanna Bond is a teaching fellow in Georgetown University Law Center's International Women's Human Rights Clinic. In 1998-1999, she received a Georgetown Women's Law and Public Policy Fellowship. She has also acted as a consultant to the United Nations Development Fund for Women (UNIFEM) and as a law clerk for U.S. District Judge Ann D. Montgomery. Her women's human rights experience includes work in Bulgaria, Macedonia, Nepal, Cambodia, and Kenya, as well research on a variety of women's human rights issues.

Jacquelyn C. Campbell is the Anna D. Wolf Endowed Professor and Associate Dean For the Doctoral Program and Research at the Johns Hopkins University School of Nursing. She has been a researcher and advocate in the area of violence against women for more than 20 years, with extensive publications, research grants, and policy positions. She has been a member of the National Advisory Committee on Violence Against Women and U.S. the Department of Defense Task Force on Domestic Violence.

Rebecca Campbell is Assistant Professor of Community and Quantitative Psychology at the University of Illinois at Chicago. Her research examines the community response to rape and ways in which the legal, medical, and mental health systems can better serve victimized women. A primary theme in this work is how rape crisis centers can work as effective liaisons between survivors and other social systems. She is

also completing a book that examines the emotional impact on investigators of studying violence against women. She received the 2000 Louise Kidder Early Career Award for the Psychological Study of Social Issues for her contributions to social science research.

Walter S. DeKeseredy is professor of sociology at Ohio University. He has written dozens of articles and several books on woman abuse. He is also the author of *Women, Crime, and the Canadian Criminal Justice System* and co-author of *Contemporary Social Problems in North American Society* (with Shahid Alvi and Desmond Ellis).

Sujata Desai is a behavioral scientist on the Family and Intimate Violence Prevention Team, Division of Violence Prevention, National Center for Injury Prevention and Control, Centers for Disease Control and Prevention in Atlanta, Georgia. Her research focus is primarily in the area of measurement and intimate partner violence. She is involved with research on effective measurement methods to study violence against women and public health surveillance of violence against women.

Jacqueline A. Dienemann is Clinical Associate Professor at Georgetown University School of Nursing and Health and Science Consultant, Shelter for Battered Women, North Carolina. She has been involved in domestic violence program development and evaluation since 1995, working with hospital emergency departments and community-based domestic violence programs. She is a coinvestigator with Jacquelyn Campbell on a study of health maintenance organization enrollees and active-duty military women regarding prevalence of intimate partner abuse. Her current research focuses on validating a tool to assess the counseling needs of women at the time they disclose partner abuse. She serves on the Maryland Family Violence Council, Cultural Diversity Advisory Committee of the American Nurses Association, and is President of the Council on Graduate Education for Administration in Nursing.

Jeffrey L. Edleson is Professor in the University of Minnesota School of Social Work and director of MINCAVA—The Minnesota Center Against Violence and Abuse (Web site located at http://www. mincava.umn.edu). He has published more than 80 articles and five books on domestic violence, groupwork, and program evaluation. He has conducted intervention research at the Domestic Abuse Project in Minneapolis for almost 17 years. He has provided technical assistance to domestic violence programs and research projects across North America as well as in several other countries including Germany, Australia, Israel, and Singapore.

R. Amy Elman teaches political science at Kalamazoo College in Michigan, where she is associate director of the Center for European Studies and chair of the Political Science Department. She is author of *Sexual Subordination & State Intervention: Comparing Sweden and the United States* and editor of *Sexual Politics and The European Union.* In addition, her articles concerning violence against women have appeared in several volumes and international journals including *Violence Against Women, Women Studies International Forum, Nouvelles Questions Feministes, and Women and Politics.*

Marie M. Fortune is the founder and senior analyst at the Center for the Prevention of Sexual and Domestic Violence in Seat-

tle, Washington. She is a pastor, author, educator, and practicing ethicist and theologian. Ordained in 1976 in the United Church of Christ, she has written numerous books including *Sexual Violence: the Unmentionable Sin, Keeping the Faith: Guidance for Christian Women Facing Abuse, Is Nothing Sacred?,* and *Violence Against Women and Children: A Christian Theological Sourcebook* with Carol Adams. She is editor of *The Journal of Religion and Abuse* and serves on the National Advisory Council on Violence Against Women for the U.S. Department of Justice.

Marissa Ghez is a White House Fellow appointed by the President of the United States and the bipartisan Commission on White House Fellowships to serve as a special assistant to the Secretary of the Navy at the U.S. Department of Defense. She served as associate director and communications director of the Family Violence Prevention Fund for several years and was the founding director of its national public education campaign, *There's No Excuse for Domestic Violence.* She has developed many innovative communications initiatives designed to advance public recognition of domestic violence as a preventable public health problem. She is coauthor of *Ending Domestic Violence: Changing Public Perceptions/Halting the Epidemic,* and she coproduced "Speaking Up: Ending Domestic Violence in Our Communities," a half-hour program distributed by American Public Television, which aired on dozens of public television stations nationwide in 1999.

Tameka Gillum is a doctoral candidate in the ecological-community psychology program at Michigan State University. Her research interests include exploring culturally specific dynamics of and interventions pertaining to intimate partner violence in communities of color, including same-sex intimate partner violence within communities of color. Her previous research includes a master's thesis, *Exploring the Link Between Stereotypic Images and Intimate Partner Violence in the African American Community.* She assisted in conducting a statewide needs assessment of survivors in rural areas of Michigan, and she is currently working on a needs assessment of African American female survivors of domestic violence in Michigan.

Barbara J. Hart is the legal director of the Pennsylvania Coalition Against Domestic Violence and associate director of the Battered Women's Justice Project. Her work includes public policy making, training, and technical assistance on a broad range of issues: crafting coordinated community intervention systems; developing and critiquing legislation, court procedures, and program standards for batterer-treatment services; collaborating between the research and practitioner communities; affecting litigation on behalf of battered women and children; and designing training curricula for effective intervention against domestic violence. She was a leader in efforts to implement the Violence Against Women Act of 1994 (VAWA).

Drew Humphries is Associate Professor of Sociology and director of the Criminal Justice Program on the Camden Campus of Rutgers University. Her publications include *Crack Mothers: Pregnancy, Drugs, and the Media.* For the journal *Violence Against Women,* she edited a Special Issued entitled, "Women, Violence, and the Media."

LeeAnn Iovanni is an independent researcher and consultant based in Denmark.

Her most recent research, which was conducted in conjunction with the Institute for Communication at Aalborg University, examined the social-psychological aspects of the acculturation of refugees and immigrants in northern Denmark. Previously, she was Assistant Professor in the Department of Criminology, Indiana University of Pennsylvania.

Jana L. Jasinski is Assistant Professor of Sociology and Anthropology at the University of Central Florida. In 1997, she was a National Institute of Mental Health Post Doctoral Research Fellow at the Family Research Laboratory, University of New Hampshire (1997). Her research interests include both lethal and nonlethal interpersonal violence (particularly intimate partner violence), substance abuse, the response of the criminal justice system to violence, and the negative consequences of child sexual assault. She has presented her research at numerous conferences, published several articles, and is the coeditor of two books: *Out of the Darkness: Contemporary Perspectives on Family Violence* and *Partner Violence: A Comprehensive Review of 20 Years of Research.*

Dheeshana Jayasundara is a master's student in criminology and criminal justice at the University of Missouri-St. Louis and is currently completing a study with Jody Miller of the commercial sex industry in Sri Lanka. She received her undergraduate degree in sociology at University of Delhi in 1998. She was formerly a research assistant at the International Centre for Ethnic Studies in Colombo, where she conducted research (with Ameena Hussein) on violence against women in Sri Lanka. On completion of her master's degree, she plans to return to Sri Lanka to work with commercial sex workers.

Kathleen A. Kendall-Tackett is a research associate at the Family Research Laboratory, University of New Hampshire. She is on the editorial boards of *Child Abuse and Neglect: The International Journal* and *Journal of Child Sexual Abuse,* and she was program cochair of the June 2000 conference, *Victimization of Children and Youth: An International Research Conference.* She has wide research interests that include family violence, child maltreatment, maternal and postpartum depression, breast-feeding, and women's health. She is author of *Postpartum Depression: A Comprehensive Approach for Nurses.* Her current research is on the health effects of victimization.

Mary P. Koss is Professor of Public Health, Family and Community Medicine, Psychiatry, and Psychology in the College of Public Health at the University of Arizona in Tucson. She is cochair of the American Psychological Association Task Force on Violence Against Women, which in 1994 published *No Safe Haven: Male Violence Against Women at Home, at Work, and in the Community,* winner of the Washington EdPress award for the outstanding book on a social concern in 1994. She served on the National Tesearch Council Panel on Violence Against Women, which in 1996 published its report, *Understanding Violence Against Women.* She received the 2000 American Psychological Association Award for Distinguished Contributions to Research in Public Policy.

Linda E. Ledray developed the Sexual Assault Resource Service (SARS) program and has been the director since its establish-

ment over 20 years ago, providing competent forensic medical services to sexual assault survivors in Hennepin County, Minnesota. She has been a lecturer at the University of Minnesota since 1976 and has taught nationally and internationally on the topic of victim assistance. She has been active in international humanitarian relief and has been involved in numerous committees and organizations that focus on topics such as mental health, child abuse, and political, social, and sexual violence. She has undertaken several research projects, the results of which have been published in her multiple articles and books.

Patricia Mahoney is a sociologist and a research associate at the Stone Center, Wellesley Centers for Women, at Wellesley College, Wellesley, Massachusetts. She is currently working on a variety of projects focused on the incidence and outcomes of family violence and sexual violence. Her main area of interest is sexual abuse by marital and intimate partners. She has led workshops and presented to local, national, and international audiences on the topics of intimate partner sexual abuse and survey methodology.

Mary Malefyt is an attorney on the staff of the Full Faith and Credit Project, a national project of the Pennsylvania Coalition Against Domestic Violence in Washington, D.C. Prior to joining that project in 1998, she was a staff member for the STOP Grants Technical Assistance Project for 3 years, where she provided technical assistance on doemstic violence and the criminal justice system to state STOP Grant administrators, criminal justice system practitioners, and advocates throughout the United States. She participated in the Domestic Violence Advocacy Project, a community legal clinic for low-income survivors of domestic violence established by the George Washington University National Law Center in Washington, D.C.

Patricia Yancey Martin is Daisy Parker Flory Alumni Professor and Professor of Sociology and Social Work at Florida State University. Her research interests are gender and organizations. She has coedited a book (with Myra Marx Ferree) on feminist organizations in 1995, *Feminist Organizations: Harvest of the New Women's Movement,* and she has written recent papers on social construction of the body, gender accounts given by people who process rape survivors, R. Connell's theory of masculinities, and a California rape crisis center that mobilized unobtrusively for 25 years. She is completing a book on the politics of rape-processing work and papers on mobilized masculinities in large corporations. She recently received the Southern Sociological Society's Jocher-Beard Award for Distinguished Research on Gender (1999).

Jody Miller is Assistant Professor of Criminology and Criminal Justice at the University of Missouri-St. Louis. She is completing a study with Dheeshana Jayasundara of the commercial sex industry in Sri Lanka, funded by a Fulbright Senior Scholar Award. She is a member of the National Consortium on Violence Research, through which she is currently researching (with Norman White) violence against urban African American adolescent girls. Her monograph, *One of the Guys: Girls, Gangs, and Gender,* was publishedin 2000. Additional publications have appeared in *Criminology, Social Problems,* and *Journal of Research in Crime and Delinquency.*

Susan L. Miller is Associate Professor in the Department of Sociology and Criminal Justice at the University of Delaware. Her research interests include gender and crime, as well as criminal justice policy issues related to domestic violence. Her recent books are *Crime Control and Women: Feminist Implications of Criminal Justice Policy* and *Gender and Community Policing: Walking the Talk.*

Phoebe Morgan teaches undergraduate and graduate courses in the Department of Criminal Justice at Arizona State University and is an affiliate of the Women's Studies Program at Northern Arizona University. She cofounded Sociologists Against Sexual Harassment and maintains the International Coalition Against Sexual Harassment Web site. She conducts research about women, crime, and justice and has published various articles about sexual harassment.

Mary K. O'Brien has more than 14 years of experience in health psychology and health communications. These efforts led to teaching medical students, residents, physicians, and other health care professionals to communicate with their patients about many issues—in particular, domestic violence. She is currently involved in several research projects in the area of teen dating violence, violence as experienced in the lives of 11-to 14-year-old girls, and program evaluation. As a core faculty member of the School of Public Health, she has integrated issues of domestic violence and communication skills throughout the curricula.

Ellen Pence has been an advocate in the battered women's movement since 1975, focusing her work on legal reform efforts.

She has developed the process of safety and accountability audits based on Dorothy Smith's institutional ethnography work. She is one of the original organizers of the Duluth Domestic Abuse Intervention Project, which serves as an international model of legal reform work for battered women.

Robin Phillips is an attorney and the director of the Women's Human Rights Program at Minnesota Advocates for Human Rights. She has investigated human rights violations against women in Romania, Bulgaria, Albania, Macedonia, Armenia, Ukraine, Moldova, and Uzbekistan. She has organized international workshops and conferences on women's human rights issues. She practiced law for several years before joining Minnesota Advocates. Her previous law practice included employment discrimination and sexual harassment litigation.

Jody Raphael has served as executive director of the Center for Impact Research (formerly Taylor Institute) since 1994. Her research has led to an acknowledgment that large numbers of women on welfare are current and past victims of domestic violence, for whom the violence serves as a welfare-to-work barrier. Since 1997, she has worked in collaboration with the University of Michigan School of Social Work. The joint Project on Welfare, Work, and Domestic Violence collects and coordinates the dissemination of research data on the relationship of domestic violence and welfare and poverty, sponsoring national research conferences on the subject. Her book, *Saving Bernice: Battered Women, Welfare, and Poverty,* was published in 2000.

Claire M. Renzetti is Professor and Chair of the Department of Sociology at St. Jo-

seph's University, Philadelphia, Pennsylvania. She is editor of the international, interdisicplinary journal, *Violence Against Women,* coeditor of the Sage *Violence Against Women* book series, and editor of the Northeastern University Press book series, *Gender, Crime, and Law.* She is the author or editor of 10 books as well as numerous book chapters and articles in scholarly journals. She is president-elect of Alpha Kappa Delta, the International Sociological Honors Society, vice president-elect of the Society of the Study of Social Problems, and a member of the Board of Directors of the National Clearinghouse for the Defense of Battered Women.

Linda E. Saltzman is senior scientist, Family and Intimate Violence Prevention Team, Division of Violence Prevention, National Center for Injury Prevention and Control, at the Centers for Disease Control and Prevention. Her work there has focused on prevention of family and intimate partner violence, public health surveillance of violence against women, and violence as it relates to pregnancy and other reproductive health issues. Recently, she has worked on the development and pilot-testing of uniform definitions and recommended data elements for intimate partner violence surveillance.

Martin D. Schwartz is Professor of Sociology at Ohio University. He has written more than 70 articles on a variety of topics in such journals as *Violence Against Women,* the *Canadian Review of Sociology and Anthropology,* and the *Journal of Interpersonal Violence.* He is also the editor of *Researching Sexual Violence: Methodological and Personal Perspectives* and co-author of *Sexual Assault on the College Campus: The Role of Male Peer Support* and

Woman Abuse on Campus: Results from the Canadian National Survey (with Walter S. DeKeseredy).

Evan Stark is Associate Professor in the Graduate Department of Public Administration at Rutgers-Newark, where he is the director of the Masters in Public Health Program. He is a founder of one of the nation's first shelters, an award-winning researcher, and a forensic specialist who has served as an expert in more than 100 cases involving battered women and their children. Coauthor with Dr. Anne Flitcraft of *Women at Risk: Domestic Violence and Women's Health,* he cochaired the U.S. Surgeon General's Working Group on Domestic Violence and Health and has served as a consultant to the Centers for Disease Control and numerous federal and state agencies.

Cris M. Sullivan is Associate Professor of Ecological/Community Psychology at Michigan State University and director of evaluation for the Michigan Coalition Against Domestic and Sexual Violence. She has been an advocate and researcher in the movement to end violence against women since 1982. Her areas of expertise include developing and evaluating community interventions for battered women and their children and evaluating victim services. She has received numerous federal grants to support her work and has published extensively in this area. She has also served as a consultant for numerous local, state, and federal organizations and initiatives.

Roberta L. Valente has written on civil legal issues in domestic violence cases, including child custody and visitation, workplace violence, attorney responsibilities,

and community responses to domestic violence. She has worked in shelter programs in the United States and the United Kingdom, for the Clinica Legal Latina at AYUDA in Washington, D.C., as the director of the American Bar Association Commission on Domestic Violence, and as attorney adviser for the U.S. Department of Justice, Violence Against Women Office. She currently works for the Battered Women's Justice Project of the Pennsylvania Coalition Against Domestic Violence.

Linda Vinton is Associate Professor at Florida State University's Institute for Family Violence Studies. Her research focus is on older women and community-based programs for elders. Prior to joining the faculty at FSU, she worked at domestic violence shelters and also as an adult protective services social worker.

Neil Websdale is Associate Professor of Criminal Justice at Northern Arizona University in Flagstaff. He has published work on violence against women, the state response to domestic violence cases, and the media portrayal of intimate partner and stranger violence. He has completed three books: *Rural Woman Battering and the Justice System, Understanding Domestic Homicide,* and *Making Trouble: Cultural Constructions of Crime, Deviance, and Control* (coedited with Jeff Ferrell). He consults for the Florida Governor's Task Force on Domestic and Sexual Violence. Part of his current work involves setting up Domestic Fatality Review Teams in selected jurisdictions in Florida.

Carolyn M. West is Assistant Professor of Psychology in the Interdisciplinary Arts and Sciences Program at the University of Washington. She completed a postdoctoral clinical fellowship at Illinois State University (1995) and was a National Institute of Mental Health postdoctoral research fellow at the Family Research Laboratory at the University of New Hampshire (1995-97). Her current research focuses on partner violence in ethnic minority families and the long-term consequences of child sexual abuse.

Linda M. Williams is director of research at the Stone Center and codirector of the National Violence Against Women Prevention Research Center at Wellesley Centers for Women, Wellesley College. She is also Research Associate Professor at the University of New Hampshire. She has conducted research on violence, child sexual abuse, partner violence, rape, and women's mental health for the past 27 years and is author or co-author of five books and many articles on violence against women and children. She has directed longitudinal research on violence against women, family violence, sex offenders, and the consequences of child abuse. She is currently principal investigator for the Navy Family Study funded by the U.S. Navy.

Oliver J. Williams is Associate Professor of Social Work, University of Minnesota, and director of the Institute on Domestic Violence in the African American Community. He previously taught at Illinois State University and West Virginia University. He has been a practitioner in the field of domestic violence for more than 20 years, including work with child welfare, delinquency, and battered women's agencies. He has created and conducted counseling groups for partner abuse-treatment programs. As an academic, his research and publications have centered on creating effective service-delivery strategies that will reduce the violent behavior of African American men who batter.

Tamar Diana Wilson is a research affiliate with the Department of Anthropology, University of Missouri, St. Louis. She has published in *Human Organization, Review of Radical Political Economics, Journal of Borderland Studies,* and *Latin American Perspectives,* primarily on international migration from Mexico to the United States and on Mexican women in the informal sector.

Seema Zeya is the senior attorney for the Full Faith and Credit Project of the Pennsylvania Coalition Against Domestic Violence. The project's mission is to promote and facilitate implementation of the full faith and credit provision of the Violence Against Women Act in states, tribes, and U.S. territories. To that end, the project provides ongoing technical assistance and training to law enforcement officers, federal and state prosecutors, judges, court administrators, private attorneys, victim advocates, and other professionals who work with victims of domestic violence and stalking. Before joining the project, she worked for Central Pennsylvania Legal Services in Harrisburg, where, among other things, she represented victims of domestic violence in civil protection order proceedings. She also participated actively in outreach and education projects to promote community awareness of legal options available to survivors of abuse.